# THE AMERICAN JAIL

*Cornerstone of Modern Corrections*

GARY F. CORNELIUS

Upper Saddle River, New Jersey 07458

**Library of Congress Cataloging-in-Publication Data**
Cornelius, Gary F.
The American jail : cornerstone of modern corrections / Gary F. Cornelius.
p. cm.
Includes bibliographical references and index.
ISBN-13: 978-0-13-114280-0 (alk. paper)
ISBN-10: 0-13-114280-1 (alk. paper)
1. Prisons—United States. 2. Prison administration—United States. 3. Corrections—United States. I. Title.
HV9469.C66 2008
365'.34—dc22
2007031490

Editor-in-Chief: *Vernon R. Anthony*
Senior Acquisitions Editor: *Tim Peyton*
Associate Editor: *Jillian Allison*
Editorial Assistant: *Alicia Kelly*
Marketing Manager: *Adam Kloza*
Production Liaison: *Joanne Riker*
Cover Design Director: *Jayne Conte*
Cover Design: *Bruce Kenselaar*
Full-Service Project Management/Composition: Integra Software Services, Ltd.

Credits and acknowledgments borrowed from other sources and reproduced, with permission, in this textbook appear on appropriate page within text.



Pearson Education LTD.
Pearson Education Singapore, Pte. Ltd
Pearson Education, Canada, Ltd
Pearson Education–Japan
Pearson Education Australia PTY, Limited
Pearson Education North Asia Ltd
Pearson Educación de Mexico, S.A. de C.V.
Pearson Education Malaysia, Pte. Ltd

ISBN-13: 978-0-13-114280-0
ISBN-10: 0-13-114280-1

*This work is dedicated to three special people who gave me the encouragement to see this through, and without their love and support this book would not have been written.*

*The first is my late wife, Nancy, who was proud of my writing and urged me to do even more, all the while helping me. Even though she has passed on, I believe that she still guides me.*

*The others are our children, Gary Jr. and Amber Beth. They always are proud when Dad tackles a new project. Thanks to all of you for being there for me.*

*This book is also dedicated to another group of people to whom all of the work will hopefully benefit. They are the new generation of jail officers, staff, and criminal justice students. Please take this book, its knowledge and experience and put it to good use.*

# CONTENTS

# PREFACE

Jail. The slammer, the pokey. By whatever name it is called, the fact is that every jurisdiction in the United States has, or has access to, a local jail. Jails are a crucial part of our criminal justice system. Every locality has to deal with crime and criminal offenders. They must deal with the questions of what to do with the law-breakers who commit crimes and either wait inside the jail for their trials or receive sentences to the jail or to the prison system. No matter what the offender has done, he or she first awaits their fate in the local jail.

This is a book about the local jail—how it developed, how they work, and what jail staffs are doing to protect the public and keep inmates safely confined. This text is based in a large part on my 27 plus years working inside a local jail and dealing with inmates.

The purpose of this book is to give the reader, whether he or she is a jail officer in training or a criminal justice student in college, a realistic view of the world of the local jail. My goal is to allow the reader to see from a practitioner's viewpoint, the development and operation of jails. Much information will be presented about both the inmates and the staff—the keepers and the kept.

While many texts discuss jails as part of a larger work, this book is designed to focus on jails in detail. I have combined data and career experience. The reader will not only see information, but will read how that information is manifested in the daily operations and administration of the jail. This book is unique because I apply over 27 years of experience and observations in several areas of jail operations to the material.

I have organized the book in a straightforward format as is possible. Each of the 12 chapters has objectives at the beginning, review questions, and a list of terms. Each term is defined in the text and also in the glossary. Photographs and forms that are used in jails applicable to the chapter concerned are in the text. Each chapter has a feature that I call "Point of View." Each Point of View is written by a jail practitioner in the field, either active or recently retired. The goal of the Point of View feature is to see the views and observations, as well as opinions of jail professionals. Reference lists at the end of each chapter can refer the reader to other sources of information.

The chapters contain the following information:

Chapter 1: *The History and Development of The American Jail*—the development of punishment systems in Europe and Colonial America; the evolution into the local jail, conditions of the local jail; an overview of jails in the United States today, their designs and architecture, population counts, strengths, weaknesses, and problems.

Chapter 2: *Jail Security*—examinations of how jail staff keeps jails secure, techniques of confining the inmates inside; keeping the public the public safe; and dealing with emergencies.

Chapter 3: *Jail Climate*—how inmates do their time, the mood of the jail, how staff can keep a positive atmosphere in the jail, thus preventing riots, disturbances, and violence, discussions of gangs and security threat groups.

Chapter 4: *Booking and Initial Intake*—booking inmates into the jail, receiving, the first hours of incarceration, handling problems of newly arrived inmates.

Chapter 5: *Classification and Inmate Housing*—proper interviewing and placement of inmates, custody levels, disciplinary proceedings, segregation, and the decisionmaking process concerning inmate housing.

Chapter 6: *Jail Programs and Services*—a description of jail programs, types and objectives, and the staffs that administer them, basic inmate services, health care services, food service, library services, recreation, and commissary.

Chapter 7: *The Jail Population: Profile and Special Categories*—a demographic look at the characteristics of jail inmates, the types of crimes, criminal histories, and an overview of the special types of inmates including juveniles, females, the elderly, substance abusers, the mentally disordered, suicidal inmates, and foreign and inmates from various ethnic groups.

Chapter 8: *Jail Staff*—information on the jail staff, plus an examination of hiring and training issues.

Chapter 9: *Jails and the Courts*—a concise view of court decisions and case law that have impacted jail inmates and operations.

Chapter 10: *Jail Standards*—an examination of the state, health, and correctional organization standards that dictate the operations of the local jail.

Chapter 11: *Jails and Community Corrections*—an examination of alternative programs operated by jails to facilitate inmate reintegration and relief from overcrowding.

Chapter 12: *The Future of the American Jail*—a discussion of issues and practices facing the American jail in the next several years.

The book concludes with a glossary that defines all terms in the text in an easy-to-use format. It is a handy reference for the instructor and the trainee/student.

This text is designed for use in a corrections academy or college criminal justice class as a supplementary text. This book can also be used for research. Information about jails covers a wide range of subjects. Due to its concise nature, researchers and students will find it useful.

In summary, this can be a useful book for many different people who are involved with the local jail: the student aspiring to have a career in corrections, the college and academy instructor, and the researcher. By using this text, all will be better informed about the American jail through clearly written, realistically presented information based on first-hand experience.

**Gary F. Cornelius**

# ACKNOWLEDGMENTS

As in any work this involved and time consuming, there are people who helped the author, both on the personal and the professional side. My late wife, Nancy, encouraged me to pursue this project. Others instilled in me a sense of commitment and a hard work ethic. I owe that to my wife, my late father, and my late mother in law, all who died before this book was completed.

My former secretary, Tiffany Watkins-Kirby, assisted me with formatting references, formatting the text, and put together the final manuscript. Also, Deborah Lenassi helped me out when the final draft was being put together.

On the professional side, I personally thank all of the active and retired corrections professionals who took time from their busy and often hectic schedules and wrote "Point of View" essays for the book. I am thankful to Dean Champion from Texas A&M International University; Mike Schmintz from the Walworth County (WI) Jail; Ed Szostak, retired warden and now correctional consultant; and Captain Sabrina Butler from the San Francisco Jail for their essays on the history of jails, today's jail, security and jail climate, respectively. Sgt. Ron Rose from Hampton, Virginia City Jail, Warden Rich Gigliotti of the Butler (PA) County Prison wrote on booking and classification, respectively.

My good friend Mondre Kornegay from the Alexandria (VA) Detention Center discussed inmate services; Wendy Jones from the Whatcom County (WA) Jail loaned her expertise on the diverse nature of the jail population; and another good friend, Mike Pinson from the Arlington (VA) Detention Center wrote on inmate rights. Chief Deputy Walter Smith wrote an excellent essay on jail staff based on his many years of experience at the Denver, Colorado Sheriff's Office.

Finally, three Point of View essays wrapped up the book: corrections consultant and expert Rod Miller on jail standards; Blake Poindexter from the Wells County (Indiana) Sheriff's Office on community corrections, and my dear friend, corrections consultant Bill Sturgeon on the future of jails.

A special thanks goes to a former inmate called Joseph R. (not his real name) who is continuing on the road to rehabilitation and recovery. He took the time to write an essay on his experiences in the jail as an inmate. My family and I continue to wish him well.

A book of this nature needs supplemental information. Forms were supplied by Mondre Kornegay, Wendy Jones, Lt. Colonel Greg Centeio of the Bristol County (MA) Sheriff's Office, and Jim LaMunyon of the Washington (State) Sheriffs and Police Chiefs Association. Material from inmate regulations was courtesy of Mondre Kornegay and Rich Gigliotti. A special thanks is in order to Sgt. Troy Sutton, Teton County (WY) who supplied information on inmate visiting. Julie Kuksa from the DuPage County Sheriff's Office in Illinois supplied Illinois jail standards and Gail Arnall, Executive Director of the Arlington (VA) Offender Aid and Restoration (OAR) supplied information on OAR jail programs. Nancy Cook sent me information on jail operations from the Corrections Corporation of America (CCA). Harry Greene, director of Good News Jail and Prison Ministry, gave permission to use Good News material. Gayenne MacNichol of the Colonial

Williamsburg (VA) jail kindly loaned me material on one of Virginia's oldest jails. One of the earliest supporters of this work was the Alameda (CA) City Jail, where Lt. Sean Lynch and Officer Barbara Leahy were extremely helpful and supplied information, as did Blake Poindexter from Wells County, Indiana Community Corrections.

Many jail and correctional organizations are doing a fine job enhancing the field. Permission to include these organizations and contact information in the text were kindly granted by Steve Ingley, former director, and Sheryl Ebersole, interim director of the American Jail Association; Nancy Cook, Harry Greene, Joe and Laura Noonan of the Corrections Connection (a great Web site), Linda Rubin, president of the International Association of Correctional Training Personnel (IACTP), which is THE best organization of correctional trainers. Alice Heiserman, a dear friend from Publications and Research of the American Correctional Association (ACA) allowed the use of ACA material.

A few folks granted permission to paraphrase and quote: Sheryl Ebersole, Alice Heiserman, Laura Noonan, Courtney Ingram of LRP Publications (home of *The Corrections Professional*), and Jennifer Whaley of Carolina Academic Press.

Photographs can speak volumes and some I took and some were supplied. I thank the following individuals and correctional agencies for either granting me permission to use their photos or allowing me to take photos inside their jails: American Correctional Association (Alice Heiserman), Bristol County Sheriff's Office, (thanks to Lt. Colonel Greg Centeio), Norfolk (MA) County Sheriff's Office (special thanks to Deputy Superintendent Dave Reilly), Ed Szostak, Butler County Prison (Warden Rich Gigliotti), Alameda City Jail (Lt. Sean Lynch), Baltimore City Central Booking and Intake Center (Warden Sue Murphy), Teton County Jail (Sgt. Troy Sutton), Central Shenandoah Criminal Justice Training Academy (former director Bill Flink and current director Tim Kindrick), and the Hampton Roads Criminal Justice Training Academy (executive director Vince Ferrara). A thank you is extended for photos allowed and/or supplied from Executive Director Michael E. Behm from the Nebraska Crime Commission, and Mondre Kornegay director of inmate services at the Alexandria (VA) Detention Center.

Finally, on behalf of my family, a special heartfelt thank you to four people; three are at Prentice Hall and the other is a dear friend. They all understood how personal loss can upset the best laid plans. They stood by me and by doing so, allowed me to focus on finishing this book. These three folks, my attorney Jim Autry, Frank Mortimer, Margaret Lannamann of Prentice Hall and Shiny Rajesh of Integra Software Services Pvt Ltd., will always have a warm place in my heart.

# THE HISTORY AND DEVELOPMENT OF THE AMERICAN JAIL

# 1

***Objectives of chapter***

The student will:

- Learn about early punishments and confinements of criminal wrongdoers
- Understand the different philosophies in corrections that guided the reform and management of prisons and jails
- Understand the history and development of jails in the United States
- Understand the current status and problems of the American jail

The current status of the American jail is a product of several hundred years of correctional philosophies and beliefs on what should be done with wrongdoers. The jail is an "off shoot" of the larger study of prisons. Prisons, in conjunction with the philosophies and beliefs of social scientists and correctional administrators, have exercised a great influence both on under what conditions offenders should be locked up and on what should be done with them *while* they are locked up.

In the overall study of jails, one has to differentiate on what is a jail as opposed to two other institutions, prisons and lockups. These three terms historically have been the most used when describing penal institutions. However, they are all different in scope, even though they all confine inmates.

In the most clear and simple of definitions, a **jail** is a correctional facility that is administered by a local law enforcement agency, such as a county sheriff's office or local department of corrections. Jails confine mainly adults, but under certain circumstances may confine juvenile offenders.[1]

Jails have several functions, namely:[2]

- Detain and confine offenders who are awaiting trial for both major and minor charges and cannot bond out or be released on their own recognizance.
- Confine criminals who are sentenced to short sentences, generally one year (12 months) or less, for nonviolent felonies or misdemeanors.
- Confine convicted inmates who are sentenced to prison terms; jails will confine these offenders pending transportation to the state or federal prison systems.
- Confine mentally ill offenders who are awaiting transfer per court order to state mental health facilities.
- Confine substance abusers who have been court ordered into an alcohol/drug treatment facility.

- Confine juveniles ordered to jail by a juvenile court or due to the jurisdiction having no juvenile facilities.
- Confine parole violators awaiting revocation hearings before the parole board.
- Confine probation violators awaiting probation revocation hearings before the court.
- Confine federal prisoners awaiting pick up by the United States Marshals Service for further action by the federal courts or the Immigration and Customs Enforcement (ICE).
- Confine criminal offenders on outstanding warrants from other jurisdictions.

What may be confusing to the student of corrections is the variety of names that jails in the United States are known by. Terms used for jails include house of corrections, county prison, adult detention center, correctional facility or correctional institution. Six states in the United States due to geographical size and/or funding operate combined jail/prison systems: Alaska, Connecticut, Delaware, Hawaii, Vermont, and Rhode Island.[3]

A **prison** is a correctional facility funded and operated by the federal government (the United States Bureau of Prisons) or a state government. A prison confines criminal offenders sentenced to longer than one year for serious offenses. Offenders in local facilities are "jailed," whereas those in state and federal prisons are "imprisoned."[4]

The third type of penal facility is the **lockup.** A lockup is a temporary holding facility used to confine offenders who have just been arrested. Lockups are generally located adjacent to or inside a police headquarters, a local police station, or a designated area of a jail. Lockups have several functions, such as holding newly arrested offenders for no more than 48 hours, excluding weekends and holidays, until such time that they appear before a magistrate or a judge, are released through posting a bond or bail, or are released on their promise to appear in court. Lockups also hold inebriated offenders until they "dry out" or "sober up" and are determined to be ready for release and pay a fine. Lockups also hold juvenile offenders pending notification of the parents/guardians while authorities arrange placement in a shelter or appropriate juvenile facility. There are approximately 15,000 lock ups in the United States.[5] The number of lockups is constantly changing due to the ongoing renovation and/or construction of police stations and holding facilities.

## EARLY PUNISHMENT AND CONFINEMENT OF CRIMINALS

In the wide spectrum of history, imprisonment of offenders has only been a viable option of authorities during the past several hundred years. Prior to that, wrongdoers suffered harsh punishment in which pain, humiliation, torture, and other forms of suffering were inflicted. Imprisonment was looked upon as places to put offenders while other forms of punishment were decided, and not as a means in itself as punishment.[6]

### Early Punishment of Criminals: Corporal and Capital Punishment

Many early punishments were swift, harsh, painful, and publicly humiliating. Until the eighteenth century, the general goal of punishing wrongdoers was

**corporal punishment,** or actions carried out against wrongdoers which were meant to inflict pain and suffering, but not death.

Societies throughout the world for the most part have had ideas on the types and severity of corporal punishment. Some examples are:[7]

- Flogged (whipped)
- Mutilated
- Put into stocks: immobilizing the feet and legs
- Put into pillories: immobilizing the head and arms
- Branded
- Forced to wear a heavy wooden collar around the neck

According to some correctional literature, the most common forms of corporal punishment have been flogging, mutilation, and amputation, often reserved for the lowest members of society and carried out before the public. The ancient Romans carried out flogging of slaves and initiated the practice of public flogging. The most feared instrument of flogging was the **flagellum,** which were ox-hide thongs knotted and weighted with bone slivers, metal balls, or hooks. The British Navy improved on this design, flogging sailors with the famous cat'o nine tails'. Flogging continued in eighteenth-century England for such offenses as stealing goods, adultery, prostitution, and offenses committed by slaves (including those in the American south) that angered their masters.[8]

Mutilation took the form of inflicting a permanent, visible reminder of the wrongdoing. Criminals would be scarred for life and would be subjected to constant derision, discrimination, ridicule, and violence from citizens. For example, in England, a criminal's ear would be nailed to the pillory and would be ripped off when he or she was released; in other cases petty thieves had their thumbs cut off. Robbery and arson were dealt with by amputating the right foot and gouging eyes. Crimes were also punished by splitting noses and cutting off ears. Mutilation, especially in public, was one step higher than branding. First practiced by the Babylonians, branding was practiced in medieval England, where brands were placed on the offender's face or body. A brand of "T" indicated a thief, a "B" defined a blasphemer, a "P" stood for perjurer, etc.[9]

Mutilation was combined with amputation in some cases as a form of graduated punishment for repeat offenders. In 1657 in Boston, first offender Quakers would suffer one ear being cut off plus jailing. The second offense would result in the other ear being amputated. Women had it a little easier; they were whipped and jailed. However, the third offense for both men and women resulted in jailing and having their tongues bored through with a hot iron. Amputation is still being carried out in some countries, such as Nigeria and Saudi Arabia. Amputation is most commonly administered in Saudi Arabia, where according to Amnesty International, 90 judicial amputations were performed on criminals between 1981 and 1999.[10]

In conjunction with corporal punishment, offenders suffered horrible deaths through **capital punishment,** or inflicting such severe punishment on offenders resulting in death. Capital punishment has existed for centuries and its methods are well known: hanging, beheading, stoning, burning at the stake, etc.

One of the earliest depictions of the death penalty was described by an explorer in Florida in the 1500s. A native town had been burned because the sentinel had fallen asleep. The sentinel was brought before the chief and the tribal elders, and ordered by the executioner to kneel down. The executioner planted his left foot on the sentinel's back and struck his head with a hard wood sharp-ended club. The blow was hard enough to split open the skull. This brutal method was also used for other crimes.[11]

Capital punishment has been prevalent in the history of many nations. The first laws establishing the death penalty were in the Babylonian Code of Hammurabi in the eighteenth century B.C.E., which contained 25 crimes punishable by death. The ancient Greeks and Romans used the death penalty; offenses punishable by death included willful homicide, witchcraft, poisoning, manufacturing poison, treason, and perjury by high officials. Brutal methods were used: crucifixion, beating, burning, beheading, and being thrown to beasts. Murdering a parent or grandparent resulted in being flogged until bleeding profusely, being sewn up in a sack with a dog, a cock, a viper or an ape, and being thrown into the sea to be tortured and drowned.[12]

In England, the number of crimes punishable by death continued to increase until the eighteenth century, where 222 crimes carried the death penalty—among them stealing, cutting down a tree, defacing the Westminster Bridge, and stealing a rabbit from a rabbit warren. Reform was present, as many juries were hesitant to convict offenders of minor crimes that carried the death penalty. Reform was called for, and between 1823 and 1837, the death penalty was removed as punishment from 100 of the 222 capital crimes.[13]

The concept of vengeance and the infliction of pain on criminals were plainly evident in both capital punishment and corporal punishment. As the concept spread, the American colonies felt the influence of Europe and adopted capital punishment. The first recorded execution in the colonies was in the Virginia colony of Jamestown, where a man was executed for the crime of spying for Spain. In 1612, Virginia's colonial governor enacted statues called the "Divine, Moral and Martial Laws" that punished by death such offenses as stealing grapes, killing chickens, and trading with Indians. In the colony of New York, one could be executed for striking one's parents or denying the "true God." Due to reformers like Thomas Jefferson of Virginia and Dr. Benjamin Rush of Pennsylvania, many states (formerly colonies) had limited the death penalty for serious crimes or had limited its use. The states started to concentrate on the construction of prisons.[14]

## Early Confinement of Criminals

As capital punishment faded in its frequency of usage and society became more organized, a critical question was asked: Where do we put wrongdoers? Once this question began to be addressed, the discipline of penology took root. There were no formal penal systems; criminals were more or less "dumped" into whatever structures were available. The history of confinement is a disorganized one among many different societies and nations spread throughout the civilized world.

Surprisingly, ancient civilizations realized that all criminals could not—or should not—be executed. In ancient Babylon, 6,000 years ago, prisons were operated for several criminal types, mainly slaves, foreigners, petty thieves, and debtors. The Greeks punished wrongdoers by crucifixion, fines, exile and **precipitation,** or throwing offenders off of cliffs. However, a powerful committee of magistrates called The Eleven supervised a system of prisons. In 64 B.C., the

Romans built a series of underground dungeons called the **Mamartime Prison** and also confined offenders in stone quarries.[15]

The idea of confinement progressed, but not the quality of the facilities. Special chambers in monasteries and abbeys were used to confine violators of church laws. One aspect was revolutionary for its time: These places were used as alternatives to capital and corporal punishments, and also as places where offenders could do penance for their criminal acts. With the development of public laws and nonchurch governments, wrongdoers were locked up in castles and other fortifications.[16]

As English society progressed, localities, or "shires," were governed by **shire reeves,** which evolved into what are now called *sheriffs*. In 1166, King Henry II of England initiated the Assize or Constitution of Clarendon. This law established the first local gaols (pronounced "jails"), which housed the misfits of society: drunkards, paupers, prostitutes, debtors, thieves, robbers, orphaned children, etc. Each shire reeve was charged with the responsibility of establishing and operating the local "gaol." To fund these institutions, inmates were charged fees by the sheriffs and jailors.[17]

While some countries wrestled with the question of where to put criminals, some nations devised some novel ways to deal with the problem. In Spain and France, criminals were sentenced to serve on galley vessels as oarsmen. Galley sentences could be for life or a specific number of years, depending on the offense. Conditions were unsanitary and brutal; offenders were shackled to their oars and branded on their foreheads in order to prevent escape. Beginning in the seventeenth century, countries such as Spain, France, and England transported offenders to their colonies abroad. French and Spanish offenders were relocated to Africa and South America; English criminals were transported to America, Australia, and New Zealand. Not only did offenders meet the labor and economic needs of the developing colonies, but the practice was viewed as a way to deal with the problems of vagrancy and overpopulation in the European nations. Transportation of offenders to the colonies was carried out by private merchant shipping companies, and upon arrival, the offenders were sold to private citizens for profit. The offender became an **indentured servant,** a convicted offender who worked off his or her sentence by serving a master. The conditions of this "imprisonment" were determined by the "master." Transportation and indentured servitude were the first combinations of corrections and private business.[18]

Prisoners have always been able to work and are a ready-made labor pool. This was recognized early in the history of penology. Inmates engaged in public works in which they performed compulsory labor through a variety of jobs. Inmates performed labor mostly in the streets or underground. Inmates worked in the local mines digging ore, repaired ramparts and walls of fortifications, built roads, constructed houses, and went from house to house collecting human waste. While public works was used prominently in Spain, it attracted the attention of the rulers of Germany and Switzerland. Imprisonment and public works became synonymous; male offenders were confined inside the prison at night and worked in chain gangs outside the prison during the day. In one city, convict labor built even the prison.[19]

The practices of transportation and galleys resulted in fewer offenders being confined; they were simply "shipped out." However, not all offenders could be sent to row in a galley or be transported to a colony. Also, as the eighteenth century drew to a close, citizens were beginning to despair of mutilations, public executions, and mistreatment of offenders. Some citizens sympathized with the plight of the criminal, and this threatened the political power of the rulers. Finally, as citizens became more educated and civilized, the gathering and watching of tortures and severe punishments were contributing to criminal behavior, namely theft, drunkenness, and fighting. Other ways to deal with criminals had to be found, and public punishments were removed from view.[20]

Places of confinement were emerging throughout Europe. During the Middle Ages, criminals were imprisoned, but not in facilities designed for confinement and administered accordingly. In the second half of the sixteenth century, prisons became identified as buildings where the purpose was to confine convicts and work them in labor pools. Jails and prisons began to take separate identities. Offenders in *jails* were primarily debtors and were under detention awaiting trial, and occasionally a sentenced offender was held. Jail inmates did not have to work, while *prisons* confined sentenced offenders whose obligations included performing forced labor. European governments began to call prisons "bridewells" or "houses of corrections" in an effort to easily differentiate them from the local jails.[21]

POINT OF VIEW

## Jails and Jail History

***Dean John Champion***
Texas A&M International University
Laredo, TX

Jails, or incarceration facilities that functioned like jails do today, have existed since Biblical times (Thompson and Mays, 1991). Prior to his crucifixion, Jesus Christ was kept in a jail-like facility operated by the Roman Empire. Although this facility was very primitive and lacked most contemporary amenities such as sanitation and heat, it was used to confine Christ and others alleged to have committed crimes. From ancient historical accounts to the present, there have always been law-breakers and places to contain them once they were captured or detained. Norman Johnston (1973) has cited the Persian Empire and its criminal code established in the sixteenth century B.C. as the first of its kind in any formal political state, although the Aryans who came to India in 2000 B.C. from central Asia brought with them unwritten codes of conduct which included a variety of punishments, including confinement. During those times, persons were banished from their cities or villages, mutilated, or detained in crude dwellings for indeterminate periods. Fifteen centuries later, the Roman Empire constructed the Mamertine Prison, which consisted of a series of interconnected dungeons under the main sewers of Rome (Kerle, 2003). Different jurisdictions throughout the Roman Empire established their own places of detention for wrongdoers for the next several centuries (Morris and Rothman, 1995).

During the period of 430–1066, the Anglo-Saxon period, contemporaneous developments were occurring in England as many wars were being fought. During these conflicts, captured soldiers and others were slaughtered, held in containment areas for indeterminate periods and released, or recruited by one warring faction to attack other factions. In 1066, William of Normandy received papal sanction to invade England and killed Harold II at the Battle of Hastings on October 14th. Known as William the Conquerer, he was crowned King of England and this period was known as the Norman Conquest. This period also prefaces the early Middle Ages, which lasted from 1100–1330 (Bradley, 2004).

The term *jail* is derived from old English term *gaol* (also pronounced "jail"), which originated in 1166 A.D. through a declaration by Henry II of England. Henry II established gaols as a part of the Assize or Constitution of Clarendon (Roberts, 1997). Gaols were locally administered and operated and housed many of society's misfits. Paupers or vagrants, drunkards, thieves, murderers, debtors, highwaymen, trespassers, orphan children, prostitutes, and others made up early gaol populations. The Church of England was powerful and influential, and many religious dissidents were housed in these gaols as a punishment for their disagreements with religious tenets.

The practice of jailing religious dissidents and others continued for several centuries. For instance, the confinement of persons unable to pay their debts in debtor's prisons commenced in 1285, and this practice was widespread during colonial times in different jurisdictions (Kerle, 2003:3). Colonel James Edward Oglethorpe, an Oxford graduate and one of the original founders of Georgia, described his own 23-year confinement in a British debtor's prison before arising to a position of prominence and power. Subsequently, he exerted considerable authority over the nature and types of confinement and helped to lead the fight for penal reforms in the newly established Georgia colony. His ideas were implemented eventually in other colonies, such as South Carolina (Evans, 1996).

Control over the administration and operation of jails was exercised by shire reeves (county chief law enforcement officers) in England, and this practice was continued in the American colonies, largely because this was the only form of local control and confinement known to colonists, most of who were from England originally. Most jails in the United States today are locally controlled and operated similar to their English predecessors (Glaser, 1970).

Jails in England were originally designed as holding facilities for those accused of violating local laws. Alleged law violators were held until court could be conducted and the guilt or innocence of the accused was determined. Shire reeves made their living through reimbursements from taxes collected in the form of fees for each inmate housed on a daily basis. For instance, the reeve would receive a fixed fee, perhaps 50 or 75 cents per day for each inmate held in the jail. Therefore, more prisoners meant more money for reeves and their assistants. Such a reimbursement scheme was easily susceptible to corruption, and much of the money intended for inmate food and shelter was pocketed by selfish reeves. Quite logically, the quality of inmate food and shelter was very substandard, and jails became notorious because of widespread malnutrition, disease, and death among prisoners. These types of conditions have slowly improved, although evidence suggests that some jail systems continue to exhibit substandard conditions for inmates (West Virginia Governor's Committee on Crime, Delinquency, and Correction, 1982). These conditions have often prompted litigation by inmates seeking injunctive relief in the courts (Gettinger, 1977).

Local political influence on jails and jail conditions is pervasive. Often, changing jail conditions are linked to local political shifts through elections and new administrative appointments. Also, the fact that local officials controlled jails and jail operations meant that no single administrative style typified these facilities. Each locality (shire) was responsible for establishing jails, and the way in which jails were operated was left up to local official discretion. Again, current U.S. jail operations in each jurisdiction are characterized by this same individuality of style (Kerle, 1998).

Cruel and inhumane jail conditions continued into the sixteenth century, when workhouses were established largely in response to mercantile demands for cheap labor. A typical workhouse in the mid-sixteenth century was Bridewell, created in 1557. This London facility housed many of the city's vagrants and general riffraff (Roberts, 1997). Jail and workhouse sheriffs and administrators quickly capitalized on the cheap labor these facilities generated, and additional profits were envisioned. Thus, it became commonplace for sheriffs and other officials to hire out their inmates to perform skilled and semi-skilled tasks for various merchants. While the manifest functions of workhouses and prisoner labor were to improve the moral and social fiber of prisoners and train them to perform useful skills when they were eventually released, most of the monies collected from inmate labor was pocketed by corrupt jail and workhouse officials. This inmate exploitation continued a pattern that was widespread throughout early European corrections (Spierenburg, 1991).

In the New England area and throughout the colonies, jails were commonplace. Sheriffs were appointed or supervise jail inmates, and the fee system continued to be used to finance these facilities. All types of people were confined together in jails, regardless of their gender or age. Orphans, prostitutes, drunkards, thieves, and robbers were often contained in large, dormitory-style rooms with hay and blankets for beds. Jails were great melting pots of humanity, with little or no regard for inmate treatment, health, or rehabilitation. Early colonial jails were simply a continuation of the practice of incarcerating persons for various offenses, either actual or alleged. Often they consisted of small rooms where 20 or 30 people could be kept under crude conditions. Private companies, such as the West India Company, often built jails constructed of wood or stone to house persons accused of crimes or convicted offenders. Many of these facilities were constructed during the period 1640–1660. In the 1690s, the Plymouth and Massachusetts Bay Colony

Courts constructed a jail facility that still exists today as a museum in Barnstable, Massachusetts (Kerle, 2003:5).

William Penn (1644–1718) and the Quakers worked tirelessly to bring about jail reforms during the early 1700s. Penn was responsible for implementing various improvements in the conditions under which jail inmates were housed during this period. When Penn died, many of his reforms died with him. But the religious influence of the Quakers in Pennsylvania remained strong. Shortly after the Revolutionary War, the Quakers were able to reinstitute many of Penn's correctional philosophies and strategies through the creation of the Philadelphia Society for Alleviating the Miseries of Public Prisons in 1787. This society was made up of many prominent Philadelphia citizens, philanthropists, and religious reformers who believed prison and jail conditions ought to be changed and replaced with a more humane environment. Members of this Society visited each jail and prison daily, bringing food, clothing, and religious instruction to inmates. Some of these members were educators who sought to assist prisoners in acquiring basic skills such as reading and writing. Although their intrusion into prison and jail life was frequently resented and opposed by local authorities and sheriffs, their presence was significant and brought the deplorable conditions of confinement to the attention of politicians. One particularly disturbing feature of both jails and prisons of that period was the extensive use of common rooms for men, women, and children. Little or no thought was given to housing these inmates in private or separate accommodations.

In 1790, the Pennsylvania legislature authorized the renovation of a facility originally constructed on Walnut Street in 1776, a two-acre structure initially designed to house the overflow resulting from overcrowding of the High Street Jail. The Walnut Street Jail was both a workhouse and a place of incarceration for all types of offenders. But the 1790 renovation was the first of several innovations in U.S. corrections. Specifically, the Walnut Street Jail was innovative because (1) it separated the most serious prisoners from others in 16 large solitary cells; (2) it separated other prisoners according to their offense seriousness; and (3) it separated prisoners according to gender. Therefore, the Walnut Street Jail was the forerunner of minimum-, medium-, and maximum-security prisons in the United States as well as solitary confinement.

Besides these innovations, the Walnut Street Jail assigned inmates to different types of productive labor according to their gender and conviction offense. Women made clothing and performed washing and mending chores. Skilled inmates performed carpentry, shoemaking, and other crafts. Unskilled prisoners beat hemp or jute for ship caulking. With the exception of women, prisoners received a daily wage for their labor which was applied to defray the cost of their maintenance. The Quakers and other religious groups provided regular instruction for most offenders. The Walnut Street Jail concept was widely imitated by officials from other states during the next several decades (Okun and Thomas, 1997). Many prisons were modeled after the Walnut Street Jail for housing and managing long-term prisoners.

Information about the subsequent growth of jails since Walnut Street in the United States is sketchy. One reason is that there were many inmate facilities established during the 1800s and early 1900s serving many functions and operating under different labels. Sheriffs' homes were used as jails in some jurisdictions, while workhouses, farms, barns, small houses, and other types of facilities served similar purposes in others. Thus, depending on who did the counting, some facilities would be labeled as jails and some would not. Limiting jail definitions only to locally operated short-term facilities for inmates excluded also those state-operated jails in jurisdictions such as Alaska, Delaware, and Rhode Island. Another reason for inadequate jail statistics and information was that there was little interest in jail populations.

Another problem was that it was difficult to transmit information from jails and jail inmates to any central location during that period of time. Often, local records were not maintained, and many sheriffs' departments were not inclined to share information about their prisoners with others. Streamlined communications systems did not exist, and information was compiled very slowly, if at all. State governments expressed little or no interest in the affairs of jails within their borders, because these were largely local enterprises funded with local funds. Even if there had been a strong interest in jail information among corrections professionals and others, it would have been quite difficult to acquire.

The U.S. Census Bureau began to compile information about jails in 1880 (Cahalan, 1986:73). At ten-year intervals following 1880, general jail information was systematically obtained about race, nativity, gender, and age. Originally, the U.S. Census Bureau presented data separately for county jails, city prisons, workhouses, houses of correction, and leased county prisoners. But in 1923, these figures were combined to reflect more accurately what we now describe as jail statistics. A special report was prepared by the U.S. Census Bureau entitled *Prisoners, 1923.* And in the same year, Joseph Fishman, a federal prison inspector, published a book, *Crucible of Crime*, describing living conditions of many U.S. jails. Comparisons with 1880 base figures show the jail population of the United States was 18,686 in 1880 and eventually reached 631,240 by mid-year 2001.

Historically, reports about jail conditions in the United States have been largely unfavorable. The 1923 report by Fishman was based on his visits to and observations of 1,500 jails, describing the conditions he saw as horrible. More recent reports suggest these conditions have not changed dramatically since Fishman made his early observations (Kerle, 1998). Of course, there are exceptions, but these are few and far between. It was not until 1972 that national survey data about jails became available. Exceptions include the years 1910, 1923, and 1933, where jail inmate characteristics were listed according to several offense categories. A majority of jail inmates each of those years had committed petty offenses such as vagrancy, public drunkenness, and minor property crimes (Cahalan, 1986:86). Even since 1972, jail data have not been regularly and consistently compiled.

There are several reasons for many of the continuing jail problems in the United States. Some of these reasons are that (1) most of the U.S. jails today were built before 1970, and many were built five decades or more before that; (2) local control of jails often results in erratic policies that shift with each political election, thus forcing jail guards and other personnel to adapt to constantly changing conditions and jail operations; and (3) jail funding is a low-priority budget item in most jurisdictions, and with limited operating funds, the quality of services and personnel jails provide and attract is considerably lower compared with state and federal prison standards and personnel.

The exact number of jails in the United States at any given time and on any given date is unknown. One reason is that professionals disagree as to how jails should be defined. Some surveys count only locally operated and funded short-term incarceration facilities as jails, while other surveys include state-operated jails in their figures. In remote territories such as Alaska, World War II Quonset huts may be used to house offenders on a short-term basis. Work release centers, farms for low-risk inmates, and other facilities may be included or excluded from the jail definition. Sometimes, lockups (drunk tanks, holding tanks) are counted as jails, although these facilities exist primarily to hold those charged with public drunkenness or other minor offenses for up to 48 hours. These are not jails in the formal sense, but rather, they are simple holding tanks or facilities.

Several different federal agencies have reported different numbers of jails for any given year. For instance, in 1970, the Census of Institutional Population estimated there were 2,317 jails in the United States, while the Law Enforcement Assistance Administration reported 4,037 U.S. jails. Furthermore, a 1923 study conducted by the U.S. Census Bureau reported there were 3,469 U.S. jails in operation. And in 1984, the Advisory Commission on Intergovernmental Relations reported there were 3,493 jails in the United States. These widely disparate figures are confusing to most readers.

There has been a substantial decrease in the number of jails in the U.S. between 1970 and 2002, with 4,037 jails reported in 1970 and 3,365 jails reported in 2002 (Beck, 2002:11). How can existing jails accommodate such greater jail inmate population increases? One answer is that many old jails have been destroyed or drastically remodeled and expanded, while many new jails have been constructed. Newer jails are generally designed to accommodate several times the number of jail inmates who were accommodated in the old jails.

It has been difficult to stimulate interest among local officials to accredit them through certification from any national organization because most U.S. jails are small. The American Correctional Association Division of Standards and Accreditation reports that often, hesitancy on the part of jail officials and sheriffs to apply for accreditation is due to a lack of funds (Thompson and Mays, 1991). The primary benefits of accreditation include (1) protecting life, safety, and health of both jail staffs and inmates; (2) assessing the strengths and weaknesses of jails to maximize their resources and implement necessary changes; (3) minimizing the potential for costly, time-consuming litigation through negligence and other liability; (4) enhancing the jail's credibility with courts and the public; (5) achieving professional and public recognition of good performance; and (6) improving staff and inmate morale (Washington, 1987:15).

Most county jails throughout the United States have sought accreditation from organizations such as the American Jail Association (AJA) and the American Correctional Association (ACA) (Bittick, 2003:8). The El Paso County, Colorado Sheriff's Office, for instance, is devising policies and procedures designed to enhance inmate programs and officer safety in compliance with nationally accepted standards evolved from the ACA (Hilte, 1998:33–34). Recommendations are solicited from both the private sector and various corrections agencies to improve jail officer effectiveness with various forms of jail training in jurisdictions such as Alameda County, California

(Ryan and Plummer, 1999). At the Albany County Jail in New York, various initiatives have been adopted to deal with the problem of chronic jail overcrowding and facility improvement (Chapman, 1998:9). Private contractors have also been consulted for their input and assistance in alleviating various types of jail problems and providing certain kinds of services for jail inmates.

## References


Beck, Allen J. (2002). "Jail Population Growth: National Trends and Predictions of Future Growth." *American Jails* **16**:9–14.

Bittick, John C. (2003). "Evolving Through Accreditation." *Corrections Today* **65**:8.

Bradley, Arthur (2004). *Jails and the Old Testament.* Roanoke, VA: Unpublished paper.

Cahalan, Margaret W. (1986). *Historical Corrections Statistics in the United States, 1850–(1984).* Washington, DC: U.S. Department of Justice.

Chapman, Jack (1998). "Bigger, Better, Safer, Faster, and Less Expensive." *American Jails* **12**:9–17.

Evans, Mark (1996). *History of Colonial Georgia.* Atlanta, GA: Freedom Press.

Glaser, Daniel (ed.) (1970). *Crime in the City.* New York: Harper and Row.

Gettinger, Stephen (1977). "Cruel and Unusual Prisons." *Corrections Magazine* **3**:3–16.

Hilte, Ken (1998). "Writing Policy and Procedures." *American Jails* **12**:33–36.

Johnston, Norman (1973). *The Human Cage: A Brief History of Prison Architecture.* Berkeley, CA: University of California Press.

Kerle, Kenneth E. (1998). *American Jails: Looking to the Future.* Boston, MA: Butterworth-Heinemann.

Kerle, Kenneth E. (2003). *Exploring Jail Operations.* Hagerstown, MD: American Jail Association.

Morris, Norval and David J. Rothman (eds.) (1995). *The Oxford Dictionary of the Prison: The Practice of Punishment in Western Society.* Oxford, UK: Oxford University Press.

Okun, Peter T.M. and Michael Thomas (1997). *Crime and the Nation: Prison Reform and Popular Fiction in Philadelphia, 1786–1800.* Ann Arbor, MI: University Microfilms International.

Roberts, John W. (1997). *Reform and Retribution: An Illustrated History of American Prisons.* Lanham, MD: American Correctional Association.

Ryan, Timothy and Charles C. Plummer (1999). "Jail Accreditation: A Panacea or Problem?" *Corrections Today* **61**:157.

Spierenburg, Pieter (1991). *The Prison Experience: Disciplinary Institutions and Their Inmates in Early Modern Europe.* New Brunswick, NJ: Rutgers University Press.

Thompson, Joel A. and G. Larry Mays (eds.) (1991). *American Jails: Public Policy Issues.* Chicago, IL: Nelson-Hall.

Washington, Jeffrey (1987). "ACA Revaluates Small Jail Standards." *Corrections Today* **45**:15.

West Virginia Governor's Committee on Crime, Delinquency, and Correction (1982). *Study of Local Jails in West Virginia.* Lexington, KY: West Virginia Governor's Committee on Crime, Delinquency, and Correction.



Thanks to Dr. Dean J. Champion, Department of Social Sciences, Texas A&M International University, 5201 University Boulevard, Laredo, Texas 78041. Reprinted by Permission; Dean J. Champion.


By the eighteenth century in England, many different punishments were used to punish criminals. Fines were imposed, the pillory and whipping were also still in use. Condemned offenders were pardoned if they agreed to be transported to the American colonies. Hanging was used. However, confinement was used and two institutions existed, the jail and the prison. The jail held petty criminals, felons, debtors, those awaiting trial, and the prison held those sentenced to short terms. Because there were no set regulations of jails, and the administration of them varied from jurisdiction to jurisdiction, the populations of these two facilities became intermingled and jails were confused with prisons.[22]

Places of confinement now numbered over 300. Jails were gatehouses, cellars, rooms, or any other convenient place to hold people. Stays were not long; only a few institutions held high populations of criminals. Judges toured the country and it was common to have trials of serious crimes only twice per year.

The problem of **debtors**—private citizens confined through a civil process until a debt was paid—plagued the operation of jails. Jailors had little or no control over them because they were not technically criminals. Debtors, who were thrown into jails with felons, were unruly and complained that jailing infringed upon their rights as English citizens. They also brought into the jail their wives and children, thus creating an operational nightmare.[23]

Jailors at this time operated the jail through the **fee system.** Due to the jail being self-financing, the money for operations and wages had to come from somewhere—the inmates. In the fee system, inmates paid the jailor for services inside the jail. Fees were charged to people for visiting the inmate and to inmates for bedding. Beer was sold in the prisons and jails. Naturally, corruption followed; it was more lucrative for the jailor to treat the "paying" inmates better than the unfortunate ones who could not pay. The courts supported this system. In 1669, an inmate who was found innocent continued to be confined because he did not have the funds to pay off the jailor. The court in this case supported the jailor. As a result, many citizens sought the position of jailor not to serve the public or to rehabilitate inmates, but to simply make money.[24]

Early jails in England did not have the regimented schedule and control of inmates that jails employ today. Jailors of the time did not have staffs; what staff members they did have were recruited from their own families or from the jail inmate population. Inmate self-government was the key—the jailors allowed the inmates to rule themselves, making their own rules and routines. The larger jails operated "courts" where inmates decided disputes, levied fines, and settled arguments and disputes among their fellow prisoners. Inmates were left to their own devices as to activity. Some worked at a trade to make money for themselves while other inmates begged. Inmates engaged in drunken behavior, gambling, and games. Curious citizens and friends of inmates were allowed to come in and mingle with the inmate population after paying a fee to the jailor.[25]

By 1775, the American colonies were engaged in open revolt against the English crown, and the subsequent Revolutionary War disrupted the practice of transportation to the American colonies. Between 1718 and 1775, approximately 30,000 criminals had been transported to the American colonies. At the same time, critics of this practice argued that transportation did not deter crime; some inmates who were transported began a new life in which they prospered. Judges began to look at confinement with renewed interest. With the prisons and jails being overcrowded and the transporting of inmates being disrupted, English authorities looked to old ships lying in harbors. Known as **hulks,** these ships served as floating prisons and jails. Inmates confined in them were subjected to restrictive diets, violence, immoral activities, and squalid conditions. Inmates in hulks were forced to clean seaports and clear the Thames River.[26]

## THE REFORM MOVEMENT IN PRISONS AND JAILS

By the 1700s, a call for reform in prisons and jails began to take hold. In many jails conditions were squalid, and because of the fee system, corruption was the norm in many institutions. Even though the operation of local jails was the responsibility of the local sheriff, there was no system of standards or guidelines. Each jail was a system in itself. Inmates were subjected to harsh conditions.

The method most preferred by jailors to maintain discipline among inmate populations was simply to beat them. Reformers thought that such practices, combined with the corruptions of jailors, degraded two groups: first, the inmates who were supposed to be punished and at the same time reformed, and second, society itself. Several famous people of the time spoke out in favor of prison and jail reform, among them Frederick II of Prussia and the French philosophers Voltaire, Montesquieu, and Diderot.[27]

Calls for reform also resulted in actions by legislatures. The British Parliament passed the Penitentiary Act of 1779. This act mandated secure and sanitary penal structures, regular inspections, and the prohibition of the inmate fee system. This had results; the Wymondham Gaol in Norfolk, England was constructed in 1785 in accordance with the Act. In France, the French National Assembly authorized similar types of institutions as described above. However, reforms were slow as several provincial French prisons failed to enact reforms per the National Assembly, and in England, many reforms were set aside in favor of the transportation method.[28]

The reform movement had several core themes dealing with the administration and conditions of jails and prisons. They were:[29]

- Punishment of criminals should not be brutal, excessive, or have an orientation toward vengeance and retribution.
- The laws—criminal codes and accompanying punishments—should be rational, clearly written, and equitably applied, and court proceedings and trials should be open to public scrutiny.
- Lawbreakers should be punished by fixed terms of imprisonment, not by open-ended sentences, torture, and executions.
- Jails and prisons confining criminals should be clean, safe, and operated in an orderly manner by honest and competent staff.
- Jails and prisons should be supported financially by the government, and not through exorbitant fees paid by inmates.
- Inmates confined in jails and prisons should be segregated by gender and the severity of their crimes; the mentally ill (insane) and sane inmates should not be housed together; and young offenders should be separated from adult offenders.

These proposals were ahead of their time, but gave a start to practices that are present in today's jails: competent staff, government funding, sanitary standards, and inmate classification. Several social reformers, government officials, and philosophers made lasting and significant contributions to penal reforms that have withstood the tests of time.

## Cesare Beccaria

Cesare Beccaria, an Italian scholar of the mid to late 1700s, expounded the views of **utilitarianism,** which says the laws should be designed to bring the greatest good or benefit to the greatest number of people. Beccaria said that the law was a contract between the state and the people, and citizens must give up some freedoms to assure that there will be peace and security in society. The laws must be understood and respected by the people if they were expected to obey. The state government must agree to serve the majority of the people and their actions must be justified. Concerning crime, the fear of punishment served to insure that each citizen kept his or her part of this contract, and the punishment for each crime must be justified by the harm done to society by the crime. More simply, the punishment has to fit the crime.[30]

Beccaria also had revolutionary ideas on the mechanics of punishment. He believed that torture should be abolished and that punishment should be certain and swift, but not necessarily severe. The certainty of punishment served as a deterrent, not capital punishment. Beccaria believed that capital punishment may convince criminals that they had nothing to lose by committing further crimes.[31]

## William Penn

William Penn was a well-known Quaker and the colonial governor of Pennsylvania. Like Beccaria and other reformers, Penn voiced definitive ideas on punishment and imprisonment. What was unique about Penn's perspectives about imprisonment is that he was imprisoned for his religious beliefs. While in prison, he became appalled at the squalid and brutal conditions he experienced. Being the first colonial governor of Pennsylvania, he was in a position to put his ideas into practice.[32]

Penn was responsible for the **Great Code,** which was a set of laws that made sweeping reforms to corrections in the colony. Among these reforms was the authorization of capital punishment only for the crime of murder. This contrasted with the mother country, which had at the time 200 crimes that were punishable by death. Each county in Pennsylvania was charged with building a house of correction because under the Great Code, imprisonment was the fundamental punishment of criminals. Each house of correction would be funded by the government, and inmates incarcerated therein would not be charged fees for food and lodging. Inmates would be required to perform useful work. Stocks and pillories were abolished and bail was introduced.[33]

The reforms proposed by Penn did not set well in England, and after his death in 1718, Queen Anne forced the repeal of the Great Code. As a result, Pennsylvania enacted the Sanguinary Laws, which contrasted the Great Code. These laws reinstated the death penalty for numerous crimes and brought back corporal punishment. Ironically, the citizens of Pennsylvania approved of Penn's Great Code and after the American colonies declared their independence from England, restored a large part of it.[34]

## John Howard

As High Sheriff of Bedfordshire in England, John Howard became aware of the horrible conditions in prisons and jails. In 1775, Howard toured European penal institutions, seeing firsthand conditions for himself. In 1777, Howard wrote and published perhaps one of the best documents recommending and justifying penal reform, *State of Prisons, 1777*. The essay had a great influence on the improvement of penal institutions in Europe and America. [35]

The essay *State of the Prisons, 1977* can serve as a blueprint and predictor for many of the practices of jails today. Howard called his recommendations "correct principles" and recommended practices for sanitation, construction, discipline, food service, inmate activities, classification, prevention of escapes, and the hiring of jailors.

Also revolutionary was that he called for inspections performed by an official outside the jail. Inspections could serve to keep the jailor honest and correct deficiencies inside the jail. Another recommendation was uniforms to be worn by inmates.

The recommendations—Howard's "correct principles"—indicate common sense and are supported by solid reasoning. Some examples are:

- *Location:* Prisons [and jails] should be built near water for cleanliness purposes, ideally near a river or brook. The stench of sewers is prevented.
- *Construction:* The "men's felons ward" should be rectangular or square, and built off of the ground on supports. The wards would be more airy and more functional in wet weather. Also, inmates have been known to escape by tunneling; raising the structure may serve to prevent escapes.
- *Living quarters:* Rooms or cells for inmates should be clean, with clean bedding, linens, and sufficient bath facilities, and should be washed daily. The quarters should be heated in winter. Men and women inmates are to be housed separately. Young offenders should be separated from "old and hardened offenders." Each group's living quarters should have a dayroom or kitchen with a fireplace.
- *Inmate management:* Each inmate sleeps alone and should engage in solitary penitence and reflection. There should be no fighting, quarreling, or abusive language in the jail. Howard believed that "gaming" or gambling caused many inmate disputes and should not be allowed. Inmates could complain to the keeper or jailor, who would hear both sides of a dispute and punish the wrongdoer by "closer confinement." More serious matters could be decided by the magistrates or inspectors. Howard advocated a jail disciplinary system of rewards and punishments. Punishments could be the abridgement of diet, hard or disagreeable labor, or solitary confinement with work. Other punishments included being treated with the silence of the keepers, wearing a collar or stripes, and marks of disgrace. The term of imprisonment could be lengthened if the inmate attempted to escape from the jail. The regulations of the jail should be made known to the inmates and "intelligibly drawn up."
- *Inmate activities:* Each jail should have the services of a chaplain, who can provide "private admonitions" (counseling) to young offenders. Inmates should be able to work according to their level of strength and "degree of criminality" or crime. Inmates could be allowed to work together and some at their trades. Inmates could keep a portion of profit made from jail-manufactured goods.
- *Security:* Inmates are to wear uniforms that would easily identify them if they tried to escape or escaped. Howard also advocated lodging upstairs or over arcades in an effort to thwart escapes. There should be alarm bells, double doors with one door being an iron latticed door, and a high wall surrounding the jail. Staffing should be sufficient as to the number and disposition (placement) of turnkeys (officers). A military guard should be used if necessary, and the jailor's windows should face the yard for easier viewing.
- *Food service:* Hot provisions should be served daily. A pound and a half of bread should be served daily, and beef should be served with broth on Sundays.

- *Medical care:* Each jail should have an infirmary, a bath, and medicines. Inmates should have medical attendance (access to doctors) and have more to eat if they are sick.
- *Staffing and operations of the jail:* Howard believed that the gaoler (jailor) should be a "good man....one that is honest, active and humane." The jailor should be sober and restrain drunkenness and vices inside the jail. Jailors and their staffs should not have any connection, concern or interest in the "sale of liquors of any kind." Jailors should be paid a salary in proportion to the "trust and trouble" of the position. The jail staff should faithfully and humanely administer the jail. The salary of the "turnkeys" or subordinate officers should not be included in the salary of the jailor. Staffing for the jail should be determined by the magistrates. Positions for the jail included a matron (female officer for female inmates), turnkeys, a manufacturer, and a taskmaster.
- *Inspections:* Jails are to be overseen by magistrates who are to visit at proper intervals without prior notice. Jails should be inspected daily by the jailors and turnkeys. The Parliament or magistrates should appoint an inspector for every prison. The inspector should make weekly inspections on different days. Inspectors should speak with every inmate, hear all complaints and grievances, and immediately correct what is "manifestly wrong." If the inspector is in doubt about an issue, he can refer it to the government authorities.

Howard stated that he was impressed by the "decency, regularity and order" of the houses of corrections that he observed in Holland, Hamburg, Berne, Ghent, and Florence. He was impressed by the "constant attention that is paid to impress the prisoners a sense of religion, by plain serious discourse, catechizing and familiar instruction from the chaplains, together with the influence of a good example, in both them and in the keepers. These circumstances make a much greater impression upon the minds of criminals...." He was critical of the penal institutions in his own country, saying that "We have too much adopted the gothic mode of correction.... by rigorous severity, which often hardens the heart; while many foreigners pursue the more rational plan of softening the mind in order to its amendment."

Howard's views could also be considered the beginning of jail standards, long before the National Prison Congress in 1870. Many of the categories of modern jail standards—namely medical care, sanitation, inmate discipline, food service, and staff hiring—are mirrored in Howard's *State of the Prisons, 1777.*

**FIGURE 1-1** The Views of John Howard[36]

## Jeremy Bentham

Jeremy Bentham's contribution to corrections is mainly architectural. A key question facing persons who build jails and prisons is how to watch and observe the behavior of many inmates with the minimum number of staff. One key factor in prison and jail staffing is that they control the movement and observe the behavior of the maximum number of inmates in the facility with minimum staffing.

A noted English scholar and philosopher Jeremy Bentham introduced a circular design for prisons called the **panopticon** in 1791, which consisted of multiple stories of outside prison cells constructed in a large circle. The cells faced inward into an interior courtyard. The design resembled a wheel, with the prison guard's station or duty post in the center of the wheel or at its hub. The station was enclosed, which protected the guard. Bentham's theory was that this design could both improve the security of the prison and enhance inmates' propensity for moral reflection on their crimes.[37]

The appeal of the panopticon design was that every cell was visible to the prison guard from a central vantage point. Constant supervision was possible, and inmates were aware that they could be seen at all times. It was hoped that the inmates would become more circumspect and thoughtful, and in time would internalize patterns of more positive behavior. The central guard station—the hub of the wheel—served also as a type of "pulpit" which allowed the staff to give sermons and address the entire cellblock at once.[38]

The panopticon design was incorporated into the following U.S. prisons: the Virginia State Penitentiary in Richmond, Illinois Stateville Penitentiary, and the Western State Penitentiary in Pittsburgh. In the Stateville prison, the panopticon design was used in the dining hall, which had inmates seated at long tables in a circular pattern surrounding a three-story guard tower in the center.[39]

Today, variations of Bentham's panopticon design are still being used in jail and prison design. In some jails, cellblocks are built in a circular design around a corrections officer post. Any design where the officer can turn 360 degrees and observe inmates owes its origins to the panopticon. Primarily the center control station is used for observation, not for addressing inmates or preaching.

## Benjamin Rush

In the early history of the United States, there was much debate on the causes of crime. The problems among lawbreakers in nineteenth-century America were alcoholism, property crimes, and dealing with emerging issues such as gangs, opium addictions, and psychic disorders. Penal reform was in the air as Americans were confident that they could perfect the prison and as a result eliminate crime.[40]

New schools of thinking concerning criminals and punishment were emerging. Crime as a product of sin was viewed as outdated, and crime as a result of free will was viewed as not being ideologically correct because the penal codes were rational, but their effect on criminals was inconsequential. Crime continued, and reformers wondered why. Inmates were interviewed for biographical information. Early penologists now believed through these interviews that crime was caused by broken families and corrupted communities where negative behaviors such as drunkenness, vice, temptations of crime, etc. were rampant and hard to resist. Using the view that the environment—home and community—was so negative that morally weakened criminals could not resist crime, crime was now viewed as a spreading moral disease.[41]

In 1787, Philadelphia witnessed the founding of the world's first prison reform organization, the Philadelphia Society for the Alleviation for the Miseries of Public Prisons, or the Philadelphia Prison Society. Its members were concerned citizens who believed in the reformation of the prisons and jails and also provide assistance to the inmate. Society members regularly visited penal institutions, inquired into the circumstances of the inmates, and reported any abuses that they discovered. An earlier organization, the Philadelphia Society for Assisting Distressed Prisoners, distributed food and clothing to inmates.[42]

The Philadelphia Prison Society owed its foundation to a prominent physician, statesman, and social reformer, Dr. Benjamin Rush. Other Society members included Benjamin Franklin. Rush's position with corrections was that prisons should perform two main functions: remove persons who are a danger to society, and strive to reform inmates into law-abiding citizens. In practice, the Society sought to improve conditions in the prisons. The Society opposed what they saw as humiliating the practice of prisoners working outside the prison, chained together in brightly colored uniforms. Inmates in these work groups begged for food, as prison rations were substandard. Inside the prisons, sanitation was lacking, inmates were inadequately supervised, and no effective system of inmate classification system existed. The Philadelphia Prison Society and Dr. Rush were effective in persuading the Pennsylvania State Legislature to pass penal reform laws in 1789 and 1790. Today, the Society is known as the **Pennsylvania Prison Society.**[43]

Rush supported the popular view at the time that crime was a spreading moral disease. He held that all habits of injurious tendency—or criminal acts—were diseases and could be cured. For example, he thought that practices such as alcoholism and masturbation could be cured by constant employment in bodily or physical behavior. Two days of solitary confinement would cause the inmate to internalize self-control because of a guilty conscience. He designed an "immobilizing tranquilizing chair" for the mentally ill and disobedient inmates.[44]

Although we know now that there are many causes of crime, Rush's efforts did spawn the correctional volunteer movement as we now recognize it in our jails. Conditions in jails did improve. The "immobilizing tranquilizing chair" gave way to more humane securing devices and restraints that are employed in our jails today.

## THE HISTORY AND DEVELOPMENT OF JAILS IN THE UNITED STATES

The methods of imprisonment and styles of correctional management in England and Europe had an influence on early jails in the United States. By the seventeenth century, very few jails were constructed with brick; most were built out of wood and were in need of constant maintenance and repair. The average size of early colonial jails was small: 15 feet by 10 feet. The colonies continued the jail customs and practices that were brought from England, where incarcerating offenders was not the norm except for certain religious, political, and debtor cases.[45]

### Walnut Street Jail and Early American Jails

With American independence and the efforts of Dr. Benjamin Rush, jail conditions improved somewhat with the construction in 1773 of the Walnut Street Jail in Philadelphia. At first, the Walnut Street Jail was a typical English jail with no classification and jailors charged fees to inmates regardless of their ability to pay. From 1790, the jail served two purposes common to the time—as a local jail and as a state penitentiary for adjudicated and sentenced inmates. Conditions at the jail began to improve resulting in many eastern U.S. states such as New York, Massachusetts, Maryland, Vermont, Kentucky, Ohio, and Virginia constructing penal facilities that were modeled after the Walnut Street Jail.[46]

The improvements in conditions at the Walnut Street Jail have evolved into practices in jails today. Specifically those improvements were:[47]

- Weekly visits by a doctor allowing inmates access to medical care.
- Religious services held every Sunday with mandatory inmate attendance (not practiced currently as all religious programs in jail are voluntary).
- Establishment of prison industries where inmates were paid wages and allowed to keep all earnings above the maintenance costs.
- Inmate discipline improved: The disciplinary system was progressive; a system of rewards and punishments was used to keep control of inmates.
- Inspections: The mayor and aldermen of Philadelphia established a Board of Inspectors who inspected the jail for deficiencies in its conditions and operations on a weekly basis, as well as provided supervision to the jail.

Not all early American jail structures were as progressive as the Walnut Street Jail. The terms *jail* and *prison* became intermingled as America struggled with what to do with criminals. Whatever the term used, the various humble and poorly built structures built in the 1600s, 1700s, and early 1800s have disappeared. Counties were ordered to build jails, but many chose to either ignore the order or build jails in a cheap, substandard fashion. For example, in Virginia, the earliest county prisons that have survived are dated from approximately 1800 to 1820, because of the reform movement. As new ideas took hold in what to do with inmates, more durable jails were built. Records of early Virginia jails are mostly obscure. Records do indicate that early Virginia jails were dwellings, storehouses, or any structure that a citizen could lease to the government for a profit.[48]

In Virginia, for example, prisons and jails were constructed for short-term stays of runaway slaves and servants, debtors, offenders awaiting trial, and those offenders who were sentenced. Separate buildings were constructed for debtors and criminals. Security then, as is now, was a major concern. Because many jails were poorly constructed, it was easy for desperate inmates to make their escape. Inmates would simply puncture the walls. Realizing the problem, authorities began to incorporate improvements as close studding in the walls, double and triple lined walls, installing iron bars, stronger locks, and building perimeter walls to make escapes more difficult. In the last 25 years of the sixteenth century, Virginia started to build brick and log prisons to improve on the trend of frame jail construction.[49]

The Colonial Jail in Williamsburg, Virginia is still standing and serves as an excellent example of early colonial jails. The jail was constructed in 1703–1704 and was in use as a prison for the colony of Virginia, the City of Williamsburg and James City County until 1910. Detainees in the jail included murderers, pirates, thieves, runaway slaves, loyalists (citizens loyal to the British Crown during the American Revolution), prisoners of war, and offenders with mental problems. Prisoners were held there until trial and if convicted, remained in the jail awaiting execution of sentence. Inmates inside the jail were subjected to harsh and inhospitable conditions, such as the use of leg irons, handcuffs, and chains. During the Revolutionary War, high incidents of illness and in-custody deaths were attributed to overcrowding. Prison food was not very palatable, described by inmates as "salt beef damaged and Indian meal." Few accounts exist from inmates who were held there, but one British prisoner incarcerated there from 1779 to 1780 described his stay: "We had for our domicile a place not ten feet square . . . the only light admitted was thro' the grating of the door . . . light and air are nearly excluded for the bars . . . were from three to four inches thick. In one corner of this snug mansion was fixed a kind of Throne [author's note: During a tour of this jail in researching this book, the jail staff defined a 'throne' as a chair toilet in which human waste was emptied through a chute to a container under the surface of the courtyard] which had been of use to miscreants such as us for 60 years past, and in certain points of wind rendered the air truly Mephitic." Gaolors (jailors) lived in separate quarters, sometimes with their families, and complained frequently that their salaries were substandard due to the responsibilities, hazards, and dangers of the job.[50]

The average length of stay at the jail was no longer than 90 days due to the General Court meeting in Williamsburg four times per year. In ideal conditions (no crowding), three to four people would be assigned to each cell. Female prisoners were kept in cells on the second floor of the jail.[51]

During the nineteenth century, three penal designs and management styles competed for prominence in the United States. While the history of jails in the United States is sketchy and varied, each made a contribution to the American jail. Several of their aspects are still present in today's jail. The three styles are the Pennsylvania System, the Auburn System, and the Reformatory System; their supporters attempted during the nineteenth century to convince state penal systems to adapt their ways of inmate management.

## Pennsylvania System

As the Walnut Street Jail became overcrowded, it became apparent that a new penal facility had to be constructed. In Philadelphia, the Eastern State Penitentiary was built in Philadelphia and incorporated the Quaker ideas about inmates being isolated. Inmates were confined in cells, approximately 8 feet by 12 feet in size. Each cell had running water and a toilet, but no windows. What was unique about this type of prison architecture was that each inmate had his own exercise yard which was a yard 8 feet by 20 feet in size. This courtyard was surrounded by a high, thick brick wall that actually rendered the area soundproof. Inmates had no contact, either visual or sound with other inmates; the only other human contact with anyone was with prison officers, chaplains, or a religious person who would pray with the inmate and offer spiritual advice and counseling.[52]

The Eastern State Penitentiary replaced the aging Walnut Street Jail in 1829. The main goals were solitude, repentance, and reflection on a life of crime. These practices included inmates spending all of their time alone except for approved contact with others as previously described, eating alone, and reading the Bible. The more bizarre practices included inmates wearing hoods and masks whenever they were allowed out of their cells. It was believed that inmates would not be "contaminated" by other inmates and widespread solitary confinement would control inmates by preventing maladaptive behavior and misconduct. For this reason, the Pennsylvania System was known as the **Separate System.** Cells were built at right angles off of long central corridors. Inmates were allowed small work projects such as making shoes, weaving and dying clothes, caning chairs, and hand rolling cigars. Products from these handicrafts were sold to help defray the

Hallway: Eastern State Penitentiary, one inmate per cell, solitary confinement. Early example of linear design.

Photo reprinted with permission of the American Correctional Association.

costs of running the prison.[53] This style of cells off a corridor at right angles was an early version of the linear jail/prison housing design.

## Auburn System

Due to overcrowding at New York's Newgate Prison, state officials authorized the construction of the Auburn Prison in Auburn, New York between the years of 1816 and 1825. Inmates were confined separately at night as in the Pennsylvania System, but were allowed to eat together and work together in shops and factories during the day. For this reason—inmates working and eating together—the Auburn System was called the **Congregate System.** Discipline was harsh; inmates were not allowed to speak to each other, and rule violations were punished by corporal punishment methods such as the pillory and whipping. Inmates wore the familiar striped uniforms.[54]

Concerning the physical plant of the Auburn type prisons, it was markedly different than the Pennsylvania System. In Auburn type institutions, cellblocks were multitiered double rows of cells that did not have exterior walls, or a type of cellblock building within a larger one. The cells on the tiers were completely surrounded by a corridor, or walkway. This type of design—cellblocks "stacked" upon one another in tiered layers—was called **inside cells** or the **interior cellblock.**[55] This type of architecture gave the prison added security as inmates were not able to tunnel through and outside wall.

Interior cellblock of the Bristol County Ash Street Facility, opened in 1826.

Photo by author, courtesy Bristol County Sheriff's Office.

Economics is an important factor in correctional management today, and the same was true in the 1800s. The Pennsylvania and Auburn Systems clashed for supremacy. In the Pennsylvania System, it was thought that the inmate could redeem himself or herself from a life of crime by reflection, solitude, and penitence. The Auburn System saw inmates as a labor pool and instituted harsh discipline to keep inmates in line.

Whereas the Pennsylvania System put inmates to work individually inside their cells, the Auburn System saw the value of congregate inmate work groups to increase production. Private businesses would pay fees to the state prisons for permission to use the labor of inmates in penal factories. Inmates in prison workshops worked for private businesses under the **contract system.** The contract system was primarily used in the northern U.S. states, while in the western and southern U.S. states, inmates were "rented" out to businesses under the **lease system.** Inmates under the lease system worked on farms, plantations, and privately owned businesses and in mines, sometimes under harsh conditions.

This also overlapped into the cost of housing. Auburn inmates were confined to their cells only at night, as opposed to Pennsylvania System inmates who spent their entire sentences inside a cell. As a result, Auburn System cells were cheaper to build and maintain. More inmates could be housed inside an Auburn System prison as opposed to the Pennsylvania System.[56]

It was no surprise to many that the Auburn type of prison management won out for economic reasons. They were cheaper to build and turned a profit, as individual handicrafts in cells could not compete with inmate factories. From the 1820s to the 1870s, almost 30 state prisons were constructed and many converted Pennsylvania System type institutions to Auburn type prisons. The interior cellblock revolutionized the way in which inmates were housed.[57]

**FIGURE 1-2** Systems in Conflict: Pennsylvania vs. Auburn

## Reformatory System

While the Pennsylvania System concentrated on the moral redemption of the inmate, and the Auburn System looked upon inmates as workers to turn a profit (along with the lease system in the West and South), a group of penal reformers attempted to try again to reform inmates and get them ready for life outside the prison.

In 1876, several years after the 1870 National Prison Congress in Cincinnati approved the reform-minded Declaration of Principles, a prison called a "reformatory" opened in Elmira, New York under the direction of Zebulon Brockway, who promised a "different prison procedure." The **Reformatory System** held that young offenders between the ages of 16 and 26 could be reformed through the efforts of personnel in education, medicine, and job training and others knowledgeable in the social sciences. Offenders entering reformatories were to be studied, classified into the proper grade, and treated by social science personnel. Inmates were given a minimum sentence, such as one year, without a maximum term indicated, called an **indeterminate sentence.** How soon they earned release depended on their efforts to reform. Reformatory prisons used parole as early release; at the end of the minimum term of confinement, a parole board examined the inmate's case to see if the inmate had readied himself or herself for early release. This readiness was determined by earning or losing credits in the reformatory and positive information about the inmate's activities (such as programs), habits, associations, and reputation. The entire case of the inmate was examined: offense, criminal record, conduct history within the prison, academic progress (such as attending school), and future plans upon release. If the inmate attended programs in the social sciences such as in education and job training, the progress was noted and the chances for parole were increased. The daily routine for inmates in reformatories included work compensated by pay, job training programs, physical exercise, and a well-planned diet. The thought among penologists at the time was that the good habits of the mind and positive behavior were best developed through the good habits of the body.[58] Indeterminate sentences today have evolved into a "carrot and stick" approach (one to five years, etc.) for inmates, based on the early Reformatory approach.

A unique feature of the reformatory prison was the method in which inmates were classified and graded. Three grades existed, and all inmates started in the second grade. At the Elmira Reformatory, an offender who abided by the prison rules for at least six months could advance to the first grade. In making progress to the first grade, inmates were rewarded by having comfortable blue prison uniforms, spring mattresses, daily writing allowances, better food, extended library hours, and extended bedtime hours. Demotion to the third grade due to bad behavior resulted in coarse red uniforms, marching in lockstep with other inmates, and the denial of mail, visiting, and library privileges. Work was regarded as a means to teach inmates good industrial habits and rewards, and there was a pay incentive for good work.[59] All of the good behaviors and incentives to change by the inmate were to be considered in weighing the possibility of release on parole.

The idea of the adult inmate reformatory prison spread in the late nineteenth century. Reformatories were built in the following states: Michigan (1877), Massachusetts (1884), Pennsylvania and Minnesota (1889), Colorado (1890), Illinois (1891), Kansas (1895), Ohio (1895), Indiana (1896), and Wisconsin (1899). State systems varied in inmate eligibility criteria such as age and offense.

Michigan adhered to a punitive type philosophy and engaged in a lease-for-profit inmate work system, which made it markedly different from other states in their reformatory practices.[60]

Though the ideas and goals of reformatories were some of the best reforms proposed in corrections in over 100 years, the reformatory idea failed for several reasons, especially with problems that became apparent at the Elmira, New York Reformatory. One was the lack of funding, not just at Elmira but also at other prisons. The reformatory prison based its philosophy on reforming inmates through programs, but it could not do so in the Auburn style architecture of Gothic and fortress-like structures. The three-grade classification system was used to punish inmates rather than to try to reform them. Also, while Brockway's targets were young, first-time criminal offenders, approximately one third of the inmates coming in were repeat and hard-core offenders. Research has revealed that Brockway permitted harsh corporal punishment at the Elmira Reformatory, surprising it appears for a progressive penal reform philosophy. There were indications that management at Elmira was substandard, medical treatment was inadequate, and weaker inmates were terrorized and harassed by stronger, predatory inmates, allegedly with staff approval.[61]

Problems existed in other reformatories, and indicate how the system as a whole crumbled. In the Colorado Reformatory, inmates were not classified or separated; young offenders were housed with the old, and sick inmates lived with healthy inmates. Supplies for educational programs such as schoolbooks were lacking. There were flaws in the work programs that were to inspire inmates on the values and rewards of hard work. Inmates through working, for example, may have earned 40 cents per day, but had to pay 32 cents for room and board. Also, there were fees charged to the inmates to see the prison doctor and dentist. Rule infractions could result in as much as 60 cents being charged. Many inmates could not pay for necessities and as a result got "written up." If they incurred too many written reprimands, they were demoted to the third grade.[62] The inmates in these reformatories were victims of mismanagement and the failure of the reformatory ideal.

While reforms were occurring in the penitentiaries of the heavily populated northern states, what remained untouched were the many local jails in the counties and towns. A census of prisoners conducted in 1880 revealed that there were 58,609 inmates in the United States, not counting juveniles held in reformatories. A further breakdown of this total revealed that penitentiaries held 30,659 inmates, 7,865 were in workhouses and houses of corrections, 12,691 were held in county jails, 1,666 were in city prisons, military prisons held 499, 350 were in hospitals for the mentally insane, and 4,879 were under lease as laborers to private parties.[63]

At the local level, jails could be described as a variety of buildings and practices, lacking in uniformity. Penal reformer Enoch Wines in 1880 described Michigan's jails as "no work, no instruction, no discipline, and no uniformity of structure." The innocent and depraved, he said, were thrown together in "intimate and continuous association," indicating that there was no classification system. In rural Iowa, the local jail was called the **calaboose** and was described as a small, or tiny, simple building. Tramps and drunks were housed there before being taken to county jails over muddy and unpaved roads. The town of Grand Mound, Iowa found a profitable use for its jail—the beds were rented out to travelers.[64]

Today the discipline of corrections is more enlightened and progressive than it was 200 years ago. The reformers and penologists who advocated the Pennsylvania, Auburn, and Reformatory Systems all had the belief that what they wanted for the inmates was the right direction. While some prisons and jails allowed harsh discipline and corporal punishment, it is fortunate that such practices have not carried over into today's jail. However, what is positively seen in jails today could be traced back to these systems:

*Pennsylvania System:* With cells off at right angles to a central corridor, this style of cell placement is similar to the linear type of jail architecture that is seen in older jails today. The idea that inmates should be alone and reflect and do penitence for their lives of crime is not practiced today, but segregating disciplinary problem inmates or inmates on administrative segregation is a viable option and in some cases today a necessity. It is hoped by veteran jail staff that the inmate while isolated will take the time to think about his actions. The religious jail and prison movement in America had its early development in the Pennsylvania System, where religious clergy and volunteer citizens were allowed to come into the institution to offer spiritual advice and prayer.

*Auburn System:* The key contribution of the Auburn System was the interior cellblock. While some older jails do not have multiple stacks of tiers containing rows of cells, the main premise—building a cellblock area *within* a building resulting in inmates not having access to exterior walls—is still a security mainstay of many jails. Another contribution of the Auburn System is inmate labor. Today inmates are not exploited as in the past; jail industries and work programs can teach inmates a trade and can benefit the jail. Today, jail inmates can work and attend programs in groups. The amount and type of jail programs varies due to funding and staffing.

*Reformatory System:* Organized jail programs most likely had their start in the Reformatory System. Today, educational and vocational instructors and volunteers come into the jails to assist inmates in preparation for release. Inmates today can be reclassified based on progressive behavior and program participation inside the jail. Jail inmates can prepare for appearances before parole boards and their representatives who come to the jail. Where recreation was offered in Reformatory Systems, recreation is offered to jail inmates today. The emphasis on a proper diet for inmates in Reformatory System prisons has carried over to inmate dietary standards today.

**FIGURE 1-3** Contributions of the Three Systems

## Northern U.S. Jails

As the new nation grew, so did the need for locally confining criminals. An example of this is Onadaga County, New York, which became the twenty-first county in New York State in 1794. The population of this developing county included two Iroquois Indian reservations and approximately 2,000 settlers. The law enforcement in this county was typical for counties that were growing in the early history of the United States; it was the responsibility of the local county sheriff. Early in its history, Onondaga County did not have a jail and prisoners were transported to neighboring jurisdictions east of the county, which meant trips of 40 to 60 miles depending on the destination. Sheriffs in the early days of the United States had primary occupations; being a sheriff was secondary. The fee system was not profitable; neither was transporting prisoners and taking time away from a primary job.[65]

Seeing the need for a jail, construction commenced in 1802. The trend in early U.S jails was to build the jail near to or combine it with the local county courthouse.

The new jail was a wooden two story building 50 feet square, with the jail and jailor's living quarters on the first floor and the courthouse on the second floor. The jailor's apartment, in which he could live with his family, was separated from the cell area by a hallway. The cells were constructed of heavy oak plank, connected by wrought iron spikes for extra security. Doors to the cells were made of the same oak plank and iron combination, and had a diamond-shaped hole in the center through which the jailor passed meals to the inmates and light could enter the cell. Grated windows were at the rear of the cells. Debtors were confined in the jail, but were not treated with the severity of felons, such as in the use of leg irons. Debtors were a concern to early jailors; in Onondaga County, the jailor was responsible for making good the debtor's debt if the debtor inmate escaped from the jail. With the rise of penal reform in the 1820s, inmates were treated more humanely. As the county grew, so did the need for a more secure jail. In 1829, a stone jail was built in Syracuse solely for incarceration and to provide jailor's quarters. A new courthouse was constructed across the street.[66]

Not all jails followed the example of Onandoga County and constructed a stone jail. In Herkimer, New York, the jail was similar to the first Onondaga jail, a combination courthouse and jail built of wood. In January 1834, inmates were lighting newspaper clippings that were pasted on a cell wall, using a candle. The resulting fire destroyed the jail/courthouse and a church located across the street. As a result, changes in jail design were made.[67]

In Barnstable County, Massachusetts the old colonial jail, described as a five-bay two-story house, was in use until approximately 1820. The old jail was built circa 1690–1700 by Barnstable County per orders of the Plymouth and Massachusetts Bay Colony Courts. Counties got a lot of use out of existing buildings and the old jail served in an auxiliary capacity until 1854–1855. In keeping with improvements in jail construction, a new stone jail was constructed in 1820. At that time, the old jail saw use as a barn.[68]

Lawbreakers could be held in cells in police stations, and the more serious offenders went to the local jail or "big house." One such lockup was described by George Walling as a place where men and women are hauled to the cells in a state of "beastly intoxication" shouting and screaming. The cells he described as "loathsome" where sleeping or just getting comfortable was difficult. Inmates with mental problems, alcohol withdrawals, and fear would be confined there, "howling" and "sobbing." At New York City's Ludlow Street Jail, an inmate of financial means could get a comfortable room instead of a cell by paying the jailor $15 per week. They could eat good meals at the warden's table; a few rich inmates paid between $50 and $100 per week for a nicely furnished room, and had their meals served to them. The nonpaying inmates had bread, soup, tea, and coffee. Inmates had to be quick and grab the bread through the cell door as fast as they could.[69]

New York City also boasted the notorious "Tombs," a four-story jail opened in 1838. The architecture of the Tombs was said to resemble an Egyptian tomb. The jail had cells for both men and women, but had a system also where inmates who could pay stayed in comfortable rooms. Conditions were squalid and the courtrooms were known to reek of the odors of Tombs inmates brought to them. Sentenced inmates, mentally ill inmates commonly known as lunatics, and inmates withdrawing from alcohol were housed on the first floor. The second floor was known as "Murderers' Row," and housed murderers, burglars, highway robbers, and other serious and desperate offenders. Persons arrested for grand larceny were on the third floor, and the fourth floor was for housing minor criminals and misdemeanants.[70]

An example of a northern U.S. jail is the Bristol County Ash Street Facility, which opened in 1826 and is still operational today.

Photo by author, courtesy Bristol County Sheriff's Office.

## Southern U.S. Jails

The Civil War devastated the Southern economy due to savage warfare destroying many businesses, farms, and plantations. Also, the mainstays of the Southern labor force, slaves, were now free. As the South rebuilt itself, it wrestled with the fundamental question of where to put criminals, and who was going to work the farms, plantations, shops, factories, etc.

The answer was to use convicts in the prisons and jails. Through the lease system, inmate leasing in the South became very profitable. Inmates were transported to work sites in crowded, filthy caged jail wagons, guarded by officers with pistols and shotguns. Dogs served as "posses" and chased down escaping prisoners. The work was back breaking: picking cotton, cutting timber, road construction, and working in quarries and canals. Relying mostly on camps, newly freed slaves and returning soldiers who were arrested were put to work in the South. The penal institutions due to damage, destruction, and disrepair could not handle the increase in the confined criminal population.[71]

The lease system proved to be a form of legalized slavery. Private businesses rented inmate labor from either state or county corrections authorities. The conditions of confinement of leased inmates were so bad that bureaucrats whose job it was to inspect the operations refused to even enter the facilities. Corruption was rampant with bribes and deals. At the turn of the century, the conditions of leased inmates were so bad that the federal government and labor unions began to strenuously object to its use. The lease system began to decline, and its negative influence helped in the creation of the United States Bureau of Prisons.[72]

Southern U.S. jail: jail wagon, inmates were kept in these wagons when not working. Conditions were squalid.

Photo reprinted with permission of the American Correctional Association.

Southern jails were Spartan and plain. However, inmates in some Southern jails were better off than other inmates in jail wagons, working in fields or on chain gangs. The Cleveland County, North Carolina jail was described in 1870 as a brick building 30 feet by 26 feet in size, three stories high, with four cells for prisoners, including a cell for debtors and an iron cage. Male and female inmates were separated. There was no way to heat the jail in cold weather except to give the inmates a heated rock. Some of the inmates suffered frostbite in cold weather. Bedding consisted of a straw bed and three blankets. Inmates could have as much fresh water and food as they wanted. Excrement was removed from the jail, and the smell of it was nullified by burning tar in the cells.[73]

## Midwest Jails

Jails in the Midwest had a colorful history, and not all of it positive. For example, in Hannibal, Missouri there were no provisions for a jail when Hannibal became a city in 1845. Before the establishment of the first local jail, the ordinances in Hannibal did not specify any punishment by placing offenders inside a jail. Unlawful acts were punished by levying a fine if the offender was white and specific lashing on the back in cases of black offenders. In 1847, a one-room building was designated as the city of Hannibal's calaboose, holding offenders convicted of drunkenness, fighting, and theft. The city ruled that slave owners could place unruly slaves in the "jail" at a fee of ten cents per day, and in 1849 a high fence to thwart escapes was built around the calaboose. The building became unfit for human habitation due to the lack of sanitary facilities. In 1851, a new limestone and cobblestone jail was built; citizens were paid to feed the prisoners for 15 cents per day at first for a daily menu of bread and water. When the fee was increased to 20 cents per day, the typical jail fare was potato, bacon, bread, and coffee served three times per day. Inmates confined in the Hannibal calaboose were required to work on streets, on curbing, in the city quarry, all under guard. Another method of security was the inmate chained to a heavy metal ball. Due to disrepair, a new jail was built in 1878, and when the land on which it stood was sold, a new stone jail was constructed and opened in 1886. The 1886 jail was used until the present Hannibal jail opened in 1976.[74]

The Midwest also has the distinction of having one of three remaining standing **squirrel cage jails** in the United States. Built in 1885 in Council Bluffs, Iowa for a total cost of $30,000, the squirrel cage jail was a three-level jail built inside a cage. Each floor had revolving pie-shaped cells that could be turned for easy staff access to inmates. Another part of the building had offices for the jailor, quarters for inmate workers, a kitchen, and living quarters for female inmates. The rotary design was patented in 1881 by William H. Brown and Benjamin F. Haugh, both from Indiana. They said that the purpose of the rotary design was "to produce a jail in which prisoners can be controlled without the necessity of personal contact between them and the jailer . . . . . . [the jail provides]

Exterior view (caged area was probably recreation yard) of the Johnson County Jail, (1872–1974) Nebraska.

Reprinted by permission: Nebraska Crime Commission, Michael E. Behm, Executive Director.

Interior cellblock view; Johnson County Jail.

Reprinted by permission: Nebraska Crime Commission, Michael E. Behm, Executive Director.

'maximum security with minimum jailer attention'. One jail deputy was reported to say "If a jailer could count . . . . . . and he had a trusty [inmate worker] he could trust . . . he could control the jail."[75]

## Western U.S. Jails

The jails of the American West have been portrayed as secure, brick structures operated by a strict, "Old West" type sheriff who took good care of the "bad guys." In reality, the jails of the old west were a potpourri of different buildings of different sizes. It is evident in American history that the western part of the United States had a history of lawlessness, booming business and development, and conflicts between social classes. The question to sheriffs in the West was essentially the same as in other parts of the United States—where do we put the criminals? Towns began to boom as miners, farmers, cattlemen, and railroaders came to seek their fortune. As always, booming development brings crime and crime brings a need for incarceration. In the American West, a guiding management principle for jails could be termed as "whatever works."

Washington State and Idaho had a history of mining in the 1880s. In Black Diamond, Washington, a very small jail was built but fortunately, the town of Black Diamond had very little crime; many of the mine workers were married and had families. The jail was primarily used for drunks, persons fighting, and petty offenses. The jail, built circa 1910, was placed on a cinder block foundation, was an all-wood structure made from two by fours laid flat on each other. The exterior walls were over the two by fours in a board and batt type of construction. The jail had two cells for offenders and a marshal's office in front, and was wired for electricity. Heat came from a wood stove.[76]

Burke, Idaho had its founding in 1884. As it is located in rich mining country, the wild antics of the miners necessitated the construction of a jail in 1888. Burke's jail was 18 feet by 30 feet and was built of wood and iron. Prisoners were transported quickly from the court to the sheriff's jail by train. Because jail inspections were virtually unknown in the late 1800s, jail sanitary conditions were handled quite differently than today. In 1893, the town marshal attached a fire hose to the water main and simply hosed out the jail, which was considered filthy and neglected. In 1923 a fire destroyed the jail; the following year a new jail measuring 10 feet by 12 feet with two cells was built of concrete. As the town became more civilized and the mine activity decreased, this jail was only 120 square feet in size, whereas the original jail was four times larger.[77]

In Echo, Oregon, the city jail was located on the first floor of city hall, and was built in 1916. Prior to placing the jail inside city hall, it is believed that a building was rented from a private citizen and used as the jail. The Echo jail was small, but was considered state of the art for the early twentieth century. The jail had two side-by-side 9 foot by 5 foot cells that were divided by a concrete wall three and one half inches thick. The room that housed the jail had walls seven and one half inches thick. The jail floor was concrete and the ceiling was plaster. Each jail cell could hold one or two inmates. The jail boasted inside plumbing and electricity, and heat was supplied from a coal-fired boiler.[78]

Another method of operating local jails was to combine the city hall and the jail such as in Park City, Utah—a mining town that had a lot of crime from miners, prostitutes, gamblers, and saloon patrons. A city jail opened in the basement of the city hall in 1885. The city jail was nicknamed the "dungeon" because of its underground location. The Park City "dungeon" jail continued to serve city residents until 1964.[79]

In keeping with the image of the Wild West, sometimes the locals may act out their displeasure with the local jail. In Prescott, Washington, a small town jail was built for confining offenders arrested for drunkenness, being disorderly, and engaging in misconduct such as gunplay. A jail was necessary because the town marshal had to take offenders on a 16-mile ride to the county jail in Walla Walla. In 1903, the City Council authorized the construction of a town jail. The jail was 10 feet by 14 feet, constructed with two by sixes that were stacked and spiked together. Floor and ceiling planks were two inches thick, and the only window was a small, barred hole situated in the heavy thick door. The Prescott jail had no accommodations such as heat, light, or water. One night, a group of cowboys attacked the jail in retaliation for their recent stay there. Using horses and lassos (ropes), the group tried to turn the jail over, but it was too heavy. In 1915 a fire destroyed most of Prescott's business district, rendering the need for a jail obsolete.[80]

Jails in the growing cities of the western United States adapted to the times. In Spokane, Washington in 1881, the Spokane jail consisted of wooden two by fours or two by sixes stacked on top of one another. Prisoners could look outside through small barred windows. A new city jail, also of wood, opened in 1888, located behind city offices and adjacent to the morgue. This jail boasted a "cage" where tramps and vagrants could meet and, as one newspaper described, "recount their sad experiences." There was an apartment for female prisoners. The old jail could not hold inmates and many escapes occurred. Circa 1894, the jail moved to a three-story brick building that also housed the fire department and the police department. Prisoners worked the "rock pile," which was a pile of rocks located behind the jail. Either for punishment or exercise, inmates would carry rocks from one pile to another and back again.[81]

By 1910, the population of Spokane was nearly 104,000 citizens and the need again became clear for a new city jail. In 1913, a new brick and stone trim jail opened in the city office building. As is the case with many old jails, this jail was used by the city of Spokane until 1960. A parallel development in the 1880s was the construction of a wooden county jail in 1881 at a price of $285.00 in nearby Cheney, to which the county government had moved. Some officials saw a need to combine the county jail in Cheney with the Spokane jail. In 1887, the Cheney jail closed, and a new county jail was built in Spokane in 1887. This jail conducted hangings until 1900 when executions were transferred to the state prison at Walla Walla.[82]

In 1895, a new county jail with a 200-inmate capacity was built as part of a new courthouse complex. Cells held four men and were 6 feet by 8 feet by 8 feet. Security was improved, but there were no dayrooms and narrow walkways containing a sink and shower. The quality of the steel was not good and was susceptible to corrosion. Inmates were locked inside their cells from 4:30 P.M. to 6:30 A.M., and the jail had a female inmate ward with two matrons on duty. The females were shifted to the city jail in 1917 because few female inmates were ever held in the jail. Misdemeanants were held in the Spokane city jail, and felons were taken first to the city jail and then to the county jail after a hearing. Female misdemeanants and felons were confined in the city jail.[83]

In many jurisdictions, combining city and county jails is a viable option that both streamlines operations and makes sense financially. Spokane serves as a good example of this. By the 1960s, Spokane realized this and opened a modern 410-prisoner capacity county jail in 1970 to replace the 1895 jail, and in 1986 opened a 483-bed facility.[84]

At the turn of the century in 1900, jails in the United States were a mixture of both different physical plants and management styles. Conditions in many were substandard, and this situation would not change until the corrections litigation explosion and the birth of jail standards in the 1960s and 1970s.

In 1923, J.F. Fishman authored *Crucibles of Crime: The Shocking Story of the American Jail.* In this landmark work, he defined the American jail as:

> An unbelievable filthy institution in which are confined men and women serving sentences for misdemeanors and crimes, and men and women not under sentence who are simply awaiting trial. With few exceptions, having no segregation of the unconvicted from the convicted, the well from the diseased, the youngest and most impressionable from the most degraded and hardened. Usually swarming with bedbugs, roaches, lice and other vermin; has an odor of disinfectant and filth which is appalling; supports in complete idleness countless thousands of able bodies[d] men and women, and generally affords ample time and opportunity to assure inmates a complete course in every kind of viciousness and crime. A melting pot in which the worst elements of the raw material in the criminal world are brought forth blended and turned out in absolute perfection.[85]

As the American West grew, primitive jails were not the only places where offenders were confined. In California, the 1849 Gold Rush stimulated the economy and development of California, especially in the cities of San Francisco and Sacramento. Tens of thousands of people came to California to "strike it rich" and seek their fortunes. As the area grew from mining and business development, crime increased also. The courts and vigilante law enforcement of Sacramento recognized the need for a place to hold lawbreakers. In 1850, authorities in the Sacramento courts authorized the building of a county jail. It is not clear according to researchers who initiated the idea of using a ship to hold offenders. The city fathers may have been influenced by the British system of the 1700s where the prisoner overflow languished in the holds of old ships. Starting as a temporary measure, the British used hulks until 1856. They may also have imitated the city of San Francisco, who bought the brig *Euphemis* and converted it [and] was a key factor as a ship could be stripped of certain fixtures and fitted with cells. No expensive and time-consuming construction was needed. British ships used to confine prisoners were termed prison hulks, while American ships holding prisoners became known as jail hulks.[86]

During the 1850s, the city of Sacramento used three jail hulks: the *Stafford*, the *Stirling*, and the *La Grange*. The *La Grange* was modified by portioning the ship into cells and adding a topside deck superstructure. Inmates were segregated according to type of crime and gender. The solid oak forward cabin was used as a dungeon. Conditions were harsh in the name of security; iron shafts were embedded in the oak cell walls and prisoners were shackled to them each night. In addition to being shackled, prisoners were outfitted with a ball and chain, riveted to their leg. Escapes did occur, sometimes at a rate of four to five per year, even though the jail hulk was advertised by officials as escape proof. In a desperate measure to stop escapes, the Sacramento County Board of Supervisors stated that for each escape, $500 would be deducted from the sheriff's office budget. As a result of this financial incentive, the number of escapes decreased. Finances then, as now, played a role in local corrections. Jail hulk inmates were used on chain gangs, doing roadwork. Inmates were confined in the jail hulk for a variety of crimes; one census conducted in 1855 revealed that the 39 inmates were incarcerated and awaiting trial for a variety of crimes including grand larceny, petty larceny, assault and battery, robbery, and keeping a gambling house open on Sunday. Four additional prisoners were awaiting transport to the state prison, which brought the total confined to 43. Sacramento built a new combined courthouse and jail in 1855 and the use of jail hulks was phased out.[87]

**FIGURE 1-4** America's Use of the Jail Hulk

J.F. Fishman was a jail inspector, and his observations and writings were based on the 1,500 jails he observed. In 1880, the United Census Bureau started compiling information about U.S. jails, noting information every ten years concerning ethnicity, race, gender, and age. In 1923, the information being compiled was combined into now what is known as "jail statistics."[88]

By 1980, conditions in jails were gaining national attention after decades of inattention and ignorance. Sheriffs did what they could to confine inmates in an era where federal and state courts took very little notice of jail conditions. The neglect of local corrections and the use of old jail buildings built in the late nineteenth and early twentieth centuries were finally being noticed. Prison riots at the Attica state prison in New York had made Americans aware of the negative state of prisons. However, prisons were located away from population centers; many were in rural settings. By contrast, every locality—cities, towns, and counties—had a local jail. In a benchmark article published in August of 1980 in *Newsweek*, the majority of U.S. jails were described as "dirty, dangerous, overcrowded, unhealthy, and stupefyingly dull." It was clear that conditions in jails varied; in a Mississippi jail, the sheriff complained of trying to operate a jail that was built in 1845 and last renovated in 1901. By contrast, a Colorado jail was described as progressive and "mellow," where programs exist for inmates and jail guards are called "corrections specialists." In Alabama, a judge ordered a county jail to cease the practice of scraping dead animals ("road kill") off of a nearby highway and serving them to jail inmates per dinner. Cases such as this resulted in jails of the time being a creation of federal and state courts.[89]

In 1979, the U.S. Supreme Court in the landmark case of *Bell v. Wolfish* ruled that inmates in jail who have not yet been found guilty, or in other words, are in a pre trail status, cannot be "punished." This surprisingly frank declaration enabled the courts to stop through court orders some practices in jail that were deemed punitive. The case also afforded jail administrators "wide ranging deference" to run their jails. The *Bell* case was a clear warning beacon for localities to clean up their substandard jails. Inmates knowledgeable in court proceedings began to sue; in Florida, inmates brought a class action suit against the state's corrections department to have that Florida law which required corrections department to have minimum standards and jail inspections had not been enforced. Other inmates protested jail overcrowding, especially convicted felons waiting in jails for bed space in state prisons. Inmates in Massachusetts, New Mexico, and Mississippi protested in efforts to get out of local jails and into state prison systems. Several sheriffs in Louisiana and Mississippi transported jail inmates to the state prisons, and upon arrival, they were greeted by officials with court orders that denied them entry.[90]

Also targeted by criminologists was the need for adequately hired and trained staff. Understaffing and poor design resulted in inmate violence. Programs and recreation began to be recognized as tools to promote more positive operations in jail and better morale among both jail staff and inmates. The mentally ill in jail finally gained recognition as a problem; in a Florida jail, mentally disturbed jail inmates were handcuffed to an elevator so they could be watched closely by a jail officer.[91]

As a result of reports in the media as previously described, criticism from criminal justice professionals, and court action, the 1980s and 1990s saw jails being renovated or new jails being constructed. These efforts, in conjunction with standards and training, have not resulted in jails moving backward, but facilitate the progress that jails have experienced.

## CURRENT STATUS AND PROBLEMS OF U.S. JAILS: AN OVERVIEW

Jails are a unique institution in U.S. corrections. With over a half million offenders incarcerated in them and their management and architecture styles varying, there are important issues facing them. Ken Kerle, Ph.D., a leading authority on U.S.

jails, managing editor of *American Jails* and author of *Who's Who in Jail Management* gives a "snapshot" based on data for the fourth edition of *Who's Who in Jail Management*, published in 2003:[92]

| | *2003* | *1991* |
|---|---|---|
| Number of U.S. jails (total) | 3,276 | 3,353 |
| Regional jails | 75 | 25 |
| City jails | 200 | 287 |
| Rated jail capacity | 741,896 | 353,409 |

The **rated capacity** is the number of beds that were placed or built inside the jail when it was designed and constructed. This number can fluctuate due to renovations and additions to the jail.[93] While the rated capacity states the number of beds that the jail was designed for, the **operational capacity** is the level of population that a jail can safely function at day to day.[94] For example, a jail with a rated capacity of 300 makes available bed space in hallways and classrooms for an additional 100 spaces. The operational capacity is now 400. The jail superintendent or chief jailor determines the operational capacity after consultation with his or her staff. The operational capacity is based on such factors as double bunking, turning recreation areas into dormitories, etc. The student of corrections must understand the difference, as the rated capacity can be easily computed, while the operational capacity can vary among jails due to overcrowding, etc.

Such factors as jail closings, new construction, and openings of jails all influence the numbers of jails from survey to survey. For example, according to Kerle, the decline in the number of city jails is due to closings of very small "Mom and Pop" jails, or small local jails with a capacity of 0–100 inmates.[95]

## Overcrowding

Based on the popular saying, one could say when discussing the problems of today's jails "If you build one, they will come." Inmates coming into jail at increasing rates forces jurisdictions to renovate their jail, to build a new jail (both at taxpayer expense), or to merely crowd the inmates in. Some jails can handle the overflow simply due to their population base such as in rural or remote areas, while other jails in growing towns, cities, and counties experience simultaneous crime and population growth.

A snapshot example of a jurisdiction grappling with a jail-overcrowding problem is Davidson County, Tennessee. According to Sheriff Daron Hall, the 2000 census estimated the county's population at almost 570,000, with a projected increase of another 40,000 citizens by 2010. The county police force numbers just over 1,300. The jail population has increased to an average of 2,941 inmates, which is an all time high for the county. In the early 1980s, the federal courts took over the supervision of the county jail due to overcrowding and unconstitutional conditions. For ten years, the county was the target of federal lawsuits, court costs, and embarrassment. Upon the reinstatement of the county charter concerning the jail, Davidson County instituted a balanced approach to crime in an effort to improve local corrections. This balanced approach balances the capacity of the jail and the alternatives to incarceration. Sheriff Hall has a philosophy that the police arrest the criminal, while the local corrections system arrests the problem. Jail programs and alternatives to corrections assist to keep offenders out of jail. One example is the Davidson County Day Reporting Center (DRC), which opened in 1998. The DRC supervises 200 eligible offenders who would normally be in jail at a cost of $55 per day. The DRC cost is $10.25 per day; the DRC requires offenders to report several times per week for participation in substance abuse classes, anger management classes, education classes, and drug testing. If necessary, offenders diagnosed with mental problems must participate in mental health counseling. Offenders at the DRC must show proof of employment, pay supervision fees, and perform community service work.[96]

Strategies for reducing overcrowding are becoming clear to jail and local criminal justice administrators. Dr. Neal Vance, jail consultant and faculty member from the University of Arizona, states that in his experience there are 14 components found in the approximately 3,000 county-based local criminal justice systems that contribute to jail overcrowding. These components must be recognized and modified. They are:[97]

1. Cite and Release Practices: Encourage the usage by police of citations for minor offenses.
2. Initial Appearance in Court: Trends such as having a judicial officer such as a magistrate at the jail, a judge available for telephonic release, and weekend,

**Overcrowding forced the use of recreation area for dormitory housing. Norfolk County Correctional Center in Dedham, Massachusetts.**

Photo by author, courtesy of Sheriff Michael G. Bellotti and Deputy Superintendent David Reilly of the Norfolk County Sheriff's Office.

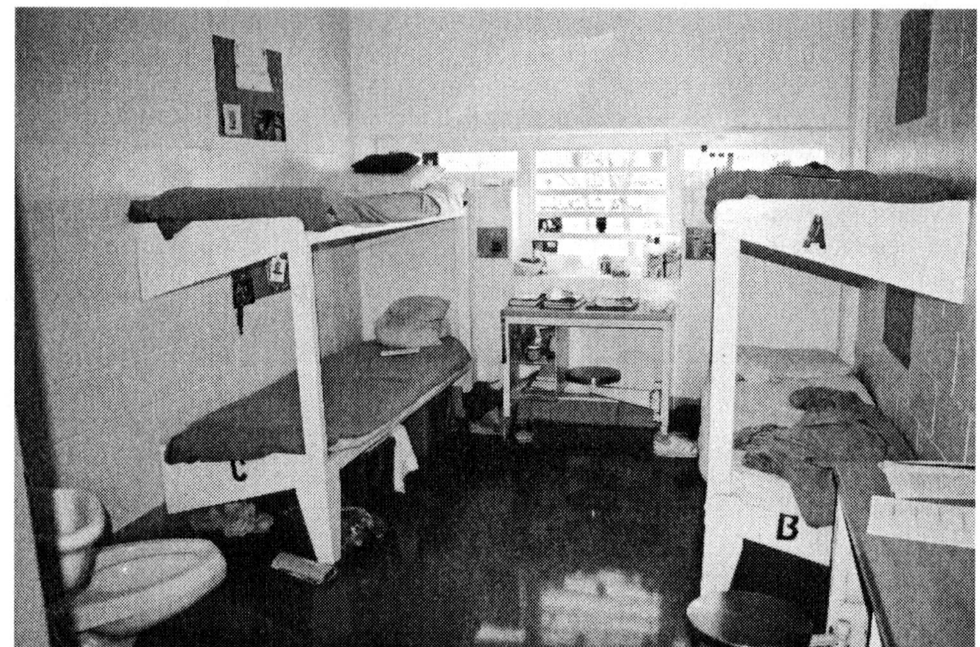


Bunking four inmates to a cell, Norfolk County Correctional Center.

Photo by author, courtesy of Sheriff Michael G. Bellotti and Deputy Superintendent David Reilly of the Norfolk County Sheriff's Office.

Coping with overcrowding: portable beds for inmates sleeping in dayroom.

Photo by author, courtesy of Sheriff Michael G. Bellotti and Deputy Superintendent David Reilly of the Norfolk County Sheriff's Office.

Dayroom area: Norfolk County Correctional Center.

Photo by author, courtesy of Sheriff Michael G. Bellotti and Deputy Superintendent David Reilly of the Norfolk County Sheriff's Office.

evening, or twice-a-day initial appearance in court can reduce the number of hours or days that misdemeanants or nonviolent felons are held in jail.

3. Bail and Pre-trial Release: Nonfinancial releases such as a supervised release program or release on personal recognizance should be more in use.
4. Prosecutors' Discretion: Some jurisdictions have a charging attorney or a representative from the district attorney's office available to make a determination to formally charge or "no paper" at time of arrest.
5. Waivers by Defense Counsel: Defense attorneys and public offenders often waive the rights to a speedy trial. Realistically, they should be encouraged to re-examine and be more active concerning in custody cases.
6. Alcohol-related Charges: An option to reduce crowding is the use of detoxification centers and treatment centers and prevention programs.
7. Mentally Ill Offenders: Mental health courts in large jurisdictions and locally funded mental health diversion programs in small jurisdictions would dispose cases of mentally ill offenders and divert them to proper treatment and not into the jail.
8. Probation Office: Local probation offices have an effect on jail overcrowding by violating clients and placing them in jail and also by conducting pre-sentence investigations (PSI) on jail inmates awaiting sentencing. Probation agencies should adopt graduated sanctions for technical violators and fast-tracking PSIs on inmates in custody.
9. Sentencing Alternatives: Minor offenders can benefit from community corrections programs, day reporting centers, etc. Not all inmates are appropriate for

inclusion in these programs, but many are which would reduce the number of inmates in the jail.

10. State Department of Correction Inmates: An inordinate number of inmates that have been convicted and sentenced are awaiting transport to state prison systems. This applies to smaller jails more than larger ones, and the process of getting these inmates to state prisons must be accelerated. In some jails "state ready" inmates make up a significant percentage of the jail populations.
11. Failures to Appear: Failures to appear (FTAs) in court does not necessarily mean that the offender is going to flee the jurisdiction. Many offenders have difficulty keeping appointment in court. For that reason, a pre-trial agency may assist offenders in keeping their court dates and avoiding jail time.
12. Warrants: Some jurisdictions have staffs that deal with the needs for warrants. In some cases, such as an offender already incarcerated in jail or prison, a FTA, or bench warrant is not necessary.
13. Court Case flow/Calendaring: Judges must be educated in scheduling court cases not so much for their personal schedule, but with the jail population situation in mind. Cases must be moved expediently through the system.
14. Management Information Systems (MIS): All jails, no matter their size, must have a system to collect and analyze data—tracking who is arrested and released. Inappropriate incarceration must be avoided.

An effort to keep inmates being released from state prisons from being re arrested and returning to local jails and thus adding to the local-jail-crowding problem is the Serious and Violent Offender Reentry Initiative Program of the U.S. Justice Department. Sixty-eight grants have been awarded to jurisdictions to develop programs in local jails and community treatment agencies. Adult and juvenile offenders coming out of prison and secure/residential juvenile facilities after being incarcerated for serious and violent crimes participate in three stages or phases: The Protect and Prepare phase consists of institutional programs in the local jail designed to get the inmate ready for release. The Control and Restore phase has the offender working with local agencies such as probation and parole and mental health. The final phase, Sustain and Support, connects the offender with agencies to assist them with problems in the long term after the offender officially has left criminal justice corrections supervision. Preparation for the program starts while the inmate is in prison and continues in the last phase of incarceration. This last phase may be at the local jail from where the inmate will be released to the community.[98] One option that the jail administrator has is in cases where the inmate is extremely hard core, noncooperative, and disruptive, the inmate will be returned to the department of corrections and not necessarily to the institution from where he was transferred to the jail. This serves to send inmates a message that if they do not cooperate with this initiative, they may not be permitted to finish their sentences in surroundings that are comfortable to them.

A simple approach to jail overcrowding is to build new facilities. It is not that easy for local jurisdictions to just build new jails. Often citizens in the community must be convinced that a new jail is necessary. Many citizens would rather spend tax dollars on transportation, education, etc. than on a jail. Town hearings and publicity campaigns take time.

In cases of extreme jail overcrowding, one option that may be necessary and not popular with the public is **early release.** Early release is the procedure where the jail relieves overcrowding by the authorized release of minor offenders, usually with the cooperation of the courts or other governmental authority.

Several jails have had to do this in the past few years either to relieve population pressure in the jail or to meet court orders, such as court-ordered population ceilings. In 2004, the Macomb County Jail in Michigan held 1,445 inmates, who were 7 inmates over capacity. Federal and state guidelines state that a jail cannot exceed capacity for more than 7 days. The jail had held as many as 70 inmates over capacity for almost 3 weeks. Sixty inmates who were confined for nonsupport, drug offenses, and nonviolent crimes were released. More alternative sentencing measures, treatment facilities, and a mentally ill offender diversion program are being considered.[99]

In Ohio, the Corrections Center of Northwest Ohio declared a state of emergency and refused to admit inmates from neighboring counties due to being over 95 percent capacity. Jail counts are in a constant state of change due to ongoing admissions and releases. The jail administrator stated that when the population drops to 90 percent of its capacity, the emergency ban would be lifted. He contacted the courts and asked the judges to consider early releases for some inmates nearing the completion of their sentences.[100]

In Colorado, the Denver County Jail in 2003 experienced an overcrowding crisis that resulted in some state parole violators being turned away. Inmates slept in hallways, in offices, and on the floor. Violence increased among inmates resulting in broken bones and a jail officer incurring a heart attack after physically struggling with a violent jail inmate. In Denver County, the jail held almost 2,000 inmates in a jail built to hold 1,350. The Denver City jail was designed to hold 158 and was confining 233 inmates. Colorado's Pueblo County Jail, built in 1980 to hold 189, was holding almost 500 inmates. Most cells at the Pueblo Jail were triple bunked and some held violent inmates; three inmates were confined in 10 foot by 10 foot cells each with two metal bunks and an army cot on the floor. In the "special needs area," an area for seriously mentally ill inmates, cots lined the length of a hallway. The staff training room and auditorium were converted to inmate dormitories. With the overcrowding, the ratio of jail inmates to one jail officer was as high as 70 to 1, which indicated a serious safety issue for the staff. Options that were explored by Colorado County officials responsible for crowded jails were building new facilities and early release. Early release guidelines for Denver County included releasing inmates being held for Denver Municipal Ordinance and County Court violations that have served over half their sentences and not incarcerating parole violators for technical violations. The Denver jail would not release inmates incarcerated for felonies, domestic violence, assault, weapons offenses, or prostitutes with over four arrests. Another option was the transfer of 200 female inmates to a nearby jail while room was added to the female unit.[101]

**FIGURE 1-5** Early Releases

The need for a new jail translating into new jail construction may take years. Planning a new jail and hiring the personnel to staff it is a long, drawn out process. Most newly constructed jails cost millions of dollars, but capital construction expenditures are only a small part of the story. Expenses laid out over 10–20 years are much more expensive and must be considered in any capital construction initiative.

POINT OF VIEW

## The Planning and Building of Jails

*Michael T. Schmintz*
Jail Administrator Walworth County Jail
Elkhorn, WI

In the last 15 years, there has been a major change in philosophy in the planning and building of jails in Wisconsin and the United States. In the past, planners and administrators would look at the increase of the jail population and make the necessary building plans to accommodate the housing of these inmates in the jail and any projected population increases. However, it has become very apparent that planning jails using just this criterion has become very inefficient for long-term use and cost efficiency. Today's modern jail needs to address philosophy of types of operation (linear, indirect, and direct supervision), space for necessary health care and mental health care issues, recreation and program space, and sufficient space for staff to be able to do their jobs in an efficient and humane manner.

The type of operation can be a very difficult decision for organizations to make. Many organizations are familiar with the "new generations jails" (direct supervision) but may find it difficult to make the transition to it due to hesitancy of staff wanting to work with no barriers between them and the inmates and also of having to spend their shift in the same living area as the inmates. The best way of making this transition is educating your staff in the benefits and the hazards of this type of operation. Visiting other facilities that use direct supervision and letting the staff speak to the officers who are already working in it can do this. You will probably find that the staff already working in this type of operation feels that they are more in charge of their post and more aware of what is happening in the jail. You will also find that building costs can be reduced because high detention doors and furnishings are not always needed in this type of facility. In the Walworth County Jail in Elkhorn, Wisconsin there are wooden cell doors and porcelain fixtures in all the living areas except the maximum security, administrative, and disciplinary segregation areas. This facility has been in operation since 1996 and has only replaced one fixture since it opened. Because the officers are in the living areas, they have better observation of inmates to prevent facility damage, something that is very difficult to do in linear and indirect supervision jails.

Health care of inmates plays an important part in today's modern jail. In the past, medical care was limited to emergency care and limited care for existing conditions. Today many larger jails have 24-hour nursing coverage, and the medium and smaller jails have nursing staffs who are scheduled shorter but still on a regular basis. Medical space needs to be planned and constructed to ensure that there is adequate space to do medical assessments and keep medical files in a secured environment so that confidentiality is not violated, and that medications can be accounted for and stored in the proper manner. A guideline for how you may want to set up your medical department may be the medical standards from the National Commission on Correctional Healthcare (NCCHC) and the American Corrections Association (ACA).

Two other health care issues that have impacts on jail operations involve dental care and mental health care. Dental care is becoming more of an issue today and will continue to be in the future. How will the jail handle the demands on their resources, both financial and personnel, to ensure that the proper dental care is provided? Some solutions are provided dental equipment in the jail (permanent or portable) so that transporting inmates to the dentist's office can be limited and in many cases eliminated.

Mental health care is important in today's jails due to the number of inmates that have mental health and behavior problems. Proper segregation cells and areas for inmates to be interviewed are important for a successful mental health program. Segregation cells for serious suicidal inmates should include provisions such as padded walls, floors, and ceilings, and also accessories that do not permit an inmate to harm his or her self by hanging or inflicting injuries to their selves. Mental health issues cannot be ignored, and properly training staff and giving them the tools to deal with these inmates in a humane manner will continue to show the professionalism that is required in the corrections field.

Jails can no longer tolerate leaving general population inmates in their cells 24 hours a day. Activities for these inmates can serve many purposes. One of the main reasons to have recreational and program activities is to keep inmates active instead of just "warehousing" them. Inmates who are involved in activities and programs can have the potential of leaving a jail facility better off than they were when they arrived. However, it does not just happen. It needs to be planned for and followed up on to be successful. Recreation areas are being included in almost all new type of jail facilities. They usually include indoor and outdoor recreational areas. They may include basketball hoops, but if they do, you should seriously consider banning competitive playing of it to prevent injuries due to not having proper foot attire and reducing risks of conflicts among inmates.

When planning programming space, a number of considerations should be reviewed. What types of programs are going to be instituted in your facility, educational, alcohol, and drug programs, religious programs, anger management, parenting skills, etc.? Is this programming going to be on an individual, group emphasis, or both? No matter what is decided, it is going to take space. This space can be the hardest justification that an administrator will have to make. The reason is that many citizens may feel it is not the objectives of a jail to provide "treatment" to incarcerated individuals. That should be done in long-term facilities such as prisons. The fault of that logic is that it may be beneficial to get people thinking about their shortcomings immediately after an arrest rather than months and in some cases years after the fact. It should also be pointed out that many individuals do not have the means to get out on bail and others do get sentenced to county jail to up to a year. In Wisconsin, individuals have been sentenced to consecutive one-year sentences, which resulted in these individuals spending close to two to three years in the county jail after sentencing.

Last but certainly not least is the space and tools that your facility creates for the staff. We all know that working in a jail can be creating stress on the staff. Proper planning for the work areas that have been identified for their duty stations can reduce this stress. This planning should include space considerations, sight lines, possible escape routes in case of emergencies, and the use of technology. The use of technology should include radios, duress alarms, computers, cameras, and viewing monitors. It should be noted here that cameras and monitors should not be used for justifying the reduction of staff. You still need them to respond to what is seen.

Special thanks to Sheriff David Graves, Walworth County Sheriff, and Michael T. Schmintz, Jail Administrator, Walworth County Jail.

Aerial view of Albany County, New York Correctional Facility. Note combination of 1930 jail with 1990 addition.

Photo courtesy of Edward Szostak.

Aerial view of Norfolk County, Massachusetts Correctional Center. Jail is built on a highway median strip.

Photo courtesy of Sheriff Michael G. Bellotti and Deputy Superintendent David Reilly of the Norfolk County Sheriff's Office.

Personnel costs alone may account for as much as 75–80 percent of an annual jail budget. However, there are new jails being planned and built; in 1994, 163 jails were under construction in the United States as compared with 89 in 2003. In 1994, 342 new jails were planned; in 2003, 241 new jails were on the drawing boards.[102]

Jails must be adaptable in terms of construction and location, and can be built in unusual places. For example, Norfolk County, Massachusetts, transitioned a 175-year-old linear facility into a direct supervision jail in 1992. A challenge in this endeavor was the staff coming up with a jail design to accommodate the logistics of the site, which is 8.2 acres of land located in the median strip of an interstate highway. This jail is currently perhaps the only jail in the United States built within a highway median strip. The 1992 facility consisted of eight two-tiered inmate-housing modules, a pre-release program building, Norfolk County Sheriff's Office administration offices, and a vehicle garage. Thanks to innovative and strategic landscaping, the pre-cast exterior buildings were concealed form the view of passing motorists on the highway.[103]

## Substandard Jail Conditions

Not all jails today are in livable condition. Some jails have problems serious enough to cause health and safety concerns. For example in 2000, court-ordered inspections and investigative reports by the District of Columbia (D.C.) government revealed an appalling state of conditions inside the D.C. jail. The reports stated that inmates routinely washed their underwear, bed linens, and jail jumpsuits in jail toilets because the jail laundry machines had been broken for 10 months. Linens and clothes were sent to the D.C. prison at Lorton, Virginia, but the service was not regular. Vermin were found in the jail kitchen areas and vents were clogged with dust and grime resulting in little air movement and the potential for spreading airborne diseases. Many showers did not function and some cells occupied by inmates had no running water. The fire marshal in his appraisal of the fire safety system said that the jail did not have emergency lighting in critical operational areas, such as evacuation stairways. In the male receiving and discharge area, the room temperature was 94 degrees Fahrenheit and the humidity was measured at 79 percent due to poor air circulation and a faulty exhaust system. Inmates complained of murky water in the shower, being bitten by insects, and seeing rats and mice. These conditions while dangerous for all who work and live in the jail were made worse by the actions of the inmates. These actions further complicated the situation: inmates tearing apart electric sockets in an effort to light cigarettes, cooling milk containers in jail toilets, and using toilets as places to burn "cook fires" in order to heat and cook food purchased from the jail commissary. As a result of these reports, D.C. had received funding to make improvements in the jail situation.[104]

In western North Carolina, a jail fire in 2002 resulted in eight inmate deaths and brought to light the plight of the county jails in that region. In 17 counties, 5 jails in operation were built in 1940 or earlier and 5 have been built since 1982. Critical life safety features such as fire sprinkler systems are present in only three jails and only eight have electronic doors. One jail has no air conditioning and also has falling plaster. Corrections officials were examining such options as ongoing repairs, opening regional jails, and trying to convince taxpayers of the necessity for jail improvements.[105]

One of the most surprising reports of the last few years has been the federal inspections and reports on the condition of the 74 detention centers and jails on Indian reservations in the United States. Released in 2004, the report was very uncomplimentary as to the management and conditions in Indian jails. Investigators visited 27 jails and found that staff lacked training and most facilities are in poor physical shape and are poorly maintained, which afford inmates easy opportunities to escape. In 2002, the 74 correctional facilities held 1,699 adult offenders and 307 juvenile offenders. Major problems cited included 209 inmate suicide attempts, 413 escapes, 5 successful suicides, and 5 inmate deaths due to medical conditions such as seizures, appendicitis, and alcohol poisoning. Reporting and inmate monitoring procedures were judged to be sloppy; in one case, a 16-year-old female died of alcohol poisoning three hours after she was discovered to be intoxicated and confined to a holding cell adjacent to an Indian boarding school. Only five deaths were reported to the Bureau of Indian Affairs. Security was a problem; in one facility a pair of handcuffs was used to lock the chain-link fence surrounding a recreation yard because the inmates had discovered the combination of the primary lock. At another facility, the wire mesh on the windows was so loose that the inmates could easily remove them.[106]

Not all Indian jails fit the negative description of the federal report. A progressive Indian jail is the Southern Ute Indian Tribal Center located on the Southern Ute Indian Reservation near Ignacio, Colorado. Recognizing that traditional county jails did not address the cultural and social needs of Native American offenders, the Ute tribe began construction in 1997 of a $8.5 million criminal justice complex, including a detention center designed to hold 55 sentenced offenders from tribal court. The detention center offers programming in Native American Indian Awareness, which addresses the development of a positive lifestyle as a Native American. Other programs include drug and alcohol therapy, group counseling, one-on-one counseling, Alcoholics Anonymous, and a General Education Development (GED) diploma program. In 2000, the facility had contracted with 11 federally recognized tribal organizations for the detention of offenders. A progressive practice is that tribal courts receive a monthly progress report on inmates held at the center who are sentenced from their jurisdictions. These reports provide in detail inmates' progress in center programs, and work details and can be used in determining whether an inmate receives a reduction in sentence or an early release for good behavior.[107]

Staffing is diverse at the Southern Ute Indian Tribal Detention Center; the staff is made up of Native American, Anglo, and Hispanic employees due to the cultural diversity of the area population. Within the first six months of hiring, staff members attend a 160-hour basic detention training course at the Federal Law Enforcement Training Center Indian Police Academy in Artesia, New Mexico. Staff members are also required to attend an annual mandatory 40-hour training session.[108]

## Regional Jails

In an effort to capitalize on resources and cut costs, jurisdictions are pooling their resources and entering into partnerships by operating **regional jails.** Regional jails are operated by several jurisdictions jointly by mutual agreement. Each jurisdiction contributes funds for operation and staffing. This makes sense both financially and operationally. A good example of jail regionalization is the state of Kentucky, which went from 120 county jails in the early 1980s to 84 jails in 1999. In enacting legislative reforms to their jails, Kentucky allowed counties to operate a regional jail shared by one or more counties, an individual county jail, a 96-hour holding facility for offenders, or a 12-hour holding facility. This assisted Kentucky counties that were financially in dire straits. The trend has spread to the West and Midwest, where sheriffs held inmates for other counties on a regular basis anyway. Ohio opened a regional jail in 1990 among fears by the citizens of lower property values and escapes. These fears never materialized. Today, more state and local governments, especially those with small jails having financial difficulties, are looking at regionalization under a jail authority or commission as an alternative.[109]

In North Dakota, the Pierce County Jail was one of the oldest jails in the state, dating back to circa 1912. In 2004, the eight-bed jail was in need of repair. The cabinet that held the mechanical levers that operated the cell doors broke down, and the sheriff had no way to repair it, as the parts dated back to 1912. As a result, the cell doors are permanently open and held in place by welds, which means that the staff cannot separate disruptive inmates or segregate an inmate if necessary. A new $7 million regional jail is planned for Rugby, North Dakota. The new regional jail has a capacity of 60 male beds, 10 female beds, and 40 beds for inmates with substance abuse problems. Four counties plan to use the jail, and the U.S. Marshals Service plans to house inmates there as well.[110]

## Privatization of the Local Jail

In discussing the status of the American jail in the last 20 years, one of the most controversial issues has been private corporations taking over the responsibility, staffing, and operations of local jails per agreement with the local jurisdiction(s), or **privatization.** During the 1980s and 1990s, companies such as the Corrections Corporation of America (CCA) made significant inroads into running jails. Additionally, some jails "partly privatize" operations by hiring private companies to operate food, jail health care, and commissary systems, but leave sworn government staff in place to perform day-to-day operations and administration.

In the *Census of Jails, 1999* released by the Bureau of Justice Statistics in August of 2001, the number of private jails in 1999 numbered 47, an increase from 17 in 1993. Most private jails hold both male and female inmates, with the population being mostly male. The number of inmates under private supervision increased rather significantly from 3,229 to 16,656 in the same period. These statistics translate into private jails being only 1.4 percent of all jails and confining only 2.4 percent of the nation's entire jail population. In mid-1999, Texas and California had eight private facilities each, followed by Florida and Pennsylvania, each with five.[111]

Privatization, either full or partial, is not without concerns for correctional professionals. In a jail that is not under private supervision, sworn staff-deputies, correctional officers, etc. generally work in the jail first in confinement, booking, etc., with the inmate population. When they transfer into commissary or in food service, they have had the training and job experience to work with inmates. In some jails, the sworn medical staff receives extensive security training. If a company is hired to supervise commissary, food, and health care systems, the staff is hired by the company, and not the agency. Jails should require these workers to receive mandatory security training; many probably have not worked with inmates previously in any type of correctional setting. The same holds true for medical services; correctional health care workers are hired by the firm and must receive training in jail security, as the jail is not the usual medical work environment.

The issue of jail privatization remains debatable now, as it has been for the last 20 years. Private correctional corporations have persuaded local governments that they can run the local jail more cost efficiently than the government civil servants can. Experts can be found on both sides of the issue. The federal government has also weighed in on the issue. In 1996, the U.S. General Accounting Office (GAO) submitted a report to the U.S. House of Representatives Subcommittee on Crime, Committee on the Judiciary. When considering privatization, two major concerns for jail authorities are the hiring of jail staff and the operational oversight of a private jail. Sheriffs and local corrections agencies are bound by laws and civil service practices in screening applicants, hiring, discipline, and retention. Also, sheriffs are constitutionally elected officials who are responsible for the jail; questions arise when they are asked to turn over that authority to a private firm. The American Jail Association (AJA) went on record as opposing the privatization of city, county, or state jails in 1985. Some studies have concluded that unless there is a significant attitude change in the corrections field, the privatization of jails will be slow in coming.[112]

One of the largest private corrections firms is the Corrections Corporation of America (CCA) that was established in 1983. CCA can contract with local governments and supply a service package or a combination of programs, medical services, training, food service, etc., designed to meet the need of a specific facility and its inmate population. CCA states that its design and construction services may be as much as 25 percent lower than public costs in obtaining a new jail. Construction may be completed in half of the time. CCA estimates its time of construction as 12–24 months as compared with the public sector's 30–60 months. CCA-managed jails are located in Florida, Indiana, Texas, Tennessee, and Oklahoma. The largest is the 1,440-bed David L. Moss Criminal Justice Center in Tulsa, Oklahoma, which serves Tulsa County. The next largest is the Metro-Davidson County Detention Facility, with 1,092 beds, in Nashville, Tennessee, serving Davidson County and Tennessee.

CCA jails offer inmate programs comparable with those of public sector jails. For example, the Hernando County Jail in Brooksville, Florida offers vocational, educational, and substance abuse programs to inmates. At the Metro-Davidson County Detention Facility in Nashville, the Theotherapy program combines faith and anger management. CCA reports that the Theotherapy program has an extremely low recidivism rate of 2 percent; the U.S. rate is 66 percent. Therapeutic programs are also in CCA jails.

Community corrections are also offered in CCA facilities. In 2000, the Hernando County Jail community service program provided 44,040 hours of community service, at cost savings of $258,240 in labor costs to county taxpayers.

CCA also recognizes the importance of correctional standards; the 40-bed Citrus County Detention Facility in Lecanto, Florida is accredited by the American Correctional Association. Thanks to Nancy Cook, Managing Director, Staff Development and Training, CCA for supplying CCA material.

**FIGURE 1-6** Corrections Corporation of America

## New Trends in Jail Population Management

Some of the most significant changes in managing jail inmates in the past 25 years have been in the design and operations of jail population living areas. While the Pennsylvania and Auburn Systems made contributions with the single cell/corridor and interior cellblock styles, respectively, jails evolved into three generation of jail design for the general population. These styles are still in use throughout U.S jails today. What style is used depends on the age of the jail, funding available to make changes and improvements, and the philosophy of the agency or sheriff.

The first generation of jail design is the traditional **linear design,** where cellblocks are aligned in rows running down a central corridor. Jail officer interaction with the inmates is limited except through a food slot located in the cellblock door for the passing through of food, mail, medications, commissary, etc. There is a dayroom or common area. The jail officer cannot see what the inmates are doing inside their cells from the hallway; the only way to personally check on inmates is to physically go inside, providing there is another officer available to stand in the doorway and "watch his or her back."[113]

The second generation of jail design uses a pod system, which is a central control booth surrounded by inmate living units, sometimes called "pods." The jail officer can turn and look into a pod to observe the inmates. While visual observation is increased, the officer can only communicate with the inmates by intercom.[114] Designed in the 1970s, this second-generation system is called **podular remote surveillance (podular).**[115] There are still blind spots in these pods where inmates have assaulted other inmates, etc. This style of supervision—the officer observing inmates "in the round"—may trace its origins to the panopticon type design by Bentham.

Jail management in both the linear and podular remote designs is usually reactive, where the jail officer reacts to situations such as arguments and fights. One jail superintendent summarized the problems with the podular remote surveillance approach. If a problem occurs, the officer in the control booth has to call the squad for assistance, and the responding officers may have a limited or no idea what they are responding to. Inmates called the surveillance officer the "puppet master" and the pod as the "fishbowl," which reduces the officer's authority. In cases of violence, the inmate(s) would be charged with a disciplinary offense; there was no opportunity to work things out. Information flow between the officers and inmates was reduced. Officers in the pod control booth would frequently overlook minor infractions and violations, thinking that it may be bothersome to the staff to frequently call for assistance. Finally, in such an environment, officers really did not know the inmates in their areas and could not relay accurate information on inmate behavior if an incident occurred.[116]

The third generation of jail design is called **direct supervision,** where the jail officer is placed *inside* the housing unit with no physical barriers such as a control booth or doorway to a secure area. The unit jail officer acts as an inmate "behavior manager" and by moving around the unit and getting to know the inmates, he or

Jail direct supervision unit; note officer post in center of dayroom.

she takes a proactive approach. The officer has more supervisory authority in the running of the unit.[117] Officers in direct supervision units exhibit a sense of pride in their units, both in its clean, orderly appearance and the manner in which the inmates behave. If low risk and cooperative inmates are placed in these units and have the socialization skills to get along with others, then the officer can spot disagreements and conflicts, counsel the inmates, and hopefully stop trouble before it starts. Classifying the right type of inmates to direct supervision units is critical.

Since the direct supervision concept was introduced in the 1980s and can trace its origins back to the early 1970s when it was used by the Federal Bureau of Prisons, more jails are adopting its principles and designs. When the jail officer has face-to-face contact with the inmates and moves around the unit, inmates must learn to function within a normalized social environment or be reclassified. Several improvements over the more traditional linear and podular remote surveillance have been noted by corrections professionals, such as violence and fear among inmates have decreased; the units have positive staff leadership which replaces the inmate predatory style of leadership; and the "normal" environment takes away the expectation that inmates are violent and cannot behave. Direct supervision units are safer, but care has to be exercised in putting competent, level headed officers in the units, as well as inmates who are mature and can get along with others.[118]

## SUMMARY

Early punishments of lawbreakers were varied and brutal. Punishment that was administered was usually of two types. Corporal punishment involved physical methods such as mutilation, torture, branding, and whipping. Capital punishment was the other alternative; early societies had numerous crimes that were punishable by death.

As society progressed, more attention was paid to the issue of where to confine lawbreakers. Early places of confinement were whatever places were convenient; very little attention was paid to standards, humane confinement, etc. Several European nations used transportation overseas colonies service in naval galleys, and indentured servitude as ways to keep the jail population in their countries down. Early jails in England were operated by shire reeves, the forerunner of the modern sheriffs, and fees were charged to inmates.

The 1700s saw several reformers come forward, voicing new philosophies about criminal punishment. Cesare Beccaria believed that punishment need not be barbaric and severe, but swift and certain. William Penn advocated a humane jail without fees, inmates were to work, and stocks and pillories were abolished. John Howard proposed far-reaching jail reforms, which laid the foundation for humane conditions in jails today. Benjamin Rush started the jail volunteer movement and Jeremy Bentham designed he panopticon method of inmate observation, whose variations are still in use today.

The American Revolution upset the plans of England concerning criminal confinement in the colonies and transportation. Early American jails followed the patterns set forth by Europe. Two penal systems vied for supremacy; the Pennsylvania System advocated complete solitary confinement and penitence while the Auburn System supported inmates sleeping alone but working in congregate groups. For economic reasons, the Auburn System prevailed. At the end of the nineteenth century, the Reformatory System targeted rehabilitation, but failed.

Throughout the nineteenth century, jails were a mixture of facilities and management. Jails in the North were first built of heavy oak and combined with a courthouse building. Conditions were not very good for the inmates. Southern jails were brutal and squalid; inmates were used in forced labor. Midwestern U.S. jails experimented with the rotary jail concept, and western jails were small and in some areas hulks of ships.

Jails in the twentieth century did not have humane conditions, but conditions changed with court intervention. Jails today are progressive and are improving. However, there are some issues such as overcrowding, substandard conditions. Privatization of jails continues to be controversial. Jails are becoming regionalized and have improved methods of jail management, namely progressing from linear and podular housing to direct supervision.

## REVIEW QUESTIONS

1. Name the functions of a jail.
2. Describe prisons and lockups.
3. Describe early punishment of criminals.
4. Describe the origin and conditions of early gaols (jails).
5. What were the views of John Howard and why were they revolutionary?
6. Define the views of the Pennsylvania, Auburn, and Reformatory Systems. What were their contributions to the field of corrections?
7. Describe nineteenth-century jails in the northern, midwestern, and western regions of the United States.
8. Why were southern U.S. jails in such poor condition after the Civil War?
9. What is the difference between rated capacity and operational capacity?
10. Explain how jails are dealing with overcrowding.
11. What are some issues that U.S. jails have dealt with recently?
12. Describe the three generations of jail design.

## TERMS TO KNOW

calaboose
capital punishment
Congregate System
contract system
corporal punishment
debtors
direct supervision
early release
fee system
flagellum
Great Code
hulks
indentured servant
indeterminate sentence
inside cells (interior cellblock)
jail
lease system
linear design
lockup
Mamartime Prison
operational capacity
panopticon
Pennsylvania Prison Society
podular remote surveillance (podular)
precipitation
prison
privatization
rated capacity
Reformatory System
regional jails
Separate System
shire reeves
squirrel cage jails
utilitarianism

## ENDNOTES


1. Gary F. Cornelius, *Jails in America: An Overview of Issues, 2nd Edition* (Lanham: American Correctional Association, 1996), p. 1.
2. Ibid.
3. Ibid., p. 2.
4. Ibid.
5. Ibid.
6. Gerald Leinwand, ed., *Prisons* (New York: Pocket Books, 1972), p. 24.
7. Ibid., pp. 13, 17, 19, 20.
8. Lewis Lyons, *The History of Punishment* (London: Amber Books, 2003), pp. 85, 87, 88.
9. Ibid., pp. 93, 94, 95, 96.
10. Ibid., pp. 95, 97.
11. Leinwand, *Prisons*, p. 16.
12. Lyons, *The History of Punishment*, p. 155.
13. Ibid., p. 157.
14. Ibid., pp. 178, 179.
15. John W. Roberts, *Reform and Retribution: An Illustrated History of American Prisons* (Lanham: American Correctional Association, 1997), p. 2.
16. Ibid., pp. 2, 3.
17. Cornelius, *Jails in America*, pp. 2, 3.
18. Thomas G. Blomberg and Karol Lucken, *American Penology: A History of Control* (New York: Aldine De Gruyter, 2000), pp. 18–20.
19. Peter Spierenberg, "The Body and the State: Early Modern Europe," in *The Oxford History of the Prison: The Practice of Punishment in Western Society*, ed. Norval Morris and David J. Rothman, p. 60 (New York: Oxford University Press, 1995).

20. Blomberg and Lucken, *American Penology*, p. 20.
21. Peter Spierenberg, "The Body and the State: Early Modern Europe," in *The Oxford History of the Prison: The Practice of Punishment in Western Society*, p. 61.
22. Randall McGowan, "The Well Ordered Prison: England, 1780–1865," in *The Oxford History of the Prison: The Practice of Punishment in Western Society*, ed. Norval Morris and David J. Rothman, pp. 72–73 (New York: Oxford University Press, 1995).
23. Ibid., p. 73.
24. Ibid., p. 74.
25. Ibid., pp. 74–75.
26. Ibid., p. 76.
27. Roberts, *Reform and Retribution: An Illustrated History of American Prisons*, pp. 14–15.
28. Ibid., pp. 17–18.
29. Ibid., p. 17.
30. James F. Quinn, *Corrections: A Concise Introduction* (Prospect Heights: Waveland Press, 1999), p. 33.
31. Ibid.
32. Roberts, *Reform and Retribution: An Illustrated History of American Prisons*, p. 23.
33. Ibid.
34. Ibid.
35. John Howard, "State of Prisons, 1777," in *Penology: Evolution of Corrections in America*, ed. George G. Killinger and Paul Cromwell, p. 5 (St. Paul: West, 1973).
36. Ibid., pp. 5–11.
37. Roberts, *Reform and Retribution: An Illustrated History of American Prisons*, p. 54.
38. Ibid.
39. Ibid., pp. 54–56.
40. Blomberg and Lucken, *American Penology: A History of Control*, pp. 47, 51.
41. Ibid., p. 52.
42. Roberts, *Reform and Retribution: An Illustrated History of American Prisons*, p. 24.
43. Ibid., pp. 24–25.
44. Blomberg and Lucken, *American Penology: A History of Control*, p. 52.
45. Tod Kemble, "Jails in America," *Texas Journal of Corrections* (May–June 1996): 14.
46. Ibid., p. 15.
47. Ibid.
48. Carl R. Lounsbury, *The Courthouses of Early Virginia: An Architectural History* (Charlottesville: University of Virginia Press, 2005), pp. 231, 233.
49. Ibid., pp. 231, 233, 237.
50. Kenney, Caroline, Gaynelle McNichols, Ginny Kauffman, John Lowe, and Linda Rowe. *Public Gaol Group Interpretations Training, Class of 2002*, Colonial Williamsburg Foundation Researcher, 1997, 29–30.
51. Ibid., pp. 31–32.
52. Carl Sifakis, *The Encyclopedia of American Prisons* (New York: Checkmark Books, 2003), p. 124.
53. Roberts, *Reform and Retribution: An Illustrated History of American Prisons*, pp. 32–33.
54. Ibid., pp. 38, 41, 44.
55. Ibid., p. 46.
56. Ibid., pp. 39–40.
57. Ibid., pp. 39, 47.
58. Blomberg and Lucken, *American Penology: A History of Control*, pp. 71–73.
59. Ibid., p. 72.
60. Ibid., p. 71.
61. Roberts, *Reform and Retribution: An Illustrated History of American Prisons*, pp. 47, 65.
62. Blomberg and Lucken, *American Penology: A History of Control*, p. 77.
63. Lawrence M. Friedman, *Crime and Punishment in American History* (New York: Basic Books, 1993), p. 166.
64. Ibid.
65. Jonathan L. Anderson, "Portrait of an Early Nineteenth Century Gaol: The Onondaga Hill Jail, Onondaga County, New York," *American Jails* (January–February 2002): 33–34.
66. Ibid., pp. 34–35.
67. Ibid., p. 35.
68. Shaun Martin, "The Old Jail," *American Jails* (November–December 1998): 49, 52.
69. Friedman, *Crime and Punishment in American History*, pp. 166–167.
70. Ibid., p. 167.
71. Roberts, *Reform and Retribution: An Illustrated History of American Prisons*, pp. 50–53.
72. Quinn, *Corrections: A Concise Introduction*, pp. 42–43.
73. Friedman, *Crime and Punishment in American History*, p. 168.
74. Roberta and J. Hurley Hagood, "Hannibal's Early Jails or Calabooses," *The Hannibal Courier Post*, http:// www.hannibal.net/visit/historicalnews/histbuild3.shtml
75. Historic Squirrel Cage Jail Museum, http://www.geocities. com/Heartland/Plains/5660/sqcgjail.htm
76. J.M. Moynahan, "Jails of the American Frontier," *American Jails* (July–August 1998): 17.
77. Ibid., pp. 17–18.
78. Ibid., p. 18.
79. Ibid., pp. 22–24.
80. Ibid., p. 24.
81. J.M. Moynahan, "Calaboose to Modules: Jails in Spokane, Washington," *American Jails* (November–December 1996): 57–58.
82. Ibid., pp. 58–60.

83. Ibid., pp. 60–61.
84. Ibid., pp. 61–62.
85. Kemble, "Jails in America," pp. 14, 19.
86. J.M. Moynahan and V.M Deitrich, "Prisoners on Ships: Sacramento County Jail Hulks (1850–1859)," *American Jails* (July–August 1999): 38.
87. Ibid., pp. 38–41.
88. Cornelius, *Jails in America*, p. 4.
89. Aric Press, Jonathan Kirsch, Vern Smith, Michael Reese, and Eric Gelman, "The Scandalous U.S. Jails," *Newsweek* (August 18, 1980): 74.
90. Ibid., pp. 74–77.
91. Ibid., p. 77.
92. Ken Kerle, Ph.D., "Jail Evolution: Rated Capacities (rc), Regional Jails, City Jails, the Growing Number of Women Jail Administrators, and New Jail Construction and Planning New Jails," *American Jails* (May–June 2004): 19, 20, 25, 26.
93. Ibid., p. 20.
94. Cornelius, *Jails in America*, p. 17.
95. Kerle, "Jail Evolution," p. 26.
96. Sheriff Daron Hall, "A Fresh Look at the Problem of Jail Crowding," *Sheriff* (March–April 2004): 32–33.
97. Neil Vance, D.P.A., "The Unusual Suspects: Fourteen Points to Consider in Reducing the Population of a Crowded Jail," *American Jails* (January–February 2003): 48–51.
98. Website: U.S. Department of Justice Office of Justice Programs: http://www.ojp.usdoj.gov/reentry/ashcroftpr.html
99. Tony Manolatos, "Packed jails give inmates early releases," *Detroit News Metro/State*, http://www.detnews.com/2004/metro/0402/01/a01–50458.htm (accessed January 30, 2004).
100. Steve Murphy, "Stryker jail bars inmates from area," *toledoblade.com* http://www.toledoblade.com/appspbcs.dll/article?AID=/20031021/NEWS17/110210108 (accessed October 21, 2003).
101. Chuck Plunkett, "Crowded powder kegs," *DenverPost.com* http://www.denverpost.com/Stories/0,1413,36~53~1586922, 00.html (accessed August 24, 2003).
102. Kerle, "Jail Evolution," p. 29.
103. Peter Pereoncello, "The Norfolk County Sheriff's Office and Correctional Center," *American Jails* (July–August 1992): 37, 38.
104. Serge F. Kovaleski, "D.C. Finds Dangers in Ailing Jail," *Washington Post Online*, Page A01, http://www.washingtonpopst.com/wp-dyn/articles/A20507–2000Sep16.html (accessed September 17, 2000).
105. John Boyle, "More WNC jails dilapidated," *Citizen-Times.com*, http://cgi.citizen-times.com/cgi-bin/story/12406 (accessed May 7, 2002).
106. Christopher Lee, "Indian Jails Need to Improve, Officials Say," *washingtonpost.com*, http://www.washingtonpost.com/ac2/wp-dyn/A634–2004Jun23?language=printer (accessed June 24, 2004).
107. Adam B. Gallegos, "Welcome to the Southern Ute Indian Tribal Detention Center," *American Jails* (September–October 2000): 25–28.
108. Ibid., p. 27.
109. Kenneth E. Kerle, *Exploring Jail Operations* (Hagerstown: American Jail Association, 2003), pp. 40–42, 46.
110. Curt Woodward, "New regional jail moving closer to construction," *Inforum Associated Press*, http://new.inforum.com/ap/index.cfm?page=view&id=D84PNCD00 (accessed August 31, 2004).
111. , James J. Stephan, U.S. Department of Justice, Bureau of Justice Statistics, *Census of Jails, 1999* (August 2001): 6.
112. Kerle, *Exploring Jail Operations*, pp. 280–281.
113. Cornelius, *Jails in America*, p. 7.
114. Ibid.
115. Kerle, *Exploring Jail Operations*, p. 238.
116. Ibid.
117. Cornelius, *Jails in America*, p. 7.
118. Kemble, "Jails in America," pp. 16–18.

## REFERENCES

Anderson, Jonathan L. "Portrait of an Early Nineteenth Century Gaol: The Onondaga Hill Jail, Onondaga County, New York." *American Jails*, January–February 2002, 33–35.

Blomberg, Thomas G. and Karol Lucken. *American Penology: A History of Control*. New York: Aldine De Gruyter, 2000.

Boyle, John. "More WNC Jails Dilapidated." *Citizen-Times.com*, http://cgi.citizen-times.com/cgi-bin/story/12406 (accessed May 7, 2002).

Cornelius, Gary F. *Jails in America: An Overview of Issues, 2nd Edition*. Lanham: American Correctional Association, 1996.

Friedman, Lawrence M. *Crime and Punishment in American History*. New York: Basic Books, 1993.

Gallegos, Adam B. "Welcome to the Southern Ute Indian Tribal Detention Center." *American Jails*, September–October 2000, 25–28.

Hagood, J. Hurley and Roberta. "Hannibal's Early Jails or Calabooses." *The Hannibal Courier Post*, www.hannibal.net/visit/historicalnews/histbuild3.shtml, copyright 2002 (accessed January 2, 2004).

Hall, Sheriff Daron. "A Fresh Look at the Problem of Jail Crowding." *Sheriff*, March–April 2004, 32–33.

"Historic Squirrel Cage Jail Museum," http://ww.geocities.com/Heartland/Plains/5660/sqcgjail.html (accessed January 10, 2004).

Howard, John. "State of Prisons, 1777." In *Penology: Evolution of Corrections in America,* edited by George G. Killinger and Paul Cromwell, pp. 5–11. St. Paul: West, 1973.

Kemble, Tod. "Jails in America." *Texas Journal of Corrections,* May–June 1996, 14–19.

Kenney, Caroline, Gaynelle McNichols, Ginny Kauffman, John Lowe, and Linda Rowe. *Public Gaol Group Interpretations Training, Class of 2002,* Colonial Williamsburg Foundation Researcher, 1997, 29–30.

Kerle, Kenneth E. *Exploring Jail Operations.* Hagerstown: American Jail Association, 2003.

Kerle, Ken Ph.D. "Jail Evolution: Rated Capacities (rc), Regional Jails, City Jails, the Growing Number of Women Jail Administrators, and New Jail Construction and Planning New Jails." *American Jails,* May–June 2004, 19–29.

Kovaleski, Serge F. "D.C. Finds Dangers in Ailing Jail." *Washington Post Online,* http://www.washingtonpopst.com/wp-dyn/articles/A20507-2000Sep16.html (accessed September 17, 2000).

Lee, Christopher. "Indian Jails Need to Improve, Officials Say." *washingtonpost.com,* http://www.washingtonpost.com/ac2/wp-dyn/A634–2004Jun23?language=printer (accessed June 24, 2004).

Leinwand, Gerald, ed. *Prisons.* New York: Pocket Books, 1972.

Lounsbury, Carl R. *The Courthouses of Early Virginia: An Architectural History.* Charlottesville: University of Virginia Press, 2005.

Lyons, Lewis. *The History of Punishment.* London: Amber Books, 2003.

Manolatos, Tony. "Packed Jails Give Inmates Early Releases." *Detroit News Metro/State,* http://www.detnews.com/2004/metro/0402/01/a01–50458.htm (accessed January 30, 2004).

Martin, Shaun. "The Old Jail." *American Jails,* November–December 1998, 49–53.

McGowan, Randall. "The Well Ordered Prison: England, 1780–1865." In *The Oxford History of the Prison: The Practice of Punishment in Western Society,* edited by Norval Morris and David J. Rothman, pp. 72–73. New York: Oxford University Press, 1995.

Moynahan, J.M. "Jails of the American Frontier." *American Jails,* July–August 1998, 16–26.

Moynahan, J.M. "Calaboose to Modules: Jails in Spokane, Washington." *American Jails,* November–December 1996, 57–63.

Moynahan, J.M. and V.M Deitrich. "Prisoners on Ships: Sacramento County Jail Hulks (1850–1859)." *American Jails,* July–August 1999, 37–42.

Murphy, Steve. "Stryker Jail Bars Inmates from Area." *toledoblade.com,* http://www.toledoblade.com/appspbcs.dll/article?AID=/20031021/NEWS17/110210108 (accessed October 21, 2003).

Pereoncello, Peter. "The Norfolk County Sheriff's Office and Correctional Center." *American Jails,* July–August, 1992, 36–39.

Plunkett, Chuck. "Crowded Powder Kegs." *DeverPost.com,* http://www.denverpost.com/Stories/0,1413,36~53~1586922,00.html (accessed August 24, 2003).

Press, Aric, Jonathan Kirsch, Vern Smith, Michael Reese, and Eric Gelman. "The Scandalous U.S. Jails." *Newsweek,* August 18, 1980, 74–77A.

Quinn, James F. *Corrections: A Concise Introduction.* Prospect Heights: Waveland Press, 1999.

Roberts, John W. *Reform and Retribution: An Illustrated History of American Prisons.* Lanham: American Correctional Association, 1997.

Sifakis, Carl. *The Encyclopedia of American Prisons.* New York: Checkmark Books, 2003.

Spierenberg, Peter. "The Body and the State: Early Modern Europe." In *The Oxford History of the Prison: The Practice of Punishment in Western Society,* edited by Norval Morris and David J. Rothman, p. 60. New York: Oxford University Press, 1995.

Stephan, James J. U.S. Department of Justice: Bureau of Justice Statistics, *Census of Jails, 1999.* Washington, DC, August, 2001.

Vance, Neil D.P.A. "The Unusual Suspects: Fourteen Points to Consider in Reducing the Population of a Crowded Jail." *American Jails,* January–February 2003, 48–51.

Website: U.S. Department of Justice Office of Justice Programs: http://www.ojp.usdoj.gov/reentry/ashcroftpr.html, (accessed October 29, 2005).

Woodward, Curt. "New Regional Jail Moving Closer to Construction." *Inforum Associated Press,* http://new.in-forum.com/ap/index.cfm?page=view&id=D84PNCD00 (accessed August 31, 2004).

# JAIL SECURITY

# 2

***Objectives of chapter***

The student will:

- Understand the meaning of security and its importance to the operation of the jail
- Understand these main components of a jail security network: headcounts, searches, tool/key control, perimeter security, patrol techniques, transportation, emergency procedures, and the gathering and dissemination of information
- Understand how security prevents of escapes

Closely related to the subject of jail security is the atmosphere of the jail—the mood of the inmates and the staff. This area, called the jail climate (Chapter 3), will tie into the discussion of the basics of jail security detailed in this chapter.

The security of the modern jail is the most important objective of the jail staff. To quote the former warden of the Bronx (NY) House of Detention, Thomas B. Barry:

> Security is the most basic function of any jail. It is almost constantly on the minds of management and line staff in the thousands of jails and remand centers throughout the United States and Canada.[1]

The **custody section** of the jail is usually composed of teams or squads, under the command of a supervisor—a sergeant or lieutenant. In some facilities, the section is referred to as security, confinement branch, etc. No matter what the name, this section and its staff are the backbone of the jail. Its operations are crucial—providing round the clock jail security, which includes keeping inmates properly confined, and the staff, jail, inmate population, visitors, and public safe. Jail security also means keeping the inmates safe from each other, from thefts, harassment, and assault. From the time a new jail officer is hired and throughout his or her career, the importance of jail security is instilled in his or her thinking. As careers develop and custody jail officers are transferred and promoted to other jobs within the agency, they realize that the security of the jail is still the primary mission. The development, maintenance, and revision of security take priority over all other jail objectives.[2] Other sections, supply, classification, programs, etc., still must operate with the security goal in the forefront. For example, the supply section will order equipment for the post officers such as pepper spray, handcuffs, and radios. The program section may not allow certain inmates to attend programs because they assault other inmates and staff, are escape risks, or are disciplinary problems.

In a broader sense, jail security focuses primarily on two areas: containment (preventing escape) and prevention of anything that could disrupt the peace and order within the jail.[3] These concerns are embedded in all security functions, operations, and procedures in the jail.

## CONTAINMENT AND PREVENTION

The containment of inmates takes two forms: containing inmates inside the facility and not allowing any escapes; and containing inmates in areas in which they are authorized to be. The jail has to be looked at a separate world in itself, a structured environment that keeps inmates inside. Inmates must live in the places that they were assigned by classification based on their custody level and behavior. Also, if inmates are cleared for work and programs, they must go to, remain, and return to their housing areas only by authorization and via areas approved by the staff for movement. These routes are direct: from the cellblocks to the classrooms, visiting areas, etc. Inmates are not allowed to wander throughout the jail; if they do, the staff can take disciplinary action. Going hand in hand is the prevention function; through searches and inspections, contraband is controlled and emergencies may be prevented.

These functions are accomplished by the confinement staff performing the following tasks:

- Use of security hardware
- Conducting headcounts
- Conducting searches and inspections
- Controlling keys, tools, and personal items
- Providing perimeter security
- Effective patrol techniques
- Properly transporting inmates
- Having emergency procedures
- Documenting and passing on critical information

### Use of Security Hardware

Security hardware is systems and items that aid the jail officer in security and safety. Included are closed circuit cameras, television monitors, electric door locks, intercoms, radio communications, alarms, and personal distress locators. These things are not substitutes for eyeball observation, but are designed to help the jail officer do his or her job. Most jails have closed circuit television (CCTV) cameras, which are monitored from a central console inside a control center. Except for jails that are very old, doors are now opened with computer "swipe" cards instead of keys. Cellblock doors are opened from a central control area. Twenty-five years ago, jail radio communications were rare due to expense and limited technology. Now, many jails use radios with a wide range of operations, multiple channels for different staff functions, and personal safety alarm buttons. If an officer is attacked or in an emergency situation where help is needed, he or she presses the alarm button, and the main control area is alerted as to who the officer is and the location. Some jails require officers to carry alarm devices on their persons, which may look like a pen. If the alarm button is depressed, sensors throughout the facility alert the control center. The newest trend in correctional officer safety is to take advantage of the technological advances available in **personal location systems**. Personal location systems use technology to pinpoint an officer's location inside the facility and can be activated to alert staff if the officer is in trouble. Ultrasonic frequencies transmit to stand alone receivers located about 80 feet apart throughout the jail. These receivers are connected to the jail's messaging systems, which pinpoint the officer's location. One type of device has a "grenade"-type pin and a "man-down" feature, which activates if the device is taken from the officer by an inmate. This is an improvement over traditional radio communications, because sound does not penetrate brick concrete or sheet rock. Another type of alarm device in use triggers an alarm when the officer, nurse, or staff member pushes a button, pulls a cord, or for a specified time there is a lack of movement due to the officer being seriously injured and/or unconscious. Also, there is a two-way speech channel on the device for voice communication. By using these devices, control centers can monitor staff safety and immediately send aid if necessary.[4]

Other security hardware can be described as more routine. Jail officers now carry "pepper spray" in belt canisters, standard handcuffs, plastic handcuffs, and flashlights. If the inmate being dealt with is a high-risk inmate (escape risk, mentally ill, or likely to commit assault), officers can use leg restraints or handcuff an inmate to a bench or chair. Gloves are also carried to prevent officers from coming into contact with inmates' bodily fluids, such as blood, semen, or urine. Not only are gloves very helpful when handling an inmate who is bleeding or throwing bodily waste, gloves when worn properly can protect the jail officer from being cut from hypodermic needles, sharp weapons, or by accident. There are also masks used on violent or irrational inmates that prevent the inmate from spitting at the officer.

## Conducting Headcounts

One of the primary duties of a jail officer is to know where the inmates are at all times, or out more simply be accountable for the inmates in his or her care. Inmates must be constantly located and counted, no matter where they are or in what activity they are engaged in. This tool is the **headcount.** One of the worst things that can occur during the daily operations of a jail is for the jail staff to lose accountability for an inmate. In such cases, the shift commander will order an emergency lockdown of the entire inmate population, preceded immediately by the cancellation of all activities and work details by ordering inmates back to their housing areas. An emergency headcount will be taken and all security doors secured. In one jail several years ago, an inmate did not return from a program and could not be located. The entire 600-bed jail was locked down, and a headcount commenced. The inmate was found talking to the program instructor inside an office. The instructor had not asked the post deputy for permission to keep the inmate after class. The point here is that all civilian staff must be instructed in the importance of inmate accountability. The instructor in this case was disciplined.

All inmate housing assignments and rosters must be kept current, to reflect new admissions, releases, transfers and changes in custody levels.

Photo by author, courtesy Butler County Prison.

Essential part of security is keeping inmates locked in and accounted for.

Photo by author, courtesy Bristol County Ash Street Facility.

In a jail's daily operations, there are these headcounts:[5]

*Formal count:* Formal counts are required by the jail's policies and procedures. They are conducted at mandatory specific times: at shift change, before securing the inmates for the night (lockdown), and before meals. One shift is not relieved until the count is taken and verified at the booking desk. The counts must match, and all inmates must be accounted for whether they are at court, on a transport to a doctor's office, etc.

*Census count:* Census counts are taken to verify inmates' presence at recreation, programs, on work details, etc.

*Emergency count:* Emergency counts are taken due to an emergency such as a power outage, fire, riot and/or disturbance, a natural disaster causing partial or full evacuation, work stoppage, or escape. Emergency counts may also be taken if the jail booking desk staff discovers that the jail inmate count is not correct.

Inmates are very ingenious and will go to any means to try to thwart a headcount. Inmates have constructed dummies (such as in the famous 1962 escape from Alcatraz Federal Prison), have had other inmates answer for them while they slip out of one authorized area into another, or have convinced staff by lying and manipulation that they should be in a particular area.[6]

It is a constant "cat and mouse" game between the staff and the inmates concerning where inmates should be and the headcount. Also, an informal headcount may be conducted at the discretion of the post officer. However, there are basic rules for jail officers to follow when properly conducting headcounts inside a jail:[7]

- *Controlling the count:* The jail officer orders the inmates to stand in front of their bunks, cells, or rooms and to be quiet while the count is being conducted. All noise and activities cease. This method is effective when conducting a count in a dormitory, direct supervision unit, or in an overcrowded area. The officer can also check off the inmate's name by confirming the inmate's identity by the use of an identification badge, or wristband containing the inmate's name, a photo, or a bar code that is read and confirmed electronically. Inmates at some jails, such as in the Rappahannock Regional Jail (VA) and the Baltimore City Central Booking and Intake Center, wear wristbands with a barcode so that staff can tell immediately who the inmate is. Technology in inmate identification is advancing. Wristbands can now be sealed by a laminator inside a plastic tube and laced on a wrist so that it they cannot be tampered with or removed by the inmate. Twenty-five years ago, jail staff could identify inmates at a glance just by getting to know the inmate. But as jail populations have increased and more duties are placed on the jail staff, it is imperative that identification methods become more advanced. In many jails, tampering with wristbands and interfering with a headcount are grounds for disciplinary action against the jail inmate.
- *Physically observing flesh and breathing:* Inmates bent on escape, trafficking in contraband, or assault want to fool the officers. Jail officers must see the inmate "in the flesh." This means at night when counting inmates in their beds, officers must see skin and breathing. Inmates know that the worst time during an officer's night shift is the 3 A.M. to 6 A.M. stretch. Officers are tired, but they must be alert.
- *If interrupted, the count must start over.* Inmates will do things to distract the officer, either to hide unauthorized activity that they are doing or maybe to engage in their idea of "fun" and to make the officer look foolish. For whatever reason, if a headcount is interrupted, the best thing for the officer to do is to start the count over.

- *Watching for behavioral changes in inmates*: Not all inmates can hide their feelings; some may be nervous for a particular reason: threats received from other inmates, being the victim of inmate assaults, knowledge of negative behavior by other inmates, etc. Officers should not only count inmates but also look at them. If something is apparently wrong with the inmate, the officer can take the inmate aside later for further investigation and follow up.
- *Document headcounts*: Jail officers should document headcounts on the proper log or roster and confirm the count with the booking desk. Headcount records are official documents and may be subpoenaed to court in the event of criminal charges against an inmate, or by investigators in the event of an escape. By documenting and signing for the count, the jail officer is taking official responsibility for its accuracy. Inmates should never conduct headcounts. Headcounts should only be conducted by sworn officers.
- *Verification of count*: The headcount from the living and working areas of the jail must be confirmed with the booking desk of the jail. The booking desk keeps a running count of all inmates in the facility and absent (for authorized reasons) from the facility, so that the exact jail population is known at a glance.

## Conducting Searches and Inspections

To prevent the introduction of contraband into the jail, the main tool of the jail officer is the search. Inmates, their living and work areas, their belongings, mail, and deliveries, must be searched thoroughly and frequently. **Contraband** is the main enemy of jail security. The basic definition of contraband is:

> Unauthorized items or materials either manufactured or introduced into the jail that could disrupt security, safety, aid escape, and facilitate criminal behavior. Items that are authorized are deemed contraband if they are possessed in excess or changed, altered or modified in any way.

Jail officers can define any item or items as contraband if they have reason to believe that it is a threat to the safety and security of the jail.[8] For example, an innocuous item such as a blanket is authorized by the jail staff and issued to inmates. But if an inmate has managed to get a hold of three blankets when he should have only one, the other two are considered contraband. Extra food and clothes can also be considered contraband. Officers discover early in their careers that inmates can become jealous of other inmates who have extra items. Fights can result over an extra blanket or hoarded food. Also such contraband can be traded for more deadly contraband such as weapons and drugs. In jail, an inmate having extra things gives that inmate "the edge," a little more status, and power. Contraband can be hidden more effectively if the inmate has many items to be searched.

Contraband may come in many shapes, sizes, and forms and have many different purposes. One jail officer during his career personally observed the following items of manufactured contraband:

- Sharpened toothbrush, designed to puncture and gouge.
- Broken razor blade sticking up inside a container of stick deodorant. (The user—the intended victim—would ultimately cut his armpit as the deodorant wore down.)

- A pen with a nickel (coin) sharpened into a point, melted on the end, similar to an arrow.
- A homemade club: a heavy sock with a metal doorknob inside; this could fracture a skull.
- A light bulb made into a homemade "bong" for smoking drugs.
- A staple melted onto a toothbrush for use as a homemade tattoo needle.
- A bent piece of metal from the bottom of a cleanser can fastened onto a toothbrush for use as a weapon.
- Wet, braided toilet paper made into a noose or rope after drying.
- A toothpaste tube with a hole punctured in the middle to be used to smoke drugs.
- A sharpened metal spoon.
- A crucifix made from sandwich wrap.
- A sharpened meat bone.
- A shampoo bottle containing bread, water, fruit, and sugar fermenting into alcohol.
- A broken mop (wooden) handle with the end sharpened.
- A martial arts "numchuk" made from empty shampoo bottles weighted down with newspaper tied together with shoelaces.
- A "club" made from tightly tied, wet magazines.
- Parts from a television with an electrical cord attached, designed to clip onto a metal jail cup and to keep coffee heated, if the inmate was lucky to keep the cup.

Ed Szostak, the former superintendent of the Albany County, New York, Correctional Facility, says that his facility

> has experienced a variety of contraband items, i.e., homemade knives **(shanks)**, homemade alcohol **(home brew)**, and in order to create contraband hiding places inmates have hollowed out books and bars of soap. We have found bars of soap carved into various shapes including the shape of a small handgun. The gun appears quite genuine once colored with a black marker or pen. Broom and mop handles can be fashioned into spears, shanks, or clubs; bed sheets braided like rope; broken Plexiglas mirrors and pens can be sharpened and made into shanks. Even harmless powdered coffee creamers can be dangerous. When the powdered creamer is blown through a hollow pen or straw-like device onto a flame, it becomes a crude flame thrower.[9]
>
> Home brew—homemade jail alcohol-is very easy to make. All inmates have to do is put water, sugar, fruit and bread into an airtight container, such as a shampoo bottle—and let it sit for several weeks. Eventually the mixture ferments into a crude alcohol.

Contraband can also be introduced through the mail, through visitors, and through property left for inmates. One jail officer found two marijuana cigarettes and three pills sewn inside the seam of a tee shirt that was being left for an inmate by his mother. The inmate's mother was immediately arrested and charged criminally. In most, if not all, states it is a criminal offense to introduce weapons, drugs, etc. to an inmate inside a correctional facility or to assist in an escape. Greeting cards must be searched thoroughly, as drugs can be hidden inside the folds of some greeting cards. In one jail, an officer inspecting a letter to an inmate discovered photos of a female inmate in the jail showing "skin" in the visiting area, and in one photo, she was apparently looking out for the officer while her visitor snapped the pictures. The photos were confiscated as contraband and she was charged with sexual misconduct—a rule violation. To an outsider, the photos may seem harmless. However, they were contraband. If they circulate through the jail via an inmate "underground" mail system, not only do they serve to titillate the male inmates, but female inmates and male inmates alike could get ideas on how to have "fun" during visiting. By doing so, an aspect of security is undermined. Another example is inmates giving themselves tattoos with tattoo needles and ink from jail-issued pens. Not only do inmates "charge" for such services by commissary, sex, or contraband, the tattoos can become infected and that undermines the inmate's health, which is all part of the security and safety aspect of the jail.

With the ever-ongoing war on contraband, searches generally take on the following forms:[10]

**Area searches and inspections:** Commonly called **"shakedowns,"** jail officers wearing protective gloves search inmate living/working areas—cells/rooms, dayrooms and common areas, kitchens, closets, classrooms, libraries, gym/recreation areas, and anywhere that inmates have access. Often inmates will leave contraband hidden in these areas in order not to be identified with it, for it to be picked up later, or it to be passed to another inmate. Even hallways are not immune. In one jail, an officer on rounds saw a crumpled up piece of paper outside a classroom where the female inmates had classes. Before he threw it away, he opened it up and discovered that it was a note from a male inmate to a female inmate. In area searches, all things should be searched: bedding, seats, books, telephone receivers, trashcans, vents, magazines, newspapers, dirty laundry, towels, nooks, crannies,

Warning to visitors against bringing in unauthorized items (contraband).

Photo by author, courtesy Butler County Prison.

cracks in walls, and all inmate property. Officers wearing gloves prevent getting stuck by needles, sharp objects, or any inmate bodily fluids.

Additionally, jail officers should regularly inspect plumbing, light fixtures, showers, etc. for any malfunctions. The jail is the inmate's home, and it should be livable. Broken fixtures, walls, furniture, etc. can add to the tension of the inmates and to the availability of hiding places for contraband and the materials to make weapons. All living areas must be inspected and any repairs expedited as quickly as possible.

**Vehicle searches:** *All* commercial vehicles such as food delivery vehicles, maintenance vehicles trash trucks, etc., should be searched when entering the perimeter of the facility. Some facilities use mirrors to sweep under the vehicle, inspection pits, or "creepers." Vehicle searches are important because in most jails inmate workers called **"trusties"** may assist staff in loading and unloading vehicles. Staff has to make sure that the trusties do not bring anything in from the vehicle. Also, staff may not know if the inmates have made arrangements to have something brought in. Any type of sensitive equipment or items such as medical supplies, staff uniforms, weapons, or security hardware and equipment should be unloaded away from inmates. In all deliveries, the contents list or manifest should be checked against the actual contents of the vehicle.[11]

Some jails do not have the luxury of storing prisoner transport vehicles inside the confines of the jail facility. In such cases where vehicles are stored in an outside parking lot, the vehicles should be frequently searched for drugs, weapons, or other contraband that could have been left in them by friends or family of inmates.

**Individual inmate searches:** Individual inmate searches consist of three types and can be performed inside the jail to general population inmates, trusties, newly arriving inmates at booking, inmates returning from transportation runs, and visitors. They are:[12]

*Frisks or "pat downs":* This is the most common type of search. The officer inspects the inmate's clothing and body by feeling through the clothing. Officers run their hand and fingers over the clothing, including the waistline and crotch areas, and collar to ascertain if any contraband or weapons are hidden. Pat downs can be performed at any time in the jail, during inmates present during area searches, or at any time an officer deems it prudent. Shoes and socks are removed, and the feet and footwear are searched. Inmates must also empty their pockets and turn them inside out in front of the officer.

*Body or "strip" search:* Strip searches examine the skin surface of the inmate without clothing. Possible hiding places for contraband include the hair, behind the ears and knees, armpits, under the breasts, under the scrotum and the genital areas, soles of the feet and between the toes, between the buttocks, inside the mouth and under the tongue. Dentures and prostheses are also removed and inspected. A proper strip search will also require searching under any hairpieces. While not as common as the frisk, strip searches are performed when an inmate is returning from an outside transportation run, from another institution and contraband is suspected, after a lengthy stay in solitary confinement, or if there is reason to believe that drugs or weapons are being concealed. The clothing is handed by the inmate to the searching officer for a thorough search. A few years ago in one jail, an inmate was discovered to have hidden drugs under the foreskin of his penis. The courts have taken the position that **reasonable suspicion** must be present in cases of a strip search. Reasonable suspicion is the existence of objective, not subjective information that could likely predict the presence of weapons, drugs, any items of contraband, or a possible plan for escape. Reasonable suspicion has these predictive elements:[13]

- Current offense that involves felony violence, such as drug charges, fugitive status, felony assault, murder, etc.
- Criminal history of offenses that involves the usage of weapons and contraband possession.
- Behavior, past or present in the facility that indicates the possession or manufacture of contraband, refusing to submit to a clothed search, or if a clothed search has proved fruitful in the suspicion or possession of contraband.
- The inmate in custody has had contact with the public, through a contact visit, a court appearance or has been transported to and from an area of public exposure.
- The inmate through court order has been committed to custody after arraignment, upon conviction, and upon sentencing.

*Body cavity search:* This is the most intrusive of all inmate searches and can result in injury if performed improperly. Body cavity searches inspect the body's openings: the anus and vagina. It is based on reasonable suspicion and should only be conducted by trained medical personnel, authorized by a supervisor, and documented in an incident report.

Although many jails have cross gender supervision, searches of inmates should be performed by members of the same gender as the inmate. As strip searches and body cavity searches are embarrassing to the inmate and seemingly undignified, they must be performed in private—a bathroom, or any closed and private space—so as to not offend the dignity of the inmate. Strip searches and body cavity searches should be documented in a report that explains the reasons for the search, who conducted it, and the results, including action taken—such as criminal or disciplinary charges. It is advisable to have two officers perform the strip search and a witness to observe medical personnel conducting a body cavity search. By doing so, staff can defend themselves against accusations of impropriety. In all cases of searching inmates, the officer should not act in an insulting, condescending, or harassing manner towards the inmate. Any search is intrusive to the basic human notion that we have space and do not like being handled.

A search of visitors to a jail is a delicate subject. Visitors can bring in contraband. Many jails have personal visiting through glass and phone, with no physical contact between visitors and the inmates. However, visitors can hide contraband in a lobby area, where trusties working to clean the lobby can bring it in later. One jail officer recalled marijuana being hidden inside the mouthpiece of a lobby pay phone. Anything that looks innocent, such as a crumpled cigarette pack or a candy wrapper, may contain drugs or messages that are swept up as trash only to be retrieved later. In one jail that was over 100 years old, visitors talk through a mesh screen to inmates on the other side. In researching this book, a senior supervisor said that the jail staff discovered that some visitors introduced contraband in rolled up in sheets of paper so small that they could fit through the holes in the mesh screen. These visitors practiced by fitting rolled up contraband into the mouthpiece holes on a telephone, whose holes are roughly the same size as the ones in the mesh screen.

As a rule, visitors receive greater protection from searches than the inmates. However, when a visitor enters the jail, some of those expectations are forfeited. The courts have approved correctional staff requiring visitors going through magnetometers, being routinely patted down, and having briefcases and purses searched.[14] In jails, notices to visitors are clearly posted stating that they may be subject to search. For a strip search to be performed on a visitor, the courts have required that reasonable suspicion must exist for a visitor to be subjected to a strip search. Reasonable suspicion in such cases means that suspicion is focused on the particular person to be searched, based on a specific fact combined with reasonable inferences drawn from experience. For example, a convicted drug dealer has been found with drugs in his cell. The only visitor on his list is a friend of his who is under investigation by the local police for drug trafficking. The drugs were discovered a few hours after the visits, and a reliable informant tells the jail staff that the drug dealer's former cellmate, now a trusty cleaning the lobby, is bringing the drugs in. This may be enough reasonable suspicion to require the visitor to be strip searched. However, as in all pat searches or strip searches of visitors, the visitor may refuse to be searched. He then must leave the facility. These are unusual cases, and high-ranking supervisors in the jail should make the final decisions. The courts take this very seriously. In one case, a New England sheriff incurred $177,000 in damages because his facility required that every visitor "agree" to be strip searched. This policy was rejected by the court who said that due to the visitor "consenting" for the search, the state was granting a privilege—visiting—at the expense of the visitor giving up a constitutional right. That right was for the visitor to be free from unreasonable searches.[15]

Non-contact visitation; by use of glass windows and telephones, prevent possible introduction of contraband.

Photo by author, courtesy Butler County Prison.

**Mail and property searches:** All incoming mail must be searched for contraband. Mail is not read, but searched to see if drugs or any small forms of contraband are hidden in the mail to undermine security. Liquid hallucinogens such as PCP or LSD can be smeared on a piece of mail. Officers must be alert to anything in a piece of mail or the envelope that looks out of the ordinary. In some jails, mail is opened, inspected in front of the inmate, and given to him or her. However, as jail populations increase, a growing trend is to enlist the assistance of civilian workers to inspect mail and then deliver it to inmates in the housing areas. Concerning property, another growing trend in jail operations is to have a **"publishers only rule,"** where if an inmate wants a particular newspaper, book, or magazine, it has to be obtained by direct purchase or subscription from the publisher. Jails are wise not to accept books and magazines left at the jail by inmates' family and friends. Donated reading material—material that is donated to the jail library by citizens—should be screened for contraband that could inadvertently be introduced and content. As was previously mentioned, if a jail does accept property such as underwear, socks, etc., it must be searched thoroughly. Jail administrations reserve the authority to restrict what types of property can be left for inmates.

**Substance abuse searches:** If inmates are suspected of using drugs, homemade alcohol, or drinking alcohol that has been smuggled into the jail, staff can utilize devices that determine the presence of drugs in urine (random urine tests) and alcohol breath tests. Courts have approved these measures, but the urine should be collected by same gender personnel. Testing should be performed by staff members who have undergone training and certification in the proper procedures of such a search and the testing of the samples.[16]

## Shakedowns

As previously mentioned, shakedowns are essential in keeping control of contraband. Shakedowns combine area searches, pat downs, strip searches, and body cavity searches depending on the circumstances and the seriousness of the contraband problem. Shakedowns can be just a few squad members searching a few cellblocks, a kitchen, an entire floor, or an emergency response team searching the entire jail. All shakedowns should have a plan—who performs the searches, in what uniform method they are conducted, how they will be documented, who collects the contraband for subsequent follow up (in house and criminal charges), how the evidence will be secured and stored, and where the inmates will be during the search. Inmates do not have a right to be present when their cells and living areas are being searched. It is not prudent to afford them the opportunity to observe staff security methods. A good example of a large shakedown is to discuss three massive shakedowns performed at the Albany County Detention Facility in 1991, 1993, and 1996—all following construction projects. The goals were to find any left over construction materials, weapons, and other contraband. Each search cost approximately $10,000 in staff and overtime costs, took 8–12 hours to complete, used teams, K-9 dogs and handlers from local law enforcement, identification officers for photographing evidence, property officers to account for all confiscated property, maintenance staff to provide access and entry, additional jail officers, supervisors, and command staff personnel. Inmates were warned before lockdown (2200 hours) that the shakedown would commence the next morning at 0700 hours. Interestingly, throughout the midnight shift, jail officers heard toilets repeatedly flushing and found items thrown and placed into common areas.[17] Inmates do not like to get caught with contraband. One veteran jail officer described how he suspected an inmate having smuggled food from the kitchen in his cell. When the inmate was out in the dayroom, and the officers appeared at the cellblock door to conduct a search, the inmate tried to get back into the cell to flush approximately a pound of smuggled coffee. It was too late for him as officers had locked his door from the cellblock lock box in the hallway, and the coffee was found in his cell. The officer goes on to describe how inmates have a "sixth sense" about shakedowns, recalling when he and a group of officers were walking down the hallway one evening to start a shakedown of several cellblocks. He recalls one inmate at a cellblock door yelling "shakedown!" and then hearing inmates scrambling and toilets flushing. Another supervisor called a team together during the evening hours, waited outside with staff members, and then entered a pre-release center unit and performed a surprise, unannounced shakedown, resulting in the removal of several trusties for possession of contraband.

Shakedowns do not always run smoothly, as inmates are being disrupted. In another incident in an eastern United States urban jail, a surprise shakedown was conducted at 11 P.M. on the main jail and four local halfway houses by teams of correctional officers. The search of the men's cellblock areas was described as subdued, while the search of the female areas resulted in angry female inmates yelling and threatening officers. Items of contraband that were found included hoarded medication, a toilet paper holder that could be fashioned into a weapon, syringes, a BB gun, a butcher knife, a pocket knife, and cash.[18] As a rule, jail inmates do not carry cash, as it can be stolen, gambled with, argued over, or paid to other inmates for favors, including assaults and sex. Some gang leaders continue their power plays from behind bars, and cash can be paid to inmates being released for tasks to be performed on the outside. Inmates are not known as being able to account for their property and may complain to the staff that they are missing money. The simplest solution is no cash allowed inside the jail.

## Security Audits

Security audits are defined as when the jail administration performs a self-analysis of all security policies, practices, and equipment as well as a close inspection of the physical plant of the jail. Its goal is to discover security weaknesses, analyze their causes, and take corrective action.

In the late 1990s, the scientists charged with protecting the United States' nuclear material and weapons at New Mexico's Sandia National Laboratory began working with prison and jail administrators in the development of security and vulnerability analyses. With funding from the National Institute of Justice, the scientists began looking at correctional facilities in Pennsylvania and Texas, and blueprints for a Nebraska prison and a Michigan jail. There are advantages to this type of analysis; it merges the scientists' expertise in examining security from a system perspective with a correctional staff's real world experience and firsthand knowledge of their staff and facilities. The lab team familiarizes itself with institutional life: staffing, security systems, inmate movement, programs, probability of escape, the surrounding community, controlling/containing inmate violence and the detection of contraband.[19]

The goal is to analyze all aspects of the correctional environment and spot and correct any deficiencies, examining three key elements: people, equipment, and policies and procedures. In one facility, the policy called for the tower correctional officer in periods of inclement weather to walk around the tower walkway every 15 minutes. He did so, and the analysis team thought that the inmates could calculate when he would be coming out. This is useful to the inmates for an escape plot or for someone to know when to throw contraband over the perimeter fence. The policy was changed to require the officer to walk around randomly within 15 minutes, and do so at no set time intervals. In another facility, an inmate escaped because of deficiencies in the security cameras, which had not been corrected due to procurement restraints and delays. Administrators said that had the security analysis been performed earlier and the cameras corrected, the escape may have been prevented.[20]

Security analysis can spot other deficiencies such as security doors that are "propped open" for staff convenience when they should be closed and malfunctioning cameras. Another key aspect is to observe staff habits in conducting inspections, counts, checks, and searches. If officers are not making thorough checks and counts, or are conducting sloppy searches, defective work habits can be addressed with those particular officers or training can be implemented. In one jail, two inmates made their escape because a door installer hung a door upside down. This caused the locking mechanism to malfunction, and the inmates used a piece of a light fixture to open the latch.[21]

POINT OF VIEW

## Correctional Security

*Edward Szostak*

Security in a correctional facility consists of a variety of electronic equipment and resources to include things such as metal detectors, iris scans, boss chairs, razor ribbon motion detectors, CCTVs, digital video recorders (DVRs), body alarms, tracking devices, communication devices, chemical agents, body armor, stun guns, electronic watch tour detectors, etc. Although valuable, the resource most important to a secure correctional facility is a well-trained professional correction officer constantly observing his or her surroundings and applying the knowledge and skills they acquired through training and experience.

During my 27 plus years in corrections, I have experienced many events testing the security of our operation. For the most part, we have been very successful in maintaining security. We did not encounter one escape during my first 26 plus years because of our corrections staff. We prevented escapes and averted many attempts. Unfortunately, during my last year as superintendent, we experienced our first escape since 1972.

### First Escape in 26 Years

On November 27, 2001, an inmate charged with bank robbery escaped from the Albany County Correctional Facility during the evening shift (3–11 P.M.) at the end of his recreation time from the outdoor yard. The escape was only discovered the next day (16 hours later) when the inmate was being sought for a court appearance. The facility was locked down immediately after the 7 A.M. to –3 P.M. tour. The tour commander was notified of a missing inmate. Officers were then ordered to conduct inmate head counts on their housing units to rule out an accounting error or an escape. That dreaded call to my boss, the Sheriff, and our law enforcement division was made for advisement. Within minutes of the head count results now known, the second call to the Sheriff, and all law enforcement agencies was made alerting them of our confirmed escape.

## Manhunt Underway

A manhunt was commenced and an investigation unfolded determining that the inmate had a 16-hour head start on us.

Preliminary information also revealed the inmate's success was partly achieved because the officers and supervisors deviated from established procedure.

Inmates acknowledged that they observed the officers' behavior for days and that they knew exactly what the officers would do routinely during their work shift.

The officer assigned to supervise the recreation yard was ignoring his duties while he played a handheld video game. That officer neglected to conduct an inspection of the recreation yard before, during, and after the inmate recreation. This inmate actually hid beneath a picnic table and remained in the recreation yard until he felt safe enough to make his escape. He climbed two 16-foot fences topped with razor ribbon. He sustained several lacerations to his hands in the process. We later learned that he protected his body by padding himself with several layers of clothing and jackets he obtained from other inmates.

The correction officer never walked the recreation yard to inspect it for security, and it was later learned that he never did so on previous security details. Having ample time the escapee; now bleeding was able to walk through the woods at the rear of the facility in his bright yellow jail jump suit and bright orange jail-issued canvas sneakers. He walked along the edge of the tree line and made his way to Albany County's Nursing Home, located approximately one mile down the road. Arriving at the nursing home, he was able to convince a nurse to call a taxi for him to travel several miles to the City of Albany to his former employer's business. He was still in his distinctive brightly colored yellow uniform labeled: Albany County Correctional Facility with fluorescent orange jail sneakers. He entered the business to obtain cash from his former boss to pay the taxi cab driver the fare. Despite all the obvious signs of an inmate in process of escaping, not one individual contacted authorities to report what they observed.

## Escapee Caught

One week later, the escapee was caught after he robbed a bank in the City of Albany, NY. He was later sentenced to 15 years in prison after admitting to two bank robberies and the escape.

The Sheriff quickly fired four correctional officers and a sergeant, after determining their responsibility in the escape. The Supervisors and Correction Officer's Labor Union promised they would fight the firings but not the disciplinary suspensions.

Within one week of discussions between the labor unions and the Sheriff, the discipline imposed was changed by the Sheriff to lesser penalties. Two of the five fired officers remained out of a job, and the remaining three were suspended for between 15 and 30 days and placed on one-year probation. The sergeant was additionally reduced in rank.

## Positive Changes

Physical changes and procedures were implemented at the Correctional Facility:

1. Installation of additional razor ribbon on the recreation yard fences and the perimeter fence;
2. Institution of a mid-shift inmate head count;
3. Revised count slip form to better distinguish and account for the inmate population;
4. Institution of 15-minute supervisory checks by correction officers;
5. Use of mechanical recording devices for all supervisory rounds;
6. Mandatory head count of inmates as they enter and exit recreation areas;
7. Mandating staff to physically count all outerwear used by inmates both prior to and after recreation period;
8. Installation of motion detecting equipment in various locations throughout the complex;
9. Rescheduling outdoor recreation to daylight hours only;
10. Unit supervisors' work area relocated to an area centrally located within the facility.

Numerous other procedures took effect that cannot be made public for security reasons.

As most corrections professionals know, change generally does not occur unless there is a major event or tragedy in our facilities. We all have been the recipient of budget cuts and have done the best we could with only limited resources. The best advice anyone could give is to keep trying to obtain the resources you need and document each and every request. It is also very helpful to have an outside authority identify the need and put it in writing to attach to your request.

## Escapee Tries Again

Once again, the inmate who succeeded in escaping from the Albany County Correctional Facility on November 27, 2001, attempted to escape from Attica State Prison in Attica, NY, 12 months later. The correctional officers were credited with following procedures when they found the inmate hiding outside the chapel. The officers while conducting a head count found him with 67 feet of rope made from bedsheets wound around his torso. He had slipped into an open area surrounded by chain-link fence open to evacuate prisoners in case officers must use tear gas in the chapel. In the inmate's cell was a convincing dummy to attempt to fool the housing unit officers. The penalty under New York Sate law for attempting escape is an additional seven years.

## Dirty Dozen Escapes

Three years before I began working in the field of corrections, 12 men escaped from the Albany County Correctional Facility who became known as the "Dirty Dozen." They took over the facility in 1972 and injured several correctional officers and supervisors in the process. After the inmates beat the officers, they secured them in locked closets or rooms. Officers' keys, money, 38 caliber revolvers, a rifle, and a 15-passenger van were stolen when they overpowered the 65-year-old officer in the main control center. Stopping before they walked out the front doors of the facility, several of the inmates returned to the cellblock with the intent to kill the cellblock officer. Fortunately, several of the inmates who did not participate in the escape convinced the others from not harming or killing that officer. Fearing the unknown the inmates departed and were then the subject of a major manhunt by the Albany County Sheriff's Department, New York State Police, City of Albany and Colonie Police Departments.

## Two Months of Freedom

It took over two months before authorities caught all of the Dirty Dozen and put them back behind bars. The escapees were each charged with felony escape or misdemeanor escape, depending on the charges they were originally committed on. Several were also charged with assaulting and robbing the officers. Two days after the escape, then-Warden Robert E. Beam said, "Every prisoner in the tier (about 50) could have walked out if they wanted to," at that point.

## Investigation

An investigation was conducted by the New York State Commission of Correction, the Albany County Sheriff's Department, and the Albany County District Attorney's Office. The conclusion of the investigation proved positive with numerous changes resulting. Security was greatly improved when locks on control gates were replaced, eliminating the problem of all locks being keyed the same. Control center security was enhanced with new security locks installed, increased officer training, and revised policies and procedures were implemented and enforced.

## Professional Officers Is Security

If there is a lesson to be learned in all of this, I think it is all summed up with the key component in any security setting: Security is well-trained, experienced, observant, diligent, contentious, **professional officers** who adhere to policy and procedure of their department. The professional officer is more valuable to any organization, well above and beyond electronic devices or equipment. One officer doing his or her job to the best of their ability may prevent a life-threatening event from occurring. It is all up to each one of us.

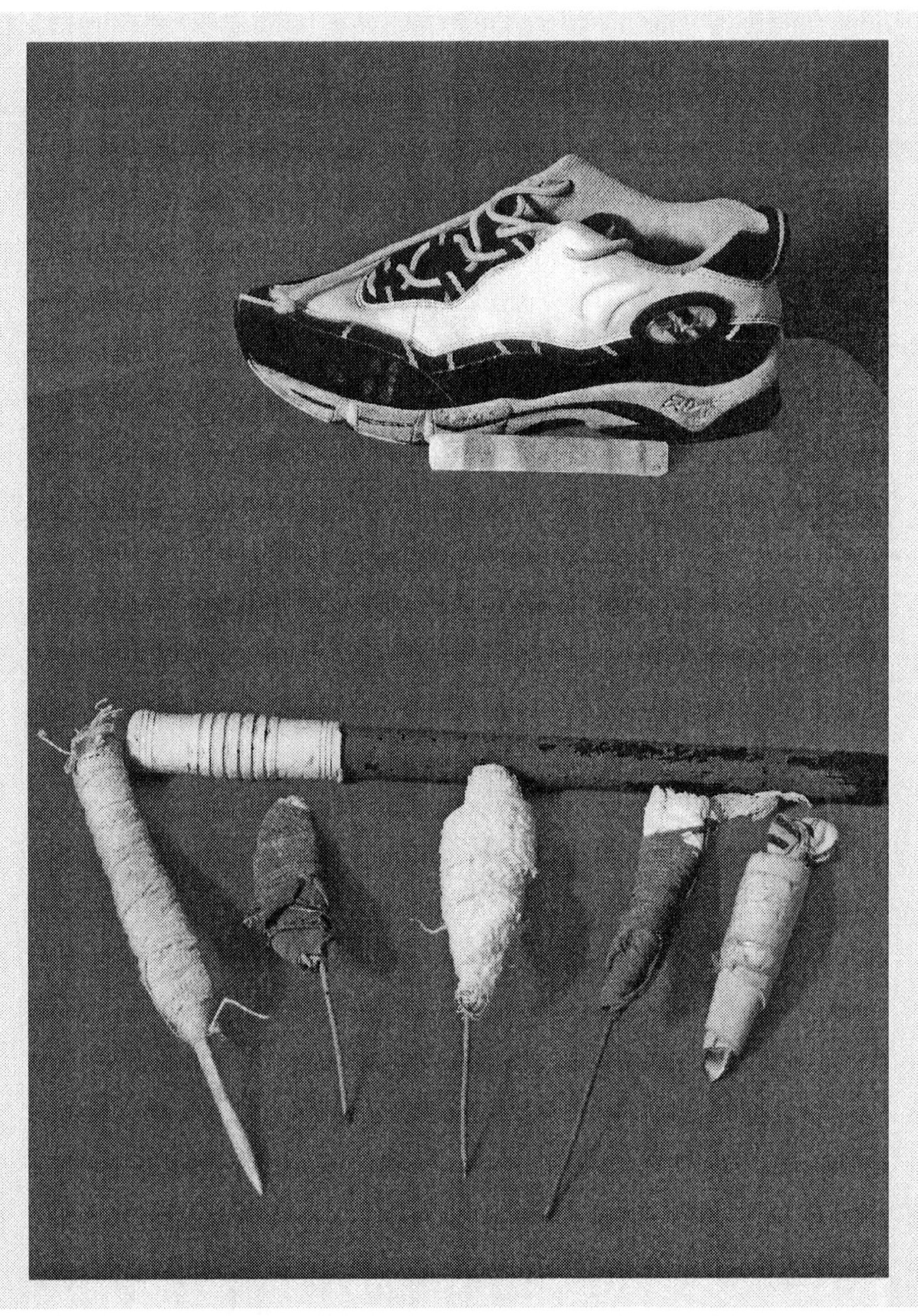

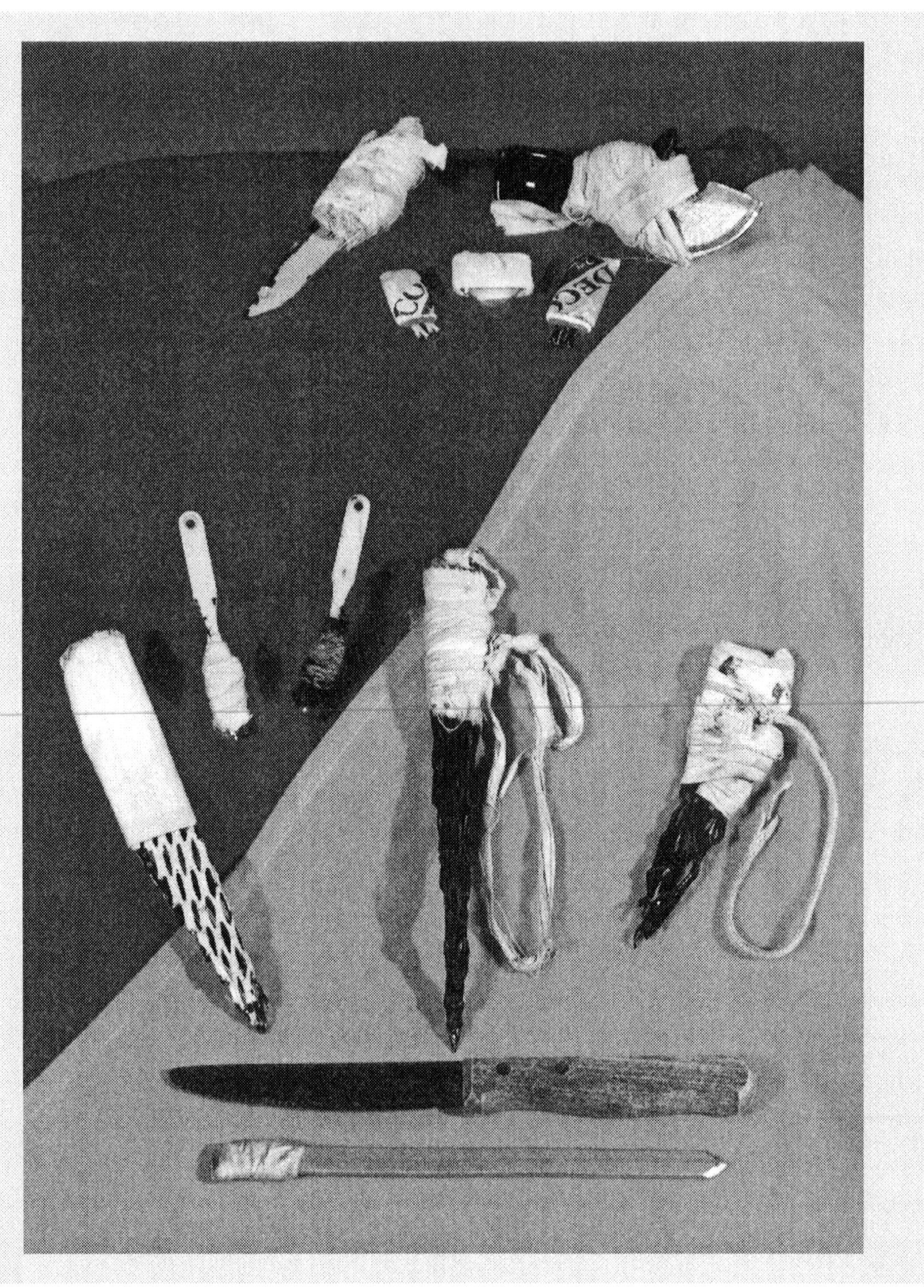

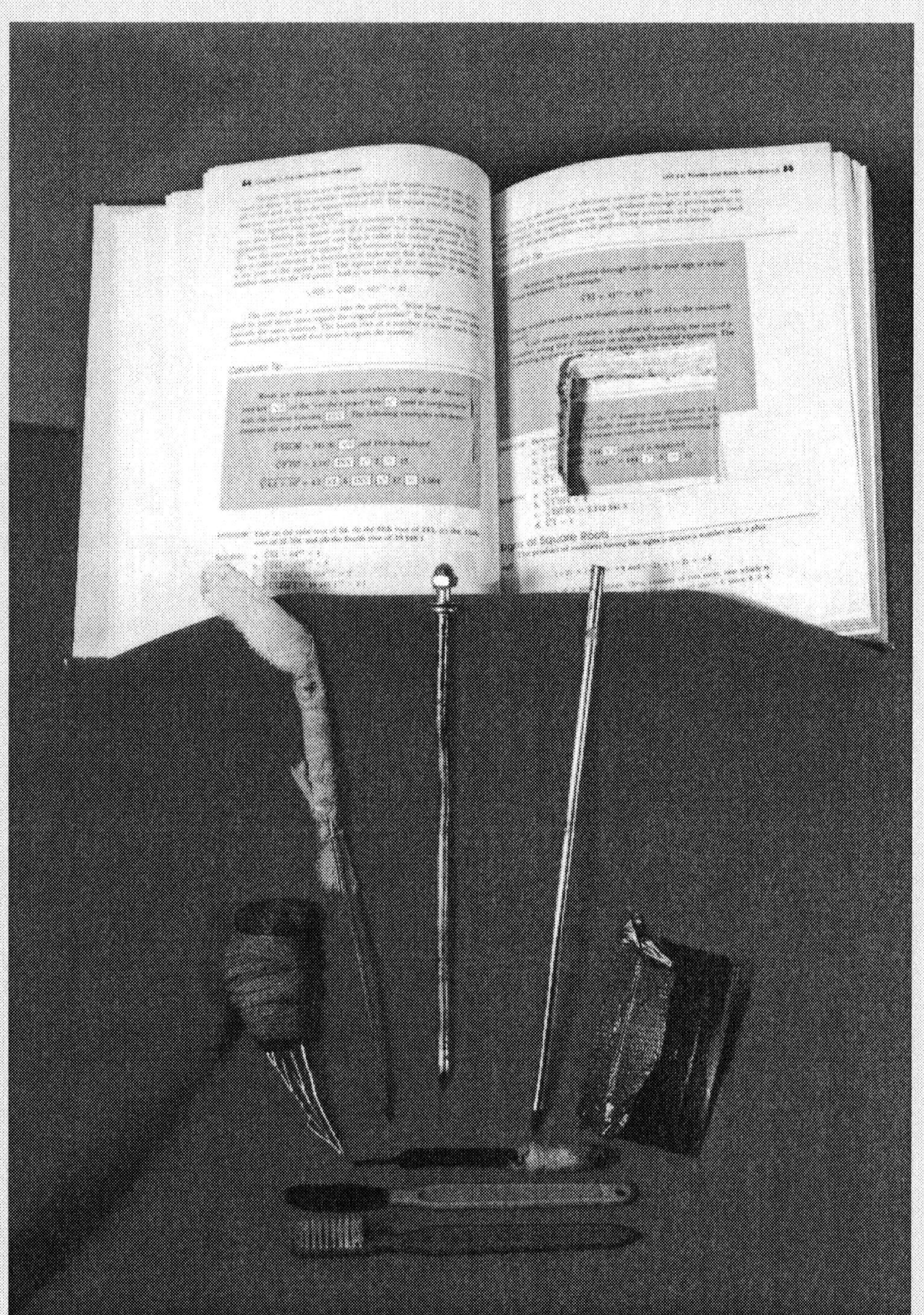

Series of photos depicting weapons (contraband) found by staff at the Albany County, NY Correctional Facility: homemade knives (shanks) made from parts of sneakers, mops, pieces of metal, and toothbrushes. Note that a hollowed our school book was used to hide weapon.

Photos courtesy Edward W. Szostak. Photos taken by Al Roland, Albany County Correctional Facility, Albany, NY. Special thanks to Edward W. Szostak, Criminal Justice Consultant and former Superintendent, Albany County Correctional Facility. Mr. Szostak can be reached at ewszostak@aol.com.

## Controlling Keys, Tools, and Personal Items

All staff, volunteers, and visitors inside a jail must learn immediately the importance of keeping control of their keys, tools, and personal belongings. Inmates are exceptionally talented scavengers, and many will pick up or steal anything that they feel is useful to them for many reasons such as escape, fashioning a weapon, tattooing themselves, etc.

### *Keys*

All jail officers carry keys. In most modern jails, the cellblock and security doors are all opened from a central control area or by the use of a computerized "swipe card." However, officers still carry keys to unlock closets, to unlock cellblock food slots for feeding and the passing of mail and commissary, to unlock offices, and operate elevators. A sacred rule among jail officers is to *never lose your keys.* In case of being attacked or taken hostage, keys that unlock outside doors are not carried by officers inside the jail. In the older type jails, large brass keys were used to unlock the **lockboxes**. Lockboxes were large steel cabinets at the end of a cellblock outside the main cellblock door. This cabinet contained all of the levers that locked/unlocked the individual cell doors by sliding them open or shut. Inmates were advised by the jail officers to keep their hands, legs, and heads clear to avoid injury. In one southern U.S. jail, an inmate managed to get a sharp piece of metal and some wood. By observing the key hanging from the officer's belt, he was able to whittle a wooden key, which was found and confiscated. When the staff tried the key inside the lock box, it worked and it could open the lock box. Some of the old jails still in operation use the levers and lockbox system. Needless to say, large brass keys should be carried in a way that the teeth of the key are concealed from inmates' view. Jail officers soon learn that inmates are very adept observers and can improvise quickly.

Key control, whether it be the actual keys or computer card "keys," is a primary duty of a jail officer. In a jail, besides regular operations or post-issued keys, there are eight types of keys:[22]

*Backup keys:* Keys to limited areas such as the armory, lock shop, maintenance shop, control centers, etc. These keys are located in a secure area outside of the main jail secure perimeter, such as in a control booth.

*Emergency keys:* These keys allow staff access to all areas of the jail in the event of a computer malfunction, where doors cannot be opened with a computer card, a riot, a disturbance, a fire, natural disaster, a power outage, or a serious emergency. For example, a master key opens all of the security doors in the jail. Emergency keys are usually kept in a secured area and are separate from all regular issue keys. If these keys are distributed in an emergency, the inmates are usually secured in their housing areas.

*Inactive keys:* Keys that are no longer used by staff and are retained as spare and backup keys for unused locking devices. They are maintained separately for areas for other uses, including storage for other parts of the agency or other facilities.

*Master keys:* Master keys are cut so that one may unlock many locks throughout the jail that are made by a single manufacturer.

*Pattern keys:* These are pattern keys from which all other keys for a certain lock or series of locks are cut. They are stored separately from all other spare or blank keys.

*Restricted keys:* Restricted keys allow access to sensitive areas of the facility, such as the pharmaceutical storage area, the evidence locker, firearms storage area, emergency response/riot gear lockers, etc. To obtain them, an officer must get special authorization from a supervisor. The following are areas of restricted key issue:

- Commissary sales and storage areas.
- Property and valuable storage areas.
- Evidence storage areas.
- Personnel records and inmate records storage areas.
- Warehouse, kitchen, and food service areas.
- Armory, weapons vault, emergency response.
- Medical areas including pharmaceutical storage.

*Security keys:* Security keys are keys that if lost or duplicated, an escape may occur or inmates would seize the opportunity to jeopardize the security of the facility, property, or anyone inside the jail. If a security key is lost, misplaced, or compromised, immediate remedial action must be taken. An example would be a fire exit door, which is designed for inmate/staff evacuation in case of fire. When open, it leads to the outside. As a rule, post officers do not carry these keys. If the doors must be opened, such as for testing, all inmates are locked in, and the area is clear of any inmate traffic.

*Vehicle keys:* Keys to vehicles, including transport vehicles, cruisers, supply vehicles, forklifts, etc. should be stored outside the jail's inner perimeter.

Another important key to keep possession of is the handcuff key. Jail officers routinely carry handcuffs and handcuff keys. If an inmate needs restrained for any reason, handcuff keys are used to double lock the handcuffs. Inmates will consider the handcuff key worth its weight in gold. However, paper clips, ballpoint pen refills, or any small piece of metal that can fit into the handcuff keyhole can be used to pick the lock of the handcuffs.

The American Correctional Association based in Alexandria, Virginia, is one of the leading organizations in corrections. They recommend these guidelines for proper jail key control:[23]

- All keys must be cross-indexed, numbered, showing through documentation where the keys fit, their use, what particular keys are on what particular ring, and what staff member uses those keys and is responsible for them.
- All keys must be checked out and returned to a secure control area, outside of the jail's inner perimeter.
- Staff members should never toss keys, leave them lying on a desk or hanging from a lock. Keys should always be retained by the staff person and if necessary to allow their use by another staff member, transferred by hand.
- Keys should never, at any time, come into contact with inmates.
- Entrance keys, grand master keys, external door keys, or any key having the capability to break the security outer perimeter and allow access to the outside should not be carried inside the jail for any reason except in emergencies, and only when all inmates are secured and officers are stationed at exit points.
- Staff members should never leave the jail with their keys or take them home.

- If appropriate, such as in work release dormitories or minimum-security institutions, inmates may have keys to their rooms. Inmates should never see staff keys or be allowed to handle them for any reason.

### Tools

Like all buildings that are lived in by many types of people, jails need constant upkeep by maintenance staff, food service staff, computer technicians, and a variety of contracted civilian workers. These workers do everything from fixing plumbing to pulling cable for computers. Often staff will have to "shuffle" around inmates to empty housing areas, so that work and repairs can be done. One key element of security is to have staff and authorized workers keep control of their tools, including kitchen utensils. Ideally, jail officers escort each worker or group of workers throughout the facility, keeping the workers away from inmates. However, a lost or misplaced tool can be very handy to the inmate as a means of escape or a weapon. Ideally, contractors and repair personnel should always be screened, authorized, and given a quick security orientation as to the type of environment that they will be entering. What is important to stress is that a jail is not like any other workplace; trash, debris, tools, parts, and miscellaneous refuse must be cleaned up, and the area inspected by the jail staff. The following guidelines are for effective control of tools:

- All construction personnel should be briefed and informed of security requirements before the work is to begin. Throughout the project, staff needs to monitor the security of the operation, review deficiencies, and correct any problems.[24]
- Contractors must be instructed not to have any contact with any jail inmate. They need to inventory and be responsible for all items: all tools, screws, nails, etc.[25]
- All tools and utensils should be controlled through a system. Some jails use a shadow board, some, number the tools, and some combine these systems with a tool-control officer who is responsible for logging in and out tools to and from authorized staff and supervised inmate workers. Daily checks and inventories are strongly recommended, and broken or discarded tools must be thrown away outside of the jail's security perimeter.[26]
- If necessary, change the makeup and composition of tools, items, and fixtures inside the jail. For example, for the inmate janitor crew, plastic mop buckets, wringers, and mop frames inside the mops are better for security than metal ones. Most jails now have stainless steel sinks and toilets with push button controls that are tamper resistant. Plastic chairs replace wooden chairs or metal folding chairs. Plastic storage lockers for the inmates can replace metal ones. Cleaning and food supplies should be in plastic containers having plastic lids and clips to replace metal lids and twist ties, which can be used by inmates to conduct electricity from an outlet. As contraband can be hidden and transported in trash bags that are often opaque, trash bags should be clear so that the jail officer at a glance can see what is inside.[27]

### Personal Items

Everyone who works inside a jail whether civilian or sworn staff is responsible for the safekeeping of his or her personal items. Personal items include but are not limited to jewelry, eyeglasses, wallets, cellular phones, pens, pencils, purses, teaching material, pagers, personal keys, etc. The best rule of thumb is to not take anything inside a jail that is not absolutely necessary. If any of these items are lost or stolen, inmates can have the upper hand. For example, an officer loses his cellular phone while breaking up an inmate fight. Once that cell phone is picked up by other inmates, they have an unauthorized way to contact the outside. If a ballpoint pen is lost, inmates may have a handcuff key or ink for jailhouse tattoos. Anything metal—a badge, a nameplate, a set of keys, etc.—can be turned into a weapon. One jail officer told the author that before entering a cellblock to subdue an inmate, officers would remove eyeglasses, pens, etc., so that they would not be lost or grabbed by the inmate for use as a weapon.

A growing trend in jail security training is to impress upon all workers not to carry personal items, especially those that are not needed, into the jail. These items should be secured in lockers or special storage rooms before entering the jail. In one southern jail, sworn staff who conduct civilian training stress this point. A locker room in the jail's outer lobby at the entrance to the inner perimeter was made available to civilians and volunteers.

Another aspect of personal items is that through observation of such innocuous items such as keys, inmates are able to tell a lot about the person. For example, a set of personal keys can tell an inmate

- The type of car that the person drives.
- Whether the person lives in an apartment or a house and if there is a deadbolt lock.
- Because of discount swipe cards, where the person shops.
- If the person belongs to a special organization, like a fitness club.
- If the person has a family, by looking at photos on a key ring.

These are pieces of information that no inmate should ever know about a staff member or civilian.

## Providing Perimeter Security

There are two perimeters in the jail compound. The **outer perimeter** encompasses the outer grounds of the jail and the approaches to it, by vehicle and pedestrian traffic. The outer perimeter may be bordered with a fence, a masonry wall, or a combination of the two. The outer perimeter line of the jail may be walled or fenced. An open space may exist between the outer border and an inner fence. Both the outer and the inner borders may use either barbed wire, **razor wire**, which is coiled barbed wire topped with razor-like blades. The American Correctional Association recommends that wherever possible, a "buffer zone" with a width of 100–150 feet should exist between the facility building(s) and the inner fence and between the outer fence and adjacent neighborhood buildings or tree lines.[28]

Some jails, because of their location in neighborhoods or congested urban areas, do not have a walled perimeter and may border a street. For example, at the Arlington County Detention Facility in Arlington, Virginia, the jail is located in a downtown urban setting, which opens up into an office plaza. In the neighboring City of Alexandria, the jail is located in an isolated setting, at the end of an access

Triple perimeter barrier.

Photo reprinted with permission of the American Correctional Association.

road on the outskirts of the city's urban area. At the Clarke-Frederick-Winchester Regional Adult Detention Center in Winchester, Virginia, the jail and the adjacent work release center are located in an open area at the end of a road, surrounded by a large field, on the outskirts of the City of Winchester. In various types of jail perimeters, security is maintained because there are a limited number, ideally no more than two, entry points for vehicular and pedestrian traffic operated from a remote location such as a tower or control center. Emergency exit doors are not able to be opened from the outside. Windows consisting of shatter-resistant glass cannot be opened and are sealed. Some jails rely on observation towers located at specific intervals around the outer perimeter.[29] The tower officer is responsible observing and visually checking the zone around his tower, both inside and outside the border, for contraband that may have been thrown over the fence, unauthorized inmate movement, inmates attempting to penetrate the perimeter and escape, and suspicious persons, vehicles, or items close to the inside or outside of the jail's perimeter.

Some facilities enlist the security method of roving **outside patrols.** These patrols can consist with an officer inside a vehicle, or by one officer or a two-officer team on foot. Jail policy will dictate how random these checks are to be conducted. In all cases, they must be logged. Outside patrol officers look for any security breaches, suspicious persons or activities, or contraband. Outside patrol officers and tower officers are in constant communication and observation with the main control center via radio, telephone, and television.

The **inner perimeter** is the next barrier inside from the outer perimeter, with controlled entrances through lobby checkpoints and sally ports into the jail work and inmate areas, or the jail proper. The **sally port** is the entrance/exit for vehicles and persons delivering supplies, doing maintenance, bringing official visitors to the jail, transporting incoming inmates to be booked in or returned and inmates under official escort to be transported out. Sally port doors can be opened by remote control from a control center after the vehicle; driver and persons are identified by a CCTV camera and through voice intercom. Emergency vehicles, such as police, fire, and rescue vehicles, may enter the jail complex through the sally port. In some jails, such as the Baltimore City Central Intake and Booking Center, a jail officer is stationed at the sally port entrance to verify the vehicle and people inside as having official business inside the jail. Sally ports connect to an inmate reception area, which is covered in Chapter 4, *Booking and Initial Intake*. Booking and intake centers can house inmates waiting processing and classification, but are usually located away from the jail's general inmate population.

Pedestrian traffic, such as the public visiting inmates, official visitors to the jail, law enforcement officers, social workers, attorneys, probation officers, counselors, etc. may also enter the outer perimeter through a lobby and check in with the jail's sworn staff or authorized civilian staff. Visitors check into the jail at an information desk in the jail lobby, similar to a lobby at a hotel, or in some jails, at the control center window. Identification is checked, and the visitor must state the purpose of his or her visit. Jails can regulate the hours of visitation, post visiting rules, and sworn staff is posted to check in visitors and observe the visiting activities. **Professional visits,** such as with attorneys, bail bond personnel, law enforcement officers, clergy, social workers, counselors, etc. in most jails take place in a secure room with the inmate. Professional visitors are required to show picture identification; some visitors such as clergy may have to be on a pre-approved list. These rooms are under visual observation by a jail officer, and an intercom call button is available so that the visitor can call an officer in emergencies or to be allowed out at the conclusion of the visit. **Personal visits** are defined as inmate visits with family and/or friends. To prevent contraband, personal visits are conducted through glass and phone, with no physical contact between the visitor and the inmate. Up until the 1980s, and still occurring in some older jails, is personal visiting through a wire screen or by sitting at a bench with a high physical barrier between the inmate and the visitor. Many jails rely on the visiting list system, where the inmate has to list the family members and friends that may come to visit; changes may only be permitted at a certain time, such as once per month.

Some jails, as a reward to inmate workers or for a verifiable good reason, will grant an inmate a **personal contact visit.** This type of visit allows the inmate to visit with a family member or significant other in the same room, with strict rules such as holding hands only, no sexual misconduct, set time limit, a kiss at the start and end of the visit, etc. The inmate is subject to strip search at the conclusion of the visit. Contact visits are not a right; they are at the discretion of the jail administration. Some jails grant them, while others do not. One veteran jail officer related several reasons for granting them that he observed in his career: death in the family, children of the inmate having adjustment problems in home and at school, or very satisfactory work performance by a trusty. It is being increasingly recognized that contact visits are one of the best ways to get contraband smuggled in: in a New England jail in 2001, an inmate's wife was charged with drug possession and delivering drugs to a prisoner. She reportedly placed a heroin-filled balloon in her nine-year-old daughter's mouth and told her that it was medicine for her stepfather. She then told her to kiss him. Jail officers intervened and caught the child passing the drugs. The stepfather was also charged.[30]

Concerning perimeter security, jail officers must expect the unexpected. In 2004, a Virginia deputy sheriff shot and wounded a man whose son had been arrested and jailed for driving under the influence. The upset father drove into the jail's parking lot and right up to the front door of the jail. He exited his vehicle brandishing an AK-47 assault rifle with a bayonet attached. He had an ammunition belt slung around his chest containing 300 rounds. The deputy tried to stop the man who turned toward the deputy, making it necessary for the deputy to open fire. The jail had received a phone call warning them of the man's plan to come to the jail, saying that the man was intoxicated, irate, and confrontational.[31]

## Effective Patrol Techniques

The containment and prevention functions of jail security depend on the effectiveness of the jail officers patrolling the areas inside and outside. Good security patrols are similar to the police patrols on the street. The same principle—making the community safer by preventing crimes and taking actions against wrongdoers—applies equally to the jail setting. Another important similarity of police patrol and jail officer patrol is to know the people—the police know the citizens—good and bad, in their area, and the jail officer knows the inmates, good and bad—in his or her area of the jail.

Good patrol techniques inside a jail means that officers are *nosey*-looking, inspecting, observing, and watching. Inmates should always be "looking over their shoulder," wondering where the officer is or where the officer may appear.

The following are tenets of effective jail security patrol techniques that security minded jail officers should follow:[32]

- *Knowing the inmates in your area*: who they are, what their normal behavior patterns are, what their problems are, any special needs that they might have, who belongs where, not only in the cellblock or dormitory, but what inmates are allowed in an area, such as trusties. Knowing certain behavioral habits can benefit the officer: which inmates are "bullies," steal, are disciplinary problems, are frightened, or follow the rules and get along with both the staff and other inmates. For example, an inmate who is normally upbeat and socially outgoing withdraws suddenly and seems irritated. This could be a sign that something is wrong at home—such as a marital problem—which could lead to a suicide attempt. Too many trusties "wandering" into your area could be a sign that messages and contraband are being passed. Besides observation, the best way to get to know inmates is to circulate and talk to them. An inmate in an area where trouble is brewing may not want to be part of it and may talk to you.
- *Preventative patrol*: Simply put, preventative patrol is visibility. Its objective is to prevent, by your presence: sexual assaults, equipment tampering, escape attempts such as digging or tunneling, gang activity, fights, manufacture and/or storage of contraband, verbal arguments, suicide attempts, and other serious incidents. Inmates are opportunists and will look for any situation (such as a lax jail officer, an officer that does not move around too much, or one that is not

inquisitive) to engage in illicit and illegal activities. Inmates will try to anticipate jail officer's movements. Signs of security problems many include:

- Blankets and towels draped across cell door/cellblock door windows or hanging from a top bunk to a bottom bunk: inmates can be covering up sexual assaults, digging, etc. In one western U.S. jail, inmates placed towels over the cell door windows, which blocked the view to tunneling; the inmate was trying to dig out through the wall. In another jail, inmates broke out a dayroom window and jumped. The view to the inside dayroom was blocked by a hanging towel.
- Inmate clothes lines strung from one side of a cell to the other: blocks the view of the interior of the cell.
- Increasing amounts of "nuisance"-type contraband, such as magazines, newspapers, books, etc., means more places to hide contraband and more time and effort needed to search through it.
- Inmate lookouts: inmate standing "guard" at cellblock doors and windows are constantly looking out for staff.
- Be alert for signs of obvious tension (see Chapter 3, *The Jail Climate*).

- *Practice officer safety*: Inmates must see that officers have good voice and visual communication with each other at all times. Officers should avoid being "blind," turning a corner too fast where inmates may be waiting to attack, reaching into a crevice or space in a cell area blindly and not knowing if a piece of sharp contraband is there, or entering a cellblock dayroom with a shower curtain closed. Inmates have been known to wait behind shower curtains and doors to attack officers. Officers should never enter cells alone; a back up officer should be summoned. Officers should expect the unexpected; they may surprise inmates in the act of doing something negative or hiding.
- *Use unorthodox patrol procedures*: The standard time frame for checking inmates is every 30 minutes or twice an hour in general population areas and every 15 minutes or less for special management inmates. Officers should be **"systematically unsystematic"** and vary their routine enough that the inmates cannot predict where they will patrol and not be able to set a "stopwatch" based on their habits. Also, during patrol, officers should use **"Backtracking"** when checking an area. The inmates may think that they are "in the clear," and the officers immediately return to the area and look again.
- *Using inmates as confidential sources of information*: Not all inmates want to engage on illegal or unauthorized activity. Many just want to do their time and be released. Some realize that if they are in an area and an event occurs, such as an escape, inmate assault or riot, they can be suspected as being part of it. Inmates want to survive. Some inmates will approach an officer on patrol and relay information that could have a serious bearing on the security of the facility. These inmates are called **confidential informants:** inmates who supply critical information to correctional officers or staff members with the understanding that the officer or staff member will not divulge the inmate's identity. The more modern term for confidential informant is the slang term, used by inmates and staff, the **"snitch."**

Care has to be exercised by the officer when working with confidential informants. The number one priority is to keep the identity of the informant secret, both verbally and in writing. It is customary to write in incident reports that information was received from a confidential informant. Also, officers are cautioned not to discuss the identity of "snitches" within earshot of inmates, no matter whom they are. In the atmosphere of a jail, the officer cannot leave paperwork, such as an incident report, lying about or be loose lipped when discussing informants. Inmates do not like informants, because it violates the "inmate code" (see Chapter 3) and any inmate who testifies against another puts him or herself in danger and subject to attack and harassment. Informants are crucial to the disciplinary process because many rules violations are witnessed by inmates.[33]

There are occasions when a serious incident is being investigated in a crowded unit, such as an assault, fight, or a serious incompatibility problem among the inmates. In such cases, a copy of the report will not be given to an inmate who is charged with an offense because other inmates, who are not necessarily confidential informants, may be mentioned in the report as giving information. This is an exception to a basic inmate right of receiving written notice of a disciplinary charge in the form of a report.

Not all informants' motives are genuine. Many jail officers rely on what may be called the **"respected informant,"** such as an older inmate who has done a lot of time in prison or jail. This type of informant basically wants to do his or her time and not get into trouble. If he or she is in a situation where this stable environment is compromised, such as being in a cellblock where an escape is being planned, the respected informant may give information to the staff asking no favor in return because he or she does not want to get caught up in any trouble.

The opposite type of informant is called the **"dubious informant."** This informant may have underlying, self-serving motives in giving staff information. Some inmates may cooperate due to a genuine "desire to reform" to gain a measure of self-respect and repay society for their crimes.[34] With some inmates, there may be opposite motives, such as:[35]

- *Revenge*: The inmate believes that he or she is being mistreated by inmates or certain staff members.
- *Fear*: The inmate may fear that he or she may be the target of another inmate or group of inmates.
- *Animosity*: The inmate may want to eliminate the "competition," such as a rival for power in a unit, an enemy from the outside, or a rival gang member.
- *Egotism*: The inmate wants staff to look upon him or her favorably. However, manipulation may also be an underlying motive.
- *Reward*: To be granted a favor, such as a privilege ranging from a phone call, special visit, or trusty job, an inmate will give the staff information.
- *Game-playing*: The inmate may want to "screw around" with the staff and confuse them (especially new officers) by giving false information.

Information from a confidential informant may be used in a disciplinary hearing or in a court of law if an inmate is charged with a criminal offense. The hearing officer must be convinced that the concerned confidential informant is reliable and not just relying on a statement just saying that that is true. The jail officer must be able to explain *why* the informant is reliable. Also, the informant must be credible due to specific, detailed information that is corroborated by facts. The more detailed the information is that is presented, the more credible it is.[36] In all cases of using a confidential informant, the jail officer should make every effort to corroborate the information.

## Properly Transporting Inmates

Inmates will use any means to escape. A situation may present itself during a transport to court, another jail, a medical visit, or any time that the inmate is officially removed from the security confines of the jail. They are out and may make a "break for it." If they escape, the public is at risk as inmates may commit new crimes to secure the means to avoid capture. In a broad sense, the taking of an inmate to the local courthouse, either through a connecting security corridor or by a short trip in a vehicle, is also an inmate transport. An **inmate transport** is defined as the removal of the inmate under correctional officer escort from the secure confines of the jail for official and authorized reasons such as court, police investigation, medical/psychiatric visits, or transfer to another jail or department of corrections facility.

Per the American Jail Association (AJA), a "routine" duty of "transporting inmates" can become "deadly." An illustration of this occurred a few years ago. Two jail inmates complained of food poisoning and were transported by an officer to a local hospital. The trip was "routine"; nothing occurred. Upon arrival, the inmates complained of diarrhea and asked the officer whether they could use the bathroom next to the emergency room. After checking the bathroom to make sure it was empty—standard procedure—the officer let them go in while he restricted access. Unobserved by the officer, the inmates secured a handcuff key and handgun that had been hidden in the paper towel dispenser by an accomplice. Coming out of the bathroom brandishing a gun, they tried to disarm the officer, who reached for his service weapon. One inmate shot and killed the officer; the other inmate took possession of the officer's gun. The two escaped into a friend's waiting car parked outside the emergency room.[37] In this case, a routine transport turned deadly in minutes, leaving an officer dead.

Such incidents can be avoided with proper preparation on all transports, from the normal groups of inmates going to court to transporting a high-risk prisoner cross country to another jail. While all inmates, no matter what their charge and sentence should be considered escape risks, a **high-risk prisoner** is an inmate or prisoner, who because of his criminal history, prior escape attempts, charge, conviction status, mental state or criminal affiliations (such as gangs) is considered especially a high risk to attempt to escape or assault a staff member. Their behavior is unpredictable. For example, an inmate convicted of capital murder and sentenced to death would be considered a high-risk inmate, as would an inmate with several escape charges and/or convictions on his record. Criminal affiliations are important. In the aforementioned example, a confederate assisted the inmates' escape. If an inmate is a high-ranking criminal gang leader, the possibility would exist that his gang may try to aid an escape. If a high-risk inmate is only going to a local court, he or she may still attempt escape. A mentally ill inmate may be unpredictable, violent or suicidal.

To maintain the security network when dealing with transports, proper attention as to the procedures, the inmate being transported, and equipment must be given.

For court in an adjacent or nearby building:

- All restraining equipments, handcuffs, waist chains, leg restraints, etc., must be checked frequently for signs of tampering and wear.
- All inmates should be searched before being taken to court. Only legal work should be allowed in the inmate's possession, and that too should be inspected.

- If the court inmates have to be moved through an open area, citizens should be kept away and have no contact with the inmates.
- Because inmates' friends and family may be in the courtroom, the courtroom should be inspected and searched before court and sufficient staff should be on hand, especially in high-profile trials for serious crimes. Inmates should never have contact with family or friends in the courtroom.
- As a precaution, inmates should be searched upon returning from court. If they are allowed to wear civilian clothes for felony trials, the civilian clothes should be immediately removed and secured.
- Jail officers should have knowledge of the inmates' behavior and charges. Many jails publish a daily escape risk list, listing those inmates with a high degree of propensity to escape. Officers should have a copy of that list with them for easy reference.

For transporting to another correctional facility, medical/psychiatric appointments, court in another jurisdiction, etc.[38]

- Planning is important; how transported (vehicle, air, etc.), destination, what route, how many officers, knowledge about the inmate as to jail history, charge, and conviction status are all important. Plan for unexpected security problems. Verify the authority to move the inmate.
- The checking of equipment including restraints, vehicles, and radio communications must be performed. There should be nothing in the vehicle to aid an escape or that may pose a safety problem, such as a vehicle breakdown. In an Ohio jail in 1989, jail personnel discovered that the inmates being transported in a van figured out how to use the seat belt clips to break the connecting chain on swivel handcuffs. Upon arrival at another jail, the transporting officer opened the back of the van to discover that 10 inmates were loose, and all of them were quite amused that they had accomplished this.
- Thoroughly search the transporting vehicle and the inmate (including a possible strip search) for contraband. Officers should not assume that the inmate and vehicle has been searched by other personnel. Also, there is always the risk of **recontamination**, where the inmate may be contraband free when the transport begins, but may pick up something such as an object that can be manufactured into a weapon, civilian clothes, drugs, etc., while out on the transport outside of the jail. Officers must search the inmate upon return. This may require a strip search.
- Properly apply all restraining devices before removing the inmate from the secure confines of the jail. Make sure handcuffs, waist chains, and leg restraints all fit properly and are double locked. The most secure way to restrain an inmate on a transport is to cuff the hands behind the back. On long trips, this may be uncomfortable. An option is to use a waist chain or type of restraint that retrains the hands onto a waist restraint so that the hands and arms cannot move.
- Make sure that the destination area is safe before removing the inmate from the transporting vehicle.
- Do not accept inmate suggestions as to where to eat, the "best" route of travel, or restroom facilities. They could be a set up.

- A female officer should be on transports involving female inmates. If this is not possible, the transporting officer should document thoroughly departure time, arrival time, and mileage directly to the destination. This helps to avoid female inmate accusations of sexual assault, misconduct, and harassment.
- Officers must remember that the time that they are most vulnerable to inmate assaults and escape attempts is when they are removing the restraining device. This task should be done by one officer with another or several officers present as backup, observing the inmate.
- At least 48 hours or more prior to an air transport, transporting officers should obtain and study the airline's policies and procedures for transporting inmates.
- Under no circumstances should an inmate or member of his family be informed of the details of the transport, including destination, date of departure, and means of travel.
- Inmates should be transported in highly visible clothing, such as red, yellow, or day glow orange. If he or she does escape, visually locating that inmate would be easier.

Additional guidelines to follow in transporting inmates would be:[39]

- Maintain a professional attitude with the inmate at all times.
- Never place an inmate directly behind the vehicle driver if the transporting vehicle is not equipped with a separation cage.
- The inmate(s) to be transported must be informed of the ground rules of the transport: no phone calls, all orders are to be followed, etc.
- In high-risk prisoner escorts, scout the route in advance, gather intelligence on the inmate, and arrange for security along the route and at the destination.

## Having Emergency Procedures

Things can go wrong in a jail, like in any building. Power outages can occur, computerized door locks can fail, and depending on the location of the jail, the effects of natural disasters such as earthquakes and hurricanes/severe weather can be felt. Every jail should have emergency plans for such serious events. These plans should include these responses based on the number one priority: security.[40]

- Make sure the security perimeters of the jail—inner and outer are intact, so as to not endanger the public.
- The crisis, fire, hostage, etc., should be contained to the smallest area possible inside the jail.
- Ensure that all staff, inmates, and visitors are accounted for and safe.
- Have up-to-date notification information (phone numbers, addresses, etc.) of staff and outside agencies so that manpower and resources can be mustered quickly.
- Ensure due process for all inmates who may be charged with criminal law violations, and take steps necessary to preserve evidence.
- During any evacuation, maintain security, including proper use of weapons and equipment.

- Ensure that appropriate information is approved by the agency head or representative and released to the media.
- Take appropriate post-emergency actions to care for inmates and staff and as soon as practicable, resume normal operations.
- Debrief, to include investigations as to what went wrong, what went right, what can be improved, and what training is needed.

It is difficult to predict what type of emergency, its location and the time it will occur. Many jails run annual drills with local fire departments or run in-house drills and training exercises. These drills include mock injuries, smoke conditions, and equipment training, such as fire extinguishers, air packs, and fire hoses. The above list is a thumbnail guide of responses based on a sound plan. A progressive jail will have a good emergency plan that is annually revised. One important component of any emergency plan is the command center. The emergency could be anything from a fire to a hazardous material spill/leak to a weather-related emergency. Generally speaking, a good jail emergency plan should contain the following components, which closely tie in to the aforementioned responses.[41]

- Definition of the emergency for each plan: Fire, hostage, weather-related emergency should all be clearly defined.
- Which areas have the potential for problems: For example, the kitchen and laundry areas are potential fire areas.
- Preventative steps to be taken: Fire inspections, etc.
- Notification system: A jail officer discovers a problem. By what means does he or she report the problem? Are there code signals to be announced and does everyone, including civilian staff and volunteers know what they mean and what to do? For example, Code Red mans fire, Code Green means clear, etc.
- Checklists to secure the facility: For example, an officer is working a cellblock post, and the escape code is announced. Is there a handy checklist for him to refer to in order to secure his area and lock the inmates down? How are programs canceled, non-emergency staff evacuated, and inmates returned to their quarters?
- Notification of command staff, especially after normal business or duty hours, when many emergencies occur. A staff directory of contact information combined with a checklist is recommended. Also important is who decides to call and who makes the calls? Usually the shift supervisor starts this sequence of events, calling a **staff duty officer (SDO).** The SDO is a supervisor of high rank, usually a captain or higher, who is on call to lend advice, take charge, or make decisions in times of critical emergency or unusual situations.
- Additional people and agencies to call: Local police, fire hospitals, transport companies, etc. all should be listed. Memorandums of agreement on the roles of outside agencies and their duties should be on file and updated annually.
- Command center: Where it should be located, who reports in, communication to and from, lines of authority to initially respond to the crisis and adapt and expand as the situation lengthens. The **command center** is a central headquarters for the staff in charge of the emergency to meet, plan, evaluate the situation, communicate with all involved and issue orders, make statements to the media and to meet with the families of staff/inmate hostages.

- Media: Only one official speaking for the jail head or sheriff should be speaking to the media, so as to not jeopardize a delicate and sensitive situation. Also, a media staging area should be set up away from the command center.
- Crisis team: If staff members are taken hostage, or are seriously or fatally injured, staff members trained in crisis intervention, and peer support should have an area to meet with other staff and the families of affected personnel.
- Position statements: A jail should include in its emergency plans policy statements on hostages, escapes, work stoppage, bombs, fires, etc. Also included in a position statement are training procedures. For example, it can be stated that there will be a joint annual fire drill involving the jail staff, the local fire department, and the local police.
- Secondary operational steps for the command staff to take to resolve the emergency.

Probably the three most important emergencies that can occur that have a detrimental effect on jail security are fires, escapes, and riots/disturbances. All can result in the security framework being compromised. Riots and disturbances, their effect on the jail climate, and staff responses will be discussed in Chapter 3. Escapes are well planned by inmates taking advantage of contraband that is either manufactured or introduced. Fires can result in confusion and staff being overloaded with tasks to keep the inmates accountable and safe, the staff safe, and the physical plant of the jail as undamaged as possible.

*Fires*: In 1982, an inmate started a fire in the top floor of a 50-year-old urban jail. He was in a dormitory cell, and all seven inmates who were locked in that cell died. Fortunately only seven died in a jail that held 500 inmates. In late 1982, an inmate allegedly started a fire in an isolation cell of a new county jail. Inmate deaths totaled 29, and 59 inmates, jail officers, police officers, deputies, and fire fighters were injured.[42] A more recent example of a serious fire involving a jail is the August 27, 1998, fire in a tobacco company building one block from the Forsyth County, North Carolina Detention Center, in downtown Winston-Salem. Thanks to an evacuation plan that outlined procedures for such an emergency, inmates, including high-risk inmates, were evacuated from the jail to a nearby sports coliseum, a vacant county prison farm, North Carolina Department of Corrections facilities, and several neighboring county detention centers. Staff involved included the Detention Center's Special Response Team, off duty deputies and staff, the United States Marshals Service, the Winston-Salem Police Department, the North Carolina Department of Corrections, and numerous federal, state, and local agencies. A private bus company assisted in transporting inmates. Normal operations resumed at the detention center after an evacuation that lasted a little over 13 hours.[43]

There are many reasons that a fire can start in jails. Even though many jails do not allow smoking or tobacco-related paraphernalia, a mentally ill inmate may start a fire if his matches were missed on a search and not confiscated. Smuggled in smoking materials can result in a fire if inmates conceal smoking activities and do not fully extinguish cigarettes. Fires can break out in food preparation areas.

As far back as 1983, the National Fire Protection Association (NFPA) foresaw the need for corrections facility fire prevention and procedures in the event of a fire and began working with the American Correctional Association and was referenced in ACA's 2nd Edition of *Standards for Adult Local Detention Facilities*. Its Fire Safety System for Correctional Facilities developed four main objectives.[44]

- *Life safety*: protection of all individuals from death or injury by fire.
- *Property protection*: protection of facility structure and contents.
- *Limited downtime*: restricting the loss of use to a part of the facility where services can be replaced or resumed easily.
- *Security*: maintaining security and inmates must be prevented for committing suicide, escape, homicide/assault, or any act that breaches security.

Jails have progressed greatly in the last 20 years concerning fire prevention. Many jails have or are eliminating smoking privileges for inmates, and staff cannot smoke inside the building. This is a key element in fire prevention—the banning of fire-starting implements. Also, it makes for a healthier environment due to the elimination of secondhand smoke. This does not completely prevent fires from occurring, but the overall chances of a fire are significantly reduced. As part of an effective fire prevention policy, the American Correctional Association recommends the following:[45]

- When storing paints, flammable materials, and combustibles, facilities must follow the local fire code and standards such as ACA jail standards (see Chapter 10), NFPA, and local fire codes.
- Inmate bedding should be fire resistant, where they cannot burn or give off toxic fumes.
- Inspections, whether weekly, quarterly, and annual, should evaluate compliance with applicable fire and safety codes, results of staff fire drills, visual observation, and checking of all emergency equipment, including replacements if necessary. Every post as part of post orders should have an inspection performed of all fire-related equipment on the post, condition logged in writing, and deficiencies repaired immediately by qualified personnel.
- Degree of readiness of all fire-fighting equipment, including air packs, hoses and extinguishers.
- Readiness and placement of alarms and smoke detectors.
- Compliance with standards as to fire-resistant furnishings and facilities.
- Trash collection and discard procedures.
- Condition of all emergency exit signs.
- Distance to travel to reach exits.
- Emergency lighting.
- Facility evacuation plans: sufficient or in need of revision.
- Procedures for safety procedures with flammable materials, trash, etc.
- Initial reaction by staff and notification procedures.
- Location and tasks of a central command center.
- Assembly areas for staff and assigned duties in case of emergency.
- Accounting of inmates and keeping the security perimeter intact.
- Investigation of a fire situation, evaluation, and reporting by qualified personnel.
- Training in the fire emergency plan, fire prevention, and security concerns such as escape.

One example of a fire due to faulty equipment happened in 2004 in a southern U.S. jail. Due to the heat, fans were placed in inmate housing areas. Three of eleven inmates assigned to the housing area suffered smoke inhalation. The fire possibly started from a frayed cord or faulty motor. A new county jail meeting state and federal guidelines was due to open, and fans were not needed.[46]

*Escapes*: When most people look at a jail, a frequent thought is "How escape proof is it?" The primary mission of a jail is to keep the inmates locked in and allow no escapes. An escape plan should clearly define what actually an escape is. For example, an inmate "out of bounds" in the institution or being found "off limits" is not an escape. An **escape** is the breach of the security perimeter of the correctional facility, an authorized extended area of incarceration (such as on work release) or custody of a correctional officer (such as on a transport or in court) by an inmate resulting in unauthorized access into the community. Escapes can be either by force or by stealth and cunning, using a combination of manipulation and contraband.

Escaping from a penal facility such as a jail is against the law, subjecting the staff to conduct a criminal investigation and bringing the inmate and accomplices to criminal prosecution if apprehended. For example, in the Commonwealth of Virginia, the criminal code thoroughly covers the escape from, communications with, and deliveries to prisoners inside correctional facilities, including jails. A thumbnail guide to several code sections reveals the details of then offenses and their punishments.[47]

CCTVs with strategically placed cameras throughout the interior and exterior of the facility are critical to good jail security.

Photo by author, courtesy Butler County Prison.

- 18.2–473: If any person conveys anything into the jail, in any way aids the prisoner to escape or attempt to escape, or forcibly takes or attempts to take the inmate there from, the person could receive a felony conviction of 1–5 years if the escape was successful, and the inmate was detained on conviction, commitment, or charge of felony. If the escape is not successful and the prisoner is not detained on conviction, commitment or charge of a felony, the person shall be found guilty of a Class 1 misdemeanor (jail imprisonment of not more than 12 months, a $2,500 fine, or both).
- 18.2–473.1: Persons other than correctional personnel outside a facility that communicate by word or sign to a confined prisoner shall be guilty of a Class 4 misdemeanor (a fine of not more than $250.00).
- 18.2–474: If a person delivers *any article whatsoever* to a prisoner without staff authorization he or she is subject to conviction of a Class 1 misdemeanor.
- 18.2–474.1: Deliveries of illegal drugs to prisoners can result in a Class 5 Felony conviction (1–10 years and a $2,500 fine). If the articles are firearms, ammunition or explosives, the conviction is a Class 3 Felony (5–20 years and a $100,000 fine).
- 18.2–475: If a jail officer voluntarily allows a charged or convicted felon to escape, he or she will be guilty of a Class 4 Felony (2–10 years and a fine of not more than $100,000).
- 18.2–476: If a jail officer voluntarily allows a prisoner not charged with a felony to escape, he or she will be guilty of a Class 2 misdemeanor (either or both imprisonment not more than 6 months and no more than a $1,000 fine)
- 18.2–477: Any inmate confined in jail after conviction of a crime and escapes by force or violence, other than setting a fire, is guilty of a Class 6 Felony (either or both imprisonment of 1–5 years, and a fine of not more than $2,500, or the court at the discretion of a jury or court without a jury, a jail sentence up to 12 months). This sentence will commence from the completion of the former sentence.
- 18.2–478: If an inmate is in jail, and not tried or sentenced on a crime, and escapes by force or violence and does not set fire to the jail, or escapes from the custody of a police officer by force or violence, he or she will be guilty of a Class 6 Felony.
- 18.2–479: If a prisoner in jail or in the custody of a law enforcement officer or court and is charged or convicted of a misdemeanor, and escapes, with no force or violence or setting fire to the jail, he or she will be guilty of a Class 1 misdemeanor. If the prisoner escapes as described above and is charged or convicted of a felony, he or she will be guilty of a Class 6 Felony.
- 18.2–480: If any person lawfully confined in jail escapes or attempts escape by setting a fire to the jail, he or she will be guilty of a Class 4 Felony.

Much insight into the inmate and his or her criminological behavior and mind set can be gained in examining his or her criminal history to see what type, if any, escape charges are on record. There are not a great number of inmates on escape status at the time of arrest: 0.6 percent of jail inmates in 2002 as compared with 0.9 percent of jail inmates in 1996.[48]

An escape from a jail is a media event. Jails are usually viewed by the community as safe, secure facilities that keep inmates locked up and the community safe. When an inmate breaches the security perimeter, it makes news and can be potentially embarrassing for the corrections department or sheriff's office. A media investigation can result in possible deficiencies and mismanagement coming to light.

A good, functional escape plan should have these elements, which parallel the components of the general emergency plan. Each of these elements has a supporting rationale. They are[49]

- *Definition of an escape:* This sets a guideline for staff. Also, it sets the parameters for the usage of deadly force in the jurisdiction involved and per agency guidelines. An inmate out of bounds wandering in another part of the jail is not an escape or off limits violating a minor rule is not an escape.
- *Reporting an escape:* Jail officers and support staff should know the proper procedure to report an escape, usually to a central control booth or control center.
- *Announcing an alert to perimeter entry and perimeter patrol staff:* Immediately when an inmate is discovered missing, all staff around the perimeter must be notified with the inmate's name, identification photograph, and description. Inmates have been known to escape wearing civilian clothes.
- *Securing and locking down the jail:* When an escape is discovered or reasonably suspected, the entire jail population should be locked down in their living areas. All civilian staff should be located, accounted for, and escorted out at the discretion of the supervisor in charge of the situation. Civilian staff may get in the way of search efforts and also may be the target of a desperate inmate hostage taker.
- *Conducting an emergency count:* An immediate count and verification of inmate identity through either by wristband, photo, etc. should be conducted. This determines which inmate or inmates are missing and whether he, she, or they are using another inmate's identification.
- *Notification procedures for command staff:* The plan should state the order of notification of command staff. It is customary to start with the warden or chief jail officer.
- *Stating hostage policy:* The hostage policy of the agency should state that no inmate will be released with a hostage and that no hostage, no matter how high in rank, has any authority. For example, if the chief jail officer is taken hostage, for practical purposes, he is no longer the chief jail officer.
- *Continuance of essential staffing:* Some staff will have to aid in the emergency counts, inmate identification, facility search, and the search outside the facility for the inmate(s). Other functions, such as feeding, custody duties, court, booking, must continue.
- *Establishment of a command center:* The command center is the central point of the emergency, with internal communications from inside the jail, and coordination through external communications with local, state, and federal law enforcement personnel assisting in the escape hunt.
- *Recalling staff:* Off duty staff must be recalled if necessary to assist.
- *Notifying local law enforcement:* Authorized staff should notify local law enforcement, by what means, and the distribution of alerts Fax, e-mail, flyers for police cruisers, etc.
- *Use of internal searches:* An inmate or inmates may be hiding inside the facility awaiting the chance to escape, aided by darkness, bad weather, fog, confusion such as in a riot, disturbance or hostage situation, etc.
- *Use of external searches:* Plans must include "fresh pursuits," use of force coordination with local law enforcement, etc.

- *Outside escape posts:* The plan should establish outside fixed or roving escape posts, equipment needed, staffing, relief, and feeding.
- *Strategies and procedures for escapee apprehension:* Staff should receive training in procedures for apprehending an escapee. Escaped inmates are desperate people and may resist capture. Officer should not search a place, residence, etc., alone, two officers should be present to search an escapee. If only one officer is apprehending an escapee, the inmate should be told to lie flat on his or her stomach in a "spread eagle" position until assistance arrives. Use of force guidelines must be included in any briefings and training.
- *Notification of capture:* Plan should outline procedures for capture notification, cancellation of lookouts, etc.
- *Proper interviewing of escapes:* Escapees should be interviewed to gain information, but not in a way that hinders criminal prosecution.

Training can include other subjects, such as gathering information on an inmate escapee. Visiting lists can indicate who has been visiting the inmate and can be a reference point for a search, and items that are left in the inmate's cell may contain information. There may be information in the inmate's classification file and administration record. Other inmates in the unit may give insight in what the escapee may have been talking about, and law enforcement personnel such as police officers familiar with the inmate may give information as to places frequented on the street, associates, etc.

## A Digest of Actual Escapes

The following escapes are true accounts of jail inmates escaping, using deception, breaches in security, contraband, and daring:

- A convicted murderer, who was confined to a wheelchair, hacked away metal bars and broke an eighth floor window of an urban jail treatment facility. He climbed out leaving the wheelchair and tried to lower himself using a bedsheet rope. The rope became unraveled, and the inmate plunged to his death. His body was spirited away and dropped off at a nearby hospital by an unidentified woman.[50]
- An inmate escaped from a courthouse by forcing a wire mesh screen and walking past officers. He was captured in a motel in a nearby community. He was taken to that community's sheriff's office, where he escaped from a courthouse conference room by punching a hole in a bulletproof dividing screen.[51]
- An inmate acting as his own lawyer in court was allowed to wear civilian clothes, which were not taken from him upon return to the jail. He wore his jail coveralls over his civilian clothes, faked an ID by cutting out of a magazine a full face movie ad photo of actor Eddie Murphy, and wearing his civilian clothes, walked out of the jail.[52]
- Three inmates wearing correctional officer uniforms walked out of a jail. The resulting investigation revealed that inmates due to their mobility inside the jail could gain access to several areas where uniforms were stored.[53]
- An inmate who escaped by hiding in a garbage can was captured after a three-day search.[54]

- In a Pennsylvania county prison in 2002, an inmate escaped by going over a wall in an outdoor recreation area. He exploited a weakness in the razor wire (coiled barbed wire topped with razor-like blades) perimeter and took advantage of it.[55]
- Two jail inmates escaped from a county jail by using a piece of metal taken from a door casing and gouging out a hole in a concrete block wall. They were captured at a nearby truck stop after the van that they were driving broke down.[56]
- A Kentucky jail officer was charged with helping two inmates escape by walking out the front door on a "break" and letting the two inmates walk out. Authorities had the jail under surveillance. They had been "tipped" by a confidential informant that the jail officer had been bribed with money and drugs. At the time of the attempted escape, police saw a car parked near the jail. It sped off breaking a barricade. Police thought that it was a girlfriend of one of the inmates.[57]
- Five federal inmates escaped from a jail in Texas several years ago by crawling through an air duct to the jail roof and made a makeshift rope using bedsheets or mattress covers and lowering themselves to the ground.[58]

## Documenting and Passing on Critical Information

With all that is going on inside a busy jail—searches, counts, rule infractions, visiting, population moves—it is asked how, considering how important security is, staff can keep up with and communicate developments and information? There are several methods that can serve to tie together staff communications in a security network. A **security network** is a system that operates jail security through staff following agency procedures, post orders, sharing information through written and verbal communications, properly using security equipment, reporting security problems for follow up, taking action on inmate problems, and enforcing discipline.

Besides routine duties such as counts and inspections, the best methods for sharing vital information about inmates and the physical plant of the jail are several forms of written communications. The **incident report** documents unusual events in the jail: inmate rule violations, security problems, critical information about an inmate received from outside sources such as another jail, and observations of inmate behavior. The report can be used for referral, such as to mental health or medical staffs, a basis for a rule violation hearing and/or a criminal charge. The report should be numbered and approved by a supervisor who may authorize further actions and instructions. Incident reports should be filed in the inmate's classification file. Incident reports should answer the following questions in as much clear and concise detail as possible:

- *WHO* was involved? What inmates and staff? What staff and inmates who may be potential witnesses were present?
- *WHAT* happened? What did the staff and inmates do? Statements should be gathered from all staff involved and inmates who are willing to cooperate. Inmates may be reluctant to put information in writing. Information that they do have, even verbally, should be documented in the report. It is advisable to keep cooperating inmates' names confidential.

- *WHEN* did it happen? Reports should be accurate as to time and date.
- *WHERE* did it happen? This should be exact as to cell location, area, etc.
- *WHY* did the event occur? Sometimes the answer is clear, but often the jail officer may have to make a reasonable conclusion based on the facts and observations at hand.
- *HOW* did the inmate do the act, or how did the event take place? A reason or condition, if known, should be reported. For example, Inmate X managed to leave his area because the cellblock door was not properly secured.
- *ACTION TAKEN*: What was the follow up? Medical attention? Block locked down? Were the inmates charged with a criminal or disciplinary violation or both?

Incident reports should be read at staff roll calls where officers can make notes on problems in their areas. The central repositories for incident reports should be with the shift commander's report where approved reports and shift activities are reviewed by command staff and the inmate's classification file. If the inmate is not classified and is released from the jail, the report should be filed in the booking jacket. Also, a central archive, either as a database or as a paper hard copy file, is recommended as a back up system.

Other methods of documentation include memorandums for the classification file, e-mails, or memos from another jail that has incarcerated the inmate. Supervisors who are of the opinion that a serious security deficiency exists, such as a weak window screen, or an inmate is labeled an escape risk based on good information, or has knowledge of *any* condition or inmate that could jeopardize jail security, should order a report or other documentation be written.

Another method of communication is **pass-on,** or more simply the passing on of vital, critical information from a jail officer on a post to a relieving officer. Pass-on is also conducted at the shift and section levels, where an ongoing shift receives information about inmates, problems, etc. from the off going shift. Also, sections in the jail such as transportation and court holding receive information about inmates that they will be taking custody of. For example, an officer is coming onto the administrative segregation unit to assume the post for the next shift. Inmate John Jones, on protective custody due to his child molestation conviction, has just discovered through a phone call to his wife that she is planning to divorce him. He has been crying and asking to see the chaplain. Mental health has been alerted and will see him that day. That information, which is very critical, needs to be passed on from the officer who is relinquishing the post to the officer coming onto the post. Although many officers pass this information on verbally, the recommended way is in writing. Some jails use a logbook or a form, for critical and sensitive information. More routine details, such as feeding, etc. are passed on verbally. Incident reports can also be used to pass on vital information.

Pass-on information is important and may figure prominently in a criminal action or lawsuit. Roll call pass on takes place at the squad or shift meetings where an oncoming squad is relieving an off going squad. Incident reports and pass-on information is read to the officers, followed by instructions from their supervisors.

Alexandria Sheriff's Office incident report form.

**ALEXANDRIA SHERIFF'S OFFICE INCIDENT FORM**

| | | | | |
|---|---|---|---|---|
| **ALEXANDRIA SHERIFF'S OFFICE INCIDENT FORM** | 1. INCIDENT TITLE | | | 2. CASE NUMBER |
| 3. DATE AND TIME OCCURRED BETWEEN AND | | | 4. DATE AND TIME REPORTED | |
| 5. SUBJECT, VICTIM OR BUSINESS (LAST, FIRST, MIDDLE INITIAL) | 6. RACE (1) ☐ WHITE (3) ☐ SPANISH (5) ☐ AMER. INDIAN (2) ☐ BLACK (4) ☐ ORIENTAL (6) ☐ OTHER | | 7. SEX ☐ MALE ☐ FEMALE | 8. AGE |
| 9. ADDRESS OF SUBJECT, VICTIM OR BUSINESS | | HOME PHONE | WORK PHONE EXT. | |
| 10. LOCATION OF INCIDENT ☐ DETENTION CENTER ☐ COURT ☐ FIELD | EXACT LOCATION (NUMERICAL DESCRIPTION) | | | |
| 11. WITNESS #1 (LAST, FIRST, MIDDLE INITIAL) | AGE | ADDRESS | HOME PHONE | WORK PHONE/EXT. |
| 12. WITNESS #2 (LAST, FIRST, MIDDLE INITIAL) | AGE | ADDRESS | HOME PHONE | WORK PHONE/EXT. |
| 13. INJURY ☐ YES ☐ No | 14. LOCATION OF INJURY | 15. CONDITION | 16. TREATMENT ☐ MEDICAL UNIT/ADC ☐ EMT/FIRE DEPT. ☐ HOSPITAL ☐ OTHER________ | |
| 17. NARRATIVE: | | | | |
| 18. INMATE STATUS ☐ PRE-TRIAL ☐ CONVICTED ☐ SENTENCED ☐ FEDERAL ☐ MISD. ☐ FELONY ☐ WORK RELEASE ☐ OTHER________ | | | | 19. ☐ ENTERED IN CJIS |
| 20. REPORTING EMPLOYEE # | 21. FILED BY (INITIALS) | 22. APPROVING SUPERVISOR # | DATE | TIME |
| 23. DISPOSITION | | 24. PROPERTY NUMBER | | 25. PAGE OF PAGES |

F-SHR-0007 Rev. 9/88

Reprinted per permission Alexandria, VA Office of Sheriff.

The incident report can be the basis or foundation of a criminal charge or disciplinary action. Quite simply, it is an official document. The content and accuracy of the report is important because the report may be introduced in a court of law through subpoena for either civil litigation against the jail staff or criminal action.

## SUMMARY

The security of the jail is the primary mission of the jail staff. Security focuses on containment of the inmates and the prevention of serious security incidents and emergencies. It is important to keep inmates inside and, while there, in their authorized areas. Security is accomplished through the proper use of security hardware, conducting different types of headcounts, searching inmates, inspecting the jail, and keeping the inner and outer perimeter intact. Security also means keeping inmates in custody during transport to different official destinations and court. Emergency plans, primarily dealing with fire and escape, are a must in a secure jail setting. Escapes are violations of the law. Information sharing through a security network is crucial to effective operations.

## REVIEW QUESTIONS

1. When discussing security, what is meant by containment and prevention?
2. What are personal locator systems?
3. Define the three types of headcounts.
4. How does contraband exist inside a jail?
5. Define the three types of individual inmate searches.
6. What should be examined as part of a proper security audit?
7. Discuss three proper guidelines for key control.
8. What is the importance of staff keeping control of their personal items while inside the jail?
9. Differentiate between the outside and inside perimeters of a jail.
10. Discuss three tenets of effective jail security patrol.
11. What are the motives of the confidential informant?
12. How can a jail officer make a transport safer?
13. List and explain the four main objectives of a good correctional facility fire plan, according to the NFPA.
14. How can jail staff gather information about an escapee?
15. What questions should be answered in a properly written incident report?

## TERMS TO KNOW

back-tracking
backup keys
body cavity search
body or "strip search"
census count
command center
confidential informants
contraband
custody section
dubious informant
emergency count
emergency keys
escape
formal count
frisks or "pat downs"
headcount
high-risk prisoner
home brew
inactive keys
incident report
inmate transport
inner perimeter
lockboxes
master keys
outer perimeter
outside patrols
pass-on
pattern keys
personal contact visit
personal location systems
personal visits
professional visits
publishers only rule
razor wire
reasonable suspicion
recontamination
respected informants
restricted keys
sally port
security audits
security keys
security network
shakedowns
shanks
snitch
staff duty officer (SDO)
substance abuse searches
systematically unsystematic
trusties
vehicle keys

## ENDNOTES


1. Thomas R. Barry, "Jail Security: A Unique Challenge," *Corrections Today* (July 1987): 16–18.
2. Ibid., p. 16.
3. Walter R. Newcomb, "Basic Security Principles," *Jail Operations Bulletin* (American Jail Association) 1, no. 7 (1989): 2.
4. Donna Rogers, "Emergency Personal Location Systems: Essential or Excessive?" *Corrections Forum* (July/August 2004): 36–38.
5. Gary F. Cornelius, *The Correctional Officer: A Practical Guide* (Durham: Carolina Academic Press, 2001), p. 141.
6. Ibid.
7. Ibid., pp. 141–142.
8. Ibid., p. 142.
9. Ed Szostak, "Maintaining Safety and Security by Managing Contraband," *American Jails* (July–August 1998): 62–64.
10. Cornelius, *The Correctional Officer: A Practical Guide*, pp. 144–145.
11. Ibid., p. 145.
12. Ibid., p. 143–144.
13. Ray Sabbatine and Don Leach, "A New Strip Search Paradigm," *American Jails*, (November/December 1996): 39–42.
14. William C. Collins, J. D., *Correctional Law for the Correctional Officer, 4th Edition* (Lanham, MD: American Correctional Association, 2004), pp. 94–97.
15. Ibid., p. 97
16. Ibid., p. 92.
17. Szostak, "Managing Safety and Security By Managing Contraband," p. 64.
18. Brian Reilly, "Officers Raid Jail, 4 halfway houses," *Washington Times*, January 8, 1994.
19. Bill Siuru, "How Vulnerable is Your Facility, Really?" *Corrections Technology & Management* (September/October 2000): 30–32.
20. Ibid., pp. 31–32.
21. The Lighter Side, *The Detroit News*, January 11, 1996.
22. James D. Henderson, W. Hardy Rauch, and Richard L. Phillips, *Guidelines for the Development of a Security Program, 2nd Edition* (Lanham, MD: American Correctional Association, 1997), pp. 95–96.
23. Cornelius, *The Correctional Officer: A Practical Guide*, p. 140.
24. Szostak, "Managing Safety and Security by Managing Contraband," p. 63.
25. Ibid.
26. Cornelius, *The Correctional Officer: A Practical Guide*, p. 141.
27. Szostak, "Maintaining Safety and Security by Managing Contraband," p. 64.
28. Don Bales, ed., *Correctional Officer Resource Guide, 3rd Edition* (Lanham, MD: American Correctional Association, 1997), 37.
29. Ibid.
30. Associated Press, "Girl, 9, Used to Smuggle Drugs to Inmate," *The Corrections Connection*, http://www.corrections.connection/news/Justin/index.html (accessed October 5, 2001).
31. Allan Lengel, "Va. Deputy Shoots Armed Man Outside Jail," *Washington Post*, http://www.washingtonpost.com/ac2/wp-dyn/A32256–2004May17?language-printer (accessed May 17, 2004).
32. Patricia C. Perrin, ed., *Correctional Officer Correspondence Course: Book III: Security Issues* (Lanham, Md.: American Correctional Association, 1999), pp. 92–104.
33. Collins, *Correctional Law for the Correctional Officer*, p. 166.
34. Perrin, *Correctional Officer Correspondence Course: Book III*, p. 102.
35. Ibid.
36. Collins, *Correctional Law for the Correctional Officer*, p. 167.
37. John M. Sells, "Transportation of Inmates," *Jail Operations Bulletin* (American Jail Association) 1, no. 10 (Hagerstown, MD, 1989): 2.
38. Ibid., pp. 2–5.
39. Peter Meringolo, "High Risk Security Escorts," *Jail Operations Bulletin* (American Jail Association) 3, no. 11 (Hagerstown, MD, 1991): 2–4.
40. Henderson, Rauch and Phillips, *Guidelines for the Development of a Security Program*, p. 180.
41. Bales, *Correctional Officer Resource Guide, 3rd Edition*, pp. 61–63.
42. David Novak, "Jail Fires: Still A Deadly Potential," *The National Sheriff* (April–May 1983): 6.
43. Michael Schweitzer, "Forsyth County Detention Center: Inmate Evacuation-The R.J. Reynolds Building 256 Fire," *American Jails* (January–February 1999): 50–57.
44. Novak, "Jail Fires: Still a Deadly Potential," p. 9.
45. Henderson, Rauch, and Phillips, *Guidelines for the Development of a Security Program*, pp. 215–218.
46. Biloxi Sun Herald, "Jail Fire that injured three inmates blamed on faulty fan,"*Corrections Connection*, http://www.corrections.com/printNews.aspx?BriefZone=This Just In (accessed August 12, 2004).
47. *Police Crimes and Offenses and Motor Vehicle Laws of Virginia 2006 Edition*, Volume 1, Title 18, Article 3, Sections: 18.2–10, 11, 473, 473.1, 474, 474.1, 475, 476, 477, 478, 479, 480.
48. Doris J. James, Bureau of Justice Statistics Special Report, *Profile of Jail Inmates, 2002*, NCJ 201932, July 2004, 6 (revised October 12, 2004).
49. Bales, *Correctional Officer Resource Guide, 3rd Edition*, pp. 66–67.
50. Bill Miller, "D.C. Inmate Dies After Jail Escape," *Washington Post*, March 15, 1999.
51. Carle Murphy, "Slippery Prisoner Succeeds Again," *Washington Post*, April 4, 1986.
52. Ken Kanowsky, "Fake ID Enables Escape," *Corrections and Technology Management* (November/December 2001): 51–52.

53. Nancy Lewis, "Inmate Access to Uniforms Cited in Jail Break," *Washington Post*, July 26, 1984.
54. *USA Today*, November 1, 1993.
55. "Recreation Suspended at Prison," *Allentown Morning Call*, http://www.corrections.com/news/justin/today.oncc.htm (accessed September 16, 2002).
56. "Jail Inmates caught in Southern Indiana," *Indianapolis Star*, http://www.corrections.com/printNews.aspx? BriefZone=Todayoncc (accessed February 3, 2004).
57. "Ky. Jailor helps inmates in escape attempt," *WTVW*, http://www.corrections.com/printNews.aspx?BriefZone=Todayoncc (accessed on February 3, 2004).
58. Houston Chronicle, "Five Federal Inmates Escape From Texas Jail," *Today on Corrections.com*, http://www.corrections.com/news/justin/todayoncc.html (accessed October 3, 2002).

## REFERENCES

Allentown Morning Call. "Recreation Suspended at Prison," *Corrections Connection*, http://corrections.com/news/justin/today.oncc.htm (accessed September 16, 2002).

Associated Press. "Girl, 9, Used to Smuggle Drugs To Inmate," *Corrections Connection*, http://www.corrections.com/news/justin/index.html (accessed October 5, 2001).

Bales, Don, ed. *Correctional Officer Resource Guide, 3rd Edition*. Lanham, MD: American Correctional Association, 1997.

Barry, Thomas. "Jail Security: A Unique Challenge". *Corrections Today*, July 1987, 16–18.

Biloxi Sun Herald. "Jail Fire that injured three inmates blamed on faulty fan," *Corrections Connection*, http://www.corrections.com/printNews.aspx?BriefZone=This Just In (accessed August 12, 2004).

Collins, William C. J. D. *Correctional Law for the Correctional Officer, 4th Edition*. Lanham, MD: American Correctional Association, 2004.

Cornelius, Gary F. *The Correctional Officer: A Practical Guide*. Durham: Carolina Academic Press, 2001.

Detroit News, "The Lighter Side: 'Hanging Helps Two Inmates Escape', January 11, 1996," http://www.detnews.com/menu/stories/31707.htm (accessed August 2, 1998).

Henderson, James D., W. Hardy Rauch, and Richard L. Phillips. *Guidelines for the Development of a Security Program,. 2nd Edition*. Lanham, MD: American Correctional Association, 1997.

Houston Chronicle, "Five Federal Inmates Escape from Texas Jail," *Today on corrections.com*, http://www.corrections.com/news/justin/todayoncc.html (accessed October 3, 2002).

Indianapolis Star, "Jail Inmates caught in Southern Indiana," *Corrections Connection*, http://www.corrections.com/printNews.aspx?BriefZone=Todayoncc (accessed February 3, 2004).

James, Doris J. Bureau of Justice Statistics Special Report, *Profile of Jail Inmates, 2002*, NCJ 201932, July 2004, 6 (revised October 12, 2004).

Kanowsky, Ken. "Fake ID Enables Escape". *Corrections and Technology Management*, November/December 2001, 51–52.

Lengel, Allan, "Va. Deputy Shoots Armed Man Outside Jail," *Washington Post*, May 17, 2004, http://www.washingtonpost.com/ac2/wp-dyn/A32256–2004May17?language-printer (accessed May 17, 2004).

Lewis, Nancy. "Inmate Access to Uniforms Cited in Jail Break". *Washington Post*, July 26, 1984.

Meringolo, Peter. "High Risk Security Escorts," *Jail Operations Bulletin* (American Jail Association) 3(11), 1991, 2–4.

Miller, Bill. "D.C. Inmate Dies After Jail Escape". *Washington Post*, March 15, 1999.

Murphy, Carle. "Slippery Prisoner Succeeds Again". *Washington Post*, April 4, 1986.

Newcomb, Walter. "Basic Security Principles," *Jail Operations Bulletin* (American Jail Association) 1(7), Hagerstown, MD, 1989, 2.

Novak, David. "Jail Fires: Still A Deadly Potential". *The National Sheriff*, April–May 1983, 6–24.

Perrin, Patricia P., ed. *Correctional Officer Correspondence Course: Book III: Security Issues*. Lanham, MD: American Correctional Association, 1999.

*Police Crimes and Offenses and Motor Vehicle Laws of Virginia 2006 Edition*, Volume 1, Title 18, Article 3, Sections: 18.2–10, 11, 473, 473.1, 474, 474.1, 475, 476, 477, 478, 479, 480.

Reilly, Brian. "Officers Raid Jail, 4 halfway houses". *Washington Times*, January 8, 1994.

Rogers, Donna. "Emergency Personal Location Systems: Essential or Excessive?" *Corrections Forum*, July/August 2004, 36–40.

Sabbatine, Ray and Don Leach. "A New Strip Search Paradigm". *American Jails*, November/December 1996, 39–42.

Schweitzer, Michael. "Forsyth County Detention Center: Inmate Evacuation-The R.J. Reynolds Building 256 Fire". *American Jails*, January–February 1999, 50–57.

Sells, John M. "Transportation of Inmates," *Jail Operations Bulletin* (American Jail Association) 1(10), 1989, 2.

Siuru, Bill. "How Vulnerable is Your Facility, Really?" *Corrections Technology & Management*, September/October 2000, 30–32.

Szostak, Edward W. "Maintaining Safety and Security by Managing Contraband". *American Jails*, July/August 1998, 62–64.

*USA Today*, November 1, 1993.WTVW, "Ky. Jailor helps inmates in escape attempt," *Corrections Connection*, http://www.corrections.com/printNews.aspx?BriefZone=Todayoncc (accessed on February 3, 2004).

# JAIL CLIMATE

# 3

***Objectives of chapter***

The student will:

- Understand the meaning of the term "jail climate" and how it relates to security
- Understand the painful aspects of incarceration to the inmate
- Learn how a jail inmate survives incarceration
- Understand what results in a "calm" or positive jail climate
- Understand what inmates and actions can have a negative impact on the jail climate
- Learn what staff can do to counteract the negative aspects of the jail climate

## JAIL CLIMATE: DEFINED

In any correctional institution, whether it be a prison or a jail, the atmosphere or mood is important. The atmosphere can be compared to weather—is the mood calm where inmates and staff are getting along, inmates are following the rules and regulations, and negative occurrences such as rule violations and violence are happening at a minimum? Or is the atmosphere stormy—where officers are filing numerous rule violation reports, inmates are not getting along with each other, and the jail is ripe for a serious occurrence such as a riot, a disturbance, or a hostage situation? Thus the **jail climate** can be defined as *the overall mood of the jail: terms of inmate behavior and actions and the level of tension experienced by both the inmates and the staff.*

To put more clearly, if the staff is experiencing increases in disciplinary actions, fights, violence, incidents of incompatibilities, inmate defiance, and overt actions against the staff, the climate is negative. Conversely, if inmates are getting along with each other, inmates are getting along with the staff, and incidents of rule violation fights, etc. are not at an emergency level, then the climate is positive. Jail staff can perform their duties and keep inmates in custody with a minimum of problems.

There are many components to the study of the jail climate. Inmates experiencing fear, frustration, and victimization by violence can result in an atmosphere so ridden with anger and frustration that it is difficult for staff to keep up security. Inmates, in their frustration, may find it satisfying to defy staff with acts of disobedience and violence. Combined with this are acts of bravado, "power plays" and "grandstanding."

**Power plays** are actions where an inmate or a group of inmates attempt, by fear, violence, and intimidation, to "run" a cellblock. This is accomplished by controlling the television, stealing food and commissary items, and making weaker inmates do their bidding such as cleaning, or in worst cases, sexual favors. Very often the jail officer in the housing/cellblock area will not be aware of this unless the inmates in the unit tell the officer verbally (usually outside the block and away from other inmates), they get a note to the officer, or the officer firsthand observes an argument or another overt act, such as a physical altercation.

**Grandstanding** involves an inmate acting "big" in front of the other inmates, or "showing off." This could be to solidify his or her reputation as an inmate leader or someone whom he or she wants other inmates to look up to. Grandstanding could involve acts such as arguing with an officer in an attempt to intimidate or embarrass the officer, or going to the defense of another inmate who may be having difficulty with an officer.

Other factors in the study of the jail climate are groups such as gangs and racial supremacist groups. These groups, which will be explored later, are a threat to security. Other inmates affecting the jail climate are sexual predators and the violently mentally disordered.

The incarceration history of jail inmates must not be overlooked. Many inmates who engage in power plays and grandstanding have done time in prison, other jails, or both. Many have a reputation of being "hard core" and try to force their will on others. For a breakdown of the incarceration history of jail inmates, see Chapter 7.

## PAINFUL ASPECTS OF INCARCERATION

When an inmate is incarcerated, he or she loses much more than just freedom. An offender entering jail for either the first time or the tenth time—it does not matter—suffers losses that we as law-abiding citizens take for granted in our daily lives. Some may seem trivial, but all have a profound impact:

- *Loss of family connection:* Quite simply, the offender cannot see his or her family or significant other (husband, wife, and boy/girlfriend) until he or she has been classified into the jail population and become eligible for visits. Visiting is generally no contact and through phone and glass for security reasons. Also, visiting restrictions may dictate a specified number of visitors during a week, and are short in duration. Phone calls are afforded, but only at the discretion and convenience (depending on workload) of the jail staff. Once the offender has access to a phone, the calls are usually collect and the phones are turned on and off by the staff. If the area is crowded, the offender must wait with other inmates for a chance to use the phone.
- *Loss of privacy:* Simple things like bathing and eliminating bodily wastes are performed around other inmates. If the innate is upset and breaks down and cries over the situation and its stresses, there is no where to go to be alone.
- *Loss of freedom of movement:* The offender, now an inmate, is confined to restricted holding areas or a cell. He or she is told where and when to go, often under staff escort.

- *Loss of personal identity items:* Wallet, photos, jewelry, clothing, etc. are taken away and inventoried.
- *Loss of job and income:* Often the offender will lose his or her job. Being incarcerated results in an uncertain future. The offender's employer may not be able to afford keeping the person on the payroll. This can lead to worry and anxiety if the offender is the sole provider for a family, his or her parents, etc. Also, bills and debts accumulate while the person is incarcerated. This may result in the offender being evicted and his or home taken away.
- *Loss of stabilizing resources:* Closely related to the loss of family, people that stabilize the offender's lifestyle are often affected. For example, if the offender is a single parent with dependent children, his or her family may have to step forward and take in the children, provide financial support, go and collect belongings, etc. Incarceration has a shocking "ripple effect."

The losses continue as the offender, who is now an inmate, copes with the negative, often despairing situation of being locked up. An offender who has never been incarcerated before and has always thought of him or herself as a rational person may be in close proximity to an offender suffering from mental illness or the effects of substance abuse. He or she wants desperately to sleep but cannot due to the fluorescent lights in the receiving holding area, being closely confined with many other offenders. Or he or she may be in a cell next to a mentally ill inmate who is verbally ranting, talking to himself, or smearing feces on himself and the cell walls.

The newly arrived offender, especially a first-time offender, may know nothing about jails except what he or she sees in movies, reads in books, or sees from news media reports that often criticize the local jail in cases of inmate illnesses, deaths, or staff misconduct. This adds to the fear and uncertainty of incarceration.

Incarceration is a form of psychological pain, according to Robert Johnson of American University. In his book, *Hard Time: Understanding and Reforming the Prison,* Johnson describes punishment in three stages, which he calls the **amelioration of pain,** based on earlier research by Gresham Sykes. This process deprives the imprisoned (or jailed) inmate of five important things in life, which are:[1]

- *Loss of liberty:* Liberty is lost by being confined to the institution (jail) and secondly by confinement within the institution. This goes beyond the jail staff taking away the freedom of movement. A deeper loss is felt by the inmate because apparently society has involuntary secluded the inmate, or outlaw, from the larger society in a form of banishment. The inmate is considered a pariah and may experience a callousness and uncaring attitude from some of the staff.[2]
- *Deprivation of goods and services:* Contrary to the misinformation of citizens, jails are not "country clubs" where inmates it idly all day watching television in relative comfort. Inmates do get food, shelter, and clothing, which are life's necessities, but do not get the amenities such as choices of food, cigarettes, liquor, and individual clothing. Self-worth is measured by what shows on the outside of the person.[3]
- *Deprivation of heterosexual contact:* Johnson terms this as a figurative castration due to the inmate being involuntary celibate. Female inmates can be looked on as wearing a form of a chastity belt.[4] Outlets for sexual tension may include inmates having homosexual and lesbian relations, engaging in sexual relations with staff,

and masturbation. All have an effect on the jail climate. Sexual activity with other inmates can be a rules violation. Also, if inmates become intimately attached to one another and break it off, arguments and jealousies can result. Not all inmates like to be near inmates who masturbate, and requests to have inmates removed from the unit and requests for transfers may increase.

- *Deprivation of autonomy:* In jails the inmate is in a regimented, authoritarian environment. There is a schedule of getting up, meals, visiting, etc. The inmate has no say in this routine and it is to be followed at all times. Also, there are rules and regulations to be followed, and inmates discover that in the majority of "write ups" the inmate is found guilty. Staff usually wins disputes and arguments. These jail rules and regulations dictate every aspect of the inmate's life inside the jail. Many inmates feel that they "have been forcibly returned to the helpless, dependent status of children."[5] Inmates do not have a freedom of movement. They are only allowed in authorized areas and are not permitted to wander through the jail.

  Autonomy also means the freedom to make choices. Jail inmates do not have a say in what unit or cellblock they will live in and who their cellmates will be. Frequently, the jail classification unit (see Chapter 5) will adjust the population of the units by moving inmates from one unit to another in order to make way for inmates coming into the population from booking and intake.
- *Deprivation of security:* Jail inmates want to feel safe in their persons and property. As a rule, they do not want to be assaulted, harassed, or robbed. However, many of them have to live with inmates whom they would not associate with on the street. While people on the outside can lock their residences at night and feel reasonably safe, jail inmates in crowded cellblocks and units often have to watch their backs against aggressive inmates, predators, and the sly types of inmates who will steal food and commissary. Many inmates know that if they engage in violent acts, it often means that they will be placed in disciplinary segregation or suffer other sanctions.

As a rule, the jail environment is the opposite lifestyle of what the normal person experiences on the street. The inmates are not only deprived of life's comforts, but their lives are disrupted by the uncertainties of both jail life and their lack of having any influence on their lives, loved ones, and resources on the outside.

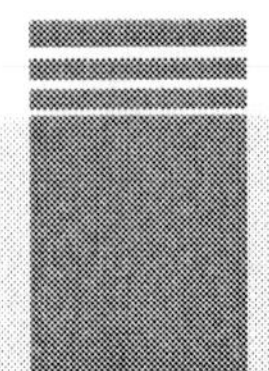

POINT OF VIEW

## Jail Climate

***Captain Sabrina Butler***
San Francisco, CA Sheriff's Department

Every person booked into the San Francisco County Jail must first process through the Intake and Release Facility. This can be a very "hair raising" experience for someone being arrested for the first time. The facility design is circular with multiple holding cells, sobering cells, and safety cells. Many newly arrested individuals are held in this area. They walk around, sit up, or sleep on floors or benches.

Once a person is booked and prior to housing, they are either pat- or strip-searched depending on their charges. "Regular" inmates are used to this process. Depending on the time of day, the facility could be very loud with numerous inmates being processed in and out. This is the first realization to most individuals that they are truly separated from society and will be locked up "in jail."

In a pretrial facility that transitions many inmates in and out on a daily basis, the environment can be very loud. Occasions of individuals not being "conditioned" to incarceration and their status, long or short term, are virtually unknown. The facility houses men and women with crimes ranging from theft and drugs to murder. Although these inmates are separated according to a classification system, they are still on the same floor and can see and hear each other. The classification system separates inmates based on a variety of factors such as their sex, type of crime, criminal sophistication, incarceration history, etc. We have to deal with a variety of people who come from a wide range of lifestyles as well as socioeconomic backgrounds and mental illness, which includes drug-induced illnesses.

The jail environment can be very chaotic. There are inmates constantly milling about with not much to do but watch television and sleep. Some inmates will take advantage of weaker inmates by taking their food or dictating where they can sit, where they can sleep, or when they can use the phone. Other inmates are angry because of their circumstances and may look for someone else to blame: another inmate or staff.

Inmates will show their anger in many ways. Some inmates who have a psychiatric history may be self-destructive and try to kill themselves by hanging or cutting their wrists. There have been occasions where a person comes to jail for the first time and are so overwhelmed, scared, and/or embarrassed that they too will try to kill themselves. Then there's the other type of inmate who is mad at everyone and wants to fight other inmates as well as staff. The latter inmate must be housed separately and whenever out of the cell, special safety precautions are used to prevent injury to staff or inmate.

The jail environment changes many times during the day. No day can ever be predicted. Staff has to be diligent when walking around the jail and must be present wherever there are inmates. Some inmates will "behave" if a staff person is in the area. Our presence alone is usually a deterrent to act out. Deputies have to learn who is housed in the area they are supervising. It is okay to familiarize yourself with the crimes the inmate is charged with. However, it is imperative that staff learn the individual inmate: learn his different moods, learn his body language, and be ever aware of his level of sophistication. Experienced deputies can "feel" when something is wrong with the inmates in their area. You are able to look into a cell and tell by the inmates' body language, movement, or lack of movement if someone is fighting, injured, or getting ready to fight. You have to be able to look at an inmate, who's just returned from court, and recognize if he's received bad news and may possibly present a danger to himself or to you, your coworkers, or other inmates. Even though "gut feelings" aren't acceptable in a court of law, it is almost 100 percent accurate in a jail environment.

To run a tier or dorm effectively, staff has to show inmates respect. The attitude of "they are just inmates" will make the job very difficult. Inmates respect an individual that "does his job." As an example, if you are writing up an inmate for a rule violation and call him several inappropriate names and make him feel degraded, he will act out based on the comments made. He knows he broke the rule and he doesn't have a problem with the consequences. His problem would be in the manner in which you issued the violation and consequences. Inmates feel that we are the professionals and we are to act in a certain way. If we deviate, we are stooping to a lower level and are treated accordingly. Our badge alone does not guarantee respect. As in every profession it has to be earned. Although the inmates are "charged" with a crime, no matter how serious, they are still human beings. We cannot treat them according to our feelings or to how we feel about the crime they're charged with. Inmates have a "job" to do and so do we. Their job is typically looking for ways to make their incarceration better, no matter what it takes, even if it violates a jail rule or the law. We are there to ensure a safe and secure jail environment.

If I was asked to give words of advice to a new officer to ensure he had a smooth transition working in a custodial environment, I would tell him to show respect to all human beings because that's the only way you will receive respect. Also, always maintain a high visible presence in whatever area you are assigned.

Special thanks to Captain Sabrina Butler, San Francisco County Jail #1, San Francisco Sheriff's Department, San Francisco, CA.

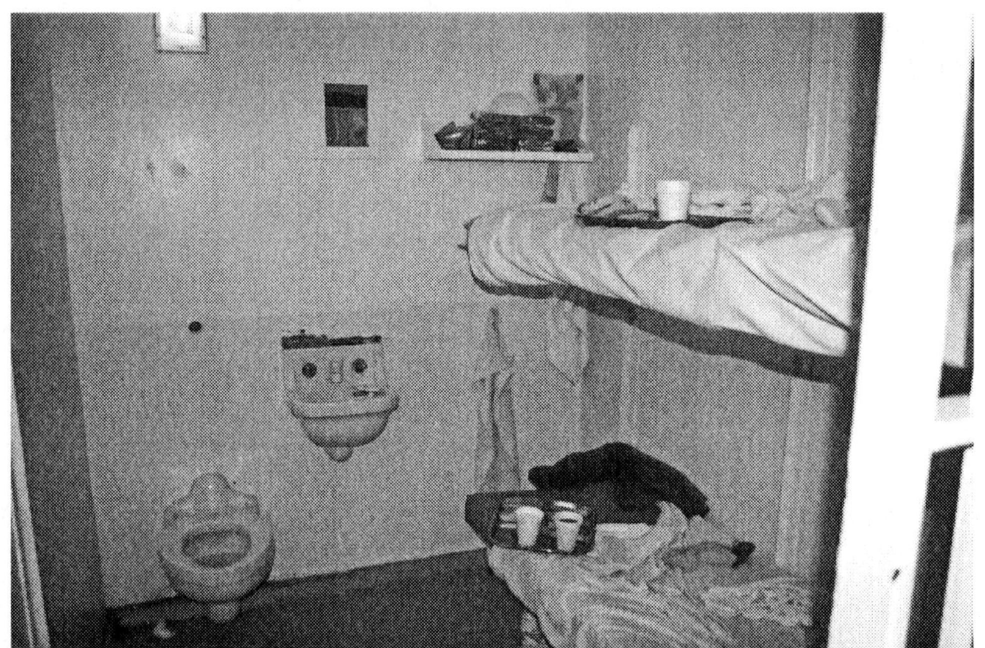

Typical jail cell, offering only bare necessities.

Photo by author, courtesy Butler County Prison.

## SURVIVING INCARCERATION

Inmates want to do time in jails as comfortably as possible. Jails are "Spartan" environments. While some modern jails appear comfortable and clean with modern lighting and institutional furniture, they are still regimented and authoritarian. All around the inmates are reminders of where they are. Door locks, cameras, officers in uniform are visual reminders as is the clothing that the inmates wear. While many jails provide colored jumpsuits to the inmates, some jails have returned to the 1940s-style prison black and white striped uniforms. This occurred in 2003 at the Norfolk, Virginia City Jail, in order not to mistake inmates for construction workers or garbage workers who wore jumpsuits similar in color to the jail inmate jumpsuits. The staff wanted to identify inmates at a glance, but some inmates felt that they were being stereotyped.[6]

The jail population is composed of a mixture of **first timers,** who are offenders experiencing their first incarceration, **jail-wise inmates,** who have done occasional periods of varying lengths of incarceration in local jails and not prison, and **prison-wise inmates,** who have done time in federal and state penitentiaries and, because they have re-offended, are incarcerated in the local jail. Due to the overcrowding demands of operating a jail, it is possible to have a mixture of these types of inmates together in a unit or cellblock.

First timers may be experiencing their first incarcerations, but their criminal records may indicate that they have lengthy arrest records and may have had exposure to the criminal justice system through arrests, probation, and participation in community corrections programs (see Chapter 11), but not inside the jail. They may be **"street wise,"** which means that they are well versed in breaking the law, the criminal lifestyle both in and out of jail, and associating with other criminals. Jail-wise inmates gain their experience through multiple incarcerations, while prison-wise inmates are the most experienced in how to do time, both negatively, such as making contraband, and positively—knowing how to stay out of trouble.

If an inmate is a first timer with no criminal justice experience, he or she may be frightened, anxious, and naïve. It may be in their best interest to bond out if possible. Jail staff can assist them by giving them access to family and friends by use of the phone so bonding can be arranged.

Once the initial shock of incarceration has worn off, and jail inmates know where they will live inside the jail and with whom, the process of **prisonization** sets in. Prisonization is the process by which the jail inmate learns the formal rules, regulations, and routine of the jail, as well as the informal values, customs, and rules of the inmate subculture. This is accomplished through socialization with inmates.[7] Through prisonization, inmates learn such coping skills as how to sleep in overcrowded conditions; how to safeguard their property; new inmate jargon and slang; which inmates to stay away from because of potential threats; and which inmates to befriend and will "watch their back." Other jailhouse "skills" that are learned include how to live in close proximity to others (for example, in a five-inmate unit holding ten inmates), how to eat with a food tray on one's knees sitting on the floor, how to share one toilet and one shower with many inmates, how to share one television and one phone, etc.

Much has been written in corrections literature about the "inmate code." Veteran jail officers will say that the inmate code does exist. The **inmate code** is a set of informal social rules that inmates learn to live by, and its violation could mean physical assault (which may have serious or fatal consequences), ostracism from other inmates, or being labeled a "snitch" or weak.[8] Inmates learn this code from living with hard-core, jail-wise offenders.

Many corrections departments have descriptions of this code, but one of the most clear is from the Kansas Department of Corrections, which reads:[9]

- *Be loyal:* Be quiet about other inmates' actions, including crimes. This means lying if you have to. Be loyal to your fellow inmates and never take a problem to the jail staff.
- *Be cool:* No matter what the pressure is from the staff, maintain calmness and control. Do not make waves: do your own time.
- *Be straight with fellow inmates and do not take advantage of them:* Do not lie, steal, or break your word. Do favors with other inmates and share with them. To get your way or avoid a problem, telling staff "half truths" is all right.
- *Be tough:* Take it. Do not whine or be weak. Inmates should not start fights, but should not run from a fight that has been started by another inmate.
- *Be sharp and never trust a correctional officer:* In inmate/officer conflicts, remember that the inmate is always wrong.

In recent years, some correctional reformers and inmates, including former inmates, have been speaking out against the code saying that by its silence, brutal inmates are protected. Also, these inmates—the ones who engage in violence—may not face the consequences of their actions. Jail officers must find ways to convince the inmates to trust them and abandon the dangers of the inmate code.[10]

In addition, the inmates will learn which officers are open to communication and will listen to problems, which officers are "hard core" and are for the most part unapproachable, and which officers are prone to being manipulated. Inmates size up their surroundings—both the physical plant and the people (staff and inmates). Some inmates prove through constant complaints to staff by themselves or other inmates that they are **incompatible,** meaning that they have difficulties living in a group setting with other inmates. This could be because of personality clashes, threats of sexual assaults or violence, an inmate attempting power plays in the unit/block, lack of personal hygiene and basic manners, gang friction, or any number of reasons resulting in inmates not getting along. Some inmates state to the staff that they prefer to live by themselves, and due to overcrowding, this is not always possible. Incompatible inmates are often shifted around to several living assignments until they "settle in." If this is not successful, then the classification staff through a formal administrative hearing will have to place the inmate in administrative segregation (see Chapter 5). In more serious cases, the problem inmate is removed from population due to breaking the rules and being placed in disciplinary segregation.

The study of the jail climate and how inmates live must include a discussion of the advice that some of the jail-wise and prison-wise inmates give to the younger, first-time inmates. One prison-wise inmate gave this advice on avoiding trouble to inmates. Calling the advice the "pitfalls to avoid," he advised inmates to avoid the following:[11]

- *Gangs:* Staff may judge inmates by the company that they keep or what inmates they associate with. Leave gang members to their own space or "turf." Inmates should not accept favors from gang members, as accepting a favor may oblige an inmate to join a gang. Inmates should know the environment and not show disrespect to a gang's colors, mottos, and emblems by humor or sarcasm.
- *Drugs:* Drugs put inmates at risk, because by taking illicit drugs smuggled into the jail, control over their judgment and behavior is hindered or lost. Inmates could be assaulted sexually, or be placed in dangerous situations by associating with drug dealers.
- *Sex:* Engaging in sex with another inmate or staff member puts the inmate at risk of sexually transmitted diseases (STDs) and punishments by the disciplinary process. Sexual behavior is not worth the risk.
- *Debts and gambling:* Inmates should not borrow or lend items to other inmates. Owing debts that are not able to be paid may result in the inmate paying with sexual favors. Inmates may be looked upon as weak, and not able to stand up for themselves.
- *Stealing:* Older inmates advise younger ones to safeguard their property. Theft of another inmate's property is comparable to stealing from survivors in a lifeboat.
- *Snitching:* Being a snitch is being at or near the bottom of the inmate population "pecking order." Inmates are advised not to believe staff promises of better treatment, transfers, early release, or protection. (Veteran jail officers are careful not to promise inmates anything for information.) The best thing to do is to stay away from unauthorized activity and not to get caught up in anything that other inmates do. An inmate does not want to be labeled a "snitch," even if he or she is not engaging in anything.
- *Trick bags:* A **"trick bag"** is an easy way for jail-wise inmates to trap naïve inmates. For example, a jail-wise inmate lends his radio to a new inmate. When it

Female housing unit. Living in jail is very tedious; inmates live in the same surroundings with same people day after day.

Photo by author, courtesy Butler County Prison.

is returned, the jail-wise inmate claims that it is broken. Now the naïve inmate must pay back in flesh (sex), commissary, etc.

- *Riots:* Inmates should avoid any riot, disturbance, or hostage situation. Emergency response teams will target inmates in a hostage holding area. Inmates who want to stay out of trouble in such situations should not talk to the media; this may lead to prosecution later as a possible riot organizer or leader.

## The Seven Needs of Incarceration

For jail inmates to do time as comfortably, safely, and calmly as possible, research by Hans Toch promulgates the seven ecological needs of inmates. Doing time within the confines of a jail does not mean that inmates just exist inside the cellblocks. Inmates' preferences and, more importantly, needs must be understood and met wherever possible in order to keep a secure, orderly, and positive jail climate. These needs are:[12]

- *Activity:* Inmates need to be distracted, active, or entertained in order to keep the tedium and boredom of jail life to much as a minimum as possible. Jails provide recreation, television, commissary (which in some jails includes sales of portable radios), library services, and rehabilitative programs.
- *Privacy:* Privacy is sought by almost all inmates, especially older ones who would like quiet surroundings. With the exceptions of behavioral problems (including mental illness), disciplinary cases, protective custody cases, high-risk inmates, and medical problems, inmates live in crowded surroundings with other inmates.

One aspect of privacy is that jail life does not allow inmates to be alone with their thoughts and problems. If an inmate wants to or needs to be alone or cry, there is really no place to go.

- *Safety:* Inmates generally do not like to be "messed with," that is to be the victims of assault, harassment, and theft from other inmates. Inmates concerned about safety may label a situation involving a threatening inmate as tense or explosive, or may write in a request that "there will be a fight in here" warning the staff to take steps to resolve the situation.
- *Emotional feedback:* Just like the normal everyday person who needs friends, love, being cared for, and intimacy, jail inmates on the inside need the same things. Friendships are formed with other inmates, and inmates strive to maintain contact with their families, friends, and significant others on the outside through mail, visiting, and phone contact. All these mechanisms of contact take on a new significance inside the jail.
- *Support:* Inmates are generally concerned about assistance from the jail for their problems including substance abuse, education, and vocational training. Some take advantage of the programs that are offered, realizing that a lifestyle of going in and out of jail is not for them, while others use programs as ways to communicate with other inmates or fellow gang members, or to escape the daily drudgery of jail life.
- *Structure:* Inmates would like the jail rules to be uniformly and fairly enforced by all of the squads or teams working. It is important to inmates that the routine in terms of policies, procedures, and discipline follows a predictable, set pattern.

Televisions in jail dayrooms can help relieve tensions and offer distractions to the inmates.

Photo by author, courtesy Butler County Prison.

- *Freedom:* Inmates, like all people, would like to be treated as adults, to have a chance to govern their own conduct, and not to be so restricted in terms of movement. However, to maintain security, staff closely controls inmate movement. Freedom simply means that the inmate wants to be treated as a mature adult, be able to make choices, and govern his or her own conduct. This approach is useful when an inmate is confronted with a disagreeable situation such as moving to another unit or not being permitted out segregation. Telling the inmate that acting in a mature manner and complimenting him or her for adult behavior and making the proper decisions can facilitate a positive atmosphere.

Inmates will form friendships and relationships with other inmates who will help them meet these needs. For example, if there is a safety concern in the cellblock about a belligerent inmate, inmates will befriend others who watch out for them and vice versa.

## A POSITIVE JAIL CLIMATE

In order to maintain a positive jail climate, staff must mentally put themselves in the inmates' place. The living conditions of the inmate areas must be properly maintained. The simple amenities that inmates are entitled to—linens, laundry, and personal hygiene items—must be delivered as expeditiously as possible and also in good condition. Plumbing and sanitation must also be in good working order. It is a negative atmosphere when ten inmates, for example, are housed in an area built for five. Many jails were not built for the amount of inmates that are currently housed in them, and overcrowding takes its toll on toilets and showers. The more inmates using the fixtures of the jail, the more that those fixtures need maintained.

Activity is important, as it is one of the seven needs of the inmates. Participation in positive activities such as programs, recreation, etc. should be encouraged by the jail staff. The main activities reported by jail inmates in 1996 were:*[13]

| Activity | Percent |
|---|---|
| Watching television | 74% |
| Reading | 68% |
| Physical exercise | 44% |
| Games, arts, crafts, and other recreation | 55% |

* Rounded percentages, based on activities 24 hours prior to the interview by staff for the Bureau of Justice Statistics profile.

Other activities that could foster a positive jail climate that were reported in the previous week prior to the survey interview were:*[14]

| Activity | Percent |
|---|---|
| Inmates having any work assignment | 26% |
| Visits from family and friends | 42% |
| Phone calls with family/friends | 77% |
| Religious activities: prayer, services, meditation | 55% |

* Rounded percentages.

Keeping inmates occupied so idleness and boredom do not materialize into fights and violence is an ongoing challenge for the jail staff. Staff cannot force inmates to participate in programs and recreation, but efforts should be made to keep them active, including encouragement to call family and friends on the outside and receive visits.

Meeting another need, safety, can also help the jail climate. In the same profile in 1996, 14.3 percent of male jail inmates had been in a physical altercation, or fight, hit, or punched since entering jail; by gender this was applicable to almost 15 percent of male and almost 11 percent of female jail inmates.[15] Perceptions and feelings of safety are important to the inmate. Interestingly, 69 percent said, when questioned about how safe they felt from other inmates, that they felt safe or somewhat safe. Conversely, 22 percent said that they did not feel safe or felt somewhat unsafe. Jails are generally safe, and the inmates know this. In the 1996 profile, 57 percent of jail inmates questioned were of the opinion that the jail was safer than or as safe as the street areas where they had lived.[16]

The perceptions of safety by inmates who are confined against their will could be the result of several staff practices. One is concern—where the jail officers watch out for the inmates, openly communicate with them, and frequently ask them if there are any problems in the cellblock. By doing so, inmates can feel that the jail officers are approachable and will take action once that they are informed that there are inmate predators and assaultive "bullies" who are taking out aggressions on inmates. Another practice is being proactive. Through documentation of inmate acts and staff knowing the inmates, aggressive inmates are carefully placed in the jail population, generally around similar inmates. The assaultive inmate may think twice before starting something. The third practice is being fair. In an inmate fight, many times both inmates are charged with fighting each other. If the jail staff holds an impartial, objective hearing with presented facts, observations, and staff/inmate witnesses, the decision can be fair due to the aggressor being punished, and the victim receiving no punishment if he or she was simply acting in self-defense.

Regarding communication, the best practice is the "management by walking around," or the MBWA approach. Jail officers must be both "nosy" and mobile. In the three types of jail design discussed in Chapter 1, the MBWA approach is the most feasible in the direct supervision type of housing, where the unit officer can walk around the entire unit and spot trouble—such as inmate arguments and aggressive body language—and take action before a fight or assault occurs. In the podular type of housing, the officer is detached from life in the unit, but can observe several units at once from a control center or booth. Communication from inmates is via a request form, which some inmates are reluctant to write or send because of possible interception by other inmates. Communication by staff is through an intercom, which broadcasts loudly for all to hear. Similarly, the linear type hides from the post officer violent behavior. The officer cannot see what is going on inside the cellblock and must rely on visual observation through cellblock windows, or reading inmate request forms. Request forms from linear blocks may not be sent frequently due to the chance, like in the podular unit, of interception. The jail officer, in order to see what is happening among the inmates, must physically enter the linear block in person, and have another officer stand by as a backup for safety. In all cases of potential violence, and regardless of the housing type, the jail officer must let the inmates see that the staff does take an interest.

Some inmates prove themselves to be inmate leaders. An **inmate leader** is defined as an inmate who becomes known to the staff and inmates as an inmate who exerts his or her will and influence over a group of inmates. They do this in order to feel that they have some control over their immediate surroundings (the jail) and strive to impress others with their importance. The types of leaders include positive leaders who serve as a positive influence on other inmates, seasoned veterans whose followers are younger naïve inmates, and jailhouse lawyers (see Chapter 9) who assist other inmates in disciplinary/administrative hearings and legal work. Unfortunately, there are negative inmate leaders such as predators, gang leaders, revolutionaries, racists, and extremists.[17] While it may be rare to see inmates in a jail expounding a political, revolutionary dogma based on politics, race, or religion, the arrest of terrorist suspects in a post 09/11 world may bring more of these inmates into jail.

The positive type of inmate leader will encourage other inmates to behave; attend programs; speak in self-help programs such as Alcoholics Anonymous, Narcotics Anonymous, and religious programs; tutor other inmates; lead discussions in therapy groups and prerelease programs; and try to defuse problems in the cellblock or unit. Positive leaders will assist programs staff and volunteers, and may decide to speak to tour groups including college students and at-risk high school students. The positive leader will file grievances or complain to staff in a dignified, respectful manner.[18] A seasoned inmate leader will advise inmates of the pitfalls of doing time, as previously discussed. Jailhouse lawyers will assist inmates in a law library.

## NEGATIVE ASPECTS OF THE JAIL CLIMATE

Inside a jail, there are many factors that can negatively influence the jail climate. These factors include many inmate types—such as gang members, negative inmate leaders, traffickers in contraband, manipulators, and violent predators. While predators have been already discussed in this chapter, this section will focus further on violence and other inmate types who have a negative influence. These types engage in such actions as hostage taking, inciting riots and disturbances, clandestine operations such as the manufacture and trafficking of contraband, assaults, and manipulating staff.

**Security threat groups** (STGs) are defined in the most basic sense as groups that, because of their organization, views, and ability to recruit new members and carry out actions/illegal activities to support their views, cause disruption to the orderly operations of the jail. To clarify, these groups fall into several categories, but the two most prevalent types are street gangs and racial supremacist groups such as the Klu Klux Klan, the Aryan Brotherhood, Skinheads, and the White Aryan Brotherhood. These white supremacist groups believe in the natural supremacy of the white race whose ancestors can be traced to Northern Europe. They exhibit an extreme viewpoint, have common enemies, and are identifiable through belief patterns, markings, and traits. By their presence in the jail population, interactions with other inmates are strained, and as a result, inmate management becomes difficult.[19]

Sometimes these racial extremist groups are referred to as prison gangs, as many of these groups have members who are incarcerated and the gang dogma parallels the extremist group views. The most recent practice has been to designate such groups as STGs. Racially extremist, hard-core STG inmates may be incarcerated in the local jail due to re-offending or through transfer in from a prison system. STG extremists may make their views known to the staff and state that they will not be housed with members of a certain race or ethnic background, such as blacks or Jews. Many jails have staff whose job is to find out as much as is possible about the inmate and the particular STG group that he or she belongs to. Classification and housing decisions should be postponed and the inmate segregated until enough information is gathered to make an informed decision. In some cases, the inmate may have been active in a STG group in the past, but is not at present. Nevertheless, the inmate's affiliation must be checked out.

Jail professionals advocate that each facility have a working definition of what exactly an STG is. A more detailed definition has been put forth by Deputy Sheriff Loran D. Hatcher, the Sheriff's Intelligence Coordinator for the Arlington County (Virginia) Sheriff's Office. He states that an STG can be "any group, gang or inmate organization that has been determined to be acting in concert to pose a threat to the safety, security and orderly operation of the correctional facility, to its staff and/or the public safety. This [STG] group may also be considered a threat to the safety and health of other inmates."[20]

Deputy Hatcher further states that another definition that would serve the security efforts by a jail staff is to consider STGs "as any formal or informal, ongoing inmate/offender groups, gangs, organizations or associations comprising three or more members who have:

- A common name or common identifying signs, colors, language or symbols;
- Members or associates who individually or collectively engage in or have engaged in a pattern of gang activity or departmental rule violations; and
- Potential to act in concert to pose a threat or potential threat to staff, visitors, inmates or the secure and orderly operation of a facility."[21]

STGs pose a definite management problem for jail officials. Racial violence with other inmates may occur, and some inmates, especially those who do not have a lot of incarceration experience, may not wish to be housed with them. STG inmates engage in such negative practices such as loan-sharking, drug smuggling and use, offers of protection, sexual prostitution, and murder.[22] Such activities may garner respect from younger, impressionable inmates and unite the inmates in a cellblock against the staff and the jail procedures.

Since 1950, the Federal Bureau of Prisons has taken steps to identify many of the more prevalent STGs/prison gangs. Four traditional STGs have been identified by the Bureau as certified disruptive STGs: the Aryan Brotherhood, Mexican Mafia, Texas Syndicate, and the Black Guerilla Family. Others that have been identified in recent years (1980s, 1990s, and 2000s) include the Arizona Aryan Brotherhood, Black Gangster Disciples, Jamaican Posse, and the Hells Angels.[23]

Some STG groups hide behind the cloak of religion, such as the Nation of Gods and Earth, also called the Five Percenters. Recognized in some correctional institutions as a prison gang, its members claim to be a religious group.[24] In the group Christian Identity, its members purport to follow a religious theology that justifies extremist views for all white supremacist groups, such as the Skinheads, KKK, and neo Nazis. By doing so, these other groups can belong to "Identity Churches." The Christian Identity beliefs are that Jews descended from Satan, Jews are imposters and the British are true Israelites, nonwhite people are "mud" people and on the same spiritual level as animals, and the Bible predicts a cataclysmic race war resulting in the destruction of all nonwhite people.[25]

STGs/supremacist groups mostly recruit along ethnic and racial lines; they have members generally over the age of 25 who have experience in the criminal justice system. This means that a hard-core STG inmate may have extensive experience in being arrested and incarcerated in both state and local correctional institutions. When an inmate joins, it is usually for life, along with strict discipline that involves assaults or death for violating the group's rules.[26]

All supremacist STGs/gangs are not white in composition. The Black Guerilla Family was derived form the Black Panthers in 1966. In the late 1990s, heavy recruitment by this group was reported occurring in the federal and California penal systems. Also, the group Black Mafia was organized in California and is a suspected reformation of the Black Guerilla Family. Two Hispanic STGs/gangs are the La Nuestra Familia and Mexican Mafia, who are composed of Hispanics from southern California cities and the barrios of southern California inner cities, respectively.[27]

Even though STG supremacist and prison gang groups can be present in the local jail, jails at this time are grappling with the street gang problem. Street gangs are prevalent throughout the United States, engaging in serious criminal activities, such as assault and murder. Its members are arrested and brought to the local jail, where the jail staff has to deal with them their philosophies, behavioral characteristics, and potential for problems with other inmates. Since about 1990, there has been much written on the gang problem and recommendations on how to handle it inside correctional facilities. The following is a summary of the current gang problem as reported in the *CQ (Congressional Quarterly) Researcher*:[28]

- There are an estimated 21,500 gangs with a membership of approximately 731,000 members in the United States; in 2002 over 40 percent of police agencies reported increased gang activity in their jurisdictions, up from 27 percent in 2001.
- Heavy immigration from Latin America and Asia has introduced several violent gangs to the United States. Two examples are Mara Salvatrucha 13 (MS-13) and the Almighty Latin Kings Nation.
- Offenders in criminal street gangs often try to thwart police investigations (and jail investigations) by threats, assaults, rapes, and killing potential witnesses.
- Crimes include illegal drugs, auto theft, extortion, property crimes, home invasions, and recently fraudulent identification papers that could be used both by terrorists and by illegal aliens.
- Gangs now include the MS-13 gang, the Bloods, Crips, Black Gangster Disciples, Almighty Latin Kings nation, several so-called Jamaican Posses, and additional motorcycle gangs and prison gangs.
- The National Alliance of Gang Investigators states that gangs have changed from an urban scourge into a nationwide threat. Gang memberships now cross all socioeconomic, ethnic, and racial boundaries. Gangs now permeate American society.
- Concerning U.S. gang membership, the National Youth Gang Center estimates that 49 percent are Latino, 34 percent are black, 10 percent are white, and 6 percent

are Asian. White gangs have expanded into the most new territory in the years 1994–2004, and Latino and Asian gangs are thought to be the most violent.

- Areas that had been thought to have a low crime rate have a gang problem. In Utah there are at least 250 gangs comprising 3,000 members operating in the Salt Lake City area.
- According to a Justice Departments survey, both gang members and at-risk youth admitted to significant involvement with firearms. Gang members were more likely to own large caliber handguns. Explosives are often used by MS-13; drug stashes are "booby trapped" with antipersonnel grenades.
- Gangs are becoming well organized. For example, during the execution of a search warrant, police discovered the organizational chart of Chicago's Gangster Disciples, which has a membership of 7,000. A federal prosecutor described the gang as "more sophisticated than many corporations." The gang has formed a political action committee, purchased legitimate businesses, and sponsored community events.
- One of the most well known gangs, MS-13, is ranked at the highest level of violence by the National Gang Crime Research Center. Youths as young as 11 years of age are members; MS-13 members range in age from 11 to 40. MS-13 members in Los Angeles sent several members to Northern Virginia with orders to randomly kill a county police officer, but this effort was unsuccessful. The Justice Department estimates that MS-13 has approximately 8,000 members in the District of Colombia and 27 states, with 20,000 more in Central America, especially El Salvador and South America.
- More research is being done on female gangs; law enforcement estimates that between 4 and 11 percent of gang members are females. Females in gangs tend to be less violent than male gang members, approximately 65 percent carry weapons, and the most prevalent crimes involve drugs. Females join gangs for the same reasons as males, seeking friends and self-affirmation. Females tend to leave gangs when they become pregnant, generally by age 18.

Members of STGs, including extremist groups, prison gangs, and street gangs, can be identified by certain behavioral characteristics and visual indicators. Jail staff, especially booking/intake staff and classification staff, should be well informed about these identifiers.

Concerning racial extremist groups, identifiers include the following:[29]

- Their views are that they are *certain* that they know the truth, the country is controlled by a conspiratorial group, they openly hate their opponents, denial of civil liberties to their "enemies," constant character assignation, and little faith in the judicial system and democratic process.
- Key statements of racism and bigotry to members of other races and ethnic backgrounds.
- Tattoos: Tattoos that appear crude in black or dark blue ink are frequently done in prison because inmates do not have access to commercially dyed tattoo ink. Tattoos to look for include: swastika (often associated with the Aryan Brotherhood), shamrock or clover, knuckles ("skin" on right hand and "head on left hand), small dots on the web between thumb and forefinger signifying murders for the "cause," and skull, demon, or serpent. The skull, demon, and serpent indicate the alienation from society's normal social values.

Prison and street gang members also display indicators and behavior. Signs that jail staff should look for include:[30]

- Tattoos and personal identifiers: Many tattoos have the gang symbol designs and may be displayed on neck, head, chest, calf, or forearms. Some gangs do not use tattoos but will use colors that are displayed in clothing or sometimes using playing cards.
- Photographs of fellow gang members on the outside displaying gang hand signs, colors, or tattoos may be in the inmate's possession at booking or be sent in the mail. Jail officers should check the inmate's property and what is displayed in his or her cell.
- Gang paraphernalia, such as letters with gang symbols, gang rules, etc.
- Code and ciphers: Gang inmates are very adept at using codes to send message to other inmates in other jails, or to gang members on the outside. Certain words may have certain meanings. For example, in the Black Guerilla Family, the term "Annette Brooks" means "Aryan Brotherhood," "kiss" means "marked for death," and "Paula" means police officer. In the La Nuestra Familia cipher, A is +, B is –, etc.
- Written or printed materials: Gang members sometimes keep the gang doctrines, constitution, insignia, publications, or "hit" lists of enemies.

A benchmark study conducted in 1994 by six university researchers and sponsored by the National Gang Crime Research Center gives a very clear picture of the behavioral traits of gang members. A total of 891 inmates in eight county jails in the Midwest United States were surveyed. The study found the following traits among gang members.[31]

- Concerning family background, gang members are more likely to come from a single parent (female parent or guardian only).
- Regarding school and education: Gang members are more likely have not completed high school or advanced to grade levels achieved by non-gang members, have been expelled from school, or have assaulted teachers at school.
- They are more likely to have never held a full-time job.
- They are more likely to have friends who are also members of gangs and use drugs.
- They have more of a likelihood to have been incarcerated in a juvenile correctional facility.
- They are more likely to have permanent tattoos.
- Concerning disputes with others, gang members are more likely to respond to a verbal insult with violence and think that they have few means other than violence to settle grievances.
- Gang members had more of a propensity to steal firearms, own and use assault rifles, use sawed-off shotguns in crimes, and carry concealed weapons.
- Gangs can originate in large cities and heavily populated suburban areas and then spread to outlying areas in a sort of "ripple effect."

What can be concluded from this study is that gang members are probably not going to respect the authority of the jail staff. Also, when coming into conflict with others—staff and inmates—violent reactions can occur. Also, gang loyalty is a critical factor, where gang members may remain loyal to the criminal ways and antisocial views of their respective gang. Some gang members may declare a truce with other rival gang members for the sake of mutual survival in the jail, but often these agreements are very weak. Rival gang members may assault each other or try to communicate with other gang members housed throughout the jail.

In the classification interview, the jail officer/counselor should be as blunt as possible when dealing with a member of an STG. Questions such as "Are you a member of —?" may result in the inmate answering that he or she is a member of an extremist group or gang. The interviewer should also ask if the inmate will freely associate with inmates of other races, etc. Another question could be if the inmate feels persecuted by a certain racial or ethnic group. Many inmates of STGs are proud of their affiliations and will admit to membership.[32] Some inmates in gangs may be afraid to enter population due to reprisals from rival gangs, they have turned informant for law enforcement, or they have made it known that they want to leave the gang. Protective custody must be examined as an option in such cases.

Since about 1990, jails are taking definitive steps to combat the STG threat to a positive jail climate. Some of these measures are applicable to both prison/street gangs and extremist groups. They include:

- Photographing all tattoos and markings.
- Recording of phone calls to the outside if STG activity is suspected, including leaders giving orders to STG members on the outside.
- Carefully searching all inmate property for gang material, photos, codes, and paraphernalia.
- Carefully observing visiting to determine if STG individuals on the outside are coming to see the inmate, and monitoring STG inmate accounts to determine if large deposits have been made as payment for illicit activities.
- Having a "zero tolerance" policy concerning STG activity in the jail. A **zero tolerance policy** means that all STG activity (as well as all inmate rule violations) will be dealt with through disciplinary hearings, administrative hearings (resulting in disciplinary or administrative segregation), and/or criminal prosecutions.
- Segregating known STG leaders and members, either through disciplinary segregation or through administrative segregation.
- Attempting as much as possible to keep rival gang members separate, and splitting up gang members throughout the jail population.
- Having an agency **"STG intelligence unit"** in the agency. This unit works with federal, state, and local law enforcement agencies and other jails to gather STG intelligence, investigate inmate STG activity inside the jail, recommend actions to staff, and provide staff training. STG unit officers can inspect inmate property for STG activity and observe which inmates are associating with whom (a sure sign of STG affiliation), etc.

Jails have progressed with the establishment of STG intelligence units. However, jails must be creative in devising methods on how to allocate both staff and material resources for such units. According to Lina Presley, a member of the National Major Gang Task Force and Director of Operational Support Services for the Indiana Department of Corrections, after the terrorist attacks of September 11, 2001, gang intelligence units suffered due to shifts in funding to homeland security.

Some gang units have been dismantled or their areas of focus have been shifted. Presley also states that gang units can learn from the effort being put into terrorism investigations and homeland security efforts. In some aspects, says Presley, there is a similarity between religious (STG) groups and gangs.[33]

For example, Benjamin Smith, a white supremacist and member of the World Church of the Creator group, visited inmates before embarking on a crime spree in which he murdered 11 people.[34]

According to former California Department of Corrections Senior Special Agent and veteran gang identification officer Joe DeLaTorre, keeping up with gang activity outside is critical. He states that street gangs are fluid and undergo change. Gangs may get along until an assault, such as a stabbing occurs, and then the two gangs are enemies. The rivalry and animosity can carry over from the street to inside the jail. He also says that many of the "shot callers" for gangs on the outside are actually inside correctional facilities. This is one of the main reasons that law enforcement—both police and corrections agencies—must pool resources and work together.[35]

In Maricopa County, Arizona, the sheriff's office has formed a jail intelligence unit comprised of 10 sergeants and 1 supervisor. The unit monitors gang activity and attempts to identify all incoming street gang members. Like in most jails experiencing a gang problem, the unit has discovered that street gang members display a tendency to group up with one another and form associations inside the jail. Frank "Paco" Marcell, the unit supervisor, states that according to research, gang members represent the highest number of repeat offenders coming out of the correctional system and then returning. He refers to a 1999 study by the National Gang Research Center that clearly shows the gang problem in corrections. From 1991 to 1999, the number of male inmates who identified themselves as gang members increased from 9.4 to 24.7 percent. By 2004, few in corrections have believed that this percentage has decreased. According to Marcell, gangs are a closed society, and when incarcerated, will continue their illegal activities.[36]

Other negative aspects of the jail climate are clandestine operations by inmates, such as the manufacture of contraband, drug smuggling, etc. The manufacture of weapons and the usage of chemical substances for ingestion—alcohol and drugs—can cause tension, fear, and the loss of inhibitions by inmates. Also, this is dangerous for the jail staff. Confronting and subduing an intoxicated or "high" inmate may result in a serious physical altercation and injury.

In contrast to positive inmate leaders, negative inmate leaders are defiant to staff, try to implement power plays, and frequently attempt to persuade young, naïve inmates or mentally disordered inmates to do their bidding or cause trouble. This type of "amusement" is dangerous, as some inmates are easily led and do not think of the consequences of their actions. As stated earlier in this chapter, inmates who are actively involved in STGs and emerge in the jail population with reputations are a danger to the jail climate.

Inmate violence can have a fallout or negative effect on the jail climate and has several aspects: inmate on inmate violence, inmate on staff violence, riots, disturbances, and hostage taking.

Inmate on inmate violence can be the result of an argument between inmates in a cellblock, in a program, or in a recreation area. Arguments among inmates vary from disputes over television programs, disputes over the availability of the phone, theft of commissary and property, racial tension, or suspicion of being an informant. Inmate on inmate violence also can be in the form of sexual assault or rape.

Whatever the reason, the consequences are multiple. Not only do inmates suffer injuries ranging from blackened eyes, broken noses, broken jaws, head injuries, but staff must afford the inmates medical attention, which means taking them to outside medical facilities such as a hospital, if the condition is too serious for the jail medical facilities and staff on site. On some occasions, inmate violence can result in death.

These two examples illustrate the range of inmate on inmate violence. Two male inmates on the Orange County, North Carolina jail were charged with assaulting each other after they argued over a toilet brush. One inmate hit the other on the head and behind an ear with the brush; the victim received stitches. The other inmate hit the brush-wielding inmate in the chest. Both were charged with criminal assault.[37] In an assault at the jail in Los Angeles, five convicted felons were charged with first-degree murder in the beating death of another inmate.[38]

Concerning jail assaults, the practice is to have the injured inmates; both victim and perpetrator receive medical attention. The incident is then investigated by the correctional agency or the police agency of the jail's jurisdiction and criminal charges are filed if necessary. In cases of criminal prosecution, evidence must be obtained and carefully preserved. In Pennsylvania in 1999 an inmate, whom jail officials described as a well-behaved inmate, was attacked while sleeping; he suffered multiple bruises, with his right eye swollen shut and a badly bruised face. Investigating jail officials reportedly were looking at athletic shoe marks on the victim's neck and chest, which could be traced to several inmates' shoes.[39]

Inmate "hazing" can also pose a problem to the jail climate. In 2005 in Pennsylvania, a county jail was under a police investigation due to an inmate ritual of hazing, or beating. Police said that there were 30 confirmed victims and 20 additional suspected inmate victims. Police stated that 40 percent of victims in the confirmed cases did not want to press criminal charges. The hazing worked as follows: "senior" inmates would administer a "shower shoeing" to newly arriving inmates by beating them with a heavy rubber-soled shower shoe. If the inmate would not submit, a more severe beating involving punches and kicks would take place. Eight male inmates and one female inmate who delivered the shower shoeing to female inmates were charged or had charges pending. Younger, small-sized inmates were targeted. Injuries ranged from broken bones including a skull fracture, lacerations, contusions, and one inmate had to have his jaw wired closed. Officials said that overcrowding may be part of the reason for the inmate rituals. The jail is 24 years old and was initially built to hold 45 inmates. The 2004 average daily population was 118 inmates, and the state approved a capacity of 136. Many inmates were sleeping in closets and hallways. Besides the negative publicity and the police investigation, the jail was in danger of not passing its state inspection and could lose its certification.[40]

For inmates who are new to a jail setting or have been in the jail for a time and want to stay out of trouble, instances such as jail violence, hazing, etc. can be unsettling. Another form of violence is sexual assault. In recent years, the corrections profession has begun to take a serious look at this problem.

In 2003, Congress enacted the **Prison Rape Elimination Act,** which is designed to combat the problem of sexual assaults in corrections facilities. The Act applies to all public and private facilities and institutions that house offenders and also applies to community-based agencies. The law creates national standards for the detection and prevention of prison sexual assault, and supplies funding to state prison systems to deal with the sexual assault problem. Its purpose is to establish within the nation's correctional systems—including local jails—a "zero tolerance" policy for prison rape and sexual assault, prioritizing prevention and the development of standards for the detection, prevention, reduction, and punishment (of perpetrators) of prison rape. This also includes the sexual abuse of female inmates by correctional staff. Through statistical survey assistance from the United States Justice Department, data will be collected and a bipartisan commission will issue a report in two years in order to make improvements in correctional facilities to combat the problem. The National Institute of Corrections is providing training to corrections facilities.[41]

The seriousness of the prison rape problem was recognized by Congress during the development and passage of the Act. Among the findings:

- In the past 20 years, the number of inmates who have been assaulted sexually probably exceeded 1 million.
- Young, first-time offenders are at increased risk for sexual assault, often within the first 48 hours of being locked up.
- Inmates who are mentally ill are at increased risk of being a victim of a sexual assault while incarcerated.
- Juvenile offenders are five times more at risk to be sexually assaulted while incarcerated than are adult offenders.
- Most staff in prisons and correctional facilities are not prepared or trained to prevent, treat, and report sexual assaults.
- Prison rape and sexual assaults are often not reported. Inmate victims suffer physical and emotional trauma, sometimes receive inadequate treatment, and have difficulty reintegrating into the community after release. This may result in new crimes (some brutal) being committed, homelessness, the inability to hold a job, and receiving government assistance.
- Prison rape and sexual assault add to the AIDS/HIV and STD problem in U.S. correctional facilities. In 2000, 6 percent of all deaths in federal and state prisons were attributed to HIV/AIDS. (Prison inmates who are AIDS/HIV positive can be transferred to a local jail for many reasons, or can be paroled, released time served, be re-arrested and committed to the local jail.)
- Closely related to the above, infection rates for diseases such as tuberculosis, hepatitis B and C, and other STDs are greater for prisoners than for the U.S. population as a whole.[42]

The Prison Rape Elimination Act is a significant step forward in corrections to positively impact the jail climate. Not only is the "zero tolerance" policy clear, but the definitions in the Act leave no room for doubt concerning the purpose of this law. The definitions used in the Prison Rape Elimination Act are wide-ranging and include the following:[43]

- *Prison* is defined as any confinement facility of a federal, state, or local government. This includes local police and jail lockups, private correctional institutions, and juvenile detention centers.
- *Rape* is defined as carnal knowledge, oral sodomy, sexual assault using an object, or forced sexual fondling against the person's will.
- *Inmate* includes any person who is incarcerated or detained in any facility—who is accused of, convicted of, sentenced for, or adjudicated as a delinquent for criminal law violations or for violating the terms of probation, parole, pretrial release or diversion program.

In July 2005, the Bureau of Justice Statistics (BJS) issued the special report titled *Sexual Violence Reported by Correctional Authorities, 2004*, which examined data relating to incidents of sexual violence reported in correctional facilities in 2004. Among the facilities selected for the survey were 404 public local jails, 5 private local jails, and 10 Indian country jails. The number of sexual violence allegations (accusations) reported in public local jails was 699, with 225 of those being reports of staff sexual misconduct. A total of 210 incidents of sexual violence were substantiated or found to be valid.[44]

The term *rape* is easily recognized and understood when discussing forced nonconsensual sexual activity whether inmate on inmate, staff on inmate, and inmate on staff. The BJS report further explained the categories of sexual violence, which include many conceivable types of sexual activity. There are four categories in measuring corrections sexual violence:[45]

- *Nonconsensual sexual act:* It includes sexual contact of any person without his or her consent, or sexual contact of a person who is unable to refuse or consent. Contact includes contact between the penis and the vagina, or between the penis and the anus. This includes penetration, however slight. Also included is contact between the mouth and the penis, anus, or vagina. Penetration includes penetration of the anal or genital opening of another person using a hand, finger, or any other object.
- *Abusive sexual contact:* Differing slightly from the above category, this defines *contact* in lieu of an overt act. Abusive sexual contact is sexual contact of any person, without his or her consent, or of a person who is unable to consent or refuse. Included is the intentional touching either directly or through clothing of genitalia, anus, groin, breast, inner thigh, or buttocks.
- *Staff sexual misconduct:* It is defined as *any* behavior or act of a sexual nature toward an inmate. Staff members as indicated here are employees, volunteers, official visitors, or agency representatives. Sexual acts–both consensual and nonconsensual—include intentional touching of the genitalia, anus, groin, breast, inner thigh, or buttocks with the intent to abuse, arouse, or seek gratification of a sexual desire. Also prohibited are sexual acts that are completed, attempted, threatened, or requested. Included also are occurrences of indecent exposure, invasion of privacy, or voyeurism by staff for sexual gratification. Included in this section are romantic relationships between staff and inmates.
- *Staff sexual harassment:* It includes acts such as repeated verbal statements or comments of a sexual nature by employees, volunteers, official visitors, or agency representatives to an inmate. These statements include demeaning references to gender, or derogatory comments about body, clothing, and any profane or obscene gestures or language.

Staff members who engage in any of the behaviors discussed in the Prison Rape Elimination Act such as engaging in sex with inmates are literally "playing with fire" and jeopardize their careers and good standing in both their professional and their personal lives. With many states adopting criminal sanctions punishing staffs who engage in sexual misconduct with inmates, jail staff members risk conviction and acquiring the status of convicted criminal. In examining the nature of these acts, staffs stating that "the inmate wanted it" or "we were in love" are not defenses.

For the benefit of local corrections, sexual misconduct by inmates and staff is taken seriously and is not without consequences. Concerning 42 jails dealing with inmate on inmate sexual violence in 2004, 76 percent resulted in legal sanctions (arrest, referred for prosecution, and receiving new sentence); 74 percent resulted in custody changes (placement in segregation or solitary confinement, higher custody level assigned in the jail, or transfer to another jail); and internal discipline (confinement to cell/quarters, loss of good time, extra work given, or loss of privileges) was imposed in 60 percent of cases. Concerning jail staff and sanctions in 2004, in 81 substantiated incidents of public jail staff sexual misconduct, 59 staff members were discharged, 17 were disciplined, and 17 were referred for prosecution. Staff sexual harassment substantiated incidents were reported to be 34; 8 staff were discharged, 22 were disciplined, and 1 was referred for prosecution. Private jails reported only 1 substantiated incident of staff sexual misconduct, with 1 staff member being discharged and 1 referred for prosecution. No staff sexual harassment incidents were reported in private jails in the 2004 study; Indian country jails were reported to have incurred no incidents of either staff sexual misconduct or harassment.[46]

Gathering of data in this area is continuing, as the BJS released its second, subsequent report, *Sexual Violence Reported by Correctional Authorities, 2005,* in July of 2006. For the 2005 survey, 347 local public jails, 5 private jails, and 7 Indian country jails were selected, and the survey was expanded to include more data on substantiated incidents. The number of substantiated incidents of sexual violence in local and private jails was estimated as 336 and 13, respectively. Concerning staff sexual misconduct and harassment, jail authorities concluded that staff had a romantic relationship with the inmate in over half of jail cases.[47]

The 2005 survey resulted in more information about substantiated inmate on inmate violence in jails. Most incidents examined had one victim (96.9%), generally male (92.4%), white (71%), and was between 18 and 24 years of age (53.4%). Most incidents examined had one perpetrator (91.4%), who was a male (98.6%), was white (48.2%), and was also between 18 and 24 years of age (30.1%). Most inmate on inmate sexual violence occurred in the victim's cell/room (60.2%) between the hours of 6 P.M. and midnight (42.4%). In most cases of inmate on inmate sexual violence, the victim reported the incident to jail authorities (90.6%). Legal sanctions, including arrest, referral for prosecution, or receiving a new sentence, were imposed on 83 percent of the inmate perpetrators of cases in jails.[48]

Collateral effects of such events include imposing in-house disciplinary punishment on the perpetrator, confinement to disciplinary segregation, staff escorts in restraints, and keeping the victim and perpetrator separate. It is important to offer the victim counseling as well as mandatory medical attention and follow up, including testing for STDs. Staff must exercise compassion and concern when dealing with an inmate victim of sexual assault, as it is a depressing and traumatic experience. Finally, the jail supervisory staff must examine in detail the incident in order to prevent a reoccurrence.

Inmate assaults on officers can occur at any time. When dealing with many inmates over a long period of time, officers soon discover that even the level-headed, apparently mature, and easygoing inmates may have a breaking point or experience frustration leading to violence. When being confronted by staff for wrongdoing or during an investigation, there is a tension. An example of this occurred in November of 2003 at the Macomb, Michigan County Jail. In one week, three jail officers were injured coming to the aid of a female officer who had been assaulted from behind by a 45-year-old inmate who was jailed for reportedly assaulting a police officer. She had just put him back in the court holding cell and turned her back and entered a doorway. The inmate forcibly knocked her over from behind. Two officers were injured when they came to her aid. Sheriff Mark Hackel was aware of the tense conditions at the overcrowded jail, saying "There's tensions that rise sometimes with the inmates when they're stuffed in a facility for any length of time....They really want to get out, they want to move, the food is not the greatest and they've got some medical and mental health issues themselves, so you're going to get that."[49]

Attacks can be spontaneous and use a variety of methods. In 2004, an officer at the Albuquerque, New Mexico Detention Center was stabbed in the hand with reportedly a pen tied to the inmate's wrist. The assault happened as the officer was attempting to search the 20-year-old inmate's cell.[50] In another incident in 2001, three murder suspects escaped from the Mower County, Minnesota Jail by kicking a male jail officer, bruising his ribs, throwing cleaning solution in a female officer's face, and beating her. Two leaped from a jail second story window, and a third also jumped from the jail but broke his leg and was captured. The local police chief stated that the escape did not appear planned and said that he thought that it was a "spur-of-the-moment, take-advantage-of-an-opportunity type thing."[51]

## Riots and Disturbances

Riots and disturbances by inmates can occur at any time in a jail, especially when inmates are in group activities such as recreation, programs, or eating. During these activities, large groups of inmates are out of their confined housing areas and outnumber the jail officers in that area.

A **riot** is defined as a series of violent acts by a large group of inmates whose purpose is to disrupt to the greatest extent possible the security and operation of the facility. For example, if a group of 30 inmates in a recreation yard overpowers jail officers and begins destroying the physical plant of the jail, while other inmates are joining them, that can be termed a riot. A **disturbance** is smaller in scale than a riot. It is defined as a disruptive or violent act or acts by a small group of inmates and is usually confined to a much smaller area. Its purpose may be short term, such as gang animosity, tension, revenge to inmate enemies, a protest, etc. An example of a disturbance may be three or four inmates engaging in a physical altercation after arguing over the use of the cellblock phone or what channel to watch on television.

The causes of a riot may vary. Overcrowding and the resulting tensions of so many inmates confined to a limited area can lead to frustrations. Inmates may riot in retaliation or because of gang violence. An example of a jail experiencing riots is what occurred at the Corrizela-Rucker Detention Center in Cameron County, Texas during the summer of 2004. In July 2004, approximately 135 inmates took part in a gang-related riot. One inmate was stabbed and 11 others were injured. In August, 11 inmates barricaded themselves in a pod of the facility and began destroying county property. They had homemade weapons—buckets, broomsticks, metal shanks, and other homemade, makeshift weapons. After an hour of holding off officers, the 11 inmates were subdued by over two dozen officers armed with pepper spray, rubber pellets, and tear gas. The 11 were acting in retaliation for being locked down after at least one of the inmates seriously assaulted another

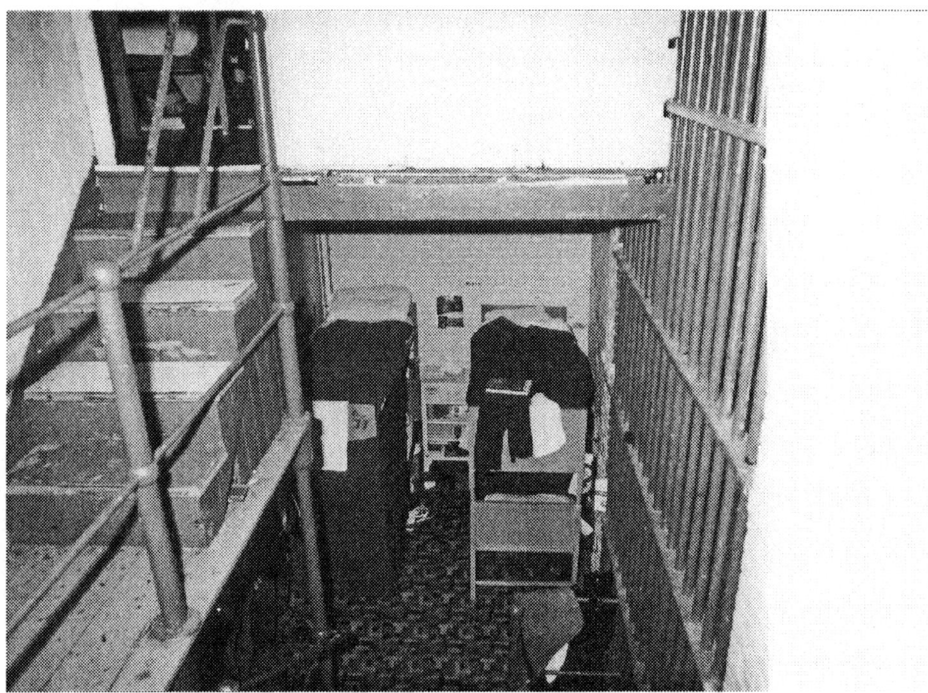

Inmate bunks under a stairway, old Norfolk County Jail, circa late 1980s.

Photo courtesy of Sheriff Michael G. Bellotti and Deputy Superintendent David Reilly of the Norfolk County Sheriff's Office.

inmate earlier in the month. The riot started when the group was ordered back to their cells after recreation in an enclosed recreation area. They refused and barricaded themselves.[52]

Minimum security facilities are not immune. In November 1998, a person threw bolt cutters over a fence at a minimum security facility in Kansas in an apparent attempt to aid an escape. When jail officers moved in, 150 inmates started fighting.[53]

## Causes of Riots and Disturbances

There can be many causes of a jail riot or disturbances. The event can either be "sparked," and erupt spontaneously, or be planned. A "spark" could be a unit erupting into violent behavior as a group of jail officers attempts to break up an argument between two inmates, enforcing the rules, or inmates seizing a set of security keys that have been left lying in the open, resulting in inmates having access to different areas of the jail. This occurred in a Georgia Jail in 2002. Over 100 inmates started some small fires, which were put out by other inmates, and temporarily seized control of the jail after jail officers tried to turn off televisions during an Atlanta Falcons-Dallas Cowboys football game between 11:00 P.M. and 11:30 P.M., enforcing the lights-out rule. When 150 sheriff's deputies and police officers showed up and entered the jail, the inmates, numbering 105, backed down.[54] A riot can also be planned by inmate ringleaders who may be in a gang. When a riot is going to occur, either by spark or through planning, is difficult for the staff to predict. What is important is that the staff recognizes certain conditions that could lead to such an event. These conditions, called **predisposing factors of unrest,** are conditions of the jail environment and population that tend to reinforce the potential for trouble in the jail. They are:[55]

- *Environment:* regimentation, lack of privacy, sexual intimacy, separation from family, friends, and loved ones, gang/STG activity, different behaviors from inmates, brutality, poor food, etc.
- *Substandard facilities:* aging buildings that need maintenance and repair.
- *Inadequate funding:* programs, maintenance, and staffing suffer due to no money.
- *Overcrowding:* resulting in tension, anger, violence, inmate predators, and jail services being taxed beyond reasonable limits.
- *Inadequate staffing:* under supervision by jail officers, lack of responses to grievances, requests, and problems that leads to a climate of depersonalization by staff toward inmates.
- *Idleness/lack of programs:* Inmate idleness and tension are not reduced because of a lack of positive activity.
- *Negative attitudes/apathy:* Public apathy and punitive attitudes toward rehabilitation and inmates may manifest themselves in some jail officers having negative views and behavior toward inmates.
- *Inadequacies in the criminal justice system:* Inmates may be frustrated when they see disparity in court sentences, parole board decisions, etc.

## Principles of Collective Behavior

Jails are a mix of different types of inmates with different types and levels of criminal behavior. Some remain incarcerated in the jail longer than others depending if their charges are felonies or misdemeanors, etc. However, there are circumstances, called the **Principles of Collective Behavior,** that may bring inmates together in a riot or disturbance situation:[56]

- *Unity:* Inmates may unite over common issues that affect all or most of the jail population.
- *Frustration:* Negative inmate leaders in riot and disturbances may find recruitment and support of inmates easier if inmates feel angry, frustrated, and their complaints are ignored.
- *Highly charged atmosphere:* Due to the presence of police, corrections, fire and rescue, and the media, the environment is one of high tension and energy. It is possible for the inmates involved in the disturbance to band together more cohesively.

Recent events in jails that have involved policy decisions, conditions, and staff practices have led to inmate unrest. In a Florida jail in 2004, the jail administration decided to end its policy of permitting contact visits with inmates. While the change affected a small group of sentenced inmates, three inmate workers threatened a work stoppage and inmates in a 32-bed unit refused to place their breakfast trays outside the unit door for pickup.[57]

In February 2002, an overcrowded and understaffed Maine county jail experienced an inmate riot where inmates clogged toilets, broke windows, and set mattresses on fire. State corrections officials inspected the facility after the riot and listed 58 code violations and blamed continuous overcrowding. A county investigation indicated the following problems: overcrowding, incorrect inmate classification, lack of recreation, inadequate staff supervision, staffing, and security. One safety deficiency found was that inmates were able to tamper with a lock cylinder, remove it, and use it as a weapon. Staff was held partially accountable. The supervisor on duty during the riot was described as showing a "lack of direct involvement" with the inmates showing signs of unrest, and resigned after the riot. Jail staff involved in the riot did not file reports until almost four days later. Maximum security inmates were reclassified to medium security despite risk factors. The jail built in 1979 was designed for 58 inmates, expanded to a 90-bed capacity, but held more than 100 inmates. A new 250-bed jail was being planned.[58]

## Riot and Disturbance Warning Signs

The signs of an impending riot or disturbance may appear before the event itself. Inmates start to "get ready to survive" by avoiding certain areas, hoarding food, or making weapons for self-protection. Levels of defiance and frustration toward staff may increase. The signs take three forms: increases, decreases, and warnings:[59]

- *Increases in:*
  - Contraband found
  - Reports on misbehavior/incidents
  - Requests for cell change
  - Assaults on staff
  - Verbal defiance of staff members
  - Purchases of food from canteen/hoarding
  - Smuggling of contraband by visitors
  - Manufacture/possession of weapons
  - Sick call attendance
  - Protective custody requests/admissions
  - Thefts of food from kitchen
  - Requests for antianxiety or antidepression medications
  - Requests to go to infirmary or outside hospital
  - Excessive or specific demands from inmates
  - Number of calls from family or friends about institution conditions
  - Number of grievances, especially about an unpopular policy change, called **grievance flooding**
  - Suicide attempts
  - Employee resignations
- *Warnings:*
  - To tell family and friends not to visit
  - To well-liked staff to take leave or a sick day
  - Anonymous warnings that something is going to happen
- *Decreases in:*
  - Attendance at movies, meals recreation
  - Number of inmate workers

(List reprinted with permission of Carolina Academic Press).

Inmates behave differently in a riot/disturbance prone atmosphere. They may be reluctant to communicate with staff, may post lookouts when groups of inmates are talking, and may even congregate along ethnic, racial, or STG lines. Inmates may also mail out cherished personal belongings to friends or family.[60]

## Hostage Situations

Jail officers fear being taken hostage by desperate and angry inmates, who may brutalize and assault them. In a jail riot situation, like in a prison riot, officers and staff are vulnerable to be taken hostage. Also, being taken hostage results in an emotional strain for the friends, families, and significant others of the hostage. Hostage situations are tense, and if force is used to resolve the situation, the hostages themselves may be seriously injured.

Not all inmates think that taking hostages is a wise course of action, as it may result in criminal prosecution and strict security conditions, such as solitary confinement. In a riot or disturbance situation, it is reasonable to believe that not all of the inmates involved wish to take hostages.

Two actual events illustrate these points. In September 2004, a Special Weapons and Tactics Team (SWAT) and other law enforcement personnel stormed the Bay County Jail in Panama City, Florida. An inmate, complaining about health hazards, had phoned the local television station and said that he was holding hostages at the jail. After 11 hours and failed negotiations, the SWAT team went in and freed three employee hostages, shot two inmates who were involved in the standoff, and accidentally shot a nurse who was a hostage. All survived.[61]

In a Virginia regional jail, inmates seized two jail officers, ages 25 and 70, and attempted unsuccessfully to escape. The local police negotiated with the two hostage takers, resulting in the older officer being released for medical reasons. Four to six inmates in an adjoining cellblock grabbed one of the hostage takers and subdued him. The event ended with the two hostage takers being charged with attempted escape, abduction, felonious assault, and other offenses.[62]

Hostage plans fall under emergency plans and preparedness procedures that all jails should have and may vary from one jail to another. However, several issues need addressed in a hostage policy:

- *Prevention and safety:* Staff should be aware of preventative measures to avoid being taken hostage. Good security procedures include proper restraint of inmates, escort and back up procedures, and how not to over react and enter an area until backup officers are present.
- *How to act if taken hostage:* Officers should remain as calm as possible, noting information that can be later used in court.
- *Negotiations:* Negotiations with inmates should be conducted only by corrections or police hostage negotiators who have received extensive training.
- *Command decisions:* Critical decisions about hostage situations should not be made by the negotiator, but by command staff personnel who have had requests and information relayed to them. This procedure may appear cumbersome, but may buy the staff time in order to plan a course of action that will provide for the safety of the hostages.
- *Hostages who have authority lose that authority:* For example, if the chief jailor is taken hostage, he loses that authority. By doing so, a hostage cannot order the jail staff to do something, such as open the front door and let the hostage takers escape.

- *Zero tolerance:* No hostage will be released while holding another person—staff, civilian, visitor, another inmate—under duress. The perimeter staff should especially be aware of this.[63]

## COUNTERACTING A NEGATIVE JAIL CLIMATE

The negative aspects of a jail climate can be counteracted in several ways. By adhering to positive, proactive practices, the possibility of violence, including riots and disturbances, can be reduced, but unfortunately not entirely prevented. As long as inmates are confined in close quarters against their will, there will always be the threat of violence and disruption.

Jail staffs are making progress in keeping the pressure of incarceration at manageable levels. An important practice for jail officers to do is to be as mobile and visible as possible in the housing areas. Not only do the inmates feel safer, but staff by circulation among the inmates can dispel rumors, answer inmates' questions, and handle problems.

### Positive Communication

Positive communication is a key factor. One veteran jail training officer advises younger officers "to think seriously about what is going to be said to the inmate before it comes out of your mouth." He also advises staff to treat the inmates with basic respect, calling them "Mr." or "Miss." Inmates are people and will respond to basic human respect that is shown to them.

Jail officers must carry themselves professionally at all times. How officers perform their duties and present themselves is called **officer comportment.**[64] If an officer's comportment is negative, this will only add to the tension of the jail climate. Inmates tend to respect officers who are "squared away," and tensions between inmates and officers may be reduced.

How officers verbally communicate with inmates can affect the jail climate. Verbal communication should have an aspect of respect and consideration. How officers get their points across to the inmate without arguments, tension, or stress, ensuring compliance from the inmate, is called **correct assertiveness.** In correct assertiveness, the jail officer balances communication with both what he/she and the jail inmate want to say and what both understood or heard.[65]

The seven components of correct assertiveness, when used properly, can provide the inmate with an adult forum for communication without embarrassment, anger, and negativity. These components are:[66]

- *Consider the context:* When engaging in serious communications with inmates, the setting should be free of distractions, noise, and other inmates.
- *Maintain calmness:* Understanding and cooperation increase if both parties are respectful and understanding. Condescending behavior, being critical, combined with fatigue and impatience does not enhance communication.
- *Consider the other's point of view:* Listening to both sides is necessary. The inmate may not get the answer that he or she wants, but will respect the officer for listening.

- *Explain your side:* Inmates should receive an answer to a question or request unless security will be compromised. They will feel like they are being treated as people.
- *Come to a solution:* Both officer and inmate should work to resolve the problem and come to a solution. Compromise is important, but the inmate may have to be told that the officer's decision is final, and the inmate can choose to go along or not.
- *Consider the consequences:* Officers will decide on a course of action after all has been discussed. He/she must weigh the consequences.
- *Do not run hot and cold:* The effectiveness of communications can be affected by mood. Officers should try to be level headed and even tempered at all times.

Correct assertiveness does not apply to all inmates; some suffer from mental disorders or are so hard core and institutionalized that any communication from the staff will be looked upon with distrust. Officers in their everyday activities should practice correct assertiveness with the inmate population who just want to do their time with as little problems as possible.

## Human Service Officers

Positive jail officers realize the precariousness of the environment in which they work. Tensions are always right below the surface, and at times jail officers feel that they are locked up the same way as the inmates. Officers who want to make a good impression on the inmates, keep them safe, and positively impact the jail climate advocate the **Human Services Officer** approach. This approach means that officers are treating the inmates like people, giving them what they need, helping them adjust, and assisting them whenever possible. There are four components:[67]

- *Goods and services:* Inmates are provided with the basic necessities and services such as towels, soap, medications, toilet paper, etc. This results in the inmate feeling less degraded in going without these items. Then officer serves to calm the inmate and make the environment habitable.
- *Referrals and advocacy:* Inmates are assisted in getting to see counselors, enrolling in programs, or getting to sick call by officers willing to make a phone call or speak in their behalf, thus cutting through the "red tape."
- *Officers and inmate adjustment:* Inmates who appear frightened, vulnerable, and easy targets for predators are looked out for by officers. Officers may use good interpersonal communication skills and speak to inmates about what may be bothering them. Anxiety and fear are lessened. Inmates are encouraged to communicate with staff.
- *Helping network:* The human service approach can be quite effective if many different staff members from many different sections of the jail work together to reduce the fears, anxiety, and tensions of the inmate population.

## Controls of Corrections Violence

There are inherent, "built in" controls for violence in a jail setting using the work practices, procedures, and policies of the jail staff combined with the beliefs and views of the inmate population. Research by Lee Bowker suggests that by staff being aware of these internal controls, inmate violence can be reduced. These controls are:[68]

- *Physical control:* The jail environment is conducive to this. Locks, cameras, security doors, legalized application of force by officers, restraints, escorts, perimeter walls, fences, towers, and uniformed staff all convey to the inmate a sense of control by the jail staff. A new trend in jails is the establishment of emergency response teams, sometimes called jail "swat" (special weapons and tactics) teams that are called upon to provide order and resolve violent and potentially violent situations.
- *Antiviolence norms, values, and beliefs:* Not all inmates agree with violence; some want to stay out of trouble. Some violent inmates are written out of units by antiviolent inmates.
- *Fear of reprisals:* Some inmates feel that if they engage in assaults and violent acts, they may be subject to reprisals by officers and other inmates. They may think that they will be unable to protect themselves.
- *Legal and administrative sanctions:* Jail inmates want to be released from jail as soon as possible and without any "hassles" that may incur additional criminal charges or lose such "perks" as **good time,** which is time off (by statute) an inmate's sentence, awarded for program participation, working as a trusty in the jail, or for general good behavior. Acquiring good time may have a positive impact on the jail climate. Other administrative sanctions could be doing disciplinary segregation time for breaking the rules, or being placed on administrative segregation, which is generally without television and social inmate contact. The jail classification section (see Chapter 5) has a lot of influence. The inmate may also be reclassified to a higher custody level within the jail resulting in more restrictive housing.
- *Profit motive:* Inside a jail, there are inmates who manufacture, smuggle, and distribute contraband. Their cells are their home bases, and if those cells are destroyed, damaged, or they are reclassified or moved due to violence, their "business" suffers.
- *Social acceptance:* Inmates need meaningful social relationships, just like people on the outside. Their sense of self-esteem is enhanced—they feel good about themselves. As a result, violence is often avoided.
- *Housekeeping considerations:* Inmates realize that for as long as they are incarcerated, the jail is their home. If violence, riots, and disturbances occur, their "homes" may be damaged. Many inmates keep their areas clean and tidy, and this is part of an orderly atmosphere and doing time as "hassle free" as possible.

## Responses to Potential Violence and Disruption

Not all interpersonal communications and built in violence controls are successful, and at times, inmate violence will have to be met with force when all else fails. Emergency equipment and protective vests are but two of the various products being made available to jail officers. In the past 20 years, the most important mechanism to responding to inmate violence, especially organized inmate violence (such as riots), has been the **emergency response team, or ERT.** Sometimes called the Sheriff's Emergency Response Team (SERT) or the Corrections Emergency Response Team (CERT), the team is defined as a carefully selected, highly trained group of correctional officers who through special tactics and security devices respond to and resolve volatile situations in the jail, in order to maintain and restore order. Under a supervisor's direction, an ERT may respond to subdue a group of inmates who are destructive, and inmates who will not obey commands to return to their cells, or extract a mentally disordered violent inmate from his cell and place him inside a padded cell. ERT members also provide escorts for extremely dangerous inmates and conduct shakedowns.

One example of an ERT is the Cochise County, Arizona Sheriff's office Detention Response Unit, or DRU. The DRU was developed in response to a hostage situation in 1994, where seven inmates seized a female officer and her radio. By having the radio, the inmates could listen in on all sheriffs' office frequencies. The weapon used to hold the officer was a mop bucket ringer fashioned into a "sharp, spike like object." After 14 hours of fruitless negotiations, a decision was made to assault the pod in the jail where the hostage was being held. The Arizona Department of Corrections emergency team and the Cochise Sheriff's Office SWAT team retook the pod in 20 seconds and freed the hostage, who was hospitalized and soon released thereafter. Fortunately, no one—inmates or staff—was harmed. The hostage takers were criminally charged and transferred to the Arizona Department of Corrections. A decision was then made to form a jail ERT.[69]

The Cochise County DRU is supervised by the detention lieutenant and maintains operational control. In a situation, a tactical unit leader will conduct operations. DRU members volunteer and must pass a basic upper-body strength test; physical fitness levels are evaluated twice annually. Applicants must have completed their probationary periods, have good performance evaluations, and have no problems in his or her job record. Officers are on probation in the DRU for six months after completing the Basic Tactical Officers Academy. Training includes being proficient in using Colt MKIV .45 semi auto firearm, Remington 870P shotgun, OC (Pepper) spray, restraints, and force. Additional training includes high-risk transports, high-profile court proceedings, basic weaponless stun techniques and procedures, tactical handcuffing, and using chemical agents, less-than-lethal munitions, M26 Advanced Taser, and the Mini 14 Rifle.[70]

Like in most ERTs, Cochise County members wear protective gear, including helmets, protective vests, and protective masks. One member during an operation is assigned to videotape the event.[71] Videotapes are useful—they can serve to prosecute the inmate in court, absolve the ERT of any misconduct, and be used for training.

One advantage to having ERT members working inside the jail is that if there is a situation, the ERT members working on shift can "suit up" and plan a course of action under the direction of an ERT supervisor. The remainder of the jail staff can operate as usual, but in some cases the jail may be locked down until the situation is resolved.

## Antiviolence Programs

Some jails are taking a proactive stance toward violence. Realizing the deadly potential if inmate violence is not controlled, jails have put forth innovative programs and practices. One example is in New York, in the New York City Department of Corrections (NYC DOC). The department operates 10 jails on the 415-acre island, with a combined capacity of over 16,000 inmates. NY DOC also operates six other houses of detention. In 1994, NY DOC implemented the Violence Reduction Initiative, which resulted in a 64 percent decrease in inmate stabbing and slashings from fiscal year (FY) 1995 to FY 1996. The numbers were impressive; in FY 1995 there were 1,124 incidents compared with only 407 in FY 1996. The program was revolutionary: supervisors were held accountable for incidents within their facilities, weapon searches increased, inmates needing to be searched more frequently carried a special red identification card, inmates prone to violence were housed in separate units, a computerized database monitored and tracked violent inmates, and a 24-hour ERT was formed.[72]

Other practices by the NY DOC have been beneficial. All front-line captains were authorized to be issued and use mace. Handheld wands and metal detectors were made available to look for weapons and contraband. With these practices, there have been fewer violent incidents resulting in injuries and costly trips to the hospital. Staff and inmates both feel somewhat safer.[73]

Concerning gangs, the New York City jail system started the innovative Gang Tracking Program, which works as a task force unit. It tracks gangs inside the jail and on the street, gathers intelligence, photos, physical descriptions, aliases, enemies, and factual data, and organizes the information into a computer database. These data allow for better decision making concerning inmate movement and housing.[74]

## Research in Jail Violence

More research is being conducted concerning jail violence. The more that is understood about jail violence, the more changes can be made in inmate management to foster a positive jail climate. Writing in the May/June 2004 issue of *American Jails,* Dr. P.F. McManimon summarized research findings:[75]

- Some research suggests that jail staff have more control over the jail environment due to high inmate turnover rates, whereas in prison, inmates develop stronger, more sophisticated subcultures because they are incarcerated there for longer periods of time.
- A consistent finding is that inmates who generally commit rule infractions tend to be younger than those inmates who commit no infractions. The inmate's age at entry to the jail increases the likelihood of that inmate breaking the rules and committing assaults on other inmates.
- Race does not appear to be a factor, due to mixed results in the research. A 1993 study found that whites and nonwhites committed acts of violence in proportion to their numbers in the jail's general population.
- Current offense: Research suggests that inmates incarcerated for violent crimes were found to be more likely to commit assaults on other inmates.
- Overcrowding does have an effect on inmate assaultive behavior. One researcher noted that as correctional facilities became more crowded, inmate on inmate assaults without weapons and inmate assaults on staff increased. Another researcher suggested that chronic overcrowding where antisocial people are gathered together could affect personal space and the occurrences of both disruptive and assaultive behavior.
- Staff factors: One study found that jail officers with less than one year of experience were more at risk of being assaulted by inmates than by experienced officers. Another study suggested that well-trained and competent staff can serve to deflect violent reactions from jail inmates.

As jail operations, architecture, and research become more sophisticated and progressive, the problem of inmate violence and its effect on the jail climate bears further scrutiny. However, innovative programs such as in the NY DOC are providing good data and a precedent for other jails to take similar actions.

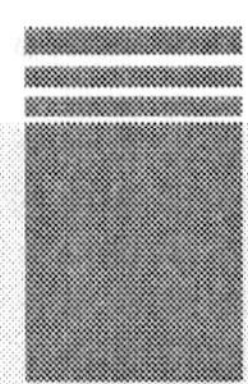

POINT OF VIEW

## Doing Time in Jail

***Joseph R.****

*Author's note:* Joseph R. is an ex jail inmate who was incarcerated in jail several years ago on drug charges.

There were no stronger feelings of shame, guilt, remorse, embarrassment, depression, fear, and shock the day my bail was revoked and I was held in the jail until sentencing for a drug distribution charge. I would certainly receive more time than the three months until the sentencing, so only God knew when I would be released. I was held for 12 hours on the night of my arrest so I knew the (jail's) procedure of getting my jumpsuit (jail uniform for inmates), and sitting in the drunk tank (holding area) until I was moved into the general population. Yet this time things were different. Nobody was "hustling" to get money together to bail me out. There was nothing anybody could do; I was there however long the judge saw fit.

My drug habit had turned into greed. Greed changed the way of life that I had lived. I neglected my family, health, and future. Who knows where I would be today had I not been arrested? Am I thankful for it? It is hard to say that I am glad for the two years I spent in jail, the pain I caused my family, and the overall horror of it all. It is something I wish no one should ever have to experience. I did learn a great deal about what I deem important in my life, and that I had no intentions of spending the rest of my time giving it to the state.

Being stuck on the "B" floor in the jail is like living as sardines in a can—uncomfortable, tight, stuffy, and plain terrible. Ten men live in an area the size of a master bedroom with one phone, one TV, two toilets in the open, a shower, and a window covered by bars. We were not permitted to go into our cells between 8 A.M. and 4 P.M. and sleep the days away, though some of us felt quite comfortable on the floor. My first three months I spent playing Monopoly, doing 2,000 daily pushups, reading John Grisham, worrying about my sentencing, praying, writing letters, and avoiding confrontations with other inmates and staff at all costs. My impressions of the other inmates were many. Some had come and gone and come back again, so this was nothing new. Some were sitting on short time (60 days or less), and took the whole thing as a joke. Some were gang members who looked for trouble. I found that there were a few like me who hated every second, and feared the future of sentencing, and spent hours trying to solve the mystery of how life turned out this way.

My family are four of the most beautiful people in the world—a father who would go into a burning building to save his children and wife; a mother who kept us together when hope was low; a sister so gifted and brilliant that she could be anything and converse with anyone; and another sister who is so thoughtful for us that she has incorporated it into her own family. Not a second passed where I did not regret the moment I decided to use and sell drugs. Why? There was no answer, just a solution that I needed to find to ensure that this would never happen again, and that one day, no matter how long it took, they could look at me and be proud of the fact I carried the same last name.

Beside the aforementioned, I signed up for church, wrote numerous letters, and called friends and family a few times a week. Phone calls were hard, because the circumstances where depressing, and hurtful to all involved. Days seemed like months and my sentencing kept getting extended in hope of me getting into a drug program. I made acquaintances with a few other inmates. One was awaiting trial on a rape charge and faced 30 years to life; the other was a barber who had six months left on a nine-month driving-while-intoxicated (DWI) charge. I learned the great calmness in meditation from the one awaiting trial, for he spent over three hours a day in prayer. I started saying the Rosary three times a day. It helped refocus my anger and sadness, pass the time, and relieve the never-ending guilt that blanketed my aura.

My thoughts of the C.O. (corrections officers) varied. They used their badge as a right to down talk the inmates, always said no to every request, would go out of the way to make life more miserable, and made fun at our situation. There were ones that helped us when our behavior was good, and in a way understood that we had nothing. I never saw any unwarranted force inflicted, or racial behavior, and for that I do give them credit. Personally I think it would not be my first or last choice of a career, but overall the job they did was respectful and well done considering the type of people in society they are dealing with. All the inmates "hate" them, because that is the "cool" thing to say, but we all knew that not one was the reason we were in jail.

I finally reached the drug program after I was in jail about three months. I was the happiest I had been since the day I got locked up. No more standing against a cellblock wall so I didn't have to watch my back, laying around waiting for the day to pass, and hope that the judge would see this as a positive step and show some leniency when judgment day came. I was introduced to my new cellblock, same amount of space, but there were four less people and lots of structure. There were classes all day, four counselors, and enough work to keep my mind off the fact I was looking at a lot of prison time. The other inmates in the program varied in crime and age—bank robbery, day-time burglary, auto-theft, assault, petty larceny, etc. But there was one constant—drug abuse. Each had a different drug, but the mission was the same, get high, stay high by any means necessary. We participated in lessons such as a family tree, a timeline; questions were asked and answered about each drug we used, each crime we committed; we attended AA and NA meetings, and were constantly reminded of the piece of garbage we were, the ones we hurt, and the destruction we had caused.

During this time my relationship with two parts of life grew to heights that have never been. They were God and my family. I felt that these two were the only ones I was sorry for, and I was on a mission to overcome all what I had done. My father was so strong. He visited, wrote letters, and stayed upbeat when I knew he did not feel that way. I turned to God more now then ever, in quiet moments when there was not a letter to write or phone to pick up or loud times when I could not scream at the others or run out the door. The goal of the program was to understand the severity of my drug use, where it had gotten me, and where I would return if I did not quit. For me it was simple: don't use, don't return. I was told that I needed meetings for the rest of my life and that God and family were not enough. Though I got positive things from meetings, something inside me knew that I had a better life ahead and the love of my family, belief in God, and pure fear of what was happening and would happen again if I did not get my life straight.

After seven months in the program, I finally faced sentencing. Nothing to this point in my life had caused me to be so scared and completely helpless. I did not sleep the night before court and I had lost over 30 pounds from worrying. The other inmates tried to be supportive, yet no such luck. I had learned a lot from the others. I was doing Yoga, meditating deeper, and felt calmer, but all that was useless at this point. It was all in the hands of the judge.

So many questions raced in my head that night! When would I get? Would I ever get out and see my family? Would I get a second chance? Would I be sent downstate to the state prison as soon as I was sentenced? I drove my self-crazy. I must have said 1,000 Our Fathers, Hail Mary's, and Acts of Contrition. I broke into sweats, got the chills, and did pushups until complete arm failure to try to knock myself out, but it was useless. The mind is too powerful when faced with fear and uncertainty.

My name was called and I was ushered with the rest of the inmates to my holding cell, shackled and scared. The quiet ones were facing the real time, the loud ones either were never getting out or were about to go home. The holding cell was dark and gloomy. Inmates compared past sentences and how strict certain judges were. After two hours my name was called. I almost threw up from the anxiety in my stomach. The door opened to the brightest light, and I saw lawyers, district attorneys (DAs), observers, and deputy sheriffs. There in the front row was my father. Tears wet my eyes as I wanted to jump in his arms, say I was sorry and wished this whole thing was a nightmare. The whole proceeding only took about ten minutes. My lawyer was saying I was deserving of a second chance, the time served was adequate, etc. Completely opposite was the DA's view. The judge asked if I had anything to say. I froze. Blacked out. My mind took me to my room when I was ten and my mother was reading me a part from my history book. My father was cooking ribs, and my sisters were talking in their rooms, enjoying each ones company with them, both being out of school for the summer. From that, I flashed through many moments in my life. Half good, half bad. The whole incident felt like an hour, though it was probably two seconds. I stumbled over a few apologetic sentences for the judges. I meant well but I am sure I was not too convincing. Ten years, eight suspended, he said. I did not know how to react—pleased I did not get 10 years or upset because I still had 13 months to go. I turned to my father to say I love you, but I was grabbed by the deputy, for it is wrong to turn your face toward the audience. I could care less; I turned back, nodded at my father, and was rushed to my holding cell. My lawyer came to visit about an hour later and promised a reconsideration hearing. (I got one and was denied about 2 months later.) I called my father who had actually predicted I would have to serve two years total. I guess we were both relieved that the hardest part was over, and now I just have to behave and wait it out.

I spent two more months in the drug program, graduated, and was sent to the hospital part of the jail for two weeks. During reconsideration, the judge was concerned about my weight and color of my skin, which had become yellow tinted. Considering that inmates at the jail spend very little time outside, it was probably lack of sun. I was monitored before being sent over to the new part of the jail, which looks like the Ritz Carlton compared to other part. Everything was new, one person to a cell, space to walk around, and freedom (or should I say access) to lie in bed all day as long as your room was clean. Two TVs, 10 phones, a full-time volleyball court, vending machines, and about 12 showers. My spirits raised for I knew what I had been through and doing my remaining 10 months in here would be a piece of cake. These inmates were all nonviolent offenders, short timers, one timers, DWIs, and drug offenders. I no longer feared getting jumped by a gang or having to defend myself. I still stuck to the same routine: prayer, pushups, reading, and sleeping.

My name was called in the middle of the night. My next biggest fear was now upon me. Downstate!! I packed my things and hurried downstairs. You called either early morning or late night when getting moved to a state jail (prison). I only asked one question. When could I use the phone to tell my father I was getting moved? They said in the morning. I said that is pretty fast, the jail must be close. They corrected me and told me I was going to PRC—the Pre Release Center. There I would be able to go to a job, wear civilian clothes, start paying my court cost, and earn unsupervised two-day release visits. I was stunned. Five days later I was wearing pants, a collared shirt, standing at a bus stop on my way to Burger King. I think that was the first time I smiled in two years. I felt like dancing, for it was the first time in two years, I felt like a person again. I had been through so much pain, misery, demoralization, and fear and never knew when it would end. At that moment, I could see the light. I would soon be out with my family and free to walk the streets. God had watched over me, protected me and my loved ones.

PRC was like a large college dorm, yet it had lots of rules. Obey and it was easy; disobey, and you were back with the inmates on the other side in the main jail. I got a job and loved every second. I busted my ass, and took full advantage of working as many hours as I could. I was rewarded a furlough every month, one 36-hour visit to my sister's house. It was great to visit her and spend time with her. I had a real bed to sleep in and time to feel somewhat normal. I ate like I was pregnant. She was so good to me, and I can never forget how loving she was for opening her home to me.

PRC was still subjected to shakedowns, searches, and your occasional deputy hostility, but I was straight as a ruler, so I never let it bother me. I just crossed the days on the calendar. I absolutely hated jail. What I went through mentally was harder than any physical pain I have ever felt. I was reduced to nothing. My freedom was taken, and my dignity was stripped away. I had no say in anything that went on. I was at the mercy of the guards, judge, DAs, and sheriffs. I was fortunate to never have had to protect myself, or go downstate. My family kept me strong, and I owe them everything. Jail makes me sick just thinking about it. I wasted years due to my own selfishness. Yet somehow I managed to understand that it could not last forever. I never wanted anyone to ever tell me I could not go anywhere, do anything, or see my family again. I guess you can say that for me, fear is a great motivator.

* Joseph R. is a fictitious name given in order to protect the ex-inmate's identity.

## SUMMARY

The jail climate—its mood, atmosphere, and whether it is positive or negative—can affect the order and stability of the jail. Incarceration in such a setting is painful to the inmate, due to deprivations of amenities, safety concerns, and loss of intimacy. Inmates learn to adjust through the process of prisonization. Inmates have several needs that when met make incarceration more bearable. Inmates also abide by the inmate code, but strict adherence to that may wane in some cases.

There are factors in the jail that may either negatively or positively affect the jail climate. Negative factors include STGs, gangs, sexual violence, and inmates who commit violence. Positive factors include staff communications, correct assertiveness, and officers taking a human services approach. Riots and disturbances and why inmates come together to engage in such behavior are a major concern to jail administrators. Hostage situations are another concern. Jails are making progress through antiviolence initiatives, ERTs, and positive work practices by jail officers.

## REVIEW QUESTIONS

1. Why is the jail climate important?
2. Discuss the painful aspects of incarceration.
3. What pitfalls should be avoided when an inmate is incarcerated?
4. Discuss each component of the "inmate code."
5. What are the seven needs of incarceration and how important is it that they should be met?
6. What factors may influence the jail climate in a negative way?
7. How can the jail climate be made more positive?
8. Explain the Principles of Collective Behavior.
9. What are some "built in" controls of inmate violence?
10. What is being done in some jails to combat inmate violence?
11. Explain the importance of the Prison Rape Elimination Act.
12. What are some results from research looking into the problem of jail violence?

## TERMS TO KNOW

amelioration of pain
correct assertiveness
disturbance
emergency response team (ERT)
first timers
good time
grandstanding
grievance flooding
Human Services Officer
incompatible
inmate code
inmate leader
jail climate
jail-wise inmates
officer comportment
power plays
predisposing factors of unrest
Principles of Collective Behavior
Prison Rape Elimination Act
prisonization
prison-wise inmates
riot
security threat groups
STG intelligence unit
street wise
trick bag
zero tolerance policy

## ENDNOTES

1. Robert Johnson, *Hard Time: Understanding and Reforming the Prison* (Belmont, CA: Wadsworth, 2002).
2. Ibid., p. 64.
3. Ibid., p. 65.
4. Ibid.
5. Ibid., p. 70.
6. Michelle Washington, "Norfolk Jail Switches to Stripes," *The Virginian-Pilot,* September 3, 2003, http://.home.hamptonroads.com/stories/print.cfm?story=59286&ran=4197 (accessed September 5, 2003).
7. Harry E. Allen, Ph.D., and Clifford Simonsen, Ph.D., *Corrections in America: An Introduction, 9th Edition* (Upper Saddle River, NJ: Prentice Hall, 2001).
8. Gary F. Cornelius, *The Correctional Officer: A Practical Guide* (Durham, NC: Carolina Academic Press, 2001).
9. Ibid., pp. 87–88.
10. Ibid., p. 88.
11. Gary Cornelius, "Advising Inmates What 'Pitfalls' to Avoid," *The Journal of Correctional Training* (Spring 1998): 37–38.
12. Johnson, *Hard Time,* pp. 168–171.
13. Bureau of Justice Statistics, *Profile of Jail Inmates, 1996,* NCJ 164620, April 1998, p. 12.
14. Ibid.
15. Ibid., p. 13.
16. Ibid.
17. Gary F. Cornelius, "Inmate Leaders," *Jail Operations Bulletin* (American Jail Association) **VII,** no. 10, (Hagerstown, MD, 1995): 2.
18. Ibid., p. 5.
19. John J. Mason III and Paul J. Beckner, "Know Your Bigots: Identifying and Supervising White Supremacists in a Correctional Setting," *American Jails* (September/October 1994): 61.
20. Loran D. Hatcher, "Security Threat Groups: It Is More Than Managing Gangs in a Local Facility," *Corrections Today* (April 2006): 55.
21. Ibid.
22. Philip L. Reichel, *Corrections: Philosophies, Practices and Procedures, 2nd Edition* (Needham Heights, MA: Allyn and Bacon, 2001).
23. Ibid., p. 375.

24. Ibid.
25. Mason III and Becker, "Know Your Bigots," p. 64.
26. Denise Orlando-Morningstar, "Prison Gangs." *Special Needs Offenders Bulletin*, no. 2 (October 1997): 1.
27. Ibid., p. 3.
28. William Triplett, "Gang Crisis: Do Police and Politicians Have a Solution?" *CQ Researcher* 14, no. 18 (May 14, 2004): 421–436.
29. Mason III and Becker, "Know Your Bigots," pp. 62–65.
30. Orlando-Morningstar, "Prison Gangs," pp. 6–8.
31. Ed Tromanhauser, Ph.D., George W. Knox, Ph.D., James G. Houston, Ph.D., James A. Laske, Ph.D., and Thomas F. McCurrie, "Gangs and Guns: A Task Force Report," *American Jails* (May/June 1995): 59, 61.
32. Mason III and Becker, "Know Your Bigots," p. 65.
33. Michelle Gaseau, "Keeping on Top of Gangs and STGs," *Corrections.com*, September 8, 2004, http://www.corrections.com/printNews.aspx?Zone=Homepage (Accessed September 8, 2004).
34. Ibid., p. 2.
35. Ibid., p. 1.
36. Ibid., pp. 2, 3.
37. Herald-Sun, "Inmates Charged in Jail Cell Fight," *corrections.com*, June 14, 2004, http://www.corrections.com/printNews.aspx?BriefZone=ThisJustIn
38. Associated Press, "Five Convicted Felons Charged in Inmate's Death," *corrections.com*, January 6, 2005, http://corrections.com/printNews.aspx?BriefZone=DidYouKnow
39. Bob Bauder, "Inmate Accused of Women's Killings Badly Beaten in Beaver County Jail," *The Times/Beaver Newspapers, Inc.*, August 15, 1999.
40. Paula Reed Ward, "Hazing Probe at Jail Widens," *Pittsburgh Post-Gazette*, March 20, 2005.
41. "NIC Assists Facilities with Prison Rape Elimination Act Compliance," *The Corrections Professional* 10, issue 3 (October 8, 2004): 1, 6.
42. "Congress passes bill to deter prison rape, mandates reforms," *The Corrections Professional* 9. 1 (August 22, 2003): 1, 8.
43. Gary F. Cornelius, "A Special Twenty Minute Trainer: The Prison Rape Elimination Act of 2003: Progressive Thinking for Corrections," *The Correctional Trainer* (Fall 2004): 21–23.
44. Allen J. Beck, Ph.D., and Timothy A. Hughes. *Sexual Violence Reported by Correctional Authorities, 2004*, NCJ 210333, Washington, DC: Bureau of Justice Statistics, July 2005, pp. 1, 3, 6, 7.
45. Ibid., pp. 3, 6.
46. Ibid., pp. 9, 10.
47. Allen J. Beck, Ph.D., and Paige Harrison. *Sexual Violence Reported by Correctional Authorities, 2005*, NCJ 214646, Washington, DC: Bureau of Justice Statistics, July 2006, pp. 3, 5, 9.
48. Ibid., pp. 6–8.
49. "Report: Inmate Attacks Guard at Overcrowded Jail," *ClickOnDetroit.com*, November 10, 2003, http://www.clickondetroit.com/print/2627149/detail.html?use=print (accessed October 14, 2004).
50. Associated Press, "Inmate Charged in Wounding of Albuquerque Officer," *corrections.com*, http://www.corrections.com/printNews.aspx?BriefZone=ThisJustIn (accessed September 13, 2004).
51. Associated Press, "Murder Suspects Escape Minn. Jail," *corrections.com*, http://www.corrections.com/news/justin/todayoncc.html (accessed March 26, 2001).
52. Ildefonso Ortiz, "No Procedure Changes Expected at Jail After Second Uprising in Two Months," *The Brownsville Herald*, August 22, 2004, http://www.brownsvilleherald.com/print.php?id=60731_0_10_0 (accessed September 1, 2004).
53. "KC Leaders Consider Jail Security," *Kansas City Business Journal*, November 18, 1998, http://kanasacity.bizjournals.com/kansascity/stories/1998/11/16/daily5.html (accessed January 11, 2004).
54. Atlanta Journal Constitution, "Inmates Temporarily Seize Control of Georgia Jail," *corrections.com*, http://www.corrections.com/news/justin/todayoncc.html (accessed August 27, 2002).
55. Gary Cornelius, *The Correctional Officer: A Practical Guide*, pp. 207–208.
56. Ibid., pp. 209–210.
57. Duane Bourne, "County Jail Inmates Protest Ban on Contact Visits," *St. Petersburg Times*, February 18, 2004, http://www.prisonsandjails.com/stories/021704/02180401.htm (Accessed August 19, 2004).
58. Associated Press, "Report: Overcrowding Led to York County Jail Riot," *corrections.com*, http://www.corrections.com/news/justin/index.html (Accessed August 5, 2002).
59. Gary Cornelius, *The Correctional Officer: A Practical Guide*, pp. 211–212.
60. Ibid., p. 212.
61. Associated Press, "Officers Storm Jail in Florida Standoff," *New York Times*, September 7, 2004, http://nytimes.com/2004/09/07/jail.html (Accessed September 7, 2004).
62. Associated Press, "Inmates Help in Rescue of Captive Guard," August 15, 2004, *Yahoo Prison News*, http://news/yahoo.com/news?tmpl=story&cid=519&u=ap/20040815/ap_on_re_us/jail_sta (Accessed August 18, 2004).
63. Don Bales, ed., *Correctional Office Resource Guide: 3rd Edition* (Lanham, MD: American Correctional Association, 1997), p. 39.
64. Gary Cornelius, *The Correctional Officer: A Practical Guide*, p. 159.
65. Ibid., pp. 169–170.
66. Ibid., p. 170.
67. Johnson, *Hard Time*, pp. 242–255.

68. Lee H. Bowker, "An Essay on Prison Violence," in *Prison Violence in America*, ed. Michael Brasswell, Steven Dilingham, and Ried Montgomery, Jr. (Cincinnati, OH: Anderson, 1985), pp. 7–17.

69. Ron Hager, C.J.M., "Cochise County Sheriff's Office Detention Response Unit [DRU]," *American Jails* (November/December 2002): 39–42.

70. Ibid., p. 42.

71. Ibid.

72. Barbara Nadel, "Care, Custody and Control: The New York City DOC," *Corrections Today* (December 1996): 90–92.

73. Ibid., p. 92.

74. Ibid., p. 93.

75. P.F. McManimon, Jr., Ph.D., "Correlations of Jail Violence," *American Jails* (May/June 2004): 41–47.

## REFERENCES


Allen, Harry E., Ph.D., and Clifford Simonsen, Ph.D. *Corrections in America: An Introduction. 9th Edition*. Upper Saddle River, NJ: Prentice Hall, 2001.

Associated Press, "Murder Suspects Escape Minn. Jail." *corrections.com*, March 26, 2001, http://www.corrections.com/news/justin/todayoncc.html (accessed March 26, 2001).

Associated Press, "Report: Overcrowding Led to York County Jail Riot." *corrections.com*, http://www.corrections.com/news/justin/index.html (accessed August 5, 2002).

Associated Press, "Inmates Help in Rescue of Captive Guard." *Yahoo Prison News*, August 15, 2004, http://news.yahoo.com/news?tmpl=story&cid=519&u=/ap/20040815/ap_on_re_us/jail_sta (accessed August 18, 2004).

Associated Press, "Officers Storm Jail in Florida Standoff." *New York Times*, September 7, 2004, http://www.nytimes.com/2004/09/07/national/07jail.html (accessed September 7, 2004).

Associated Press, "Inmate Charged in Wounding of Albuquerque Officer." *corrections.com*, http://www.corrections.com/printNews.aspx?BriefZone=ThisJustIn (accessed September 13, 2004).

Associated Press, "Five Convicted Felons Charged in Inmate's Death." *corrections.com*, January 6, 2005, http://www.corrections.com/printNews.aspx?BriefZone=DidYouKnow (accessed January 6, 2005).

Atlanta Journal Constitution, "Inmates Temporarily Seize Control of Georgia Jail." *corrections.com*, http://www.corrections.com/news/justin/todayoncc.html (accessed August 27, 2002).

Bales, Don, ed. *Correctional Office Resource Guide: 3rd Edition*. Lanham, MD: American Correctional Association, 1997.

Bauder, Bob. "Inmate Accused of Women's Killings Badly Beaten in Beaver County Jail." *The Times/Beaver Newspapers, Inc.*, August 15, 1999, Sec. A.

Beck, Allen J., Ph.D., and Timothy A. Hughes. *Sexual Violence Reported by Correctional Authorities, 2004*, NCJ 21033, Washington, DC: Bureau of Justice Statistics, July, 2005.

Beck, Allen J., Ph.D., and Paige Harrison. *Sexual Violence Reported by Correctional Authorities, 2005*, NCJ 214646, Washington, DC: Bureau of Justice Statistics, July 2006.

Bourne, Duane. "County Jail Inmates Protest Ban on Contact Visits." *St. Petersburg Times*, February 18, 2004, http//:www.prisonsandjails.com/stories/021704/02180401.htm (accessed August 19, 2004).

Bowker, Lee H. "An Essay on Prison Violence." In *Prison Violence in America*, eds. Michael Brasswell, Steven Dilingham, and Reid Montgomery, Jr., pp. 7–17. Cincinnati, OH: Anderson, 1985.

"Congress Passes Bill to Deter Prison Rape, Mandates Reforms." *The Corrections Professional* 9 a (1), August 22, 2003, 1, 8.

Cornelius, Gary F. "Inmate Leaders." *Jail Operations Bulletin* (American Jail Association) VII (10), 1995, 2.

Cornelius, Gary. "Advising Inmates What 'Pitfalls' to Avoid." *The Journal of Correctional Training*, Spring 1998, 37–38.

Cornelius, Gary F. *The Correctional Officer: A Practical Guide*. Durham, NC: Carolina Academic Press, 2001.

Cornelius, Gary F. "A Special Twenty Minute Trainer: The Prison Rape Elimination Act of 2003: Progressive Thinking for Corrections." *The Correctional Trainer*, Fall 2004, 21–23.

Gaseau, Michelle. "Keeping on Top of Gangs and STGs." *Corrections.com*, September 8, 2004, http://www. corrections.com/printNews.aspx?Zone=Homepage (accessed September 8, 2004).

Hager, Ron, C.J.M. "Cochise County Sheriff's Office Detention Response Unit [DRU]." *American Jails*, November–December 2002, 39–43.

Harlow, Carolyn Wolf, Ph.D. *Profile of Jail Inmates, 1996*, NCJ 164620, Washington, DC: Bureau of Justice Statistics, April 1998.

Hatcher, Loran D. "Security Threat Groups: It Is More Than Managing Gangs in a Local Facility." *Corrections Today*, April 2006, 54–58.

Herald-Sun, "Inmates Charged in Jail Cell Fight." *corrections.com*, June 14, 2004, http://www.corrections. com/printNews.aspx?BriefZone=ThisJustIn (accessed June 14, 2004).

Johnson, Robert. *Hard Time: Understanding and Reforming the Prison*. Belmont, CA: Wadsworth, 2002.

"KC Leaders Consider Jail Security." *Kansas City Business Journal*, November 18, 1998, http://kansascity.bizjournals.com/kansascity/stories/1998/11/16/daily5.html?t=printable (Accessed January 11, 2004).

Mason III, John J., and Paul J. Beckner. "Know Your Bigots: Identifying and Supervising White Supremacists in a Correctional Setting." *American Jails*, September–October 1994, 61–65.

McManimon, Jr. P.F., Ph.D. "Correlations of Jail Violence." *American Jails*, May–June 2004, 41–47.

Nadel, Barbara. "Care, Custody and Control." The New York City DOC, *Corrections Today*, December 1996, 94–95, 156.

"NIC Assists Facilities with Prison Rape Elimination Act compliance." *The Corrections Professional* 10 (3), October 8, 2004, 1, 6.

Orlando-Morningstar, Denise. "Prison Gangs." *Special Needs Offenders Bulletin*, no. 2, October 1997, 1–12.

Ortiz, Ildefonso. "No Procedure Changes Expected at Jail after Second Uprising in Two Months." *The Brownsville Herald*, August 22, 2004, http://www.brownsvilleherald.com/print.php?id=60731_0_10_0 (Accessed September 1, 2004).

Reichel, Philip L. *Corrections: Philosophies, Practices and Procedures, 2nd Edition*. Needham Heights, MA: Allyn and Bacon, 2001.

"Report: Inmate Attacks Guard at Overcrowded Jail." *ClickOnDetroit.com*, November 10, 2003, http://www.clickondetroit.com/print/2627149/detail.html?use=print (Accessed October 14, 2004).

Triplett, William. "Gang Crisis: Do Police and Politicians Have a Solution?" *CQ Researcher* 14 (18), May 14, 2004, 421–444.

Tromanhauser, Ed, Ph.D., George W. Knox, Ph.D., James G. Houston, Ph.D., James A. Laske, Ph.D., Thomas F. McCurrie, "Gangs and Guns: A Task Force Report." *American Jails*, May/June 1995, 59–63.

Ward, Paula Reed. "Hazing Probe at Jail Widens." *Pittsburgh Post-Gazette*, March 20, 2005, Sec. B.

Washington, Michelle. "Norfolk Jail Switches to Stripes." *The Virginian-Pilot*, September 3, 2003, http://home.hamptonroads.com/stories/print.cfm?story=59286&ran=4197 (Accessed September 5, 2003).

# BOOKING AND INITIAL INTAKE

# 4

***Objectives of chapter***

The student will:

- Learn the importance to jail operations of booking, the initial intake process, and proper release procedures
- Understand what procedures are necessary to gather accurate information on newly admitted inmates, safeguard their well-being and property, and coordinate with other key sections of the jail staff
- Understand what problems may occur in the jail booking area and how the jail staff deals with them

The booking and intake area of the local jail is a key area that is crucial to the mission of the jail. Jail staffs are at the mercy of whatever types of inmates are arrested and booked, as well as the effects of court actions on inmates.

Due to jails performing a duty to the public by properly incarcerating offenders and releasing them, the procedures of jail intake must be as error free and exact as possible. As the local jail is part of the community, the taxpaying citizens look at the local jail for assurance that offenders are properly booked in, securely confined, and cared for. Also, the public does not want offenders being released into the community by mistake or escaping from the booking area.

## JAIL BOOKING: IMPORTANCE TO JAIL OPERATIONS

Jail booking personnel do not know from day to day the types of inmates who will be brought to the jail by local, federal, and state law enforcement agencies, be received from the state, local, and federal courts, or be received via transfer from other correctional institutions such as juvenile centers, local jails, out of state jails, or federal or state prisons. Some inmates who are accepted as transfers may stay for one day, a week, or a month or more depending on their particular situation. In any event, the jail booking desk is the main entry point. Practically speaking, the majority of offenders passing through the booking desk are offenders who are placed under arrest or are being received from the courts. All offenders who have dealings with the local jail pass though the booking desk.

There are miscellaneous types of offenders who also pass through the booking desk such as the witness who is being held in protective custody. This is based on such occurrences as homicides or serious assaults occurring in nearby correctional institutions. Inmates who are witnesses to these acts may be placed "incognito" into a nearby local jail under protective custody. This could be at the request of a federal, state, or local law enforcement agency. Staff may be given instructions *not* to release the inmate's name under any circumstances to the public; the inmate may also be immediately assigned to administrative segregation by the convening of an emergency Institutional Classification Committee (ICC), as is discussed in Chapter 5.

Another type of offender is an inmate from the jail system who violates a rule of a work release or home incarceration program, or a criminal statute that dictates that inmate's removal from such programs pending further criminal action. For example, an inmate in the jail's work release center may be arrested and criminally charged for burglary. This action makes it necessary to remove the inmate from the work release program and place him or her into the local jail, through the booking desk. Or the inmate may be charged with violating a rule, such as withholding wages from the staff, and the penalty is removal from the program, which is also accomplished through the booking desk. In both cases, the inmate must be cycled back through the booking desk into the jail population. Whatever the circumstances of a special inmate, the booking desk must communicate that information to the key sections of the jail: confinement, classification, and medical.

Jails may hold inmates who are serious security risks or management problems as a favor to other jails. For example, if inmates in an old jail are discovering tunneling in an effort to escape or have tried to get contraband smuggled into the jail, the sheriff or jail administrator may contact a nearby jail that is newer and more secure and request that the inmates be **farmed out** to that jail. Farming out is jail jargon for the transfer of inmates to another jail due to security reasons or due to overcrowding. Another type of farm out is an inmate who is charged with the homicide or serious assault of a jail or police officer. Another jail may agree to take the inmate so as the inmate cannot claim harassment, revenge, or mistreatment from the first jail's staff. Farming out inmates requires the jail staff to photocopy records and prepare documentation that will provide much needed information to the receiving jail.

The jail booking staff must be constantly on guard concerning volatile inmates, mentally ill inmates, high-profile inmates (such as gang leaders), inmates in possession of weapons, etc. The jail booking area can be viewed as a sort of "crossroads" where a variety of inmates enter and leave the jail, and in realistic terms, "anything can happen."

## Jail Booking and Relations to Other Sections

Jail booking encompasses two operations—the legal commitment of offenders and the proper release of jail inmates. The admittance of an offender to a local jail has several implications. Offenders have to be admitted and confined legally, they have to be held under strict security, and many have serious health problems that need further examination and attention. Jail booking impacts jail transportation officers, classification officers, and the medical staff. Jail booking officers must have a thorough understanding of proper admittance/release procedures, the law, and human relations.[1]

The jail booking desk is the "anchor" of the jail, just as classification is the "nerve center." The jail booking area can be compared to the "swinging door" of the jail, the only stipulation being that offenders must properly come through the door and exit out that door. Another part of this "anchor" analogy is that in the jail, the booking desk is the focal point of the jail count. Depending on the operational makeup of the jail, the jail booking desk serves as the main checkpoint for the jail count and inmate roster, and keeping both accurate are two key functions of the confinement section. The count is confirmed by jail officers calling the inmate count on their respective posts to the booking desk. If the count is in error and inmates are not accounted for, the booking desk can request that inmates stop movement through the jail supervisor. The jail booking desk must be appraised of all inmate moves inside the jail, both routinely scheduled by classification and unscheduled emergency moves, such as an inmate immediately being placed in segregation due to assaulting an inmate or staff member, or when a search uncovers contraband in an inmate's cell and he is moved to a more secure area. The physical locations of all inmates must exactly match in the computer inmate database and the jail post rosters. Paper files, such as classification and medical, should also reflect accurate cell locations. The jail booking desk also generates inmate court lists and schedules inmates for transportation to state departments of corrections, courts, transfers to other correctional facilities, and medical appointments.

Jails rely primarily on documentation. The jail booking record is important for several reasons. The commitment record is the foundation for all of the other jail records that comprise the inmate jail record. From the jail booking record stems the inmate's administrative record, the classification record, and the medical record. The booking record generally is the first record that the various staff consults in preparation for their interactions with the inmate. In jails that have computer networks, staffs who are responsible for the confinement, classification, and medical care of the inmate have access to the jail booking record. Another reason for the importance of the jail booking record is that as the inmate's stay at the jail goes on, new charges may be added, charges may be dropped by the court or dismissed, detainers may be filed, court dates are scheduled/rescheduled, and most importantly any sentences imposed are entered into the record. This information can impact custody assessments by classification, housing, trusty selections, security safeguards, etc. For example, an inmate may be booked into the jail on a charge of burglary, and a few days later, a warrant for rape is served on him. This has a definite impact in classification, which may have been considering him for a trusty job, based at first on a non-violent property crime charge. The seriousness of a rape charge may make the inmate ineligible for a trusty position. The classification level of the inmate most likely will change due to the seriousness of the rape charge.

Another important aspect of the jail booking record is the listing of crimes that occur inside the jail. For example, an inmate may be booked into the jail for possession of drugs and assault. He or she becomes involved in a fight in a cellblock, and other inmates or the staff files charges. The new charges are listed on the booking record, which impacts classification. Other jail charges that may be listed on the booking record include escape, attempted escape, sexual assault, drug possession, etc.

The "anchor" of the jail paper record is the **jail booking form.** This form contains crucial information that is obtained from the offender, arresting/transporting officer, court, etc. by the jail booking officer who establishes legal commitment and the official jail record. While booking forms vary from jail to jail and most are automated, the following types of information should be recorded on a newly admitted inmate at a minimum:[2]

- General data: date, time of booking and release, booking number (or inmate number), case number, court number if committed from court, booking officer initials or badge/employee number.

- Information on offender: full name, alias (other names used, street names, etc. if known), date of birth, driver's license state and number, social security number, Federal Bureau of Investigation number (in criminal history), home address, telephone number, emergency contact, next of kin, employer (if known), attorney (if known), occupation, height, weight, hair color, eye color, scars, marks or tattoos.
- Charge information: charged crime, bail type and amount, charge status in cases of transfers or holds, **detainers** (charges on file in other jurisdictions; the inmate is held pending transfer to that jurisdiction), arresting officer and agency, case number, committing agency (in case of transfer/holds), court of jurisdiction, warrants, and any special instructions from the court (such as victim notification).

Much of this information can be obtained from the arrest warrant obtained by the arresting police officer after appearance in front of a local magistrate, who can set the bond and the next date of court appearance. If the offender has been committed to the jail previously, the information should be updated. Critical information that impacts other sections of the jail must be communicated in writing to these sections. Such information can include:

- Offender who is extremely violent, intoxicated, under the influence of drugs, or is severely mentally ill.
- High profile security risk: charged with a capital crime, has assaulted police officers, gang member, or leader.
- Offender is uncooperative.
- Offender is suicidal.
- Offender has a serious medical condition.

Magistrate's window for new admissions.

Photo by author, courtesy Baltimore City Central Booking and Intake Center.

Report Number ____________

# ALAMEDA CITY JAIL

## BOOKING CHECKLIST

Name: ____________

DOB: ____________

Sex: M F

Arrival Date/Time ____________

Intake Time: ____________

**Confirm Identity:**

Verification Prints Sent: ________

CCR Confirmation Rec'd: ________

PFN: ______

Booking Officer: ____________

*VIOLENT OFFENSE?* ________

**Intake:**

Searched by ________

Medical Intake Screening ________

Classification ________

Jail Rules / Phone Calls ________

Property ________

Fingerprints ________

Photograph ________

Arm Band ________

TOT Housing ________

**Warrants Check:**

Check ________

Confirmed ________

Updated ________

**Housing Assignments:**

Cell # _____Date: ________Time: ________

Cell # _____Date: ________Time: ________

Cell # _____Date: ________Time: ________

Separated: ____________

Segregated: ____________

Reasons: ____________

**Disposition:** *Circle one*

TOT AMC

TOT Santa Rita

TOT OPD

Cite / Release

Bailed

849b

Other ____________

Departure Date / Time: ____________

Removed for CORPUS: ____________

Distribution Copies: ____________

CPAP____ CUAP____ CPQU____ CBTE CPAA____ CCQD____ CBAO____

CBAD____ CBQU____ CBAW____ CBAE CBAC____ CBPP____ CBPM____

Reprinted by permission, Alameda City (CA) Police Department.

The arrestee must be photographed, and any distinguishable scars, marks, and tattoos must also be photographed. This is especially true in cases of gang members and any members of a security threat group. If the offender does not cooperate initially with being photographed or being booked in properly, these actions must be delayed until such time as the offender is cooperative. Jail inmates must not be released without an accurate and detailed booking record, plus a clear photograph.

The purpose of the jail photo is to match the inmate to the photo, so that there are no doubts as to the offender's identity. Also, the physical condition of the arrestee's face is recorded. The main booking file must contain a photo, and a photo can be made available to an inmate identifier, such as an identification badge or a wristband. Another use of the jail booking photo is to place the photo next to the inmate's name on a roster or status board or in a file.[3] By doing so, the inmate can be identified at a glance. The arrestee may be injured, intoxicated, or under the influence of drugs. This should be noted along with the known circumstances, which may clarify the situation in case the arrestee, his or her attorney, or his or her family claims mistreatment.

Part of the accurate information contained in the booking record is fingerprinting. As jails modernize, many are obtaining automated fingerprinting systems that directly link with their state's **criminal justice information system.** This system links to state computerized criminal records, warrant databases, identification data, and to the national, federal system, and the National Crime Information Center (NCIC). If the jail is not linked to NCIC, the jail booking staff will have to submit a separate inquiry. If the offender is discovered to have a warrant on file, there should be procedures in place to notify the appropriate agency for verification and extradition.[4]

Intake area; inmates will be restrained on bench with handcuffs, awaiting booking.

Photo by author, courtesy Baltimore City Central Booking and Intake Center.

POINT OF VIEW

## Intake and Booking

*Sgt. Ron Rose*
Hampton Sheriff's Office, Hampton, Virginia

Remember the days of the old keys sticking, letters missing on a typewriter that had been around forever, card files, 35-mm cameras, ink fingerprinting, and the huge teletype machine that was consistently printing out on the large, wide paper? Those were the days that remind me just how far we have come.

Modern technologies have made our job easier in the booking and tracking of our inmate population. The automated computer booking with video imaging gives our department and police department the ability to review any and all arrests with a photo at any time just by a key stroke. Computerized fingerprints (Livescan) have been my favorite tool. The days of rolling the black ink and waiting for the post office to deliver the prints are over. With the Livescan machine, it has improved the quality of prints the State Police receive. If you make a mistake, all you have to do is re-roll the finger you messed up and not the whole card again. Within 15 minutes, you will know who you are dealing with. We had an inmate get arrested for a robbery who refused to answer any questions. I took him to the Livescan machine and rolled his prints. The State Police advised us within 15 minutes whom we had in custody and he had escaped from the city jail in an adjoining city.

The workload in booking has increased over the years, with the deputies taking on the role of a classification officer. Deputies need specialized training in areas of inmates' needs. Sheriffs and administrators understand the importance of training for the officers working in their facilities. This helps in lowering the threat of legal liability in the intake areas. Most intakes are now becoming classification units, thus requiring extensive training in administrative paperwork.

### Entry and Rear Doors

While observation is a very important part at intake, it all starts at the entry door. You will make a judgment about the person you are about to receive. Is he or she injured? Can you see any injuries? How is his or her demeanor? Is he or she loud, crying, or very quiet? Is he or she suicidal? Is the person walking by himself or herself or being assisted by the arresting officers? What is the demeanor of the arresting officer? Remember you should never accept an unconscious person. This is all part of reducing your department's liability. You will determine in the first two minutes whether to receive this prisoner, based on the answers to your questions and your observations. I remember once that we received a prisoner for drunk in public, the shift we relieved told us she did not walk in on her own; she was carried in by the arresting officers. She could not answer any of our questions. The intake officer accepted her and placed in a cell. She was charged with drunk in public. I was making rounds and noticed she was still lying in the same position she was in about six hours earlier. I tried to wake her with to no avail. I checked her pulse, and it was very faint. I called for assistance, and we sent her to the hospital. We were later advised she had a blood alcohol level above 5.0. She could have remained in the cell and died from alcohol poisoning.

### Professionalism

In this day and time, it is all-important in the way we carry ourselves on and off the job. Any negative actions reflect badly on you and your department. We have a hard enough time as it is doing our daily routine; we do not need the general public looking at us as the enemy. Sometimes when an officer brings in a combative arrestee, it is good to be calm and not to raise your voice; this will calm most people down but will not work on all prisoners. Remember the rules about escalating force, only going to the next level when the prisoner takes you there. If the arresting officer is not helping the situation, separate the officer from the prisoner. Some intake officers have a tendency of letting their adrenaline get the best of them, instead of calming the situation. This has a tendency of shortening their careers. Always use the minimum force necessary when trying to get control of a situation. If you find yourself getting frustrated, secure the situation and "take five". A five-minute walk outside with fresh air will always do some good. This will usually make you feel better, refreshes you, and allows you to re-focus on the task in front of you.

### Medical Questionnaire

In this day of civil litigations, people are always looking for some reason to sue. When a prisoner comes to jail, their medical problems and medications become the new focal point. Even while on the street, dealing with health problems was the last thing on their minds. All departments have some form of medical questionnaire. We have a pretty intensive set of questions. While asking these questions, you should be listening not just typing their response in to the computer. There may be something the prisoner says that you will need to act on right away.

### Maintaining Contact with the Inmate

When dealing with inmates off the street, you really do not know who you are dealing with. Think security at all times, and do not be distracted. Searching is all so important, you have to learn a system that works for you. Doing the search the same way every time will help you be consistent and you will make fewer mistakes. I know first hand how busy it can get in intake. The old joke "it's feast or famine" applies. It is always famine when the lieutenant comes around. One day I received a teletype, which said that a man had killed a deputy sheriff in another state with a gun while in a lockup. The story said the man was charged with driving while intoxicated (DWI) and was brought in to the lockup. The deputy started the process on the man, when the phone rang. He turned and answered the phone, when he turned back around, the inmate was pulling a gun out of his boot and shot and killed the deputy. This really disturbed me, because I can remember doing the same thing, taking my eyes off the prisoner. The man's charge was a minimum one; he would be out in four hours. That could have been me, and that day I learned a valuable lesson. You really do not know who you are dealing with. Treat all inmates as if they are a threat; never let your guard down. It could mean the difference between life and death for you or your partner.

### Suicidal Inmates

We are dealing with special inmates when it comes to threats of suicide. You really cannot separate them into groups because as soon as you do, you will regret it. We deal with the inmate who comes through the back door screaming he wants to kill himself. These inmates want special attention. Do you take their threats lightly? No! How about the inmate, who comes in lockup, is quiet, not answering any questions, and just seems like the whole world is against him? He follows your instructions, but will not talk to you. Is he a threat? Yes! Then we have the polite inmate who feels he has disgraced his family by being arrested. Is he a threat? Yes! How about the first time drunk? Alcohol has affected his judgment. I could go on and on. Any of these inmates can and will try to kill themselves. This is why we cannot get distracted in our work; we must make sure we are checking on these inmates and are taking all threats seriously.

### Prisoners

I have noticed over the years that population of inmates get younger. Our society has become more violent: kids killing kids, guns everywhere, problems in schools, bullies, and peer pressure. Some inmates put a lot of faith in their lawyers. I remember accepting a kid through the rear door. He was with two detectives and just laughing and having a good old time. When I asked the detectives what the charges were, they told me murder. I was shocked; I could not believe this kid. The way he was taking the news, you would think he just won the lottery. It really bothered me that he showed no remorse. I asked the inmate if he knew what his charges were. He said "yes, but my lawyer will get me off these charges. They have nothing on me." I told him they have enough to put you in jail, and you must have a lot of faith in your lawyer.

### DNA Buccal Swab

A new tool, the DNA Buccal Swab, was introduced to law enforcement this year. Samples are taken at the time of arrest from persons with certain serious charges such as rape, robbery, breaking and entering, murder, etc. The samples are then logged and sent to the state lab for analysis. This is helping law enforcement open unsolved cases that were closed 10, 15, and 20 years ago. In the future, I can see a buccal swab being done on every person arrested.

In my 21 years as a deputy sheriff, I have seen a lot of improvements in the way we are trained. We are given the tools and knowledge to perform our duties. We are driven to be at the highest level—to be on top of our game. We are held accountable for when we do not perform at our best.

Thanks to Sgt. Ron Rose, Hampton Sheriff's Office, Hampton, Virginia.

## Transactions

A **transaction** is simply the act of booking an offender in or out of the jail. The number of transactions varies from jail to jail depending on the activity of law enforcement, the courts, the size of the jurisdiction, and other factors such as the time of day, whether it is a holiday, etc. For example, if police presence is heavy in the jurisdiction, there may be an increase in the arrest rate and subsequently an increase in the number of offenders placed under arrest. Other events may preclude an increase, such as mass arrests during a large protest or demonstration. The local police chief may decide over a specific time period to establish several sobriety checkpoints. The rate of driving under the influence (DUI) arrests most likely will increase, as will the number of transactions at the local jail. A series of drug raids by undercover police officers may also increase the number of transactions.

On the other hand, the time of day such as the early morning hours of a weekday may result in very little or slow arrest rates. Holidays usually find empty streets and closed business establishments, resulting in little street activity and many police officers on leave. The local jail can be impacted by this. Whatever the activity is on the street can affect how busy the jail booking desk can be. Jails are open 24 hours per day, 7 days per week, and 365 days per year—they never close.

Transactions are also actions such as recommitting an inmate coming back from the local court, returning from another jail after court, returning to the jail after being taken by the local police for interrogation, etc. If the inmate is confined to a local hospital, the booking desk may keep the inmate "on the count," depending on the booking desk general orders or procedures. Weekenders—community corrections offenders doing time on the weekends—are booked in and out every weekend, which adds to the total number of transactions per year.

The booking area also "funnels out" inmates to the local court, and in some jails, the court is located adjacent to the jail for better security. While these inmates may not be off the count because they are in the custody of court security personnel, they are secured and escorted in groups by jail officers or court security officers to the court. High-risk inmates are escorted singly in restraints. It is common to see in a jail booking area a variety of offenders: new arrestees, newly transferred inmates from other correctional facilities, inmates being released, and inmates going to court. This environment can be stressful and hectic for the jail booking staff.

There is no way to predict the number of transactions annually that are performed by the nation's jail booking desks. According to the *Census of Jails, 1999,* 2,610 jail jurisdictions, which represented 85 percent of the jails in the census, reported 193,880 new admissions during the last week of June 1999. This figure excludes such transactions as returns from escape, work release, medical appointments, treatment facilities, bail, and appearances in court. During the same time period in 1999, the number of new admissions in all jails—reporting and non-reporting in the census—was estimated at 219,408.[5]

In large urban jurisdictions, the number of inmate admissions can be significantly high. For example, the San Diego Central Jail handles adult male offender bookings for the greater San Diego metropolitan area. This results in an annual rate of 65,000 offenders being processed into the jail, 44 percent of these offenders coming from the San Diego Police Department. Female inmates are booked into a separate facility, the Las Colinas Detention Facility, and in the northern San Diego County area, adult male offenders are booked into the Vista Detention Facility. In FY 2001–2002, 26,612 offenders were booked into the Vista Facility.[6]

The above represents a new trend in jail booking—the **central intake processing** center for a jail system. This centralization in a specific facility of jail booking procedures, inmate processing, and transfer to the main jail system can concentrate more staff and effort on booking, the safe processing, and proper release of inmates. For example, Baltimore, Maryland, has a central intake center for the city jail. The county of Denver, Colorado, operates the PADF, or the Pre-Arrangement Detention Facility, which is the prisoner intake center. Inmates arrested in Denver are processed into the system, booked, fingerprinted, and housed there temporarily until they make bail or bond, or have been given an advisement by the court. Depending on the outcome of their court appearance, inmates are booked out of (released) from the PADF or are transported to the main county jail to serve their sentence or be incarcerated pending trial. The Denver Health Medical Center also has a Sheriff's Office, which is part of the PADF division of the Sheriff's Office. Like many jails, the Denver PADF is experiencing the high rates of incarceration over the last several decades. The PADF was completed in 1978, with the goal of processing 12,000 inmates per year. Currently, the PADF is processing over 60,000 inmates per year.[7]

The statistics of jail admissions and releases vary from jail to jail. Compare the above mentioned jails to the city of Roanoke located in southwest Virginia in the Shenandoah Valley. The Jail Security Division of the Roanoke Sheriff's Office reported that in fiscal year 2000–2001, the Roanoke City Jail committed 8,649 inmates at an average of 24 inmates admitted per day.[8]

Another new trend in jail intake is **regional processing,** or the booking of offenders into the jail system from locations in the community such as police substations or processing centers. This relieves the load on the central jail booking area and uses correctional personnel in the field. This concept has been initiated in Prince Georges's County, Maryland. Regional processing allows the police to process an arrestee (photographs, fingerprinting, and taking/inventorying property) at one of three strategically located regional processing locations, instead of at multiple police facilities. This initiative allows any federal, state, or local law enforcement agency placing an offender under arrest to deliver the arrestee for processing by county Department of Corrections staff at each regional processing center. An automated booking system has an interface with all police agencies, district court commissioners, state records, and corrections. This system, which is integrated with Maryland's Automated Arrest Booking System, includes inkless fingerprint scanning with simultaneous transmission to the state fingerprint repository, the county's Regional Area Fingerprint Identification System and the Federal Bureau of Investigation. The traditional "mug shot" was replaced by video imaging that is stored locally, as well as transmitted to the state. Video images and arrest information are accessible to any police facility. The data screen from this system is used by the county corrections department and the county courts.[9]

Procedures for both police and the county corrections department are streamlined. The arresting officer brings the arrestee to a regional processing center. The correctional staff initiates the automated booking system, takes fingerprints and photos, collects the offender's property, and records data about the offender. The police officer is free to write reports, perform related police duties, and return to street patrol. The correctional staff checks the offender's criminal history and takes the offender to the district court for an initial appearance hearing. If the offender is to be committed to custody, the corrections officer arranges for transport to the jail. If the offender is not to be incarcerated, the correctional officer checks the criminal history for a second time to ensure that there are no outstanding warrants or other charges, returns the offender's property, and releases him or her.[10]

There are several other important advantages to regional processing. In Prince Georges County, the quick return of police officers to street patrol has resulted in increased arrest rates (as much as 25%). The potential for use of force complaints against police officers by offenders has been reduced due to a "neutral" corrections officer processing the offender. Many arrestees are upset with the arresting officer when being booked in. Booking by a corrections officer can reduce friction and conflict. Finally, an automated prisoner processing system linked to all concerned criminal justice agencies ensures the positive identification of offenders and reduces inaccuracies and mistakes.[11]

Jail admissions and releases vary annually, but in some jails, figures are relatively close from year to year. Jail administrators, for budgeting and funding

The following figures represent the admissions or receptions into the Allegheny County Jail in Pittsburgh, Pennsylvania, from 1995 to 2005:

| *Year* | *Total Offenders Received* |
|---|---|
| 1995 | 21,172 |
| 1996 | 21,097 |
| 1997 | 21,974 |
| 1998 | 22,881 |
| 1999 | 22,858 |
| 2000 | 24,278 |
| 2001 | 26,351 |
| 2002 | 27,219 |
| 2003 | 24,599 |
| 2004 | 24,961 |
| 2005 | 26,947 |

The Allegheny County Jail is located in downtown Pittsburgh, Pennsylvania, and was opened in 1995. It opened with a capacity of 1,850 inmates and in 2005 housed over 2,000 male and female inmates, with an average daily population that year of 2,394 inmates. An expansion allows a jail population up to 2,400 inmates. The Allegheny County Jail also serves as a lockup for the City of Pittsburgh. Approximately 80–100 arrestees per day are held pending formal identification for the Bureau of Criminal Identification, the Pittsburgh City Magistrate and District Justice Pre Arraignment Hearings. These arrestees appear in hearings that determine the probable cause for arrest and the amount of bail. If an arrestee can meet the bail, he or she is released. If bail is not met, the offender is sent to the jail.

The Allegheny County Jail handles over 350 temporary and permanent movements in and out of the jail daily. The daily average of arrestees coming into the jail intake area is 100. After arraignment, about 60 offenders per day who do not bond out are committed to the jail. Additionally, other offenders apprehended by federal authorities, constables, and sheriff's deputies add to the daily influx of inmates. Overall, offender commitments to the jail range from 50 to 70 per day. The number of permanent jail releases is slightly less than the number of daily jail admissions. Over 100 inmates move daily in and out of the jail to and from criminal court hearings and trials.

**FIGURE 4-1** Jail Admissions and Intake: Allegheny County Jail[12]

purposes, can work out an average of jail admissions and releases in order to obtain booking staff and equipment, such as computers, cameras, and fingerprinting apparatus.

Jail booking staff has to be exact in both work habits and procedures. No matter how many transactions occur during a particular day in the jail, the count has to be exact, and the amount of the in and out transactions must accurately match the jail count. Previously many jails could operate with one booking officer, but with the advent of technology and to ensure accuracy and continuity in the booking and release process, many jails assign more than one officer to the booking desk. Depending on the agency staffing, the jail booking staff can be part of a confinement squad where certain officers are designated booking officers, or the booking desk staff may be a separate section of the jail staff. The volume of inmate admissions and releases dictates that a busy booking desk should be staffed by several officers under the supervision of a veteran jail supervisor.

## BOOKING PROCEDURES

The booking area has to operate under strict, accurate procedures with very little room for error. The procedures at booking set the stage for the safe incarceration of the jail inmate. In jails, the booking desk is supported by **receiving** a post manned by jail officers who take control of the inmate as soon as he or she enters the jail, and process the inmate after the booking procedure is completed. Receiving officers also assist in releasing the inmate and assisting the court security officers in getting inmates to court and receiving inmates upon their return from court.

### General Duties of Booking/Receiving

To understand the procedures of booking and receiving, one must have insight into the general duties of this area of the jail. As has been mentioned, all jails vary somewhat in their procedures, but the following encompasses the general duties of jail officers assigned to the booking/receiving area:[13]

- Determine that the offender is legally committed to the jail: the warrants and committing paperwork are filled out correctly, and all is in order. Court commitments require some type of paperwork from the court. Inmate transfers also must have a transportation order or some other type of documentation.
- Determine immediately if the offender is a high-risk inmate (security risk, suicide, gang member, assaultive, escape risk, mentally ill, etc.) or if the inmate has enemies or keep separates in the jail; take immediate steps to segregate inmate, place under high observation, and notify the appropriate jail staff and supervisors.
- Assign a **booking (inmate) number** or an inmate identification number to the inmate. That is the official number that will appear on all jail paperwork relating

to that inmate. Inmates should be required to write their booking number on all correspondence to the jail staff. This keeps confusion at a minimum when several inmates have the same name.

- Complete the booking record: charge, arresting officer, court date, bond, commitment times, the booking officer, address of the inmate, etc.
- Take a booking photograph and fingerprint the inmate.
- Perform a complete search of the inmate and his or her possessions.
- Store all allowed property, dispose of forbidden property, and issue a property receipt to the inmate, carefully noting all damaged property.
- Issue a money receipt for any funds in the inmate's possession.
- Properly mark contraband, such as weapons, illegal drugs or alcohol, and process it according to jail policy, dispose of it, or retain it as evidence if inmate is charged with a criminal violation.
- Dispose of medications in inmate possession according to jail procedures or notify medical staff and turn medications over to them for follow up.
- Allow the inmate to make at least one or several telephone calls to secure a bail bondsman, to notify friends, family, or next of kin of incarceration, to notify an attorney, and to give the jail's address.
- Assign the inmate to a housing or holding area.
- Properly identify inmate for release, verify release orders and paperwork, and issue funds to inmates being released.
- Arrange for a shower and change into jail clothes.
- Arrange for medical and dental screening and if applicable due to the charge and inmate's behavior, mental health screening.
- Conduct an orientation for new inmates and provide written orientation materials such as an inmate handbook, mail and visiting procedures, etc.

The last three procedures may or may not be part of the jail procedures in the booking and receiving areas, depending on the staffing of the jail and the operations approved by the command staff.

For these procedures to be effective, the area of booking and receiving operations must be functional and at the same time provide for staff and inmates the utmost in physical security, as many types of inmates—new admissions, inmates being released, and inmates going to and from court and returning to the jail from outside activities—all merge into this area. As jails vary in physical plant, so do the receiving/booking areas. In some jails, visitors are escorted through the booking/receiving area while offenders are being processed. The ideal situation is to have receiving and booking completely separate from both personal and professional visiting. The only exception to this is to have a professional visiting area to enable attorneys, probation/parole officers, and law enforcement officers to meet with their clients and offenders.

The following features of a well-run and designed booking/receiving area have been recommended by corrections professionals:[14]

- Area designed to separate newly arriving inmates from classified jail inmates and inmates being released. Inmates who have been searched *must* be separated from unsearched inmates.

- Holding cell hardware should be tamper resistant. For example, it should be very difficult for an inmate to break off a piece of a light fixture, etc. in order to obtain a weapon or means of suicide.
- Viewing windows in holding cell walls and doors should allow for the maximum view inside by the jail staff.
- An adequate number of toilets, sinks (with hot and cold water), soap and towels should be in holding areas. Shower stalls should be available if necessary.
- Property areas should adequately allow for the inventory and storage of inmate property, the careful disposal of contraband, and the securing of cash and monies found on inmates. Procedures should allow for the release of clothing and property by inmates to their families and the acceptance of civilian clothes for court.
- Jail officers working in the receiving/booking area should wear a radio, an alarm device, a set of handcuffs, possess a handcuff key, carry pepper spray if authorized, and have access to protective gloves to guard against contamination from blood-borne pathogens through punctures, needle sticks, etc.
- Jail booking/receiving procedures should allow for additional staff coverage and security in the event of mass arrests, high volume of incoming offenders, and the processing of inmates with extremely dangerous records.

## Processing of Inmate Property

Jail booking/receiving officers are responsible for the confiscation and inventory of everything the offender has with him or her when being booked into the jail. Records of the inmate property, including money must be accurate. All inmate property must be recorded in detail—no matter how small or seemingly insignificant in value. For example, if an inmate has a key ring with five keys, all keys should be recorded. The **property receipt** states what items and monies were taken from the inmate at intake.[15] These items minus any contraband found or released items must be returned to the inmate when being booked out. Also, if the inmate is transferred to a prison or another jail, the property will be transferred also.

Items should be described by its color, make, and condition. Incomplete, inaccurate, and vague descriptions of property may target jail officers by inmate "con artists". For example, an officer should not list a "man's brown suit" but a man's "brown jacket and pants, stained, pocket and lapel torn." A watch should be described by its make and color, such as a "watch, brand —, gold colored, and watch crystal face cracked." If the officer writes a gold watch, the inmate may complain that he is not receiving a gold watch when being released. The condition of the items should be noted. In the above examples, the clothing condition and the condition of the watch were noted accurately. Special engravings, markings, and colors should also be noted, in order to facilitate identification. The inmate should sign the completed property receipt, be given a copy, advised not to lose it, and the property should be sealed and stored in a secure area with limited access by staff.[16] No trusties should be permitted to enter the inmate property room unless under staff escort.

Inmates may be allowed to keep some property. If jewelry, such as a ring cannot be removed from the inmate's finger due to risk of injury, the staff may allow the inmate to keep it, but that fact should be noted on the property receipt.[17]

While being booked in, the inmate may retain such items as legal material related to ongoing litigation, court actions, or pertaining to his or her case. Inmates who are married may also keep wedding bands if they are plain metal and contain no precious stones. Depending on the jail regulations, inmates may keep religious medals, medallions, and pendants (such as a crucifix) if worn in an appropriate manner, and cannot be fashioned into or used as a weapon or used to disrupt security.[18]

Property receipts are also given to inmates' family members and friends when they bring property to the inmate that is allowed by the jail. Though seemingly insignificant, good property records are a good defense against charges of mishandling inmates' property and money.

## Searching Inmates

Once the inmate is booked in by the booking officer and released to the receiving officer, the inmate must be thoroughly searched for weapons, contraband, and unauthorized items, even though as a general rule, the offender has been previously searched by the arresting or transporting officer. A good jail officer will not take prior searches for granted and will search the offender again. Law enforcement officers are human, and mistakes in searches have been made on the street and have been caught by an alert and thorough jail officer.

Searches of newly admitted offenders or returning inmates employ the frisk (or pat down), the body (or strip search) and the body cavity search, depending on the circumstances of the arrest. Jail regulations may specify under what conditions a strip search or body cavity search may be conducted and the supervisory approval that is needed. Every search of an offender coming into the jail must not be a cursory search—it must be thorough; even "delicate" areas such as the groin must be examined. Clothing, pockets, wallets, purses, even shoes, and socks must be thoroughly examined. A thorough search of any arrestee, offender, newly sentenced inmate, or returning inmate who comes through the jail booking/receiving area is the first line of defense in the battle against contraband.

A precautionary note about jail booking is necessary. People generally do not like being handled, and inmates coming through the jail booking/receiving area are no exception. Emotions and anxiety levels are high, and this situation could be compounded by the effects of illegal drugs, alcohol, and the presence of mental illness. An officer can set a positive tone and keep the inmate calm by being thorough but professional while booking and searching the inmate and inventorying his or her property. Officers should attempt to maintain the inmate's dignity and keep tension levels low.[19] Strip searches and body cavity searches should be performed in secure, private areas.

## Housing of Newly Arrived Offenders

Newly arrived inmates may be held with other inmates in a holding area (sometimes called the "drunk tank") waiting to be booked in, processed, and searched if their conduct and behavior is calm. Unruly inmates such as mentally disordered inmates must be segregated away from other inmates for the safety of themselves, other inmates, and the staff. This may delay the booking process until such time that the inmate is manageable. However, in the case of mentally ill offenders, only a qualified mental health staff person should advise the confinement staff and classification on the initial housing of the inmate. Any jail officer who segregates an inmate should file a report and start an observation log (see *Glossary*).

Normally, after booking and processing, newly arrested inmates make their initial appearance in court to set a court date and bail. In some jails, this is accomplished through video communication, enhancing the safety of the court staff. If video is not available, the inmate is taken to court the morning following his or her arrest. The inmate may remain in the receiving holding area until seen by Classification for an initial interview (see Chapter 5).

## Medical Screening

It is imperative that the newly admitted inmate—whether an arrestee from the street, newly sentenced inmate from court or a transfer from another correctional facility—be given a medical screening by the medical staff as soon as possible. Not only is the inmate checked for diseases, but he or she is also checked for injuries, wounds, and any apparent mental disorder or behavioral problem.

Realistically, the process of medical and mental health screening begins at the booking desk with a series of questions and observations by the booking officer. In small jails where full-time medical staff are not available, or the medical staff is short handed and not immediately available, initial medical screening may be performed by the jail booking officer. In such cases, the booking officer should have some training and instruction from medical personnel.[20]

At the Hampton Correctional Facility in Hampton, Virginia, the first duties listed in the Booking/Receiving Security Post Procedures is for the booking officer to "look over the person [detainee] to ensure that he/she does not need medical emergency attention." Subsequent procedures call for notification of the medical staff if the booking officer is unsure whether there is a medical problem. All medical assessments that are conducted by the medical staff are logged.[21]

One of the best benchmarks for initial jail medical screening is Standard J-E-02, Receiving Screening, of the *2003 Standards for Health Services in Jails* by the National Commission on Correctional Health Care (NCCHC). It states that all inmates should have receiving screening performed immediately upon arrival at the intake facility. Standard J-E-03 concerns transfer screening and requires that all inmates being transferred from one correctional facility to another or inmates being booked in with an established medical record for their incarceration be screened within 12 hours. Standard J-E-04 requires that inmates receive an initial and periodic health or medical assessment in the facility, including a physical exam, a test for tuberculosis, and laboratory and diagnostic tests for communicable diseases, including sexually transmitted diseases. This initial health assessment should be conducted as soon as possible, but no later than 14 calendar days after the inmate's arrival at the jail.[22] This coincides with the inmate being placed in temporary classification housing pending an orientation. Generally, during this waiting period, the medical staff is able to complete their assessment and conduct the physical exam before the inmate is assigned to housing in the jail's general population.

The NCCHC intake screening is very detailed and listed in standard J-E-02. There are three goals to this standard: the identification and treatment of any urgent health needs of newly admitted offenders, the identification and treatment of any easily identifiable health needs before the health assessment is performed, and the identification and isolation of any inmates who are potentially contagious. Receiving medical personnel or trained jail booking personnel should use a form approved by a health authority. Immediate health needs, especially communicable diseases, are addressed by appropriate medical treatment or medical isolation. Inmates who do not speak English should have the assessment done in their native language as the information obtained is of vital importance. Inquiries should address:[23]

- Illnesses: current, past, health conditions or health requirements such as special diets, etc.
- Past serious infectious diseases.
- Recent symptoms of communicable diseases: coughs, coughing up blood, lethargy, weight loss, appetite loss, fever, night sweats, etc.
- Current or past mental illness, including psychiatric hospitalizations, treatment history, and psychotropic medications.
- Current or past history of suicidal ideation.
- Dental problems.
- Allergies.
- Illegal and legal drug use, including the last time used.
- Any symptoms of drug withdrawals.
- Recent or current pregnancy.
- Observations of appearance (sweating, tremors, anxious, disheveled), behavior (insensible, odd, appropriate, disorderly), state of consciousness (level of alertness, responsive, or lethargic), ease of movement (any deformities, gait, difficulty walking), breathing (cough and/or hyperventilation), and the condition of the inmate's skin (lesions, rashes, sores, jaundice, bruises, scars, infestations, tattoos, needle marks indicating drug use, indications of drug abuse or self mutilation).

Once the jail booking desk personnel accepts the offender, the jail assumes responsibility for the inmate, including dealing with any medical problems. With this responsibility comes potential liability if something goes terribly wrong, such as the inmate becoming extremely ill, further aggravating their wounds or injuries, or death. The jail is responsible for providing medical treatment and attention to any offender being accepted with a serious medical condition. A basic fundamental rule that most if not all jails follow is to not accept any offender who is seriously ill, injured, unconscious, or in critical need of medical attention.

The American Medical Association (AMA) recommends that offenders with any of the following problems be taken by the arresting or transporting officer before being booked into the jail:[24]

- Unconscious offenders.
- Offenders currently or recently experiencing convulsions.
- Offenders having significant external bleeding.
- Offenders having obvious fractures, arms and legs that are severely swollen, deformed, or not functioning properly.
- Offenders having any type of head injury: cuts and bruises on the head, clear or bloody fluid coming from the nose and eyes, one eye larger than the other, dizziness, difficulty walking, extreme or forced vomiting, noted confusion, or appear in a semiconscious state.
- Offenders with neck or spinal injuries: walking difficulty, pain or deformity in the spinal area, numbness in arms and/or legs, loss of muscle function.
- Offenders with possible internal bleeding: paleness, cold skin, clammy, blue or gray in color, sweating, rapid pulse, fainting, vomiting, nausea, weakness, feelings of confusion, agitation, restlessness, or appear frightened, blood present around the eyes and ears.
- Offenders showing signs of alcohol and drug abuse: confusion, disorientation. Hallucination, delirium, cannot stand or walk, slurred speech, rapid or shallow breathing, lethargic, severe depression, severely agitated, having cramps, nausea, vomiting, diarrhea, pupils are dilated or pinpointed, restlessness, or feelings of being very hot or cold. Inmates who suddenly collapse should not be admitted; neither should an offender who claims to have overdosed, even if he or she exhibits no symptoms.
- Pregnant women with serious problems such as cramps, abdominal pains, headaches, blurred vision, vaginal bleeding, or having strong uterine contractions less than two minutes apart; the stress of being brought into a jail has been known to trigger women into going into labor.
- Inmates who claim to be on a medication but do not have it with them; the medical staff must call the offender's doctor or pharmacy for verification.

The last recommendation may be somewhat controversial. The jail booking and medical staff will have to look at the circumstances of the medical condition. If the condition is not life threatening and the offender can function without it, the offender may be admitted. For example, an offender on medication for a head cold would not be necessarily prohibited from being booked into the jail.

Also many medical symptoms are not present at booking. For example, an inmate may not exhibit symptoms of drug withdrawal right away; they may become present later. Also, inmates are not known for being entirely honest and truthful. They may inform the staff of a medical problem after being incarcerated in order to gain better housing, such as a bed in the dispensary. In any case, constant observation by staff on all inmates is a must. The classification interview, with its medical questions, provides a good back up to the initial booking and medical screening.

WHATCOM COUNTY JAIL
SCREENING-RECEIVING RECORD

Booking # ______________ Date ________________ Time __________

Property # _________ Booking Officer ________________________

INMATE NAME ______________________________________ DOB ________________ AGE __________

RACE _______ SEX _________ HEIGHT _________ WEIGHT __________

I hereby acknowledge that I am not ill or injured at this time. X ______________________________

| # | QUESTION | Y | N | # | QUESTION | Y | N |
|---|---|---|---|---|---|---|---|
| 1 | DR CARE / OR SPECIAL DIET? | | | 24 | FAINTED RECENTLY? | | |
| 2 | ILLNESS / INJURY? | | | 25 | PREGNANT? | | |
| 3 | PAIN / BLEEDING? | | | 26 | CURRENTLY TAKING BIRTH CONT PILLS? | | |
| 4 | FEVER / INFECTION? | | | 27 | GYNECOLOGICAL PROBLEMS? | | |
| 5 | MEDICATION? | | | 28 | SUICIDE ATTEMPT? | | |
| 6 | DIABETES? | | | 29 | HISTORY OF MENTAL ILLNESS? | | |
| 7 | EPILEPSY / SEIZURES? | | | 30 | BODILY DEFORMITIES? | | |
| 8 | RECENT HEAD INJURY? | | | 31 | ARTHRITIS / MOVEMENT DIFFICULTY? | | |
| 9 | HEART TROUBLE/HIGH BLOOD PRESSURE? | | | 32 | SKIN RASH / INFESTATION? | | |
| 10 | ULCERS / STOMACH PROBLEMS? | | | 33 | OTHER HEALTH PROBLEMS? | | |
| 11 | ALLERGIES / ASTHMA? | | | 34 | NEED TO SPEAK TO MEDICAL STAFF? | | |
| 12 | ALLERGIC TO MEDICINES? | | | 35 | HEALTH INSURANCE? | | |
| 13 | HEPATITIS / JAUNDICE? | | | 36 | MEDICARE / PUBLIC ASSISTANCE? | | |
| 14 | EVER BEEN TOLD YOU HAVE TB? | | | 37 | WELFARE / DISABILITY COVERAGE? | | |
| 15 | HAD BAD COUGH FOR LAST 3 MONTHS? | | | 38 | OFF OBS: COUGHING / SPITTING? | | |
| 16 | LOST WEIGHT LAST 3 MONTHS? | | | 39 | OFF OBS: ALCOHOL ON BREATH? | | |
| 17 | SYPHILIS / GONORRHEA? | | | 40 | OFF OBS: NOT ALERT? | | |
| 18 | OTHER STD OR ABNORMAL DISCHARGE? | | | 41 | OFF OBS: DISORIENTED? | | |
| 19 | DRUG WITHDRAWAL PROBLEM? | | | 42 | OFF OBS: OTHER MENTAL PROBLEMS? | | |
| 20 | ALCOHOLISM / SHAKES / DTS? | | | 43 | OFF OBS: ABNORMAL SKIN COLORING? | | |
| 21 | HAVE YOU BEEN DRINKING? | | | 44 | OFF OBS: APPARENT POOR HEALTH? | | |
| 22 | PAINFUL DENTAL PROBLEM? | | | 45 | BOOKING OFFICER COMMENTS: | | |
| 23 | BODY LICE / OTHER VERMIN? | | | | | | |

Enter details of questions answered yes (use back of form if more room needed):

I authorize the correctional staff to make available summaries and/or copies of my jail medical records to attending health care staff and/or other facilities to which I may be transferred. Additionally, I understand that my health information may be disclosed if that information is necessary to: Provide health care to me, provide for the health and safety of others, or for the administration and maintenance of the safety, security and good order of the Institution. I also understand that once information is disclosed, it may no longer be protected information and the person or organization it is released to, may redisclose it. Further, my health information may only be provided to others while I am an inmate in this facility, unless I sign a release of information.

Signature ________________________________________ Date ____________

Next of kin or whom to notify in an emergency:

Name ________________________________ Relationship ____________________

Address ______________________________ Phone __________________________

Disposition of Booking Officer:

( ) Fit for Jail
( ) Referred to Nurse's sick call
( ) Sent to Med Services prior to jail
( ) Isolated for Medical/Mental reasons

Reprint by permission, Whatcom County (WA) Sheriff's Office.

## Releasing Inmates

One of the nightmares for a sheriff, a jail squad supervisor and the booking officer is the improper release of an inmate, or quite simply, letting an inmate go by mistake that has outstanding charges or has been convicted and is supposed to be serving a sentence. Jail booking areas are busy areas, and even with technology, jails are operated by people who make mistakes.

If the inmate is a new arrestee (pre-trial detainee) and has an amount of **bail**, he or she can post that bail and be released. Bail is an amount of money set by the court that the offender pays to ensure his or her appearance in court. Bail can also be paid by offenders' family members or friends.[25] Courts set the procedures of posting bail. Generally, the arrestee is brought by the arresting officer before a magistrate (an officer of the court) who hears the probable cause of the arrest and sets a bail amount before the offender is taken to the jail for booking. If the charge is especially serious, it is possible that no bail will be set.

Closely related to bail is the offender posting a **bond.** A bond is a written agreement by a bonding company pledging that the offender will appear in court. Bonds can be posted by an authorized bonding company in the jurisdiction.[26] Usually a bond is a percentage of the bail amount that the offender, his or her family or friends pay to the bondsman in order to secure release. Most jail booking officers know the bonding companies and their personnel and have a good relationship with them.

If the offender fails to appear in court, a warrant is issued for his or her arrest. Additionally, the bondsman can apprehend the offender and return him or her to jail in cases of violations of the conditions of the bond. This is commonly known as **bond surrender.**

In the cases of offenders released on bail or bond being returned to the jail, they must go through the same booking process on the original charge and bail with the information on file being updated. The court has to be notified that the inmate has been returned to the custody of the jail.[27]

Offenders may be interviewed by representatives from the court to ascertain if they would qualify as a good risk to be released without posting bail or bond. Jail personnel are not directly involved in this decision process and release the offender only after the court representatives have approved a release without bail or bond. This release is known as **personal recognizance.** This type of release is not in effect if the offender has detainers from other jurisdictions or bail on additional charges that has to be posted in order to be released.[28] A personal recognizance release is simply a promise of the offender that he or she will appear in court.

The jail booking officer must work closely with the jail records section to ensure that inmates are properly released. Release dates have to be correct, with the proper amount of earned good time calculated if applicable. All jails have procedures to ensure that an inmate is being properly released to another jurisdiction through a detainer, to the state or federal department of corrections, or another jail through a farm out.

In 2002, an inmate accused of robbery, being a fugitive and failing to appear on a domestic violence case, was released by mistake from the District of Columbia (DC) jail because the jail records office did not notice an outstanding warrant from a neighboring county, Prince George's (PG) County, Maryland, when his file was reviewed before his release. He was to be held at the DC jail until PG County authorities were to transport him to the PG County Jail. The director of the DC Department of Corrections said that preliminary findings indicated staff negligence and instituted corrective measures to include severe disciplinary action including termination. In 2001, the DC jail processed in 12,501 inmates and released 10,800, which is a substantial workload. In 2001, jails in the United States logged 20 million transactions. Mistakes do occur, with severe consequences.[29]

In Allegheny County, Pennsylvania, law enforcement officials reported that four inmates were released by mistake in 2001. An inmate released previous to that was charged with shooting two police officers after authorities tried to apprehend him. In Oklahoma in early 2001, a female jail inmate charged in one jurisdiction with assault with a deadly weapon was released mistakenly by another jurisdiction. A clerk failed to enter the additional charge in the jail's computer system.[30] An inmate who was mistakenly released from a North Carolina jail in 2005 had a prison sentence of 11–14 months for numerous vehicle break-ins. He was arrested after being charged with robbing one bank and attempting to rob another.[31]

Some jails use checklists. Common sense should dictate the proper release of inmates, using these steps:[32]

- Comparison of photograph: photos of the inmate at booking should be compared to the inmate being released. Many jails use an identification system such as a wristband containing the inmate's photo and identification number. These must be verified.
- Verification of inmate's signature.
- Comparison of fingerprints taken at booking.
- Checking for identifying features such as scars, marks, tattoos, etc.
- Asking the inmate questions about his or her personal history, including social security number, place of birth, emergency contact, next of kin, home address, etc.

Many jail booking desks in order to guard against human error use checklists. The booking officer simply performs the procedures listed in the checklist when booking the inmate in and out.

Booking technology is improving. In Tarrant County, Texas, jail booking staff scans the offenders' irises, using handheld devices resembling a video game. Both eyes are scanned, and jail staff believes that iris scan identification is more reliable than fingerprint identification in verifying that the right inmate is being released. The entire iris scan technology takes approximately 30 seconds, which is less time than the fingerprint analysis process, which was performed by hand. The system costs $45,000, which included software interface, computer server application, and video game sized handheld scanning devices for officers to use in an expedient manner. During the booking process, the inmate being scanned has to be cooperative in having their eyes scanned. In the first seven months of operation, almost 16,000 inmates had been entered into the iris scan database. The database is expanding, as approximately 30,000 offenders are booked into the jail annually. The only major disadvantage is that the iris scan database cannot be integrated into the jail's information management system.[33]

Holding inmates beyond their release dates is an embarrassment and a serious liability issue for any jail. In one case, a female jail inmate, aged 46 years, was held on a misdemeanor conviction five months longer than her release date, due to a corrections worker incorrectly calculating her sentence. In another case, a deaf and mute inmate was held in jail without a conviction for 22 months.[34]

Even miscellaneous inmate types such as weekenders (see Chapter 11 *Jails and Community Corrections*) are booked in and out. Booking weekenders involves the same procedures as booking on new or returning inmates. Weekenders mean exactly that doing time from Friday evening through Sunday. Some jails house weekenders in holding areas, dormitories, or other minimum-security housing.

## PROBLEMS IN THE JAIL BOOKING AREA

The jail booking area can be compared to a busy bus or train terminal—the shuffling of people, checking paperwork, phones ringing off of the hook, and staff being constantly at the mercy of incoming volumes of inmates going to and from the street, the courts, and other institutions. This is a volatile area, and the safety of staff and inmates are of high priority. Anything can happen, from suicides to assaults to escape attempts.

### Differences between Jail and Prison Intake

The issue of how the jail booking area is much different from a prison area has been recognized by corrections professionals. This is not to say that prisons are not safe, but the jail booking area is an example of the unpredictable dangers of correctional work.

Safety is priority number one in both prisons and jails, but a main difference between the two is the number of offenders coming through the front door every year. According to Peter Perroncello, Detention Division Superintendent for the Bristol County Massachusetts Sheriff's Office, "there is more turnover based on admissions, [meaning] more people [in] a 24 hour period . . . while some prisons get 2,000 inmate admissions per year, some local jails can get up to 100,000." Perroncello also says that increasingly higher number of admissions means a lot more bodies need to be thoroughly searched for contraband and other dangerous items upon entry to the jail.[35]

According to Anthony Callisto, Chief Deputy of the Onondaga County (N.Y.) Sheriff's Office Custody Division, prison inmates have previously been incarcerated in a jail, and their behavior is on record and can be a prediction of future behavior in the facility and can be a valuable classification tool. However, with jails, the offender is brought in "fresh" from the scene of a crime and may be fearful and resentful of authority. The jail staff must take the following three to five days to gather information and observe the offender's behavior for classification purposes.[36]

Offenders may also be under the influence of drugs and alcohol or suffering from mental disorders, which adds to the unpredictability of what may happen in the booking area. Coupled with suicidal behavior, the booking area deserves a lot of staff attention.

### Jail Booking: The Danger Zone

Veteran jail officers take nothing for granted. The jail booking area can be quite and calm one minute and noisy and disruptive the next minute. Consider these examples:

### Booking Area Inmate Suicides

The last example in Figure 4.2 illustrates one of the most serious problems in jail booking areas and police lockups—suicide. A common practice is to place the inmate in isolation and remove all items that could be potentially used in a suicide attempt. Suicidal inmates are supposed to be closely observed until they are seen by qualified mental health staff.

The essence of jail suicide prevention is teamwork and concern for the offender by the uniformed jail staff and mental health. This concern has to be shown from the moment the offender is incarcerated.

In Orange County, California, the jail system consisting of five facilities has maintained a record of effective suicide prevention. The Orange County jail system

Consider these occurrences:

- In a Kentucky jail in 2005, an offender being booked in for drunk driving attacked jail officers with a knife, which had been missed by the police officer in the search incident to the arrest.[37]
- An inmate on suicide watch was left unsecured in a Michigan jail's booking area, slipped into a closet containing jail officers' uniforms, put on the uniform of a jail supervisor and nearly escaped. He was supposed to be handcuffed to a bench in the booking area before being sent to his floor or housing area. He was dressed in a jail suicide prevention smock.[38]
- Two inmates, each charged with serious felonies, hit a jail deputy with a sock filled with batteries and bars of soap. They then hit the deputy again with a mop handle, took his keys, and jumped over the booking desk counter. They went to the exit door, but got trapped between two doors where they were recaptured. An alert was broadcast to sheriff's road units, and a deputy sheriff responding to the call for assistance to the jail suffered a fractured skull in a car accident.[39]
- An offender was brought into a Louisiana jail by police after being subdued with a "Taser" stun gun. He was booked into the jail on disturbing the peace, resisting arrest, and misrepresentation during booking. Shortly after booking, the offender was placed on medical observation and later was transported to a local hospital where he died. According to a coroner's report, the inmate died from cocaine and alcohol poisoning.[40]
- An offender died a few hours after being booked into a California jail after he had stopped breathing while being subdued by correctional officers. The offender was reported to be combative and had been in an auto accident. He received medical treatment for head injuries and had been booked into the jail for charges relating to the accident, outstanding warrants relating to DUI, battery, and driving on a suspended license. He was handcuffed to a chair and fell to the floor. Jail officers and medical staff tried to help him, but he became combative. Resuscitation efforts were commenced, and paramedics were called and transported the offender to a local hospital where he was pronounced dead.[41]
- A woman was arrested in Louisiana for attempted murder and tried to kill herself just prior to her arrest. The arresting state troopers informed a sheriff's investigator of her suicide attempt, and the sheriff and his deputies were also aware of her suicidal risk. The arrestee was noted as being on suicide watch, but was placed in a detox cell that had a serious blind spot and was not visible from the jail's control room. The cell had several **tie off points:** points such as light fixtures and bars where a noose could be tied off for hanging or strangulation. Previously, another arrestee had successfully killed himself in the same cell by hanging himself with a sheet from a tie off point. Despite this information, the offender was given a sheet by the jail staff on the second night of her incarceration. She was last observed in her bunk and awake at 2:00 A.M.; she was discovered dead at 2:44 A.M. She committed suicide by using a string from the bunk mattress and a rope fashioned from the sheet.[42]

**FIGURE 4-2** Serious Incidents in Jail Booking

is the fourth largest in California and the thirteenth largest jail in the United States. The mega jail "Orange County Complex" books an average of 60,000 offenders per year. Over a ten-year period prior to 2003, only five suicides occurred in a jail system that houses between 5,000 and 5,500 inmates per day.[43]

As increasing jail suicide rates became a national concern for jail staffs during the 1980s, the Orange County Sheriff's Department (OCSD) and the Correctional Mental Health (CMH) staff collaborated to develop a jail suicide prevention program. The development of this program coincided with the commencement of operations in the OCSD Intake and Release Center (IRC) in the Orange County Jail Operations Division. The command staff at OCSD communicated to the jail staff that suicides are not acceptable.[44]

Jail staff suicide prevention training is important; many local correctional agencies conduct jail suicide training as part of the basic recruit curriculum, but not all offer it as in service training. Some jails only deal with suicide prevention training only after an inmate has killed him or herself.

The OCSD approach is both unique and humane. Besides the standard academy training, jail staff members carry a pocket suicide prevention card (see Figure 4.3), which serves as a constant reminder that jail suicide prevention is everyone's job. Mental health staff is on site at the Central Jail Complex 7 days per week, 24 hours per day, which gives effective crisis intervention and assessment. A 76-bed unit (IRC mental health unit) for inmates identified as significantly mentally ill or at high risk for suicide is staffed by deputies specially trained to deal with depressed and/or mentally ill inmates. Deputies sign on for a one-year commitment to staff the unit. In 2000, the utilization of the beds in the mental health unit was 98 percent; the average length of stay in the unit was 10.4 days for males and 17.7 days for females.[45]

The IRC books in 150–200 offenders per day. Offenders are screened by medical prior to admission, and the risk of suicide is assessed. This is a triage approach; a nurse asks the offender a series of questions designed to determine medical and mental health status. Once booking is approved, classification staff reviews the offender's past criminal and jail history. If at any time, a staff member—classification or medical—feels that there is a risk factor, the offender is immediately referred to the mental health team, whose staff is stationed inside the medical triage area.[46]

In 10 years, from 1993 to 2003, the Orange County Jail system had booked in approximately 800,000 offenders, and only five inmates killed themselves. Due to effective intervention by deputies and CMH teams, 85 inmates were prevented from committing suicide. Inmates with depression problems are referred to rehabilitative programs, such as drug treatment, anger management, general education, and parenting skills. These programs and others serve as an effective follow up and give depressed and suicidal inmates hope.[47]

## Modern Improvements to the Jail Booking Area

Jails are making improvements to the critical area of booking. In Finney County, Kansas, the following improvements were made to improve booking:[48]

- Open concept intake and booking area: two booking spaces with space for a third; serves to introduce the offender to the concept of direct supervision at an early stage.
- Live scan fingerprint machine.
- Photo system: produces inmate "mug shots" for a plastic inmate identification card.

Of use for jail officers is the **pocket guide,** a compact summary of vital information and procedures concerning inmates in the jail. Examples of pocket guides are law enforcement commands translated into another language such as Spanish and criminal constitutional rights (Miranda warnings). Officers carry these guides, and they may prove useful time savers.

In the Orange County jail system, each custody deputy carries a "Suicide Prevention Card," which has been described in the magazine of the American Jail Association, *American Jails.* It serves as an instant guide to the signs and symptoms of suicidal behavior, high-risk times and situations, and symptoms of Sudden Custody Death Syndrome. Please note the text of the card:

A suicidal inmate will:

- Look sad
- Not sleep
- Feel hopeless
- Withdraw
- Give things away
- Suddenly "improve"
- Look tired
- Not eat
- Feel worthless
- Refuse treatment
- Write a will

Inmate is at high risk of suicide if:

- First offense
- Long sentence
- Violent history
- Family suicide
- Stigma
- Drugs/alcohol
- Culture considers suicide honorable
- First 24 hours
- Personal tragedy
- Suicide history
- Mentally ill
- Publicity
- Pillar of society

Symptoms of sudden custody death syndrome:

- Bizarre and aggressive behavior
- Dilated pupils
- Fear
- High body temperatures
- Irrational or incoherent speech
- Panic/paranoia
- Profuse sweating
- Disrobing
- Self-inflicted injuries
- Shouting (frequently, irrationally)
- Unexpected strength
- Violent behavior towards other/objects

CMH: 647–6055, 6030, 4158, 4159

**FIGURE 4-3** The Use of Pocket Guides: Orange County Jail[49]

- Padded cell for violent and self-destructive prisoners.
- Property room: conveyor belt and numbered garment bags.
- Video arraignment system.

## Handling of Problems

Due to the uncertain nature of booking and the potential for serious problems, procedures must be in place to guide the jail staff in handling such unexpected problems. Jail supervisors must frequently be in the area, as suicides, assaults on staff, and medical emergencies can occur at a moment's notice. In booking, jail staff must:

- Expect the unexpected. Offenders do not like to be locked up and may take advantage of a security breach in order to escape, as simply as "slipping out of the front door," or joining a line of inmates waiting to be processed out. Offenders may resist being searched and escorted by staff. For this reason, staffing in the booking area cannot be short; this is one area where new offenders and returning inmates should immediately see "a lot of uniforms."
- Offenders with any medical problems, whether observed or reported, should be seen by the medical staff as soon as possible; offenders with serious medical problems such as loss of consciousness, bleeding, etc. should be treated at a medical facility before admittance to the jail.
- Offenders who do not answer booking questions and refuse to cooperate should have their records noted for staff information and be segregated from other inmates until a decision is made on housing guidelines or until such time that they do cooperate.
- Offenders who appear to be suicidal or mentally ill should be referred to mental health staff for assessment and follow up. Unstable prisoners should be segregated for the safety of both staff and inmates and be observed every 15 minutes or less. The agency mental health staff should be very involved in drafting the policy on the handling of mentally ill and suicidal inmates. Options for suicidal inmates include restricted issue, isolation, wearing suicide-resistant garments, or placement with other high-risk inmates if authorized by the mental health staff. In all cases such as these, an observation log should be started and a report filed with the proper staff referral.
- Any prisoner who is known to be an escape risk, assaultive, charged with a particularly serious crime, is on death row and is brought to the jail, a member of a security threat group or gang, or is a possible security risk should be segregated until a decision is made by classification and the jail command staff on how to confine the individual.
- Carefully document and follow procedures concerning the use of force in cases of unruly and violent inmates. Starting in the booking area and throughout the jail, officers may have to use force to make inmates comply with orders and regulations, protect other inmates, the public, staff, and visitors from harm, protect the inmates from harming themselves, prevent escape, prevent criminal acts, and prevent damage/destruction to jail property. It is always hoped that unruly and uncooperative inmates will comply with verbal commands, but in some cases, especially if the inmate is under the influence of drugs and/or alcohol, is mentally unstable, or very angry and upset, force may have

to be used. The Supreme Court in 1992 listed five factors that courts will use in deciding whether force used against an inmate or inmates is excessive. These guidelines can serve as a "common sense" checklist in justifying the use of force anywhere in the jail—from booking to housing areas. They are:[50]

1. Was here a need for the use of force? Was the inmate uncontrollable? Was anyone in imminent danger? Was immediate action necessary?
2. What was the amount of force used? A good rule to follow is to use only the force necessary to control the situation or bring the inmate under control.
3. What was the extent of the inmate's injuries? Were they excessive? Was medical attention given as quickly as possible?
4. What was the threat perceived by a reasonable officer? Did the officer feel that he or she would be seriously injured? Did he or she fear for his or her life?
5. What were the efforts made to temper the use of force? Was the inmate warned of the consequences? Did the staff try to "talk him or her down" by persuasion, etc.? This is important. Any reasonable jail officer does not want anyone—themselves, the inmate, or anyone in the area—to be injured. In some instances, persuasion may take a few minutes, but it may result in the situation getting under control without force.

Documentation of use of force is critical. An inmate may be controlled by force anywhere in the jail and may incur injuries ranging from cuts, bruises, or worse. A well-written and reviewed report that explains why staff had to take forceful action may be useful in defending the jail from a lawsuit, sometimes years after the incident.

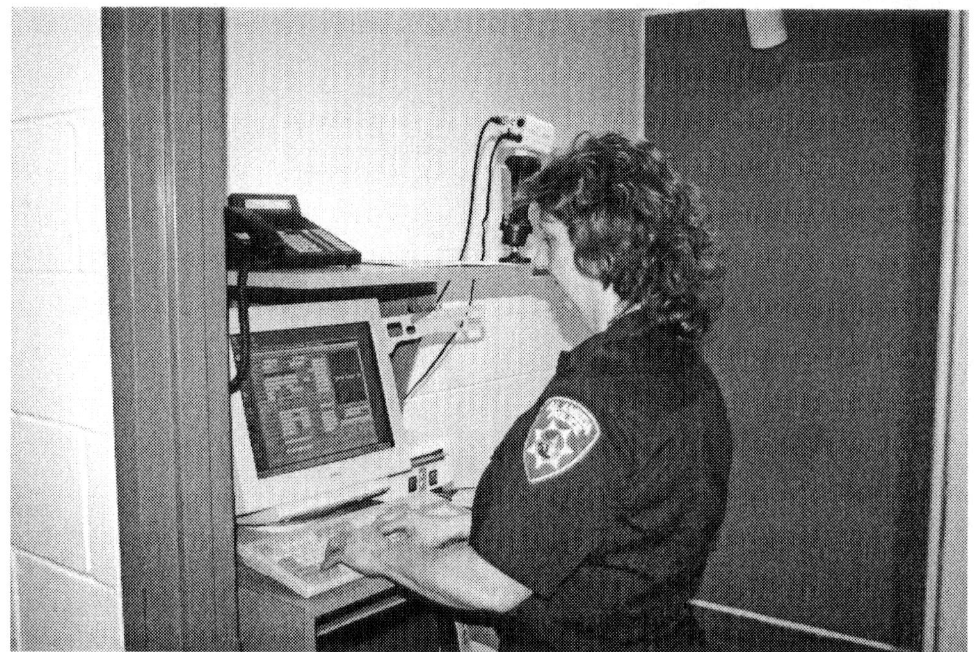

Many jail admissions and release procedures have been improved with the use of computer software and networking.

Photo by author, courtesy Alameda City Jail.

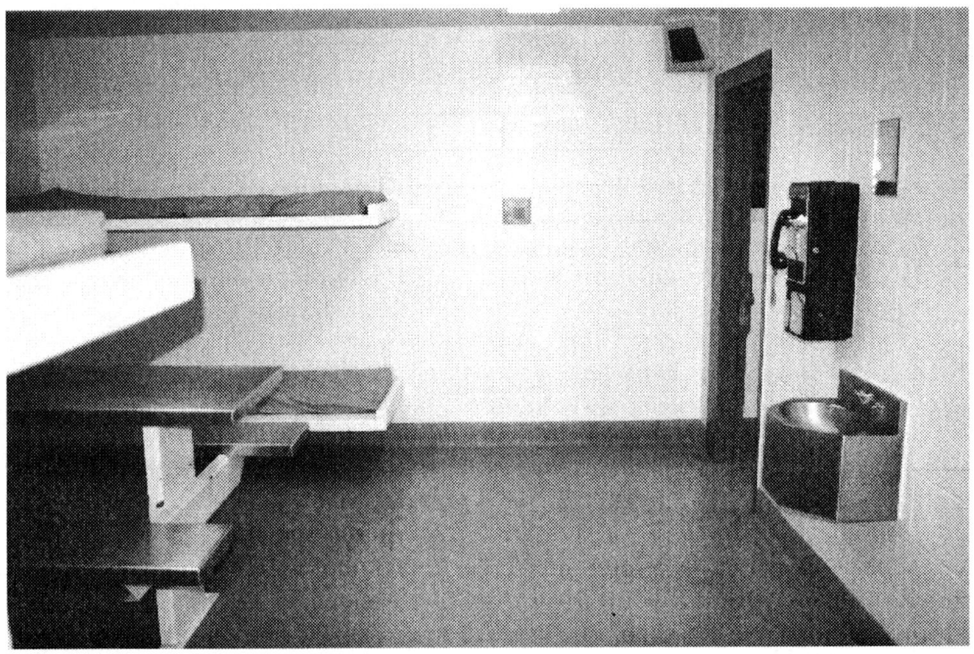

Inmate housing area.

Photo by author, courtesy Alameda City Jail.

## SUMMARY

The jail booking area, or booking desk serves as an important gathering point for information on inmates as well as coordinating such activities as the initial screening, headcount, and the intake and release of a variety of offenders. Jail booking receives and releases newly arrested offenders, transfers (farm outs) from other jails, inmates coming from or going to court, etc.

The jail booking record provides the foundation of the inmate's jail record, and information has to be accurate; all other jail staffs base their record on the booking record. New trends to facilitate this process include central intake and regional processing where new offenders are booked into the jail system at outside locations that are linked to the jail.

Jail booking staff deals with many inmate problems such as escape attempts, mentally disordered offenders, suicidal inmates, high-risk inmates, etc. The use of force must be justified and not excessive. The jail booking physical plant must be secure and provide a safe environment, and staff procedures must give the tools to address these problems. New and improved screening, staff training and physical plants are improving the booking process and making it safer for staff and inmates.

## REVIEW QUESTIONS

1. Why is the jail booking process so important to jail operations?
2. What information should be obtained from the offender as part of the booking process?
3. What types of offenders are processed in and out of booking?
4. Discuss the new trends in jail intake and booking.
5. What features should be present in a properly run and staffed jail booking area?
6. Discuss the proper release of jail inmates.
7. How should offender's property be properly accounted for and safeguarded?
8. Discuss several problems with inmates in the jail booking area.

9. How should booking and receiving staff deal with jail suicide?
10. Discuss ways that jail booking staff can deal with safety and security problems in booking.
11. What medical conditions may prevent an offender from being booked into a jail?
12. What are some "common sense" guidelines concerning use of force?

## TERMS TO KNOW

bail
bond
bond surrender
booking (inmate) number
central intake processing
criminal justice information system
detainers
farmed out
jail booking form
personal recognizance
pocket guide
property receipt
receiving
regional processing
tie off points
transaction

## ENDNOTES


1. Debra Goldentyre, "Booking and Admissions," Mark Schaeffer, ed., *Jail Operations Bulletin* (American Jail Association) 3 (4) (1990): 2.
2. Mark D. Martin and Thomas Rosazza, *Resource Guide for Jail Administrators* (Washington, DC: National Institute of Corrections, 2004), pp. 195, 196.
3. Ibid.
4. Ibid.
5. James J. Stephan, *Census of Jails, 1999,* Bureau of Justice Statistics.
6. San Diego Sheriff's Office, http://www.sdsheriff.net
7. Denver Sheriff Department, http://www.denvergov.org/Sheriff/template14453asp
8. http://www.roanokegov.com/WebMgMt/ywbase61b.nsf/nsf/vwContewntByKey/063B2C8F5AB
9. Milton M. Crump, "Keeping Cops on the Street with Regional Processing," *LJN Exchange Annual Issue 2003*, pp. 35–37.
10. Ibid., p. 37.
11. Ibid., p. 36.
12. http://www.county/allegheny.pa.us/jail/
13. Don Bales, ed., *Correctional Officers Resource Guide, 3rd Edition* (Lanham, MD: American Correctional Association, 1997), pp. 111, 112.
14. James D. Henderson, W. Hardy Rauch, and Richard L. Phillips, *Guidelines for the Development of a Security Program, 2nd Edition* (Lanham, MD: American Correctional Association, 1997), pp. 107, 108.
15. Goldentyre, *Booking and Admissions*, p. 5.
16. Ibid.
17. Ibid.
18. Henderson, Rauch, and Phillips, *Guidelines for the Development of a Security Program*, p. 109.
19. Goldentyre, *Booking and Admissions*, p. 5.
20. Ibid., p. 4.
21. *Security Post Procedures, Receiving Detainee/Inmate,* Hampton Correctional Facility.
22. *Standards for Health Services in Jails 2003* (Chicago: National Commission on Correctional Health Care, 2003), pp. 58–62.
23. Ibid., pp. 58, 59.
24. Goldentyre, *Booking and Admissions*, pp. 3, 4.
25. Debra Goldentyre, *Releasing Inmates*, Mark Schaeffer, ed., *Jail Operations Bulletin* (American Jail Association) 3 (5) (1990): 3.
26. Ibid., p. 2.
27. Ibid., p. 3.
28. Ibid.
29. Serge F. Kovaleski, "Another D.C. Jail Inmate Released by Mistake," *Washington Post*, July 5, 2005, http://www.washingtonpost.com/ac2/wp-dyn/A25878–2002Jul4?language=printer (accessed January 15, 2005).
30. Ibid.
31. Associated Press, "Inmate Let Out by Mistake Accused in Robbery," http//:www.corrections.com/printNews.aspx?BriefZone=This Just In (accessed March 2, 2005).
32. Goldentyre, *Releasing Inmates*, p. 4.
33. Meghan Mandeville, "Keeping a Closer Eyeon Offenders in Tarrant County," *corrections.com*, http://www.corrections.com/printNews.aspx?Zone=Technetwork (accessed September 4, 2004).
34. Kovaleski, "Another D.C. Jail Released by Mistake."

35. Keith Martin, "Maintaining Staff Safety in Jails," *corrections.com,* April 28, 2003, http://database.corrections.com/news/results2_new.asp?ID=4751 (accessed September 12, 2005).
36. Ibid.
37. WKYT, "Inmate Attacks Jail Employee," *corrections.com,* June 22, 2005, http://database.corrections.com/news/results2_new.asp?ID=13334 (accessed September 12, 2005).
38. Associated Press, "Genessee Inmate Nearly Makes Escape," *corrections.com,* May 23, 2005, http://database.corrections.com/news/results2_new.asp?ID=13148 (accessed September 12, 2005).
39. Associated Press, "Two WBR Parish Inmates Attempt to Flee, Deputies Injured," *corrections.com,* May 9, 2005, http://database.corrections.com/news/results2_new.asp?ID=13040 (accessed September 12, 2005).
40. Associated Press, "Coroner: Inmate Death Due to Cocaine and Alcohol, Not Taser," *corrections.com,* November 22, 2004, http://database.corrections.com/news/results2_new.asp?ID=11924 (accessed September 12, 2005).
41. San Jose Mercury News, "Calif. Man Dies After Being Booked into Jail," *corrections.com,* March 29, 2005, http://database.corrections.com/news/results2_new.asp?ID=12753 (accessed September 12, 2005).
42. *Sheriff Was Deliberately Indifferent to Suicidal Arrestee,* The Corrections Professional, Lawsuits and Readings, October 20, 2000, p. 13.
43. Erin Giudice, "Inmate Suicides at a Record Low for Orange County, California, Jail System," *American Jails* (January–February 2003): 69.
44. Ibid., pp. 69, 70.
45. Ibid., p. 70.
46. Ibid.
47. Ibid., pp. 70, 71.
48. Mark Welch, CJM, "The Finney County Jail: Then and Now," *American Jails* (January–February 2003): 31.
49. Ibid., p. 70.
50. William C. Collins and John Hagar, "Jails and the Courts . . . Issues for Today, Issues for Tomorrow." *American Jails* (May–June 1995): 27.

## REFERENCES


Allegheny County (PA) Jail, http://www.county/allegheny.pa.us/jail/facility.asp

Associated Press, "Genessee Inmate Nearly Makes Escape," *corrections.com,* May 23, 2005, http://database.corrections.com/news/results2_new.asp?ID=13148 (accessed September 12, 2005).

Associated Press, "Inmate Let Out by Mistake Accused in Robbery," http://www.corrections.com/printNews. aspx?BriefZone=This Just In (accessed March 2, 2005).

Associated Press, "Two WBR Parish Inmates Attempt to Flee, Deputies Injured," *corrections.com,* May 9, 2005, http://database.corrections.com/news/results2_new.asp?ID=13040 (accessed September 12, 2005).

Associated Press, "Coroner: Inmate Death Due to Cocaine and Alcohol, Not Taser," *corrections.com,* November 22, 2004, http://database.corrections.com/news/ results2_new.asp?ID=11924 (accessed September 12, 2005).

Bales, Don, ed. *Correctional Officers Resource Guide, 3rd Edition.* Lanham, MD: American Correctional Association, 1997.

Collins, William C. and John Hagar, "Jails and the Courts . . . Issues for Today, Issues for Tomorrow." *American Jails,* May–June 1995, 18–28.

Crump, Milton M. "Keeping Cops on the Street with Regional Processing," *LJN Exchange Annual Issue 2003,* 34–40.

Denver Sheriff Department: http://www.denvergov.org/Sheriff/template14453asp

Giudice, Erin. "Inmate Suicides at a Record Low for Orange County, California, Jail System." *American Jails,* January–February 2003, 69–71.

Goldentyre, Debra. "Booking and Admissions," Mark Schaeffer, ed., *Jail Operations Bulletin* (American Jail Association) 3(4), 1990.

Goldentyre, Debra. "Releasing Inmates," Mark Schaeffer, ed., *Jail Operations Bulletin* (American Jail Association) 3(5), 1990.

Hampton Correctional Facility, *Security Post Procedures, Receiving Detainee/Inmate.*

Henderson, James D., W. Hardy Rauch, and Richard L. Phillips. *Guidelines for the Development of a Security Program, 2nd Edition.* Lanham, MD: American Correctional Association, 1997.

Kovaleski, Serge F. "Another D.C. Jail Inmate Released by Mistake," *Washington Post,* July 5, 2005, http://www.washingtonpost.com/ac2/wp-dyn/A25878–2002Jul4?language=printer (accessed January 15, 2005)

Mandeville, Meghan. "Keeping a Closer Eye on Offenders in Tarrant County," *corrections.com,* http:// www.corrections.com/printNews.aspx?Zone=Technetwork (accessed September 4, 2004).

Martin, Keith. "Maintaining Staff Safety in Jails," *corrections.com,* April 28, 2003, http://database.corrections.com/news/results2_new. asp?ID=4751 (accessed September 12, 2005).

Martin, Mark D. and Thomas Rosazza. *Resource Guide for Jail Administrators.* Washington, DC: National Institute of Corrections, 2004.

Stephan, James J. U.S. Department of Justice: Bureau of Justice Statistics, *Census of Jails, 1999.* Washington, DC, August 2001.

Roanoke, http://www.roanokegov.com/WebMgMt/ywbase61b.nsf/nsf/vwContewntByKey/063B2C8F5AB

San Diego Sheriff's Office, http://www.sdsheriff.net

San Jose Mercury News, "Calif. Man Dies After Being Booked into Jail," *corrections.com,* March 29, 2005, http://database.corrections.com/news/results2_new.asp?ID=12753 (accessed September 12, 2005)

*Sheriff was Deliberately Indifferent to Suicidal Arrestee,* The Corrections Professional, Lawsuits and Readings, October 20, 2000, p. 13.

*Standards for Health Services in Jails 2003.* Chicago: National Commission on Correctional Health Care, 2003.

Welch, Mark, CJM. "The Finney County Jail: Then and Now." *American Jails,* January–February 2003, 28–32.

WKYT, "Inmate Attacks Jail Employee," *corrections.com,* June 22, 2005, http://database.corrections.com/news/results2_new.asp? ID=13334 (accessed September 12, 2005).

# 5 CLASSIFICATION AND INMATE HOUSING

***Objectives of chapter***

The student will:

- Understand the definition of classification, its goals, its procedures, from the initial interview through the decision-making process, and how they relate to jail operations
- Understand the importance of properly housing inmates in the local jail and risk assessment, including an examination of the three custody levels in the jail's general population
- Learn how the jail classification staff deals with inmate problems

When offenders enter the local jail, some very important processes swing into action. Booking officers properly and legally book the inmates into the jail, medical staff begins a screening, and the classification staff interviews the inmate for proper housing and custody levels. Classification is a vital function of the jail; every inmate has to be housed in an appropriate setting based on his or her charge, criminal background, and behavior. Classification also performs other critical functions, such as conducting disciplinary hearings, conducting administrative hearings, reviewing the status of inmates on administrative or disciplinary segregation, providing jail adjustment reports to probation officers, adjusting the inmate population, arranging for inmate transfers, etc.

Classification can be called the "nerve center" of the jail due to the importance of its many functions. Whenever an inmate is interviewed, assigned to a housing area, relocated, reassigned from segregation, or cleared for general population or his or her special category status is reviewed, the classification section personnel are the ones who take action in these matters. Classification is notified of problems in the inmate population, and takes appropriate steps in the cases of high-risk and high-profile inmates. In many ways classification is a "catch all" of many problems and events that happen inside a local jail.

# CLASSIFICATION: DEFINITION, GOALS, AND PROCEDURES

## Definition of Classification

There is no simple definition of jail inmate classification. Probably the best definition is by Carl R. Peed, former sheriff of Fairfax County, Virginia. Writing in 1989, Peed defined **classification** as:[1]

> An ongoing process and management which is based on the staff's analysis and diagnosis of information gathered about an inmate; staff will have the tools to predict and control the inmate's behavior while he or she is incarcerated.

Classification is a key management tool, where the jail staff can make educated, reasonable decisions about inmate housing decisions, custody levels, staff precautions, work assignments, and program involvement. When the classification process is well staffed and well executed, the safety, security, and integrity of the jail are safeguarded, and all staff, visitors, and inmates are protected from potential harm. Jail classification is the "central focus" of all staff decisions pertaining to inmate security, housing, programs, and assignments.[2] In other words, classification is the procedure by which inmates are confined in ways that are best for the jail and best for the inmate population.

Inmate behavior must be controlled, and classification is a very important inmate management tool. First, the classification staff through interviewing and assessment can determine the proper security level that best fits the inmate. Second, the same tools with supporting documentation can determine the appropriate housing type for the inmate: dormitory, direct supervision, cellblock with other inmates, or segregation. Finally, inmates may behave more positively if they know that the classification staff can reassess or reclassify them, resulting in less restrictive housing, more program participation, more privileges, and possibly a trusty or program cellblock assignment.[3]

POINT OF VIEW

### The Importance of Jail Classification

*Richard P. Gigliotti*
Warden, Butler County Prison,
Butler, PA

As all correction professionals know, the art of classification in any jail or prison is key to a well-run, safe, and secure institution. When I first became Warden of the Butler County Prison in 1988, we were not overcrowded and we would classify inmates based on the normal criteria consisting of the seriousness of the charge, aggressiveness of the defendant, level of bond set, whether the defendant was sentenced or unsentenced, any known medical condition, known criminal history, etc. Once we felt that we had determined what classification level this particular inmate required, we then had to make a determination on which range in that particular security level the inmate could be placed. In our main prison, which was built as a "linear design prison" approximately 50 years ago, we have ranges

"A," "B," "C," "D," "E," "F," "G," "H," "I," "J," the Restrictive Housing Unit (RHU), which the inmates affectionately called "the hole," the Diagnostic Classification Unit (DCU), and the Behavioral Adjustment Unit (BAU), which the inmates referred to as the padded cell or simply "the pad." Because all Pennsylvania county jails and county prisons are required to hold female inmates as well as male inmates, "F" range was designated as our female inmate housing area. This female range consisted of two large separate locking dormitory rooms. In one of these rooms, we built a lockdown cell for disciplinary status female inmates. There was also one "day space area room" that the female inmates were permitted to use to eat their meals, watch TV, read books, work out, etc. Our secondary building was located approximately 50 yards from our male prison. This secondary building was called the Butler County Prison Annex. This prison annex was a three-floor building that housed a very well designed direct supervision medium classification level on the second floor. A minimum security level dormitory-style area was on our first floor that housed our work release inmates, community service inmates, and other inmates who were classified as "low risk offenders." The ground floor was used as a "day space area" that inmates from the first floor only were permitted to use to eat their meals, watch TV, read books, write letters, or exercise on work out stations. This prison annex building has recently been demolished as it now serves as the site for the construction of the new Butler County Prison that is currently being built. In replacing some of the bed space that was lost in the demolition of the prison annex, we now have a new area located across the street of the main prison on the bottom floor of a five-tier public parking garage. This new area is called the Butler County Prison Tier Inmate Housing Area. It was designed to hold our work release inmates, community service inmates, and other low-risk offenders. These areas have served us well over the years except now our prison has become extremely overcrowded to the point it has severely restricted our ability of utilizing our classification system to its fullest extent. In an ideal situation, good classification can be accomplished in an institution until the institution begins reaching a point of 80–85 percent capacity. When we reached that point we began realizing that we did not necessarily have the accommodating bed space in the right areas to accomplish a proper classification system. The overcrowding forced us to make some hard decisions on where we were placing individuals that we did not feel fully comfortable that they should be placed. Although we may have had some bed space available in our minimum security level areas, our medium and maximum security levels may have been filled. In some instances, we were forced to begin using portable plastic bedding the inmates called "boats" that were placed on the floor, and an inmate mattress was placed on the portable bedding so that additional inmates could be placed in the medium and/or maximum security ranges, thereby meeting the classification level but now creating a new problem of being over the 100 percent capacity for that range. Our decision at the time was that it was less of a risk to be overcrowded in a particular range than running the risk of putting an overly aggressive inmate into a group of inmates, whom the aggressive inmate may try to take advantage of, or worse, putting a less aggressive inmate into a range suited for more aggressive inmates. We further progressed in our problem as our inmate count has continued to rise as a result of our growing civilian population. We are one of the few counties in western Pennsylvania where our civilian population has been growing for the last 30 years. Our 20-year future projection shows continued growth in each of the years with no slow down in growth indicated at this time. Although this causes us to continue to experience problems with our classification system, we do feel that we have light at the end of the tunnel with the building of the new Butler County Prison, which is expected to be open in the summer months of 2007. In explaining the classification levels in our institution, ranges "A," "B," "C," "D," "H," and "I" are all cellblock areas and by definition and by design are considered maximum security ranges. However, even with our maximum security ranges, we have developed a variation of security levels within the maximum security level which has aided our classification and security throughout our building. Our "A" range is designated for our most aggressive inmates. Ranges "B" and "C" we use for our more medium level maximum security inmates. Range "B" also happens to be a range that gets the most visibility by corrections staff mainly due to its location of being close to the kitchen and doorway to the outside exercise yard. Because of its close proximity to these doors, more officers travel this route more so than some other corridors within our building. Because "B" range gets this added visibility, we place some of more younger, immature inmates who have a tendency to have a little too much energy in this block. Our "D" range is used as our disciplinary lockdown range or RHU. The inmates in "D" range are locked in their cell 23 hours a day, Monday through Friday. The one hour they are provided outside of their cell is for them to use our outside exercise yard. Saturday and Sunday "D" range inmates are in lock-down status 24 hours a day. Our "H" and "I" ranges are also used in our medium level of our maximum security classification and because these last two ranges are smaller than the other maximum security ranges, we are able to isolate some inmates away from others who either need protection from other inmates or perhaps are codefendants who may be testifying against one another who we need to keep apart. We also get requests from outside law enforcement personnel to intentionally keep inmates apart from one another so that they cannot formulate a fraudulent story to use in court of law at a later date. This also serves the purpose that one inmate does not know if the other inmate may be meeting with the police and/or District Attorneys Office and making a plea with them before the first inmate does. Range "E" is a large dormitory range that is set up the same as "F" range, which has already been explained. Range "G" is also a smaller dormitory range and is where we keep our "inmate workers." Please note that we do not use the term "trustee," or "trusty." Too many corrections personnel have been embarrassed over the years by some facilities that have designated some of their above average inmates or worker inmates as "trusties." Our last range, "J" range is also set up in dormitory style. Our current use for this range is to keep most of our "sexual offender" inmates. As you can see, we have maximized the different areas for inmate classification. Without a proper classification process, chaos would develop and a warden would soon find himself in trouble. For the safety of his staff, inmates, and local community, a good classification system is a must in the field of corrections.

Prepared by Richard P. Gigliotti, Warden, Butler County Prison, 121 W. Vogely St., Butler, PA. 16001. Warden Gigliotti can be contacted through e-mail at rgigliot@co.butler.pa.us or by phone at 724-284-5257.

Special thanks to Warden Richard P. Gigliotti, Butler County (PA) Prison, Butler, PA.

Example of inmate artwork; Teton County Jail.

Photo by author, courtesy Teton County Jail.

## Goals and Benefits of Classification

More specifically, classification has several goals and benefits, and the greatest benefit is the handling of problem inmates. The three most primary benefits of an effective classification system are:[4]

- Classification is a guide for the separation of predatory inmates from weaker inmates.
- Classification serves as a valuable tool for the correct handling of special category inmates such as pregnant females, suicidal inmates, mentally ill inmates, elderly, etc.
- Classification assists in the management of security risks—such as escape risk inmates, traffickers in contraband, security threat groups, and other inmates who pose a threat to the jail climate and security.

Besides these benefits, there are secondary benefits that impact favorably on the institution and involve other staff besides the classification officers. They are:[5]

- *Improved security and control of inmates:* With the classification staff working as a team with the custody staff, problem inmates are identified and correctly handled. For example, an inmate who is interviewed upon arrival to the jail makes threatening comments to the interviewing officer and spits at the staff in receiving. The classification officer recommends housing in receiving until the inmate behaves, and the jail staff—medical and confinement—is alerted and takes the appropriate precautions. Another example would be a disciplinary problem inmate being reassigned to general population after 45 days in disciplinary segregation. His classification level could be adjusted to a higher level of security and housed in maximum security.
- *Fewer escapes, suicides, and arsons:* An inmate can be designated an escape risk due to his or her current charges, such as a capital murder charge, etc. that could indicate that the inmate has nothing to lose by attempting escape. Another indicator of an escape risk could be in the inmate's criminal history, where escape offenses from jails and/or police custody could be listed. In some jails, a list is generated to the staff listing which inmates are escape risks. Suicidal inmates can be identified through the classification interview, mental health interviews, etc. Classification can house them in special observation housing until cleared by mental health. Most jails have gone to nonsmoking, which lessens the chances of arson. However, mentally ill inmates can still set fires, providing they have secreted, smuggled, or obtained matches or lighters. The classification staff through interviewing and obtaining information from other sources (such as the arresting officer or another jail) can identify these types of inmates.
- *Fewer assaults on inmates and staff:* Assaultive inmates, once identified, can be segregated or requiring a **staff escort.** A staff escort means that the inmate is escorted by staff whenever he or she is out of the cell. Depending on the inmate's behavior and attitude, the staff escort may require two deputies and hand and leg restraints.
- *Early recognition and isolation of mentally ill offenders:* Mentally ill offenders can be housed in segregation and high observation areas per the classification staff until cleared by mental health.

- *Separate housing for codefendants:* **Codefendants** are inmates who are involved in the same offense. It is not recommended to house them together due to the potential damage to the district attorney's case, and in many cases, one may be cooperating with the police and district attorney by testifying against the other(s). Codefendants are identified by classification via information from the district attorney, police, or booking desk and placed on a **keep separate list.** This list identifies inmates who should be kept separate in all housing assignments and activities due to being codefendants, gang members, or members of a security threat group, or because they have assaulted each other or have been proven incompatible and not being able to live together. Any section that is responsible for assigning inmates to programs, running sick call, transporting inmates, taking them to court, or running recreation *must* use an accurate and up-to-date keep separate list to avoid conflicts. It is necessary at times to restrict inmates from activities if he or she has numerous keep separates, such as five or more inmates. The chance of a fight or altercation is too great. However, staff must be sure that when restricting privileges or programs in such cases, the inmate incurs no violation of his or her constitutional rights.
- *More effective use of resources:* If problem inmates are identified and housed appropriately, staff is used more effectively. Also, the classification file is a resource; it is a central repository for much crucial information such as the initial interview, criminal history information, mental health reports, incident reports, housing assignments, and miscellaneous information from the courts, law enforcement agencies, other jails, etc.
- *Use of data for facility planning and the evaluation of program goals:* Classification can supply data as to how many inmates are interviewed and what housing is necessary. This can assist in planning jail renovations and the construction of new facilities. Programs such as antigang initiatives and suicide preventions can be monitored and evaluated through the use of classification data.
- *Provides for an equal, consistent decision-making approach:* Classification decisions excluding emergencies should be a team's decisions getting input from confinement, mental health, etc.
- *Improved morale, efficiency, and effectiveness:* The classification staff operates at "crossroads," where they must act on the requests of the inmates (such as work requests, changes in housing, etc.) and staff requests for actions such as moving a particular inmate because he or she is disruptive. If inmates see that *legitimate* requests are acted upon and problems are addressed, and the staff sees that their concerns are addressed by classification, this can improve effectiveness and morale.
- *Reduced liability for the jail:* If the classification staff is treating and housing inmates in accordance with case law and court decisions, the opportunity for inmate litigation is reduced. For example, if safeguards are consistently taken to ensure that weak inmates are not placed in housing areas where they would be assaulted, then the windows for an inmate assault victim to successfully sue the jail are reduced. The key word is consistent.

## Classification Procedures

Classification procedures in a jail follow a logical progression of events that are happening with the inmate: booking, initial placement in a housing area, determination of eligibility of release, behavioral observations, classification interview, change-up, placement into temporary housing, placement into general population or assigned to segregation, and ICC review/initial placement. Following these basic procedures are such aspects of reassessment of custody level, placement in segregation, and population adjustments. Due to these last few procedures, the process of classification is a flexible, changing one.

The booking procedure supplies the basic information about the inmate such as the charge, bail, detainers, as well as address, height, weight, and emergency contacts (see Chapter 4). For the classification officer, this serves as the foundation. Other information that is useful includes the details relayed to the booking staff from the arresting or transporting officer. For example, if an offender is charged with felony assault on a gang member in the community, the arresting officer can inform the booking staff that the inmate should not be housed near any gang members such as his own gang or the victim's gang. Another situation is when inmates are disruptive at another jail and the jail administrator or sheriff agrees to hold them. Their behavior could involve an escape attempt or the introduction of contraband. The mental state of the behavior observed by booking, arresting, and transporting staff can also be relayed to the classification officer. In summary, any critical information about an inmate must be documented and relayed to the classification staff.

The circumstances surrounding an inmate when first booked in will determine what type of temporary housing the inmate will be placed in. If no problems are observed, and circumstances warrant it, the inmate may be placed in a general holding area with other inmates. If the inmate poses a threat or risk, he or she may be segregated until seen by classification or mental health. This includes placement in a restraining cell, such as a padded cell. The classification officer must have all information before going to the inmate and attempting an interview.

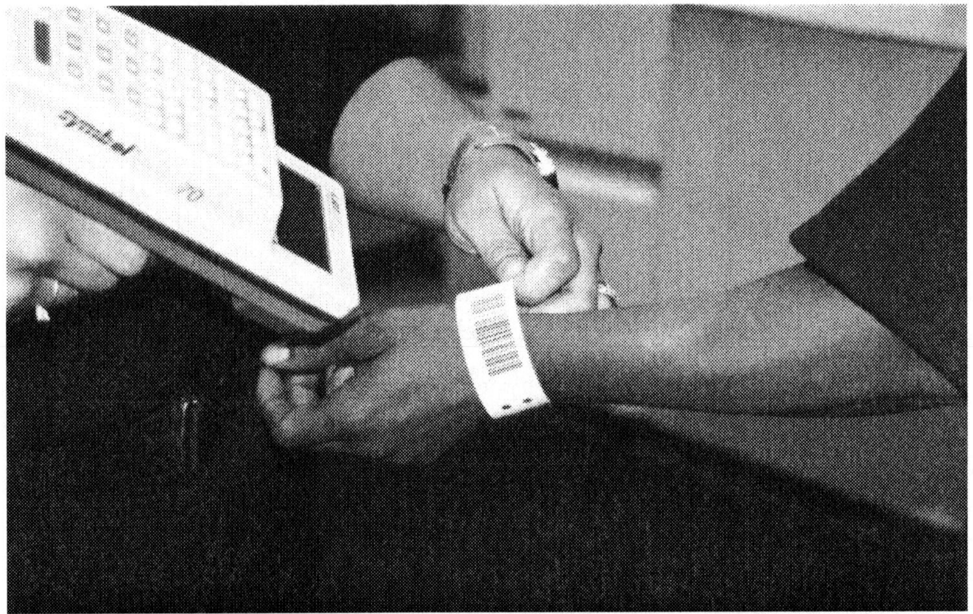

Inmate identification wristbands with bar codes contain critical information to assist staff in accounting for all inmates.

Photo by author, courtesy Baltimore City Central Booking and Intake Center.

### *Classification Interviews*

Before jails were automated with computers at various workstations, classification initial interviews were performed by hand using a standardized form approved by the agency in accordance with state and professional organizational standards. However, with the advent and progress of computer software, the classification interview can be conducted at a personal computer terminal where the inmate's answers can be filled into a computer screen containing information fields. If the computers are down, a paper form can be used. Classification staff usually has some latitude in deciding who will be interviewed. Inmates who have serious charges with high bonds, have detainers, have no bonds, or are transferred from other jails or correctional facilities will be interviewed. Inmates who have lesser charges and have a chance of bonding out may be lower on the interview priority list and will be interviewed if they do not bond out in a reasonable length of time. It is very important that no inmate is overlooked by the classification staff and left in the receiving area.

The setting of the interview is important. Some inmates, especially sex offenders, are reluctant to talk about their charges in front of other inmates and jail staff. The interview is a key way to gain the inmate's confidence in the professionalism of the jail staff. If the classification officer is rushed, brusque, or rude, any trust or rapport from the inmate will be lost. This is especially true of inmates who are depressed, despondent, anxious, and afraid. Besides booking and the medical prescreening, the classification interview gives the inmate a first impression of the jail staff and how mature they are.

Inmate behaviors must be consistently documented in classification files.

Photo by author, courtesy Baltimore City Central Booking and Intake Center.

Interviews may be delayed for several reasons, which the classification officer has no control over. If the interview is not conducted right away, the jail officers in that area should be notified and the inmate made as comfortable as possible until such time he or she is interviewed. Interviews may be postponed or delayed for the following reasons:

- *Uncooperative inmate:* Inmate may be uncooperative due to anger at being incarcerated, or shows a type of resistance in a form of "bravado"; inmate may refuse to be interviewed, to give information, a medical or mental health screening, or a shower or changing into the inmate uniform. The inmate may be also making a self-styled "political statement," especially if arrested of part of a demonstration, etc. One tool to use in such cases is for the classification officer to inform the inmate of the consequences of such behavior: remaining segregated in receiving, no recreation, no program participation, no visiting from family and friends, no television, no commissary, etc. Many inmates will give up after a few days.
- *Unstable behavior due to apparent mental illness:* Due to mental illness, the inmate may not be functioning in reality; the interview is pointless. This condition may be relieved somewhat with medication after an evaluation by the mental health staff. Also, as with cooperative inmates, the actions of the inmate are unpredictable and staff must use caution.
- *Court:* High-profile inmates such as those charged with a capital crime or multiple crimes, gang members, witnesses, etc. may be in court frequently, and as a result the interview may be delayed.

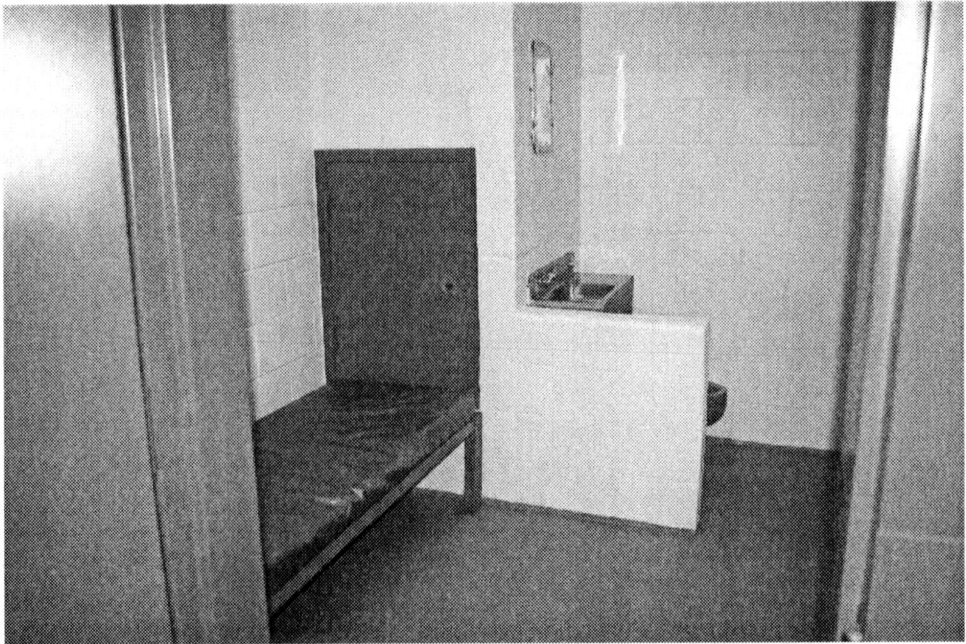

High-observation cell.

Photo by author, courtesy Teton County Jail.

- *Communication barriers:* The inmate may not speak English or may be hearing impaired. It is important to have a cross-cultural staff who mirrors the inmate population: civilian and/or sworn staff members who speak several different languages. Concerning hearing impaired inmates, staff members who have had training in sign language have proved valuable. This training is available through agencies that assist the hearing impaired and should be encouraged.

The **classification initial interview** is defined as an interview conducted by a classification officer who obtains detailed social, criminal, substance abuse, medical, mental health information, and any information about the inmate that can be used to formulate classification decisions.

The classification interview is one of the most important functions in the jail. Safety and security depends on what is found out by the classification officer. It is important that jail classification officers have the following traits: good writing skills, good interviewing skills, patience, good verbal communications skills, maturity, the ability to be proactive concerning potential problems, and the ability to relay the information gained from inmates to other jail staff. The classification officer should be a veteran officer who is very familiar with inmates and the jail.

The classification interview obtains information that is necessary for housing, custody level determination, treatment, and program needs. Many jails have the classification interviews conducted with the data entered into an online form.

No matter what the format, the following information and supporting rationale should be part of a jail classification interview:[6]

*Inmate's full name:* proper identity and can be compared with criminal history.

*Alias:* can assist in determining identity and can be matched to names in the criminal history; important to obtain all nicknames and street names; aliases are often abbreviated as **AKAs (also known as).**

*Race and sex*

*Age and date of birth (DOB):* can also be compared with criminal history date of birth.

*Place of birth (POB):* can also be compared with place of birth listed on criminal history.

*Criminal history:* including crimes, dates, sentences, and prior incarcerations.

*Size:* small, medium, large (based on height and weight).

*Charges:* felony or misdemeanor.

*Detainers:* in-state or out-of-state charges that hold the offender.

*Status:* pretrial or if post-trial, indicate awaiting sentencing, sentenced, etc.

*Substance abuse:* substance (drug of choice and/or alcohol: how much per day).

*Medical alerts:* diabetic, epileptic, pregnant, handicapped, heart condition, or any condition of note.

*Mental illness:* observations of inmate, any history of psychotropic medications, hospitalizations, and treatment, with dates if known.

*Sexual preference:* homosexual, heterosexual, bisexual.

*Educational background:* can be useful in placement in population and if inmate applies for a trusty position in programs, etc.

**FIGURE 5-1** Continued

*Employment/vocational history:* the type of job or occupation and the length of time at a job indicate the stability of the inmate and community ties.

*Marital status (married, separated, widowed, divorced, and single):* ascertain if spouse or significant other is also incarcerated if involved in arrest.

*Military history and type of discharge:* can give an indication of inmate's character if dishonorably discharged.

*Keep separates:* includes codefendants, enemies in jail and from the street: assists in housing placement.

*Gangs or security threat groups:* important for confinement staff to know, information needed for housing.

*Religious preference:* may be useful to the programs staff, to the chaplain, or in any crisis intervention if the inmate is suicidal.

*Recommendations:* This should be a narrative in which the officer states his observations, his housing recommendations, and any precautions that should be taken. His or her assessments are important: Is the inmate an escape risk, a management problem, assaultive, a potential assault victim, or a potential suicide risk? Also important is the recommendation, based on the information gained in the interview as to what type of housing would be suitable for this inmate. Finally, the classification officer can recommend segregation. Also important is to state if the inmate is being referred to mental health or medical. However, in a teamwork approach between medical, mental health, classification, and booking, the inmate may have been already referred. The classification interview can serve as a referral backup.

**FIGURE 5-1** The Classification Interview

The classification interviewer at his or her discretion may ask the inmate about the offense for which the inmate is being incarcerated. This cannot be viewed as an interrogation, because the inmate is not being advised of his constitutional rights as a police officer would advise under the Miranda decision. Depending on the personality of the inmate, he or she may relate details of the offense. Probably the best way to approach this subject is for the interviewer to ask the offender what the police say that he or she did to get arrested.

The classification interviewer may feel that the offender is not suitable for the jail environment. This may be true in cases of petty crimes and misdemeanors. The inmate may be emotionally upset, fearful, or weak. He or she may have a bond that is affordable or has ties with the community such as employment, residence, or family that may assist in obtaining a release. The classification interviewer may permit the inmate to make more than the one customary phone call in order to get bonded.

After the interview, if the inmate is suitable to be removed from the receiving area, he or she may be moved to an area for observation and orientation. During this move, the inmate will undergo a **change-up,** where the inmate showers and civilian clothes will be exchanged for the jail uniform. After the change-up, the medical staff may conduct an exam to follow up on the screening that was conducted when the inmate was first incarcerated.

### *Placement into Temporary Classification Housing*

It is a good practice not to move a newly interviewed inmate into the general population of the jail immediately. An exception would be when the inmate has recently left the jail, such as to go to court in another jurisdiction, and has returned. In that case, the interview information is updated and the inmate can be reassigned to the inmate population if the information and/or the inmate's behavior have not changed.

When assigned to temporary classification housing, the inmate can begin adjusting to the jail, routine, rules, and procedures and to see if he or she can get along with other inmates. This is important—if the inmate cannot get along with a small group of inmates, then there is a good chance that the inmate will not be able to survive without incident in the inmate population. The duration of this temporary housing can be 48–72 hours, depending on the space available in the jail housing areas.

Also, during this period, the new inmate will receive an **inmate orientation** about the jail that informs the inmate as to what is expected, such as behavior, respecting others, and following the rules. Other aspects of the jail that are covered include how to notify medical staff if the inmate has any medical problems, how to request assistance from the jail staff, mail, visiting, and programs. Orientations may be in the form of a video or conducted in person by a jail officer. It is important that jail personnel who personally conduct orientations be veterans whose knowledge about the jail will enable them to answer various questions from an inmate. In addition, the officer must appear no-nonsense, security minded, and professional, and be able to verbally communicate clearly to the inmate and be able to handle the occasional sarcastic or grandstanding inmate. Inmates who do not cooperate during orientation may either remain in the temporary classification unit or be moved back to receiving until they do cooperate.

In conjunction with the orientation, inmates receive an **inmate's handbook,** which contains detailed information about everything in the jail that they need to know. Information useful to the inmate in this handbook includes:

- how to contact staff in an emergency (medical or personal safety issue).
- laundry services.
- how to file a grievance.
- filing a request form.
- trusty assignments.
- programs and recreation.
- commissary.
- rules and regulations.
- disciplinary proceedings.
- mail.
- use of the telephone.
- jail routine.

The officer conducting the orientation can refer to the handbook, but it is the responsibility of each inmate to read it. The reality is that probably very few

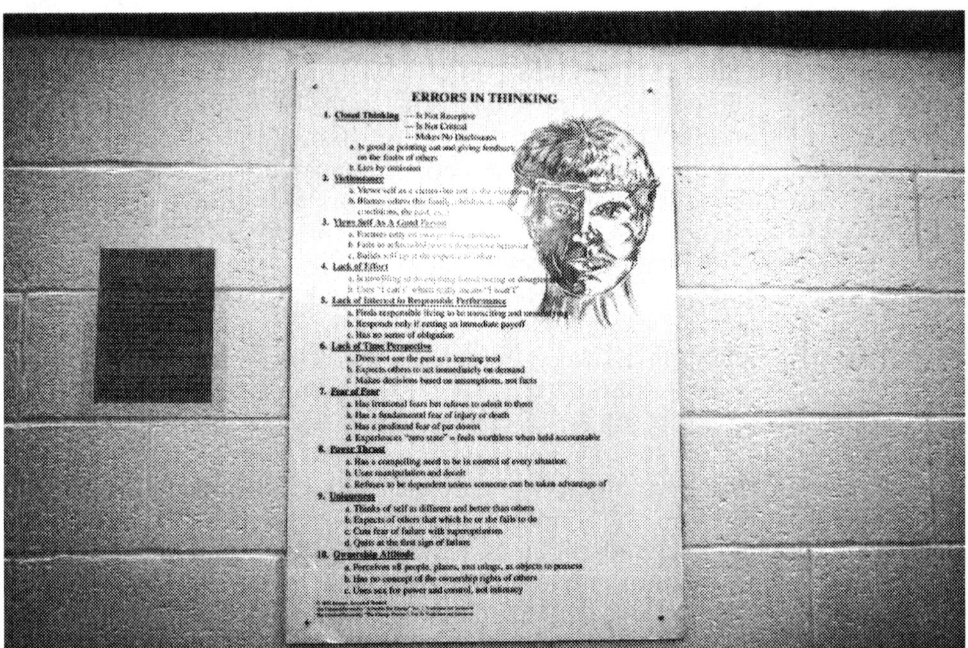


Advice for inmates, posted in Teton County Jail.

Photo by author, courtesy Teton County Jail.

inmates do. With the influx of non-English-speaking inmates into our nation's jails, it is becoming necessary to have inmate handbooks published in other languages and the orientations conducted in languages that mirror the jail's ethnic makeup.

If the inmates read the inmate's handbook and follow its guidelines, then serious incidents in a jail would hopefully be at a low level. The handbook and the orientation both attempt to convey to the inmates that they will be treated humanely and with dignity, but jails are places run by schedules and procedures.

## Decision Making in Classification

The decision of where to house inmates and under what conditions must be a team decision, looking at all of the data from the perspective of different jail staff sections. In emergencies, such as the jail booking in a known gang leader on a weekend or after normal working hours, the shift supervisor or booking officer can segregate an inmate. However, when deciding on more permanent housing that will be in the jail's best interest, the decision is best made by a team in accordance with departmental policies based on standards and case law. Jails vary by design, size, procedures, and staffing. As a result, the methods of classification decision making may also vary depending on how the jail is set up.

When the inmate is ready to be placed into the jail population, in many jails a committee meets and reviews the entire inmate classification file for

An example of a very detailed inmate's handbook is the one given to inmates at the Butler County Prison, in Butler, Pennsylvania, located north of Pittsburgh. Its preface reads:

> This book will explain the rules, regulations and guidelines of the Butler County Prison. Although you are expected to follow the living pattern set for you, we fully realize that each inmate here is an individual and possesses the dignity inherent in every human being. Each of you will be treated with fairness and respect and you will be expected to obey the rules and regulations of this institution. We feel that it should not be necessary to make rules governing every small detail of your stay here; therefore, you are expected to be governed by the basic rules of common sense and decency, having proper regard of other inmates and the personnel of this institution.
>
> Remember, you are here through no fault of any prison staff member, but, we are responsible for your care, custody and control until the charges holding you are resolved. Be of good behavior, the benefits will be to your advantage.
>
> Inmates wishing to talk with the Warden or Deputy Warden privately, must file a written request.[7]

From: Preface, in INMATE RULES, REGULATIONS AND GUIDELINES FOR THE BUTLER COUNTY PRISON *Revised January 2002.* Reprinted by Permission, Butler County (PA) Prison.

It is divided into two sections; Section I lists and explains in detail everything that affects the inmate from the daily routine of the jail to the general rules of the law library. Also included are rules of behavior during fire drills and a copy of the local court order stating the conditions under which selected inmates can obtain "Earned Time," or sentence reductions from good behavior and program participation.

Section II contains rules that are specific to the female inmate housing areas. Section I rules also apply. Contained in Section II are rules governing proper dress, cosmetics allowed for jury trial only, and the proper disposal of sanitary napkins.

Special Thanks to Warden Richard P. Gigliotti, Butler County Prison.

**FIGURE 5-2** Inmate Rules, Regulations, and Guidelines[8]—Butler County Prison, Butler, Pennsylvania

placement in the jail population. This committee is called the **Institutional Classification Committee,** or **ICC.** It is comprised of staff supervisors from the following sections:

- Classification section (chair).
- Confinement section.
- Mental health section.
- Medical section.

Other staff can sit in and have input, such as the programs staff or any staff having critical information about the inmate. The daily meeting of the ICC where routine assignments are made and files are reviewed is an informal

ICC meeting. A formal ICC meets as an administration hearing panel to place inmates on administrative segregation or authorize other special procedures.

The purpose of the ICC is to make proper housing assignments, change housing assignments for valid reasons, reassign inmates to the jail population when being released from disciplinary segregation and/or administrative segregation, place inmates on administrative segregation, place certain restrictions on inmates such as staff escort and restraints, and remove inmate from participation in programs and recreation for a valid reason. The ICC can also recommend programs for inmates, especially in cases of inmate assignments to specialized programs or cellblock-based programs such as therapeutic communities.

The ICC can also review reports from the confinement staff and make recommendations to the jail command staff on the housing and conditions of confinement concerning an inmate. Of all of the meetings that take place inside the jail during a typical day, the ICC's meeting is the most important. In a well-operated jail, any section—mental health, confinement, medical, and programs—can bring matters of importance to the ICC for further action, including reassessment of inmates to higher or lower levels of custody.

Another method that is found in some jails is **unit management,** where the jail's housing unit is divided into smaller areas that are supervised by staff, handling much of the same problems and tasks that the ICC does. Confinement staff rotates in and out of the unit, and classification decisions are handled by the unit management team, which is authorized to make classification, programs, and inmate housing decisions in the unit. The teams' membership consists of a unit manager or supervisor, a case manager, an education or programs staff person, a mental health staff member, and a secretary/administrative assistant. The benefit to this type of management is that the inmates get to know the staff in the unit, and the unit management team can make very informed decisions concerning the inmates.[9]

An important staff in the unit management concept is the **case manager,** who is the liaison between the inmates, the jail staff, rehabilitative agencies, and the unit management team. A key function is the realistic assessment of inmates entering the unit. The duties of the case manager range from dealing with inmates in the unit to getting them ready for release. The following is a general description of the duties of a case manager:[10]

- Performing intake and screening of newly admitted inmates.
- Classifying inmates by security and/or custody level, work assignment, and housing assignment.
- Assisting the confinement staff with the supervision of inmates.
- Participating in administrative hearings, including disciplinary hearings.
- Performing ongoing needs assessment of inmates and assigning them to programs.
- Monitoring of progress of inmates for reclassification.
- Approving inmates' personal visitors.
- Providing counseling and support for inmates.
- Preparing inmates for release.

Two-level housing unit, recreation machines (lower half), and inmate library (upper half).

Photo by author, courtesy Teton County Jail.

## PROPER HOUSING OF INMATES IN THE JAIL POPULATION

### Subjective Classification vs. Objective Classification

Jail classification can be subjective or objective. **Subjective jail classification** is a system that relies on the "gut" feeling of the classification staff when making decisions, especially housing decisions. This approach relied on a review of jail records (especially if inmate had been incarcerated before), current charge, criminal history (including prior incarcerations), social history, substance abuse history, mental health history, and the impressions of the classification staff interviewer to make placements. Subjective jail classification has been described as an "ad hoc, clinical, intuitive, seat-of-the-pants approach."[11]

This approach relied on opinions and feelings instead of objective criteria. Much weight was given to the comments of the interviewer, such as "inmate acting all right, placement recommended in a quiet group." However, what are the criteria for acting "all right"? What is a quiet group to one classification officer may not be such a quiet group to another. Decisions are made subjectively by the classification staff, and during the ICC meeting, placements are usually given a cursory review as the decision has been made beforehand. The ICC supervisors may just sign off on the placement without looking at it in depth.

Supporters of the subjective classification system argue that it is faster, is flexible, is economical, and requires less classification staff. However, the courts have found that inmates classified under this system have not been equally protected per constitutional mandates.[12]

Subjective jail classification does not stand up under close scrutiny. Housing and other classification recommendations, such as trusty assignments, have a tendency to reflect the opinions and orientation of then officer. Required due process—an informed objective decision—is not provided. The validity and value of the system cannot be shown because it is inconsistent.[13]

For example, two classification teams staff the classification section at a jail, and work opposite shifts from each other. One team may have different opinions where "jail wise" inmates should be placed, especially if the inmate "knows the ropes" about being in jail. When making a trusty, an inmate candidate may be "okay" to one officer and not acceptable to the other team. Inconsistencies such as these can result in a fragmented system where decisions are questioned and mistakes must be corrected.

**Objective jail classification** uses measurable factors and applies them in the same way to all inmates by a scoring method. Objective jail classification has replaced subjective classification in almost all prison systems, and does the following:[14]

- Uses classification and assessment instruments that have been validated on inmate prison populations.
- Uses the same components and scoring methods for all inmates.
- Reaches decisions through a straightforward, rational process that is based on factors related to successful classification placement decisions.
- Assigns inmates to the appropriate security levels that are consistent with their background.
- Promotes the use of similar classification decisions on comparable offenders, resulting in consistency.
- Minimizes the use of assessment overrides.
- Uses a process that involves inmates and staff, and is readily understandable to both groups.
- Uses a process that can be monitored systematically and efficiently.

An objective classification system involves **risk and needs assessment,** or measuring the level of danger an inmate poses to him/herself and to others, in conjunction with the likelihood of attempting to escape (risk). The inmate's needs are also measured by examining the inmate's physiological and psychological needs in terms of medical care, mental health care, and educational/vocational needs.[15]

To accurately assess the risk and needs factors with an inmate, classification staff commonly uses the following criteria:[16]

*Risk:*

- Current charge: severity.
- Warrants and detainers.
- Status: pre- or post-sentencing.
- Criminal history and the possibility of additional charges.
- History of escapes and attempted escapes.
- Correctional institutional disciplinary history.
- History of substance abuse.
- Social characteristics: age, employment, residence, and family ties.

*Needs*

- Medical problems or conditions.
- Mental health condition.
- Intellectual capacity.
- Substance abuse.

Because of its objectivity, the objective classification system withstands three key tests. First, it is reliable, because different classification staff using the system will get the same assessment result for a given inmate. Second, the system is valid where the risk level and need of an inmate are accurately predicted. Third, it is equitable—the system is applied the same way for each inmate who is classified.

Before the inmate's classification file is presented to the ICC with the risk assessment and housing assignment recommendation, a process must be in place so the staff can arrive at the decision. One is the **decision-tree instrument,** where the inmate is asked a series of yes or no questions containing risk factors. The more popular method is the **point additive instrument,** where the classification staff assigns weights and numbers to a variety of risk factors and a score is computed. The inmate is placed onto a custody level based on the total score.[17]

There are three levels of jail custody classifications, based on scoring from the objective classification system:[18]

- **Maximum custody**: Requires constant supervision in the most secure general population housing possible. Inmates designated as maximum custody are considered hard core, violent, very institutionalized, dangerous, and potential escape risks.

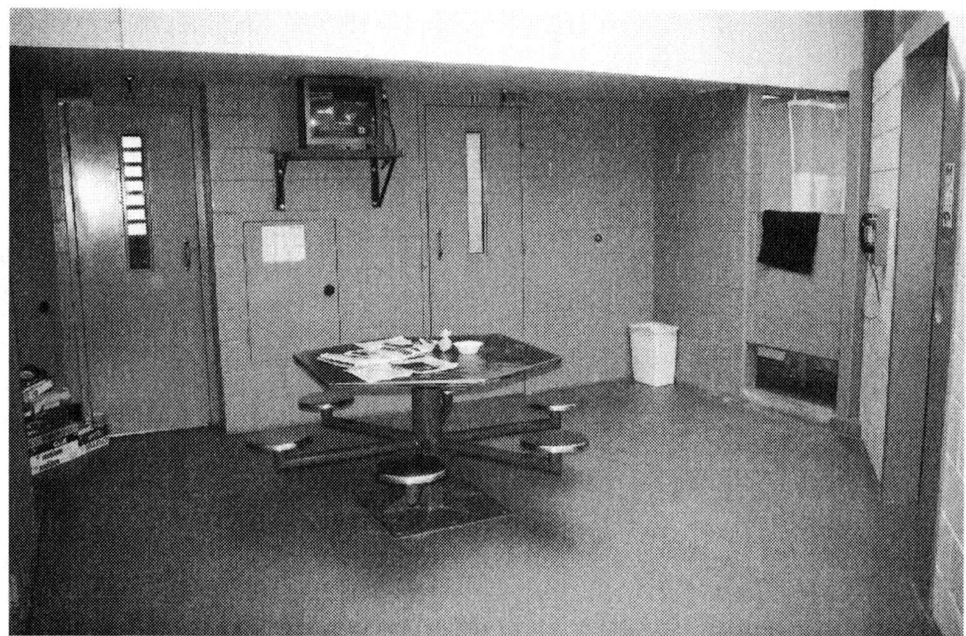

Inmate dayroom.

Photo by author, courtesy Teton County Jail.

- **Medium custody**: Constant supervision is present, but the inmate is allowed some freedom of movement, can apply for trusty assignments, and are not considered as a potential problem as the maximum security inmate. Medium custody inmates are usually nonviolent, are charged with lesser offenses, and are not viewed as serious escape risks.
- **Minimum custody**: Periodic supervision is required, and inmates are allowed maximum freedom of movement. Minimum custody inmates are not viewed as security risks, and many have nonviolent misdemeanor offenses and are sentenced to short terms. Examples of minimum custody inmates are traffic offenders, trusties, nonsupport inmates, etc.

Reassessment, as well as initial assessment, is an important component of the objective jail classification system. Reassessment benefits both the jail security needs and the inmates' needs. As inmates remain incarcerated, their behavior, charge disposition, and programs may change. If their behavior is positive, they may be reassessed to a lower custody level, making them eligible for less restrictive housing and programs. If circumstances change in a negative way, such as incurring many disciplinary infractions, the reassessment can increase their custody level.

To ensure uniformity in the system, inmates should be reassessed at regular 30-, 60-, or 90-day intervals, so as to not overlook any inmate. Events that would necessitate the reassessment of inmates outside of a routine reassessment are:[19]

- Deterioration or improvement of an inmate's behavior, such as becoming a housing problem, a disciplinary problem, or committing a new crime inside the jail such as attempted escape or assault.
- Crisis involving the inmate: sentencing, conviction, personal problem, denial of parole.
- Medical or mental health emergency.
- Information received from court or law enforcement: new charges, new detainers being filed, under police investigation, long sentence, or death sentence.
- Inmate's request for reclassification.
- Staff request from an inmate to be reclassified.

An objective classification system also takes into consideration what some researchers have called the **dimensions of classification.** This theory states that there are five areas along which new offenders are classified in the jail. Each relates to the other. They are:[20]

- *Custody*: Each inmate receives an assignment to a specific custody level that determines the level of staff supervision and privileges. An inmate with a maximum custody level grade may not be assigned to a trusty job, participate in a program that handles tools, or be placed in certain programs.
- *Security:* New inmates are classified based on security needs, and especially into certain types of jail housing design. For example, an inmate with a high custody score (maximum) should not be placed in a direct supervision unit.
- *Housing:* The days of staff just putting an inmate in the next available bed and hoping that the inmate will get along and not be hurt are gone. An approach that is being used now is **internal classification,** or placing an inmate with other inmates like him or herself. If an inmate has a medium custody level assigned, has done a few months in local jails for minor, nonviolent offenses, and has a

Bristol County Sheriff's Office

**Inmate Classification Form**

**CIN#:** [redacted] **Book#:** [redacted] **Location:** ASH-GB -144

**DOB:** 06/18/1970 **DOC:** 06/30/2004 **J/C:** 94 **S/E:** 03/28/2004 **P/E:** 03/27/2005 **EOS:** 03/12/2006

**Caseworker:** [redacted] **Level:** 5 **Open Cases:** Yes **Court Rec. DRNCAC:** No

## Review Information

**Date Seen:** 09/13/2004 **Next Review Date:** 11/12/2004 **Vote Made In Absentia:** No

**Review Type:** 60 Day **Board Members:** [redacted]

## Recommendations

| Rec | Cur | Programs |
|---|---|---|
| X | X | 1) Values |
| X | X | 2) Spiritual |
| X | X | 3) Substance Abuse |
| | | 4) Vocational Ed. |
| | | 5) Reintegration |
| X | X | 6) Health Issues |

| Rec | Cur | Education |
|---|---|---|
| | | 1) SPED |
| | | 2) GED |
| | | 3) ABE 1 |
| | | 4) ABE 2 |
| | | 5) ESOL |
| | | 6) Title 1 |
| X | X | 7) Post High School |
| | | 8) Carpentry |
| | | 9) Print |
| | | 10) Pre-GED |

| Rec | Cur | Work |
|---|---|---|
| | | 1) General |
| | | 2) Laundry |
| | | 3) Kitchen |
| | | 4) Maintenance |
| | | 5) Auto Shop |
| | | 6) Woodshop |
| | | 7) Work Details |
| | | 8) Greenhouse |
| | | 9) Unit Cleaner |
| | | 10) Outside Detail |
| X | X | 99) Other |

| Recom-mended | Inmate Request | Movement/Phase |
|---|---|---|
| | | 1) DRNCAC |
| | | 2) Pre-Release |
| | | 3) Modular Units |
| X | X | 4) Ash Street |
| | | 5) Bootcamp |
| | | 6) Dartmouth |
| | | 7) A-Phase |
| | | 8) Complete T-Phase |
| | | 9) Dartmouth EA |
| | | 10) Dartmouth EB |
| | | 11) Dartmouth EC |
| | | 12) Dartmouth ED |
| | | 13) Dartmouth EE |
| | | 14) Dartmouth FA |
| | | 15) Dartmouth FB |
| | | 16) Dartmouth GA |
| | | 17) Dartmouth GB |
| | | 18) Dartmouth HA |
| | | 19) Dartmouth HB |
| | | 20) Dartmouth HSP |
| | | 21) Dartmouth HSU |
| | | 22) Other Facility |
| | | 23) Remain |
| | | 99) Other |

**Comments:**

IT IS THE SOCIAL WORKER'S RECOMMENDATION THAT INNMATE [redacted] REMAIN AT ASH STREET. HE IS ENCOURAGED TO CONTINUE WORKING IN THE PROPERTY DEPARTMENT AND HE IS ALSO ENCOURAGED TO CONTINUE ATTENDING PROGRAMS AND SERVICES.

**Approved** ✓ **Denied** ______ **Modified** ______

***Reasons/Conditions:***

**A.D.S. Classification:** [redacted] **Date:** 9/15/04

**Approved** ______ **Denied** ______ **Modified** ______

***Reasons/Conditions:***

**Asst. Dep. Superintendent:** ____________________ **Date:** ____________________

I have been advised of my right to appeal the classification decision in writing within 5 days of receipt of the decision to the Deputy Superintendent or his/her designee.

I have received a copy of my completed Classification Review Form.

**Inmate Signature:** ____________________ **Date Received:** ____________________

## WASPC OBJECTIVE JAIL CLASSIFICATION
## INITIAL CLASSIFICATION INSTRUMENT

Inmate Name: ______________________ Current Cell: __________ New Cell: __________

Inmate ID#: ____________________ Reassessment Date: ____________ Date: __________

**REASSESSMENT REASON:** **1 - ROUTINE** **2 – DISCIPLINARY** **3 - OTHER** __________

**CUSTODY EVALUATION**

| | | | | |
|---|---|---|---|---|
| 1. | SEVERITY OF CURRENT OFFENSE * | | | |
| | Class "A" Felony | 7 | | |
| | Class "B" Violent Felony | 5 | | |
| | Class "B" Non-Violent Felony | 2 | | |
| | Class "C" Violent Felony | 2 | | |
| | Class "C" Non-Violent Felony (includes drug charges) | 1 | | |
| | Gross Misdemeanor, Misdemeanor, Traffic | 0 | SCORE | ______ |
| 2. | ADULT CONVICTION HISTORY * (Official data, e.g. NCIC; and/or Self-Report) | | | |
| | Class "A" Felony (within the last 10 years) | 7 | | |
| | Class "B" Violent Felony (within the last 10 years) | 5 | | |
| | Class "B" Non-Violent Felony (within the last 10 years) | 2 | | |
| | Class "C" Violent Felony (within the last 10 years) | 2 | | |
| | Class "C" Non-Violent Felony (within the last 10 years) | 1 | | |
| | Gross Misdemeanor, Misdemeanor, Traffic, or No History | 0 | SCORE | ______ |
| 3. | ESCAPE HISTORY (Excluding Current Charges) 10 YEARS * | | | |
| | Escape or attempted escape from secure facility | 7 | | |
| | Walk-away or attempted escape from non-secure facility or failure to return from authorized absence | 3 | | |
| | No escape or attempts | 0 | SCORE | ______ |
| | **MAXIMUM CUSTODY SCORE (Add Items 1-3)**<br>**SCORE OF EIGHT OR HIGHER – ASSIGN TO MAXIMUM CUSTODY:** | | **TOTAL** | ______ |
| 4. | PRIOR INMATE INSTITUTIONAL BEHAVIOR * | | | |
| | One or more (within the past 3 years) Major / Serious Incidents | 3 | | |
| | Four or more (within the past 3 years) Minor / General Incidents | 1 | | |
| | None or Minor Incidents (with no segregation time) | 0 | SCORE | ______ |
| 5. | PRIOR FELONY CONVICTIONS (Excluding Current Charges – past 10 years) | | | |
| | Two or More Violent | 4 | | |
| | One Violent | 3 | | |
| | One or More Non-Violent | 2 | | |
| | None | 0 | SCORE | ______ |
| 6. | ALCOHOL / DRUG ABUSE | | | |
| | Abuse Resulting in Social or Legal Problems | 1 | | |
| | No Abuse Problems / Unknown | 0 | SCORE | ______ |
| 7. | CURRENT AGE | | | |
| | 24 or less | 2 | | |
| | 25 -39 | 0 | | |
| | 40 or more | -1 | SCORE | ______ |
| | **COMPREHENSIVE CUSTODY SCORE (Items 1-7)** | | **TOTAL** | ______ |

* Single most serious, not accumulative

Revised 10/26/01

## WASPC OBJECTIVE JAIL CLASSIFICATION RECLASSIFICATION INSTRUMENT

Inmate Name: ______________________ Current Cell: __________ New Cell: __________

Inmate ID#: ______________________ Reassessment Date: __________ Date: __________

**REASSESSMENT REASON:** **1 - ROUTINE** **2 – DISCIPLINARY** **3 - OTHER** __________

**CUSTODY EVALUATION**

1. SEVERITY OF CURRENT OFFENSE *

| | | |
|---|---|---|
| Class "A" Felony | 5 | |
| Class "B" Violent Felony | 3 | |
| Class "B" Non-Violent Felony | 2 | |
| Class "C" Violent Felony | 2 | |
| Class "C" Non-Violent Felony (includes drug charges) | 1 | |
| Gross Misdemeanor, Misdemeanor, Traffic | 0 | SCORE ______ |

2. SERIOUS CONVICTION HISTORY * (Official data, e.g. NCIC; and/or Self-Report)

| | | |
|---|---|---|
| Class "A" Felony (within the last 10 years) | 5 | |
| Class "B" Violent Felony (within the last 10 years) | 3 | |
| Class "B" Non-Violent Felony (within the last 10 years) | 2 | |
| Class "C" Violent Felony (within the last 10 years) | 2 | |
| Class "C" Non-Violent Felony (within the last 10 years) | 1 | |
| Gross Misdemeanor, Misdemeanor, Traffic, or No History | 0 | SCORE ______ |

3. ESCAPE HISTORY (Excluding Current Charges) 10 YEARS *

| | | |
|---|---|---|
| Escape or attempted escape from secure facility | 7 | |
| Walk-away or attempted escape from non-secure facility or failure to return from authorized absence | 3 | |
| No escape or attempts | 0 | SCORE ______ |

**MAXIMUM CUSTODY SCORE (Add Items 1-3)**
**SCORE OF EIGHT OR HIGHER – ASSIGN TO MAXIMUM CUSTODY:** **TOTAL** ______

4. PRIOR INMATE INSTITUTIONAL BEHAVIOR *

| | | |
|---|---|---|
| One or more (within the past 3 years) Major / Serious Incidents | 3 | |
| Four or more (within the past 3 years) Minor / General Incidents | 1 | |
| None or Minor Incidents (with no segregation time) | 0 | SCORE ______ |

5. PRIOR FELONY CONVICTIONS (Excluding Current Charges – past 10 years)

| | | |
|---|---|---|
| Two or More Violent | 4 | |
| One Violent | 3 | |
| One or More Non-Violent | 2 | |
| None | 0 | SCORE ______ |

6. CURRENT INSTITUTIONAL BEHAVIOR
(Problems during the last 30 days or since most recent classification)

| | | |
|---|---|---|
| One or more Major / Serious Incidents | 3 | |
| Four or more Minor / General Incidents | 1 | |
| None or Minor Incidents | 0 | SCORE ______ |

7. CURRENT AGE

| | | |
|---|---|---|
| 24 or less | 2 | |
| 25 -39 | 0 | |
| 40 or more | -1 | SCORE ______ |

**COMPREHENSIVE CUSTODY SCORE (Items 1-7)** **TOTAL** ______

* Single most serious, not accumulative

Revised 10/26/01

Jails in Washington State use an objective classification system based on the initial assessment and reassessment instrument recommended by the National Institute of Corrections. The custody evaluation based on information from jail booking and the classification interview is computed into a custody score. Minimum, medium, and maximum custody levels are indicated based on the custody score. Built into the system are "checks and balances" custody-override factors. Discretion plays a limited role here; the rating officer can raise the level based on serious charges and management problems or lower it due to such factors as short-term sentence, good behavior, or special housing factors. The final assessment is signed off and reviewed by a supervisor.

Reassessment or reclassification rates the inmate in seven areas based on current charges, criminal history, past and current institutional behavior, and age. The override scale is similar to the initial classification scale and is also reviewed by a supervisor.

It is important to note that the Washington instruments are very detailed, which may minimize mistakes.

Special thanks to Wendy Jones, Chief of Corrections, Whatcom County Sheriff's Office, reprinted by permission of Washington Sheriffs and Police Chiefs Association (WASPC).

**FIGURE 5-3** Jail Classification in Washington State

high school educational level, he or she could be assigned to a medium custody area with other inmates having the same background.

- *Programs:* Based on data from the initial interview, such as educational background or a need for substance abuse treatment, the inmate could be assigned to a trusty job or a drug program. For example, a trusty opening exists in the jail law library. An inmate with a medium or minimum custody level and a bachelor's degree can be assigned there.
- *Reclassification:* This gauges the inmate's progress or lack thereof in the jail. Reclassification could be a "carrot and stick" approach. If the inmate receives a lesser sentence, he or she behaves well, and moves within the population are at a minimum, then the custody level could be lowered. This would open up new program and housing opportunities for the inmate.

## *Jail Housing Areas and Custody Levels*

The jail inmate population outside of the receiving and classification temporary housing areas can be divided into the following areas, each housing a particular type of inmate for a special purpose:

- *General population:* Sometimes generally called the jail population, the **general population** houses all inmates who are classified and are found suitable by the classification staff and/or ICC to live with other inmates. Inmates in general population are eligible for program and recreation participation. The type of jail architecture and design: linear, podular, and direct supervision can all be used for general population. The general population can also include programs blocks. General population areas also include the separate housing of female inmates in areas away from and not very accessible by male inmates who are trusties, going to programs, etc. Care has to be exercised in housing pregnant females, who should be housed in lower bunks due to safety reasons.

- *Segregation areas:* Inmates on disciplinary status or segregated for security or mental health reasons must be housed separately from the jail's general population. Although receiving can be used for these inmates, jails may convert units to segregation space.
- *Medical dispensary:* The **medical dispensary** can be termed as a "mini-hospital" inside the jail. Inmates are housed here on the authorization of the medical staff, sometimes before the classification interview is conducted. This type of decision is based on the inmate's medical condition or a critical need for treatment. It is incumbent on the classification staff to get an interview and find out information about the inmate as soon as possible. The medical staff also has the authorization to clear any inmate from the dispensary for housing in the general population. One current problem in jails is how to safely house inmates in the dispensary who are a security risk and pose other difficulties. For example, an inmate is admitted to the jail charged with assaulting police officers, attempted escape, and drug possession. On the street, he tried to run from the police in a stolen car and was involved in a serious accident as a result of a high-speed chase. He has serious injuries from the accident, but the charges definitely suggest that he is a security risk. A check of his criminal history reveals that he has done prison time for serious felonies and has escaped from a jail several years ago. The ICC has a problem: the inmate's injuries, though serious, can be treated in the jail's dispensary. The medical needs of the inmate dictate that he should be housed in the dispensary, but the jail's security needs indicate a need for *very* secure housing, such as in receiving or another area of isolation. Special alerts and procedures will have to be set in motion to care for this inmate and provide for jail security. Another problem is suicidal inmates, who may have serious medical problems and require close observation. Jail staffs must be creative in caring for these inmates and keeping the jail safe from the risks that they present.
- *Community corrections:* Depending on the size and age of the jail, community corrections inmates such as those on work release may be housed inside the main jail, in specially designated units or dormitories. Security is crucial, as these inmates have access to the outside community and the potential for smuggling contraband such as drugs into the jail is great. In more modern jail, community corrections inmates are housed in separate facilities from the jail proper. Other community corrections inmates include **weekenders,** or inmates under court order to do time on the weekends from Friday to Sunday, each weekend served being credited toward the completion of their sentence. Weekenders may in some jails just spend time inside the jail, or they may perform community service under the direction of jail staff in other jails. In whichever case, if they have access to the outside, they should not be housed in the jail's general population.[21] Some jails have placed weekenders in a section of classification temporary housing because space is limited.
- *Inmate work force (trusty) population:* Inmates found eligible for trusty work by the classification staff/ICC are housed separately from the jail population. The main reason for separate housing is security: trusties have access to kitchen, laundry, and maintenance areas due to their work assignments. Besides these assignments, trusties also work in education and programs. Contraband and unauthorized items such as food, linens, and messages from one inmate to another can be delivered by trusties because they have freedom of movement throughout the jail. In fact when trusty starts complaining about an assignment and becomes very interested in another job, staff should wonder if he or she has a hidden reason, such as gaining greater access to contraband.

One of the primary duties of any classification staff is the selection of jail inmate workers, or **trusties.** Selection of good trusties requires the input of the following jail staffs:

- Classification section.
- Confinement section.
- Medical section.
- Counseling staff (if part of the decision-making process).
- Jail records section.

While jails vary in their selection criteria for trusties, the following is a good "thumbnail guide" for the proper selection of inmate workers:[22]

- No current charge of a violent crime, including assault.
- No detainers.
- No history of assaultive or violent behavior.
- Minimum custody level.
- No history of escape, or attempted escape, from police or correctional custody.
- No recent serious or pending disciplinary charges.
- No medical problem that would impede the work assignment or tasks.
- Satisfactorily passed medical exam.
- Suitable for the task, has the capability to do the work, and is neat, clean, and well groomed.
- Have a positive jail record, with no adjustment and/or disciplinary problems, and is known to staff.
- Be from the local jurisdiction and not out of state—reduces risk of escape.
- Be required to undergo a job orientation, be informed that he/she is subject to strip/pat search at any time and will receive no special privileges.
- Be informed in writing of consequences and punishments of abusing inmate worker privileges and breaking jail rules.

Often trusty candidates are well known to the jail staff as they have been incarcerated in the jail previously and may be former trusties. However, sentiment must not outweigh good, common sense. In jail with objective classification systems, inmates who have maximum custody scores are not used as trusties.

The term "trusty" is misleading; it implies a level of trust with the inmate. Selection is critical, and the classification staff should be aware of what veteran jail administrator Carl Frick terms the Fifteen Worst Characteristics of Inmate Workers (the official name for trusties):[23]

1. Most always, inmates have ulterior motives to join the work force.
2. Inmate workers have a tendency to feel "equal" with staff due to being less restricted throughout the jail; they may acquire a sense of entitlement.
3. Inmate workers' loyalties most always lie with the inmate population rather than with the jail staff.
4. Inmate workers have a great communication system, and knowledge gained is their power—what the trusties see and hear in the jail, the entire jail population will also see and hear.

**FIGURE 5-4** Continued

5. Inmate trusties can be "schmoozers" and manipulators: They will try go gain personal knowledge about staff's private lives; they have face-to-face communications with staff, not communications from behind bars.
6. Trusties believe that staff trust them over general population inmates and will try to "get over" on the staff at every opportunity.
7. Inmate trusties will try to gain authority over other inmate workers, and under no circumstances should they be permitted to.
8. Inmate trusties will try to play games and pit staff against staff, or staff against the administration.
9. Inmate workers stake steps to hinder staff reprimands by doing favors, stroking egos, and patronizing staff.
10. Inmate workers will mislead staff by giving out false information, which will divert staff attention from their own wrongdoings.
11. Inmate workers move and trade contraband inside the jail.
12. Inmate workers know the location and status of all supplies and equipment in the jail, as well as the status and shortcomings of all jail security measures and procedures. As they know, as does the rest of the inmate population.
13. Inmate trusties will "test" security procedures and will "shop for staff"—finding out who they can and cannot manipulate.
14. Inmate trusties will feel indebted and obligated to other inmates and will pay debts by gathering information, running messages, and providing warning signals whenever staff is near.
15. Because of their being mobile throughout the jail, inmate workers will "set up" staff members or inmates whom they do not like.

**FIGURE 5-4** Selection of Trusties

## CLASSIFICATION: DEALING WITH INMATE PROBLEMS

### Administrative Segregation

The goal of objective jail classification is to put the right inmate into the right place, based on certain criteria. In some cases, inmates cannot and should not be placed in general population and must be segregated. Inmate types who should be segregated are:[24]

- Juveniles: if not certified as adult, must be housed out of sight and sound from adult inmates.
- Protective custody inmates.
- Behavioral problems.
- Disciplinary problems.

There are two types of segregation. **Administrative segregation,** or **A/S,** is defined as the placement of inmates in segregation, or isolation, after being removed from the inmate general population for reasons that are not disciplinary.[25]

Inmates on A/S are not on a punishment status. Within limitation, inmates on A/S can receive commissary, can attend programs if their situation warrants it, can attend recreation, and receive the same services as inmates in general population.

The limitations of certain inmates on A/S are directly related to the reasons that they have been placed in that status. Correctional researchers Martin and Rosazza list three primary reasons for inmates to be placed on A/S: [26]

- Through behavior, threats, or other actions, present a clear danger to the well-being of staff, self, and other inmates.
- For medical reasons such as communicable diseases, injuries, and other medical conditions.
- Due to developmental disabilities and mental illness, cannot function appropriately and safely in the jail's general population.

A trend currently in jails is segregating witnesses, sex offenders, transsexuals, informants (especially on gang members), and assault victims in **protective custody,** or **PC.** PC is a nonpunitive form of A/S where the inmate is isolated for his or her safety. Inmates on PC include inmates whose notoriety of their charges (such as the homicide of a child, a pedophile, etc.) may make them a target of harassment or assault, codefendants who are testifying against other inmates, witnesses to a serious crime (such as a gang homicide), or inmates who are weak and vulnerable.

Inmates on PC should be afforded the maximum protection by staff as possible. In jails holding gang members, inmates who are in rival gangs and swear out warrants on gang members who have assaulted them, and inmates testifying in open court against gang members, PC poses a logistical problem. PC inmates are not generally permitted to attend programs, are escorted by staff every time that they leave their cells, attend recreation alone, and see visitors alone.

A/S can also be used for high-risk inmates such as offenders charged with capital crimes and facing the death penalty, gang leaders who would cause security unrest in the general population, current or former law enforcement personnel charged with a crime, or high-risk inmates transferred to the jail per an agreement between sheriffs, or per an agreement between the jail and another law enforcement agency. In those cases, inmates can be transferred from one jail to another for security reasons: attempted escape, contraband smuggling, assault, or inciting a riot. Inmates also may be transferred due to testifying or being a defendant in a highly publicized trial. It is customary in some jurisdictions that in the event of a homicide of a law enforcement officer, the jail of that officer's jurisdiction will transfer the suspect to a neighboring jurisdiction. By doing so, the defendant has less cause to claim mistreatment or harassment from staff.

Inmates should not be placed on A/S without some type of due process hearing. Exceptions to this would include incidents that occur after normal hours or emergencies. For example, an offender who is a known gang member is booked into the jail, who is charged in a homicide of another gang member. He is booked in on a Saturday, and interviewed by the weekend classification staff. Due to the nature of his charge, he is changed up and immediately placed on A/S pending a formal hearing. Another example may involve an inmate whose cell is searched and a homemade knife and a list of inmate enemies are found. He is moved to isolation pending a hearing. In such emergencies as these, the jail supervisory staff should review the action as soon as possible and make sure all documentation is submitted requesting a hearing. The notice of the due process can be served on the inmate after the fact.

Inmates should never be moved to A/S—unless in emergency situations as previously described—or otherwise, without authorization from a jail supervisor or classification. If a jail officer takes it upon himself or herself to move the inmate to A/S without authorization, this is called **backdoor classification**.[27] This may be viewed by the inmate as a form of harassment, or the officer may not be aware of facts surrounding the inmate, such as who his enemies are, etc. Backdoor classification is dangerous and can open the jail to grievances by the inmate and litigation over a lack of protection and due process.

Inmates with medical or mental health problems are an exception to the normal procedures involving A/S inmates. At the informal ICC meeting, mental health and medical inmate cases can be reviewed, but the decisions for A/S should be left with the mental health and medical staffs. They have the expertise to place the inmate on A/S, and the decision to place the inmate in general population or have him or her remain on A/S can be discussed later, when the inmate is cleared by those staffs.[28]

The reasons for this course of action are clear. An inmate entering the jail suffering from a severe mental disorder is not going to comprehend what a formal ICC is, what A/S is, etc. This should be discussed if the inmate stabilizes and is responding to medication, and the mental health professional recommends to classification what a course of action should be. The same holds true for medical problems; the inmate's medical conditions—drug withdrawals, gunshot injuries, etc.—make it clear that dispensary housing is necessary, and the classification status can be worked out once the inmate is cleared by the medical staff.

A/S means that the inmate, while not in a punishment or disciplinary status, will lose some liberty and privileges in the jail and be subject to some limitations. Inmates should be afforded basic due process whenever placed in A/S, incur restrictions of privileges such as programs, or any special security conditions are imposed that are outside of the ordinary.[29] For example, a jail isolation area may not have access to television, which is a minor privilege and not a right. More importantly, an inmate on A/S may lose access to programs and social contact with other inmates. If the inmate is a security risk, a formal hearing may dictate the use of staff escorts and hand and leg restraints when out of the cell.

An administrative due process hearing to place an inmate on A/S is termed a **formal ICC,** because an ICC formally convenes a hearing to discuss the inmate's status and housing and to decide if A/S or any other restriction or condition is justified. To ensure fairness and due process, the inmate receives a written prior notice of the hearing, can ask for assistance, and present his or her position. The ICC will decide the case and notify the inmate in writing as to the decision and the reason(s) and evidence relied on for the decision. The inmate should be afforded the opportunity to appeal the decision to a higher authority, such as the jail administrator.

The placement of an inmate on A/S, P/C, removing privileges, and placing any type of restrictions should be based on documented information that is clear and accurate, and supports the need for formal ICC action. Documentation can come from incident reports, police information, reports from other jails (in cases of transfers), mental health observations, etc. Even if the inmate requests PC, a hearing still should be conducted, and the inmate should sign a written consent for PC placement.[30]

Inmates facing formal administrative hearings for A/S should be made aware of what is involved. This can be written in the inmate's handbook, such as this section from the Alexandria, Virginia Detention Center's *Inmate Handbook:*

> Administrative Segregation/Maximum Custody
>
> If you are in Administrative Segregation, you will stay in your cell most of the day. You will receive breaks according to a break schedule that the Deputies follow. During your break, you may make personal telephone calls and attend to your hygiene needs. You will be able to go to a limited number of programs and get all services unless we think you will cause safety or security problems. Inmates are put in Administrative Segregation for the following reasons:
>
> - Incidents that occurred during prior incarcerations.
> - You are a safety risk to other inmates or to staff.
> - You are a security risk.
> - There are concerns about how well you can handle being in jail.
> - You have an extensive criminal history.
> - We do not have enough information about you.[31]

## Disciplinary Segregation

Placing inmates on **disciplinary segregation,** or **D/S,** is a primary duty of the classification staff. Inmates on D/S are housed in isolation or segregation without privileges in order to punish for rule breaking. Due to the factor of punishment and removing privileges, the disciplinary process must be objective, nonarbitrary, non-biased, and supportive of jail security. Inmates on D/S must be housed in a way that protects other inmates and the jail staff from negative actions. Inmates charged with serious offenses, especially if the offense is serious enough to result in criminal charges as well as disciplinary charges, can be placed in A/S pending a disciplinary hearing.

All disciplinary actions in a jail do not have to take the form of putting an inmate in isolation or the "hole." In cases of minor infractions, officers can use discretion and counsel the inmate. Sometimes, advising the inmate not to behave in a certain manner is sufficient, depending on the maturity level of the inmate.

Jail discipline is in the form of three levels. The first level can be an **oral reprimand,** where the inmate is verbally counseled by the officer in private and no written documentation is generated. The officer explains the reason for the rule, its consequences if broken, and advises the inmate not to repeat such conduct. The second level can take the form of a **written reprimand,** where documentation is generated that the inmate has been warned; the documentation is placed in the inmate's classification file. The third level is a written incident report charging the inmate with an infraction and referring the matter to a disciplinary hearing officer or committee. The level of discipline is determined by the nature or seriousness of the offense, the inmate's record of prior infractions and conduct, and the length of time since the last disciplinary infraction.[32]

Reprimands are forms of **positive discipline,** where the jail officer attempts to teach and instruct the inmate. It takes a "training approach," treats the inmate as an adult, and encourages the inmate to think maturely and use common sense. The other form of discipline is **negative discipline,** where the teaching is conducted through the use of sanctions and punishments, such as a stern lecture, loss of privileges, and time in D/S. In both forms of discipline, the approach used by staff is that of reprimanding children—the worse you behave, the more punishment you will receive.[33]

Offenses are generally divided into two categories: major and minor. Each has a different set of punishments in the case of a finding of guilty. An excellent illustration of major and minor offenses can be found at the Alexandria, Virginia Detention Center (see Figure 5-5).

Inmate disciplinary procedures must be written so that inmates can understand the offenses, procedures, and punishments. At the Alexandria, Virginia, Detention Center, inmate rights are clearly written in the *Inmate Handbook*. Also, inmates are informed that information from a confidential source or informant may be used in the proceedings, and that his or her identity will remain anonymous. Inmates are also informed that witnesses may also be questioned outside of their presence. Inmate rules are divided into major and minor violations, all which are clearly written. The major offenses also address sexual misconduct, disruption of security procedures, and criminal activity. Personal or social visiting is taken as part of the disciplinary punishment in some jails; in the Alexandria jail an inmate may lose social visitation privileges for 30 days, or may keep them, depending on the hearing results and the circumstances of the violation.[34]

Major violations—violations that threaten safety and security, and are considered serious. The following are examples of major violations:

- Any criminal violation such as stealing, setting fires, attempting escape, destroying property, gang tagging, etc.
- Possession of any item that can be used as a weapon.
- Entering another inmate's cell.
- Interfering with the inmate headcount.
- Planning to break facility rules.
- Failing to follow staff's instructions, resulting in a security issue.
- Tampering with any equipment, locks, etc.
- Throwing any objects around a housing unit.
- Engaging in sexual activity involving another person.
- Possessing alcohol, nonprescription drugs, or any dugs; belonging to another inmate, and/or hoarding your own medication.
- Fighting or assaulting another person.
- Possessing an item with the intent of using it as a weapon, i.e., razor, pen, shank.
- Indecent or inappropriate exposure.
- Creating a security disturbance.
- Interfering with normal operations of the facility.

If you are found guilty you may receive any of the following sanctions:

- Written or verbal reprimand.
- Loss of privileges and programs for no more than 60 days.

- Disciplinary segregation for no more than 60 days for all violations arising from a single incident, with no more than 15 days per offense. No good time is earned while on disciplinary segregation.
- Loss of all or part of your earned "good time."
- Payment for Detention Center property damaged by your actions.
- Any combinations of these sanctions.

If you are found guilty of assault or fighting, you will automatically receive 15 days on disciplinary segregation for each rule violation.

During the time that you are serving sanctions in disciplinary segregation, your canteen items will be stored for you. You may purchase only hygiene and stationary items. You may receive professional and social visits. Your hearing results, however, will determine any limitations on your programs and social visitation privileges.

Minor violations—any incidents that interfere with the Detention Center's normal operations. The following are examples of minor violations:

- Failing to follow staff instructions and causing an operational problem.
- Failing to follow rules or planning to break rules.
- Yelling, cursing, verbal abuse, screaming, threat.
- Possession of contraband.
- Passing notes or objects.
- Gambling.
- Lying to staff.
- Using intercoms when an emergency does not exist.
- Running in your dayroom or housing unit.
- Loaning, trading, or giving anyone food or Detention Center property.
- Wearing any headgear outside your cell.
- Hanging clothing over furniture, lights, or the window in your cell.
- Attempting to communicate with anyone outside the Center through the windows.
- Harassing staff.
- Profiteering—trading or lending items/food and receiving more in trade.
- Trading personal items.
- Damage to Detention Center property of less than $25.00 value.

If found guilty of a minor violation, you may receive:

- a written or verbal reprimand.
- lockdown in your cell up to five days.
- loss of privileges for up to 30 days (excluding hygiene and sanitary items on canteen)
- payment of up to $25.00 from your inmate account for Detention Center property that was damaged.

From: Detention Center Rules Violations, in *Inmate Handbook*, Alexandria Detention Center, Alexandria, VA Office of Sheriff, 2004. Reprinted by Permission, Alexandria Office of Sheriff.

**FIGURE 5-5** Alexandria, Virginia Detention Center: Rules Violations

Care has to be exercised in the administration of inmate discipline. If handled incorrectly and with malice, the inmate population may feel that the jail staff is not fair and may become argumentative, the charges may be dismissed, and grievances may result. This is not conducive to a positive jail climate.

Inmate disciplinary hearings may be conducted by either the confinement staff or the classification staff, or both, depending on the staffing organization and workload of the jail. Until the hearing is conducted, inmates segregated pending the disciplinary hearing should be housed on A/S until the determination of guilt is or is not determined. Although the inmate may be found not guilty, or the charges may be dismissed, the ICC can still look at the entire case and the inmate's history and decide if the inmate should be placed on A/S in the best interest of the jail.

An important aspect of the disciplinary process, especially if the inmate (or inmates) is moved to segregation pending a hearing, is the proper gathering of facts and an examination of the offense. The jail officer who is administering the discipline or "writing up" an inmate needs to determine the answers to the following questions:

1. *What is the specific rule/rules that has/have been broken?* All disciplinary actions must be based on a specific rule or infraction that is listed both in the standard operating procedure for staff *and* in the rules for inmates listed in the *Inmate Handbook.*
2. *Does the inmate's rule breaking appear to be deliberate or accidental?* Is an inmate fighting as part of a malicious assault or in self-defense? Did the inmate throw the food tray or drop it accidentally?
3. *Did the charging officer or staff member witness the incident?* If he or she did not, who witnessed it? Are written statements available?
4. *How do the inmate's explanation compare to witnesses or the observations of the officer?* In complex charges, statements from all present should be obtained.
5. *What is the seriousness of the infraction?* Is an oral reprimand sufficient? Is the charge serious enough to justify a hearing and/or criminal action?
6. *Does the inmate in question have a history of disciplinary actions or is this the first offense?* This is crucial in determining future management of that inmate. If there is a history of disciplinary problems, then A/S after D/S is a viable option.
7. *Was the rule violation in question due to ignorance?* Did the inmate know that the rule existed? Does the inmate read and write? Does the inmate understand English?
8. *Did the inmate in question violate the rule as a result of poor staff supervision?* Have officers ignored violations of this particular rule in the past? In some cases, sloppy staff practices may lead to a situation where inmates see the opportunity to break the rules. This does not condone the rule breaking, but inmates should not see a "green light" to break the rules. For example, an area that is off limits to inmates, such as a hallway by the kitchen, is not patrolled by officers. Inmates coming back from visiting stop and talk to the kitchen trusties and receive food and other contraband. Although this conduct is not allowed, what is the staff doing to correct the situation?
9. *Does the rule violation seriously jeopardize the safety and security of the jail staff and inmates?* Examples of such violations include criminal assault, sexual misconduct, arson, manufacturing contraband, etc.[35]

As inmates are released from disciplinary isolation, the ICC will examine the circumstances of the disciplinary record and reassign the inmate to appropriate housing, or recommend a formal ICC to keep the inmate segregated on A/S. This should be a team decision.

## Segregated Inmates: Conditions of Confinement

Inmates on D/S and A/S (sometimes called **special management inmates**) can be housed in the same unit or area, but each has a status that dictates that they be handled differently in terms of privileges. A/S and PC inmates should have approximately the same privileges as inmates in the general population, depending on the circumstances. Inmates on PC may have to be housed in cells as far away from other inmates as possible and inmate access is restricted in that area.[36] The following conditions of confinement in housing special management inmates are recommended:[37]

- *Housing:* Housing for special management inmates should be clean, sanitary, well maintained, well equipped, well ventilated, and with adequate lighting. All fixtures in the cells should work perfectly.
- *Food:* Special management inmates should receive the same food service as the rest of the inmate population. The exception may be if the jail command staff authorizes the feeding of D/S inmates with **nutra loaf,** a baked mixture of vegetables, bread, and fruit, designed to meet daily nutritional requirements. Care must be exercised, as inmates on D/S devise unique methods (such as hooking another inmate's lunch bag or commissary with homemade "fishing line" made from clothes).
- *Personal property:* Excess personal property of special management inmates should be placed in storage; inmates on A/S and PC should be allowed the amount of personal property that is possessed by the general population.
- *Personal hygiene:* All inmates in segregation should have the same opportunity to maintain personal hygiene by showering at least three times per week and by receiving laundry services, and should be issued ample supplies of personal hygiene items: toothpaste, toothbrush, towels, soap, toilet paper, towels, and washcloth.
- *Clothing and bedding:* In some jails, bedding during the day is taken from D/S inmates; otherwise all segregation inmates should have the same clothing and bedding as the general population. Exceptions to this would be if there are medical or mental health reasons. For example, if an inmate is considered suicidal, mental health may restrict the inmate from having bed linens, which could be made into a noose.
- *Medical care:* Special management staff should be visited by the jail medical personnel at least three times per week. If the jail does not have full-time medical staff, jail officers trained in health care should check on the inmates regularly and refer any problems to health personnel.
- *Exercise:* Recreation is important to segregated inmates, and they should be afforded the opportunities for indoor and/or outdoor recreation unless their behavior does not warrant it. One hour per day, five days a week is recommended,

but that may not be possible due to staff shortages, PC inmates having to attend gym alone, etc.

- *Correspondence, telephone, and visitation:* A/S inmates should be afforded the same opportunities for mail, personal visiting, and telephone use. Inmates on D/S may be restricted to legal calls and professional visits only.
- *Access to courts and legal materials:* Special management inmates should have access to the courts through telephone, attorney visits, the jail law library, and the mail. Inmates on disciplinary should be allowed access to the law library unless their behavior is disruptive.
- *Programs and services:* Inmates on A/S and PC should be afforded the same opportunities for programs, counseling, library, religious services, commissary, education, etc. as the general population on a case-by-case basis, in consideration of their behavior or reason that they are segregated.

A key to the safe and effective management of special management inmates is frequent communications. Jail classification, mental health, confinement, and medical staff all should regularly make rounds in the segregation units to check on the status of these inmates. This is proactive as it may head off any problems and keep a lid on inmate frustrations.

## File Reviews

**File reviews** are necessary in any jail in the handling of inmates on segregation, whether administrative or disciplinary. File reviews by the informal ICC can serve several purposes. First, file reviews combined with staff interviews of segregated inmates can determine if the inmate behavior has changed enough to have the inmate come off A/S. To remove an inmate from segregation and reassign him or her to the jail's general population, ICC should hold a formal ICC hearing. File reviews ensure that the inmate on segregation is not forgotten in the busy workload of the jail.

Second, any special requests from the inmate can be addressed and not "fall through the cracks." For example, a high-profile inmate's status as an escape risk precludes him from frequent trips to the law library. In a staff interview to check and see if he has any problems or requests, he communicates the need for several court cases that he needs. By periodically seeing the inmate and reviewing his file, this request can be accommodated. Other concerns that can be addressed are health concerns, requests to see mental health, etc.

Third, file reviews by the ICC ensure that information from medical and mental health staffs concerning inmates on medical or mental health segregation is reviewed thoroughly. They have the final determination in recommending to the ICC if the inmates in their areas can be removed from segregation. Other sections of the jail staff such as confinement should not decide to relocate these inmates unless there is an emergency and only after documented consultation with the medical and mental health staff.

File reviews assess the need for continued segregation or restrictions. Professional standards require a classification or ICC review of an inmate's segregation status every 7 days during the first 30 days of segregation and every 30 days thereafter.[38] A review should not be a "gloss over" sign off; it should be an in depth discussion of the case so that all information is examined and weighed. File reviews are also important when an inmate's status changes. Inmates found guilty of serious disciplinary infractions should be on A/S while on appeal, and their status should change to D/S if the appeal is denied.

## Classification Documentation

Like in other areas of jail operations, classification requires exacting and accurate documentation. Besides the classification interview, the following paperwork exemplifies the importance and diversity of classification:

**Inmate request form**: This is probably the most common form of communication from jail inmates to various sections of the jail staff. A common version contains checklists or boxes of sections to which the inmate can address his or her message and a space for staff response. Inmate request forms are given to the jail officer in the area where the inmate resides. Inmates are advised to write clearly and be specific. A good rule for the classification staff is to keep copies of inmate request forms, especially if they contain in writing staff actions and responses. Inmate request forms can be used for disciplinary hearing appeals, requests for grievance forms, or requests to see a staff member privately if there is a problem.

The investigation of problems that are sent to the staff by inmates via request forms is a crucial function. The jail command staff may decide to have problems investigated by the on duty confinement squad or the classification staff. However, the classification staffs in larger jails are often overwhelmed by interviews, placements, and hearings. The jail officers in the squads get to know the inmates and are familiar with inmates living together. The most expedient way to prevent incompatibility problems is to have any problems in housing areas investigated by the squads and the results turned over to the classification staff for ICC follow up.

**Inmate move list**: This list shows where the inmates are moving from, their destinations inside the jail, and the reason for the move. Move lists must be approved by a supervisor. Inmate moves are scheduled at certain times during the day; it would be too chaotic to do otherwise. However, emergencies occur in a jail, and inmates may be moved upon the order of a supervisor if necessary in the event of a fight, escape attempt, sexual assault, or any other emergency or inmate actions that compromise the security of the jail. Moves may take place for several reasons, such as for maintenance in a cellblock where the inmates have to be removed for security reasons, moving inmates into available bed spaces, moving inmates to trusty areas, moving inmates to segregation for disciplinary or ICC reasons, or due to a **population adjustment.** It is necessary to adjust the inmate population due to balancing a cellblock at a custody level (such as making a new maximum security cellblock), or separating inmates who are not getting along. Other reasons may include balancing the age range in a cellblock, or balancing the racial makeup of a cellblock to relieve racial tension.

At a minimum, move lists should require the following information:[39]

- Inmate name and number.
- Present cell assignment of inmate.
- New cell assignment.
- Reason for transfer.

**ALEXANDRIA DETENTION CENTER**
**INMATE REQUEST FORM**

NAME ______________________________

DATE ____________________ HOUSING ____________________

**INSTRUCTIONS:** Please check the problem or request area **Be specific** about what action you want. This is **not** a grievance form.

- ☐ Appeal of Discipline
- ☐ Classification Appeal
- ☐ CDI - Community Diversion
- ☐ Waive 24 hour hearing
- ☐ Waive hearing appearance
- ☐ Inmate Housing Unit Worker
- ☐ Inmate Work Force
- ☐ Property Bin No ____________
- ☐ Special Canteen
- ☐ Special Visit
- ☐ Inmate Accounts
- ☐ Hearing Assistant
- ☐ Other, Specify ____________

Request: ______________________________

Staff Receiving the Request ____________________ Date __________

Supervisory Review ____________________ Date __________

Action Taken: ______________________________

Response: ______________________________

Signature ____________________ Date __________

Original - Completed form forwarded to appropriate file
Copy 1 - Completed form returned to Inmate with Action Noted
Copy 2 - Retained by Inmate at Time of Request

F-SHR-0016 Rev. 2/91 Initials DLP

Reprinted by permission, Alexandria Detention Center.

- Jail supervisor authorizing the transfer.
- Jail officer completing the transfer.

**Special housing roster**: Jails may employ the use of a document that is distributed to the jail that lists the inmates on special segregation, what types of segregation (A/S, PC, D/S), the reason for the segregation, the authority placing them in segregation (such as "per ICC," "per Medical"), release dates from D/S, caution alerts for staff, and the dates of file reviews. This log can be part of a larger log listing inmates with medical problems, escape risks, recreation restrictions for medical and disciplinary reasons, keep separates, etc. In this age of computers, this information can easily be entered into a computer network, and printed and distributed daily.

**Observation log**: The observation log contains such information as status (A/S, D/S, PC, etc.) documenting showers, meals, medical staff visits, any staff precautions, reasons for segregation, other staff visits with the inmate, D/S release dates, keep separates, etc. This documentation clearly states that the inmate is being properly housed and cared for, and is posted on the cell door or kept in a binder at the jail officer's post where the inmate is housed.

**Classification file**: The advantage of the inmate classification file is that it is a central repository for much information about the inmate. The inmate classification file is generated by the classification staff and contains the following critical information:

- Initial classification interview.
- Booking information.
- Criminal history.
- Record of inmate transfers and/or ICC file reviews.
- Mental health reports: observations and recommendations.
- Medical reports placing/clearing inmate in or from A/S.
- Incident reports.
- Records of disciplinary hearings/appeals.
- Record of formal ICC hearings/appeals.
- Signed jail orientation form.
- Custody level scoring, reassessments, and overrides.
- Programs information.
- Good time paperwork.
- Inmate request forms.
- Grievance forms, responses, and appeals.
- Miscellaneous information: memos from jail administrator, jail command staff, gang unit reports, reports from other jails, information from outside law enforcement agencies, court orders concerning the custody and housing of inmates, letters from attorneys, etc.
- Any counseling notes and staff observations (may be in memo form).
- Special diet needs/request.
- Visiting list: if additions/deletions handled by classification section.
- Observation logs.
- Keep separates.

The classification file is invaluable to the jail staff. Access should be limited to the classification staff, supervisors, and the jail command staff. Internal affairs may also need access and the jail's policies and procedures should be very clear on access and the safeguarding of these files. In emergencies, these files should be removed from the jail, or at a minimum be protected from fire and water damage. The information contained in these files would be difficult to reconstruct or replace.

## SUMMARY

Classification, often referred to as the "nerve center" of the jail, is an ongoing process of managing inmates. Classification procedures enhance security through the proper assignment of inmates to living quarters, the handling of special category inmates, and dealing with security risks.

Classification decisions should be team decisions; the most effective way is the Institutional Classification Committee, or ICC, comprised of staff from the key sections of the jail. Unit management is another method of reaching classification decisions of inmates housed in a unit, based on input from a case manager.

Classification procedures consist of an initial interview, assignment of the inmate to temporary housing to determine adjustment, an orientation to the jail rules and regulations, and custody scoring. The custody scoring determines the level of custody—minimum, medium, and maximum. Scoring criteria is known as objective classification, which is more accurate than subjective classification, which was previously used in many jails. Objective classification is also based on a risk–needs assessment, which ascertains risk factors with the inmate, and assesses what needs the inmate has. This is useful in housing and program assignments.

Classification determines whether the inmate will be housed in general population, A/S, medical dispensary, or in some jails, community corrections. Medical and mental health staff should determine the housing of inmates with medical and mental health problems. Problem inmates are housed in D/S if they are found guilty of breaking the rules and A/S if they are considered a behavioral problem or security risk. Placement in segregation requires either a disciplinary or administrative hearing, or inmates in segregation should have their files and status regularly reviewed. Conditions in segregation must not be substandard, and inmates on segregation should be afforded the same conditions as those in the general population, except if disciplinary circumstances dictate some restrictions.

Discipline in jail is progressive, using the "carrot and stick" approach, and can be compared to the discipline administered to small children. Its goal is to influence inmate behavior and encourage inmates to think and act more appropriately.

Documentation is important in classification. The classification file is a central reference point of critical information on inmates in the jail. The file contains a variety of information ranging from the initial classification interview to grievances.

## REVIEW QUESTIONS

1. Name the three primary benefits of good jail classification.
2. Name four secondary benefits of classification.
3. What information should be obtained in a classification interview?
4. What is the function of the Institutional Classification Committee, or ICC?
5. Which is more effective in the jail: subjective classification or objective classification and why?
6. What are the dimensions of classification and why are they important?
7. Besides receiving and temporary classification housing, describe population areas on the jail.
8. What are the criteria for the proper selection of trusties?
9. Why should jail inmate discipline be progressive?
10. Describe proper conditions of confinement in segregation.
11. What is the purpose of file reviews?
12. Name eight components that should be part of a jail inmate classification file.

## TERMS TO KNOW

administrative segregation (A/S)
AKAs (also known as)
backdoor classification
case manager
change-up
classification
classification file
classification initial interview
codefendants
decision-tree instrument
dimensions of classification
disciplinary segregation (D/S)
file reviews
formal ICC
general population
inmate move list
inmate orientation
inmate request form
inmate's handbook
Institutional Classification Committee (ICC)
internal classification
keep separate list
maximum custody
medical dispensary
medium custody
minimum custody
negative discipline
nutra loaf
objective jail classification
observation log
oral reprimand
point additive instrument
population adjustment
positive discipline
protective custody (PC)
risk and needs assessment
special housing roster
special management inmates
staff escort
subjective jail classification
trusties
unit management
weekenders
written reprimand

## ENDNOTES

1. Carl R. Peed, "Inmate Classification Procedures," *Jail Managers Bulletin* (American Jail Association) 1, (6) (1989): 2.
2. Ibid.
3. Richard P. Seiter, *Corrections: An Introduction* (Upper Saddle River: Pearson Prentice Hall, 2005), p. 324.
4. Ibid., p. 74.
5. Peed, "Inmate Classification Procedures," pp. 2, 3.
6. Ibid., p. 4.
7. *Inmate Rules, Regulations and Guidelines for the Butler County Prison,* Revised January 2002, p. 5.
8. *Inmate Rules, Regulations and Guidelines for the Butler County Prison,* Revised January 2002.
9. Peter M. Carlson, "Case Management/Unit Management," in *Prison and Jail Administration: Practice and Theory,* ed. Peter M. Carlson and Judith Simon Garrett (Gaithersburg: Aspen, 1999), p. 85.
10. Ibid., pp. 84, 85.
11. Robert B. Levinson, "Classification: The Cornerstone of Corrections," in *Prison and Jail Administration: Practice and Theory,* ed. Peter M. Carlson and Judith Simon Garrett (Gaithersburg: Aspen, 1999), p. 265.
12. Ibid.
13. Ibid.
14. Ibid.
15. Mark D. Martin and Thomas A. Rosazza, *Resource Guide for Jail Administrators* (Washington, DC: National Institute of Corrections, 2004), p. 139.
16. Ibid., p. 140.
17. Ibid., p. 142.
18. Peed, "Inmate Classification Procedures," p. 4.
19. Martin and Rosazza, *Resource Guide for Jail Administrators,* p. 141.
20. Levinson, *Prison and Jail Management,* pp. 262, 265.
21. Peed, "Inmate Classification Procedures," p. 4.
22. Carl F. Frick, "Selecting and Supervising Inmate Workers," *Jail Operations Bulletin* (American Jail Association) 2, (4) (1990): 4, 5.
23. Ibid., p. 4.
24. Peed, "Inmate Classification Procedures," p. 4.
25. Martin and Rosazza, *Resource Guide for Jail Administrators,* p. 166.
26. Ibid.
27. Debra Goldentyre, ed., "Administrative Segregation," *Jail Operations Bulletin* (American Jail Association) 2, (5) (1990): 3.
28. Martin and Rosazza, *Resource Guide for Jail Administrators,* p. 167.
29. Ibid., p. 166.
30. Ibid.
31. Office of Sheriff, Alexandria Detention Center, *Inmate Handbook* (Alexandria, VA: Alexandria Detention Center, August 2004), p. 4.
32. Mark Fitzgibbons, "Inmate Disciplinary Principles," *Jail Operations Bulletin* (American Jail Association) 1, (5) (1989): 4.

33. Ibid., pp. 2, 3.
34. Alexandria Office of Sheriff, *Inmate Handbook*, pp. 20, 21.
35. Fitzgibbons, "Inmate Disciplinary Principles," p. 3.
36. Martin and Rosazza, *Resource Guide for Jail Administrators*, p. 167.
37. Ibid., pp. 167, 168.
38. Ibid., p. 167.
39. Peed, "Inmate Classification Procedures," p. 5.

## REFERENCES


Alexandria VA Office of Sheriff, Alexandria Detention Center. *Inmate Handbook*. Alexandria, VA: Alexandria Detention Center, August 2004.

Carlson, Peter M. "Case Management/Unit Management." In *Prison and Jail Administration: Practice and Theory*, ed. Peter M. Carlson and Judith Simon Garrett, pp. 82–86. Gaithersburg: Aspen, 1999.

Fitzgibbons, Mark. "Inmate Disciplinary Principles." *Jail Operations Bulletin* (American Jail Association) 1, (5) (1989): 4.

Frick, Carl F. "Selecting and Supervising Inmate Workers." *Jail Operations Bulletin* (American Jail Association) 2, (4) (1990): 4, 5.

Goldentyre, Debra, ed. "Administrative Segregation." *Jail Operations Bulletin* (American Jail Association) 2, (5) (1990): 3.

*Inmate Rules, Regulations and Guidelines for the Butler County Prison*, Revised January 2002.

Levinson, Robert B. "Classification: The Cornerstone of Corrections." In *Prison and Jail Administration: Practice and Theory*, ed. Peter M. Carlson and Judith Simon Garrett, pp. 260–267. Gaithersburg: Aspen, 1999.

Martin, Mark D., and Thomas A. Rosazza. *Resource Guide for Jail Administrators*. Washington, DC: National Institute of Corrections, 2004.

Peed, Carl R. "Inmate Classification Procedures." *Jail Managers Bulletin* (American Jail Association) 1, (6) (1989): 2.

Seiter, Richard P. *Corrections: An Introduction*. Upper Saddle River: Pearson Prentice Hall, 2005.

Washington Sheriff & Police Commission, Classification Form.

# 6 JAIL PROGRAMS AND SERVICES

***Objectives of chapter***

The student will:

- Understand the purposes and goals of jail programs
- Describe the types and examples of programs available to inmates in the local jail
- Understand the importance of good custody and program staff relations
- Understand what services are provided to jail inmates

In our nation's overcrowded jails, the idea that inmates can apply for, be screened for, and attend programs can be viewed as a shining light. In the overcrowded, tense, tedious world of the jail inmate, getting out of the unit and attending a program is not only a welcome break away from the cellblock, it can also serve as a beacon of hope. Inmates who seriously attend programs are in a positive frame of mind and are engaging in a positive, healthy activity. If enough inmates have this mind set, the jail climate can be safer and positive.

Not all of the inmates in our nation's jails take programs seriously, and staff would be foolhardy to think otherwise. However, as programs staff in jails will say, some inmates actually *do* get something out of programs, and some *do* use these acquired skills to stay out once released. Others use programs as a convenient way to not only get out of the cellblock for a while but also use programs to manipulate, to "check out" new programs staff and volunteers, and try to acquire some "freedom" by roaming the jail.

Not all inmates qualify for programs. Some due to their mental state, charges, institutional records in the current jail or in other jails are not eligible for participation due to security and staff/inmate safety concerns. Just because an inmate wants to attend a program does not mean that he or she automatically goes. In some cases, the jail classification staff will have a great influence on decisions concerning problem inmates and programs.

## PURPOSES AND GOALS OF JAIL PROGRAMS

**Jail programs** are defined as rehabilitative programs that eligible inmates can attend at specific times and in specific places in the jail. Programs in jails have four major goals that involve inmates, the courts, and the staff. The most important goal of providing programs to inmates incarcerated in a local jail is to give them the tools to stay out of jail once released. The tools are the programs that deal with many problems. Ideally, local corrections staff wants inmates to correct and change their criminal behavior, so that they will not re-offend. However, realistically speaking, many inmates continue to return to jail. But, jail staffs who support programs feel that while the jail has the inmate in custody, opportunities should exist for inmates to improve themselves. The inmate can benefit my reversing all or part of the criminal behavior that has resulted in a criminal record and a history of incarceration. To most staff in a local jail, the goal of inmate programs is simply one of **rehabilitation.** For example, a jail Alcoholics Anonymous (AA) group in a jail classroom led by a trained volunteer is a jail program. Other examples would be a **General Educational Development** (GED) program or English as a Second Language (ESL) program.

Rehabilitation for the purposes of the local jail means for the inmates to change their criminal behavior through programs that help them to:

- identify their needs, weaknesses, and problems.
- attempt to strengthen the weaknesses through law abiding behavior.
- improve abilities to solve problems and meet future challenges in life.[1]

Second, if not trying to manipulate the court system and "pull the wool" over the eyes of the sentencing judge, involvement in programs may result in a more favorable sentence for the inmate from the judge or the increased chance of a plea bargaining or suspended sentence and placement in a treatment center.

Third, programs can serve in the preparation of the inmate for his or her eventual release back into the community. Programs can also assist the inmate in earning **good time** off their sentences. Good time is time off the sentence granted to eligible inmates that successfully participate in programs over a period of time. Successful participation must be documented and agreed on with the jail programs staff.

A fourth goal of jail programs is to keep inmates occupied in a productive way, thus decreasing the tension in the jail population (see Chapter 3, *Jail Climate*). Inmates for the most part do welcome the chance to get out of close living conditions, if even for a short while. One value of jail programs that can never be measured is how many arguments and fights are avoided by the separation of two inmates who are argumentative and abrasive. When one inmate goes out of the cellblock to a program, several things occur: the situation is defused, the block calms down, and the inmate may have the time to reflect on the situation. This is true especially if he or she is in a program that deals with inappropriate behavior or is in counseling/mentoring with a programs staff person or volunteer.

According to Lt. Lance Bohn, a jail administrator at the Chester County Prison in Pennsylvania, programs, activities, and services assist the jail staff by filling an inmate's time constructively; this is called the **pacification of inmates.** This pacification process gives inmates incentive and motivation to follow the jail rules, so that they do not lose privileges (such as programs). Program participation does reduce inmate misconduct and allows for a less punitive jail atmosphere.[2]

Programs in jails are the result of **judicial intervention** that occurred between 1970 and 1990. Judicial intervention is defined as courts, through court orders and consent decrees, dictated change in local jails in terms of overcrowding,

According to the Bureau of Justice Statistics *Census of Jails*, 1999, released in August 2001, the following are the number and percentage of jails in the United States that have a program or policy for education and counseling:

| | Number of jails | Percentage |
|---|---|---|
| *Education* | | |
| Secondary | 1,545 | 55 |
| Basic adult education | 696 | 25 |
| Special education (learning disabilities) | 303 | 11 |
| Study release (community corrections) | 260 | 9 |
| Vocational education (trade, etc.) | 182 | 6 |
| College | 94 | 3 |
| *Counseling* | | |
| Religious/spiritual | 1,960 | 70 |
| Alcohol abuse counseling | 1,724 | 61 |
| Drug abuse counseling | 1,528 | 54 |
| Psychological/mental health | 1,306 | 47 |
| Life skills | 601 | 21 |
| Domestic violence | 488 | 17 |
| Pre-trial services | 468 | 17 |
| Job seeking | 411 | 15 |

Using statistics to illustrate, the majority of jails surveyed had education, religious programs, and substance abuse counseling. However, to attack the multiple problems that inmates have, programs in vocational, mental health, life skills, and domestic violence will need to expand and develop.[4]

**FIGURE 6-1** State of Jail Programs: 1999

staff increases, and services. Twenty years ago, jail expenditures were mandated by federal court orders and rulings.[3] Jails have improved in both facilities for programs and the type of programs that they offer to the inmates.

## Guidelines for Effective Jail Programs

Operating jail programs requires coordination among the sworn jail custody staff, classification staff, programs staff from outside agencies that are approved to enter the jail, trained volunteers, and the inmates. It is one of the most important team efforts that can occur in the local jail. This coordination and cooperation is included in the following principles of jail programs, as discussed by Dr. Mark Kellar:[5]

- *Programs in the local jail must be basic and straightforward:* Because jails hold pretrial detainees and convicted inmates awaiting releases or transfers, it is impossible to predict how long inmates will be incarcerated in the jail. The jail count is always changing. Some inmates enrolled in a GED program, for example, may be bonded out, released after trial with time served or transferred to another jail or the prison system. They may only be halfway through the GED program.

In such cases, programs staff can recommend to them that they continue the program on the outside, and specifically recommend local adult programs, adult education centers, etc. Some avail themselves of the opportunities and contacts; many probably do not. The same is true for substance abuse programs. An inmate who has a severe dependence on alcohol may be getting to the causes of her addiction and coming out of the denial stage, but then is released. If released to probation or some type of supervised release, a probation/parole officer may make the completion of rehabilitative programs a condition of supervision. Long-term-type programs (such as auto/diesel mechanics and cosmetology) that are very detailed and involved may not be offered due to the short-term stays of inmates.

- *Jail programs should be conducted inside the security perimeter of the facility:* While some inmate programs are termed work program and are part of community corrections (see Chapter 11), jail programs are conducted inside the jail in designated classroom areas or inside units that have rooms for studying or counseling. Inmates that are selected to attend inmate programs should be screened for security problems by both classification and the programs staff. Jail classrooms should be equipped with video monitors and intercoms, so that instructors and volunteers can be watched by staff, and two-way communication can take place. Jail officers should check the classroom areas very frequently.
- *Jail programs should take advantage of all available resources:* Local colleges, school districts, local social service agencies, private organizations, and churches can be of assistance in providing instruction, curriculum, books, materials, and volunteers. Jails may also apply for grant funding. It is advantageous to the jail program section to have **memorandums of agreement (MOA)** with the jail and local school boards, religious organizations, substance abuse services, mental health services, inmate assistance groups, etc. The MOA specifies in writing the goals of the jail program, the responsibilities of the program staff agreeing to work inside, the jail staff, what agency will supply such items as computers, audio–visual equipment, classroom materials, etc. Due to changing needs and security concerns, the MOA should be reviewed annually and updated as needed.
- *Jail programs should have multiple objectives (inmate and staff) and interagency cooperation:* Inmates have a variety of needs, which can be addressed by programs. For example, programs are beneficial for **dually diagnosed** inmates. Dual diagnosis means that the inmate has a substance abuse problem combined with a diagnosed mental problem. Treatment programs for this problem must address two areas—the mental illness and the substance abuse. County agencies supply therapists who are qualified to conduct a program in dual diagnoses. Inmates may also lack life skills and education. Or they may lack vocational/job skills and not know how to read and write. A jail job-hunting program may work in conjunction with literacy teachers from the local school district. Other objectives may involve the jail staff. For example, programs that teach inmates cleaning skills, custodial procedures, and food preparation may result in those inmates becoming better trusties who perform those jobs inside the jail as well as being prepared for a marketable trade on the outside after release. Another objective is incentive—if inmates successfully participate in programs, it appears more advantageous for them in court, if transferred to the prison system or another jail, or in earning good time.

- *Jail programs must be fiscally responsible:* Spending large amounts of money does not guarantee program effectiveness. Jails are beholding to the taxpayers, who appreciate financial responsibility with public funds. One way to achieve this is to use **inmate commissary funds.** Inmate commissary funds are monies that are made from the inmates buying items in the commissary. This money is then earmarked for inmate use in programs, recreational services, the leisure, law libraries, etc. A jail programs staff may get a set amount of money from the inmate commissary fund and can use it to buy educational materials, videos for the classes, pencils, notepads, Bibles, etc. Also, the recreation staff can use the money to buy new exercise machines, board games, basketballs, volleyballs, etc., and to repair existing machines. The jail staff has procedures and bookkeeping in place to track the money and to make sure that it is appropriately spent.
- *Jail programs and services must be acceptable to the community:* Jails are generally operated by sheriff's offices or county corrections departments. Both are government agencies that are accountable to the citizens. The public wants to see programs that will turn inmates' lives around. Programs must have an element of hard work, be no nonsense, and administer discipline. The recent "tough on crime" trend is being reflected in some jail programs. The public wants the inmates to get out of jail and not commit new crimes. At the same time, the public wants practical programs that teach the inmates how to be law abiding citizens using basic skills such as reading, financial planning, keeping sober, etc.

Many inmate programs and services are funded through the inmate commissary.

Photo by author, courtesy of Sheriff Michael G. Bellotti and Deputy Superintendent David Reilly of the Norfolk County Sheriff's Office.

## TYPES OF PROGRAMS AVAILABLE TO INMATES

Programs in jails deal head on with the various problems that inmates have: mental disorders, substance abuse, lack of life skills, literacy, deficiencies, etc. While the public wants to see inmates get "treatment" in jail, many problems are complex, and cross over into other areas. An inmate may have a drinking problem resulting in arrests and also cannot keep a job, or is illiterate. Treatment programs concern psychological and substance abuse problems, while skills programs target educational, vocational, and life skills problems. Religious programs that stress positive living could be termed a skills program.

Psychological or therapeutic programs generally consist of the following subcategories, each with its own approach to the inmate's problems:[6]

- *Individual therapy:* The client, or inmate, enters a therapeutic relationship with a trained and qualified therapist or counselor. The goal is for the therapist to encourage the inmate to set aside the denial and psychological defense mechanisms that are a hindrance to treatment. This involves structured meetings and appointments in meeting rooms, offices, etc.
- *Group therapy:* A group of clients with similar problems works together with the therapist, who leads the group. Clients give each other support, advice, and challenge each other's defense mechanisms.
- *Behavior modification:* This approach sets out to change the offender's criminal behavior. It resorts to a system of rewards and punishments that the offender receives that facilitates him or her relearning behaviors. It does not believe that criminal behavior is a defect in the offender's psychological make up, emotions, etc., but is the result of a defect in learning. One could say: "Behave badly (criminally) and this happens; behave well and this happens." Use of "good time" for positive behavior, working in the jail, and program participation is a form of behavior modification.
- *Social therapy:* Social therapy combines traditional therapy and behavior modification in a unique way. The offender must exist within a pro social environment and is rewarded for such traits as honesty and taking responsibility for his or her actions. Acting irresponsibly or dishonestly is met with challenges. Group therapy and educational programming is used to give the offender assistance in dealing with his or her behaviors. Another name for a social therapy setting is the **therapeutic community.** In a therapeutic community, a unit is designated as a "program unit" for a select group of inmates needing or requesting treatment, such as substance abusers. Inmates live inside the unit under rules set down by the programs staff. Programming can be conducted by staff inside the unit. Projects are given to the inmates, which they must complete. If an inmate disobeys the rules, does not participate in the program, or causes disruptions or incompatibility, he or she is removed from the unit. The removal can be permanent or temporary, depending on the inmate, the circumstances of the removal, or the views of the staff. An important advantage of therapeutic communities is that inmates do not have to be escorted to a classroom for a majority of the programming, and many inmates in these settings are well behaved.

Jail programs consist of these general categories:

### *Mental Health Programs*

Much has been written and researched on the issue of jail inmates in U.S. jails with mental health problems. According to the Bureau of Justice Statistics (BJS) Special Report released in September 2006, at midyear 2005, a reported 479,000 inmates with mental health problems were incarcerated in jail, representing 64 percent of the jail population. Nearly 49 percent of inmates in local jails were reportedly found to have *both* a mental health problem *and* a substance abuse problem. It should be also noted that jail inmates reporting a mental health problem had a higher rate of binge drinking (48%) than inmates without a mental problem (30%). For those inmates in jail identified as having mental health problems, 17.5 percent received some type of treatment after admission to the jail, or approximately one in six. After booking, a reported 2.2 percent had an overnight hospital stay, 14.8 percent used prescribed medications, and 7.3 percent were afforded professional mental health therapy. Another indicator of the severity of mental illness in jails is the reported statistic by BJS that approximately 24 percent of jail inmates had at least one symptom of psychotic disorder. Psychotic disorders are considered to be hallucinations (inmates seeing and things that are not seen and heard by others) and delusions (inmate believing that their brains and thoughts were controlled by others, other people were reading their minds or spying on them).[7] This translates basically into one in four inmates entering jail with a severe mental health problem.

Many mentally ill inmates inside jail do not behave in ways that would allow them to attend programs. If funding and staffing allow for mental health staff to operate daily inside the jail, mentally ill inmates are monitored, seen frequently, and their progress is reported to the jail classification staff. If they are violent or irrational, security takes priority, and they will not be cleared by mental health for general population or attendance at programs or recreation. If they become stable and communicative with the jail staff, it is possible that they will be classified to the general population and/or be able to attend programs only after the programs, classification, and custody staffs consider the inmate's suitability either by discussion or through an Institutional Classification Committee (ICC) hearing (see Chapter 5).

There are some jails operating programs for the mentally disordered inmate. As the population of the jail is transient, long-term therapy for mentally ill offenders is not very feasible, as opposed to a prison setting where inmates with mental problems will spend years in the institution. The best that a jail mental health unit can do—and this is important—is to stabilize the inmate to the point where the inmate adjusts to jail life, can live with other inmates, and takes part in programs and activities. As a result, there are programs for mentally ill inmates, but they frequently consist of small groups inside special units, or groups of inmates on psychotropic medications meeting with the mental health staff either one on one with a therapist or in groups.

One progressive jail that took on the difficult task of providing programming and treatment for mentally ill inmates was the Albany County (NY) Correctional Facility. In 1975, the jail had a small staffed Albany County Mental Health Center's Adult Forensic Unit. Staffing then consisted of a part-time psychologist and full-time social worker who performed court evaluations and limited services. By 1997, the mental health staff had expanded to the inclusion of a psychologist, several forensic (mental health) social workers, and a contracted psychiatrist. By 2001, the unit consisted of mental health workers and behavioral health care providers working on weekdays, part time, and on weekends. Two psychologists and several forensics social workers are on staff resulting in a 24-hour presence of mental health staff. All jail staff who interacts with mentally disordered inmates receives specialized training in handling the mentally ill and suicide prevention.[8]

The Albany facility as of 2001 was the fifth largest jail in New York State, with an average daily population of 719 and a 1,005-bed capacity. The need to provide treatment, programs, and services to mentally disordered offenders and developmentally disabled offenders was critical. By 1997, the Adult Forensic Unit was providing the following services: suicide screening and prevention, crisis stabilization, counseling (both individual and group), diversion of mentally ill inmates into appropriate community-based treatment programs, and discharge planning. Mental health and medical staff, along with trained jail officers, provide a good model for teamwork. The discharge planning not only addresses issues such as housing and medication in the community but also plans discharges of mentally ill inmates into the New York Department of Corrections.[9]

Mental health programs for mentally ill inmates are unique, as there is no set traditional curriculum. Each mentally ill inmate is an individual treatment problem. Jails must enlist the help of community mental health professionals and merge them with the jail staff. Mental health programs work differently than what has been traditionally viewed as a classroom setting.

Several jails are doing this. In Philadelphia, where 1,600 of inmates have been diagnosed with some type of mental illness, it was recognized by jail administrators and community mental health staff that these offenders have great difficulty transitioning back into the community. A collaboration resulted between the jail and Philadelphia Behavioral Health Services. Through a grant from the National Institute of Corrections (NIC) and the Council of State Governments (CSG), computer access and databases are being improved, so that information can be shared, mental health staff can do more work inside the jail, and more offender pre-release planning can be accomplished. The jail administration feels that this approach will help the mentally ill offender, and if all of the programs and services cannot be made available inside the jail, the community resources can be identified. In Orange County, Florida, improvements have been made to the jail (mentally ill offender) diversion program that works with the county's only community mental health agency. With funds for an NIC/CSG grant, existing mental health services inside the jail will work more cooperatively with community mental health in getting mentally ill offenders help on the outside. The advantage is that assistance and programs start on the inside and can have a positive impact on the outside.[10] This approach is called **mentally ill diversion,** or evaluating and diverting out of the jail low risk mentally ill offenders and placing them with treatment resources in the community.

Another example of a jail doing something about the mentally ill offender is the Macomb County, Michigan jail. For the last two years, the jail, which had been designed to hold 1,438 inmates, has been struggling with overcrowding. The Michigan Department of Corrections has funded a pilot program for part of 2004 and all of 2005. Called the Jail Mental Health Reduction Program, funding is funneled through the jail's community corrections program. A case manager works inside the jail and is a liaison to the court and community providers. The mentally ill offender is evaluated in the jail, a criminal background check is conducted, and a determination is made if the offender can be safely released back into the community. The court is asked to either amend the offender's sentence (post-sentence) or do a conditional bond release (pre-sentence). Both methods make it mandatory for the offender to enter the program. Once in the community, diverted mentally ill offenders can be placed in a variety of treatment programs, such as residential treatment, intensive or regular outpatient treatment, and dual diagnosis treatment programs. A psychiatrist evaluates released inmates for medication issues. The program hopes to take steps to reunite mentally ill offenders with their families. The original goal was to divert 100 offenders per year put off the jail, and if successful beyond that amount, more funding is possible.[11]

Programs to provide better treatment for mentally ill offenders inside jails are due to responses to this problem from the state and federal levels. With jails releasing over 7 million inmates per year and approximately 16 percent of these offenders have a mental illness, something had to be done. Minnesota, Texas, and New York have passed legislation that aids the process of connecting eligible mentally ill offenders to certain benefits upon their reentry to the community. For example, New York's Medication Grant Program is a county-based program that provides to mentally ill offenders psychotropic medications in the community. The program also assists mentally ill offenders by referring them to Medicaid, food stamps, and cash assistance. At the federal level, the House of Representatives passed in October 2004 HR 2387, the Mentally Ill Offender Treatment and Crime Reduction Act. This Act authorizes $50 million over the next two years in federal grants to assist state and local criminal justice and mental health agencies to improve responses and services to mentally ill people.[12]

The legislation became law in late October, 2004. Included in the Act is funding through a federal grant program. This funding gives states and countries the ability to establish mental health courts, permit better access by incarcerated offenders and those being released to mental health treatment, to implement pre trial diversion programs, and to develop cross training for mental health personal and law enforcement staff, including correctional officers. Its aim is to identify mentally ill offenders and provide treatment for adult and juvenile non violent Offenders.[13]

## *Substance Abuse Programs*

Jails offer a variety of substance abuse programs, depending on staff and volunteer availability, and funding. Besides therapy approaches and behavior modification, substance abuse programs use education, where staff attempts to educate the inmates on the dangers of substance abuse.

Many citizens that are not familiar with substance abuse programs think that AA and Narcotics Anonymous (NA) programs are treatment programs. In reality, AA and NA are self-help groups facilitated by recovering alcoholics and drug users. The advantage to AA and NA is that the selected and trained volunteers who run many AA and NA meetings in jails are people with criminal histories, including jail records. They are able to see through the inmates' denials and manipulations.

AA has five tenets for sobriety, and the popularity of AA has led to other groups "spinning off" from AA that could assist inmates. Two are NA and Cocaine Anonymous. The five sobriety tenets are commonsense approaches to staying clean and sober:[14]

- Alcoholism is a disease.
- Recovery only begins after one hits "rock bottom."
- There is a "higher power."
- One must look at oneself and confess the problem.
- The message of AA must be carried to other alcoholics.

At the Allegan County Jail in southwestern Michigan, the problems of drugs including methamphetamine ("meth") labs were being recognized by the Allegan County Sheriff's Office as a major concern. An estimated 15–20 percent of the jail inmates are incarcerated for methamphetamine-related offenses. Due to a high repeat offender rate of drug offenders, the sheriff's office took action with the community. A task force was created in 2002 consisting of corrections, law enforcement personnel, drug treatment personnel, circuit and district court staff, and citizens. As a result of the ideas and research of the task force, a five-phase cognitive and behavioral substance abuse program began at the Allegan County Jail in 2004.

The first step is for a circuit court probation agent to identify all methamphetamine offense offenders, conduct criminal history checks, consider the offenses, and decide whether to recommend or not to recommend offenders to the program. A judge has to agree to offenders being placed in the program, and a review team (a smaller version of the task force) votes whether or not to accept offenders into the drug program. During this process, offenders undergo screening to see whether they recognize that they have a serious problem and whether they are willing to receive help. Other eligibility guidelines are that offenders must be non-violent and are eligible under Michigan sentencing guidelines and laws. Because of recent grants, eligibility protocol may change to include offenders who are not normally eligible. Offenders who are accepted into the drug program begin a five-phase process:

*Phase 1*: Offenders accepted into the drug program begin Phase I upon incarceration in the jail. For a minimum of 45–60 days, inmates receive individual and group counseling three times per week and must complete homework assignments.

*Phase 2*: Inmates who finish Phase 1 are eligible to be released. They enter Phase 2, where they come back to the jail to receive services for a minimum time frame of five months. This is required. Services include individual and group treatment sessions, community program meetings such as AA and NA. Offenders must provide documentation that proves attendance at these meetings. Offenders must submit to random drug tests and have a plan to pay court fees and restitution. Offenders must be employed or be in school. Some inmates remain incarcerated in Phase 2, while some live outside in the community.

*Phase 3*: After the successful completion of Phase 2, offenders enter Phase 3. Phase 3 is no more than six months in duration. Offenders are to focus on the changes in their behavior that they made in Phases 1 and 2, plus maintaining the skills that they have developed. Offenders return to the jail at least once a week for group sessions. They also meet with a case manager and are required to keep journals to monitor their daily activities.

*Phase 4*: After completion of the first three phases, offenders enter Phase 4, which is a three-month period that has the offender reinforcing the positive things learned in the program.

*Phase 5*: The offender graduates from the program and is released from its requirements. However, offenders are still monitored and evaluated until the 24th month of their program participation even if they have completed Phases 1 through 4 in less time.

Offenders can be sent back to previous phases if they do not make progress. The program review team must approve the offender advancing through each phase. At the end of 2004, there were only six offenders in the program, and the program had spared them an average of 90 days incarcerated in the jail. The future of the program looked promising with additional grant money from the state. Plans called for the program to increase its capacity to 20 offenders and the hiring of a full-time case manager.[15]

**FIGURE 6-2** Allegan County Jail, Michigan: Dealing with Drugs

At the Albany county facility, the Intensive Corrections Addiction Residential Education or ICARE program was re-commenced in 1997, consisting of 16 beds for male inmates. In April 2001, a female 8-bed ICARE program was added. [16]

Some substance abuse programs incorporate the aspect of shame into treatment, taking the view that addiction to drugs and alcohol is a disease that is reinforced by a cycle that includes self-destructive behavior resulting in despair, violence, criminal activity, and self-hatred. Shame, which results in incarceration, is a part of this process and must be addressed. At the Montgomery County Correctional Facility in Boyds, Maryland, a state of the art addictions program was developed in 1991. The Women's Program addresses the shame factor in the context of the inmate engaging in the continuous addiction of drugs and alcohol. Female inmates in the program are asked to write an autobiography about their life and how they became addicted and incarcerated. They present the autobiography to the group in an effort to become aware of patterns of self-destructive behavior. Other aspects of the program include strength building, which counteracts both low self-esteem and poor health coping skills. Inmate groups and the program therapist work with the females to get them prepared to deal with their shame. Additionally, movement therapy and yoga serve to educate the addicts about positive health, physiological recovery from addiction, managing stress, and good decision making.[17]

## Education Programs

Jail inmates do on occasion take advantage of the educational opportunities that are offered to them inside the jail. To survive on the outside, inmates must be made to realize that a basic education can be the key to success. Inmates realize that even rudimentary jobs require at least a General Equivalency Diploma or GED. Even with a criminal record, inmates who show self-discipline, perseverance, and a propensity to do the work required have a better chance of "making it" on the outside than inmates who are lackadaisical where education is concerned. Literacy and education rates of jail inmates are low (see Chapter 7). Inmate writing skills many times are lacking in spelling, sentence composition, and punctuation. Jail staffs see this when inmates take educational tests, complete program assignments, write request forms or file grievances.

The standard jail education program is the **GED** program or General Equivalency Diploma. This is recognized nationally as an alternative to the high school diploma. The test to obtain the GED consists of five sections: Reading, Science, Social Studies, Math, and Writing. A practice GED test is given to see if the inmate qualifies to take the formal GED test and to hopefully correct and strengthen any deficiencies. If the inmate passes in all areas of the Practice GED, he or she is ready for the formal GED test. Most GED test centers, jails included, use a **TABE (Test of Adult Basic Education),** which is an initial assessment tool of student math and reading proficiency.[18]

To prepare for the GED test in a jail does not mean that inmates take one or two classes and then take the exam. Jail education programs also require support programs in math, reading, writing, etc., which gets the inmate ready for the GED or continue in a specialized education plan or curriculum. As a result, an inmate in a GED preparation program or curriculum could be enrolled in several classes, referred to as **Adult Basic Education** (ABE). Education staffs may consist of several teachers, either full or part time, teaching several different subjects.

Teachers in jails also communicate with high school teachers in the community if an inmate is incarcerated and is currently enrolled in high school. To continue education from the outside requires the approval of the jail programs staff. In some jurisdictions, inmates who have been enrolled in a specialized education plan on the outside are given the opportunity to continue learning inside the jail. These inmates may have learning difficulties that require a teacher well versed in learning difficulties and inmates requiring special education.

The Incarcerated Education Program in Syracuse, New York, is a good illustration of jail inmate education. The program is a joint, cooperative effort between the Syracuse City School District and the Onondaga County Sheriff's Office. It serves approximately 610 incarcerated youth and 600 adult offenders per year. The program offers a variety of classes and is staffed by 8 full-time and 14 part-time teachers. About 25 percent of the jail inmates participate in one or more education classes, and graduation/certificate ceremonies that honor the inmates who complete the program are held every two months.[19]

One of the teachers, Lynn Olcott, described working with a female inmate group between January 11 and June 20, 2003, for *American Jails* magazine. The ABE/GED preparation classes were offered to the inmates in their general residence pod and in the behavioral health pod. Class size averaged eight students, which is manageable. She estimated that 33 percent of the females had learning disabilities and should be referred for educational testing. Of the inmates tested, 73 percent scored below 10th grade in reading and 84 percent were below the 10th grade level in math. Twenty-nine percent had math levels at or below the third grade. The lack of education among jail inmates is a serious problem, as illustrated by Ms. Olcott's group.[20]

The inmate mind set and culture can hinder learning. Some inmates go to an educational program to "check out" the teacher, manipulate the staff, and escape the boredom of cellblock life. Ms. Olcott in her teaching experiences has heard inmate remarks about learning. Inmates would say "I hate math," or "I can count my money and that's all the math I need to know." Another inmate said to the teacher "Miss, you don't need a GED on the streets."[21] These attitudes combined with being out of learning environment such as public schools for a long period of time makes the job of teaching inmates difficult.

Another jail that has a GED program is the Alvin C. Glenn Detention Center, a modern direct supervision jail in Richland County, South Carolina. In cooperation with Richland School District One, the Pre-GED/GED program started in September 2000. Two state-certified teachers instruct three days per week to separate male and female groups. Three different levels of classes are taught. All program materials are provided free to the inmates except the Pre-GED/GED books that cost $12.00. That fee is taken out of the inmate's commissary or canteen fund. If the inmate has no money, the book is still provided, and the school district pays for it. Initial testing of the inmate's literacy level is accomplished by the administering of the AMES (Adult Measure of Essential Skills) series of tests, established by the United States Department of Education. The GED test is given once the teachers have determined that the inmate is ready.[22]

Additional education programs that many jails offer include ESL. ESL programs are conducted by bi-lingual paid teachers or volunteers. They are designed to assist inmates who do not speak English to learn the basics in reading and writing English. A barrier to inmates staying crime free on the outside is the inability to speak and read English.

## Health Education

Offenders who enter jails do not exercise the best judgment and behavior concerning their health. Many, due to poor life skills choices, immaturity, or ignorance neglect their health. Jail programs in health care and awareness can provide some education to the jail inmate. Staffing for these types of health programs can come from staff in the local county health department or from retired health service volunteers. Also, local college nursing and health care programs of study may use the jail for internship sites, and requirements for interns may include providing health care education for inmates.

An example of health education for jail inmates can be found in Alabama, where female jail inmates across the state can attend an outreach program designed to educate them about early detection of breast cancer and cervical cancer. Through the Alabama Breast and Cervical Cancer Early Detection Program's Butterfly Project, low income, uninsured, and underserved women obtain access to life saving screening services for breast and cervical cancer. Physicians' visits and tests are paid through the program, which does not impact the jail's budget. The state program is part of the national initiative, the Centers for Disease Control and Preventions' National Breast and Cervical Cancer Early Detection Program, which is available in every state. By late 2004, approximately 350 female jail inmates in Alabama had been educated through the state program. There are other benefits besides education about self-exams; inmates are educated about their health and the services available through health services in the community that they can go to if necessary upon release.[23]

## Life Skills

Many offenders on the street do not know how to function in responsible ways and resort to criminal behavior to survive. With their lives consisting of a "revolving door" going in and out of jail, many do not develop the skills—the "right things to do" as normal citizens do. As a result, they do not know how to manage money, apply for a job, etc. These skills are called **life skills,** or more simply the proper, correct things that law-abiding citizens do every day in order to provide for themselves and their families. These things include completing a job application, opening up a bank account, acquiring insurance, balancing a checkbook, working out a budget, paying bills, etc. The more serious life skills include such things as child care and parenting.

At South Carolina's Alvin C. Glenn Detention Center, Life Skills classes for males and females include how to write a resume, how to open and maintain a bank checking account, developing a budget to live on, and proper childcare. A unique part of the life skills program is a fatherhood program sponsored by the Columbia Urban League, Inc. Part of the League's Fatherhood Engagement Initiative, it targets male inmates between 18 and 30 years of age who have children up to 12 years of age.[24]

An important factor in jail programs for inmates is the equal opportunity to participate in parenting and life skills programs with male and female inmates. Parenting is a major life skill, and inmates must realize that a criminal lifestyle is not conducive to raising children. At the Santa Rita Jail in Alameda County, California, the Alameda County Sheriff's Office instituted the Maximizing

Opportunities for Mothers to Succeed (MOMS) program in 1999, for pregnant and parent female offenders. The program, in collaboration with several community-based organizations, was created to enhance mother/child bonding, reunite mothers with their children, and hopefully will reduce repeat jail incarcerations by female inmates. The program is designed to encourage the female offenders to be self-sufficient, learn parenting skills, provide access to substance abuse treatment, and assist the offenders in finding stable and affordable housing. The curriculum includes parenting, personal skills training, addiction, literacy, and mental health education—all designed to help the offender. Community case managers provide both individual and group case management. Education and services are provided during incarceration in the jail and up to one-year post release. With the cooperation of the Oakland, California Housing Authority, a MOMS transitional housing complex consisting of 12-unit apartments was set up for MOMS participants, where they could live and receive services as they transitioned from jail to the outside.[25]

## Criminal Thinking

This is a challenge for jails program staff—how to change an offenders' thinking to positive law abiding behavior from criminal negative behavior. The pull of the "street" is strong, especially where substance abuse is concerned. Many offenders find the criminal lifestyle glamorous and appear not to mind coming to jail occasionally. However, with the advent of the "three strikes and you're out" legislation, truth in sentencing, mandatory sentencing and the abolition of parole in some states, it is hoped that jail inmates realize that the odds are against them if they continue criminal behavior.

There are many programs that attempt to get the jail inmate to realize that his or her ways of thinking must change. The challenge in this type of programming is to integrate other programming factors into this one process. Criminal thinking is influenced by such negative factors such as substance abuse, lack of educational skills, and little or no vocational skills. The problem must be attacked from many angles, using a combination of programs and resources.

One such program is the "Recovery in a Secure Environment (RISE)" program at the Henrico County (VA) Regional Jail East, located near Richmond, Virginia. The jail is one of two in the system, (the other is the Henrico Regional Jail West) with a total average daily population of 1,100 inmates. The inmate population of the Regional Jail East is approximately 400 inmates. A survey indicated that 74 percent of inmates in the two jails were incarcerated as a result of drug and alcohol involvement. The RISE program is described as a "social model recovery" program and helps inmates in changing destructive lifestyle patterns. The program owes its success and development to a progressive sheriff with a master's degree in rehabilitative counseling, cooperation with Henrico Mental Health and Substance Abuse Services, a new jail designed for rehabilitation, professionally trained jail deputies, and an effective vocational/educational staff. Inmate involvement is voluntary, and inmates can ask to leave at any time. As long as an inmate meets minimal standards of program involvement and participation and also obeys the rules of the jail, he can remain in the program for the duration of his jail stay.[26]

The RISE program commenced in August 2000 with the start of a 36-bed direct supervision pod housing the "Project Fresh Start" program. In this separate program unit, a 12-hour day schedule includes activities and daily community (in unit) meetings where constructive behavior, civility, and recovery from addictive behavior are discussed. Six senior member inmates are democratically elected by the inmates in the pod. Inmates get a sense of ownership and empowerment in the program. As it is a direct supervision unit, a deputy sheriff is assigned to the unit at all times to ensure compliance with jail rules and security procedures. Henrico Mental Health/Substance Abuse jail team members conduct activities with the inmates throughout the week.[27]

As the waiting list grew for the program, the sheriff approved another 44-bed pod opening up in March 2002. The new six-week program was named "Project Hope" and is a 14-hour per day program, facilitating many groups developed from the leadership from Project Fresh Start. Over time, Project Hope with its Intensive Addiction Focus program became Phase 1 and Project Fresh Start became Phase 2. Both pods became filled, and a 36-bed unit was added in August 2002. This program that became Phase 3 was called "New Direction: A Successful Living Program" and primarily focuses on life skills, transition and reentry back into the community, preventing relapse, and contributing to the community. To help the inmate reenter the community, a Phase 4 was begun for the work release unit at Henrico Jail West. Phase 4 includes involvement with Henrico County's drug court, outpatient services by Henrico Mental Health and Substance Abuse Services, and an alumni group of offenders who have completed the program called "The Going Home Group." [28]

One program that has a good relationship with jails in its jurisdiction is Offender Aid and Restoration, Inc. (OAR), of Arlington County, Virginia. OAR is a private, non-profit organization and has been assisting inmates, ex-inmates, and their families since 1974. OAR provides a wide range of services: alternative sentencing options, programs for inmates and ex-inmates, and a volunteer program. OAR's goal is to reduce recidivism, build family stability, and enhance the life of the community by turning inmates' lives around. The OAR movement started in Richmond, Virginia, in 1968 and was incorporated as OAR/USA in 1973. OAR/USA has affiliated, but autonomous offices in four states. OAR of Arlington conducts programs and coordinates volunteer services in the Arlington County (VA) Detention Center and the Alexandria (VA) Detention Center. OAR programs for inmates are diverse, non-traditional, revolutionary, and reflect a proactive approach to the problem of inmate recidivism. Jail programs include the following:[29]

- *Impact of Crime:* The Impact of Crime (IOC) program takes a restorative justice approach to criminal behavior, bringing together the inmates and crime victims. Inmates are then required to understand the consequences of what they have done and crime's impact on victims and the community. Each IOC group completes a community service project both to provide restitution and educate the public on the consequences of crime.
- *Employability Readiness Program:* This jail-based vocational skills program teaches inmates how to find employment, how to keep a job, how to be a good employee, problem solving, budgeting, goal setting, and planning a future career.

- *Women Empowered for Change:* This program (WEC) is designed to assist women inmates in overcoming barriers that lead them to being rearrested and reincarcerated. Female inmates have different treatment needs than men. WEC programs are offered inside a 14-bed living unit. Female inmates attend groups and classes dealing with such topics as anger and stress management, domestic violence, parenting, assertive communication, substance abuse and recovery, AA and NA meetings, women's health, employment readiness, legal issues/rights, managing money, parenting, assertiveness training, conflict resolution, building self esteem, and using community resources. After release, female offenders continue to receive support through domestic violence programs, substance abuse recovery programs, public assistance, housing and shelter, assistance with transportation and employment, and identification services.[30]
- *MASTERS:* This program, offered in a 36-bed housing unit, is designed to assist male offenders in pursuit of physical, mental, and social stability. The "Men Acquiring Skills to Evolve and Return to Society" (MASTERS) program includes presentations, classes, and groups on many of the same topics as in the WEC program, but from a man's point of view. Also, MASTERS' participants are required to attend GED and ABE classes. Aftercare services are also similar to what is provided for WEC participants.[31]

OAR is a visionary organization, and through excellent working relationships with the Arlington and Alexandria jails, quality inmate programming and assistance are possible.

Thanks to OAR of Arlington, Inc. Gail Arnall, Executive Director.

**FIGURE 6-3** Offender Aid and Restoration: Fighting Crime by Changing Lives

One unique service for jail inmates soon to be released is the jail job fair, where prospective employers from the community meet with inmates in the jail who are in need of employment when they are released.

Photos by author, courtesy Alexandria Detention Center.

## Religious Programs

The freedom to practice and observe the religion of one's choosing is one of the most cherished rights that we have. Courts have been very protective of this right when it concerns jails. Jail security and safety still takes priority. However, jails do allow inmates to practice their faith and attend religious programs within reason.

As inmates of different faiths enter the jail, it is important that the chaplaincy services and programs afforded to inmates are from a **non-denominational chaplain's staff.** Non-denominational simply means that the jail chaplain does not promote one particular faith and is knowledgeable in all religions. For example, a jail chaplain may be Baptist by faith, but when ministering to jail inmates, he or she is neutral. This neutrality also means that the chaplain encourages inmates to practice their faith and take advantage of the chaplain's programs and services, all in an effort to facilitate behavior in the inmate who respects others, encourages spiritual growth, and leads to self-reflection on their acts that led them to jail.

The chaplain's office provides to the inmate population many different religious programs in the forms of Bible studies, worship services, etc. Due to being non-denominational, many chaplain's programs are of recognized faiths, such as Roman Catholic, Protestant, Islam, and Judaism. Programs of this nature must be approved not only by the chaplain but also by the jail programs staff, who also schedules them throughout the week.

One important factor in the chaplain's programs is equal opportunity. While in a jail, it is not possible to have all of the programs and services that inmates of a

Inmate Chapel, used for religious services.

Photo by author, courtesy of Sheriff Michael G. Bellotti and Deputy Superintendent David Reilly of the Norfolk County Sheriff's Office.

particular faith would like, it is important to offer a variety of programs to inmates of different faiths. For example, a jail religious program schedule may offer Catholic Mass and Protestant Worship for Christian inmates, a Hebrew service on Saturdays for Jewish inmates, and a Friday Jumah service for Muslim inmates. Supporting these worship services are religious education programs such as Bible studies, Islamic study or prayer programs, Catholic Rosary, etc. At times of religious holidays, such as Christmas, Easter, Ramadan, etc., the jail chaplain may coordinate special religious programs such as Christmas services, a special Catholic Mass, Easter Service, and Islamic services at Ramadan.

Some jails have only one chaplain, depending on funding and the size of the jail. Large jails may staff the chaplain's office with two chaplains. As a rule, chaplains are ordained clergy and must supply credentials attesting to this. Chaplains and their staffs undergo security jail training, as they are a part of the jail's security network. Besides coordinating religious programs, jail chaplains perform a variety of functions inside the jail, including

- Performing death notifications to inmates.
- Performing spiritual counseling to inmates.
- Providing religious reading material of all faiths to inmates.
- Working with the jail administration and local clergy concerning clergy visits, donations of religious materials, and recruitment of volunteers.
- Approving all material and curriculum for religious classes.
- Helping troubled inmates to adjust to jail life.
- Assisting staff in working with suicidal inmates.
- Aiding jail staff in times of crisis, such as a death in the family.

- Advising staff of observed or suspected security concerns.
- Conducting cell visitation to inmates who cannot attend religious activities.
- Confirming and approving inmate requests for special religious diets.

In order to keep the jail climate positive, chaplains should approach inmates with acceptance, understanding, and compassion, and not one of harsh judgment. Through the activities of chaplains, visiting clergy, and religious volunteers, inmates can feel that someone cares, someone will listen to what they have to say, and may express feelings of guilt and shame about their crime. In terms of rehabilitation, the chaplains and staff attempt to instill within the inmates what all a religions desire: a message of divine grace, reconciliation, sincere repentance, forgiveness, a life of moral discipline, ethical behavior, and being personally responsible to oneself, friends, and loved ones. If inmates can be made to see those qualities and live by them, while inside the jail or upon release, the chaplain can be a powerful correctional tool.[32]

Chaplains, their staffs, and volunteers can be targets of inmate manipulators, who feign good behavior and intentions by attending numerous religious programs. They may appear devout and sincere, but secretly have an agenda to persuade a religious volunteer to bring in contraband, perform favors, or bend the rules. Some inmates may be called **copycats,** imitating what religion other inmates are practicing. They also may want rosary beads, religious books, prayer rugs, etc. that other inmates have. It may be a form of status to be part of a religion that is being practiced by others. Chaplains, through their education, are familiar enough with many religions, so that the copycat can be asked questions to ascertain their sincerity. A good rule of thumb is to ask the inmate the requirements of the religion, its sacraments and liturgy. Local clergy can assist the jail chaplain in doing this.[33]

The chaplain's office at the Jefferson County Detention Center in Golden, Colorado, handles many important duties concerning religion and inmates that illustrates the important role that chaplains perform in the local jail. Community religious practitioners are recruited from the major and minor faiths in the community. Through a month long process involving a criminal history background check, integrity interview, training and orientation, personal references, ordination certificate, and medical information, the person is designated a chaplain's volunteer. Inmates entering the jail and request a visit with a clergy person from his or her faith receive a visit from a clergy volunteer within one to two days. Some clergy who work with the chaplain are trained in pastoral psychology, have masters' degrees in social work, or doctorates in psychology. They perform one-on-one counseling and teach classes in parenting, addiction recovery, meditation, effective communication, spiritual formation, and anger management. When an inmate requests to see a particular priest, imam, pastor, etc., the clergy resource person will ask the inmate-specific questions to see whether they are legitimate members of that faith.[34]

All chaplaincy classes conducted at the jail are ecumenical and interfaith, and the Bible classes are of a generic Judeo-Christian perspective and not extreme. The purpose of the chaplain's office is to educate, share information, to help inmates develop their faiths, but not to have any particular religious group proselytize. Sincerity is important and must be shown by the inmates if they want to learn about a faith. Knowledge of a religion is critical. If inmates want to attend a Catholic Mass and receive rosary beads, they are asked when they were baptized

*Providing Chaplains to America's Jails and Prisons*

There are many organizations in the United States providing religious services to inmates in jails and prisons. One of the oldest is the Good News Jail and Prison Ministry, based in Richmond, Virginia. Originally formed in December 1961, the Good News Ministry had its beginnings with one chaplain at a jail in northern Virginia. It has now grown to provide over 400 staff chaplains to 276 jails and prisons in 23 states, plus 19 countries and one U.S. territory.[36]

Good News Ministry works with local churches, other religious organizations, and volunteers. It is funded not by tax dollars but by donations from grants, churches, individuals, businesses, and foundations. Thanks to the support and participation of clergy and citizen volunteers, inmates who participate in numerous jail religious activities. Two such activities are the Bible Correspondence Course and the Life Learning Block.

The Bible Correspondence Course was developed by Good News and consists of 184 individual Bible studies, each having four pages of questions. The inmates look up the answers in the Bible and will gain a greater understanding of the Bible and how it can help them.[37] The Life Learning Program is a Biblically centered program designed to bring about positive change in inmates and showing them that thoughts, attitudes, and actions that they have exhibited can be turned around. It can be housed in a unit and uses the services of clergy and volunteers. Topics of the program include getting along with people, forgiveness, handling being in jail/prison and getting out, and responsibility and accountability to family and authority.[38]

Organizations such as the Good News Jail and Prison Ministry, its affiliated churches and organizations, and religious volunteers serve two valuable purposes: inspiring hope in inmates who are serious about changing their lives and helping to maintain a positive climate in the jail.

Thanks to Good News Jail and Prison Ministry, Harry L. Greene, President and CEO at www.goodnewsjail.org.

**FIGURE 6-4** Good News Jail and Prison Ministry

and confirmed, to what parish they belong, who their priest is, and to recite the Lord's Prayer and say the "Hail Mary's."[35]

Some religious groups are aggressive and wish to enter a jail, make the rounds of the cellblocks and recruit inmates into their faiths, forgetting that a jail is a secure confinement facility and non-denominational. If a clergy member from such a group wishes to see an inmate of that faith, the jail staff can authorize certain protocols under which such a visit can take place, the main protocol being if the inmate actually is of that faith and wants to see the clergy member.

## Vocational Programs

Inmates can learn a trade in jail, even though the media has portrayed prison shops and factories as the main vocational opportunities for inmates. In some jails, inmates have learned cooking, custodial/cleaning skills, upholstering, and have found jobs on the outside through such services as job fairs, where prospective employers come to the jail and meet with inmates. The ability of a jail to sponsor a vocational program depends on the availability of instructors knowledgeable in the field, the funding available to purchase equipment and class materials, space available to house the program, and most importantly, the ability to provide security and supervision. These programs use tools and items that could become useful to inmates as weapons if they are lost, misplaced, or stolen.

A partnership with a local college and a jail resulting in an inmate vocation program is in Harris County, Texas. Nearly 30 years ago, the Harris County Sheriff's Office teamed with the Houston Community College Northeast to form the Harris County Inmate Education Program. The program enrolls approximately 3,500 inmate-students per year and was the first county jail to receive national certification from the Correctional Education Association. Program instructors come from the college, and the sheriff's office staffs the program with a director, assistant director, and security personnel. Classroom space is provided by the sheriff's office and a multi-million dollar vocational facility was built in 2000 for the program. The Inmate Education Program offers ABE classes, GED preparation classes, a Workforce Literacy Course, and vocational Workforce Training Classes.[39]

Each vocational training course is 11 weeks long, and the inmates who successfully complete the course are awarded a certificate that they can use to be marketable and find gainful employment in the community. Inmates who attend classes for six hours per day, five days per week can earn certificates in more than one trade if they are incarcerated for a length of time. Vocations include heating and refrigeration, graphic arts, welding, sewing, cooking, construction, horticulture, upholstery, auto bodywork, offset printing, and building maintenance. Inmates perform work for the sheriff's office by reupholstering furniture and printing, which saves the county money.[40]

A barber program is offered at the Prince George's County Correctional Center in Upper Marlboro, Maryland. As of 2002, the program had a spotless infraction record and was strongly supported by the security staff. It is self-supporting because of fees charged to the inmates for receiving haircuts from the trainees. The program has a low recidivism rate of 15 percent. Every inmate-student is placed in a full-time job upon release, and most pass the state licensing examination. The instructor interviews all applicants and works with each inmate-student for approximately 850 hours of the 1,200 hours needed to apply for a state barber's license. Working in a local barbershop after release makes up the rest of the 1,200 hours.[41]

Inmate applicants are screened by the jail's treatment assessment board for suitability. Inmates enrolling in the barber program must have four to five months of incarcerated time remaining to serve, must be a non-violent offender (if a violent offense was omitted over ten years ago, the inmate may be considered for the program), no outstanding warrants or detainers (which could hinder job placement), and a good jail record free of infractions. The instructor, Phil Mazza, tracks inmates for 18 months in the community following their release and keeps in close contact with community barbershop owners.[42]

Inmates can learn a trade while producing goods for the private sector. This is possible due to the **Private Sector Prison Industries Enhancement Act Certification Program (PIECP).** Created by Congress nearly 20 years ago, it is based on 18 U.S.C. 1761 (c), which authorizes correctional agencies to engage in the shipment of goods made in jail or prison for sale on an open market. Inmates must be paid at a similar wage not less than the wage for the same work in the community; inmate employment does not displace workers outside the correctional facility and does not occur in occupations where there is a surplus of jobs in the community. Participation in PIECP cannot impair or harm existing contracts for services. Local labor organizations and competitor manufacturers must be told of the jail/private business partnership before work begins. Jails in Stafford County, New Hampshire and Utah County, Utah, have experienced financial success with the programs, each earning over $1 million in inmate wages and generating hundreds of thousands of dollars in room and board fees paid by inmates. Not only do inmates learn a trade, but they can use their wages to make restitution to victims, support their families, and pay state and federal taxes.[43]

### Health Programs

Due to the dangerous practices of the inmate lifestyle, such as intravenous drug use, sexual promiscuity, and lack of hygiene and health care, inmate health programs are important. Inmates see first hand how their lives are endangered through the lack of good judgment when it concerns their health. Health care staff can be recruited from the local health agency to provide instruction. One method is the use of a health and wellness fair, which has been conducted in the Palm Beach County, Florida jail. The main goal of the fair was to inform inmates about resources in the community that would benefit their health and medical needs. Twenty-eight exhibitors attended the February 1999 fair. Organizations and agencies on hand included the American Red Cross, the American Lung Association, the American Diabetes Association, Nutrition Services, Healthy Mothers-Healthy Babies, and the Center for Information and Crisis.[44]

There are factors that affect programs that the programs staff has little or no control over. One is the lack of classroom space. There may not be enough classrooms for the amount of programs desired. Classrooms may be used for multiple programs—church, substance abuse, etc. A programs schedule with specific times during the week is necessary to ensure that classrooms are getting the maximum use possible. All programs staff has to work together on sharing of classrooms.

Lack of funding is another factor. The inmate commissary fund is a good way to equip programs, and that money cannot be wasted. Only materials that are both absolutely necessary and will be used extensively should be used.

Another hindrance to inmate programs is the varying length of time that inmates stay in the jail. Some stay for 90 days, some six months, etc. or are transferred to other jails and to the departments of correction. As a result, they do not finish programs. The best that can be hoped for is that they continue with rehabilitation efforts once released to another facility or into the community.

## CUSTODY AND PROGRAMS STAFF RELATIONS

For jail programs to work, three groups of jail staff must work together: the custody staff, the civilian programs staff, and the volunteers. Volunteers can be considered staff due to receiving clearances, specialized security training, identification, and access to certain areas of the jail. Volunteers, however, have no authority inside the jail other than supervising inmates inside the classroom or vocational training areas.

Custody staff, including classification, can determine whether an inmate is eligible to attend programs and can write rules and regulations governing inmate conduct while attending programs. With the exception of court orders, program attendance by inmates is generally voluntary. The general guidelines are

- Inmate is in general population, on administrative segregation with clearance to attend, or a member of the work force (trusty).
- If on Administrative Segregation, the reason does not preclude program attendance (such as protective custody, mentally ill and not cleared by mental health, has serious medical problem, etc.)
- Inmate is not a disciplinary problem, a behavioral problem, or have adjustment problems concerning other inmates, staff, and authority.
- Inmate is not an escape risk.
- Inmate is not a high-risk prisoner (examples include gang/STG member, violent crime, facing a long sentence, the death penalty, serious detainers, etc.)
- Inmate has a critical need for the program.
- Program is court ordered.

In special cases such as behavioral problems, high-risk inmates, etc., the ICC determines whether the inmate can attend programs (see Chapter 5). For example, a leader in a street gang or security threat group requests to go to education classes. The custody or program staff can recommend a formal ICC hearing to decide the matter. The critical issue is if the inmate attends, other inmates use this as getting together for meetings. Or, if an inmate is charged with murder and is facing the death penalty or a life sentence, the issue is staff safety over the needs and wants of the inmate. In such a case, the inmate may look for means to escape, obtain contraband, or take a hostage. The ICC may deny program involvement, as staff safety is the overriding priority. In such cases where high-risk inmates cannot attend programs, programs staff can take programs material and work to their cell, with custody/program sworn staff approval.

In cases of court orders, if the inmate is not eligible because of a disciplinary problem for example, the programs or classification staff must notify the sentencing judge in writing of the reason(s) that the program is denied. Judges usually leave these matters to the jail staff but should know in detail that the inmate is a problem, etc. Normally an ICC hearing is held to discuss the situation, and the decision of the ICC is included in the letter to the judge.

Inmates can remove themselves from a program, or be removed by the programs staff, the custody staff, or at the request of a volunteer conducting a program. Some inmates think that programs are too much work, a "hassle," or a waste of time. Conversely, an inmate can be removed if he or she is not putting forth any effort, are misbehaving, being disruptive, or not following the programs rules.

Custody staff and programs staff must work together. Jail officers must be made aware of the positive effects that programs have on the jail climate and the inmate sense of well-being. Jail officers have the responsibility of letting inmates out of their housing areas for programs, escorting them to the programs area, and monitoring the classes for signs of inmate misconduct. Programs civilian staff must closely supervise inmates in their classes, report any misconduct, send inmates back to their housing units on time, and obey the security regulations of the jail. Also important is both staffs engaging in mutual reporting of inmate actions. If the inmate's classification file contains reports of maladaptive behavior or unusual conduct filed by both staffs, well-informed decisions can be made about inmates' suitability for participation in programs.

Not all jail officers think that programs are worthwhile. Due to the stress of the job, manipulative inmates, and seeing the same inmates return over and over, hard-core attitudes may take form among the jail staff. Supervisors must ensure that these attitudes do not manifest themselves in such actions as not getting inmates for programs, condescending remarks to inmates and programs staff, etc. Programs staff should include custody supervisors at staff meetings, present programs information at roll call training, and introduce themselves to the jail officers in their areas. Program staff and volunteers must remember that the security of the jail is the jail officers' primary function and must obey without reservation all security regulations.

Programs staff through two-way communication with the custody staff and, in observations about their jobs, must understand that discipline plays a key role in jail security. If an inmate breaks the rules, a punishment that he or she may experience is the removal from inmate programs. If an inmate is halfway through the GED program course of study and incurs a serious infraction, is found guilty, and receives disciplinary segregation time, he is removed from the GED program. The same is true for AA, NA, and other programs. If the inmates break the rules, then all of the work that they have done in programs is for naught. Programs staff may find it useful to instill in the inmates attending programs the importance of adhering to discipline.

## Volunteers: A Valuable Resource

A primary reason that jail programs are very successful is due to the involvement of citizen volunteers. Volunteers come from all walks of life, and lend their life experiences to helping inmates stay crime free. Programs that volunteers are active in include AA, NA, GED Preparation, ESL, church programs, worship services, Bible Studies, Life Skills, vocational training, etc. The jail may require volunteers to complete an application, have references, and be subject to a background/criminal history check.

Ex-offenders can be a valuable volunteer resource, if the jail administration allows their entry. Ex-offenders see through the inmate manipulations, game playing, and denial. Many AA and NA group leaders are ex-offenders because of having an arrest record for substance abuse and related crimes. While some jail officials do not want ex-offenders inside the jail, they can be a valuable resource and get the message of rehabilitation through to the inmates. If they are allowed in, the jail may place requirements on them such as being crime free for a long time, be off of probation or parole, have no outstanding court cases pending, be substance abuse free, and have supporting documentation from probation or parole officers, community and program leaders, corrections officials, etc.

Training is critical to be an effective volunteer and must be conducted by veteran sworn and programs staff. The training agenda may include such topics as:

- Jail security procedures and staffing.
- Jail emergency procedures.

- Jail operations and program schedules.
- Proper use and retention of identification badges.
- Jail areas approved for volunteer entry.
- Retention of belongings.
- Inmate sub-culture and criminal thinking.
- Inmate manipulation.

Jail-sworn staff may set the frequency of volunteer training, the maximum number of volunteers, volunteer rules and regulations, and reasons for suspending, reprimanding, or terminating a volunteer.

POINT OF VIEW

## Quality Jail Services: Keeping Jails Secure

*Mondre Kornegay*
Commander, Inmate Services, Alexandria (VA) Detention Center

Jail services strengthen jail security. The effectiveness and efficiency in which jail services are delivered impact immeasurably the secure operation of any jail facility. Quality jail services enhance inmates' quality of life, and therefore, reduce stress, anxiety, and resentment. Without the quality jail services, inmates are left to languish in their cells and dayrooms with little to do other than contemplate how to circumvent facility security, create conflict or inflict injury on staff and other inmates.

Well-run facilities take seriously their mandate to offer satisfying meals and quality medical services, recognizing that through the adequate provision of these basic services, inmates are reminded of their humanity and their value as human beings. Well-run facilities provide a myriad of inmate programming that meets the needs of their populations, recognizing that the seeds for change can be planted through jail incarceration. According to the BJS in 1999, more than half of the jails in this country addressed inmates' needs for secondary education and provided in-house substance abuse programs. Two-thirds of jails offered religious or spiritual counseling programs. Why do such facilities choose to provide these services to their inmates? They do it because they recognize the value of investing in activities, resources, and systems that enhance inmate satisfaction, reduce conflict, and create an environment for positive change.

Yet still, some jail facilities fail to provide adequate medical services to its inmates. They fail to recognize their mandate is to provide inmate access to quality services as well as the benefits to the secure operation of their facilities once those services are provided. According to the National Commission on Correctional Health Care's website, "based upon more than 20 years of intensive evaluation of health care systems in jails and prisons, [the] lack of access to health care is a serious problem in detention and correctional institutions."

### Why Provide Quality Jail Services?

Providing quality services such as food that tastes good and is filling and medical care that is compassionately and competently given lets inmates know that they are indeed human beings worthy of receiving the quality of life that mainstream citizens enjoy every day. Inmates are, after all, the mothers, fathers, sisters, brothers, neighbors, and cousins of people we know. Outside of their jumpsuits, they are likely to be at the local movie theater and eat at your neighborhood McDonalds. They are our waiters, cooks, construction workers and janitors, and sometimes our teachers, lawyers, doctors, and government workers. As citizens of our localities, inmates have similar expectations for respect and access to those good things that society provides its citizens. Their expectations do not fade away into a nebulous cloud of smoke once they become incarcerated. Indeed, inmates often come to jail with expectations that far exceed what they should expect or what they are entitled to. One thing is clear—inmates desire that their basic needs will be met and that they will be treated in a manner that esteems their personhood.

Quality services enhance a secure facility by providing a structure for inmate behavioral change. Most individuals booked into jail do not wish to be there and often resent the exercise of authority over them by jail staff. They are separated from family and friends and locked into a routine that takes away their basic freedoms and right to choose. They are angry.

Inmate programs help diffuse inmate anger at the criminal justice system and their personal circumstances. Programs enhance positive behavioral adjustment and serve a strong behavioral modification function. Inmates who participate in programs are working on issues that brought them into the criminal justice system. They are achieving educationally, developing life skills, and building for the future. They are learning to work with people without conflict. Without these opportunities, inmates have no stimuli to challenge them to do better or be better. Without this challenge, they have only street behavior to mimic during their incarceration, behavior that is self-destructive and disruptive to jail operations. Jail programs, then, serve an important purpose by creating opportunities for inmate behavioral modification and positive jail adjustment.

Quality health care and food services, while they do not create the infrastructure for change in the same manner as inmate rehabilitation programs, do affect strongly the ability of security staff to manage inmates. Inmates often come to jail after ignoring health problems evident prior to their incarceration. These reasons include active substance abuse, lack of money to pay for services and ignorance as to how to access those services. Once incarcerated, however, inmates have the time and inclination to seek help for their medical woes. Without the stimuli of street life, inmates can concentrate more on what is happening with and to their bodies. Fear and concern now drive them, and such emotions heighten their anxiety and defensiveness. They not only seek medical care; they demand it, expecting services above and beyond that which they could expect in the community, and on unrealistic timetables. If they had a doctor on the outside, they want the exact medicine their community doctor prescribed and are convinced that if the jail physician prescribes anything else, the medication will not work, and they are being inadequately treated. They look for next day test results when those tests, if taken at the community clinic, would take two weeks to receive the results.

Notwithstanding the constitutional safeguards concerning inmate medical care, it is incumbent upon jails to provide medical services that are timely, efficient and that allow for full communication between the inmate and the medical treatment providers. Timely, so that inmates have test results and follow-up care on timetables that are reasonable and, as much as possible, consistent with what was told the inmate. If medications prescribed are different from that which the inmate was taking on the street, medical staff are open to explaining why this new medication is being prescribed, and if applicable, its benefits. Yes, this does take a little more time, but the cost is reasonable given the benefits reaped in fewer inmate assaults, complaints, and conflict.

The same goes for food services. Portions that are too small or inconsistent and poor food quality create housing unit beggars, gamblers, and conflict. Caloric portions must meet dietary guidelines for the populations housed at the jail, and meal preparations overseen by trained food services staff. Food must be palatable, fresh, and with variety.

## Jail Services and Inmate Accountability

While jail administrators have the responsibility to provide services that are fit for use by their inmates, quality services does not require the burden for their provision to rest solely upon jail staff. Inmates must accept accountability for their own health and welfare just as free citizens, although that accountability takes a different form while incarcerated. One such example is the fee for service medical care program. While it is an established practice to have inmate workers in kitchens preparing facility meals, the debate continues as to whether inmates should "pay" for medical services under fee for service programs. Both create opportunities for inmates to assume shared responsibility for the services they consume. Structured correctly so that services are provided despite the inmate's ability to pay, medical fees for service programs do not hinder access to services, but rather force the inmate to make mature choices as to the services they receive. They reduce frivolous complaints and overuse of services while at the same time cut the costs for providing services, because the burden on the medical provider systems is reduced.

### Quality Jail Services: A Description

What do quality jail services look like? How can jail managers be confident that what their jail offers meets standards of acceptability?

All services, whether mandated food, medical or mental health services, or rehabilitative or recreational programs, must meet the identified needs of the particular jail's inmate population. Periodic assessments must be made of inmate use patterns of the jails' programs and services. Jail administrators should be able to identify what service needs tax their service delivery systems, what services are underused as well as the efficiency and efficacy of those services. Such assessments help ensure that the services provided match the identified needs of the inmates housed in their facilities. Targeting services accurately and appropriately delivering them result in lower costs and higher service efficacy.

Services must be held against industry standards. Food services, for example, should meet local health codes governing their preparation under staff trained, and preferably certified, in food service management. Caloric values and menus should be established by acceptable national or state dietetic standards. Such reviews ensure that the facility meets correctional standards governing the provision of the reviewed service. Standards set by the American Correctional Association, for instance, provide acceptable guidelines for jail administrators to ensure that their service and program delivery systems meet levels of acceptability by corrections professionals and constitutional mandates. Similarly, the National Commission on Correctional Health Care governs the provision of medical services, providing standards for health care delivery systems. Local jails are encouraged to adopt standards set by these national accrediting agencies and/or in-state accreditation programs.

Lastly, jail services should be augmented by volunteers. This is especially true for rehabilitative and recreational programming, although trained volunteers can assist medical and mental health staff in their areas of certification to reduce costs and provide a wider range of services. Volunteers bring the community into facility and keep the inmates connected with the outside world. They provide social civility that many inmates lack due their current lifestyles and prior life experiences.

### Summary

Jail services are essential for secure and orderly management of jail facilities. They soften edges, soothe fears, meet the physical, emotional, and spiritual needs of inmates, and provide for their very sustenance. If done right, jail services create an environment that transforms an inmate's jail time to one of self-reflection and opportunity for change. Without adequate services, jail environments become hostile places of punishment that become unsafe for jail staff and inmates. Ideally, jails have the power to transform lives or at least plant the seeds for change. I challenge jail practitioners to create in their facilities, through their jail services programs, environments that enhance positive behavioral change, that recognize the humanity of all inmates, and that create a safe environment for both staff and inmates. Providing quality jail services can do just that.

Thanks to Mondre Kornegay, Commander, Inmate Services, Alexandria Detention Center. Also, special thanks to former Sheriff James Dunning and current Sheriff Dana Lawhorne.

## JAIL SERVICES

There is a difference between the terms jail programs and jail services. Popular thinking dictates that jail programs and jail services are one in the same. **Jail services** (as differentiated from programs, but related) are services offered to inmates to aid in their rehabilitation or to assist them in some way. Examples of jail services include health care services, food services, recreation, mail, commissary, laundry, barber, property, the leisure library, and the law library.

According to the Bureau of Justice Statistics *Census of Jails*, 1999, released in August 2001, the following are the number and percentage of jails in the United States that have a program or policy for health care and mental health services:

| | Number of Jails | Percentage |
|---|---|---|
| *Health Care Delivery Systems* | | |
| Inmate fee for service | 1,101 | 39 |
| On site health/medical staff | 882 | 31 |
| Managed care | 500 | 18 |
| Local government physicians | 338 | 12 |
| *Mental Health Services* | | |
| Intake screening | 2,152 | 78 |
| Psychotropic medication | 1,832 | 66 |
| 24-Hour care | 1,309 | 47 |
| Routine therapy and counseling | 1,283 | 46 |
| Psychiatric evaluation | 1,044 | 38 |

A new trend in jails is charging the inmate a fee for medical services such as sick call. The 1999 figure will most likely increase in future jail surveys. A positive note is that most jails have some type of mental health screening at intake and have access to psychotropic medications to make them more manageable for the jail staff.[45]

**FIGURE 6-5** State of Jail Services, 1999

## Health Care Services

When inmates are incarcerated in the local jail, they are deprived from the opportunity to seek and choose medical care. The jurisdiction, i.e., the local jail assumes responsibility for their physical, dental, and mental health needs. Failure by the jail to adequately care for these needs may be viewed as cruel and unusual punishment. Each jail should have some type of health authority. As all jails are different, the health authority could be a physician, health administrator, government agency, or a private health service contractor.[46]

No two inmates entering the jail are alike medically. Inmates have been booked in having substance abuse withdrawal, skin disorders, cancer, diabetes, heart conditions, malnourishment, dental problems, ear infections, colds, influenza, ear, nose and throat infections, kidney problems needing dialysis, nausea, diarrhea, broken limbs, scabies, crabs, lice, and so on—the list is endless. Some inmates are handicapped physically, visually and have hearing disorders. Some have more serious conditions that can be contagious to other inmates and staff, such as HIV, tuberculosis, hepatitis B and C, or some other type of communicable disease. Inmates may also be suffering from injuries that are not life threatening but need medical attention.

Due to these factors, it is imperative that all inmates are screened by the medical staff as soon as possible after arrival. Medical screening determines the overall state of their health, whether any conditions exist that need treatment and whether the staff and/or inmates are in any danger health wise from a disease or condition that they may be suffering from. Other issues are whether the inmate requires medication, whether he or she has medication with them, etc.

Not all jail medical facilities are spacious; many have to make do with space available.

Photo by author, courtesy Bristol County Ash Street Facility.

With female inmates, pregnancy is a major concern. The jail environment is not conducive to a normal, healthy pregnancy. As much information as possible must be found out about the female's pre-natal condition, so that the baby is not in danger in any way. The pregnant female inmate may be experiencing drug withdrawals or may not have been taking proper care of herself on the outside. With many inmates engaged in the criminal lifestyle, proper medical and dental care is not a priority.

Jail medical staffs try to keep track of incoming inmates and see them to least get an initial intake screening as soon as possible. The initial medical screening can take place in several areas—at the booking desk where booking staff first meets the inmate, the first contact with the medical staff, and the classification interview.

A full medical screening is conducted as soon as possible after the inmate arrives. This is a combination of specific questions about the inmate's current and past medical history, tests (such as tests for sexually transmitted diseases and tuberculosis), a physical exam, and observations.[47] The medical staff may also inquire about the mental state of the inmate—whether he or she is acting irrationally or dangerous. If a mental condition is observed or suspected, the inmate is referred to qualified mental health staff. If the inmate refuses to cooperate with the screening, he or she will not be permitted to live in the jail's general population until they do cooperate. Some inmates refuse due to mental illness, while some do as a sign of defiance. If an inmate commences a hunger strike, jail medical staff regularly weighs the inmate and monitors his or her condition.

Medical staff can authorize the inmate to be segregated due to a mental or medical condition, pending follow up by staff. Medical staff keeps informed on inmates on segregation. This segregation may be in the jail intake/receiving area a special unit or a dispensary. An up-to-date jail dispensary is a type of mini hospital with separate, secure rooms, examining rooms for medical and dental exams, secure storage for pharmaceuticals, and negative pressure rooms to guard against airborne spread of disease. Jail dispensaries are also staffed by jail officers—just because an inmate in the dispensary does not mean that he or she is any less an inmate and not wanting to escape.

Two important medical services are sick call and medication runs. **Sick call** is a designated time in the jail operational schedule when inmates see the medical staff, nurse, and/or doctor for any observed or reported (by staff or inmate) medical problem. Medication can be prescribed, the inmate may be moved to the local hospital, jail dispensary, or be approved to see an outside doctor. **Medication runs** take place when the medical staff makes its rounds in the jail living areas to dispense medications. Jails with large inmate populations find it more feasible to take the medication cart around to the inmates; while jails with small inmate populations may call inmates to the dispensary to receive medications. When dispensing medications, the medical staff must ensure that the inmate actually took the medication and will not hoard it later for a suicide attempt.

Medical personnel also respond to medical emergencies involving staff, inmates, or visitors. In cases of inmates being restrained due to an assault or fight, medical staff will check the inmates' restraints, treat any injuries, and authorize transport to the local hospital.

Jail medical staff must meet the guidelines of the local health care authority and state jail standards. More jails are being accredited by the American Correctional Association and the National Commission on Correctional Health Care (see Chapter 10).

Jail medical emergencies can be other than inmate fights and injuries. In 2003, the Manatee County, Florida Jail had a staph (*Staphylococcus aureus* bacterium) infection to deal with. Only two of the 1,000 inmates in the jail at the time tested positive, 83 other inmates were quarantined and were observed for signs of infection. Inmates showing signs of possible staph infection were isolated in one of the jails' "pods" and placed on a 10-day antibiotic regimen. The jail's health service, Prison Health Services, handled the situation.[48]

Medical staff also attends the daily meetings of the ICC where housing assignments, trusty assignments, and other inmate issues are discussed. Medical staff also medically approves all inmate work (trusty) assignments. They may request housing assignments for medical reasons such as low bunks due to pregnancy, physical handicaps, and seizures. Medical personnel also clear inmates from administrative and medical segregation if their medical conditions improve or if they cooperate in their screening and physical exam.

As local jails become more crowded and sophisticated, jail medical departments will come under increasing scrutiny. The standards of inmate health care must continue to be high. The following statistics can gauge the effectiveness of a jail's inmate health care:[49]

- Number of intake screenings, inmate physical exams, sick call (nurse, nurse practitioner, doctor), dental calls, encounters with physiologists and psychiatrists, medications prescribed to inmates, and inmates on psychotropic medications.
- Number of offsite (out of jail) visits: scheduled visits, emergency room visits, hospitalizations.
- Number of inpatient hospital days and psychiatric inpatient days.

In smaller temporary holding jails, meals are microwavable and ready to eat, which eases the staff workload.

Photo by author, courtesy Alameda City Jail.

- Number of inmates seen for chronic (ongoing) care clinics or appointments: hypertension, seizures, diabetes, pregnancy, infectious diseases, respiratory ailments, blood-borne pathogen exposures, tuberculosis (TB) test performed, number of positive TB tests.
- Number of grievances: received, resolved, and pending.

Other areas that jail medical staff should examine in an effort to provide quality medical care are policies and procedures, which should be revised annually if necessary. Current licensing status should be reviewed, and educational opportunities must be made available to the medical staff to keep up with health information, treatment methods, local, state, and federal laws concerning inmate health care, and ACA and NCCHC standards. Medical staff can also conduct informational programs to the inmates and the staff.

## Food Service

Another priority service to the jail is food. Meals are a temporary relief from the monotony of jail life. Inmates eat three meals per day, they get what is on the food tray, and there are no seconds. Breakfasts can be hot (such as pancakes or eggs) or cold (cereal and milk). In many jails, lunch is a simple sandwich, fruit, and a drink. Soup may be served on occasion. Inmate trusties assist the dieticians and cooks in preparing meals for the inmate population and the staff. Trusties eat better than the general inmate population, and inmates in the units may try to get trusties to smuggle food to them.

In some jails, a vendor is contracted to provide food service to the jail. It is important that all food service operations meet the requirements of the state and local food service guidelines, including those pertaining to jails. Menus are usually prepared under the supervision of a registered dietician at least one week in advance. Food supplies should be of the best quality possible, from approved vendors. Food should be stored properly in secure areas, and there should be a cold food storage locker on site. Sanitation is critical in the food preparation areas, and inmates who do not meet cleanliness guidelines should be removed from the kitchen. Adequate facilities to keep the area and the staff clean are a must.[50]

Food should be served as soon as possible after it is prepared. Warmers are used to bring the food to the housing areas. Even though many jails have dining areas, it is not feasible security wise to bring a large inmate population together as a group. Fights and arguments may occur, and jails generally do not have the manpower to adequately supervise large groups of inmates. There must be a control and accountability system for utensils, eating trays, cups, etc.[51] Jails may serve meals that require the minimum usage of utensils, such as sandwiches, fruit, cookies, etc. Regardless of what is used, the disposal by inmates of food utensils or collection by staff should be expedient, easily observed, and controlled.

Also, the jail custody staff cannot take the chance that inmates who should be kept separate from each other may end up in the same room at the same time. While the best security practices may be followed, one mistake in an inmate dining hall can be catastrophic where an inmate assaults, maybe fatally, his or her enemy.

## Recreation

**Recreation,** or more commonly called "gym," is an opportunity for inmates to engage in physical activity, sports, and games that are approved by the jail staff. Inmates' engaging in physical activities is called **active recreation.** Not every recreational activity is conducive to a jail setting. Team sports such as basketball and volleyball are usually allowed, but caution has to be used. Inmates have been known to argue while playing those games or use the physical contact and close proximity with other inmates to deliver clandestine assaults on other inmates. Physical activity can include exercise equipment such as aerobic treadmills, steppers, and stationary bicycles. Weight equipment can result in the inmates "bulking up" and contain many parts that if broken off or stolen could be used as weapons or as a means to tunnel, etc.

Recreation services to inmates also include what is termed **passive recreation.** Passive recreation services include board games such as checkers, chess, playing cards, etc. that are supplied to the inmate housing areas. Staff must ensure that these items are "tamper resistant," and game pieces that could be fashioned into items of contraband are removed. This is inconvenient to the inmates, but they usually find ways to adapt.

## Library Services

Another important area of inmate services is the library, which comprises two distinct parts. Reading material is important to inmates. Glancing through a magazine or reading a book is a distraction from the monotony of jail life. Leisure library services are usually included in jail programs sections, but they are actually a

Inmate recreation is a valuable service, relieves tension within the inmate population.

Photo by author, courtesy Baltimore City Central Booking and Intake Center.

related service. **Leisure library** services make quality reading material available to general population and administrative segregation inmates, usually through donations from citizens, civic groups, or through an acquisition agreement from the local library. Inmates may also receive reading material directly from the publisher (see Chapter 9). As a safety precaution, many jails allow inmates to have only paperback books. The weight and hardness of hardback books can be used by inmates to assault other inmates. Also, inmates have been known to place hardback books in laundry bags and use them as makeshift weights.

Magazines can be used by inmates for other purposes than for reading. Magazines can be "wet down," hardened and be used as a striking weapon. When searching and inspecting inmate property and living quarters, magazines and books must be inspected for unauthorized altering and hiding contraband. *All reading materials*, whether donated from citizens, the local library, or received from the publisher, *must* be searched and inspected for contraband and content. Reading material sent to inmates by inmates' families and friends should not be given to them for security reasons. Exceptions may be made for educational material if the inmate is in school and the material is coming from a teacher on the outside or the inmate's family. However, these requests must be looked at very carefully and documentation may be required. Generally, jail programs directors will have the authority to approve such material.

It is important that all reading materials—books and magazines—be screened for content and anything that can be used inappropriately by inmates. For example, inmates can take the "scratch and sniff" perfume and cologne advertisements out and use them on themselves. Content prohibitions in books and magazines include pornography, nudity, and strong sexual content, material that glorifies the criminal lifestyle or violence, and any content that the jail staff feels that are inappropriate for inmate reading.

Three other concerns concerning leisure libraries are space, demand, and foreign inmates. One is space. Many jails have limited space for the organization, storage, and categorization of reading material. Because of space and staffing limitations, reading material is brought to inmate housing areas by a volunteer, staff librarian, or inmate trusty. The second is the demand—many inmates request certain types of reading material or books. If the jail population is small, the administration may allow the granting of such requests. In large jails, inmates may only pick the reading material that is available on the book cart. The third concern is providing reading material to foreign inmates. Reading material must be obtained in languages such as Spanish, Farsi, Vietnamese, Chinese, and Korean. Jail librarians must take a look at the ethnic makeup of the jail population and obtain appropriate reading material in the languages that are represented.

The law library will be discussed more in detail in Chapter 9. The **law library** is a library that affords the inmates access to up–to-date legal references, court decisions, statutes, and opinions, so that they can participate in their own defense in court, file motions, pursue civil rights litigation, and conduct legal research. The jail staff can decide the hours of operation, group size of inmates, rules for the law library, etc. Jails may either use computers that hold legal data or stock the law library with printed volumes. Copy services are provided to the inmates using the law library. The jail staff can make copies of legal material or legal work that the inmates have done and may charge the inmate a fee for copies. If the inmate is segregated for administrative or disciplinary reasons, and cannot go to the law library, he or she may have upon written request, legal material brought to the cell. Legal forms may also be available to the inmate. It is imperative that the jail staff keep abreast of court rulings and opinions concerning the inmate law library. Materials must be kept current; the law library should be stocked with current state law, legal reference books and dictionaries, forms, state and federal cases, including appeals cases. There should be either typewriters or word processors with printers, plus adequate workspace for the inmate.

## Mail Service

While case law through the courts has determined guidelines for inmate mail, the jail has great flexibility concerning regulations how the mail is to be delivered, such as the publisher's only rule. Like food, mail call is a welcome change in the monotony of jail life. Mail is delivered throughout the day. Many jails have designated officers or civilians who sort the mail and deliver it to the inmate housing areas. Incoming mail, including legal mail, is opened and checked for contraband. This is done either in the jail mail room or in front of the inmate, and the jail staff handling mail does not read the mail. Mail, incoming or outgoing, should never be handled by inmate workers, as some would undoubtedly try to get contraband sent through the mail. Outgoing mail is stamped with the name of that jail, so that the recipient can see that it came from the jail. All packages intended for inmates are inspected before delivery. If the contents are permissible for the inmate to have, the items should be inventoried, and the inmate should sign a form stating that he or she received the item(s). If the item is prohibited, it should be placed in the inmate's property and a property receipt given.[52] The jail should have a service to inmates that allows for the special mailing of legal documents.

### Commissary

Inmates may order and receive commissary with funds that they had when incarcerated or from money that friends and loved ones bring to the jail for deposit in each inmate's individual accounts. **Commissary** or canteen is a privilege by which the inmates can purchase snacks, over-the-counter medications, or toilet articles. For example, inmates may purchase candy bars, cookies, etc. Commissary relieves the monotony and can be taken away as a punishment for rule breaking. Commissary money collected from the inmates is put into the inmate commissary fund for purchases of recreation and programs materials and equipment.

### Fees for Services

To offset the rising costs of operating jails, several jurisdictions have begun to charge inmates fees for housing and services such as haircuts, sick call, etc. In Marion County, Florida, the sheriff charges inmates for meals and medical care. This process at the Marion County Jail survived a 1997 court challenge. The court said that even though inmates are entitled to adequate medical care and nutritious meals, the bill does not have to be paid by taxpayers.[53]

In Henderson County, Kentucky, in 2003, inmates owed the Henderson County Detention Center approximately $1.5 million. County jail inmates paid $17.00 per day housing fee for every day that they were in the jail. They also paid for medical bills and booking fees. When being released, inmates had to sign documents promising to pay what they owed. A system to collect these fees was under development by county authorities.[54]

## JAIL PROGRAMS AND SERVICES: REDUCE OR NOT?

Are jail programs effective and should inmates have access to a variety of services? This is the debate among many professionals—both management and line staff—in corrections. Some feel that inmates should be subjected to a harsh, "no frills" environment where programs are few, and some services that are considered "plush" should be curtailed. One sheriff or warden may differ in his or her views about programs in jail than another; this tone could change from election to election and may be considered the view of the citizens.

### Operational Concerns

The jail programs staff may be directed to curtail the number of volunteers and sessions of programs based on the following operational reasons:

- Increase in inmate population: more inmates means more staff have to be put on posts in housing areas to observe them and keep control.
- Increase in inmate movement: Some jails have correctional officers escort inmates to program sessions, especially females; others allow inmates from general population to go to classrooms unescorted. More programs sessions either way means

that more inmates have to be escorted or are allowed to walk the halls to the classrooms. If the jail is short staffed, these procedures may cause security concerns.

- Lack of attendance by inmates at specific programs: Each class has a specific program area such as a classroom, and if a program listing 20 inmates is attended only by a few, management usually concludes that the program is not popular with the inmates and staff should be put to better use.
- Rule violations/security breaches by programs staff: Security breaches by programs staff and volunteers are not only cause for concern, but may be embarrassing in the media. A serious security breach, especially involving staff/inmate sex or an inmate escape, may cause management to shut down programs and re-evaluate procedures.
- Lack of confinement staff to supervise inmates at programs: In some jails, there exist specific posts in program office and classroom areas. Inmates are walking through those areas; if insufficient staffing cannot man those posts, programs will be curtailed.

The central theme of jail programs is to prepare inmates for eventual release back into the community. Programs inside the main jail facility can work with programs in a community corrections facility. For example, a GED program being offered to inmates in the main jail can work with a GED program in an adjacent work release section/facility or a day reporting center (see Chapter 11). This is also true for such programs as mental health, substance abuse, religious services, AA, and NA, as volunteers and staff can be screened and cleared for both sections/facilities.

Funding, or lack thereof, can have a serious impact on local correctional programs. Jails are competing for tax dollars with other government entities—schools, transportation, health care agencies, etc. In Waukesha County, Wisconsin, in 2006, the sheriff of the newly expanded county jail was denied staffing in the 2007 budget by the county board of supervisors. The sheriff stated that he would be forced to close half of the jail's work release facility and shift staff into the main jail facility. The sheriff has under consideration a move to free approximately 100 inmates and switching non-violent offenders to electronic monitoring. A day reporting center is being considered for funding in 2008, and a former county nursing home is being considered to house both the work release and day reporting programs. Some county officials were of the opinion that the partial closure of the work release facility would better manage the county's offender population while at the same time save the taxpayers' money. Also, as part of the funding debate, county officials were going to look at the types of programs available to inmates.[55]

## The "No Frills" Jail

In the past 20 years, there has been much media coverage and popular discussion about the "no frills" jail or jails where programs and services are drastically reduced or cut to make jail life undesirable for the inmates. The hope is that inmates, once released, will take steps not to get rearrested and return to the jail. Measures may include, besides the reduction of programs, a limited canteen/commissary selection, a small number of television channels available to inmates, and a modification of the menu such as a reduction in beverage choices and hot meals. This could include the replacement of regular meals with nutra-loaf for inmates on disciplinary segregation.

One such jail is the "Tent Jail" in Maricopa County, Arizona, where some of the inmate population is housed in tents. Sheriff Joe Arpaio announced in 2003 his intent to reduce the approximately 8,700 inmates' daily caloric intake from 3,000 calories to 2,500 calories. Inmates are fed in the Maricopa jails twice per day, and the calorie reduction will save the county taxpayers $300,000 annually. Inmates are not served coffee, mayonnaise, ketchup, and salt. In answering his critics, Sheriff Arpaio said that the new meal system meets federal dietary guidelines for sedentary adults, which stipulates 2,200 calories per day.[56]

However, even in "no frills" jails, there is room for programs. In the Maricopa County Jail system, Sheriff Arpaio praised federally funded substance abuse programs in his jail in a report released by the Arizona Criminal Justice Commission in 2006. He stated that his correctional philosophy is to mainly make his jail system austere enough to discourage recidivism and has banned smoking, pornography, access to most commercial television, rental movies, and operates a kitchen that puts out inmate meals at a cost of approximately 15 cents each. He realizes, however, that there exists a recidivism rate of 60 percent. The exception is the drug and alcohol treatment program in his jail, which has resulted in only 15 percent of its graduates being rearrested. Reducing its funding, he stated, will result in more crimes in the community.[57]

Another example of a "no frills" jail is the Benton County (Arkansas) Jail, which describes itself as the only no frills jail in the United States. According to its Internet Web site, inmates do not receive the following:[58]

- Television
- Coffee
- Radios
- Milk
- Chewing tobacco
- Razor blades
- Weight lifting equipment
- Hair cuts
- Deodorant
- Magazines
- Commissary
- Hot meals
- Soft drinks
- Shank [handle] toothbrushes

The verdict is not in as yet on the effectiveness of the "no frills" jail. However, on the surface, it is pleasing to the eyes of the citizen. Budget cuts, short staffing, and a strict "punishment" correctional philosophy can all have an impact on programs and services.

The question is what programs to cut and reduce, and whether by doing so the public is endangered by releasing inmates who have not learned to deal with problems and the criminal lifestyle. Progressive corrections professionals are wondering why jurisdictions are cutting educational opportunities for inmates in favor of allowing a jail inmate population to sit idle.

Stefan LoBuglio, Deputy Superintendent for the Suffolk County (Massachusetts) Sheriffs Department and former county detention center education director, stated in

2003 that inmates are distracted by television and idle activities. These tend not to motivate the inmates into participating in organized classroom instruction that is "forward-thinking in their plan for release and focuses their attention on what they need to do before they leave." Deputy Superintendent LoBuglio believes that corrections agencies also have to make tough choices, but the effects may be more severe. Discretionary line items, such as treatment and programs are cut back more than the more necessary items such as food, security equipment, and uniforms. In addition, managers and agency heads retain the mandatory programs such as juvenile education and eliminate more traditional adult programs such as ABE. The agency head may decide to retain lower cost programs under the heading of "education and/or treatment." For example, a jail may keep a program called "Crime Free Thinking" or other cognitive behavior-based programs. The problem is that these types of programs are designed to be taught by lower skilled instructors and volunteers—not professional educators.[59] The same is true for AA and NA—a jail head may say that his or her jail offers these programs, and hence, we have substance abuse treatment. AA and NA are self-help programs and not in depth substance abuse treatment and education.

The focus may be on trimming budgets, more than trimming programs, according to Steve Steurer, Executive Director of the Correctional Education Association. However, he advises local correctional agencies to gather their own data and show that inmates are getting help and becoming employed. This shows the public that correctional programs can work, giving the public more "bang for its [taxpayer] buck." Ideally the data must be on going and recent, not data that is 5–10 years old.[60]

An example that illustrates what programs may have priority are programs that have value in labor and other markets, according to Superintendent LoBuglio. Programs such as GED and literacy skills show prospective employers that inmates have worked to better themselves by getting an education and changing their ways. This can have a favorable impact, more so than with cognitive skills programs, although they too are important. Data in this area can show county and state legislators that these programs can have a good community impact.[61]

## SUMMARY

Most jails have programs that offer inmates chances to rehabilitate themselves. Programs assist inmates in changing behavior and overcoming numerous problems ranging from substance abuse to mental health problems. The purpose of rehabilitative programs is to identify these needs and change behaviors.

Programs have a pacification effect on the jail climate. Sound program guidelines include calling for programs to be basic, straightforward, adhere to jail security, and to use available resources. Programs, particularly substance abuse and mental health programs, use four different therapy approaches.

Security (custody) staff and programs staff must work together. Programs can be hampered by negative attitudes of jail officers and disciplinary actions by inmates.

There are many unique and revolutionary programs in the areas of mental health substance abuse, life skills, and job skills (vocational). Some jails have formed partnerships with the local community and colleges. Religious programs and educational programs are widespread in our nation's jails. Many programs use volunteers as a valuable resource, and they must be trained thoroughly in jail security issues.

The two most important jail services are medical care and food. Other services include library services, commissary, and recreation. Future trends in inmate programs and services include manufacturing goods for private businesses and requiring inmates pay fees for services to offset jail costs. However, the "no frills" jail movement can result in a cutback in programs and services that are viewed as making inmates too comfortable. Programs can be reduced and scaled back due to a variety of operational reasons. The value of programs cannot be ignored, and this is seen by many correctional administrators.

## REVIEW QUESTIONS

1. Name three ways that rehabilitation programs helps inmates with their problems.
2. How do programs impact the jail climate?
3. Discuss guidelines for effective jail programming.
4. Describe three types of jail programs.
5. What are the values of volunteers?
6. How does the jail fund programs?
7. Define the different types of recreation and library services.
8. What is involved in checking an inmate medically when booked into a jail?
9. Name five statistical evaluators of a jail medical department.
10. Why are inmates being charged fees for programs?

## TERMS TO KNOW

active recreation
Adult Basic Education
behavior modification
commissary
copycats
dually diagnosed
General Educational Development (GED)
good time
group therapy
individual therapy
inmate commissary funds
jail programs
jail services
judicial intervention
law library
leisure library
life skills
medication runs
memorandums of agreement (MOA)
mentally ill diversion
non-denominational chaplain's staff
pacification of inmates
passive recreation
PIECP
recreation
rehabilitation
sick call
social therapy
TABE (Test of Adult Basic Education)
therapeutic community

## ENDNOTES

1. Richard P. Seiter, *Correctional Administration: Integrating Theory and Practice* (Upper Saddle River, NJ: Prentice Hall, 2002), p. 106.
2. Lt. Lance Bohn, "Pacification of inmates holds necessary place in programming," *The Corrections Professional* 10, (14) (2005): 10.
3. Mark Kellar, "Responsible Jail Programming," *American Jails* (January–February 1999): 78–91.
4. James J. Stephan, Bureau of Justice Statistics. *Census of Jails, 1999*, NCJ 18663, August 2001, p. 10.
5. Kellar, "Responsible Jail Programming," p. 79.
6. Stan Stojkovic and Rick Lovell, *Corrections: An Introduction, 2nd Edition* (Cincinnati, Ohio: Anderson, 1997), pp. 210–214.
7. Doris J. James and Lauren E. Glaze, Bureau of Justice Statistics Special Report. *Mental Health Problems of Prison and Jail Inmates*, NCJ 213600, September 2006, pp. 1, 2, 5, 6, 7, 9.
8. Edward W. Szostak and Janet Mattox, "From Conflict to Mutual respect: Programs for Offenders with Mental illness and/or Substance Abuse Disorders in Albany, New York," *American Jails* (September–October 2001): 43.
9. Ibid.
10. Micelle Gaseau, "Building Bridges: Jail Partnerships," *corrections.com,* http://www.corrections.com/printNews.aspx?Zone=Homepage (accessed February 24, 2004).
11. Meghan Mandeville, "Making Room at the Macomb County Jail," *corrections.com,* http://www.corrections.com/printNews.aspx?Zone-HealthNews (accessed September 24, 2004).
12. Denise Tomasini and Karen Imas, "Collaboration Among State and Federal Agencies Benefits Mentally Ill Offenders Reentering Society," *Corrections Today* (February 2005): 52.
13. Mentally ill Offender Treatment and Crime Reduction Act Becomes Law: APA On Line: http://www.apa.org/releases/S1194 law.html (American Psychological Association) accessed August 29, 2007.
14. Stojkovic and Lovell, *Corrections: An Introduction, 2nd Edition*, p. 206.

15. Meghan Mandeville, "Dealing with Meth in Michigan: Allegan County Targets Addicted Inmates for Treatment," *Corrections.com,* http://www.corrections.com/printNews.aspx?Zone=HealthNews (accessed December 26, 2004).

16. Szostak and Mattox, "From Conflict to Mutual Respect," p. 44.

17. Rebecca Milliken and Sandra Strickler, "Treatment of Shame in a Jail Addictions Program," *American Jails* (September–October 2004): 9–14.

18. Lynn Olcott, "The Best Teaching Job in the World," *American Jails* (March–April 2004): 45.

19. Ibid., p. 44.

20. Ibid., p. 46.

21. Ibid.

22. Michael F. Higgins, "The Modern Detention Center-Progress Through Programs," *American Jails* (September–October 2002): 29.

23. Linda Bryant and Brooke Thorington, "Breast and Cervical Cancer Detection Program," *American Jails* (September–October 2004): 16, 19.

24. Michael F. Higgins, "The Modern Detention Center-Progress Through Programs," p. 30.

25. Barbara Bloom, Joan Johnson and Elizabeth Belzer, "Effective Management of Female Offenders: Applying Research on Gender-Responsive Correctional Strategies to Local Jails," *American Jails* (September–October 2003): 32.

26. V. Morgan Moss, Jr., "Recovery in a Secure Environment (RISE): Changing the Culture of Incarceration," *American Jails* (September–October 2003): 15, 16.

27. Ibid., p. 16.

28. Ibid.

29. Offender Aid and Restoration, *Programs and Services,* Brochure, Arlington, Virginia: 2004.

30. Offender Aid and Restoration, Alexandria Detention Center, *Women Empowered for Change Program,* Brochure, Arlington, Virginia: 2004

31. Offender Aid and Restoration, Alexandria Detention Center, *MASTERS PROGRAM,* Brochure, Arlington, Virginia: 2004.

32. Robert Toll, "How a Multifaith Chaplaincy Program Operates in a County Detention Facility," *American Jails* (January–February 2004): 20.

33. Ibid., pp. 20–21.

34. Ibid., p. 22.

35. Ibid., p. 23.

36. Good News Jail and Prison Ministry. About Us. http://www.goodnewsjail.org

37. Good News Jail and Prison Ministry. Programs. http://www.goodnewsjail.org

38. Ibid.

39. Meghan Mandeville, "County Inmate Education Program Becomes First of Its Kind to Earn certification from CEA," *corrections.com,* http://www.corrections.com/printNews.aspx?Zone=Edunetwork (accessed December 28, 2004).

40. Ibid., pp. 1, 2.

41. Vicki Duncan, "Jail Barber Training Program Hits a High Note," *American Jails* (March–April 2002): 45, 46.

42. Ibid., pp. 46, 47.

43. Barbara Auerbach, "Private Sector Jail Industries," *American Jails* (May–June 2003): 15, 16.

44. Susan Dean and Harold B. Wilber, "Health and Wellness Fair at the Palm Beach County, Florida Jail," *American Jails* (May–June 1999): 67, 68.

45. James J. Stephan, *Census of Jails, 1999,* p. 10.

46. Don Bales, ed., *Correctional Officer Resource Guide, 3rd Edition* (Lanham, MD: American Correctional Association, 1997), p. 89.

47. Ibid.

48. Herald Tribune, "Another Inmate has Staph at Fla. Jail," *The Corrections Connection,* http://www.corrections.com/news/justin/index.html (accessed August 30, 2003).

49. Susan Laffan, "Evaluation of Your Medical Department," *American Jails* (September–October 2002): 33, 34.

50. Don Bales, *Correctional Officer Resource Guide*, pp. 75, 76.

51. Ibid., pp. 76, 77.

52. Ibid., pp. 128, 129.

53. *Washington Post,* "Florida Jail Allowed to Keep Charging for Meals," August 30, 1997.

54. The Gleaner, "Ex-Inmates Owe Jail $1.5 Million," *The Corrections Connection,* http://www.corrections.com/news/Justin/index.aspx (accessed November 2, 2003).

55. Scott Williams, "Waukesha inmates may be freed; Sheriff considers reducing work," *Milwaukee Journal Sentinel,* November 17, 2006, http://www.findarticles.com/p/articles/mi_qn4196/is20061117/ai_n16862854/print (accessed January 18, 2007).

56. Associated Press, "Sheriff to put inmates on 2,500-calorie diet," *The Corrections Connection,* http://www.corrections.com/news/article_print.aspx?articleid=611 (accessed January 18, 2007).

57. Arizona Criminal Justice Commission, *Residential Substance Abuse treatment FFY 06 cuts Impact on Arizona,* March 30, 2006, http://216.239.51.104/search?q=cache:PdS3E3ZGUJ:azcjc./gov/pubs/RSAT_cuts.pdf+Ma (accessed January 18, 2007).

58. Website: Benton County Jail, www.co.benton.ar.us/Sheriff/Inmate.htm (accessed January 17, 2007).

59. Keith Martin, "Preventing Budget Cuts From Erasing Inmate Education," *correctios.com,* July 28, 2003, http://www.corrections.com/news/article_print?aspxarticleid=9029 (accessed January 18, 2007).

60. Ibid.

61. Ibid.

## REFERENCES


Auerbach, Barbara. "Private Sector Jail Industries." *American Jails*, May–June 2003, 15–18.

Arizona Criminal Justice Commission, *Residential Substance Abuse treatment FFY 06 cuts Impact on Arizona*, March 30, 2006, http://216.239.51.104/search?q=cache:PdS3E3ZGUJ: azcjc. /gov/pubs/RSAT_cuts.pdf+Ma (accessed January 18, 2007).

Associated Press, "Sheriff to put inmates on 2,500-calorie diet," *The Corrections Connection*, http://www.corrections.com/news/article_print.aspx?articleid=611 (accessed January 18, 2007).

Bales, Don, ed. *Correctional Officer Resource Guide, 3rd Edition*. Lanham, MD: American Correctional Association, 1997.

Benton County Jail, www.co.benton.ar.us/Sheriff/Inmate.htm (accessed January 17, 2007).

Bloom, Barbara, Joan Johnson and Elizabeth Belzer. "Effective Management of Female Offenders: Applying Research on Gender-Responsive Correctional Strategies to Local Jails." *American Jails*, September–October 2003, 29–33.

Bohn, Lt. Lance. "Pacification of Inmates Holds Necessary Place in Programming." *The Corrections Professional* 10, (14) (April 15, 2005): 10.

Bryant, Linda and Brooke Thorington. "Breast and Cervical Cancer Detection Program." *American Jails*, September–October 2004, 15–20.

Dean, Susan and Harold B. Wilber. "Health and Wellness Fair at the Palm Beach County, Florida Jail." *American Jails*, May–June 1999, 67– 68.

Duncan, Vicki. "Jail Barber Training Program Hits a High Note." *American Jails*, March–April 2002, 45–49.

Gaseau, Micelle. "Building Bridges: Jail Partnerships," *corrections.com* http://www.corrections.com/printNews.aspx?Zone=Homepage (accessed February 24, 2004).

The Gleaner. "Ex-inmates Owe Jail $1.5 Million." *The Corrections Connection*, http://www.corrections.com/news/Justin/index.aspx (accessed November 2, 2003).

Good News Jail and Prison Ministry. About Us. http:// www.goodnewsjail.org

Good News Jail and Prison Ministry. Programs. http://www.goodnewsjail.org

Herald Tribune, "Another inmate has staph ay Fla. Jail." *The Corrections Connection*, http://www.corrections.com/news/justin/index.html (accessed August 30, 2003).

Higgins, Michael F. "The Modern Detention Center-Progress Through Programs." *American Jails*, September–October 2002, 28–31.

James, Doris J. and Lauren E. Glaze, Bureau of Justice Statistics Special Report. *Mental Health Problems of Prison and Jail Inmates*, NCJ 213600, Washington, DC, U.S. Department of Justice, September, 2006.

Kellar, Mark, "Responsible Jail Programming." *American Jails*, January–February 1999, 78–81.

Laffan, Susan. "Evaluation of Your Medical Department." *American Jails*, September–October 2002, 32–34.

Mandeville, Meghan. "County Inmate Education Program Becomes First of Its Kind to Earn Certification from CEA." *corrections.com*, http://www.corrections.com/printNews.aspx?Zone=Edunetwork (accessed December 28, 2004).

Mandeville, Meghan. "Making Room at the Macomb County Jail." *corrections.com*, http://www.corrections.com/printNews.aspx?Zone=HealthNews (accessed September 24, 2004).

Mandeville, Meghan. "Dealing with Meth in Michigan: Allegan County Targets Addicted Inmates for Treatment." *corrections.com*, http://www.corrections.com/printNews.aspx?Zone=HealthNews (accessed December 6, 2004).

Martin, Keith. "Preventing Budget Cuts From Erasing Inmate Education," *corrections.com*, http://www.corrections.com/news/article_print?aspxarticleid=9029 (accessed January 18, 2007).

Mentally ill Offender Treatment and Crime Reduction Act Becomes Law APA on Line, http:/www.apa.org/releases/s1194 law.html (American psychological Association) (accessed August 29, 2007).

Milliken, Rebecca and Sandra Strickler. "Treatment of Shame in a Jail Addictions Program," *American Jails*, September–October 2004, 9–14.

Moss, V. Morgan, Jr., "Recovery in a Secure Environment (RISE): Changing the Culture of Incarceration," *American Jails*, September–October 2003, 15–18.

Offender Aid and Restoration, *Programs and Services*, Brochure, Arlington, Virginia: 2004.

Offender Aid and Restoration, Alexandria Detention Center, *Women Empowered for Change Program*, Brochure, Arlington, Virginia: 2004

Offender Aid and Restoration, Alexandria Detention Center, *MASTERS PROGRAM*, Brochure, Arlington, Virginia: 2004.

Olcott, Lynn. "The Best Teaching Job in the World." *American Jails*, March–April 2004, 44–51.

Seiter, Richard. *Correctional Administration: Integrating Theory and Practice*. Upper Saddle River, N.J.: Prentice Hall, 2002.

Stephan, James J. Bureau of Justice Statistics, *Census of Jails, 1999*, Washington, DC: August 2001.

Stojkovic, Stan and Rick Lovell. *Corrections: An Introduction: 2nd Edition*. Cincinnati, Ohio: Anderson, 1997.

Szostak, Edward and Janet Mattox. "From Conflict to Mutual Respect: Programs for Offenders with mental Illness and/or Substance Abuse Disorders in Albany, New York." *American Jails*, September–October 2001, 42–47.

Toll, Robert. "How a Multifaith Chaplaincy Program Operates in a County Detention Facility." *American Jails,* January–February 2004, 19–24.

Tomasini, Denise and Karen Imas. "Collaboration Among State and Federal Agencies Benefits Mentally Ill Offenders Reentering Society." *Corrections Today,* February 2005, 50–53.

*Washington Post,* "Florida Jail Allowed to Keep Charging for Meals." August 30, 1997, Sec. A.

Williams, Scott. "Waukesha Inmates May Be Freed; Sheriff Considers Reducing Work." *Milwaukee Journal Sentinel,* November 17, 2006, http://www.findarticles.com/p/articles/mi_qn4196/is20061117/ai_n16862854/print (accessed January 18, 2007).

# 7 THE JAIL POPULATION: PROFILE AND SPECIAL CATEGORIES

***Objectives of chapter***

The student will:

- Understand a concise profile of the national jail population as to its status concerning criminal justice issues: type of crime, violent/nonviolent charges, detention status, and histories of arrest and incarceration
- Learn demographic data about jail inmates such as age, sex, race/ethnic background, educational level, vocational level, citizenship status, and residence/family environment
- Learn about special categories in the jail population such as the mentally ill, inmates with medical concerns, substance abusers, the elderly, juveniles, suicidal/self-destructive inmates, foreign inmates, and females
- Learn how jail staffs manage special categories of inmates

This chapter will provide two concise, overall views of the jail inmate population in the United States, based on official statistics by the United States Department of Justice, Bureau of Justice Statistics (BJS). The BJS view can be described as an official, formal view of the jail inmate population. The other view—a "special" view—is of the special categories in the jail population. By combining these views, the criminal justice student will be provided with an overall look at the types of inmates in our jails and the crimes that they commit. This chapter will also provide in combination with the look at special populations, guidelines on how special category inmates should be managed and supervised.

## THE JAIL OFFENDER: CRIMINAL JUSTICE INVOLVEMENT

In any study of the jail population, the entire picture of the involvement in the criminal justice system must be included, including both the current types of offenses and the prior involvements in the criminal justice system. Probably the best benchmark for such data is the statistical reports published by the United States Bureau of Justice Statistics.

## Type of Crime

In any jail the types of crimes among the inmate population vary from misdemeanors such as petty theft to felonies such as rape. Jails get all types of inmates who are involved in all types of crime. Officially, according to the 2002 BJS *Profile of Jail Inmates,* the categories of offenses of jail inmates are as follows:

The trends between the last two jail profiles are clear. The percentage of inmates in jail for violent offenses remained relatively the same, as do the percentages for public-order offenses and juvenile and nonspecific offenses. Property offense rates dropped slightly but the drug offense rates showed a marked increase.

According to the BJS profile, each category has specific crimes. Violent crimes are murder, negligent manslaughter, kidnapping, rape, other sexual assaults (such as sexual battery, etc.), robbery, assault, and other violent crimes. The "other" violent crimes are blackmail, extortion, vehicle hit-and-run with bodily injury, child abuse, and criminal endangerment.[1]

Property offenses include the well-known burglary (sometimes called "breaking and entering"), larceny/theft, motor vehicle theft, arson, fraud, stolen property, and other offenses such as vandalism, destruction of property, hit-and-run without bodily injury, trespassing, and the possession of burglary tools. Public-order offenses cover a wide range of crimes: weapons charges, obstruction of justice, traffic offenses, driving under the influence (DUI), drunkenness/morals offenses, probation and parole violations, immigration violations, and other miscellaneous violations. Included in the drunkenness/morals crimes are such offenses as vagrancy, disorderly conduct, unlawful assembly, morals charges, and commercialized vice offenses. The final "other" category in public-order offenses includes rioting, abandonment, nonsupport, invasion of privacy, violations of liquor laws, and tax evasion. Finally, the last category includes juvenile crime and unspecified offenses; the rate has remained the same.[2]

A unique factor in the discussion of jail inmates and their charges is that some enter the jail arrested for one charge, while others come in on a combination of charges, both felony and misdemeanor. Frequently, one incident can lead to several charges. For example, a traffic stop by police results in an arrest for driving while intoxicated (DWI). While searching the offender, burglary tools, concealed weapons, or drugs are found. Another example could be an obstruction of justice charge. This type of charge could result from someone present at the scene of arrest interfering with the police, subsequently impeding the police in the performance of their duties. An assault on the police may also result, or the arrestee kicks out a cruiser window incurring a destruction of property charge. In other words, one jail inmate can have multiple charges in several different categories. Each event of arrest by police is different.

**TABLE 7–1 Categories of Offenses: Jail Inmates, 1996 and 2002[3]**

| | *1996* | *2002* |
|---|---|---|
| Violent offenses | 26.3% | 25.4% |
| Property offenses | 26.9% | 24.4% |
| Drug offenses | 22.0% | 24.7% |
| Public-order offenses | 24.4% | 24.9% |
| Other: juvenile/unspecific | 0.5% | 0.5% |

Concerning the violent crime category, the most frequent violent crime in 2002 was assault, at 11.7 percent. The most frequent property offenses were burglary (6.7%) and larceny/theft (7.0%). In the drug offense category, the most frequent charge was drug trafficking (such as sales) at 12.1 percent, followed by possession at 10.8 percent. The highest percentage of public-order offenses was in the DWI or DUI category, at 6.4 percent. In summary, the top five offenses among jail inmates statistically are assault, burglary or larceny, drug trafficking, drug possession, and DUI.[4]

In looking at these statistics, one can assume that most inmates confined in local jails *are not* incarcerated for the high-profile crimes of murder, rape, armed robbery, kidnapping, etc. True, these criminals when arrested for these high-profile crimes do enter the local jail, but for the most part, jail inmates are arrested the most often for the above offenses. What is interesting about jail inmates is that many have varying criminal histories. For example, an inmate may be currently incarcerated for simple assault in a domestic dispute and has an arrest or incarceration history for abduction (kidnapping), sexual assault, or rape. These charges must be taken into account when the jail classification staff classifies the inmate into the jail population.

Due to the nature of the charges and circumstances of the arrests, it is difficult to divide jail inmates into either a convicted or an unconvicted (pretrial) status. When inmates' charges are adjudicated, they are in a **convicted status**, which means that they are waiting to be transferred to a penal system, state or federal, and they are finished with court. In jail, an offender can enter jail in a pretrial or **unconvicted status**, have his or her case go through the court system, and be in a convicted status. However, a jail inmate with several charges can be convicted on one and be in an unconvicted status on others. Charges can have different court dates assigned, so it is not uncommon to look at a jail inmate's record and see several charges, some felonies and some misdemeanors, all with different court dates in several courts. As a result, a jail inmate can be in both a convicted and an unconvicted status.

Another factor is the detainer—a charge from another jurisdiction that is pending. An inmate in jail may be finished with all charges for which he or she was incarcerated but may be awaiting transfer to another jail in another jurisdiction to face other charges. The most recent profile of jail inmates concerning conviction status is illustrated below.

When arrested, the jail inmate may be already involved in the criminal justice system to some degree. This is called the **criminal justice status**, and it indicates if an inmate is already in the criminal justice system.

In 1996, 46.4 percent of jail inmates were not involved in the criminal justice system at the time of arrest, and that was unchanged in 2002 with 46.8 percent

**TABLE 7-2 Conviction Status: Jail Inmates, 1996 and 2002[5]**

| | *1996* | *2002* |
|---|---|---|
| Unconvicted | 26.1% | 28.2% |
| Convicted | 47.9% | 54.8% |
| Both convicted and unconvicted | 22.1% | 16.0% |
| Other: protective custody, witness, etc. | 3.0% | 0.9% |

of inmates reporting noninvolvement. Also, the rates of being involved in the criminal justice system remained the same in the 1996 and 2002 profiles, with 53.6 and 53.2 percent reporting being on any criminal justice status, respectively. The clear indication is that slightly over one half of inmates arrested and sent to jails are already involved in the criminal justice system: on probation or parole, out on bail/bond, on a form of pretrial release, or out on an alcohol and/or drug diversion program. Other forms of involvement are on work/study release, on electronic monitoring status or house arrest, on furlough, or in a day reporting or weekend confinement program. Inmates on escape status only totaled 0.9 percent in 1996 and 0.6 percent in 2002. The highest reported status of inmates was being on probation (31.7% in 1996 compared with 33.6% in 2002). Followed closely was being on parole (13.1% in 1996 compared with 12.6% in 2002).[6]

The high rates of jail inmates being on probation and parole at the time of arrest is a clear problem. The rates are a little over ten percent, but are not a negative indictment of the probation and parole system. Probation and parole agencies are engaged in a difficult battle against recidivism. It is unfortunate that some clients slip through the cracks and re-offend. New methods of surveillance such as intensive supervised probation, electronic monitoring, etc. may have a favorable impact on this statistic in future BJS profiles.

An important factor in a profile of jail inmates and their involvement in the criminal justice system is recidivism—repeat offenders coming back into jails. According to the BJS 2002 profile, 24 percent of jail inmates in 2002 had 3 or more prior incarcerations. This is a marked decrease from the 32 percent figure reported in 1996. In the intervening years between the profiles, the number of inmates reporting one prior sentence to probation was stable from 1996 to 2002 (34.6% to 32.6%, respectively). The reporting of one prior sentence to probation or incarceration was about the same in 1996 (17.4%) and in 2002 (17.5%).[7]

It is no surprise to a jail staff that the same offenders seem to be coming in over and over. When criminal histories are run on jail inmates as part of the classification process, it appears that most have criminal histories. Statistically, that is true:

Taking all of these profile statistics into consideration, the criminal justice involvement of the overall national jail population is as follows:

- Statistically, the jail population is incarcerated with equally proportionate percentages of violent crime, property crime, drug offenses, and public-order offenses. Each category is at approximately 25 percent.
- Slightly over one half of inmates in jails are incarcerated on a convicted status.
- Well over one half of the inmates in jails have a criminal history.

**TABLE 7-3 Criminal Histories: Jail Inmates, 1996 and 2002[8]**

| | *1996* | *2002* |
|---|---|---|
| No prior sentence | 29.1% | 38.1% |
| Violent recidivists | 34.3% | 28.3% |
| Nonviolent recidivists | 36.9% | 33.6% |

- Slightly over one half of jail inmates were already involved in the criminal justice system at the time of arrest.
- Approximately one of four jail inmates had three or more previous incarcerations.

The last three observations indicate in general terms that jail offenders are no strangers to the criminal justice system. Significant numbers have a criminal history, are involved already in the system, or have been incarcerated previously. This is no surprise to jail staff who books inmates in, classifies them, and deals with them in the housing areas. These statistics indicate that a substantial number of jail inmates are well versed in crime, arrest, involvement with the police and the courts, and experiencing life inside jails and prisons.

What is indicated in the national profile may not hold true for all jails. Many jails, large and small, keep statistical data on the inmates in their custody. A good example of this is the state of Ohio, which operates a jail system with 252 jails classified into four types: full service jails (FSJ), minimum security jails (MSJ), five-day jails (5-D), and eight-hour jails. All are inspected by the Bureau of Adult Detention. In a 2001 article in *American Jails,* a 1999 inspection reported that 50.1 percent of jail inmates were awaiting court on current charges, and 46.1 percent were convicted and serving sentences imposed by the courts. The remainder of the inmates, 3.8 percent, were being housed temporarily in Ohio jails per agreements with other law enforcement agencies such as the Ohio Department of Rehabilitation and Correction (such as in the case of parole violators), the United States Marshal's Service, and the Immigration and Custom Enforcement, or ICE.[9] This is opposite to the 1996 profile for national conviction rate for jail inmates.

Another example of a detailed jail population profile is the Spokane County, Washington jail. In 2003, the average daily population was 603 in a 519-bed capacity jail. Pretrial inmates (felons and misdemeanants) totaled 371, or 61 percent of the population. The entire breakdown of the pretrial population was 225 pretrial felons, 66 pretrial misdemeanants, 5 pretrial DUI, 10 pretrial traffic, and 65 pretrial miscellaneous or other. Post-trial offenders totaled 149: 68 post-trial felons, 57 post-trial misdemeanants, 2 post-trial DUI, 8 post-trial traffic, and 14 post-trial miscellaneous or other. Post-trial offenders totaled 25 percent of the population. The remainder of jail offenders totaled 90 offenders or 15 percent in the following categories: probation hold (34), parole hold (1), felons awaiting transfers (5), immigration (3), holds for U.S. Marshals (25), federal hold (1), inmates held for other counties (3), and other (18).[10]

Local jails do hold inmates for the state departments of corrections (DOCs) per contract. To do so requires the involvement of six "actors": the governor, the state legislature, the state DOC, elected local government officials such as mayors, county commissioners, etc., county/city sheriffs, and the jail staff. Contracting state inmates has many benefits for all concerned including the inmates. The state as the contractor benefits financially as does the local jails. Jail per day inmate costs are lower than if the inmates were housed in the state system. Also, if enough state inmates are housed in local jails, the state may be able to avoid or delay the construction of new penal facilities, which can cost in some jurisdictions as much as $75,000 per cell in design and construction costs, minus the cost of staffing. State inmates can be housed closer to their communities and families, and they can be better protected in smaller local facilities than in the state prison system.[11]

State inmates may get impatient due to being incarcerated in a local jail instead of a state facility. This frustration may be due to the rules, regulations, and routine

POINT OF VIEW

## The Variety of the Jail Population

*Wendy Jones*
Chief of Corrections Whatcom County,
Washington Sheriff's Office

Several years ago, I read a description of a big city emergency room. The doctor, describing what it was like to work in the E.R., said it was like the u-trap under a kitchen sink; the last chance for all the flotsam and jetsam to be saved before it was washed away. It occurred to me at that time that the description would also fit where I have worked for over 20 years, a medium size jail in Washington State.

When I began working there in 1981, I had no idea of the wide variety of people whose lives would intersect mine. Television and movies had influenced my imagination, and I anticipated, given the size and semi-rural nature of my community, it would simply be a somewhat larger version of the jail in Mayberry. The first few days served as vivid illustration of the difference between fantasy and reality.

Inside the jail, I found people seriously affected by mental illness, developmental disabilities, medical problems made worse by homelessness and lifestyle choices, single moms, community elders, and, overlaying it all, people with significant chemical dependency issues. Over the past 20 years, the challenges posed by these growing numbers of "special needs" offenders have increased both in size and intensity.

Jails have basically become the last safety net for the forgotten and ignored in our communities. When psychiatric services are cut, our populations increase; when residential housing for developmentally delayed clients is cut, our populations increase; when drug and alcohol treatment dollars are eliminated, our populations increase. When people living on the margins lose medial assistance, they know that they can get help if they come to jail. It says something about our world that in order for someone to get insulin for their diabetes, they feel they have to toss a cinder block through a bank window and get arrested.

In 2004, it was estimated that 16 percent of all offenders incarcerated in the United States have some type of serious mental illness. Another 2–10 percent can be classified as having some type of developmental disability. Also, 20–45 percent of the offenders have been diagnosed with a serious medical problem. A rapidly growing percentage of the incarcerated population is now over the age of 65. Nationwide, the issues of geriatric offenders are becoming so prevalent that some facilities are being designed and built just to handle their growing numbers. Add these populations to the "normal" inmates with impulse control problems, attention deficits, and social–behavioral issues, and it is easy to understand why officers frequently see themselves as social service workers in addition to law enforcement officers.

Each of these groups present distinct, and sometimes almost insurmountable, challenges to the jails in which they live. Yet there are some overarching issues that apply regardless of the type of special needs the offender may have. The first and foremost is education for the staff. With knowledge, comes the understanding and creative problem solving that are essential in working with these diverse groups and offenders.

The first hurdle is often accurate information. Having been around corrections for over 20 years, I vividly recall the hysteria surrounding the new disease that appeared to strike people at random, and resulted inevitably in their death. That disease we now know as autoimmune deficiency syndrome (AIDS). The amount of misinformation that was originally propagated is mind-boggling: Rumors abounded that you could catch AIDS from using the phone, getting a mosquito bite, or merely touching someone with the disease.

We now know that was all untrue; the modes of transmission are well understood, and there are some very simple precautions that can usually prevent the disease from being passed. Back then, however, we first had to get through the fear and misperceptions. I remember the first class we gave to corrections staff, providing factual information and emphasizing the importance of Universal Precautions in the prevention of disease transmission. The information had to be repeated over and over, for several months, and in several different forms, before all staff was solid in their understanding of the disease and the response.

We have found the same phenomenon with our special needs offenders, whether the needs are due to disability, disease, or mental illness. Part of the process often has to replace long-held, but erroneous, beliefs with fact. The payoff, however, is remarkable.

Educating staff on signs of drug and alcohol withdrawal, for example, makes them aware of the symptoms, so they can alert the health care staff. Reminding staff that if someone is fully deaf, not hard of hearing, and simply speaking loudly to the inmate will not do much to gain compliance, whereas facing the inmate and speaking clearly may.

With knowledge comes power to manage this diverse community. When an officer understands that a schizophrenic inmate cannot control the delusion that the kitchen trusty is poisoning their food tray, the officer can avoid engaging in a useless argument that the poisoning is all in the inmate's head. Instead, the officer may elect to simply allow the inmate to choose whichever tray he or she would like, assuring the inmate that because no one could not know which tray the inmate would select, the tray would be safe. The officer simply adapts standard procedures, based on good information.

A jail's single best resource is its staff. Providing them with the tools they need to manage these special populations is critical. These tools can be provided via classroom training, shift-briefings, video training, or on-the-job experience with skilled senior staff. We must continue to educate our officers that while "firm, fair and consistent" are our watchwords, those watchwords must be used within the context of an offender's abilities and capacities to understand and comply.

The second issue is the need to maintain contact between these offenders and the community. Far too often, jail is seen as a place "those people" can be sent, and then ignored. This philosophy becomes formally sanctioned via government polices, as well as community behavior.

One example is the federal and state Medicaid policies that stop benefits for folks with chronic medical or mental health issues if they are arrested, regardless of the reason, or length of stay. The need hasn't changed, but once they become "inmates" they are apparently less deserving of care. We see it on a local level when practitioners won't see "inmates" even if they saw the same individual the week before. As long as our communities can view these special needs inmates as separate and distinct from themselves, rather than as community members in crisis, this disparity in treatment can continue.

On an operational level, we have been fighting this for a number of years. Historically, offenders who received mental health treatment in the community would lose any contact or services with caseworkers if they were arrested. We found the same thing happened with offenders who had chronic medical conditions such as AIDS, or who were significantly affected by some type of developmental disability. Slowly, over the years, we worked with community providers to create the understanding that while the person's physical location may change, their needs did not. This had led to a series of collaborative efforts that, while not perfect, have begun to bridge the gaps in services both in the community and in the jail.

Once the community "discovered" that mentally ill consumers do wind up in jail, the decision was made to blend some local funding with money from the jail budget to pay for full-time case managers in the jail. This case manager can provide for a continuity of the care started in the community. Conversely, the case manager can also provide a connection to community services for mentally ill offenders who had not known how to access services prior to their incarceration. The end result? A slow, but steady decline in the number of mentally ill offenders who are returning to jail. The jail benefits by a lower recidivism rate, and the community and consumers benefit by providing the services needed to maintain the person in the community.

We can argue that there should be other facilities and options for these offenders. We can argue that it is not the core duty of a jail to work as that "u-trap" mentioned at the beginning of this essay. The reality is, however, that for reasons too numerous to discuss here, jails will remain the last safety net for many, many people. We must continue to accept the responsibility to see to it that the net doesn't fail.

Thanks to Wendy Jones, Chief of Corrections, Whatcom County, WA, Sheriff's Office.

of the jail. Generally, jails are more restrictive concerning inmate freedom of movement. Jail cellblocks may be more confining than state penal camps where inmates have more room to move around. Some jails, such as the Fairfax County, Virginia, Adult Detention Center, engage in the practice of **lockout**, where inmates are locked out of their cells from after morning inspection to after the collection of the dinner meal units, or from approximately 9:00 A.M. to approximately 5:00 P.M.

Inmates are restricted to the cellblock or unit dayroom areas during those hours. Inmates must bring everything that they need out for the day. The idea of lockout is to have general population inmates both visible and accessible for visiting, recreation, programs, sick call, etc. Inmates with state or federal prison experience or having done time in other jails may not like this type of practice and may get their attorneys and/or families to get the jail to send them to the state system. If these inmates have negative attitudes toward the jail, the jail staff has no choice but to deal with them in a way that they are controlled and follow the jail rules. Additionally, state inmates housed in the local jail must follow the rules and regulations of the local jail. Some may try to convince new or inexperienced jail officers that the jail rules do not apply to them.

## THE JAIL INMATE: DEMOGRAPHIC DATA

It is important in the study of jail inmates to examine the demographic data: race, sex, age, marital status, educational history, vocational history, and status of citizenship. Some of these statistics can tell us a lot about the offender and can be useful in planning by jail administrators. These demographic factors have an important impact on the jail:

- *Race:* If many of the jail inmates are from a foreign ethnic group whose English skills are lacking, both verbally and written, steps may have to be taken to provide them with information that is both crucial to their incarceration and protects the staff from liability. Bilingual staff will have to be identified, listed, and available to interpret. Rules and regulations such as an inmate handbook may have to be translated to other languages. Forms may also have to be translated into the languages reflected in the racial make up of the jail population. Other services affected are medical—where staff must be aware that it may be more difficult to get medical information from non-English-speaking inmates. Also, in cases of inmate assaults and suspected wrongdoing, such as rule violations and incompatibility complaints, language barriers hamper investigations by the jail staff. Most areas of the jail such as booking, medical, and classification are affected if the number of non-English-speaking inmates increases. Programs may have to be developed to address the needs of this population.
- *Sex:* It is important to note if a trend exists such as an increase in the female population. If so, more bed space will have to be found. An increase in female inmates could bring more pregnant inmates into the jail. This would impact where pregnant females would be housed, under what conditions they would have to be housed, and the availability of prenatal and postnatal medical care. To assist the female inmate population, staffs may have to develop more programs for females dealing with issues unique to the gender—such as parenting, etc.—in order to have program accessibility on as an equal level as possible with the male inmate population.
- *Age:* Older inmates can affect the medical staff and the classification staff. Inmates in their 40s, 50s, and older may have medical problems associated with aging that will have to be dealt with by the medical staff. Suitable housing will have to found by the classification staff. Conversely, younger inmates, especially juveniles being held in jails, must be planned for in terms of behavioral problems and housing.

- *Educational and vocational histories:* This information can be useful to the programs staff when asking for more civilian programs staff, funding to develop more programs, and more programs materials, and in recruiting volunteers.
- *Citizenship status:* The problem of illegal immigration is under increasing scrutiny since the terrorist events of September 11, 2001. More illegal immigrants in jails can result in increasing numbers of detainers being placed on them by ICE.

The demographic profile is best viewed in the data collected in the 2002 jail inmate profile. It provides a reasonably accurate snapshot of the jail population.

**TABLE 7-4 Jail Inmates in the United States: Demographic Characteristics, 1996 and 2002[12]**

| | *1996* | *2002* |
|---|---|---|
| Sex/gender | | |
| Male | 89.8% | 88.4% |
| Female | 10.2% | 11.6% |
| Race/ethnic origin | | |
| White (non-Hispanic) | 37.4% | 36.0% |
| Black (non-Hispanic) | 40.9% | 40.1% |
| Hispanic | 18.5% | 18.5% |
| American Indian/Alaska Native | 2.4% | 1.3% |
| Asian/Pacific Islander | 0.9% | 1.1% |
| Multiracial | — | 3.0% |
| U.S. citizenship | | |
| Citizen | 91.8% | 92.2% |
| Noncitizen | 8.2% | 7.8% |
| Age (years) | | |
| 17 or younger | 2.3% | 1.8% |
| 18–24 | 28.5% | 28.1% |
| 25–34 | 37.4% | 31.9% |
| 35–44 | 23.9% | 26.0% |
| 45–54 | 6.3% | 10.0% |
| 55+ | 1.5% | 2.2% |
| Marital/significant other status | | |
| Never married | 58.6% | 60.1% |
| Separated | 8.7% | 6.7% |
| Divorced | 15.6% | 15.7% |
| Widowed | 1.4% | 1.2% |
| Married | 15.7% | 16.2% |
| Education | | |
| College graduate+ | 3.2% | 2.9% |
| Some college education | 10.3% | 10.1% |

| | | |
|---|---|---|
| High school diploma | 25.9% | 25.9% |
| GED | 14.1% | 17.1% |
| Some high school education | 33.4% | 31.6% |
| 8th grade or below | 13.1% | 12.3% |
| Vocational/employment* | | |
| Employed | 64.0% | 71.0% |
| Not employed | 35.6% | 29.0% |
| Income: sources* | | |
| Salary/wages | 74.7% | 63.2% |
| Money from family/friends | 16.2% | 15.8% |
| Illegal means | 15.2% | 11.8% |
| Welfare | 13.8% | 6.3% |
| Compensation** | 7.4% | 9.1% |
| Other sources of income*** | 5.6% | 4.7% |
| Residence | | |
| Homeless in past year | 19.2% | 14.3% |
| Family background | | |
| Growing up: both parents | 39.7% | 43.6% |
| Mother only | 43.3% | 39.2% |
| Father only | 4.9% | 4.4% |
| Grandparents | 7.0% | 10.3% |
| Other relatives, etc. | 5.2% | 2.5% |
| Foster home, etc. | 13.6% | 11.5% |
| Family member incarcerated | 46.1% | 46.3% |
| Substance abuse by parent or guardian | | |
| Alcohol | 23.1% | 19.9% |
| Drugs | 1.3% | 2.1% |
| Alcohol and drugs | 6.9% | 8.6% |
| Prior abuse | | |
| Physical or sexual | 16.4% | 18.2% |

* The month previous to arrest.

** Sources such as Social Security, unemployment insurance, Worker's Compensation, etc.

*** Sources such as pensions, alimony, investments, education assistance, etc.

In the BJS report *Prison and Jail Inmates at Midyear 2005,* further data were reported concerning recent statistics in gender, race, and conviction status of jail inmates in midyears 2003, 2004, and 2005.

This table of the U.S. jail population illustrates some interesting trends that impact the operations of our nation's jails that have been mentioned. Each category can educate the students of jails and the staffs as to what is occurring in the jail population.

Concerning sex or gender, from 1996 to 2005, the trend is that more female offenders are being incarcerated in jail. However, jail offenders are predominantly males.

**TABLE 7-5 U.S. Jail Inmates: Gender, Race, and Conviction Status, 2003 through 2005[13/14]**

| | *2003* | *2004* | *2005* |
|---|---|---|---|
| Gender | | | |
| Male | 88.1% | 87.7% | 87.3% |
| Female | 11.9% | 12.3% | 12.7% |
| Race | | | |
| White | 43.6% | 44.4% | 44.3% |
| Black | 39.2% | 38.6% | 38.9% |
| Hispanic | 15.4% | 15.2% | 15.0% |
| Other* | 1.8% | 1.8% | 1.7% |
| Two or more races | | | 0.1% |
| Conviction status | | | |
| Convicted | 39.4% | 39.7% | 38.0% |
| Unconvicted | 60.6% | 60.3% | 62.0% |

Report based on midyear data.

* Includes these groups: Asians, American Indians, Alaska Natives, Native Hawaiians, and other Pacific Islanders.

The percentage of whites in jail is hovering at 44 percent. The percentage of black jail inmates remained in the 39 percent range, and there was little change in the number of Hispanic inmates. The percentage of American Indian/Alaska Native inmates reduced slightly, but the number of Asian/Pacific Islander inmates is low. What is interesting is that multirace inmates are now being included in the BJS profile. Although these are national statistics, these are not definitive in comparison with some jurisdictions. For example, a jail in a county with a high Hispanic population may reflect a higher Hispanic percentage of inmates in the jail. Jail populations are to some extent a reflection of the surrounding community.

Concerning citizenship, the vast majority of jail inmates are U.S. citizens, which is not surprising. This percentage may vary very slightly, being affected by the arrest and incarceration rate of illegal aliens (especially along U.S. border areas).

In terms of age, less than 2 percent of jail inmates in 2002 were under 17 years of age, and the percentage of inmates aged 18–24 only slightly changed from 1996 to 2002. However, the jail population is getting older. The percentage of inmates aged 25–34 decreased, while in all of the remaining age categories, 35–44, 45–54, and age 55 plus, there were significant increases. A combination of truth in sentencing and longer court sentences resulting in more time to serve may impact the overall age of jail inmates. Improved communication between law enforcement agencies can lead to better law enforcement techniques, convictions, and subsequent incarcerations.

In terms of counseling services, it should be noted by jail professionals that most (60.1%) inmates in jail in 2002 had never been married. Slightly over 16 percent were married. To the jail staff, significant others—wives, husbands, girlfriends, and boyfriends—play an important role in stabilizing inmates in the jail. For example, if a jail inmate is in personal crisis due to the legal situation, being victimized by another inmate, or is contemplating suicide, the fact that a significant other is on the outside can be crucial in how the inmate gets through the crisis. Significant others can also be communicative with the inmate through visiting, mail, and phone calls. Jail officers will admit that inmates who are suicidal may not commit suicidal acts due to the influence of people important to them on the outside who can lend moral support. In a related note, these significant others frequently call jail personnel, such as those of programs, classification, and mental health, and inquire about inmates or give the staff valuable and critical information concerning mental state, mental history, and suicidal tendencies.

Jail inmates are for the most part undereducated. Only 13 percent have some college or a college degree, while 43 percent have either a high school diploma or a GED. Almost 44 percent (43.9%) have some high school education or have a level of 8th grade or below. Some jail inmates will take advantage of a jail's GED program. In some jails, college-educated inmates, with or without degrees, may be screened by programs staff and used as tutors in jail education classes. The classification interviews can supply to programs staff and teachers information about a jail inmate's educational level. In classification interviews, jail inmates may give a variety of reasons for quitting high school: peer crime involvement, dysfunctional family environment, substance abuse, or having disciplinary problems in school.

In regard to the vocational aspect of the jail population, most jail inmates (71%) are employed and receive money in the form of wages or salaries. Surprisingly, almost 12 percent of inmates reported in 2002 that they received income from illegal means. Concerns of newly arriving jail inmates include wondering the status of their jobs and the effects of arrest and incarceration on the

When dealing with special category inmates, jail officers must be ready to expect the unexpected at all times. What seems to be a peaceful tour of duty may turn violent in a matter of seconds.

Photo by author, courtesy Butler County Prison.

financial situation of their families. These concerns can cause stress and worry, especially as inmates find out that their cars have been repossessed, their families evicted from their homes, and their bills are unpaid. As a result, phones get shut off, possessions are lost, and spouses with children turn to family members or government agencies for assistance.

Inmates do come from all vocational areas, from white-collar professional jobs (such as computers, college jobs, law, medicine, business, etc.) to blue-collar jobs, such as restaurant workers, landscapers, etc. Many employers will not hold jobs on the outside for inmates due to their being incarcerated and not being able to bond out or be released on their own recognizance. Also of note is the fact that almost 16 percent of inmates in 2002 reported getting funds during the month previous to arrest from family and friends. These same family members and friends usually supply the inmate with money for commissary items.

## SPECIAL CATEGORIES IN THE JAIL POPULATION

Along with the criminal justice status of jail inmates, there are the special categories of offenders who must be dealt with by jail staff. These types of offenders have problems that are unique, unusual, and must be handled carefully in very specific ways. These problems can make supervising them very difficult and challenging for jail officers. Jails do not have a say in what types of inmates that they take in.

The following groups represent the "special categories" of inmates with problems who are housed in our nation's jails:

- Mentally ill
- Medical concerns
- Substance abuse
- Elderly or mature inmates
- Juveniles housed in adult jails
- Female offenders
- Suicidal/self-destructive inmates
- Foreign/culturally diverse inmates

### Mentally Ill

It is becoming clearer that local jails confine offenders who suffer from a variety of mental disorders and also commit a variety of crimes. Mentally disordered offenders cannot be "locked in" to a specific group of crimes and can be arrested for crimes in all categories, ranging from assault to trespassing. Once arrested for a charge and booked into the jail, the mentally disordered offender must be cared for and dealt with by the jail staff. Unfortunately, jails are the largest, most convenient mental health facilities in the community. Even if an offender is mentally ill, the facts that take precedence are that a crime has been committed, the offender is in custody, and his or her welfare and safety becomes the responsibility of the local jail until whatever disposition occurs from the court system.

In September 2006, the BJS released in depth statistics on mentally disordered offenders in federal prisons, in state prisons, on probation, and in local jails (see Chapter 6). These findings give an informative view on the seriousness of the situation involving mentally disordered offenders in jails. Included in the findings of this report were:[15]

- Concerning jail inmates: A reported 64 percent had any mental problem, and of these 21 percent reported a recent mental history and 60 percent reported symptoms of mental problems. Out of the symptoms of major depressive or mania symptoms, jail inmates with mental problems experienced persistent anger and/or irritability (49.4%), psychomotor agitation or retardation (46.2%), and thoughts of revenge (34.1%). Concerning suicide, 12.9 percent had attempted suicide.
- An estimated 479,900 mentally ill offenders were incarcerated in U.S. local jails in mid-2005.
- In 2005, 26.5 percent of jail inmates with mental problems were held for violent offenses, mostly for assault (12.5%). Among jail inmates with a mental health problem, 26.9 percent were held for property crimes, 23.4 percent for drug offenses, and 22.6 percent for public-order offenses.
- Concerning jail inmates identified as mentally ill, 62.8 percent were male, compared with 75.4 percent who were female.
- Concerning age and race, mental health problems were most prevalent in inmates aged 24 or younger (70.3%) and white (71.2%).
- The majority of mentally ill jail inmates are not new to the criminal justice system. A reported 42 percent of jail inmates with a mental problem had served three or more sentences of incarceration or probation.
- Among mentally ill jail offenders, nearly 32 percent were repeat violent offenders.
- Regarding substance abuse, 89.9 percent of jail inmates with a mental problem regularly used drugs or alcohol; 62.1 percent used any drug. The most popular drug of choice was marijuana or hashish (43.4%) followed by cocaine or crack (24.2%).
- Concerning sentencing, approximately 55 percent of jail inmates with a mental problem were expected to serve 6 months or less in jail as compared with 54 percent of jail inmates without mental problems serving the same amount of time.
- Mentally ill inmates in jails can be management or disciplinary problems: It was reported that 9.3 percent of jail inmates with mental problems were injured in a fight since admission, and 19 percent were charged with breaking the rules of the institution.

In recent years, there has been much discussion in the correctional field about the problem of jails housing high numbers of mentally ill offenders. The actions of a mentally ill person such as violence can result in arrests. This can be further complicated by the presence of a substance abuse problem in conjunction with the mental disorder. While many say that mentally ill offenders belong in treatment, such as a mental hospital, the truth is that the police arrest mentally ill people and their cases must be adjudicated. As a result, they are placed in the local jail.

When jail staff has to deal with mentally disordered inmates, often they are dealing with inmates who have little or no sense of reality, or may be suffering from

Jail officers, at times, must place unruly inmates in padded cells for their own protection and for the protection of other inmates and staff.

Photo by author, courtesy Butler County Prison.

hallucinations and delusions, are hearing voices, or are angry, agitated, irritable, or suicidal. They may not trust anyone in a uniform and may resist obeying orders or following simple instructions, sometimes to the point of violence. For example, a mentally ill inmate may process communications from officers very slowly, or may stare blankly for a time until he decides what to do. Others may shout and scream, and be totally out of touch with their surroundings. Jail is a regimented environment, and a mentally disordered inmate may not process the meanings of regulations, the jail routine, expected responsible behavior, and the consequences of rule breaking. Some may act calm and may not be violent or irrational. The most reliable clues that a jail officer has in determining the mental state of an inmate:

- The inmate is acting like he or she is not in touch with reality. For example, the inmate may say that he or she is a space traveler and will be "beamed up" at any moment, or that he or she is a person of high importance, such as an advisor to the President of the United States and will be released; the inmate reports that "God is in my cell," etc.
- The inmate is not acting appropriately for the situation. Being incarcerated is stressful and traumatic. It is somewhat normal to act worried or be upset. The inmate may just sit and stare, not exhibit any emotions, etc.

Mental illness is a serious problem in jails, and inmates must be referred to qualified mental health staff for follow up, evaluation, and recommendations for housing. There is no way to accurately predict how many inmates suffering from specific types of mental illness will be incarcerated in a local jail.

While it is impossible to specifically predict the types of mental illness that jail officers and staff deal with inside the jail, it is realistic to say that jail staffs see most if not all of the types of mental disorders exhibited by offenders at one time or another. Jail staff should trust their instincts or, as commonly termed, their "gut." If an inmate is acting in a bizarre manner, staff should observe and document the behavior—and not diagnose. That should be left up to qualified mental health professionals. If none are available, the inmate should be referred to medical staff. According to Virginia mental health therapist Gary L. Lupton, the following disorders are commonly seen in a jail setting:

- **Substance abuse disorders:** The criterion for this disorder is the offender having a dependency on a substance (drugs or alcohol) and the effects that the substance has on functioning. Depression may be exhibited due to the use of *sedative-hypnotics* (alcohol, barbiturates, and benzodiazepines), *inhalants* (glue, aerosol propellants, Freon, gases, and gasoline), and *narcotics* such as morphine and morphine derivatives such as heroin, codeine, etc. In depression, the offender thus appears not to care, has a lack of energy, and wants to sleep. Mania or manic symptoms can be induced by the use of *stimulants* such as cocaine (powder or "crack," and amphetamines, or "speed." Mania exhibits itself by rapid speech, agitation, energy, and not sleeping. *Hallucinogens* (LSD, peyote, psilocybin, and phencyclidine or PCP) lead to symptoms of schizophrenia: hallucinations, delusions, and paranoia. *Marijuana* and *hashish* (its derivative) can cause depression-like symptoms. However, over time, the symptoms of these disorders will disappear as the inmate sobers up. While sobering up, the inmate may experience physical discomfort, nausea, vomiting, shaking, stroke, seizures, or death, depending on the substance used. Substance abuse disorders are the most common mental disorders encountered in a jail. If the symptoms of a mental disorder persist once the inmate has undergone withdrawals and sobers up, the jail staff should assume that a mental disorder does persist.
- **Mood disorders:** Most likely, the most common non-substance-abuse disorders, mood disorders are characterized by the offender having extreme mood changes that are not considered normal. These disorders are well known to jail staff: *depression* (sadness, little energy, sleeping a lot, no motivation, occasional anger and aggravation, and gloominess), *mania* (high energy levels, talkative, unfocused in activities, and little or no sleep), and *bipolar* (going back and forth between mania and depression, formerly called "manic depressive"). To the jail officer, these can be red flags—depression can be worsened by events such as arrest, being cut off from the family, sentenced to do time, lack of sunlight, etc., resulting in suicide. Manic inmates may not think things through and use bad judgment, resulting in high-risk behavior and suicide. Depression can be caused by a chemical imbalance. Both depression and mania can be treated with medications.
- **Anxiety disorders:** Inmates appear overly anxious and engage in repetitive behavior. *Generalized anxiety disorders* display fear, anxiety, and worrying that appear out of control. *Obsessive compulsive disorders* result in the inmate repeating behaviors to eliminate intrusive thoughts such as washing hands, counting, or doing something only in a certain way. *Post-traumatic stress disorder* (PTSD) is caused by the inmate going through trauma that is out of the ordinary—sexual assault, being in combat, being molested as a child, etc. A stimulus similar to the event

**FIGURE 7-1** Continued

triggers a flashback, an anxiety, or a break from reality. *Phobias* are fears of certain situations or things. Inmates may fear insects, being confined in a small space (like a cell), etc. resulting in inability to do tasks and being immobilized. Inmates may appear noncompliant with instructions from staff, and may be ridiculed, harassed, and victimized by other inmates. Anxiety disorders can be treated with certain interventions by mental health staff and antianxiety medications.

- **Thought disorders:** Thought disorders are identified as schizophrenia, delusional disorder, and related mental illnesses. Inmates with thought disorders will not respond when spoken to, may talk to someone or something that does not exist, or may talk to themselves. *Schizophrenia* involves hallucinations, delusions, or "flat effect" (no emotions). Inmates with this mental disorder may not care for themselves—they may not bathe or keep good hygiene. They may choose not to use toilets and may not wear clean clothes, preferring dirty clothes. They may have paranoid beliefs, such as the jail staff is "out to get me," or unrealistic beliefs such as someone important or famous loves them. Inmates suffering from thought disorders may resort to violence if they feel threatened or in danger. Thought disorders are treated with medications.
- **Personality disorders:** Caused by environmental influences over a lifetime and inherited traits, personality disorder behaviors become part of who the inmate actually is. How the inmate perceives the staff and other inmates is clouded by the disorder. They may manipulate others. The *antisocial personality disorder* involves nonconformity to society's rules and norms, deceit, lying, lack of guilt, lack of remorse, and no empathy for others. The *borderline personality disorder* is characterized by unstable personal relationships, poor self-identity, ongoing suicidal gestures, self-mutilation, unstable moods, empty feelings, inappropriate feelings of anger, and stress to the point of paranoia. Inmates having the *histrionic personality disorder* have to be "in the spotlight," and draw attention to themselves through dramatic behavior, and seductive dress and behavior, or quickly shift emotions. The *narcissistic personality* inmate believes that he or she is special, has a sense of extreme self-importance, has unrealistic fantasies, has no consideration of others, and is arrogant. Inmates having a *paranoid personality disorder* think that they are under attack, bear grudges, look for hidden meanings in communications from staff, and will not trust people. Personality disorders do not respond well to medication, counseling can help, but the fact is that inmates having personality disorders will change only if they want to change.
- **Sexual disorders:** In any discussion of jail inmate mental disorders, sexual disorders must be mentioned. This is not to say that these disorders may take place inside the jail—that is possible—but offenders do get arrested for exhibitionism (exposure of the sex organs), pedophilia, voyeurism, frotteurism (sexual rubbing and friction on someone), and sadism. Engaging in these behaviors can lead to arrest. Inmates have been known to expose themselves to visitors, other inmates, or staff. While criminal charges can be placed, jail staffs often charge the inmate under the disciplinary code of the jail.

Adapted from: "Identifying and Referring Inmates With Mental Disorders: A Guide for Correctional Staff," by Gary L. Lupton, in *American Jails,* May–June 1996, 49–52, copyright 2005, the American Jail Association. Used with permission.

**FIGURE 7-1** Types of Mental Illness Found in Jails[16]

In March 2002, the National Commission on Correctional Health Care (NCCHC) released a report titled *The Health Status of Soon to Be Released Inmates,* a study of the mental and physical health concerns of inmates being released from correctional facilities back into the community. The research, conducted in the mid to late 1990s, serves as a benchmark in examining the mental and physical health status of inmates in prisons and jails. Among the mental health findings regarding jail inmates:[17]

- Approximately 1 percent of jail inmates suffer from schizophrenia or another type of psychotic disorder.
- Approximately 8–15 percent suffer from major depression.
- Between 1 and 3 percent of jail inmates have bipolar disorder.
- An estimated nearly 2 percent and less than 5 percent of jail inmates have less severe but longer term depression called dysthymia.
- Between 14 and 20 percent of jail inmates have some type of anxiety disorder.
- Post-traumatic stress disorder is estimated to be present in between 4 percent to less than 9 percent of jail inmates.

Jail staff should be trained in the identification, referral, and handling of mentally ill inmates. While this is covered in basic training, more is known about mentally ill offenders now as was known 25 years ago. The above information indicates that mental illness has different forms with different behaviors. Jail officers can deal with a paranoid inmate, an inmate who thinks that she is the First Lady, and a demanding narcissistic inmate all in one tour of duty. However, training in this area should be ongoing in roll calls, in staff meetings, or as in-service classes. Secondly, documentation is important in the form of incident reports and logs that describe inmates' appearance, behavior, and interactions with staff. The report should be written in a way that would provide a clear description to the mental health staff or the court. The inmate's behavior may be so dangerous to himself and to others that commitment by the court to a mental health facility for further treatment and evaluation is warranted. The mental health staff will make housing recommendations to classification. If the inmate is manageable due to intervention by the mental health staff and by the use of medication, housing in general inmate population is possible. Otherwise, the inmate will be placed in administrative segregation pending follow up and monitoring by the mental health staff until general population housing is recommended. Some mentally ill offenders are never placed in general population due to bizarre behavior and the possibility of violence toward other inmates, themselves, and staff.

Other practices by the jail staff when dealing with mentally ill inmates include the following:

- *Observation:* Mentally ill inmates are often unpredictable and may behave in a bizarre fashion. While the standard jail officer check on an inmate is twice per hour or every 30 minutes, mentally ill inmates housed in segregation should be checked at least every 15 minutes or less in some cases. Segregated mentally ill inmates should be housed as close to staff, such as adjacent officer posts or nurses' stations. If the inmate is cleared for population, post officers should know who they are and should frequently talk to them to see how they are adjusting. Mental health staff should follow up, also.

- *Communications and referral:* Mental health staff and jail housing staff should keep the lines of communication open with mentally ill inmates. Each should know each other's roles in jail operations and consult each other concerning the best ways to handle mentally disordered inmates.
- *Caution:* Mentally ill inmates may change behavior rapidly especially if they have refused their medications. All staff members who interact with them should be cautious, using backup procedures, emergency response teams if warranted, and exercise careful security during transports.
- *Documentation:* All important interaction with and activities of mentally ill inmates should be documented in detail on observation logs, medical records, post logs, etc. in addition to incident reports. Under no circumstances should a jail officer attempt to diagnose the inmate's mental condition; that is the job of the mental health staff.

## Medical Concerns

Because jail staffs have no control who is incarcerated inside their facilities, they must be prepared for not only all types of behavioral problems, mental illnesses, criminal backgrounds, etc., but also for medical problems. Each inmate is unique. Some are relatively healthy, and some have medical concerns ranging from minor ailments to communicable diseases to being physically handicapped. Other health concerns are venereal diseases such as syphilis and gonorrhea, influenza, skin diseases, lice, ear, nose, and throat infections, dental problems, diabetes, heart conditions, injuries from resisting arrest, assaults, car accidents, etc.

A benchmark report by the BJS released in 2006, *Medical Problems of Jail Inmates,* reported that over a third of inmates in jail reported having a current medical problem. Dental problems were reported by 26 percent of convicted and 25 percent of unconvicted jail inmates, respectively. Female medical statistics stated that 5 percent reported being pregnant when admitted to the jail, and that the rate of medical problems was higher than male inmates—53 to 35 percent, respectively. Age was also a factor; approximately 61 percent of inmates aged 45 or older reported having a current medical problem. Concerning disabilities, about 1 in 5 jail inmates claimed to have a disability. In all, an estimated 229,000 jail inmates in 2002 reported having a medical condition, excluding colds or viral infections. Over one third, or approximately 227,200, of jail inmates reported having an impairment, including learning, speech, hearing, vision, mobility, or a mental impairment.[18]

Some injuries and ailments are readily visible, but others may not be. Jail staffs are concerned about inmates being human immunodeficiency virus (HIV) positive, having "full blown AIDS," being positive for hepatitis B and C, or having tuberculosis (TB). These medical conditions can be easily transmitted to jail staff through exposure to bodily fluids of the infectious person or, in the case of TB, through airborne contamination.

Concerning chronic diseases, according to the aforementioned NCCHC Report, in 1995 an estimated 8.5 percent of inmates in prisons and jails had asthma, an estimated 4.8 percent had diabetes, and 18.3 percent were suffering from hypertension. These chronic illnesses can be serious burdens on inmate health care systems. Inmates with poorly managed or untreated diabetes may require emergency room visits for glucose and sugar problems, dialysis due to kidney failures, and amputations of limbs in severe cases. Untreated hypertension, which the report calls the most common chronic illness among adults and inmates, can subsequently require costly health care services due to it being a risk factor for other ailments such as coronary heart disease, stroke, renal (kidney failure), and diseases of blood vessels and the circulatory systems.[19]

Several serious diseases that come to mind concerning inmates in jails and prisons are HIV infections, AIDS, hepatitis B and C, and TB. The BJS bulletin *HIV in Prisons and Jails, 2002,* released in December 2004, stated that:[20]

- Almost two-thirds of jail inmates interviewed in 2002 reported ever being tested for the HIV virus, and 1.3 percent of the inmates stated that they were HIV positive.
- AIDS-related deaths in local jails in 2002 totaled 42, a decrease from 55 deaths in 2001 and 58 in 2000.
- Female jail inmates were more likely to be HIV positive than males (2.3% of tested inmates to 1.2%, respectively).
- Concerning the age of HIV-positive inmates, the lowest rate was among jail inmates aged 24 or below (0.2%). Only 1.1 percent of HIV-positive inmates were aged 25–34. Jail inmates aged 35–44 years of age had a rate of 2.1 percent, and those inmates 45 and older had a rate of 2.7 percent.
- The rates of jail inmate deaths were highest in the 35–44 age group: 22 in 2000, 26 in 2001, and 21 in 2002.
- Inmates injecting drugs by use of a needle in the month prior to the offense accounted for 3.2 percent of HIV-positive inmates, and inmates who shared a needle made up 7.5 percent of the HIV-positive total.

The criminal lifestyle—intravenous drug usage, sharing needles, and unprotected sex—can lead to HIV infections, which the jail staffs have to deal with once the inmate is incarcerated. While HIV-positive inmates are afforded some degree of confidentiality about their condition, it is not wise to have the inmate population know which inmates are HIV positive. The jail staff is too busy dealing with numerous inmates to think that inmate X or inmate Y is HIV positive. The best rule that jail staffs follow is the **universal precautions rule**. This rule simply means that *all* inmates are to be treated as if they do have a communicable disease, such as AIDS. Twenty-five years ago, very few jails supplied protective equipment such as gloves to officers. Now items such as gloves are readily supplied to jail staffs and are used when searching inmates and dealing with inmates who are sick or injured and have exposed wounds or bodily fluids.

Another health concern that came more to light in the past decade was TB, a disease spread through the air; when the infected inmate sneezes or coughs, he or she is spreading tuberculin bacteria. It is not definitively known how much exposure a noninfected person needs to endure in order to contract the disease, and correctional staffs TB cases occur on average at least three times more in prisons and jails among inmates than in the outside general population. In 1995 the Center for Disease Control and Prevention reported that in some urban correctional institutions, the rate of TB was 500 percent higher than in the outside general population.[21]

Jails are at risk of TB for many reasons including poor ventilation, inmate overcrowding, and the fact that inmates come from lower economic groups where health care and taking care of oneself are not high priorities. Jail populations have inmates who are HIV positive and are more likely to contract TB. Also, histories of drug injections and/or the use of "crack" cocaine are also found to be related to TB. The death rates of TB have increased due to some strains of TB being resistant to multiple drugs.[22]

The NCCHC recommended in 1993 that inmates exhibiting symptoms or are suspected of having TB should be isolated in single housing in a negative pressure room (if available) until the jail's medical authority clears the inmate for housing in general population. All jail staff should be tested for TB both initially when hired and annually. All inmates should be screened for TB when being booked in. If an inmate refuses TB testing or treatment, there should be written policies to address such a problem. Education—for both staff and inmates—is necessary. Staff must know infection control procedures and inmates should know what TB is and how it is treated. Inmates being released from the jail should have referrals for follow up treatment and medications in the community.[23]

Much concern among jail workers involves exposure to hepatitis. Viral hepatitis is caused by five viruses. Hepatitis B (HBV) and hepatitis C (HCV) are transmitted by needle stick (the most efficient route of infection), such as being cut with a needle that had an infected inmate's blood on it, by exposure to an infected person's blood, and through sexual contact. Hepatitis D (HDV) is also transmitted by these aforementioned methods, but only to persons who are infected with the HBV virus. Chronic hepatitis infection can result from HBV, HCV, and HDV, while viruses hepatitis A and E are transmitted by the fecal/oral route and do not cause chronic infections. HCV damages the liver. Jail staffs, besides exercising the universal precautions, should get the HBV vaccine if available through their agency.[24]

Inmate medical concerns also include emergencies. The jail medical staff responds to inmate and staff medical emergencies and notification of nearby hospitals and rescue personnel form further medical care if necessary. Jail training and standards now include procedures for emergency medical care and training in cardiopulmonary resuscitation (CPR) and first aid.

The placement of an inmate in the dispensary (the jail's "mini hospital") per the instructions of the jail physician or the jail's medical staff does not lessen the need for security. In many jails, a sworn jail officer is posted in the inmate medical housing area; the inmate is checked and the room searched for contraband. Inmates have been known to fake illnesses in order to get to a hospital or doctor via transport and increase the possibility of escape while outside the jail. Jail officers may also encounter inmates who are behavioral problems (possibly due to mental illness) disciplinary problems, and high security risks, and may also be medically ill. In such cases, the medical staff and the confinement staff must work together to maintain security of the jail while not compromising the medical care that is due to the inmate. The inmate may require additional staff presence when out of his or her dispensary room. In some cases, the inmate may be so unmanageable that the medical staff will have to provide care in a secure housing area in the jail that is not in the dispensary.

## Substance Abusers

Substance abuse among jail inmates continues to be a problem. Jail inmates who are "hooked" on drugs can complicate to a degree the operations of the jail. First, incoming jail inmates on drugs must be searched thoroughly, and occasionally a strip search is necessary or required, depending on the jail policy. For example, an inmate is booked in for possession of LSD, or drugs are discovered hidden on the inmate when he or she was searched by the arresting police officer, both requiring a strip search. Second, jail inmates on drugs may have medical problems such as withdrawals or exhibit bizarre behavior resulting from the effects of the drugs and/or alcohol. Third, the "pull" of street drugs and alcohol abuse are very powerful, and inmates are reminded of that because of living with other substance-abusing inmates and having visitors from the outside who are substance abusers. As a result, there are always schemes and plans circulating in the jail population to either manufacture homemade alcohol or smuggle in illegal substances.

The 2002 BJS *Profile of Jail Inmates* gives a clear picture of substance abuse among jail inmates:[25]

- In 1996 and 2002, approximately 77 percent of convicted jail inmates could be characterized as alcohol- or drug-involved offenders.
- In 1996, 64.2 percent of inmates used any type of drug regularly. In 2002 that increased to 68.7 percent.
- Concerning types of drugs, in 1996 the three most regularly used drugs among jail inmates were marijuana or hashish (54.9%), cocaine or crack (31.0%), and stimulants (16.5%). In 2002, the three most regularly used drugs remained the same: marijuana or hashish (58.5%), cocaine or crack (30.9 %), and stimulants (17.1%).
- Marijuana, cocaine or crack, stimulants, and hallucinogens were the most common drugs that were ever used by inmates in 1996 and 2002.
- In 2002, 50.2 percent of convicted male jail inmates and 46.3 percent of convicted female jail inmates reported using alcohol or drugs at the time of the offense. This shows a decline from 1996 convicted males (58.9%) and females (58.4%).

Jail officers when dealing with substance-abusing inmates must keep in mind at all times that the substance-abusing lifestyle can look very appealing to the inmate. They may try to get drugs smuggled in or, on a related note, be resistant to either attend substance abuse programs or actively participate once enrolled.

Jail officers when booking in substance abusers should recognize possible symptoms of drug abuse, such as an inmate who is on hallucinogens talking "crazy" or an inmate complaining that he or she is sick. Usually when asked if they have been abusing drugs, most inmates suffering withdrawals will be open and honest and tell the jail officer that they are withdrawing from drugs or alcohol. These inmates should be seen by the medical staff immediately for treatment and medical housing. Serious medical problems and in some cases death can occur during substance abuse withdrawals.

## Elderly or Mature Inmates

There has been much speculation among corrections professionals as to what exactly an "elderly offender" actually is. Like in any group of people, there are some older inmates who are in reasonably good health and are able to withstand the jail environment. However, there are offenders who become incarcerated in local jails who are older. This is a special group that has health concerns—both physical and mental. A jail officer may assume a post and discover that there may be a 55-year-old inmate in a housing unit incarcerated for child pornography, a 62-year-old female locked up for assaulting a police officer during a domestic dispute, or a 70-year-old retiree arrested for drunk driving. **Elderly or mature inmates** may be termed as offenders who are aged 50 and older, the age where some health conditions become more serious, visible, and chronic. Research has suggested how older offenders find themselves incarcerated in jail, but a simple approach suggests that some older people become arrested for the first time when they are older due to various crimes such as child pornography, embezzlement, DUI, fraud, assault, etc. They have been law abiding all of their lives, but an error in judgment resulting in arrest has placed them in jail at a mature age. Another group of mature offenders in jail are inmates who may have been arrested for serious crimes when very young, such as an inmate, for example, who was arrested for multiple felonies at age 25, received several sentences totaling 50 years, and will be literally "growing old in prison." Where this type of inmate will be transferred to the DOC, he or she may be brought back to the local jail for court motions, retrial, as a witness, etc. The group of mature offenders in jails are inmates who have been getting arrested all of their lives—off and on—and find themselves at an advanced age coming back into the local jail. He or she not only may be very familiar with the layout of the jail, but also may be on good terms with the jail staff with whom he or she has interacted with over the years. It is no surprise to a jail officer to see coming down the hallway a familiar inmate who is older, grayer, and aged.

Elderly or mature inmates may seek out the jail staff and ask for more comfortable living quarters, saying that they cannot take the noise and immaturity from younger offenders. Some mature offenders have serious health problems which may pose a problem at any time—such as having a dizzy spell in a jail hallway to having to be escorted to visiting and programs by staff due to being an amputee in a wheelchair.

Jail staff should be aware of the following problem areas in the handling of elderly/mature inmates inside the local jail:[26]

- *Physical health needs:* Many older offenders live a negative lifestyle in and out of jail. This lifestyle, combined with poor health habits and lack of medical care, can result in serious illnesses such as ulcers, heart disease, smoking-related illnesses, arthritis, hypertension, hearing impairments, cataracts and poor eyesight, sleep disturbances, incontinence, diabetes, back/joint pain, orthopedic problems, and gastrointestinal disease. Many older inmates may have more than one ailment and require prescription medications. Older inmates may require frequent trips to the medical dispensary or transports to doctor's offices and hospital facilities for treatments.
- *Mental health needs:* As in all inmates, older inmates may suffer from a mental disorder. The most common mental health problem involving older inmates is depression. Families may disown the offender or abandon him or her. Reflecting on his or her past life may lead to despondency, shame, and guilt. Older offenders may be separated, divorced, or widowed. Their medical problems and the fact that they are in jail compound the problem. Suicide is a possibility. Some older inmates may be somewhat confused, and it is possible that diseases such as Alzheimer's may be present. In all cases of apparent mental difficulties in older offenders, they should be referred to the mental health staff. If the mental disorders are severe or advanced due to the inmate's age or due to chronic substance

abuse over a long period of time, he or she may have to be segregated away from other inmates for his or her safety and the safety of other inmates.

- *Housing needs:* Older inmates may have special housing needs, due to mental health and physical conditions. If an offender is infirm or has difficulty walking or moving around, a cell with a low bunk on a bottom tier (no stairs to climb) is advisable. A handicapped inmate may require the use of a handicapped cell if he or she is confined to a wheelchair. Crutches and walkers may pose a problem in the housing area, as they could be taken away from the inmate and used as a weapon by other inmates.
- *Protection needs:* Elderly/mature inmates can be the target of youthful, aggressive inmates who may ridicule them, assault them, and steal their food or commissary items. Older inmates should be placed very carefully in the jail population and not live with younger, aggressive inmates. Protection and safety is a serious concern of elderly inmates.
- *Programming needs:* Elderly inmates need physical activities like any other inmate. In recreation, they may just walk around. Recreational activities may be limited due to their physical condition, but just getting out of the housing area and being active is beneficial. Elderly inmates can also perform work as trusties, tutors, etc. Their self-esteem can be increased, and activity can help to ward off depression.

## Juveniles in Adult Jails

Offenders under the age of 18 can be housed under certain condition in adult jails. Statistically it is very low (see Table 7–4). However, jail staffs find themselves booking in and housing offenders under the age of 18.

In the early 1990s, there occurred a significant increase in juvenile crime. Most states, in accordance with the "get tough" philosophy, enacted laws to facilitate the placement of serious juvenile offenders in adult jails. In 1980, the Juvenile Justice Delinquency and Prevention Act was amended to include a mandatory provision that all states that were in receipt of federal funding would take steps to remove all juveniles from local adult jails by 1985. Because there occurred a juvenile crime wave, which was covered by the media and bolstered by get tough legislation, a trend occurred resulting in 38 states allowing the jailing of juvenile offenders in adult jails. This was due to the fact that the juveniles were going to be tried as adults in criminal courts or have been adjudicated in criminal courts.[27]

In managing and housing offenders under 18, jail staffs are faced with a challenge. The first is proper documentation for the court that the offender is **adult certified.** This means that a court order from a judge states that the offender is certified as an adult—either to be tried as an adult or is sentenced as an adult. The youth can be housed in the jail's adult population.

If the youth is not certified and is held in the jail, he or she must be separated from adult inmates by sight and sound. This means that the youth will be housed either alone or only with other juveniles until he or she reaches the age of 18. An exception may be a jail trusty—an adult inmate—who may be serving food or cleaning the hallway area where the juvenile is housed. However, that trusty should be escorted by a jail officer. Recreation will be attended alone, as are any programs. Signs must be posted that separate the area from any adult inmate traffic. Transports to court will not be with other inmates.

In handling juvenile offenders who are either certified as adults or held as juveniles, jail officers must be cognizant of the following:

- *Emotional age vs. chronological age:* Even though an inmate may be aged 16 or 17 and be certified as an adult, emotionally they may be much younger and being in jail may result in the youth being very upset and emotional. The jail officer must have patience and be a good listener in dealing with juveniles who may have trouble adjusting to jail. They may be impulsive, and due to age and limited life experience, they may not handle their situation in a mature manner. Suicidal behavior may be a definite possibility.
- *Incarceration/criminal experience:* Many youthful offenders have had brushes with the law before coming into a jail. Juvenile detention homes and boot camps may have introduced the youth to the "street smarts" and hard-core incarceration survival tactics. Juveniles can be members of street gangs, and may have learned criminal activity.
- *Physical restraints:* Some juvenile offenders are muscular, in good physical shape, and may know fighting techniques from the street environment. Officers can be attacked by juvenile offenders or may have to protect other inmates from a hard-core juvenile. Officers should not assume that just because the offenders are in their teens, they are not dangerous.
- *Substance abuse:* Juveniles have been known to use illegal drugs and alcohol. They are prone to withdrawals just as in adult inmate substance abusers.
- *Mental problems:* Juveniles may have mental disorders and should be screened in the same methods as are adult offenders.

## Female Offenders

The majority of offenders in jails are male. However, this does not minimize the importance the jail staff being aware of the problems and needs of female inmates. The BJS Special Report *Profile of Jail Inmates, 2002* gives a clear picture of female offenders in jail:[28]

- From 1996 to 2002, the number of female offenders rose from 10.2 to 11.6 percent, respectively.
- Concerning abuse, 55.3 percent of female offenders reported ever having been physically or sexually abused, increasing from 47.5 percent in 1996.
- Property offenses accounted for 32.4 percent of female offenders in local jails, followed by drug offenses at 29.2 percent, public-order offenses at 20.8 percent, and violent offenses at 17.1 percent. Out of the public-order offenses, DWI accounted for 4.9 percent.
- Concerning alcohol or drug usage at the time of offense, in 1996, 58.4 percent of female jail inmates reported using alcohol or drugs; that statistic dropped to 46.3 percent in 2002.
- Concerning criminal histories, 48.7 percent of female offenders reportedly had no previous sentence, 16.0 percent were violent recidivists, and 35.3 percent were nonviolent recidivists.

The BJS report *Women Offenders,* released in 1999, found that females who were under the supervision by criminal justice system agencies were the mothers of approximately 1.3 million minor children, and in local jails, 70 percent of women inmates had minor children.[29]

Data on female inmates are improving. Two of the most serious concerns about female jail offenders are pregnancy and the inmate having dependent children. Medical care and housing have to be careful to provide the best prenatal care and nonintrusive housing (reduced chances of injury and assault). A female inmate worrying about dependent children can result in depression, worry, and near hysteria.

To veteran jail staff, it may seem that female jail inmates do time differently than male inmates. In the area of "keep separates," it may be more difficult to be flexible in keeping female enemies apart than male enemies. This is primarily due to the limited housing areas for females. In one jail the male housing units (both general population and segregation) vastly outnumbered the female housing units. Female keep separate lists grew to be very long, and the staff encountered increasing difficulty in housing flexibility in keeping females separate who were on the list. The classification staff finally had to personally speak to female inmates on the list and ask them if they could try to get along. All females who were on the list for reasons other than physical assaults and criminal codefendants were required to sign documentation that they would try to coexist, thereby reducing the female keep separate list and allowing some females to move out of segregation. This approach made many female receiving and segregation cells available.

Where male inmates are often physically aggressive, female inmates tend to be more verbally aggressive. They do get into physical altercations, but for the most part, most disciplinary hearings for fighting in a jail are most likely to involve male inmates. Female inmates have different issues than males, such as worrying about dependent children on the outside and medical issues, especially if pregnant.

Marilyn Brooks, Superintendent of the SCI (State Correctional Institution), Cambridge Springs, Pennsylvania stated in 2002 based on her 20 years of correctional experience that female inmates do have different issues than male inmates, and as a result, do time differently. One example is when a female inmate asks the correctional staff for something or makes a request, they may be more emotional and demand a quick response, whereas male inmates are satisfied generally with an "I'll look into it" or that a response will be forthcoming. In her experience, female inmates are "definitely appreciative" when things are explained to them so that they understand the situation. She feels that staff has to earn the respect of female inmates. Male inmates seem to respect titles and know how to interact; females may be more verbally abusive, calling staff names behind their backs, and be more verbal. This difference could be due to the fact that in society, many males are raised around authority figures such as coaches, sports, etc. and act accordingly, respecting titles and authority. It may take more time for staff to earn respect from females.[30]

Also, according to Superintendent Brooks, female inmates when incarcerated tend to emotionally bond with other female inmates. This may be due to the need for females who are incarcerated to have a partner, just like in marriage in outside society. Females may want to talk more about their problems. According to Brooks, "Women will tell you that they have a grandmother in the hospital, that there is no one to watch their kids [and other details about their lives]—you are going to have to answer them. . . . They have a lot of issues and everything that affects them, affects their child, their husband or significant other, their grandmother, their sister [and more]. Women are caregivers—they look after everybody."[31] Jail staff must be aware of these issues when dealing with female inmates, especially those in crisis.

Many jails have gone to the **cross gender supervision** type of housing supervision, where staffs of opposite genders supervise inmates. For example, a male jail officer will be assigned to the female general population housing area and the female inmate receiving area. He can assist with processing duties such as inventories of property, getting inmates on the phone, etc., but searches of female inmates will be performed by female officers. Conversely, the same methods of operation allow female inmates to work in male inmate areas.

In cross gender supervision, there are several areas of concern. The first is that female inmates are subjected to a lack of privacy because male staff members have to observe them at any and all times. Inmates may be observed and checked while showering, using the toilet, dressing, etc. This does not violate any right concerning proper privacy as long as the action is not occurring in an intrusive and/or harassing manner. Also, there have to be some accommodations made for the inmates' privacy—such as shower curtains, some physical partition for the toilet, and the jail officer announcing his or her presence.[32] This can be simply accomplished by calling out "Man [or woman] on the floor." Another way this proper supervision can be accomplished is by having detailed orientations with the inmates and informing them that they will be supervised by staff of the opposite sex and proper conduct and appearances will be maintained at all times.

Another area of concern is if the female inmate accuses the male staff member of improper conduct. Female inmates can be very manipulative, and may try to initiate a romantic and flirtatious relationship with a male officer (and vice versa). Officer training and supervisory practices in the agency should address this issue. Male staff should strive to act professional at all times and not be overly friendly with female inmates. Supervisors should be mobile and keep in mind that female inmates have a lot to gain and nothing to lose by manipulating staff to bring in contraband, have a sexual relationship, or perform other favors. An effective strategy is for staff to be aware of these efforts from the inmates, investigate all allegations of misconduct, conduct themselves properly, and take disciplinary action against staff members who sexually abuse or harass female inmates. As a matter of policy in many agencies, all allegations of staff misconduct are referred to an internal affairs section or supervisor, who will investigate further.

Pregnant female inmates must be cared for not only by the medical staff but also by the officers working in the housing units. Pregnant females must be observed for any difficulties with other inmates that may result in assaults or injuries. Assignments to low bunks for pregnant females are recommended to reduce the discomfort and possible injuries from climbing up and down. Programs in prenatal care, postnatal care, and parenting are vital for female inmates. Even if a female is not pregnant, a parenting class could assist her in the proper raising of her children. Pregnancies may be difficult depending on the health of the female inmate, especially if she has abused alcohol and/or drugs.

In the past several decades, more attention has been paid to the problems of female inmates: substance abuse, pregnancy, being mothers of children, etc. At the Cumberland County, Maine jail from July 2002 to April 2003, 100 female inmates in the jail population were interviewed by Jo Kurzmann, MSW, of the Family Crisis Services (FCS), a nonprofit agency assisting women who are the victims of domestic abuse. The following data give a picture of a jailed female population:[33]

- Age range: 18–51 years.
- Race: 93 percent white, rest were black, Hispanic, biracial, Native American.

- Marital status:

| | |
|---|---|
| Single | 48% |
| Divorced | 22% |
| Married | 18% |
| Separated | 05% |
| Live in partner | 07% |

- Education:

| | |
|---|---|
| High school diploma | 30% |
| GED | 26% |

- Dependent children:

| | |
|---|---|
| Two children, average age 10 | 71% |
| Mother has custody | 41% |
| Father has custody | 13.2% |
| Joint custody | 10.4% |
| State has custody | 11.8% |
| Remaining children are in the custody of aunt, grandparent, etc. | |

- Homeless: 66%
- Abuse:

| | |
|---|---|
| During childhood (sexual) | 70% |
| Childhood physical abuse | 44% |
| Average age of first assault | 7 |
| Physical and emotional abuse | 93% |
| Sexual abuse | 49% |
| Average age when entering abusive relationship: | 20 |

The abuse that was described was severe, as many of the female inmates surveyed reported being pushed, shoved, choked, strangled, slapped, grabbed, kicked, assaulted with fists, or bitten. Some were deprived of sleep, were stabbed, or were shot. Many females reported being threatened with a firearm, ridiculed, and insulted. Many of the females were placed under arrest when their abuser was arrested, and some said that they were afraid to call for assistance because they thought that their probation would be violated. In the jail culture, it is a sign of weakness if female inmates speak of their abuse or being battered. Two drop-in support groups were formed so the female inmate population could learn to deal with such issues as domestic abuse.[34]

Focus groups were then formed to determine the types of reentry programs and advocacy that female offenders at the jail would need. Their needs during incarceration and upon release included:[35]

- Proper medical care, especially in pregnancy cases.
- Access to attorneys.

- Access to probation officers.
- Parenting classes.
- Counseling both in jail and when released.
- Support for admittance to long-term residential halfway houses.
- Support for admittance to residential substance abuse programs.
- Protection from abuse orders.
- Safety planning.
- Long-term transitional housing.
- Housing and shelters.
- Jobs.
- Receiving clothing upon release.

If the Cumberland County Jail female population is an accurate "snapshot" of a female jail population, then much has to be done by the local jail and supporting agencies to assist female offenders. The aspect of dependent children with relatives who are caregivers illustrate that there are other people affected by the incarceration and jailing of females. The population of females in jail will most likely continue to grow as females receive longer sentences due to the courts "getting tough" with criminals, no matter the age or gender.

## Suicidal/Self-Destructive Inmates

An inmate death in a local jail is a traumatic event—for the family of the inmate, the other inmates who may have lived with that inmate, and the jail staff who discovers the inmate. An inmate suicide also can draw media attention and scrutiny of the jail and its practices.

Jail staff has a duty to keep inmates safe from harm, including harm from themselves. The stress of incarceration and being confined can have a depressing effect on an inmate to the point where suicide appears to be a solution to solving one's problems. Related to inmate suicide is the aspect of self-destructive inmates, who may not necessarily want to die, but engage in such practices as cutting themselves, etc. They are no less a concern for the jail officer, as such behavior may lead to serious injury or death.

Jail statistics are constantly changing, and data concerning suicides are no exception. Officially, the BJS reported in the *Census of Jails, 1999* (released in August 2001) that inmate deaths by suicide totaled 328. Male inmates accounted for 304 suicide deaths, and female suicides totaled 24.[36] Between October 1 and November 5, 2004, over two dozen inmates committed suicide in U.S. jails and prisons, and over 100 inmates attempted suicide during that same period of time. Suicide is attempted monthly on average by 20 inmates in U.S. lockups, and only two attempts are successful each month.[37]

Suicides in jails can occur both when the inmate is booked in and when the inmate is living in general population. Being in jail is depressing and stressful. Some inmates do not handle it too well either in the receiving area or in general population.

The rate of suicide rates in correctional custody ranges from two to nine times the rate in the outside community. The risk of suicide is greater in short-term facilities such as jails, than in long term facilities (prisons). Also at high risk are juveniles—juveniles commit suicides nearly eight times higher in adult jails than in separate juvenile detention facilities. One theory that supports this is that with the sight and sound separation requirement for juvenile offenders, the resulting isolation and little or no contact with staff may result in sensatory deprivation and depression, which leads to suicide. Pretrial detainees have a highest suicide rate due to being under the influence of drugs or alcohol when arrested, being incarcerated for the first time, and having a history of social problems, economic problems, emotional problems, and mental illness.[38]

The issue of jail suicide is one of the most researched and written about topics in jail management. Numerous training seminars are conducted annually in training academies and jail staff roll calls. Suicide prevention is a recognized and vital part of any good jail training curriculum.

Preventing jail suicides is one of the most critical duties for jail officers. To do so, a jail officer has to be aware of factors of the jail environment that can predispose an inmate to suicide, stress factors—both external, affecting the inmate, and internal, what is going on inside the inmate. The jail officer has to be aware of the variety of methods used by inmates and the symptoms of suicidal behavior that inmates may display. Finally the jail officer needs to know effective intervention and monitoring strategies to hopefully prevent a suicide. The following factors play key roles in jail suicides:

- *Jail environment:* Upon incarceration, inmates experience a lack of control over the future. They cannot control events such as what will happen in court and what is going on at home, their job, family concerns, etc. Added to this is the feeling of shame of being incarcerated, especially for a heinous crime such as murder, rape, or a sex crime against children. Misdemeanants commit most of jail suicides. Jail is a dehumanizing environment, where there is a lack of privacy, including no privacy when using the toilet, etc. The inmate may be fearful of assault, or think that the jail is what they have seen portrayed negatively in the news or in movies. Jail is a regimented, authoritarian environment that runs on a schedule; inmates are told what to do and when to do it. These factors, coupled with insensitive or condemning jail staff members, can add to the depression and despair of a potentially suicidal inmate.[39]
- *Stress factors:* Internal stress factors that may lead to suicide include prior incarcerations, reluctance to face new charges, previous/recent suicide attempts or thoughts, possibly a victim of a same sex rape or other assault, theft, harassment, impulsivity, especially in a young inmate, history of mental illness or current mental illness (including any type of depression), history of substance abuse, substance abuse withdrawal, guilt/shame, and terminal or chronic illness. Over 60 percent of suicides in jail are committed by offenders who when admitted were under the influence of alcohol and/or drugs. External stress factors include being a first-time arrestee, being under the influence of drugs or alcohol when incarcerated, loss of a stabilizing resource such as job, home, finances, or loved one(s), rejection from family or a loved one, in jail for a heinous crime, prominence in the community, family history of suicide, long sentences under adverse conditions (violence, overcrowding, etc.), and a recent suicide attempt in the jail which may lead to a "copycat" attempt.[40]
- *Methods of suicide:* Common methods of suicide include hanging with material from clothing or bed linens, overdosing on medication that has been hoarded, jumping from a tier, cutting with any sharp object including razors issued for shaving, or banging one's head against the wall. Some methods are ingenious such as inmates going on a hunger strike or trying to drown themselves in the toilet.
- *Signs or symptoms of suicidal behavior:* Often inmates may exhibit signs that they are contemplating ending their lives. The best sign is depression—it is estimated that

70–80 percent of suicidal individuals show signs of depression. Other signs include mood/behavior changes, crying, packing belongings, giving away possessions, calm after agitation (the decision to commit suicide has been made), unusual concern about what may happen in court, statements of dying, such as "the world will be better off if I am dead," lethargy, problems sleeping, high anxiety, tense, neglect of appearance and hygiene, loss/increase of appetite or weight, silence, and withdrawal.[41]

- *Intervention strategies:* Jail officers have to be ready to observe for suicidal behavior and intervene at any time. *All* threats of suicide should be taken seriously until the inmate is seen by a mental health professional. Even after that, the inmate may still be at risk. These strategies include removing any items from the cell that the inmate could commit self-harm with, or putting the inmate in a high observation area, such as a holding area directly across from a post directly in the line of sight from staff. Other methods are to refer to mental health staff, and document the inmate's actions indicating what was done to protect the jail from liability. The most important thing for the officer to do is to show concern to a fellow human being and get the inmate to talk about his or her problems. Many inmates do not want to die and will act in a suicidal fashion in the hope that a jail staff member will care about their welfare enough to try to help them, or "throw them a lifeline." Many jails perform the standard checking on a suicidal inmate every 15 minutes, but veteran jail officers may recommend every 5–10 minutes or less, as suicidal inmates are unpredictable and cannot be trusted. Jail officers must learn to "trust their gut" and check inmates as often as they think necessary—this may mean every 5 minutes if needed. One continuous debate in jail suicide prevention is whether to place a suicidal inmate in isolation or put him or her in a holding area with other inmates. If there is a question of violent or incompatible behavior, isolation may be best. However, isolation may magnify the feelings of despair and depression. Occasionally, it is feasible to place suicidal inmates around others as suicide is a private act and the inmate may be less prone to end his or her life if others are present. One method being used is to place the inmate on **restricted issue (R/I)**. This means that nothing is given to the inmate that could be used for self-harm—no sheets, towels, pencils, pens, etc. The inmate may have a suicide-resistant blanket that is tear resistant. Jail officers may place an inmate on suicide watch and on R/I with a supervisor's approval in an emergency, but only qualified mental health staff should clear the person to be taken off suicide watch/RI and be considered for general population. Some inmates are so much of a risk that they may be on R/I and suicide watch indefinitely.
- *Critical times:* There is no way to accurately pinpoint the times of inmate suicides. Research has reported that critical times for inmates are during the first 24 hours of being incarcerated in jail, and one third of suicides in jail occur within three hours after the inmate is booked into the jail.[42] The initial hours in jail are important because it is a transition period. The inmate has to adjust to jail and mental health staff may not see him or her for several hours or the next day. Other critical times are "after" times when the inmate may have received bad news. These include after visiting, after court (especially sentencing), after a personal phone call, or after receiving mail.
- *Manipulative inmates:* Some inmates do not really want to die, but want to manipulate the staff by engaging in suicidal behavior. The goal may be to elicit sympathy from the staff or the court, to be placed away from other inmates, or to enjoy

seeing what the staff does in suicidal cases. There is a danger with this type of behavior—an inmate tries a suicide attempt thinking that he or she will be discovered by the staff. If the jail officer does not find the inmate in time, for example, in a hanging, the inmate could die.

- *Self-destructive inmates:* Closely related to the manipulative inmate are self-destructive inmates who will engage in cutting themselves or engaging in other forms of self-mutilation and pain. They may be suffering from a mental disorder; only a qualified mental health professional can make an informed determination. These types of inmates are in our prisons and jails, and this behavior can occur both when first incarcerated and in prison. Inmates have been known to cut open their stomachs and remove intestines, insert objects such as oranges, apples, razor blades, pencils, pens, knives, etc. into the rectum, cutting themselves regularly with a razor, or removing an item such as a window frame screw and sticking it into a vein.[43]
- *Restraints:* If the inmate is seriously bent on killing himself or herself, or is engaging in self-mutilation and self-destructive acts, it may be necessary to forcibly move the inmate to a high observation cell, such as a padded cell ("rubber room"), and restraints may or may not be applied depending on the situation. Emergency response teams may be activated to make sure the move is accomplished and the restraints are applied.

## Foreign/Culturally Diverse Inmates

Just as jail staffs have no control over the types of behavioral problems, health problems, crimes, or mental disorders of inmates being incarcerated in the local jail, the same is true of inmates from foreign countries or culturally diverse ethnic groups. Almost 24 percent of inmates in jails in 2002 had a racial/ethnic origin of other than white and / or black; in 2004 it was 17 percent (see Tables 7–4 and 7–5).

Jail staffs have to be prepared for foreign offenders (those not U.S. citizens and have immigrated to the United States) and offenders from different ethnic groups and nationalities. The most effective way of dealing with these inmates is to have the jail staffing mirror the ethnic makeup of the jail inmate population. If Hispanics, Asians, etc. are represented in the inmate population at a significant level, there should be jail staff on duty not only to translate in cases where the inmate does not speak English, but to advise staff (classification, mental health, medical staff, etc.) about the cultural customs and habits of the inmate in order to resolve any miscommunications, to get the inmate's cooperation, and to lessen the inmate's fears. Also, if the inmate is having difficulty with other inmates, accurate translation and communications may avoid a serious incident.

Probably the language barrier is the most difficult problem for an inmate from another country or an ethnic group. In the confusing and fast moving world of the jail, he or she may not clearly understand orders, instructions, orientations, or how to communicate with staff. Also, all the offender knows about law enforcement is how the police and jails are in his or her native country, which usually are quite different from the humane jails we have in the United States. If an interpreter is to be used, jail officers must realize that this may take time and patience. Jail staff must make it clear to the interpreter, especially if he or she is a civilian, the importance of getting exactly correct what the inmate and staff are trying to say to each other. For example, in one southern U.S. jail, an offender who had recently arrived in the United States and was arrested for assault was not eating. The classification staff was concerned for two reasons—first, they could not effectively interview the inmate because he did not speak English, only Vietnamese, and second, it could not be ascertained if the refusal to eat was suicidal ideation. An interpreter was called in from a local refugee organization to translate the classification and mental health interview. It was discovered that the inmate had difficulty eating American food, and preferred rice. A dietary substitute was arranged and he was cleared for general population housing.

Training in cultural diversity is essential, as the United States experiences more foreign people entering the country and sometimes being arrested, as well as inmates from different cultural backgrounds. Most county agencies have staff liaisons that assist immigrants in the community; these agencies can assist in training jail staffs in dealing with inmates from another country. Another good practice is to have the jail administrator publish an annual listing of jail staff proficient in foreign languages. This proves useful in critical situations, such as a suicidal inmate, where translation plays a vital role.

## HANDLING SPECIAL CATEGORY INMATES

Jail officers and staff have to be a type of "jack of all trades" concerning special category inmates, ranging from the mentally disordered to pregnant females. The following are some basic, generic guidelines in addition to the practices that have been discussed in this chapter:

- *Knowledge and training:* Jail staff must be up-to-date on recent developments and information on special category inmates. Ongoing training is important, as more emphasis has been placed on mentally disordered inmates, females, foreign inmates, etc. in the last several years. Jail officers and staff are not experts, but should have a good working knowledge of dealing with these inmates.
- *Documentation:* If an inmate has a mental problem, a medical problem, exhibits odd behavior, etc., accurate documentation is crucial. If an inmate is segregated, a log should be kept stating the inmate's problem, when he or she is fed, when he or she is allowed to shower, when he or she sees the medical staff, etc. This log is called an **observation log**, a document where all vital information and staff observation and interactions with an individual special management inmate are documented (see Chapter 5 for definition and explanation). Serious incidents such as medical emergencies, suicide attempts, etc. should be documented in reports that are approved by a shift supervisor and made available to all staffs who deal with the inmate. Other important documents are mental health consultations, recommendations, and medical notes, etc. that must be accurate and properly filed.
- *Expecting the unexpected:* Special category inmates are often unpredictable and staff should use caution. A mentally disordered inmate may be calm and an hour later may be acting totally irrational. Jail officers should use basic, sound safety principles such as backup, etc. Jail officers should also know what to do if they encounter an inmate hanging, slashing, ingesting medications, etc. Jail staff should be trained in up-to-date first aid procedures. Care must be taken to preserve inmate life.
- *Networking:* All important information about special category inmates should be shared with staff at classification meetings, roll calls, etc. One effective method being used is a **special housing roster** (see Chapter 5 for definition and explanation)

Even though inmates in jail have many problems, many are artistic. These inmate "soap sculptures" were found in the Albany County, NY Correctional Facility.

Courtesy Edward W. Szostak.

that is generated daily to staff. This log lists the inmate, his or her location, the authority who places the inmate on segregation, the reason for segregation, and the dates that his or her file will be reviewed by classification. Also, the log may note advisories such as using caution, the inmate is suicidal, may assault staff, on R/I, escape risk, etc. This type of log can also list any medical restrictions for recreation, keep separates, etc.

## SUMMARY

The jail population is a diverse group in terms of both criminal justice involvement and demographic data. The offense categories of jail inmates are evenly distributed among violent offenses, property offenses, drug offenses, and public-order offenses. Statistically most jail inmates are convicted and over one third have no prior sentence.

Demographically, most jail inmates are male and almost are evenly distributed between white and black. Most jail inmates are between 25 and 44 years of age. Most have a GED, high school, or some high school education. Most jail inmates are employed. Concerning family involvement, over one half of jail inmates were raised by either one parent or guardian.

Inmates with mental illness continue to be a concern for jail staffs. The disorders vary and require special handling. Inmates also may suffer from a variety of medical problems including HIV infection, AIDS, TB, and forms of hepatitis. To be safe from exposure to these diseases, staffs use universal precautions.

Marijuana, cocaine/crack, stimulants, and alcohol are substances that are used at a high rate by inmates. Elderly or mature inmates have physical health needs, mental health needs and must be housed carefully so as not to be victimized by predatory inmates.

The continuing trend is for the criminal justice system to place juvenile offenders in adult jails. Jail staffs need to exercise caution and patience in dealing with youthful offenders, as the adjustment may be difficult and the rates of suicide are high. Female offenders have a unique set of problems, including being the mothers of young children, pregnancies, and histories of abuse. Many jails use cross gender supervision in dealing with female offenders but must be wary of accusations of improper conduct by female inmates.

Suicides in jail are problems as jail staff must protect inmates from themselves. Suicidal inmates may exhibit symptoms that officers see and will place in high observation areas, document behavior and observations, and refer to mental health staff. Training in inmate suicides including signs, methods, and intervention strategies is a must for any jail.

Dealing with foreign inmates may be difficult. The composition of the jail staff should mirror the ethnic background of the jail population, and staff should undergo cultural diversity training, which is becoming more widespread.

## REVIEW QUESTIONS

1. Describe the types of crimes in each jail offense category.
2. Explain the statement that"jail inmates are not strangers to the criminal justice system."
3. What does statistical data say concerning female offenders and the age of offenders?
4. Describe the clues that indicate to the jail officer that an inmate may be mentally disordered.
5. Describe three mental disorders and how each is a concern for jail staff.
6. What is the importance of universal precautions?
7. What are some problems of female offenders in jail?
8. How does the jail environment influence jail suicides?
9. Discuss suicide intervention strategies that can be employed by jail staff.
10. What are the four generic guidelines in handling special category inmates?

## TERMS TO KNOW

adult certified
anxiety disorders
convicted status
criminal justice status
cross gender supervision
elderly or mature inmates
lockout
mood disorders
observation log
personality disorders
restricted issue (R/I)
sexual disorders
special housing roster
substance abuse disorders
thought disorders
unconvicted status
universal precautions rule

## ENDNOTES


1. Doris J. James, U.S. Department of Justice, Bureau of Justice Statistics Special Report, *Profile of Jail Inmates, 2002*, revised 10/12/04, Washington, DC: GPO, 2004, p. 3.
2. Ibid.
3. Ibid.
4. Ibid.
5. Ibid., p. 2.
6. Ibid., p. 6.
7. Ibid.
8. Ibid., p. 7.
9. Scott E. Blough and Joyce Davenport, "State of Ohio Annual Jail Report 1999," *American Jails* (March–April 2001), 47, 48, 50.
10. Washington Association of Sheriffs and Police Chiefs, *Washington Jails: Jail Statistics: WASPC Spokane County Jail Average Daily Population"* http://www.waspc.org/jails/JailStats/2003/Counties/Spokane.html
11. Michael D. Norman, Ph.D., and Hazen L. Locke, "Housing State Prisoners in Local Jails: The Utah Experience," *American Jails* (January–February 2002), 14, 15.
12. Doris J. James, U.S. Department of Justice, *Profile of Jail Inmates 2002*, 2, 9, 10.
13. Paige M. Harrison and Allen J. Beck, Ph.D., U.S. Department of Justice, Bureau of Justice Statistics Bulletin. *Prison and Jail Inmates at Midyear 2004*, Washington, DC: GPO, 2005, p. 8.
14. Paige M. Harrison and Allen J. Beck, Ph.D., U.S. Department of Justice, Bureau of Justice Statistics Bulletin. *Prison and Jail Inmates at Midyear 2005*, Washington, DC: GPO, 2006, p. 8.
15. Doris J. James and Lauren E. Glaze, U.S. Department of Justice, Bureau of Justice Statistics Special Report. *Mental Health Problems of Prison and Jail Inmates*, Washington, DC: GPO, 2006, 1, 2, 4, 6–8.
16. Gary L. Lupton, "Identifying and Referring Inmates With Mental Disorders: A Guide for Correctional Staff," *American Jails* (May–June 1996), 49–52.
17. National Commission on Correctional Health Care. *The Health Status of Soon to Be Released Inmates: A Report to Congress, Volume 1*, Washington, DC: GPO, March 2002, p. xi.
18. Laura M. Maruschak, U.S. Department of Justice, Bureau of Justice Statistics Special Report, *Medical Problems of Jail Inmates*, Washington, DC: GPO, pp. 1, 3.
19. National Commission on Correctional Health Care, *The Health Status of Soon to Be Released Inmates, Volume 1*, Washington, DC: National Institute of Justice, 2002, pp. 20, 21.
20. Laura M. Maruschak, U.S. Department of Justice, Bureau of Justice Statistics Bulletin. *HIV in Prisons and Jails, 2002*, Washington, DC: GPO, 2004, pp. 1, 9.
21. National Commission on Correctional Health Care, "Position Statement: Management of Tuberculosis in Correctional Facilities," *American Jails* (November–December 1966), p. 95.
22. Ibid.
23. Ibid., p. 96.
24. Don Bales, ed., *Correctional Officer Resource Guide: Third Edition* (Lanham: American Correctional Association, 1997), pp. 93, 94.
25. Doris J. James, U.S. Department of Justice, *Profile of Jail Inmates (2002)*, p. 8.
26. Edith E. Flynn, Ph.D., "Working With Elderly Inmates," *Jail Operations Bulletin*, VII (7) (1995): 3–6.
27. Frances P. Reddington, Ph.D., "An Issue Worth Revisiting: Juveniles in Jails," *American Jails* (September–October 2002), 58–60.
28. Doris J. James, U.S. Department of Justice, *Profile of Jail Inmates 2002*, 2, 4, 7, 8, 10.
29. Lawrence A. Greenfield and Tracy L. Snell, U.S. Department of Justice, Bureau of Justice Statistics Special Report, *Women Offenders*, Washington, DC, 1999, pp. 7, 8.
30. Keith Martin, "Managing Female Offenders: Principles and Practices," *corrections.com*, December 8, 2002, http://www.corrections.com/news/article_print.aspx?articleid = 8023 (Accessed January 27, 2007).
31. Martin, "Managing Female Offenders: Principles and Practices," *corrections.com*.
32. Sarah Manning, "Women In Jails" (Research paper, George Mason University), November 2004.
33. Jo Kurzmann, "Advocacy for Women in a Jail Setting," *American Jails* (March–April 2004), 18.
34. Ibid.
35. Ibid., p. 20.
36. James J. Stephan, U.S. Justice Department, Bureau of Justice Statistics. *Census of Jails, 1999*, Washington, DC: GPO, 2001, p. 42.
37. "Suicide on the Rise in U.S. Prisons, Jail Facilities," *The Corrections Professional*, 10, (6) (November 19, 2004): 1.
38. Joseph R. Rowan, *Suicide Prevention in Custody: Self Instructional Course* (Lanham, MD: American Correctional Association, 1998), pp. 13, 14.
39. Ibid., pp. 26–28.
40. Ibid., pp. 37–39.
41. Ibid., pp. 46–48, 50.
42. Ibid., p. 59.
43. Sgt. Gerald Berry, "Focus on Training: How to Effectively Deal with Self Mutilators Behind Bars," *The Corrections Professional*, 9 (18) (June 18, 2004): 5.

## REFERENCES


Bales, Don, ed. *Correctional Officer Resource Guide: Third Edition.* Lanham, MD: American Correctional Association, 1997.

Berry, Sgt. Gerald. "Focus on Training: How to Effectively Deal with Self Mutilators Behind Bars." *The Corrections Professional,* 9 (18) (June 18, 2004): 5.

Blough, Scott E. and Joyce Davenport. "State of Ohio Annual Jail Report 1999." *American Jails* (March–April 2001), 47–52.

"Suicide on the Rise in U.S. Prisons, Jail Facilities." *The Corrections Professional,* 10 (6) (November 19, 2004): 1, 6.

Flynn, Edith E., Ph.D. "Working with Elderly Inmates." *Jail Operations Bulletin* (American Jail Association) 7 (7) (1995).

Greenfield, Lawrence A. and Tracy L. Snell. U.S. Justice Department, Bureau of Justice Statistics. *Women Offenders.* Washington, DC: GPO, 1999.

Harrison, Paige M. and Allen J. Beck, Ph.D. U.S. Department of Justice, Bureau of Justice Statistics. *Prison and Jail Inmates at Midyear 2004.* Washington, DC: GPO, 2005.

Harrison, Paige M. and Allen J. Beck, Ph.D. U.S. Department of Justice, Bureau of Justice Statistics Bulletin. *Prison and Jail Inmates at Midyear 2005.* Washington, DC: GPO, 2006.

James, Doris J. U.S. Department of Justice, Bureau of Justice Statistics. *Profile of Jail Inmates, 2002,* revised 10/12/04. Washington, DC: GPO, 2004.

James, Doris J. and Lauren E. Glaze. U.S. Department of Justice, Bureau of Justice Statistics Special Report. *Mental Health Problems of Prison and Jail Inmates.* Washington, DC: GPO, 2006.

Kurzmann, Jo. "Advocacy for Women in a Jail Setting." *American Jails* (March–April 2004), 17–22.

Lupton, Gary L. "Identifying and Referring Inmates with Mental Disorders: A Guide for Correctional Staff." *American Jails* (May–June 1996), 49–52.

Manning, Sarah. "Women In Jails." Research paper, George Mason University, 2004.

Martin, Keith. "Managing Female Offenders: Principles and Practices." *corrections.com,* December 8, 2002, http://www.corrections.com/news/article_print.aspx?articleid = 8023 (Accessed January 27, 2007).

Maruschak, Laura M. U.S. Department of Justice, Bureau of Justice Statistics. *HIV in Prisons and Jails, 2002.* Washington, DC: GPO, 2004.

Maruschak, Laura M. U.S. Department of Justice, Bureau of Justice Statistics Special Report. *Medical Problems of Jail Inmates.* Washington, DC: GPO, 2006.

National Commission on Correctional Health Care. "Position Statement: Management of Tuberculosis in Correctional Facilities." *American Jails,* November–December 1966, 95–96.

National Commission on Correctional Health Care. *The Health Status of Soon to Be Released Inmates: A Report to Congress, Volume 1.* Washington, DC: National Institute of Justice, 2002.

Norman, Michael D., Ph.D., and Hazen L. Locke. "Housing State Prisoners in Local Jails: The Utah Experience." *American Jails,* January–February 2002, 13–17.

Reddington, Frances P., Ph.D. "An Issue Worth Revisiting: Juveniles in Jails." *American Jails* (September–October 2002), 58–61.

Rowan, Joseph R. *Suicide Prevention in Custody: Self Instructional Course.* Lanham, MD: American Correctional Association, 1998.

Stephan, James J. U.S. Department of Justice, Bureau of Justice Statistics. *Census of Jails, 1999.* Washington, DC: GPO, 2001.

Washington Association of Sheriffs and Police Chiefs. *Washington Jails: Jail Statistics: WASPC Spokane County Jail Average Daily Population.* http://www.waspc.org/jails/JailStats/2003/Counties/Spokane.html (Accessed May 8, 2005).

# JAIL STAFF

# 8

***Objectives of chapter***

The student will:

- Identify the staff structure of a jail
- Learn the importance of proper jail staff recruitment and effective retention
- Understand how good training helps jail officers in the performance of their duties
- Learn new trends concerning jail staff: training resources, dealing with problems, emerging issues, and staffing analysis

A jail cannot be operated without a staff who is properly recruited, screened, and trained. Operating a modern jail requires more than officers walking around with keys, feeding inmates, and taking headcounts. A century ago, jails were staffed by a minimal number of jail officers whose main concern was to prevent escapes. Jails were overcrowded in some jurisdictions, but there was no concern as to the welfare of inmates, programs, special problems, etc.

Now, jails are staffed by both sworn, or uniformed staff, and civilian staff. Also, volunteers ands other personnel who assist the jail operations are cleared to come into the facility. The modern jail staff is a hybrid of sworn staff, civilian staff, and outside personnel. To further understand the machinery of jail operations, it is imperative to understand the men and women who make up the jail staff.

## STAFF STRUCTURE OF THE MODERN JAIL

Surveys conducted by the Bureau of Justice Statistics illustrate generally the number and types of jail staffs nationally. In the *Sourcebook of Criminal Justice Statistics 2002,* released in 2004, the national estimate of jail staffing as of June 30, 1999, was as follows:[1]

| | |
|---|---|
| • Total jail staff | 210,600 |
| • Correctional Officers | 151,200 |
| • Administrative staff | 14,600 |
| • Clerical and maintenance | 25,400 |
| • Educational | 2,100 |
| • Professional and technical | 11,500 |
| • Other | 5,800 |

## Total Jail Staff

A local jail may also be operated not by a sheriff's office but by a **local county corrections department.** The sheriff's office may be responsible for the service of court papers, and the safety and security of county courthouses, the courts, judges, and court staff, but the corrections department is responsible for the operation of the local jail. The local corrections department and the sheriff's office must have a good working liaison because their functions are closely linked, such as the safe transport and security of inmates from the jail to the local court.

The jail staff contains two groups: sworn staff and civilian staff. **Sworn jail staff** is uniformed personnel who have law enforcement powers, such as arrest powers, and receive law enforcement training that meet state and agency standards. The "sworn" simply means that the officer has taken an oath swearing to uphold the laws, etc. They may be called deputies, detention officers, or correctional officers. **Civilian jail staff** is staffs who have no law enforcement authority, but provide services to the jail such as medical services, food service, programs, substance abuse counseling, mental health, maintenance, etc. All personnel, sworn or civilian, must be qualified to work in the jail through applicant screening and good hiring procedures.

In some local correctional agencies, the jail staff is composed of sections that are part of a larger part of the agency called a division. An agency such as a sheriff's office may have several divisions, each with its own specialized function that supports the mission of the sheriff's office. For example, a sheriff's office may consist of an administration division, a court division, a jail division, and if applicable, a community corrections division. Each local corrections agency is somewhat unique.

The branch or division of the agency that operates the jail is generally composed of several sub-sections. As jails are part of sheriff's offices or local corrections departments, it is impossible to provide one description of an organizational chart that fits all. For the sake of illustration, the total jail staff will be explained as part of a division of either a local corrections department or a sheriff's office. The sub-sections of this division contain groups of personnel, each with its own responsibilities and job titles.

## Command Staff

At the highest level of the jail organizational chain is the head of the jail, or the **jail administrator.** Frequently called the warden or chief jailor, his or her responsibility is the supervision of all the sections and staff who work in the jail. In some agencies, the jail administrator is called captain or major depending on the rank structure of the jail. If the jail is very small, such as in a rural area, the jail administrator may be a lieutenant or sergeant. The head of the jail may also be called superintendent, depending on the agency.

An interesting situation is the state of Kentucky, which is the only state in the United States that elects jail administrators. Jail administrators, called jailors, supervise the jail and overshadow the local sheriffs, who are held to only one four-year term and focus on non-jail issues, such as tax collections. Many of these elected local jailors have strong community ties and live with their families in very close proximity to the jail.[2] However, for the most part, jail administrators are appointed by elected sheriffs or are hired to supervise a local corrections department.

Immediately under the jail administrator are the section or branch supervisors who may be captains, lieutenants, or sergeants. Each of these supervisors reports to the jail administrator. This small group of senior supervisors is known as the jail

**command staff.** The functions of the jail command staffs are to, through supervision and guidance, ensure that the policies of the agency as pertaining to the jail are carried out. Each of these supervisors also performs these duties:

- Reads daily shift reports from each section if applicable.
- Disciplines and counsels subordinates if necessary.
- Conducts jail inspections.
- Serves as staff duty officer on a rotating basis (see Chapter 3).
- Holds meetings and briefings of subordinate supervisors.
- Prepares budget submissions.
- Responds to inmate grievances.
- Any other duties from the jail administrator as required.
- Submits new or revised policies and procedures.
- Acts as jail administrator during his or her absence
- Acts as agency representative as directed (i.e., media spokesperson).

### *Confinement Branch*

A key branch in the jail staff is the **confinement branch, or custody branch.** This branch is responsible for the 24-hour a day, 7 days per week, 365 days per year operation and security of the facility. Also, it is charged with the enforcement of all laws of the jurisdiction in the jail as well as all of the jail rules and regulations. This involves such tasks as booking offenders in and out of the jail, moving them inside the jail, searching inmates and their living/working areas, jail inspections, etc.

The confinement branch has four teams or squads that work a rotating schedule in order to provide the round-the-clock coverage of the jail operations. Generally jails have a day/night rotation, either 8 hours or 12 hours for a specific period of a time such as a month of day work and a month of night shift. Some jails have adopted the **short/long schedule,** which consists of a short week and a long week of 12-hour days. This schedule works as follows, based on a two-week pay period of at least 80 work hours:

*First Week:* Monday, Tuesday, Friday, Saturday, Sunday at 12 hours per day = 60 hours

Wednesday and Thursday Off = 0 hours

*Second Week:* Wednesday and Thursday at 12 hours per day = 24 hours

Total for a Two-Week Pay Period = 84 hours

For many jail officers, this is a popular schedule because every other weekend the officer is off duty, allowing a break from the stresses of the jail and allowing for time with the family. Also, the officers are usually rotated to another post every six hours. If the officer is assigned to a high-stress area such as disciplinary segregation, a break after six hours is welcome especially if the officer is rotated to a post away from inmates such as the control center.

Operationally, the squad or team's tour of duty is preceded by a **roll call.** This is a meeting, usually 20–30 minutes in length, where command staff directives and memos are read to the officers, post assignments are announced, training is conducted, agency announcements are read, special assignments are announced, and any questions about operations or inmates are answered. Additionally, all incident reports of note are read and discussed concerning problems in the jail, such as gang activity, mentally ill inmates, escape risks, etc.

The team or squad has a rank structure and officers that are assigned to perform specific tasks:

- *Squad leader:* Supervises the operations of entire squad, has final authority on assignments, authorizes officers taking leave (vacation time), carries out instructions from branch supervisor, ensures accuracies and signs off on shift reports, logs, and incident reports, recommends or authorizes further disciplinary/criminal actions on inmates if necessary, takes whatever action necessary to fulfill the mission of the confinement branch (i.e., ordering searches), responds to emergencies, initiates calls to staff duty officer, counsels, disciplines, and evaluates subordinates. Usually serves at rank of sergeant or higher and may delegate these duties to other supervisors on the squad, especially in case of absence.
- *Assistant squad commander:* Serves as assistants to squad commander including supervising the squad, assists in review and signing off on incident reports, shift logs, etc. May relieve officers on post and participate in officer evaluations, disciplinary actions, and counseling. Usually serves below squad commanders' rank at sergeant, corporal, etc. Other duties include taking charge in emergency cell extractions, acting as liaison to Classification, etc.
- *Jail correctional officer:* Officer assigned to a specific area of the jail (post), responsible for security and smooth operations at that post, safeguards the welfare of all inmates, staff and visitors in his or her area. Conducts counts, searches, and inspections. Enforces jail rules, regulations, and policies, takes actions in emergencies including documenting rule/law violations and unusual occurrences. Responsible for completing post logs and other documentation relating to his or her assignment. May perform other duties as assigned such as booking, receiving, classification, transportation, and training. May also serve as team member on the squad's emergency response team. If certified, may act as cardiopulmonary resuscitation (CPR)/first aid instructor and field training officer (FTO).
- *"Floater:"* Jail correctional officer who moves about the jail performing such duties as post relief, transporting inmates, searches, inmate/staff/visitor escorts, inspections, special tasks, tours, etc.

In times of short staffing, supervisors may have to take over posts. It is not uncommon to see an assistant squad commander working inside a control booth or assisting booking staff. Correctional staff follows four levels that delineate the top of an agency to the bottom: leaders, managers, supervisors, and line staff.[3]

- *Leaders:* sets the direction and policy for the organization, empowers personnel, and deals with external agencies. Example: Sheriff, Director of Corrections, Chief Deputy Sheriffs, Under Sheriffs, Associate Directors, etc.
- *Managers:* sets department and division goals and objectives, controls resources such as budgets and staff allocations, disbursing those resources in a way to "get the job done." Example—Division supervisor: jail administrator, majors, etc.
- *Supervisors:* direct the line staffs, provide close supervision of daily operations, ensure efficiency and compliance with agency policies and procedures. Example—captains, lieutenants, sergeants, corporals, etc.

Some jail officers, in smaller facilities, are "jacks of all trades," where they perform various duties in different sections of the jail.

Photo by author, courtesy Teton County Jail.

- *Line staff:* personnel responsible for close, daily supervision of inmates or daily operations in their work assignments, and carrying out agency policies and procedures. Examples—correctional officers, cooks, laundry staff, etc.

## Diagnostic and Treatment Staff

The **diagnostic and treatment staffs** are the classification, medical, and mental health staff who works inside the jail diagnosing inmate characteristics and problems, and makes decisions on housing, medical care, and mental health intervention. In order of importance, medical staff screens the arriving inmates for any medical problems and arrange for treatment if necessary. Also, the medical staff takes care of inmate medical problems from illnesses and injuries incurred in general population.

The classification staff (see Chapter 5) conducts initial interviews of new offenders and constantly adjusts the inmate general population due to housing needs, offender friction, security issues, behavior problems, and disciplinary issues.

The medical staff is responsible for the medical needs and dental needs of the inmate population. The medical staff screens inmates for health problems when they are booked into the jail, performs physical exams, conducts specified tests, dispenses medications, supervises inmate sick call with a physician, coordinates basic inmate dental treatment, responds to medical emergencies, schedules medical treatment outside the jail, and is responsible for the medical care of inmates housed in the infirmary.

The mental health staff, or sometimes called Forensics, screens inmates for mental health problems, acting on referrals from booking, the confinement post officers, classification or medical. A well-funded jail unusually has an on-site mental health staff, consisting of a supervisor (psychiatrist) and several clinical psychologists. Mental health staffs *must* work closely with the entire jail staff, due to the critical nature of inmates' mental health problems and the potential for bodily harm and self-injury.

Depending on the jail organization makeup, programs staff may be included in either the diagnostic and treatment group or the support services group. Programs staff are clearly divided due to the diverse nature of their tasks. On one level, there are substance abuse counselors who not only teach substance abuse classes to inmates but also provide different forms of therapy and counseling, which regulates them into a treatment role. However, other programs staff, such as social workers, education teachers, chaplains, etc., and volunteers may be in a support role. Probably, the best way is to include all staff who has anything to do with inmates' problems into a treatment section as to not confuse them with other support staff.

## Support Services

Support services staffs are those workers who provide services to the jail in the areas of food service, sanitation (janitorial), laundry, handling property and mail, and maintenance. These are for the most part civilian staff who is hired to perform these tasks or are workers in a private sector firm that has contracted with the jail. For example, food service workers who are registered dieticians and cooks may be civilian staff working for the county or may be part of a private company. Maintenance personnel are usually county employees who are constantly performing tasks that keep the jail systems—lights, power, air conditioning, heat, plumbing, etc.—in operation.

Handling of inmate property, laundry, and mail are tasks that are slowly being turned over whenever possible to civilian workers, either contracted or as members of the agency. With the need for jail officers to be on posts, provide security such as on transportation runs, etc., the arduous tasks of receiving and releasing inmate property, and sorting and searching mail may better be left to civilian staff. However, these workers are frequently supervised by sworn staff who can take authoritative disciplinary and criminal action in times of serious incidents.

## Administration Staff

Usually composed of civilians, administration workers perform a variety of duties: clerical support, inmate records, public information, accreditation, and technical support. Almost all branches in the jail need clerical support due to increasing workloads and the need to keep good records. A key function is inmate records—such as ensuring that all jail actions and court actions are properly filed and accessible. Inmate records must be completely accurate, so that inmates have their sentences properly computed. Also inmate records staff keep track of warrants served on the inmate after he or she is booked into the jail.

Public information is another task that is performed by civilian administrative staff. As jails expand in population capacity, increasing numbers of citizens will come to the jail to visit inmates on personal and professional levels, receive property from the inmate, bring property such as court clothes (civilian clothes for felony trials, socks, underwear, etc.), leave the inmate money, inquire about the welfare of an inmate and/or his or her charges, sentences, housing status, etc. Jails use a variety of methods to deal with the public ranging from windows at the main control booths to information desks or booths in the jail lobby. On "heavy" personal visiting days, such as on weekends, civilians and sworn officers may work together to deal with the visitors.

Another administrative staff member is the **public relations officer.** Sometimes called the public information officer, this person may be either civilian or sworn. His or her duties are to serve as the agency representative to the media and the public. Such duties include press conferences, public events, media presentations, public speaking, etc. One of the key duties of the public information officer is to convey to both the public and the media how jails are different than what is portrayed in movies and television. Also, it is important to illustrate how jails are staffed by competent correctional officers.

As more jails become accredited through various organizations, an important staff person will be the **accreditation manager.** This position is explained in detail in Chapter 10. This position is either sworn or civilian and requires exemplary writing and organizational skills.

Finally, as jails become more "modernized" in terms of computer systems and state-of-the-art surveillance and communication equipment, the modern jail will most certainly have to have a technical support staff, who may be either civilian or sworn personnel proficient in the installation, usage, and repair of computer systems, radios, and video equipment. In jails on a restricted budget where staff cannot be hired easily, officers proficient in these areas may be placed on "special assignment," which may cause staff shortages in one area of jail operations while they are helping in another.

## Auxiliary Staff

In recent years, jails have used the services of volunteers, college interns, and auxiliary deputies/officers. These are considered auxiliary staff. They have limited staff privileges such as being allowed in some areas of the jail, receive training in jail security, and when dealing with inmates, they are to be respected and their instructions are to be followed.

A volunteer is a private citizen who provides services to the jail for no compensation. Jail volunteers come from all cultural and economic areas of the surrounding community and aid in conducting programs, assisting in commissary, one-on-one mentoring, and assisting staff. Jails save thousands of dollars in labor costs every year due to the use of volunteers.

College interns are students who work for the jail staff as part of a paid or unpaid internship program. Like volunteers, they should receive a detailed orientation, undergo similar training in jail security procedures, and receive limited staff privileges. College interns may be paid or unpaid, depending on the funding available, and work for academic credit. The jail staff person who supervises the intern is usually required to write an evaluation for the college faculty. College interns perform work in many areas in the jail from inmate records to the medical office to programs and classification. In Virginia, for example, interns from George Mason University (GMU) and Old Dominion University have worked in local jails. A popular time for intern involvement is during the summer, when college students are home and can work in a jail for several months. College interns should also have a criminal history check performed on them and should be interviewed for suitability to work inside a jail. Internships are valuable as they afford the student to earn college credit, gain valuable work experiences, and promote good public relations.

Many jails are open minded to the use of volunteers in assisting the jails staff, especially in programs. Not every citizen who wishes to be a volunteer is the right type of person for the job. Many citizens want to help but may not have the personality to follow security regulations and resist manipulation by inmates. Additionally, volunteers are extra "eyes and ears" and can report problem inmate behavior and information that they may come across to the jail staff. Many inmates would rather talk to a volunteer than to a uniformed staff member, as they may feel more comfortable with someone who is a non-uniformed civilian. The following steps are a guide for jail staff in the proper recruitment, training, and use of volunteers:

- Use a written application to gather as much information about the person, including occupation, special interests, education, life experience, and talents they can offer. Also determine whether the person has volunteered successfully in another facility and get references to check. The volunteer should be a citizen in the community in good standing.
- Conduct a criminal history check on the applicant. Ex-offenders who are sincere about helping inmates may be authorized to come in if they meet special criteria such as non-involvement with the criminal justice system for a long period of time, have reference letters from probation/parole officers, are clean and sober, were not management problems, etc.
- Interview the volunteer applicant carefully; asking questions about how they view inmates, their views on jail security, etc. until you are comfortable with the applicant.
- All volunteers should be given an orientation and carefully trained in the areas of inmate behavior, contraband, and resisting inmate manipulation. Most volunteers have never dealt with the criminal element.
- All volunteers should be familiar with the jail's policies concerning mail, items that inmates may and may not possess, being subject to search, identification badges, checking in and out of the jail, and bringing in guest speakers.
- Volunteers should also know what to do in emergencies, how to report problem inmate behavior, and how to conduct their one-on-one session and programs in accordance with jail security policies.
- Volunteers should clearly understand that any violations of jail rules or laws will lead to being terminated from coming into the jail and possible criminal prosecution.
- Even though the training is strict and the jail environment is regimented, volunteers should be thanked and recognized for their service.

Volunteers should adhere to the following 10 *Don'ts:*

1. Do not engage in discussions with inmates about their sentences, their trials, or the criminal justice system.
2. Do not bring your personal views inside the jail.
3. Do not bring unauthorized people into the jail, or anyone who has not been cleared and authorized by the jail staff.
4. Do not use "street talk" or slang; always use proper grammar and appropriate language.
5. Do not accept telephone calls from inmates or correspond with them.
6. Do not be late for a program or class that you are conducting.
7. Do not allow inmates to handle *any* of your personal belongings.
8. Do not allow inmates to handle any keys, NEVER.
9. Do not allow inmates to come and go from the classroom during your program.
10. Treat all inmates fairly—do not play favorites.

**FIGURE 8-1** Jail Volunteers[4]

Auxiliary deputies or reserve deputies are a new trend in the staffing of sheriff's offices. Auxiliary deputies or reserve deputies are concerned citizens who are recruited or apply to the agency, receive training and perform various duties for the sheriff's department in both the law enforcement and jail areas. They are uniformed, receive special security training, but do not have full law enforcement powers. Reserve deputies can assist jail staff in inmate records, classification, and performing special duties.

An example of a successful reserve deputy program is San Diego County Sheriff's Reserve Support Detail. Consisting of both sworn and non-sworn members, personnel reserves assist in patrol, off-road enforcement, underwater recovery, administrative, and search and rescue. Non-sworn volunteers also assist the department. There are specialists in the reserve ranks, such as members of the clergy and counselors. San Diego also has an Explorer program for young male and female citizens ranging in age from 16 to 21 years. Explorers are assigned to various tasks throughout the San Diego Sheriff's Department. Thousands of hours annually are put in by reserves, and they save San Diego County taxpayers over $2 million per year. Reserve applicants have to pass a written, oral, and physical exam and a background investigation. Depending on the role that the reserve deputy will fill, certain courses from the Basic law Enforcement Academy are required.[5]

What is important to remember is that the safe operation of a jail is a joint operation—where different staffs come together and work with each other. Deputy sheriffs, correctional officers, civilians, contract staff, and administrators working together will determine three things: the safety and security of the jail, the extent of changed inmate behavior, and the culture and atmosphere of the jail work environment.[6]

## THE IMPORTANCE OF PROPER JAIL RECRUITMENT

The recruitment of jail officers has improved over the past several years, along with the pay, benefits, and training. The recruitment of jail staff depends on the same things that attract workers to a job in the private sector: wages and benefits.

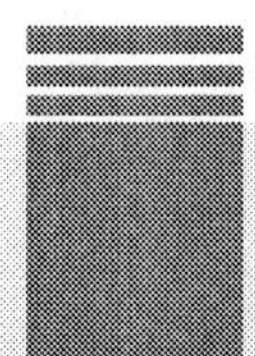

POINT OF VIEW

### A Look at Jail Staff

*Walter R. Smith*
Division Chief, Denver, Colorado Sheriff's Department

(Walter Smith is a 33-year veteran of the Denver Sheriff Department having come up through the ranks and worked all areas of the department including running their Training Academy and Division for 10 years. He is active in numerous law enforcement, corrections, training, and other professional associations including being a past president of the American Jail Association.)

First, we must clearly understand that steel bars and locks do not equal security. It is alert and competent staff in any facility that makes it safe and secure. Having said that, what makes staff good, and what positive traits do we look for when hiring and screening?

Self-motivating, self-starting, curious people with good communications and interpersonal skills are significantly more successful in this line of work. It is critical that they have a high degree of maturity, emotional stability, self-confidence, personal integrity, and responsibility. It is also important that these people be able to demonstrate good problem solving and judgment.

While good assessment center type testing can help determine the skill levels in some of these areas, a close examination of the applicants' previous work experience and history may be the best predictors of future performance. However, we often are unable to obtain accurate and reliable work history information on everyone. We also need to use some sort of psychological screening process that not only examines use of power, authority and force questions but also examines the applicants' judgment in ethical concerns and in dealing with people of different and diverse cultures, races and backgrounds.

In addition to the routine hiring screening concerns of honesty, etc. the following are some additional negative behaviors we are trying to identify and avoid in employees: Lack of commitment and dependability, lack of maturity, low self-esteem and self-confidence, emotional instability and low stress tolerance. These negative behaviors also include the inability to operate and use good judgment effectively in dynamic, uncertain and changing situations relying only on general guidelines and remote supervisory support.

So how do we find and hire the good quality people we need? Hiring starts with recruitment. We cannot hire good quality people if they do not apply for the job. With the increased competitiveness and decreased pool of high-quality applicants, we cannot rely on happenstance to bring good quality people to our doors. More than ever we need to actively seek out the type of people we want and recruit them for our jobs. We need to participate in job fairs at colleges, we need to advertise and recruit from people getting out of the military or being downsized from companies and industries. These people bring maturity and some job experience and training to us and have a previous work history we can evaluate for the points identified above.

We also know that word of mouth and personal contact methods of recruitment are often one of the best means of getting qualified and quality people to apply. Using current employees, friends, and family of employees is an excellent way of getting the word out in a personal and meaningful manner, especially to target groups representing the diversity of our communities. Several recent surveys of newly hired employees in my department as well as others has shown that a high percentage of new employees heard about and were encouraged to apply for the job through contacts with neighbors, relatives, and friends who worked on our departments. While some of this occurs normally, progressive departments may want to consider a referral bonus paid to current employees for each referred applicant who is hired and passes probation. Another idea that has been tried in some fields having a shortage of good applicants is a signing bonus. Recruiting quality people often means relocation plus if the department does not supply a weapon, leather, etc., it may mean the initial outlay of money that the person in transition between jobs may not have immediately available. A $500.00 signing bonus paid when hired shows a department's care and concern, and helps the new employee make the transition to the new job. It is also reasonable to make the bonus conditional on the new employee successfully passing probation. Some places even have a hiring contract where the new employee must repay part of the costs of hiring and training if they quit or leave within a set period time, such as two or three years of the hiring date.

Another recruitment idea could be having a part time or even a cadet entry program that works with local colleges. Allowing students who otherwise meet hiring requirements to work part time can be a real benefit. It gives them money to help pay for their education, gives them experience in our field to help them decide whether this is the right field for them, and gives us an idea of how they perform before they become full employees. Often these people can perform valuable work for us at a less costly level than full employees and they may not need to go through the full initial training program until hired as full time.

The idea of having some type of part time, cadet, reserve or other initial trial entry program is to test the person under real job conditions. Our jobs and duties are not something that most people understand unless they have some previous experience. We have all had people who were hired only to find the job not a good match. Because of the costs of recruitment and initial training of new full-time employees, this turnover in staff is very expensive. Plus, we have people slide by during the probationary period and then present problems later. The more and better we can examine their work performance on the job before we put them on full-time permanent status, the better we can weed out problems.

The last piece in hiring good officers is their initial training. State law and professional standards will dictate a lot of the training, but it is important that each department analyze the training needs in their own sections to make a good judgment on what additional or specific initial training is needed above that required by law or standards. I will not attempt to discuss specific class topics here, but I will suggest training methods, which have been successful. Good trainers need to understand Adult Learning Theory and use that in designing classes. Adults learn better with hands on training and the more practical and job specific the better. We need to hold the lecture style of classes to a minimum. Tell them briefly what to do and why; why with today's employees is that important? Staff should then spend time showing them and letting them practice and demonstrate the expected knowledge, skills, and abilities. Adults learn by doing. And our end desire is that the newly hired officer can successfully demonstrate and explain what, why, and how we want things done. Not only do they learn better, but we then have a record to show that they were successfully able to perform their required duties and tasks correctly during the training.

Thanks to Division Chief Walter Smith, Denver Sheriff's Department, Denver, Colorado.

## Pay and Benefits

The amount of wages that can be paid to jail personnel, both sworn and civilian, is dependent on funding from the local jurisdiction or jurisdictions, such as a county or a group of counties and/or towns and cities, in cases of a regional jail. Jail funds are in competition with other public areas of government such as transportation and education. In the civilian sector, an alcohol and drug services department of a county may have to cut funds due to a loss of revenue, and staffing in the local jail may take a "hit."

Jails vary in size, staffing, and funding. The salaries paid to jail officers reflect this. An examination of correctional literature, specifically job openings illustrate this. For example, an advertisement for a Texas county sheriff detention officer, the pay scale is $27,560 to $28,663 per year. In a Virginia jail in the vicinity of Richmond, the starting pay is $26,000 per year. In a small western United States jail, the starting pay for a jail officer is $10.84 per hour.[7]

Even though the salaries may appear low due to the widespread short staffing in a jail, officers may supplement their income by working overtime. An officer may work on his or her days off for a full shift or only for a few hours. Also, some jails announce daily to the on duty staff that officers are needed to work overtime in booking, transportation, etc. Some officers find it easier to work a double shift, especially if they reside far from the jail and are there anyway.

To enlist good help for the jail, jurisdictions provide benefits such as medical insurance, dental insurance, group life insurance, retirement, etc. For young people entering local corrections, this is very important—but it does depend on the financial situation of the agency. One example of a good starting salary and benefits is in Gwinnett County, Georgia. The following is their job announcement:[8]

| | |
|---|---|
| *Job title:* | Deputy Sheriff/Jailer (full time) |
| *Salary:* | $31,315.00 per year |
| *Location and department:* | Sheriff Department, Lawrenceville, Georgia |
| *Benefits:* | $2,000 hiring incentive, life, health, dental, and disability insurance; pension (retirement) plan; paid holidays; annual and sick leave; deferred compensation; and tuition reimbursement. |

What is unique about this agency is that it offers two important benefits: tuition reimbursement for those officers wishing to pursue or continue a college education and a $2,000 hiring incentive. With jobs in jails becoming more specialized, such as specially trained jail officers working posts housing mentally ill offenders or working with computer systems, being able to continue college is an attractive incentive. In some cases, officers are allowed to take leave during their shift, attend a class, and return to the jail.

However, not all jails have these wages and benefits. This leads to stress among the jail staff as they struggle with low incomes and try to pay their bills. This frequently is mentioned by jail staff at stress training seminars. Recent research released in 2005, conducted by this author with the assistance of GMU, found that over 40% of jail officers surveyed listed low salaries as a major cause of stress.[9] Many jail officers cope with this problem by working overtime, which can lead to fatigue, or moonlighting, working a second job. To protect the agency from liability, jails can initiate a policy where off duty employment, especially law enforcement related (such as a security guard) is investigated and approved by the agency head.

## Recruitment

The old adage "you get what you pay for" applies to the hiring and recruitment of good jail staff. In the Information Age, job announcements concerning local jails are posted on the Internet, on cable television, etc. Another avenue of recruitment is participation in **job fairs**, where representatives from the local correctional agencies attend employment activities on local college campuses and in the community. The idea is to meet prospective applicants, inform them about their department's career opportunities, wages, benefits, etc.

The key questions in recruiting local correctional officers are where can you find good applicants and how can you maintain their interest enough to keep them? To answer this question, a retreat was held in North Carolina in 2000 to ascertain what does work in hiring jail personnel. A 22-item survey by three agencies—the North Carolina Criminal Justice Education and Standards Commission, the North Carolina Sheriff's Education and Training Standards Commission, and the North Carolina Governor's Crime Commission—shed some light on what works in the way of recruitment, retention, and attrition. The survey was sent to a randomly selected sample of 100 sheriffs in North Carolina and each respondent self-reported an effectiveness rating for recruitment and retention techniques.[10]

Local corrections have come a long way from the days when a relative or friend of a county official or the sheriff was able to be easily hired on to work at the local jail. Using a variety of both recruitment and retention techniques, more qualified and educated people are being hired to work the jails. This is illustrated by the North Carolina study.

The following recruitment techniques were examined along with how many agencies were using that method and how its effectiveness was perceived:[11]

| *Method* | *Percentage of Agencies Using/Number* | *Average Effectiveness Rating (0–9)* |
|---|---|---|
| Word of mouth | 93.9%/46 | 6.8 |
| Community College | 83.7%/41 | 6.2 |
| Auxiliary/Reserves | 75.5%/37 | 6.2 |
| Local personnel listings | 67.3%/33 | 3.9 |
| Use of Internet | 61.2%/30 | 2.4 |
| Newspaper announcement | 61.2%/30 | 4.6 |
| Job Fairs | 61.2%/30 | 3.4 |
| Police Corps | 51.0%/25 | 1.2 |
| Radio and TV | 44.9%/22 | 0.8 |

While the effectiveness of a jail officer can only be shown with the satisfactory completion of training and time on the job, word of mouth and appearances of agency staff at community colleges—in criminal justice programs—can serve to draw the types of persons who are extremely motivated and educated enough to apply for a career in local corrections.

The retention of qualified jail staff is critical. Sometimes a new officer, right out of the academy will discover that the jail is not the right career path for him or her and may decide to leave or transfer to the local police department. After months of training, salary, and benefits, the agency stands to lose if this individual leaves. Good retention is important.

The North Carolina study found the following concerning retention of sworn officers:[12]

| *Method* | *Percentage of Agencies/Number* | *Average Effectiveness Rating (0–9)* |
|---|---|---|
| Promotions | 77.6%/38 | 5.0 |
| Education & training* | 75.5%/37 | 6.0 |
| Annual Pay increase** | 73.5%/36 | 5.8 |
| Annual Pay increase*** | 63.3%/31 | 5.3 |
| Formal awards/recognition | 61.2%/30 | 4.3 |
| Favorable work shift | 61.2%/30 | 4.5 |

* At agency expense.

** Irrespective or regardless of job performance.

*** Job performance based.

Promotions are major incentives to keep good people. Not all jail officers want to work in the cellblocks for their entire career. Moving up in the department is important, especially if the officer has various interests in correctional work. Promotions also mean increased salary and benefits such as a transfer to non-shift work positions, etc. If officers can see a potential for promotion, their likelihood of remaining with the agency as a valued employee increases.

However, not all jail officers stay. Jails, like other agencies, experience staff attrition for many reasons. The North Carolina study found that the following factors contributed to staff leaving:[13]

| *Reason* | *Percentage of Agencies Reporting/Number* |
|---|---|
| Budget restrictions | 91.8%/45 |
| Transfer to another law enforcement agency | 83.7%/41 |
| Retirement | 63.3%/31 |
| Take job in private sector | 57.1%/28 |
| Cost of living | 55.1%/27 |
| Decertification* | 46.9%/23 |
| Job duties | 46.9%/23 |
| Size of agency | 46.9%/23 |
| Lack of fringe benefits | 46.9%/23 |
| Location of agency | 44.9%/22 |
| Unrealistic expectations | 42.9%/21 |
| Residency requirement | 40.8%/20 |

* Officer is decertified by state or having a current or prior criminal history.

One can only surmise as to the reasons that a jail officer leaves for another law enforcement agency. It may be closer to his or her home, the duties may be more interesting, the pay is better, etc. Retirement is always a factor. Some jurisdictions are offering incentives to veteran jail staff that are retirement eligible to remain longer.

Leaving for the private sector may be due to the jail officer having certain skills, such as computer skills, and the private sector may pay more. Unrealistic officer expectations may be that the officer, after working with inmates, being exposed to critical incidents such as suicide, and dealing with special populations, may decide that correctional work is too dangerous or not worth the stress. Closely related to this are job duties, where dissatisfaction in assignments may result in the officer leaving.

Another way of leaving the agency is to be fired or forced to resign. This can occur for a variety of reasons, such as a breach of the agency code of conduct, failure to complete basic training, committing a criminal act, or being found liable in a civil action and incurring punitive damages.

## Interviewing

An effective jail staff applicant screener and interviewer may determine whether an applicant is right for working in the jail. Often, jail supervisors will remark after letting a jail officer go or firing one, "Is this [the problem] something that could have been picked up in the screening or interview process?"

According to correctional consultant and veteran Oregon jail inspector Jerry Hawley, applicant screeners can overestimate their abilities to understand everything that is important to know about the jail officer applicant after a short job interview. The interview is just part of a comprehensive screening that should include a ten-year employment history, a computerized criminal history check, a driving record check, a check via teletype to city or county for input as well as looking for family members with legal problems, and a credit check. While on site and in depth background checks are time consuming and costly, a standard check is conducted by telephone, written correspondence, e-mail and computer.[14]

Hawley suggests that **daily life questions** be asked of applicants—questions that ask them about themselves, their views of life, and how they would respond to obstacles and opportunities in real life. The answers are what the applicant screener is looking for, what he or she would want them to be.[15]

Daily life questions could be in seven categories, each with supporting questions. They should not intimidate, but should be blunt and direct. A good applicant screener and interviewer should take the information such as job history, credit check, etc., and compare them to the answers in the following categories:[16]

- *Career motives:* Please tell me why you want to be a correctional officer, where do you see yourself on the career path in five years, ten years, etc. Do you wish to be a correctional officer for your entire work life? Do you believe that discipline for inmates is important, and why?
- *Personal perspective:* Please explain the difference between the importance of your home life and your work life. Which would you rather do—wear your uniform back and forth from home each day or change clothes at work? Do you routinely pay your bills, including paying your credit card balance off every month? What do you think is an answer to the high crime rate in our country?
- *Antiauthority outlook:* What aspects of your private life do you think are the business of your employer? You are assigned to a supervisor whom you think that he or she knows more than you. How would you handle such a person? Describe the most important roles of a supervisor. What type of supervisor would you find is the most difficult to work with?
- *Maturity:* Please explain what you would do in the following scenarios: You are standing in line at the Department of Motor Vehicles and a man crowds into line, right in front of the person in front of you. What would you do? You are driving on the interstate at 70 miles per hour and notice a vehicle "tailgating" you and blowing the horn. What would you do? Do you think that it is all right to drive five miles over the posted speed limit? Ten miles? Fifteen miles?
- *Propensity for substance abuse:* Have you used illegal drugs in the past five years? (Hawley advises not inquiring about current substance abuse because that is a protected disability.) Do you have friends who use illegal substances? Do you think that by using drugs, mental performance is improved? Regarding alcohol, do you think that you can hold your liquor better than most people?
- *Propensity to violence:* Is it important to know how to fight? Do you have friends who fight frequently? What would you do if an inmate threw food on you, threw urine on you, spat in your face, threw feces on you, or cursed you? Do you feel that you can handle yourself in a street fight?

- *Open-ended questions:* Is there something else about you that you would like us to know? Is there something about yourself that you feel that we should know about?

These answers, the demeanor of the applicant, and the information discovered in the background check can give a realistic picture of the applicant and also give a sense of appropriateness for the job. For example, a person who has credit problems and has trouble managing anger could be trouble in the jail—inmates could persuade him or her to bring contraband in for money, or if an inmate performs an aggressive act against the officer (such as spitting), the officer may react with excessive force.

## PROPER TRAINING AND ITS BENEFITS FOR LINE STAFF

In order to face the critical problems in our nation's jails, today's jail officer must have good, positive traits in handling both people and the job.

### Jail Officer: Traits and Skills

Although much has been written about what makes up a good jail correctional officer, the list of good traits should include but not be limited to the following characteristics:[17]

- Exhibit a desire to help people (inmates) and show a concern for their welfare.
- Have an ability to create and maintain an orderly environment in inmate living and work areas.
- Exhibit an ability to work with inmates without fear, anxiety, or timidity—the officer must be able to be assertive, not sarcastic and heavy handed, in order to maintain positive control.
- Have an insight into human behavior and personality.
- Have an ability to maintain good mental and physical health.
- Handle the stresses, pressures, and physical and mental rigors associated with jail work.
- Have an ability to perform duties among staff and inmates in an organized, clear, and attention-getting manner.
- Have an ability to maintain order, control inmates, and administer inmate discipline in a professional manner.
- Be accessible to inmates, answering requests, questions, and responding to grievances.
- Have an ability to be personally credible with inmates and be able to develop an ongoing rapport with them.
- Have the ability and talent to resolve inmate conflicts and problems in a fair and prompt manner.
- Maintain effective relations with jail supervisors, fellow officers, and other law enforcement personnel in an efficient, teamwork manner.

To be an effective jail officer and to get the job done, skills must be mastered in two areas: **Security/ procedural skills** or skills dealing with the carrying out of procedures of day-to-day operations, and **human relations skills,** or how to interact with the inmate population in a positive way. Although first described by correctional researchers Michael Gilbert and Jack Riddell in 1983, they have withstood the test of time. Together, they further narrow and hone the traits described above and combine to make the exemplary jail officer. Security and procedural skills include:

- Having both the knowledge of jail procedures and policies and the skills to apply them to the post or assignment.
- Being able to locate and identify contraband, whether smuggled in or manufactured.
- Having the ability to maintain control of inmates without hostility or the compromising of jail security.
- Taking steps to prevent or properly intervene in inmate escapes, any type of assaults, predatory sexual behavior, harassment, riots, disturbances, inmate arguments, and confrontations.
- Knowing the proper usage of lethal and non-lethal weapons, and when to apply physical and deadly force.
- Safeguarding, evacuating, and rescuing inmates, staff and visitors from fire, smoke, or any catastrophic emergency, including the proper use of emergency equipment.
- Being able to protect the lives of injured or sick inmates and staff by summoning emergency medical aid, and applying correctly emergency first aid and lifesaving techniques.
- Being able to correctly and accurately document all actions taken inside the jail in the performance of duty, including incident reports, memoranda, logs, etc. and also to clearly verbally communicate with inmates and staff.
- Know inmate rights and not violate them.
- Having the physical ability and stamina to carry out these tasks.

Human relation skills include the following:

- Ability to be consistently non-judgmental, non-prejudiced, humane, treating inmates impartially, honestly, and fairly.
- Establish and maintain positive relationships with inmates without losing objectivity.
- Caring about inmates by watching and listening to them, remaining non-defensive, open, and objective to honest dialogue in determining through an interview what the inmate may think is a crisis.
- Use polite and understandable verbal communication.
- Ability to handle inmate problems calmly in a non-abusive manner, and offering advice, mediating disputes and interpersonal conflicts between inmates.
- Ability to recognize both physical and behavioral changes in inmates as signs of potential problems that may require assistance; defusing and/or de-escalating a crisis.
- Ability to refer an inmate with a serious personal problem to the proper staff for assistance.

**FIGURE 8-2** The Skillful Jail Officer[18]

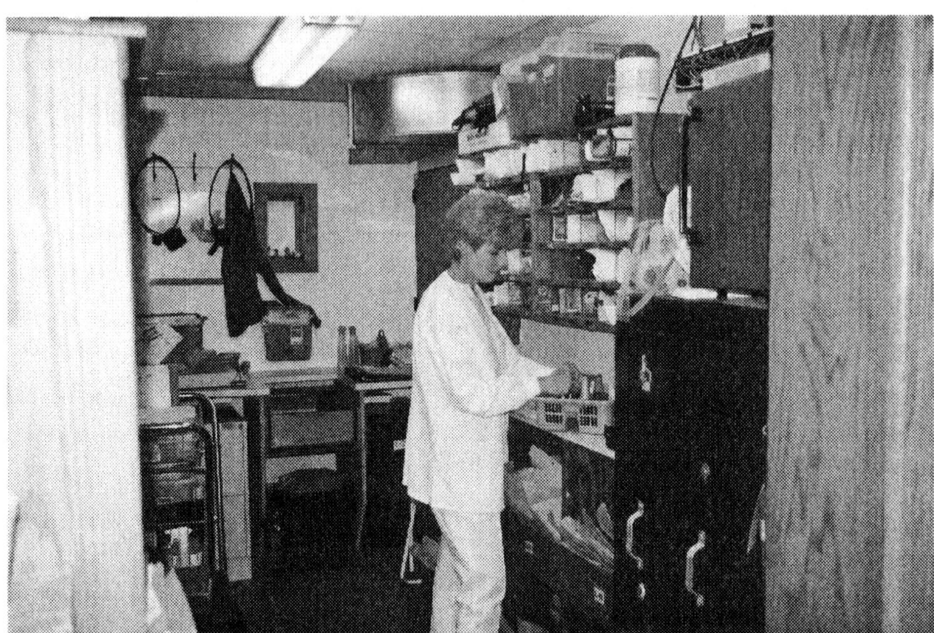

All jail staff, including medical staff, need jail security training.

Photo by author, courtesy Butler County Prison.

## Training

Training is important in the development of both the new jail officers and the skills retention of the veteran jail officer. In recent years, jails training has evolved out of the traditional classroom setting and entered the world of online Internet training, scenario-based training, self-instructional training, technological training, and the employment of outside consultants. However, jail training is anchored on four basic types of training: basic training, on the job training (OJT), roll call training, and in-service training.

## Basic Training

**Basic training** is defined as training that newly hired jail officers undergo within their first year of employment. In basic training, the new officer develops skills for job performance and is instilled with the organizational culture and makeup. Required basic skills that are taught include technical skills and human skills (similar to those in Figure 8-2).[19]

The agency determines the topics, the number of hours and objectives of basic training in accordance with standards set down by the state. In some jurisdictions, the jail officer may go through the academy and graduate with both jail and police certification, which means that some of the curriculum is police oriented.

The "new hire" or recruit receives training at an academy, where he or she is supervised by carefully selected veteran staff. To be certified as jail officers in accordance with the state and to be enabled to carry out duties inside the jail, the recruit must pass subjects taught in a traditional classroom setting and performance skills exercises. Examples of traditional training may include constitutional rights of inmates, and performance or skills subjects may include driver training, handcuffing techniques, qualifying with firearms, and defensive tactics.

Academy training includes dividing the class into squads supervised by a staff member, wearing uniforms, inspections, and conducting academy activities in a paramilitary atmosphere. The length of time of basic training among jails varies depending on the state standards and agency requirements. The agency may add other subjects at the end of an academy basic session for familiarization purposes and not for testing. Once the new officer satisfactorily completes the academy course of study, he or she graduates and is able to work inside the jail under the supervision of a training officer.

## Scenario-Based Training

**Scenario-based training** is non-traditional training in which the trainee is placed into a certain situation, either by electronic means, such as video, etc., or involved with role players. For example, in firearms training, the trainee may be facing a screen on which an offender is coming at him or her with a weapon. Deadly force is justified, and the trainee draws an electronic firearms instrument and fires. Special computer software judges the accuracy of the "hit." A video may portray an inmate acting unruly, depressed, etc., and the trainee has to describe how he or she would handle the situation.

Academies can make use of scenario-based training for both in service and basic. Firearms scenario-based training involves trainees taking part in simulated gunfights using special non-lethal ammunition. Some academies have mock houses, streets, and booking areas where selected veteran staff serves as **role players,** meaning that they take on different roles to enhance the reality of the training scenario. For example, a deputy may play a distraught inmate, an inmate hiding contraband, a mentally ill inmate, etc. The idea of using role-playing is to see how the jail officer trainee handles a particular situation with a real person.

Jails can experience fires, and one very realistic scenario is the simulated jail fire. In this training, the local fire department fills a chamber or building with thick smoke, simulating a fire condition. New jail trainees and in-service trainees don breathing apparatus and work their way from one end of the building to another, eventually exiting the building. To make this exercise more realistic, furniture can be placed in locations where trainees have to navigate through the smoke, and mannequins can be used to simulate smoke/fire victims that need evacuation. In some jails, the medical staff sets up a medical area where staff members with simulated injuries are "triaged" and treated.

Another useful training scenario is the **mock cellblock.** Inside an academy, a room or set of rooms can be remodeled and redecorated to look like a jail cellblock area, complete with inmate possessions—laundry, magazines, clutter, etc., and jail furnishings. The training staff hides contraband on role players acting as inmates and in the cellblock area. The trainees must take charge of the inmates, secure the area, and search for the contraband.

Simulation training has proven to be an effective training tool, such as this mock cellblock that is searched by trainees.

Photo by author, courtesy Central Shenandoah Criminal Justice Training Academy.

Scenario-based training can also be with groups of jail staff. A serious event such as an escape, a mass arrest, a missing inmate, a riot or disturbance can all be incorporated into a scenario for training. A new trend is a terrorist act such as a bomb threat or toxic substance mailed to the jail.

## On the Job Training

Graduation from a training academy does not mean that the officer is trained sufficiently enough to work in the jail. Jails who consider training important and critical assign the officer to a **field training officer (FTO)** for a specified number of hours. The FTO will be the training supervisor of the new officer, requiring him or her to perform tasks such as headcounts, searches, log entries, etc., which will be observed and rated. It is important that the best veteran staff be selected as FTOs, because the safety and security of the jail is dependent on the quality of training of its staff.

Once the jail officer satisfies the requirements of his or her FTO and upon review by the supervisory staff is deemed proficient enough to work on his or her own, the officer is "cut loose" to work without training supervision. This does not mean that the officer is seasoned; it means that the officer is still new but can work independently. It takes time for the officer to reach the point of being confident and comfortable as a result of experience. It also takes time to develop the security and procedural skills and the human relations skills necessary for the job.

OJT, when done correctly, can mold the trainee into a competent jail officer. Thirty years ago, the "old boy" staff might have said to throw the new officer a set of keys, have him work with another officer and eventually he or she will "catch on." Now, all staff should take a hand in training new employees, such as human resources staff, department heads, etc. The goal of a good OJT program is to supplement academy instruction with staff interaction, practical, realistic work, and preparing the trainee for the "pitfalls and perils" of working in the jail. However, due to those staff having their own workloads and priorities, new trainees may be placed in groups and receive only the basic foundational information.[20]

Some jails assign trainees to assist staff in the jail before they start at their basic training at the criminal justice academy. This serves a dual purpose—the jail may have some administrative work completed, and the trainee sees first-hand things such as searches, inmates being restrained, etc. This may show the trainee the realistic side of jail work and make him or her think if the field is the career that they actually want to work in.

There are several key elements to effective training of new jail staff, where they are both exposed to jail work, but are nurtured and guided by veteran staff and supervisors. According to Peter Wittenberg, Deputy Chief Policy Analyst of the U.S. Bureau of Prisons, these elements are:[21]

- *Supervisory Guidance:* Lieutenants, sergeants, the FTO, etc. are the supervisors who are mobile throughout the facility and will have frequent interaction with the jail officer trainee. These supervisors must closely monitor and observe the training and how the new officers handle themselves in situations such as searches, counts, directing inmates, etc. These supervisors should have a priority of instilling the importance of training to the staff.
- *Senior Correctional Line Staff:* Veteran correctional line staff has been called the "heart" of any correctional workforce. They can pass on skills that have been finely tuned from many years of experience working with inmates. Supervisors should select the best veteran staff, not staff who is unprofessional, cynical, and sloppy.
- *On the job training:* OJT must be training, not the "warm body on the post" syndrome, or using new staff as "gofers" or "fill ins." OJT must take place no matter how short staffed the jail is and must not be put aside because it may be perceived as a bother by some staff. Good OJT has a potential payoff in that it results in well-trained staff.
- *Inmates:* Inmates "teach" the new officers by manipulating them. To counteract that, new officers should be under intensive guidance by training officers and supervisors. Interacting with inmates will give the new officer experience, but manipulators are hesitant to challenge or try to fool officers who appear competent, have knowledge of how to perform their duties, and are comfortable in their job assignments.
- *Other elements:* FTOs can be authorized through selection and training to supervise and certify new staff; they may also have assigned to them several trainees. **Staff support groups** allow new officers to discuss among themselves training issues, concerns, problems, and ways to deal with them, including feedback to supervisors. These groups are good for morale and help to build good relations with fellow trainees. Labor and management in facilities that have unions can work together by forming partnerships that facilitate training. Some jails engage in **inter-facility training programs** where several jails in the same area or locality can assist each other in training staff. For example, a neighboring jail experiencing a contraband problem can ask for staff to be sent there to assist in shakedowns. Trainees will get a broader picture of how other jails operate.

## Probationary Period

For a specific time period after being hired (generally 12 months), the new jail officer is in a **probationary period.** During this time, if the agency supervisors, including the training staff, feel that the person is "not quite right" for jail work, he or she can be dismissed. Reasons for dismissal may include failure to complete a training exercise in the academy, failure of a test in the academy curriculum, failure to qualify with firearms, fail to pass driver training, poor performance while being supervised by a FTO, etc. For example, a new officer demonstrates an inability to control the movement of a group of inmates and they wander into an unauthorized area. Or a new officer is reluctant to pat down inmates during a shakedown. If enough of this behavior is observed and documented, the FTO will recommend to the agency management that this officer is not suitable to work around inmates, and jail staff and inmates may be in jeopardy. In such a case, the officer must be terminated.

An example of jail officer basic training hours and subjects can be found in the Denver, Colorado Sheriff's Department. The hiring criteria for new officers include the applicant having no criminal history of felonies, no drug involvement, a GED or high school education, a good driving record, and a general good, clean employment history. The applicant must also pass a psychological test, a polygraph, a physical exam, and a drug test. The new officer must undergo 12 weeks of training, 40 hours per week, for a total of 480 total basic hours. After the trainee is assigned to the field, they are under the supervision of a FTO for 4–6 weeks. The first year is the probationary year. Career status is obtained after the probationary year, and 40 hours of in-service training each year plus any specialized or additional training that may be required for their duty assignments.[22]

The breakdown of the basic training curriculum in the Denver Sheriff's Department is as follows:[23]

| *Academic Training Topics* | *Hours* |
|---|---|
| Communication, conflict management, human relations | 20 |
| Contraband detection and control | 14 |
| Department rules, policies, and professional standards | 16 |
| Emergency procedures | 24 |
| General operations and security (additional covered elsewhere) | 48 |
| Restraints | 8 |
| Prisoner handling | 24 |
| Classification, etc. | 6 |
| Law and legal issues | 30 |
| Unusual and suicidal prisoner behavior | 18 |
| Use of force (practical and other information covered elsewhere) | 8 |
| Miscellaneous | 20 |
| *Skills Training* | |
| Firearms and related weapons (shoot/do not shoot, use of force) | 95 |
| Defensive and practical driving | 19 |

| | |
|---|---|
| Incident evidence/scene preservation/report writing* | 22 |
| CPR, first aid, life safety skills | 30 |
| Physical fitness, defense, and control tactics | 62 |
| Inmate supervision | 16 |
| TOTAL TRAINING HOURS | 480 |

* Covered also in testifying.

## Roll Call Training

**Roll call training** is one of the most basic forms of training in a jail and helps in several areas. Conducted during a 20- or 30-minute roll call, subjects can be discussed in components, or shown in a video format. Roll call training is inexpensive; it can be done on site using staff or easily accessible guest speakers from the community or neighboring agencies. For example, if a jail is experiencing a gang problem, the local police department could send gang intelligence officers to the jail roll calls to conduct short training sessions on not the whole gang problem, but on certain components: tattoos, slang, etc. Another subject is suicide prevention, where roll call training sessions could break the subject matter down into objectives: rate of suicide, methods, symptoms, etc.

Ongoing staff training is necessary for an efficient well run facility.

Photo reprinted with permission of the American Correctional Association.

## In-Service Training

**In-service training** is designed to maintain the law enforcement/correctional certification of the jail officer by requiring that a specific number of training hours in applicable subjects are attended during a specific time. For example, to maintain state jail officer certification or law enforcement officer certification, an officer may have to attend 24 or 40 hours of training in an academy every two years depending on the state training standards and type of certification. To maintain the high level of in-service training so that it will not be limited, jail and academy training staff have to be innovative in developing the subject matter.

The longer a list of in-service subjects, the more choices a jail officer will have in selection and ultimately keeping an interest in jail work. In-service training subjects include pertinent subjects such as gangs, riot/disturbances, legal rights of inmates, defensive tactics, proper use of force, standards and accreditation, interpersonal communications, hostage negotiations, firearms qualification, suicide prevention, high-profile prisoners, transporting inmates, driver training, etc.

Besides maintaining certification, in-service training in certain areas can enhance career development and special assignment skills. For example, classes teaching word processing, use of computer programs, etc. may help officers in getting promoted. Classes in basic supervision, advanced supervision, and performance evaluations can also assist the jail officer and supervisor. Officers selected for special assignments such as the corrections emergency response team can attend training in state or out of state in cell extractions, emergency responses, etc. Sending officers to schools away from the agency has to be carefully thought out due to budget and staffing concerns.

The new jail training standards from the American Correctional Association (ACA) extensively addresses the subject of what topics to cover in training at all levels of jail staffing, from new employee orientation to part-time and contracted employees, which may be overlooked. The ACA standards can serve as a good model for all jail trainers. According to the standards, a qualified individual coordinates and plans the jail training and employee development program. Full-time training staff must at a minimum complete a 40-hour training for trainers course, which is reviewed annually and updated as necessary.[24]

The ACA training and development standards distinguish orientation from training, due to the new staff members getting information on the setting of their employment. Minimally, the orientation should include working conditions; the agency's code of ethics; staff rules/regulations; personnel policies, employees' rights and responsibilities; an overview of the criminal justice system (emphasizing their jail); facility tour, goals and objectives; agency/facility organization; and program overview.[25]

Clerical and support staff must also receive training according to ACA. If they have minimal inmate contact, they should receive at least 16 hours of training during the first year of employment and 16 hours every year after that. New full-time health care employees receive a formal 40-hour orientation including jail key control, security, and contraband policies. Appropriate conduct with inmates and medical care precautions are also covered. All part-time jail staff and contract personnel should receive formal orientations of jail procedures applicable to their work assignment, plus additional training if necessary.[26]

ACA has recommended that training hours cover many areas applicable to working inside a jail. All new professional, support, and contracted employees who

Strength in numbers—the more subjects the better—describes an effective training curriculum. The following is a non-inclusive list of correctional jail topics in the basic, roll call, and in-service areas:[27]

- Agency policies and procedures
- Budget preparation
- Criminal code
- Crisis intervention
- Cultural diversity in the jail population
- Defensive tactics
- Direct supervision
- Documentation: report writing, logs, etc.
- Emergency motor vehicle operation
- Emergency procedures
- Escapes
- Ethics/code of conduct
- Fire safety
- Firearms training
- First aid/CPR
- Gang/security threat groups
- Inmate manipulation
- Inmate rights, due process and discipline
- Juveniles in jail custody
- Lethal/non-lethal use of force
- Pathogens: blood borne and air borne
- Physical fitness and agility
- Security: counts, searches, key and tool control
- Sexual harassment
- Special category inmates
- Stress management and wellness
- Suicide prevention
- Supervision: middle management and advanced
- Supervision of inmates
- Verbal and non-verbal communication

**FIGURE 8-3** The Variety of Correctional Training

have regular and/or daily contact with inmates should receive training during the first 12 months of their employment. Before being assigned independently to a job, 40 hours of training must be completed, and each subsequent year should include an additional 40 hours. New correctional officers receive 160 hours of training during their first year, and at least 40 of these training hours are completed before being independently assigned to a jail post or assignment. During each following year of employment, jail officers must receive at a minimum 40 training hours. All jail security personnel are trained both in self-defense tactics and use of force in order to control inmates.[28]

Staff who are not line officers also have requirements under the ACA standards. Jail supervisors and managers must receive at least 40 hours of training dealing with management and supervision issues during the first year in a management position and 24 hours of training in every subsequent year.[29] This may take the form of special seminars at conferences, classes given by professional organizations, and seminars at the local training academy. A jurisdiction may participate in management training with a local law enforcement agency, such as a combined command staff seminar. However, ACA urges employees through its standards to continue education and training through agency incentives such as administrative leave to attend college or other training, salary enhancement, and tuition or cost reimbursement.[30]

Officers assigned to a special emergency unit, such as an emergency response team, must be on the job as a correctional officer for at least one year. Before taking part in an assignment, 40 hours of specialized training must be recorded. Emergency unit officers receive 40 hours of training every year, and 16 of those hours must be specifically related to the function of the emergency unit.[31]

Officers authorized to use firearms receive appropriate training, including having to qualify every 12 months showing their proficiency and competency. Firearms training include the use, care, and constraints of agency-issued firearms. Officers authorized to use chemical agents, such as pepper spray, tear gas, etc., are trained in their proper usage *and* in the treatment of persons exposed to the agent.[32]

The minimum list of training topics for professional, support, and contracted employees and for new and veteran officers is very applicable for jail work. ACA recommends these topics:[33]

- Security procedures and regulations
- Supervision of inmates
- Signs of suicide risk and suicide precautions
- Use of force regulations and tactics
- Report writing
- Inmate rules, regulations, rights, and responsibilities
- Key control
- Safety procedures
- All emergency plans and procedures
- Interpersonal relations (with inmates) and communication skills
- Inmate population: social and cultural lifestyle
- Cultural diversity: staff and inmates
- Counseling techniques
- CPR and first aid
- Sexual harassment, sexual abuse, sexual assault, and sexual misconduct awareness (author's note: includes inmate/staff fraternization)

In summary, the ACA jail performance-based training standards are essential in building a good staff. Documentation of all training classes, instructor certifications, and participating staff is essential.

The various training curriculum and the skills needed to implement them are part of both the formal and the informal duties of a jail officer. While the formal duties are structured and are per jail policies, informal duties ensure good relations with inmates while attending to their needs. Formal duties include:

- Conducting headcounts and perform regular checks of inmates at either 30-minute intervals of general population or 15 minutes or less intervals of special category inmates.
- Searching of inmates' persons, living and work areas for contraband, and unauthorized activity.
- Properly processing inmates into the facility.
- Observing the behavior and activity of all inmates in the facility.
- Supervising inmates on work assignments, programs, and recreation.
- Enforcing all facility rules, regulations, procedures applicable to inmates and criminal laws.
- Inspecting daily the jail security system and inmates and staff environments.
- Escorting and transporting inmates, admitting authorized visitors.
- Participating in disciplinary and administrative hearings, which determine penalties and housing status of inmates.

Informal duties of jail officers are

- *Psychologist:* referring inmates to the mental health staff based on recognitions of the symptoms of mental illness.
- *Legal advisor:* answers when appropriate inmates' questions concerning court date, sentence, bond, plus being requested by inmates to assist them in disciplinary, and administrative hearings.
- *Parent:* acting as a positive role model for immature inmates, providing guidance and advice in behavior, hygiene, etc.
- *Information agent:* responding to inmates' questions about the jail, such as programs, visiting, etc.
- *Counselor:* advising inmates on how to handle personal problems and problems in the jail.
- *Diplomat:* intervening and defusing disputes and arguments between inmates before they escalate into physical altercations.

It can be argued that working in a jail and performing both formal and informal duties prepares an officer to handle many types of problems and to calmly handle many types of people.

**FIGURE 8-4** Formal and Informal Duties of Jail Officers[34]

## NEW TRENDS CONCERNING JAIL STAFF

As the modern jail moves into the twenty-first century, there are some positive trends on the horizon concerning the training of staff, getting information that can be used in jail operations, dealing with several "dark clouds," emerging issues regarding the jail workforce, and new ways for management to look at a jail's most valuable resource—its staff.

## Professional Associations and Resources

For the first time in jail history, there are several excellent resources for jail line staff, jail supervisors, and any staff who performs services in a local jail. These resources can assist in the development of training curriculum and meeting state and professional association (such as ACA) training requirements. These resources include

- *American Jail Association (AJA):* This organization is the premier organization dealing with issues facing our nation's jails. AJA, based in Hagerstown, Maryland, is a national non-profit organization working to support those staffs who operate and work in our nation's jails and focuses exclusively on issues and problems specific to local correctional facilities. AJA provides excellent resources for jail personnel. Its magazine, *American Jails,* provides timely and well-written articles on a variety of jail issues. AJA offers a Certified Jail Manager (CJM) program in which jail professionals can gain certification and national recognition in the field. Also offered is a Certified Jail Officer (CJO) program in which jail officers can be certified as professionally proficient and knowledgeable in jail work and operations. AJA provides technical assistance and, through its Board of Directors and staff, assists jails throughout the nation. AJA also holds an annual conference. Two publications from AJA provide an extensive learning forum for line staff and managers. The *Jail Operations Bulletin* (JOB) is published in seven volumes that deal with such subjects as report writing, inmate discipline, use of force, classification, work release, transportation of inmates, etc. The *Jail Manager Bulletin* (JMB), published in five volumes, is written for jail supervisors at all levels in subjects that include ethics, autonomy for line staff, progressive staff discipline, jails standards and inspections, etc. The *Write It Right Quarterly* assists jail staff at all levels and assignments to become better communicators to their staff. Other AJA publications include the book *Exploring Jail Operations* by *American Jails* editor Ken Kerle, *Who's Who in Jail Management Jail Directory,* and the *Legal Issues Manual.* AJA can be accessed at www.aja.org. [35]
- *International Association of Correctional Training Personnel (IACTP):* IACTP is affiliated with the AJA, the ACA, and the American Probation and Parole Association. IACTP was founded in 1974 and works to improve and enhance correctional training. IACTP hosts an Annual Trainer's Conference where correctional trainers from the United States and abroad meet, network, share information and ideas, and present training seminars. IACTP offers a voluntary Trainer Certification Program and publishes a very informative journal, *The Correctional Trainer.* The IACTP Web site can be found at www.iactp.org.[36]
- *American Correctional Association:* ACA was founded in 1870 and was originally called the National Prison Association and is the oldest association developed to assist correctional practitioners, including those in probation/parole, jails, juvenile corrections and prisons. The *Declaration of Principles,* published in 1870, evolved into the correctional guidelines for corrections in the United States and Europe. ACA was also formerly called the American Prison Association and took the name of the ACA in 1954. ACA today has over 20,000 members. Its vision is to shape the future of corrections through progressive leadership that brings corrections professionals together. ACA's standards for correctional facilities are recognized as visionary and help to maintain professionalism in corrections. ACA

publishes the magazine *Corrections Today,* numerous books in many areas of corrections, the *Corrections Compendium,* and assists staff through regional and on-site training and technical assistance. ACA offers a Correctional Certification Program, the On-Line Corrections Academy, lesson plans and workbooks. ACA's Web site is www.aca.org.[37]

- *The Corrections Connection:* This Web site represents the "cutting edge" in on line correctional information. It features in depth articles, an on line correctional news service, interviews with correctional professionals on a variety of topics, information on corrections products, corrections advertisers, and links to many national and state corrections organizations such as ACA, IACTP and AJA. It is planning a resource for college students called "Straight Talk from America's College Students" where students design a Web page on a corrections topic for credit. The site also features an extensive directory of corrections subjects. A unique feature is a discussion forum where correctional workers in the field can voice their opinions on a particular subject. The Web site is www.corrections.com.[38]
- *The Corrections Professional:* Published twice per month, *The Corrections Professional* is an excellent resource for correction news, feature articles, opinions from corrections professionals, job opportunities, and lawsuits and legal information. Subscribers also receive another publication, *Inside Corrections Technology.* This journal is one of the best ways for jail staff to keep up to date on correctional issues. LRP also publishes several books on corrections issues. For more information on *The Corrections Professional* or other products published by LRP Publications, staff should call customer service at 1–800–341–7874 or visit the LRP Web site at www.shoplrp.com.[39]

## Emerging Staff Issues

### *Females*

In one U.S. jail in the late 1970s, there was not a housing unit for female offenders, and after booking they were transported to a neighboring county for holding. As a result, female deputy sheriffs assigned to squads had little to do after booking and transport.

In the past 25 years, the number of females working in jails has increased significantly. Jails have been viewed as predominantly male work environments and in the 1980s and 1990s; research indicated that female jail officers were in a workplace dilemma where many male jail officers viewed as threatening female jail officers who could do a good job. This was reinforced by viewing female officers who could not perform as typical of the female jail officer. It was thought that the better those female officers performed their jobs and conducted themselves in the jail, the more they posed a threat to the male-dominated jail workplace. This sexualized work environment resulted in female jail officers feeling inferior, unwelcome, and constricted.[40]

Now, sex-based discrimination is barred under Title VII of the U.S. Civil Rights Act and includes provisions against sexual harassment. Many jails now have general orders outlining what constitutes sexual harassment, reporting procedures in cases of victimization, and penalties for violations. In professional development training for staff, the reasoning behind sexual harassment laws should be clearly explained to the jail staff.[41]

Sexual harassment laws only represent one improvement in the situation of the female jail officer. There are female division heads, sheriffs, jail administrators, squad leaders, etc. More female jail officers exercise cross gender supervision. Clearly, a positive trend in jail staffing has been the abandonment of old male stereotyping concerning female jail staff.

Some jails are proactive, recognizing how sexual harassment toward female jail staff can have a severe negative impact on the working jail environment. As reported by noted jail authority Ken Kerle in his book *Exploring Jail Operations,* the Rappahannock Security Center in Fredericksburg, Virginia, decided several years ago to step up efforts to recruit good female staff and to increase staff awareness about sexual harassment. The result was impressive: 51% of the jail's general staff were females, and 38% of the security staff—the backbone of the jail—were females. To combat sexual harassment, employees were encouraged to report to management any sexual harassment activities as part of an aggressive sexual harassment policy.[42]

The changing traditional view of males in society of females can have a controlling effect in a jail setting. Kerle relates how in 1991 he was touring the Prince Georges' County (Maryland) jail and was in an overcrowded unit staffed by two detention officers, one a slightly built female who was in charge. The normal housing capacity was 50 inmates; on this day there were 100 inmates. A fight broke out between two inmates. The female officer stepped into the altercation, took one inmate by the arm and ordered him to go into his cell and ordered the second inmate to stand in a corner while she proceeded to write up the incident. The remaining inmates in the unit did not become involved in the fight, and it was clear that they recognized the authority of the female officer. Kerle concluded that the officer was mature, well trained, and knew her job. Also, many males are beginning to accept that with good interpersonal communication skills, flexibility in thinking, and problem-solving skills, female jail officers can do just as good a job at managing inmates as males. A Hispanic female jail officer commented that when dealing with physical altercations between inmates, she relies on the cultural tradition that a man will not usually strike a woman and thinks that male inmates may see her like their wife or sister.[43]

## Back to Basics

Jail training subjects are becoming more sophisticated, such as training in computers; firearms (such as agencies graduating to semi-automatic handguns and phasing out revolvers), stun devices, pepper spray, cell extractions, etc. Also, in light of the terrorist attacks of 2001, jail staffs are receiving training in weapons of mass destruction (WMD) drills, holding high-profile inmates such as terrorists and gangs; the list continues to evolve.

The basics of correctional management are the foundational processes and beliefs that are shared by all corrections officers and staff no matter in what institution they are working, their rank, or their job assignment.[44] The basics are what jail security and operations rest upon.

The following are examples of the basics: searches, headcounts, protecting inmates from predators, and providing medical care. Examples of "non basics" are providing inmates with cable television, paroling an inmate, answering a letter from an inmate's family, etc.[45]

Recent literature has described corrections, including jails has being reactionary to the point of responding "to the idea of the moment."[46] For example, in the wake of the terrorism of September 11, 2001, jails have engaged in antiterrorism training—terrorist attacks, bombs, chemical weapons, etc. But the *basics* are still in need of being included in the training. In this example of guarding the jail against terrorist acts, the basics—the foundations—that need to be reiterated are:

- Checking visitor identification.
- Checking suspicious or out of place vehicles near the jail.
- Making perimeter checks.
- Being on the lookout for suspicious looking packages or mail.

Another example is technology. In suicide prevention training, the instructor can comment on the benefits of audio and visual technology—intercoms and closed circuit television—to assist in observing suicidal inmates. However, the basic principle of talking to the inmate and observing by "eyeball" is still the most important suicide prevention tool.

Leadership is another area where the basics are important. Leadership involves both the processes of the organization (management), creating a future direction and team building. Leadership deals with the mission of the agency and its purpose. The following basics should be in any jail leadership style that is adopted: listening to the staff, walking around, observing the staff, plus observing routine duties and responding to emergencies, seeing how the employees handle situations. Second, the jail staff should not be allowed to take "shortcuts:" Faster does not mean better. Competent team building with a sense of vision is a basic, and requiring all new staff to receive training in basic correctional management techniques before jobs are assigned is recommended.[47]

Ethics should also take a basics approach. Correctional officers, like other law enforcement personnel, are sworn to uphold the public trust. In management and supervisory development of staff, the principles of honesty, trustworthiness, and fairness must be exhibited by the supervisors of the jail.[48]

## *Autonomy in Line Officers*

With more and more jails going to direct supervision, increasing attention is being paid to the autonomy of line officer thinking. This does not mean that line officers are "out on a limb" without guidance but means that they are being entrusted by the supervisory staff to handle more inmate issues independently, without being over supervised.

The basic premise of autonomy in jail officers is for the jail supervisor to allow officers to make routine decisions concerning inmates and events on their posts in order to gain the respect of inmates in their charge and to counteract challenges to authority.[49]

Autonomy serves two purposes in the development of jail staff: first, the jail officer gains confidence in his or her ability to handle inmates and situations. Second, in an era where more attention is being paid to the development of the new generation of jail officer, being able to assert oneself, and make decisions can prepare the officer to be a supervisor.

In a more practical sense, line officer autonomy can benefit the jail environment, including inmates and all staff, for these reasons:[50]

- Line officer autonomy can gain the respect of inmates who see that the post officer does not have to contact a supervisor for every decision.
- Line officers are on the front lines; they know what is going on. They have the information necessary to make good decisions.
- Autonomous officers can demonstrate leadership and good communication with inmates. They are highly motivated as to the success of the jail mission. Also, their levels of commitment, motivation, and morale are high.

It must be noted that line officer autonomy does not mean that there is no need for the squad supervisor. Emergencies and critical incidents such as inmate assaults, suicides, escapes, etc. will always require the guidance of a senior level supervisor. Also, supervisors must step in and see how the officer is doing. If an officer is running a unit with an "iron hand," lacking good interpersonal communications and discretion, inmates may resent this, and trouble in the unit may start to brew.

## "Dark Clouds" in Jail Staffing

### *Stress Management Training*

More emphasis has been given in recent years to the top twelve stressors that correctional officers face, including officers and staff in our nation's jails. Although there has been some training in stress management beginning in the 1980s, there has developed an increasing awareness in training and such services as peer counseling and employee assistance programs.

Correctional officers are not the only staff who works in a jail that experience stress. Medical staff, counselors, and civilians are all "under the gun." Stressed out staff may decide that jail work is not worth it and decide to quit. Staffs who are stressed out may not be up to their peak job performance and may cause friction with colleagues and inmates.

According to research conducted by the ACA and GMU in 2002, the top ten stressors that cause stress in jail, prison, and probation/parole staffs are as follows:[51]

- Short staffing
- Lazy colleagues
- Conflicting decisions from supervisors
- Poor communication
- No recognition for hard work
- Lack of support from supervisors
- Conflicting operations among shifts
- Large caseload
- Tight deadlines
- Lack of input in decision making
- Low salary
- Bureaucratic red tape/paperwork

According to this research, stressors are mostly organizational; the management, supervisors and agency practices are causing the stress, not the inmates. As careers progress, officers get to know the inmates and the type of inmates whom they are dealing with. By doing so, they learn strategies how to handle them. However, if they perceive that the agency management is not taking their views and workload into consideration when decisions are made and recognition is rarely given, then the management will be considered the cause of stress.

These stressors and the stress that they produce cause physical and behavioral symptoms that affect both the personal and the professional lives of a jail worker. In the same research conducted by ACA and GMU, the most frequent stress symptoms reported by the same groups were as follows:[52]

- Headaches
- Impatience
- Anxiety
- Sleep difficulties
- Fatigue slow/energy
- Cannot relax
- Anger
- Poor concentration
- Back and neck pain

Stress symptoms such as anger and poor concentration are dangerous in jail work. In an environment where interpersonal relations with inmates should be positive and non-threatening, anger and impatience shown by a stressed out officer to jail inmates may result in escalating tension, arguments, resentment, and negative communications. Sleep difficulties, fatigue, and poor concentration may cause officers to miss contraband on a search, signs of digging in a jail wall, and not checking to see whether inmates are in their assigned areas.

Correctional stress can be counteracted. Jail officers can now obtain information on what stress is, what it does, and how to lessen its effects. In the ACA/GMU research, the following were reported by correctional staff as the top six stress management techniques:[53]

- Exercising
- Engaging in a hobby
- Talking to friends
- Family activities
- Relaxing
- Talking to family

### *Inmate Manipulation*

Another "dark cloud" area in jail staffing is the jail staff falling victim to the inmate manipulator. The jail staff controls the environment; no items such as drugs, etc. that would be welcomed by the inmate are allowed into the facility. Offenders in jail generally resent the rules, regulations, and confines of their existence. Staff is then targeted by the inmates to persuade them to bring in contraband, help them escape, perform favors, look the other way when rules are broken, or to have sexual relations. Inmate manipulation can undermine the security network of the jail, and some jails and correctional academies are offering training to jail staff (civilian and volunteers) in how to combat it.

Effective training in inmate manipulation addresses the three components of the manipulative act:[54]

- *To control or play upon:* The jail environment is regimented and under the authority of the jail staff. Inmates want to do time on their terms as comfortably as possible.
- *By artful and unfair means:* Inmates may observe selected staff members over a period of time in order to confirm that the targeted staff member will bend the rules, play favorites, and will not pay attention to security procedures. Inmates will use many ploys involving acting, befriending, or "hooking staff." Acting may involve an inmate shedding tears and acting depressed to gain sympathy, getting personal information about an officer and using it to befriend that officer in order to ask for favors, or getting the staff member to break the rules and then "hooking" that staff member by threatening to expose the wrongdoing. The ploys may involve schemes and games performed over months to try to convince the staff member that they (the inmates) are not really bad at all. Inmates may offer to "look out" for the officer, spreading rumors that other staff is talking about the officer behind his or her back.
- *Especially to one's own advantage:* Jail staff through training must realize that every successful act of manipulation has a payoff for the inmate. Drugs and other contraband may be smuggled in by a jail staff member, inmates may roam into areas where they are not authorized to converse with or deliver messages to co-defendants, gang members, etc., receive extra phone calls, getting into living areas of their choice, etc. Another result is the power that an inmate gains by successfully manipulating a staff member.

### *Inmate-Staff Fraternization*

One of the most serious "dark clouds" over corrections, including the local jail, is the problem of inmates and staff members engaging in sexual relations, or **inmate-staff fraternization.** The problem is closely related to the problem of inmate manipulation. While inmates do use sex as a way to persuade staff members to do their bidding, some staff members engages in this behavior, and disregard the agency rules of conduct and proper ethics. There are serious repercussions to this behavior—embarrassment of the agency due to media coverage, the possibility of escape, new crimes being committed and contraband smuggling, and the breakdown of staff efficiency, pride, and morale.[55] Staff may contract a sexually transmitted disease, or an inmate may file a rape charge.

Examples of inmate staff fraternization illustrate how staff can get disciplined or fired. In one facility, a female corrections officer/nurse persuaded an inmate to have sex with her while on duty. The two were caught in the act by another officer, and she was fired after four years on the job. In an urban jail, a male corrections officer allowed a male inmate to have unauthorized contact with a female visitor. The favor to the officer was to engage in sexual activity with a second

Resisting inmate manipulation is being recognized more as a subject that needs to be expanded in jails training. Due to the psychopathic personality of many inmates, their lies and stories can be quite convincing. For example, in one facility, two correctional officers were fired after being convinced by inmates to deposit $1,500 into a bank account to purchase a motorcycle from an inmate. The motorcycle was fictitious.

Civilian staff, volunteers, and sworn staff are all vulnerable to the inmate manipulator. Some schemes take months to develop, as inmates befriend the officer. Training in resisting the manipulator is needed for new staff, veteran staff, civilians, volunteers, and *any* staff members who have daily contact with inmates. The ultimate goal of the inmate manipulator is to persuade the jail staff member to see the inmate not as a criminal but as a poor unfortunate person who needs help.

One tactic to resist manipulation is the **"CHUMPS"** approach. Inmates think that staff and civilians are "chumps." This inmate slang can be turned into an easy-to-remember acronym outlining strategy to resist manipulation:

- *Control yourself and do not be complacent:* Officers and staff must be "nosy" and know what is going on in inmate living and working areas. Staff should also say no when applicable to inmates firmly and assertively. Rules should not be bent, and procedures should be consistently followed. Inmate movement and activities should be strictly controlled by the staff.
- *Help the inmates help themselves:* Inmates must be discouraged from "shopping for staff," or going from staff member to staff member looking for the answer that they want. Inmates should follow the chain of command in the jail as staff does. Inmates must learn proper procedures in solving their problems, which is one of the keys to rehabilitation.
- *Understand the offender sub-culture and understanding yourself:* Staff should be well read and informed about the inmate personality, how they do time, how they manipulate, etc. Good veteran staff members should teach other staff and volunteers how inmates scheme and fool people, sometimes enlisting their friends and families to assist them.
- *Maintain a safe distance:* All personnel should never give their home/work addresses, any phone numbers, e-mail addresses, or *any* personal information to any inmate. Personnel should not have any contact with inmates' families, or buy for or receive any gift from an inmate.
- *Practicing professionalism in adhering to policies and procedures:* Personnel should be professional at all times in work habits and appearance. Personnel should follow the agencies polices, procedures, and code of conduct.
- *Stop yourself from being stressed out so you are not vulnerable:* Personnel should be aware of their strengths and maintain them. Weaknesses must also be recognized and overcome. For example, a jail officer should know whether he or she lets him or herself be too social with inmates and should take measures to prevent that. Most importantly, staff should practice effective stress management techniques. If inmates see a jail staff member showing signs of stress, inmates will become a sympathetic support group, while attempting to lure the staff member into being a friend, instead of a professional jail staff worker.

**FIGURE 8-5** The "CHUMPS" Approach[56]

female visitor in a stairwell. When the officer did not repeat the favor, the inmate turned him in. The officer was fired after two years on the job.[57]

Staffs who have sex with inmates may think that they are "in love," but in reality the risks of this behavior have serious legal repercussions. The laws are getting tougher with staffs who engage in any type of sexual behavior with inmates, probationers, parolees, etc. In Virginia, anyone having carnal knowledge of any person that he or she has authority over (including institutional custody) can be convicted of a felony and be sentenced to one to five years in prison. In Georgia, which has a similar law, the penalty is one to three years in prison. Corrections management is using the law to combat this problem, as there are laws dealing with this on the books in many states.

## Staff Analysis

A century ago, jails were very simply built and operated. It was not until 1870 with the National Prison Congress was any type of professional attention paid to improving the operation and staffing of jails. But jails continued to operate mostly on a "lock them up and guard them" type of approach. Even as recently as the 1970s, many jails were staffed according to the "warm body [jail officer] on the floor" approach. The modern jail is a complex facility, no matter the geographic location and size. In both large and small jails, the types of inmates, their problems, and security technology have made analysis of jail staffing needs imperative. Jails operate on budgets, and attention must be paid to getting the best operations for the money.

Some jail operations may be sacrificed at times for the sake of operations that have higher priority. For example, in a large jail, full-squad staffing may require 50 officers to be posted and on floater duty throughout the jail. If the agency that is responsible for the jail, such as the sheriff's department, is short staffed and does not have enough trained deputies to fill all of the post assignments on a shift, deputies will be either offered overtime or instructed to be accessible on a call in basis. **Mandatory overtime** occurs when officers are held over for the next shift either for a few hours, must work a special detail such as a hospital run, or for a few hours on days off. Overtime pay costs money and can eat into an agency's budget.

In the same hypothetical jail, some operations may be shut down in order to better use the staff on hand, without calling any officers in or holding any over. Recreation may be closed for the day and the deputies reassigned to squad posts. Visiting for families and friends (personal visiting) may also be closed due to staff shortages and the deputies who would be assigned to visiting reassigned to posts.

In 2001, the National Institute of Corrections (NIC) looked at the need for effective jail staffing analysis, based on the following characteristics of jail operations:[58]

- Jails are continuously in operation: 24 hours per day, 365 days per year.
- Jails provide to inmates a wide variety of services, activities, and programs.
- Jails operate in a high-risk environment, where inmates can be dangerous to other inmates, themselves, and to staff.
- Jail inmate populations fluctuate day to day.
- Many jail inmates spend only a few days confined in a jail; in some jails up to 90% of all inmates are released from jail within 72 hours (3 days) of being incarcerated.
- Much staff effort is required to operate admissions and release procedures (booking desk). Peak times of admissions cannot be specifically predicted.

- Jail staff must extensively and accurately document all activities and procedures in the jail.
- Jail perimeter security and internal circulation (by inmates and staff) must be controlled at all times.
- Inmate supervision needs vary due to different classifications of inmates.
- The jail inmate population consists of both pre-trial detainees and sentenced (convicted) inmates. Each group has its own operating needs and constitutional guarantees.
- Jail staff turnover is high in many jails.
- Jail staff, administrators, and funding officials are subject to liability due to their responsibility for jail operations and conditions.

In summary, jails operate round the clock, with much staff responsibility. Admissions, security, and internal movement of inmates must be controlled and dealt with at all times. Extensive documentation is required from staff.

In properly analyzing staff and providing the best operations in a jail, court decisions that have affected staff cannot be discounted. Recent and past court decisions have set parameters for staffing and operations. Due to court actions, jails, or more specifically staff, are required to:[59]

- Protect inmates from themselves and from other inmates (assaults, self-destructive behavior, etc.).
- Ensure the safety of staff and inmates at all times.
- Make special provisions for the processing, supervisions, and meeting the needs of female inmates.
- Communicate and visit regularly with inmates.
- Respond to inmate request for assistance.
- Classify separate and properly house inmates.
- Ensure the delivery of required services, programs and activities to inmates, such as medical care, visiting, recreation, programs, etc.
- Provide properly trained jail staff.

Standards are also important, as many are based on court rulings. Local health, safety, fire, and building code standards are frequently applied to jails, and this must be documented. In cases of state jail standards, many states have established jail standards that are mandatory and inspect jails to measure compliance. The ACA establishes professional jail standards and makes available to jails an accreditation process.[60]

The NIC jail staff analysis process consists of ten steps that examine the jail, jail activities, how they are scheduled, and allows for the development of a schedule and calculations of operational costs. The crucial first step is to profile the jail, including its capacity, the average daily population over several years, data on admissions and length of stay, jail design, inmate population profiles, applicable standards, serious incidents, inspections, staffing, and problems in jail operations.[61]

The entire analysis process is as follows:[62]

- Developing a detailed profile of the jail.
- Calculate the net annual staff work hours, looking at training, light duty, court, etc.

- Develop a facility activity schedule, looking at *all* activities and tasks occurring in the jail. This has to be detailed: shift changes (roll calls), formal counts, lock-downs, service of meals, visiting-personal and professional, sick call and medical activities, court appearances, commissary deliveries, recreation (indoor and out-door), counseling activities, and program sessions.
- Developing a staff coverage plan, identifying minimum coverage for staff and inmate safety, based on fixed posts and job classifications.
- Completion of a staff summary based on a summary of staff necessary for each job classification.
- Developing a schedule: this could vary depending on what staff is assigned to what tasks. Approaches could include: four workdays at 10-hour shifts, (the **4/10 approach), flex time** (if a staff member works late, he or she can leave early one day within the pay period, or a staff member can come in later and leave early, or work overtime and leave the same number of hours earlier in the pay period), variation in shift assignments, having part-time staff, split shifts, or use the 12-hour approach.
- Evaluating the plan, using a brainstorming team.
- Calculating operational costs: overtime must be factored in. Also, it must be noted that jail staffing costs can run between 70 and 80 percent of a jail's operational budget. Throughout the process, costs must be constantly considered.
- Preparation of a report that justifies the plan in an easy-to-read narrative form.
- Implement the plan and monitor the progress and results every six months.

State of the art corrections training classroom.

Photo by author, courtesy Hampton Roads Criminal Justice Training Academy.

## SUMMARY

Staffing in the modern jail is more than just having officers watch inmates. Jail staff consists of both sworn and civilian workers. The jail may be either operated by a sheriff's office or a local corrections department. At the top of the staff structure is the command staff, and the main section of any jail staff is the custody or confinement section.

Squads provide the security in the jail and each squad has its supervisors. Squads meet in roll call where directives, reports, and training are discussed. Other sections of the jail staff include the diagnostic and treatment, support services, and administrative staff. Volunteers, reserve deputies, and interns are all gaining importance in the staffing of a jail.

Proper recruitment is a key factor in having a good jail staff. According to one key study, word of mouth remains a popular recruiting method, and promotion opportunities help in the retention of a good staff. Budget problems cause staff to leave the agency. Recruitment can be enhanced by interviewing candidates using true life scenarios and questions.

Training, using a variety of subjects and methods, can bring out the best traits and skills in the jail staff. The ACA has taken the lead by requiring sufficient hours of training in numerous subjects for all staffing levels.

The future of jail staffing appears to be positive, using staffing analysis, professional resources, and addressing such issues as stress management, the emergence of female staff, inmate manipulation, and staff/inmate fraternization.

## REVIEW QUESTIONS

1. Discuss the duties of a member of the jail command staff.
2. What is the rank structure of a confinement squad?
3. Discuss the value of jail volunteers, reserve deputies, and college interns.
4. Name the most effective recruitment and retention methods in the hiring of jail staff.
5. Explain the "daily life question" method of interviewing jail staff applicants.
6. Name six topics in jails training and explain their importance.
7. Why is the training position of the American Correctional Association so important?
8. Explain the importance of jails dealing effectively with these issues: inmate manipulation, stress management, and staff/inmate fraternization.
9. Why is jail staffing analysis important?
10. Why is line officer autonomy important in jail staff development?

## TERMS TO KNOW

4/10 approach
accreditation manager
assistant squad commander
basic training
CHUMPS
civilian jail staff
command staff
confinement or custody branch
daily life questions
diagnostic and treatment staffs
field training officer (FTO)
flex time
floater
human relations skills
in service training
inmate-staff fraternization
inter-facility training programs
jail administrator
jail correctional officer
job fairs
local county corrections department
mandatory overtime
mock cellblock
probationary period
public relations officer
role players
roll call
roll call training
scenario-based training
security/procedural skills
short/long schedule
squad leader
staff support groups
sworn jail staff

## ENDNOTES


1. Kathleen Maguire and Ann L. Pastore, eds., U.S. Department of Justice, Bureau of Justice Statistics. *Sourcebook of Criminal Justice Statistics 2002* (Washington, DC: GPO, 2004), p. 91.
2. Kenneth E. Kerle, *Exploring Jail Operations* (Hagerstown, MD: American Jail Association, 2003), pp. 40, 41.
3. Richard P. Seiter, *Correctional Administration: Integrating Theory and Practice* (Upper Saddle River, N.J.: Prentice Hall, 2002), pp. 4, 5.
4. Gary F. Cornelius, "Volunteers in Jail," *Jail Operations Bulletin* (American Jail Association) 6 (1), (1994): 2–5.
5. San Diego County Sheriff's Department, "Sheriff's Reserve Support Detail," http://www.sdsheriff.net/patrol/reserves/reserve1.html
6. Robbeye Braxton-Mintz and Major Mike Pinson, "Personnel: Your Most Important Resource," *Corrections Today* (October 2000), 96.
7. "Job Bank," *The Corrections Professional*, 10 (19) (July 22, 2005): 16.
8. Gwinnett County, GA, Careers, http://agency. governmentjobs.com/gwinnett/default.cfm?action=viewjob&JobID=11535
9. Gary F. Cornelius, *Stressed Out: Strategies for Living and Working in Correction: 2 Edition* (Lanham, MD: American Correctional Association, 2005), p. 40.
10. Douglas L. Yearwood, "Recruitment and Retention of Sworn Sheriff's Personnel: What the Research Shows," *Sheriff* (March–April 2004): 24, 25.
11. Ibid., p. 24.
12. Ibid., p. 25.
13. Ibid., p. 26.
14. Jerry R. Hawley, "Success In Interviewing Correctional Applicants," *American Jails* (March–April 1998): 74.
15. Ibid., p. 74.
16. Ibid., pp. 74, 75.
17. Gary F. Cornelius, *The Correctional Officer: A Practical Guide* (Durham: Carolina Academic Press, 2001), pp. 34, 35.
18. Ibid., pp. 35, 36.
19. Seiter, *Correctional Administration*, p. 321.
20. Peter M. Wittenberg, "Field Training New Correctional Staff," *American Jails* (March–April 1996): 48.
21. Ibid., pp. 48–50.
22. Chief Deputy Walter Smith, Denver Sheriff's Department, letter to author, July 26, 2005.
23. Ibid.
24. *Performance-Based Standards for Adult Local Detention Facilities, Fourth Edition* (Lanham, MD: American Correctional Association, 2004), pp. 113–116.
25. Ibid., p. 113.
26. Ibid., pp. 113–116.
27. Cornelius, *The Correctional Officer*, pp. 30, 31.
28. Ibid., pp. 114, 115, 117.
29. Ibid., p. 116.
30. Ibid., p. 117.
31. Ibid., p. 116.
32. Ibid.
33. Ibid., pp. 114, 115.
34. Cornelius, *The Correctional Officer*, pp. 27, 28.
35. American Jail Association Web site: www.aja.org
36. International Association of Correctional Training Personnel Web site: www.iactp.org
37. American Correctional Association Web site: www.aca.org
38. Corrections Connection Web site: www.corrections.com
39. LRP Publications Web site: www.lrp.com; information from LRP Product Group Manager Courtney Ingram, April 06, 2006.
40. Mark R. Pogrebin and Eric D. Poole, "The Sexualized Work Environment: A Look at Women Jail Officers," *American Jails* (July–August 1997), 9, 20.
41. Ibid., p. 22.
42. Kerle, *Exploring Jail Operations*, p. 69.
43. Ibid., pp. 67–69.
44. Peter M. Wittenberg, "Leadership, Ethics and Training: Why the Basics Count," *American Jails* (May–June 1998), 58.
45. Ibid.
46. Ibid.
47. Ibid., pp. 59–61.
48. Ibid., p. 61.
49. Sally Chandler Halford, "The Autonomy of Line Officers: Making Decisions," *Jail Managers Bulletin* (American Jail Association), 5 (5) (1995): 3.
50. Ibid., pp. 2, 3.
51. Cornelius, *Stressed Out*, p. 39.
52. Ibid., p. 38.
53. Ibid., p. 65.
54. Gary Cornelius, *The Art of the Con: Avoiding Offender Manipulation* (Lanham, MD: American Correctional Association, 2001), pp. 46–64.
55. Ibid., p. 65.
56. Ibid., pp. 57, 112–116.
57. Ibid., pp. 65, 66.
58. Dennis R. Liebert and Rod Miller, *Staffing Analysis: Workbook for Jails: Second Edition* (Washington, DC: National Institute of Corrections, 2003), p. 3.

59. Ibid., p. 4.

60. Ibid.

61. Ibid., pp. 6, 7.

62. Ibid., pp. 6–8, 11, 13, 16, 17, 20–23.

## REFERENCES


American Correctional Association Web site: www.aca.org

American Jail Association Web site: www.aja.org

Braxton-Mintz, Robbye and Major Mike Pinson. "Personnel: Your Most Important Resource." *Corrections Today* October 2000, 96–98.

Cornelius, Gary. *The Art of the Con: Avoiding Offender Manipulation.* Lanham, MD: American Correctional Association, 2001.

Cornelius, Gary F. *The Correctional Officer: A Practical Guide.* Durham: Carolina Academic Press, 2001.

Cornelius, Gary F. *Stressed Out: Strategies for Living and Working in Correction: 2nd Edition.* Lanham, MD: American Correctional Association, 2005.

Cornelius, Gary F. "Volunteers in Jail," *Jail Operations Bulletin* (American Jail Association) 6 (1), (1994): 2–5.

Corrections Connection Web site: www.corrections.com

Gwinnett County, GA, Careers, http://agency. governmentjobs.com/gwinnett/default.cfm?action=viewjob&JobID =11535

Halford, Sally Chandler. "The Autonomy of Line Officers: Making Decisions," *Jail Managers Bulletin* (American Jail Association), 5 (5) (1995): 3.

Hawley, Jerry R. "Success In Interviewing Correctional Applicants." *American Jails* (March–April 1998), 73–75.

International Association of Correctional Training Personnel Web site: www.iactp.org

"Job Bank," *The Corrections Professional,* 10 (19) (July 22, 2005): 16.

Kerle, Kenneth E. *Exploring Jail Operations* Hagerstown, MD: American Jail Association, 2003.

Liebert, Dennis R. and Rod Miller. *Staffing Analysis: Workbook for Jails: Second Edition.* Washington, DC: National Institute of Corrections, 2003.

LRP Publications Web site, www.lrp.com

Maguire, Kathleen and Ann L. Pastore, eds. U.S. Department of Justice, Bureau of Justice Statistics, *Sourcebook of Criminal Justice Statistics 2002.* Washington, DC: GPO, 2004.

*Performance-Based Standards for Adult Local Detention Facilities, Fourth Edition.* Lanham, Md.: American Correctional Association, 2004.

Pogrebin, Mark R. and Eric D. Poole. "The Sexualized Work Environment: A Look at Women Jail Officers." *American Jails,* July–August 1997, 9–23.

San Diego County Sheriff's Department, "Sheriff's Reserve Support Detail," http://www.sdsheriff.net/patrol/reserves/reserve1.html

Seiter, Richard P.. *Correctional Administration: Integrating Theory and Practice.* Upper Saddle River, NJ: Prentice Hall, 2002.

Chief Deputy Walter Smith, Denver Sheriff's Department, letter to author, July 26, 2005.

Wittenberg, Peter M. "Field Training New Correctional Staff." *American Jails* (March–April 1996), 47–50.

Wittenberg, Peter M. "Leadership, Ethics and Training: Why the Basics Count." *American Jails* (May–June 1998), 57–62.

Yearwood, Douglas L. "Recruitment and Retention of Sworn Sheriff's Personnel: What the Research Shows." *Sheriff* (March–April 2004), 24–28.

# 9 JAILS AND THE COURTS

***Objectives of chapter***

The student will:

- Understand how the courts have played a major role in improving the conditions of jails and impacting the rights of inmates
- Gain insight as to the basic rights of inmates under the Constitution as decided by the courts
- Understand how legislative acts in recent years have had an impact on inmate rights
- Learn recent trends in inmate litigation and protective measures for staff

The courts have had a major impact on the operations of jails and the rights afforded to inmates. Jail staffs do not have to be legal experts, but should understand the influence that the court has on a jail. Inmates enjoy more rights—limited rights—now more than any other time in the history of jails in the United States. Many of these rights are the result of several actions—decisions and decrees by local and federal courts, litigation by inmates, and acts of legislation concerning the rights of offenders who are incarcerated in our nation's corrections facilities. This chapter is not designed to be a legal treatise on these subjects, but an overall, concise guide to inmate rights and how the courts impact the jail. The area of jails and the courts is an evolutionary, ongoing process; for one to understand where jails stand concerning inmate rights, one must understand where this process has been.

This chapter will relate how the courts became involved in correctional facilities, the rights that inmates have under the Constitution, how inmates get their complaints to court, recent acts by Congress that dictate the rights of inmates in certain areas, and recent trends in court decisions in inmate rights and management.

The last four decades—the 1960's through the present—has resulted both in inmates gaining more rights from the courts *and* in jail staffs becoming more adept at defending themselves against litigation filed by inmates or filed on the behalf of inmates. In a well-run jail, lawsuits are rare for anything but catastrophic incidents such as serious illness, injury, sexual assault, felony assault, or inmate suicide. By adhering to good practices and up-to-date standards, jails are avoiding being drawn into court by inmates who are very talented in filing and pursuing litigation. Perhaps the greatest tool in avoiding inmate lawsuits in the past 20 years is the grievance procedure, which evolved as a result of courts and jails engaging in "trial and error" practices—finding a common ground to examine inmate rights while at the same time protecting the jail staff and public by adhering to security practices.

The risk of being the target of an inmate lawsuit is an "occupational hazard"; all jail officers are subject to being targeted. Filing a lawsuit is one thing; an inmate being successful is another. Jail staffs have to be practiced for recognizing the circumstances that could to lead to inmate litigation, such as an inmate reporting to the staff that he or she has been threatened by other inmates, or an inmate having a medical condition that needs immediate treatment. Also, jail officers must have a basic understanding of what rights are afforded to inmates and ensure that the inmates are allowed to exercise their rights. An example of this may be an inmate who has a pending court case or is working on an appeal and requests the use of the law library.

The average jail officer is not concerned with how the mechanics of the court system works. What is important to the jail staff is that inmates are afforded opportunities to research the law, court cases, and legal procedures. These opportunities lead inmates to file legal actions that are part of the defense in their criminal cases as well as lawsuits alleging that they have been denied civil rights under the Constitution and the Bill of Rights. These lawsuits have resulted in cases granting inmates limited rights under the Constitution, and jail staffs need to know what these basic rights and limitations are.

Studies of the courts and inmate rights can become confusing for the average jail staff member. What is important to know is the United States has two court systems: state and federal. State courts, state courts of appeals and state supreme courts, have jurisdiction in only their respective state. Federal trial courts, or United States District Courts, are divided into 94 districts; each state has at least one district court. U.S. District Courts can hear cases involving the U.S. Government, federal laws (including the U.S. Constitution), and federal agency regulations. Decisions can be appealed to the United States Circuit Court of Appeals, each of which covers a geographic region. The highest court in the federal system and the nation is the United States Supreme Court. Its decisions are binding in all state and federal jurisdictions. Many cases that are appealed to the Supreme Court come from state supreme courts because they involve rights under the Constitution.[1]

Generally, inmates file litigation that is included in the following categories:[2]

- **Habeas corpus actions:** In habeas corpus actions, inmates claim that they are being held illegally, and attack a court action or agency responsible for the inmate being in custody. Habeas corpus actions can name jail personnel.
- **Torts:** Torts are actions usually filed in state courts that seek damages. The plaintiff (inmate) in a tort alleges that he or she is owed some duty by the defendant (correctional personnel). Tort claims have included medical malpractice, staff failing to protect the inmate from harm, and lack of training and assignment of staff resulting in the inmate being harmed in some way.
- **Civil rights actions:** Inmates prefer filing actions alleging that their civil rights under the Constitution were violated. The preferred method by many inmates is to file under **42 United States Code 1983** or 42 USC 1983. "Section 1983," as inmates call it, states that if a government official, such as a correctional officer, denies an inmate protections under the constitution, the injured party (inmates) can sue for liability and monetary damages. Inmates have preferred to file Section 1983 suits in federal courts than to file torts in state courts, where the scope of relief is less broad. Also, the federal courts through the hands on era to now have shown more sympathy at times to inmates' claims.[3]

A 1992 study by the National Center for State Courts (NCSC) with assistance from the Bureau of Justice Statistics studied Section 1983 cases disposed of in the U.S. District Courts in Alabama, California, Florida, Indiana, Louisiana, Missouri, New York, Pennsylvania, and Texas. Nearly 50 percent of the nation's Section 1983 litigation is located among these states. The Second, Third, Fifth, Seventh, Eighth, Ninth, and Eleventh Circuits of the United Sates Courts of Appeals were included in the study. The study was also representative of the Northeast, Southeast, Midwest, and West regions.[4]

Inmates in litigation can allege that staff is negligent if their medical conditions are not treated, if they are attacked in cellblocks which they should not have been placed in, etc. There are degrees of negligence. **Gross negligence** involves actions that take place in reckless disregard of the consequences. For example, two jail inmates who are on a jail keep separate list are placed by jail officers in the same

Section 1983 litigation in the 1992 NCSC Study targeted these areas of prison operations:

- Medical treatment (17%)—examples: failure to provide back brace, corrective shoes, dentures; failure to perform necessary surgery.
- Physical security (21%)—examples: use of excessive force by correctional officers, failure by staff to protect inmates from attacks and sexual assaults by other inmates, failure to prevent theft of an inmate's property, unreasonable body cavity searches, threats and harassment by correctional officers.
- Due process issues (13%)—examples: improper intra-prison transfer, improper placement in administrative segregation, improper classification, improper conduct of disciplinary hearings.
- Living conditions (4%)—examples: diets are nutritionally inadequate, exercise is denied or extremely limited, inadequate clothing.
- Physical conditions (9%)—examples: overcrowding, inadequate showers, inadequate toilets, inadequate sanitation, excessive noise, failure to protect inmates from tobacco smoke exposure and inmates with AIDS.
- Denial of religious expression, visitation, and assembly; racial discrimination (4%).
- Denial of access to the courts, lawyers, law libraries, and staff interference with mail and telephone calls (7%).
- Assault and harassment by arresting officer (3%).
- Challenges to conviction (12%).
- Miscellaneous remaining issues (11%)—examples: denial of parole, denial of trial, appellate attorney's refused to correspond with the inmate.

Most Section 1983 lawsuits end with the court dismissing the case (74%) or granting a dismissal on the defendant's motion.

A term widely used in inmate litigation is **negligence.** Negligence is the failure to exercise such care as a reasonably prudent person would under the same or similar circumstances. Legally, negligence is doing something that would not be done by a prudent, reasonable person. It also means the failure to do something that a prudent, reasonable person would do. Negligence is the failure to adhere to the standards of conduct that are expected by law to protect other persons from unreasonable risk and or harm.[5]

**FIGURE 9-1** A Look at Section 1983 Litigation: 1992[6]

court holding area. One is testifying against the other, and a fight with serious injuries occurs. A more serious form of negligence is **willful negligence,** when a staff member intentionally does something that causes harm. For example, a jail officer is spat upon by an inmate. The next day, the same inmate is having a seizure. To "get back" at the inmate, the officer delays calling the medical staff. The inmate suffers serious injury due to the prolonged seizure.[7]

## THE ROLE OF THE COURTS AND INMATE RIGHTS

The evolution of inmate rights is an interesting one, involving three periods or eras. A student of corrections must realize that the unsettling history of the American jail from the colonial period well into the twentieth century was characterized by different jails, different philosophies of corrections, and different staff approaches to inmates. Sheriffs and wardens had an independent, "free hand" in how they ran their jails, usually with little or no interference with the citizens, let alone the courts. For simplicity, this evolution involved jail and prison inmates, so as to clarify the evolution of inmate rights; the groups will not be differentiated and categorized.

### The Hands Off Era

The name of this era is very clear in its representation of the thought that the courts had about inmates in general. In the **hands off era,** courts took no action concerning inmate complaints filed in court about treatment or conditions in jails and prison. According to Professor Michael B. Mushlin of the Pace University Law School and an expert on the rights of prisoners, the U.S. Constitution did not cross over prison and jail walls for more than 170 years. For most of that time, a question was asked—do inmates have *any* constitutional rights at all?[8]

One case described inmates as **"slaves of the state"** and its ruling clearly answered the question if inmates have rights. The case was *Ruffin v. Commonwealth of Virginia*, 62 Va. 790 (1871), a case of the Court of Appeals in Virginia. A state prison inmate named Ruffin was convicted of killing a corrections officer. Ruffin filed litigation claiming that his trial should have taken place in the county where the crime occurred, rather than before a jury in the state capital, which was the practice at the time required by Virginia law for inmates.[9]

The opinion of the court in *Ruffin* stated that a convicted felon while incarcerated is subject to laws enacted by the legislature for the government of the prison and the control of the inmates. Further, while confined or serving his term in the penitentiary, "he [the felon] is in a state of penal servitude to the state. He has, as a consequence of his crime, not only forfeited his liberty, but all his personal rights except those which the law in its humanity accords to him. He is for the time being the slave of the state." The opinion goes on to say that the bill of rights is intended to be a declaration of principles to govern a "society of freemen, and not convicted felons and men civilly dead."[10]

This case clearly indicates the thought at the time: because of being convicted of a crime, an inmate automatically gives up the rights and protections given to them by the courts and Constitution. All personal rights are also forfeited, and the bill of rights is only for free people and not for the imprisoned. The subject of inmate rights continues to be a "hot" one. A citizen on the outside of a correctional institution or a staff member inside may remark that "they [the inmates] have committed a crime—they do not deserve any rights . . . . ." or "they [the inmates] gave up their rights when they did what they did to end up in jail."

As the courts took a "hands off" position, leaving the operation of the jails and prisons to the sheriffs and the wardens, the question was never answered as to what rights an inmate should have while incarcerated. Federal courts held fast to the position that the only intervention into the realm of correctional institutions from the courts should be to free inmates who are confined illegally.[11] As a result, jail administrators could rule with an iron hand and do things their way. Humane treatment and efficient jail operations took a secondary role.

Over time, practices in jails and prisons began to illustrate the aloofness of the courts and the subsequent terrible results. Several cases brought these issues to light. One of the best examples is the case of *Ex Parte Pickens*, 101 F.Supp. 285 (D. Alas. 1951). An Alaska court examined the conditions of a federal jail located in Anchorage in 1951. Forty inmates were housed in a room inside a wood frame jail, resulting in less than 19 square feet per inmate. Bunks, tables, and benches crowded the room. Sleeping arrangements were that only 20 bunks were available for the 40 inmates. Recreational capacity was nonexistent, and there were only one shower and one toilet. This, combined with inadequate ventilation and crowding, resulted in numerous health hazards. There was a serious fire hazard due to an old coal burning stove located in the room for heat, there was only one exit, and it was not possible to add another exit.[12]

The jail was described by the judge as not fit for human inhabitation and agreed with a description of the jail as a "fabulous obscenity." He noted that the conditions were bad, but the soldiers fighting in the Korean War were enduring far worse conditions. The court found that the only relief that could be granted was simply to release inmates, and did not find the jail in violation of the Eighth Amendment under the Constitution—cruel and unusual punishment.[13]

By the late 1960s, cases were being brought to the courts that showed the most basic, decent, and humane rights of inmates were being ignored in the areas of security, medical care, and housing. Noted correctional law expert William C. Collins cites these examples of how bad the conditions had become by the late 1960s into the early 1970s:[14]

- As recently as 1965, inmates in the Arkansas penal system were tortured by an electronic device called the **"Tucker Telephone,"** which punished inmates by delivering electric shocks. Inmates were whipped, sometimes by inmate trusties [*Jackson v Bishop*, 404 F.2d 571 (8th Circuit 1968)].
- A group of Alabama inmates filed suit in 1966 complaining that the state laws in Alabama segregated inmates by race in state correctional institutions and local jails. The correctional administrators said that the policy was necessary for security and discipline and the courts had no business inquiring into the practice. The court found the segregation practice unconstitutional and ordered the correctional facilities desegregated [*Washington v. Lee*, 263 F.Supp. 327 (M.D. Ala., 1966), aff'd. 88 S.Ct. 994 (1968)].
- In Arkansas, armed inmate trusties guarded fellow inmates, and in a prison with 1,000 inmates, only two correctional officers were on duty during the night shift. As a result, the trusty system was characterized by extortion, bribery, and smuggling.

Placement of inmates in dormitories was based on race and "rank" in the facility. Because inmates were supposed to provide supervision, sexual assaults and stabbings were common occurrences. Sanitation and medical practices were substandard [*Holt v. Sarver*, 309 F.Supp. 362 (E.D. Arkansas., 1970)].

- In Alabama, inadequate medical care resulted in an incontinent patient being forced to sit on a bench as to not soil his bed; he fell frequently, resulting in the amputation of his leg. An inmate waited 21 days before his wound was cleaned and disinfected, but by the time that was performed, maggots had set in. Inmates handled medical treatment and medical records. The correctional medical system lacked qualified staff including doctors [*Newman v. Alabama*, 503 F.2d 1320 (5th Circuit, 1974)].

The courts at the time were wrestling with several concerns that prevented proper intervention in corrections cases. Most of these centered around the concept of **federalism**—the belief by the federal courts that whenever possible, federal courts should not involve themselves in the affairs of state and local governments, like in the operations of state prisons and local jails.[15]

There were other concerns besides federalism. Corrections were unknown territory for the courts, much to the pleasure of jail administrators. Other concerns were:[16]

- *Separation of powers:* Management, control, and operations of jails are considered to be functions of the executive and legislative branches of government, and the courts during this era were of the opinion that they should not tell administrators how to run the jails. Also, legislatures appropriated monies for the operation of correctional facilities, and this tied into the legislative branch, into which courts were also reluctant to intervene.
- *Lack of expertise:* The courts assumed that the management of correctional facilities required knowledge, skills, training, and experience. In addition, the courts thought that intervening in correctional operations would undermine the authority of staff and disciplinary systems that administrators used to control inmates.
- *Increasing workload for the courts:* Inmates as a rule are always willing to file litigation or at a minimum file complaints. Courts in the hands off era thought that if hearings were granted to inmates filing suits, then the floodgates would open. Some suits were frivolous no doubt, but it was easier for a court to determine that the litigation came from a prison or a jail, and summarily dismiss it. As a result courts never heard litigation filed that involved serious matters that needed resolution.

As the civil rights movement took hold in the 1960s, the American landscape was changing concerning the rights of minorities and the underprivileged. African Americans protested racist segregationist policies in the South, and civil rights leaders such as Dr. Martin Luther King were emerging. The Vietnam War brought protesting into a new light. The news of protests transcended the walls of prisons and jails, and inmates, armed with a new tool, began filing grievances and lawsuits.

Into this volatile situation, four forces and events appeared resulting in the demise of the judicial positions of the hands off era. First, inmates were becoming active, and as corrections law authority Michael Muslin indicates, militant and assertive. Complaining that the right to practice their religion was being deliberately ignored by correctional administrators, the Black Muslims began to file lawsuits—some successful—challenging prison conditions and practices, opening the door for other inmate suits. Secondly, lawyers who supported the civil rights movement emerged, taking inmate cases to court. These cases with advice and counsel from experienced attorneys were more successful in court than poorly written inmate lawsuits. Third, the courts began to take an interest in the situation of society's underprivileged and unfortunates—which many in the courts considered to be inmates. Finally, the shocking, sordid and squalid conditions in prisons and jails came to light due to the media, books written by inmates (such as Caryl Chessman, Bill Sands, and Eldridge Cleaver), and inmate actions such as the Attica prison riot. Even though many correctional facilities were remotely located and tightly run, news of conditions and mistreatment of inmates was spreading.[17]

## Hands on Era

With the demise of judicial aloofness and refusal toward the ways in which corrections facilities were being run, courts in the 1970s entered what has been called the **hands on era,** a time when courts took a very active and some say overbearing, "micromanagement" role concerning corrections. The problem was the lack of precedent, or **case law,** or law made by court rulings rather than the legislature. In the hands off era, courts generally ignored inmate complaints and most never made it to court. Judges often look to see how other courts have ruled; it gives them ideas and guidance. With the lack of correctional case law, judges were for the most part on their own, blazing into new uncharted territory.

The number of inmate civil rights suits increased dramatically during the years 1970–1980. In 1970, for example, 2,030 civil rights actions were filed in federal courts by state prison inmates. In 1975, 6,128 such actions were filed, and that increased to nearly 12,400 by 1980. In the courts, defendants—jail and prison administrators—could put up little defense against these suits, and the courts, lacking precedent, began to make rulings concerning inmate rights and the management of prisons and jails. The rulings were so detailed that in the case of *Smith v. Sullivan*, 563 F.2d 373 (5th Circuit, 1977), a district court judge ruled (and later was reversed on appeal) that inmates be served one green vegetable and one yellow vegetable per day.[18] This "micromanagement" approach was typical of how detailed court decisions were in the operational areas of jails. However, during this period several advances were made in critical areas of inmate rights including medical care and overcrowding. For inmates, this was "The Golden Age" of filing lawsuits because they discovered that many of the courts would give them a hearing.

## One Hand On–One Hand Off Era

By the end of the decade from 1970 to 1980, the courts realized that micromanaging correctional institutions was not very practical. The Supreme Court recognized this in the landmark case of *Bell v. Wolfish*, 441 U.S. 520 (1979), saying that the lower courts had overstepped their boundaries concerning inmate rights.[19] Using a **"restrained hands approach,"** or getting involved only if absolutely necessary and leaving the administration of jails and prisons to qualified staff, courts began to "back off." This is the era where corrections is now.

POINT OF VIEW

## Constitutional Rights of Inmates

***Major Michael Pinson***
Chief Correctional Officer
Arlington County (VA) Sheriff's Office

Inmates generally confuse constitutional rights with privileges or fail to realize how certain rights change as a result of being incarcerated. It's common and sometimes comical how they go on about things. Freedom of speech, privacy, cruel and unusual punishment, disciplinary procedures, access to medical care or the law library are just some examples. In the course of managing or dealing with inmates, there is a difference; correctional officers and employees can expect encounters like the following.

An inmate upset with something curses out loud. The officer hears this and challenges what the inmate said. The inmate responds negatively with I wasn't cursing at you. I have the right to free speech. Wrong—facility rules do not permit this and you should correct this behavior of the inmate.

You go to conduct a cell search and the inmate tells you he has a right to be present during the search. He then points at a stack of papers and says you can't search that. Tell the inmate he does not have the right to be present and instruct him to move where you want him to. Then, search that stack of papers. Basically all possessions and contents of the cell are "free game" with the exception of legal mail and paperwork. With that, if it's open, you can look through it for criminal contraband. Just don't read it, learn about the inmate's defense, or destroy it. If it's not open, say it's addressed to the court, then you can feel or squeeze it to make sure there is no weapon concealed inside and then just put it back as you found it. If you have probable cause that it is criminal in nature, say an escape plan, "hit" order, or involves some other crime, then when the inmate returns open it in his or her presence and proceed as mentioned before. A supervisor should be involved by this point to handle anything you find that is criminal, or if it's clean to replace the opened envelope and postage if necessary and then leave it with the inmate.

Inmates do have the right to be free of any cruel or unusual punishment or circumstances. You can't internally create or let happen a situation that could physically harm someone. This includes physical beatings, dangerous situations, and also some environmental issues. You can't use force as punishment or use force excessively knowing that the inmate will be harmed. You can't place an inmate in a cell, or other place where you know he would be subject to physical harm by other inmates. How long would you say, you can leave an inmate in a cell with a broken toilet? If there is waste in it, you should move the inmate when you can or within a few hours or have it repaired. If not, then I would say by the end of your shift you should have taken steps to correct it.

Sometimes an inmate wants his lawyer to represent him or be present at a disciplinary hearing. Officials are under no obligation to allow this. However, there are constitutional protections for inmate discipline and they have pretty much remained the same. Most all of them can be found in *Wolff v. McDonnell* along with some elements of *Bell v. Wolfish*. Most agency policies and procedures as well as national and state standards include these. An inmate does have the right to be provided notice of the charges brought against him and has at least 24 hours in advance to prepare for the hearing. We are talking about an administrative disciplinary hearing where the sanctions carry liberty interests or a substantial change in status like segregation. The hearing board can with good cause limit or exclude witnesses, accept written testimony, and decide on other evidence and uses the preponderance of evidence rule to decide guilt or innocence. Sanctions are usually detailed in procedures for each degree of charges. Also, there is no double jeopardy, an inmate can be charged and convicted by a disciplinary hearing and a criminal court.

Inmates do have constitutional safeguards with respect to access to the courts and medical care. Access to courts is usually provided by representation of a lawyer and in some cases that is enough. Most facilities also provide a law library or electronic access to criminal code, federal supplements, and circuit court and Supreme Court decisions. Usually problems will arise when an inmate is acting pro bono (as his or her own attorney), and you have to decide matters of access. This you have to approach differently. As far as medical care, this is an area that is routinely problematic especially for jails and I am including mental health as medical. The Supreme Court ruled 30 years ago in *Estelle v. Gamble* that basically if you incarcerate someone, then you have to provide for their medical care. That does not mean you provide every aspect of health care, but you do need to if it's life threatening or urgent, or otherwise would be reasonably expected.

In conclusion, you need to uphold the oath you took to protect and enforce the law. Know what your agency policies and procedures are and make sure you perform your duties in accordance with them. Conduct yourself in a reasonable manner, meaning your actions would not shock anyone hearing about what you did. Finally go about your job using your best knowledge and work, enthusiasm, and integrity. This way you will be respected and appreciated for who you are and the job you do.

Special Thanks to Major Michael Pinson, Chief Correctional Officer, Arlington, VA, Detention Center.

By the beginning of the 1980s, several things had happened in corrections that made this restrained approach by the courts possible. The professionalism in federal, state, and local corrections was becoming more apparent. These events included:[20]

- Improved operations in prisons and jails: better equipment and procedures.
- A Supreme Court that was conservative, saying in several rulings that lower courts had gone too far in defining and enforcing inmate rights. Most likely the common phrase of "inmates have more rights than officers" was born during this time.
- Increased professionalism in the corrections work force: improved hiring and firing practices.
- Increased staffing, improvements in salary and training: Pay scales increased, attracting a better correctional worker, and the amount and subject matter of training improved.
- Improved correctional facilities: New jails were being built or renovated.
- Professional standards were being drafted, approved, and accepted by jails. These standards came from such organizations as the American Correctional Association. States began to write correctional standards and enforce them.
- Improved funding from the state and federal levels, which made many improvements possible.
- Threat of litigation: Valid inmate lawsuits and grievances caught the attention of jail administrators.

The one hand off, one hand on era resulted in a basic, fundamental test used by the courts that serves as a guide for both jail supervisors and line staff. In the 1987 case of *Turner v. Safley*, Missouri prison inmates filed suit, challenging the constitutionality of prison restrictions on inmates from different institutions from writing to each other and getting married only with the prior approval from the warden. The inmates felt that these restrictions violated the right to free speech and freedom of religion, respectively. The defense of the prison officials was based on the premise that the restrictions were necessary to maintain security and order in the prison environment. The case reached the U.S. Supreme Court on appeal. The Court found valid the rule that prohibited inmates from writing to each other, but found invalid the rule prohibiting marriages.[21]

To make this decision, the Supreme Court applied what has become known as the **balancing test.**[22] This test is applied when a court is looking at cases in which inmates are alleging that their rights are being violated. The court *balances* the needs of the correctional facility against the constitutional rights and needs of the inmate. The test asks four basic "common sense" questions:[23]

- Does a valid or reasonable connection exist between the regulation, rule, or restriction and a legitimate penological interest?
- Are inmates permitted to exercise their civil or constitutional rights in other ways?
- If inmates are allowed to exercise their rights in the facility, how much will this affect other inmates?
- Do alternatives exist to accommodate both the inmates' rights and the legitimate penological interest of the facility?

Areas of vital concern to the operation of the correctional facility—security, order, discipline, etc—are called **legitimate penological interests.** Jails are in the business of keeping order and discipline in a secure environment.

For example, a group of Catholic jail inmates wishes to meet for a Rosary prayer session. There is a vacancy for a jail chaplain, and there are no priests or Catholic volunteers trained in jail security available to come in and conduct a prayer session. The inmates say that they would like to meet in a classroom by themselves (alone) and pray. The jail warden denies the request. The inmates sue claiming that their rights of freedom of religion under the First Amendment are being violated and the case goes to federal court. The jail warden says that due to security concerns, inmates are not allowed to be in a program unsupervised; there is always an officer, a jail chaplain, or approved clergy or volunteer who is trained in security measures present. The suit is dismissed, but the judge orders the jail staff to come up with a solution. The jail warden arranges for one time per week that Catholic inmates can pray under the supervision of a jail officer. Efforts are to be undertaken to hire a jail chaplain and recruit and train volunteers.

In this hypothetical case, the right of the inmates to practice the Catholic religion is *balanced* against the security need to supervise inmates. The *Turner* case said that future cases dealing with inmate rights should have the balancing test applied to the case, and those correctional rules, regulations, and procedures that limit inmate constitutional rights are reasonable, as long as such rules, etc. are reasonably related to legitimate penological interests. In other words, if a jail is going to limit inmates' rights, they must clearly show that there is a very good reason.

These three eras served to shape the nature of inmate rights that jail staffs see today. While some litigation has been vindictive and frivolous, there have been many court decisions that have given inmates limited rights. Also, the landscape of inmate rights is changing, and staff must, through training and briefings from the legal community, keep up with new developments and changes.

## JAIL INMATES: BASIC RIGHTS

Since 1970, many rulings have been handed down concerning inmate rights. For jail staff and the student of penology, these landmark cases, mostly from the U.S. Supreme Court, clarified how rights under the Constitution are granted in limited fashion to inmates. These rights involve areas derived from the following amendments to the U.S. Constitution:[24]

- First Amendment: freedom of religion, speech, press, and association, and the right to petition the government for redress of grievances.
- Fourth Amendment: freedom from unreasonable searches.
- Eighth Amendment: no excessive bail or excessive fines, no infliction of cruel and unusual punishment.
- Fourteenth Amendment: no deprivation of life, liberty, or property without due process of law; grants equal protection of the law.

## First Amendment: Freedom of Speech, Religion, and Association

The First Amendment encompasses some very sacred freedoms that we enjoy. In jail, however, such areas as mail, telephone, visiting, and religion need to be restricted in a fair manner. To the inmate, freedom of speech means communications, and in the study of inmate rights this involves mail, publications, telephone, and visiting. However, it is not difficult for jail administrators to restrict these four factors due to security needs. Nor is it difficult to restrict religious activities if the rules can be supported by security needs.

### *Mail*

Concerning mail, jail officials may search incoming mail and publications for contraband. The standard from the Supreme Court is that mail can be inspected due to possible interference in the security interests of the jail.[25] Letters, cards, magazines, packages, etc. can all be searched for contraband and for anything that may have a negative impact on security. Drugs can be hidden in greeting cards, for example. One trend is the security threat group or gang trend as described in Chapter 3. It is advisable that staffs who inspect mail be on the alert for gang symbols, graffiti, or codes that are plainly evident in letters, etc. Incoming mail is not read, but inspected. Jail officials may restrict the nature of things that inmates can receive. For example, an inmate may send away for a science correspondence course from a college and when the material arrives, a compass (for drawing circles, etc.) is included. The jail staff can confiscate it and place it with the inmate's property.

### *Publications*

Publications is another area where the jail staff can exercise security prerogatives. If an inmate receives a magazine containing an article on how to make homemade weapons, for example, the entire magazine is subject to confiscation; the jail does not have to cut out the questionable article and give the remainder of the magazine to the inmate. Nor does a jail have to give inmates publications that contain racist material, which could cause unrest, tension, and possibly violence in the inmate population. Even though there have not been many decisions concerning sexually oriented material, courts since the late 1990s have upheld correctional officials banning sex magazines that can be commonly obtained by subscription.

The main case continues to be *Thornburgh v. Abbott*, 109 S.Ct. 1874 (1989), where the Supreme Court reversed a lower court case of *Abbott v. Thornburgh*, 824 F.2d. 1186 (D.C. Circuit, 1987) that said a correctional facility had to show that the material actually posed a threat.[26] The Supreme Court ruling gave the correctional facilities broad latitude to restrict incoming publications.

There are some "gray areas" concerning mail. Legal mail is privileged, but should be opened in the inmate's presence and checked for contraband. Media mail—letters to radio stations, television stations, newspapers, etc.—has no special privilege. If a letter is rejected, the Supreme Court requires that the inmate—whether sender or recipient—be given notice. The sender of the mail is also to be given notice and an avenue of appeal to the institution officials. Finally, in the interests of furthering security and making the job of handling mail easier, courts are supportive of **publishers only rules,** which require that inmates *only* obtain publications from the publisher.[27]

Another area of controversy is jail inmates writing to other inmates in other jails. The Supreme Court has upheld security bans on this, and this correspondence does not have to be treated the same as other outgoing mail from inmates. This can cause security disruptions such as criminal plans, escape plans, losing control of inmate gang members, etc.[28] Jails generally have a security method where outgoing inmate mail is stamped with the name of the jail, so the recipient of the mail—whether a private citizen or the mail officer in another jail—can see at a glance from where the mail has originated. Inmates know this, and will not write the jail name on the envelope, or may "con" a staff member or volunteer into taking out a letter and mailing it, thus circumventing the mail system in the jail. Inmates may try to write threatening letters to court witnesses and victims of their crimes.

Handling mail is common sense—the jail administration does not want anything coming in with the mail to threaten security. For example, if a jail allows inmates to have books sent to them, they can require the books to be paperback only, as inmates have been known to use hardback books for weapons and makeshift weights—hardly for reading and education. The main theme is to be able to support these restrictions or the denial of an inmate's mail with sound reasons concerning security.

## Telephone

Verbal communications can pose a problem such as inmates plotting in visits, or over the phone, anything from assaults, criminal activity, escapes, or contraband smuggling. Use of the telephone must be subject to regulation. Generally, the courts have ruled that inmates have a general right to speak to family and friends on the outside via the telephone. Incoming calls are not received by the inmate; they can make collect calls. Phone restrictions on special management inmates, such as those on administrative or disciplinary segregation, are permitted. Also, personal—not attorney—phone calls can be taped or monitored. The commonsense approach of the Supreme Court *Turner* decision applies—the restriction on phone use must serve the security and maintenance of discipline in the jail.[29]

The monitoring of inmates' telephone calls is an important security tool. A jail may get a call from a citizen complaining that he or she received a threat from an inmate over the phone, or a report may come in from the local police department saying that an inmate—a known gang leader—is ordering criminal gang activity in the community. Monitoring phone calls may confirm these allegations and the jail may have to take steps in such cases to restrict phone use by the inmate concerned.

### Visiting

According to prison rights experts John W. Palmer, J.D. and Stephen E. Palmer, J.D., the right of inmates to receive visitors while they are incarcerated has been strictly controlled by institution officials. The courts have said that controlling inmates' visitation is within the discretion of correctional authority. The courts will not reverse this control unless there are two factors: a clear abuse of visiting rules is shown, and the visitation polices are *not* related to a legitimate penological or government interest. Also, pretrial detainees, while not in a convicted status, are subject to visiting restrictions if the institution can show a justification for a compelling interest, such as security.[30]

Jail officials can control the days and hours that visiting is available to inmates, how many people each inmate can have on his or her visiting list, and how long each visit can last. Inmates on disciplinary segregation can have personal, not attorney, visitation taken for the duration of their isolation time. To relieve the stress on the inmate on disciplinary segregation, jails can allow a personal visit after a specified time on disciplinary segregation. Many jails allow a **status call,** in which the inmate entering disciplinary segregation is permitted to call his or her family informing them that they will not be permitted to visit during the time of the inmate's disciplinary segregation. Although contact visits and conjugal visits are popular with inmates, there are no rights to either type of visit.

### Religion

This nation was founded on freedom of religion, and the courts have been supportive of inmates' right to choose what faith they will follow and opportunities are afforded to practice that faith. The key factor in any discussion of inmates and religion is when the security needs of the jail begin to interfere with religious activities. Obviously, there has to be a middle ground that satisfies security and the religious needs of the inmates that result in a positive jail climate. Jail cannot be similar to churches in the community.

Some veteran jail officers become skeptical of the inmates attending religious services in the jail. A common view is that religious people do not get arrested, and it is interesting how some inmates who are street and jail wise become interested in religion. However, the courts have ruled that inmates are free to practice their chosen faith. Religious issues in correctional facilities have in recent years led to controversy where some inmates try to "push the envelope" concerning restrictions placed on their religious activities by jail administrations.

Characteristics of some of these cases are controversial groups claiming to be followers of legitimate religions, and seeking status and the exercising of religious freedoms while incarcerated. These types of cases have "bewildered" the courts and have involved such groups as the Black Muslims, Rastafarians, Five Percenters, and the Aryan Brotherhood.[31]

Inmates have also sued over the establishments of "new" religions, religious diets, and grooming.

There are several important questions to be answered in any study of inmates' religious freedoms, due to the numerous cases that have been brought before the

An example of a detailed visiting policy that addresses security issues while allowing inmates to have ample opportunities to visit is the following:

## JAIL VISITING POLICIES

Teton County Jail, Jackson Hole, Wyoming

### Adult Visiting

The Teton County Detention Facility will allow inmates visiting privileges with family and friends on a regular basis. Certain limitations are needed to maintain safety and security and prevent the introduction of contraband. Visiting must take place within the secure visiting area.

- Personal visits will be noncontact in nature.
- Personal visits are limited to 20 minutes.
- Visitors traveling over (150 miles one-way) may receive a 30-minute visit.
- If a lower volume of inmates/visitors permits, longer visits may be allowed.
- Inmate workers will be allowed 30-minute visits.
- Anyone under the age of 18 will not be allowed to visit, unless members of the immediate family.
- Children under the age of 8 must be accompanied by an adult in the visiting booth.
- Inmates with spouses under age 18 will be allowed to visit, providing they have proper ID and proof of marriage.
- Only money for deposit on an inmate's account or legal documents for signing will be accepted from visitors for inmates. Documents are subject to inspection by staff in presence of the inmate. NOTHING else will be accepted.
- Special visits can be allowed if the visitor lives more than 150 miles one-way from Jackson. These visits must be approved by the Sheriff, Support Captain, Jail Administrator, or Detention Sergeants prior to the visit.

### Contact Visits

Allowed only to attorneys, clergy, medical personnel, and approved counselors.

### Visiting Hours

Adult male: Wednesdays 7:30–9:30 P.M. and Sundays 3:00–6:00 P.M.
Adult female: Fridays 7:30–9:30 P.M. and Sundays 1:00–3:00 P.M.

### Visiting Restrictions

Restrictions to visitors and inmates are implemented for the security of the facility. These restrictions shall include, but not be limited to, the following:

- Inmates have the right to refuse any visitors.
- Inmates are required to be dressed in a complete blue, orange, or yellow uniform, including shoes (no shower thongs), while downstairs visiting.
- Adult visitors must produce a pictured ID card written in English.
- Visitors shall not take any container, handbags, etc. into the visiting area.
- Visitors are not allowed to bring food or beverages into the building.
- Visitors having a contagious disease will not be admitted.

**FIGURE 9-2** Continued

- Visitors shall not be disruptive, verbally abusive, disorderly, or assaultive prior to or during any visit. They may be required to leave or be subject to arrest.
- Anyone under the influence of alcohol or drugs will not be allowed to visit and may be subject to arrest.
- Visitors may be subject to a "pat down" search if reasonable suspicion exists as to officer or public safety.
- Violation of any of the above regulations may result in loss of visiting privileges for both inmates and visitors.

From: Teton County Jail, Jackson Hole, Wyoming: *Inmate Rules and Regulations*, Revised 05/12/03. Thanks to Sgt. Troy Sutton and Sheriff Bob Zimmer. Reprinted by permission.

**FIGURE 9-2** Jail Visiting

courts. These questions will serve to keep this vast area of inmate rights in some sort of perspective. The information dealing with each one comes from the most noted experts in correctional law and inmate rights. These questions are:

- *What is a religion, especially inside a jail?* If something is recognized as a religion, the inmate can practice it, subject to security restrictions under the balancing test. If something is not considered a religion, then the jail does not have to justify any restrictions imposed on the inmate. Courts use different tests to decide if the concept is a religion, saying a range of things such as a religion addresses deep, imponderable matters to men standing in relation to whatever they believe is divine. Some courts ask if something looks like a religion such as sacraments, liturgy, ordained clergy, affiliations with a church, teachings, etc. Courts will not judge the merits of the beliefs or decide if the beliefs are the "proper or correct ones." Some examples are bizarre—such as the famous case of the "Church of the New Song," or more widely known by its interesting acronym "CONS," or an inmate who claimed that he was the Reverend of the Church of Marijuana. In the "Church of Marijuana," one could use, possess, and distribute cannabis for Earth's and mankind's benefit. To prosecute him, he argued, violated his First Amendment rights under freedom of religion. In the "CONS" church, a "sacrament" was the serving of steak and wine occasionally. Both arguments were refused by the courts. In the "Church of Marijuana" case, the court stated that the inmate may sincerely believe in his faith, but those beliefs were not a religion.[32]

  The problem is that many inmates are manipulative and use the guise of religion to "play" the staff and make incarceration more comfortable and entertaining. Also, the jail administration can hire a nondenominational chaplain who does not advance any one religion. Also, a chaplain can work with the jail administration in developing guidelines for recruitment and training of religious volunteers, and the screening of clergy who wants to visit. Jail is not an "open door" for clergy to come in and see inmates of their faith or who are members of their churches; the jail can impose reasonable security guidelines.
- *What is sincerity of belief?* To practice a religion, an inmate must demonstrate a **sincerity of belief**—he or she should be well acquainted with the religion's teachings, tenets, and basic foundations. If the inmate sues and in court cannot

demonstrate this knowledge, the court may doubt that he or she is not a devout follower of that religion.[33] If sincerity of belief in a religion cannot be shown by an inmate, the jail is not under any obligation to accommodate any request by the inmate to practice his or her religion. In one case, officials in a prison refused an inmate's request for a prayer rug until they received a request for a non-pork diet consistent with the Muslim religion. In another case, the court found that the inmate did not show a sincerity of belief. No requests for religious services had been filed in 12 years, the institution's request to the inmate asking for information about the religion were not answered, the inmate did not file an appeal about being denied religious services, and a general ambiguity about the nature of the religion's beliefs contributed to this finding.[34]

- *Can jail religious services be held?* Yes, but they are subject to guidelines set down by the jail due to security. Regulations saying that inmates are prohibited from leading their own services and requiring that all facility religious services be held in a nondenominational, interfaith chapel or room are not unconstitutional. Being allowed to have access to clergy from the inmate's faith satisfied the constitutional requirements in one case. In this 1970 case, a court ruled that formal religious services are not necessary for inmates in correctional custody.[35] One alternative is **religious cell visitation,** where jail chaplains and approved clergy can go to a segregated inmate's cell and tend to the inmate's spiritual needs.
- *Can inmates wear religious medals, emblems, etc.?* The courts have ruled that Black Muslims can wear and possess religious medals. But more recently, courts have ruled that if there is a possibility that a religious item, such as a medallion, can be used as a weapon, prohibiting its being worn is justified. The security concern should be clear.[36] Jails can prohibit Muslim and Jewish inmates from wearing head coverings based on security (contraband can be hidden and moved around the jail in a head covering) and sanitary grounds (jails are not the cleanest places and head coverings will need frequent washing).
- *Can an inmate request a special religious diet?* Yes, but that does not mean that they can get everything that they ask for. When a substantial number of inmates have a special diet request due to religious reasons, courts have favored the institutions supplying the diet. An example of this would be Muslim inmates asking for a non-pork diet. One method would be to offer a variety of foods where the inmate could have a nutritious diet without any violation of his or her religious beliefs. There are several concerns in the religious diet area. One is that courts do not require accommodating an inmate's religious diet request if it imposes a significant administrative or financial hardship on the facility. The second concern is that if a special diet request is granted to an inmate, it may open a floodgate of similar requests.[37] Inmates in jails have been known to "copy" other inmates, and having a special request due to religion can be a "status symbol." Jail administrators have learned to adapt. For example, during Ramadan, Muslim inmates fast during the day, eating before sunrise and after sunset. A jail can have a list of inmates participating in Ramadan approved by the chaplain and take meal trays to them before regular breakfast feeding times and after sunset.
- *Can inmates receive religious literature?* Yes, but the justification for suppressing any religious material is if the material is inflammatory, and may lead to breaches in security, unrest, and disruptions among the inmate population.[38] For example, a religious volunteer passes out pamphlets stating that another religion contains false teachings and does not adhere to the true meaning of Christianity. Inmates

in the targeted religion begin to complain and argue with other inmates. The jail would be justified in barring such pamphlets. A good practice is to have *all* religious material approved by the jail chaplain or if he or she is not available, the jail programs director. On a related note, video presentations should also be screened for content.

- *Can inmates groom themselves in accordance with their religious beliefs?* This is more of a problem in prisons than in jails where inmates remain in the institution for years at a time. There have been cases over haircuts and beards being worn by inmates based on religious beliefs. However, all inmates, whether they are confined in a jail or prison, must be identifiable at all times. The courts' position is that an inmate can adhere to a religious belief, but those beliefs are superseded by legitimate needs of security and inmate identification. Alternative measures such as requiring an inmate to tie his hair back instead of cutting it so a photograph could be taken were approved by one court.[39]

A current controversy concerning inmates' practicing religion involves certain groups that could be identified as security threat groups that disguise illegal activity and recruitment under the guides of religion. They hope that if their activities are combated by correctional authorities, they can say that they are members of a religious group and seek protection by the courts. Criminal plans being devised inside jail walls, and orders to commit crimes being given to individuals in the community, easy recruitment of isolated, "loner" and disenfranchised inmates are threats to security. Some groups, such as the World Church of the Creator and the Five Percenters, can threaten prison security as they attempt to expand their activities by claiming religious status. Dealing with this problem has led to management inconsistencies—one correctional system allows inmates to lead inmate religious services; another does not allow any unsupervised gathering of inmates for any reason whatsoever, *including* religion.[40]

The most effective way to prevent these groups from hiding under the religion disguise is for correctional authorities in prisons and jails to have strategies in place that both recognize inmates' rights to choose a faith *and* monitor carefully such groups' actual behaviors. This also includes staff using a proactive view—looking ahead to see how the jail would respond in court to inmate litigation. Violations and threats to security must be clearly shown and documented. A practical, commonsense approach has been taken by the New York State Department of Correctional Services, which treats each inmate as individuals. The agency does not concern itself with what group an inmate belongs to, it focuses on individual behaviors and actions. If an inmate is considered a risk, it listens to phone calls, reads mail, and maintains lines of communication with fellow law enforcement agencies.[41]

What does this mean for jail programs directors who are responsible for inmate religious activities? If confronted with an inmate grievance or complaint about a suspect group practicing religious activities, a lawyer well versed in correctional law should be consulted to research case law and rulings concerning this issue. Also, a response to the inmate(s) should wait until the problem is thoroughly researched—for example, what are some other jails doing and why? Has the group or inmate done anything to disrupt security? Who are the religious clergy or volunteers who want to come in? Are they thoroughly screened for a criminal history? Have they been to other jails? The request must be looked at from a proactive security standpoint—safety and security comes first. If a suspected security threat group is barred from religious activities due to security reasons, the matter could end up in court. If it does, jail managers must have clear facts and incidents concerning security to make their case.

## Fourth Amendment: Freedom from Unreasonable Searches

Inmates do not have the expectation of privacy that ordinary citizens enjoy outside of jail. As decided in the 1984 case of *Hudson v. Palmer*, 468 U.S. 517 (1984):[42]

- Prison inmates have no reasonable expectation of privacy in their cells which would give them Fourth Amendment protection from searches and seizures that are unreasonable.
- If inmates had a right of privacy inside their cells, it would be impossible for corrections officials to meet the objectives of preventing weapons, drugs, and other contraband from being introduced into the facility.
- Random, unpredictable searches are the most effective weapon of officials in the fight against contraband.
- Corrections officials must be free to seize any articles from inmates' cells that in their opinion undermine legitimate institutional interest (such as security).

The 1984 case of *Block v. Rutherford*, 468 U.S. 576 (1984) stated that pretrial detainees do not have a due process right to observe jail staff performing random searches of their cells.[43] An inmate and his or her cell and property are subject to being searched at any time.

However, there are commonsense parameters both to protect the dignity of the inmate and to guard against grievances and lawsuits. For example, an inmate who is repeatedly singled out and searched in a harassing manner may file a civil rights action alleging harassment. This may also be true if an inmate is awakened in the wee hours of the morning. Of course, if there is a good reason to conduct repeated and off-time searches of an inmate in this manner, jail supervisors should have a good reason, such as catching the inmate off guard based on reliable information that he or she has contraband and could dispose of it quickly. Several areas that have been contested concerning searches and inmates have fallen in the areas of seizure of property, namely legal material, religious material, cross gender searches, body cavity searches, and strip searches.

Inmates are allowed to possess legal material and religious material. If that material is seized, the jail may be liable in a suit. In one case, prison officers were held liable after they seized an inmate's copy of his trial transcript. The central issue is not the inmate complaining that he or she is free from searches, but the constitutional protections afforded the inmate based on the material that was seized.[44] If jail inmates are allowed to possess Bibles or Korans, jail officers can search them but should be careful as to not unreasonably seize them.

Cross gender supervision where officers of the opposite sex supervise and search inmates has spurned controversy. Several cases have discussed this. In one case female inmates complained that their religious beliefs prohibited men who were not their husbands from touching them—in other words male officers could not search them. Their arguments were in vain, as a single-sex policy would create labor problems, including collective bargaining difficulties. Also, if a requirement was made to have only female officers conduct pat searches, the inmates could predict the searches and contraband could thus be moved throughout the facility.[45]

In another case, the court upheld a policy where female officers pat searched male inmates. The inmates were clothed, and even though the groin areas were searched, there was no intimate contact. However, the courts have said that there is a diminished expectation of privacy in prison (and jail) and there should not be "unwanted intrusions" by members of the opposite sex—such as dressing, defecating, showering, and sleeping partially undressed.[46]

## Eighth Amendment: No Cruel and Unusual Punishment

The Eighth Amendment contains the right to be free from cruel and unusual punishment. In the study of inmate rights, this has included overcrowding, conditions of confinement, lack of medical care, and excessive force. The term "cruel and unusual punishment" can mean any number of things, especially to disgruntled inmates bent on complaining about their incarceration. Over time the Supreme Court has adopted several tests to determine if a situation or condition violates the Eighth Amendment.

This test has four components:[47]

- The facts of the case shock the decency of the Court.
- The facts of the case violate society's evolving standards of decency.
- The inmate is suffering a punishment that is disproportionate to the offense.
- The actions of the defendant involve the wanton and unnecessary infliction of pain.

While the first two components of the test could be easily shown in cases such as the "Tucker Telephone," flogging, sexual assault, etc., the "wanton and unnecessary infliction of pain" has surfaced in medical care cases and use of force cases. "Wanton and unnecessary infliction of pain" is discussed differently depending on the situation. Concerning basic human needs of inmates, it is termed as **deliberate indifference** to the serious needs of the inmate. These serious needs include medical care, safety, sanitation, etc.[48] The term was defined by the Supreme Court in *Farmer v. Brennan*, 114 S.Ct. 1970 (1994). What a jail official "should have known" is not enough to be proven deliberately indifferent. An official must "both be aware of facts from which the inference could be drawn that a substantial risk of serious harm exists and (the official) must also draw the inference."[49]

For example, an inmate is injured on a work detail. The medical staff is notified, is made aware of the situation, and knows that an infection is possible, but little or nothing is done to treat the wound. The inmate incurs an infection. Another example may be a frightened inmate who tells a jail officer that he has been threatened with rape by inmates in his cellblock. The officer tells the inmate to "suck it up" and takes no other action, knowing that a rape is possible, but thinks that it may not happen. The inmate is raped later that night and contracts HIV. Sanitation may involve inmates filing a suit over conditions such as the plumbing backing up, there are vermin in the cells, ventilation is inadequate, etc. The staff is aware of both the conditions and the possible consequences, but nothing is done.

In the cruel and unusual punishment area, jail officials have to be careful about the use of force. In responding to an inmate alleging that excessive force was used and an injury was incurred, the court will look at the circumstances and ask if the actions of staff were proper, excessive, or maliciously intended to harm the inmate.

A test is used to determine cruel and unusual punishment in medical complaints, use of force cases, and any time an inmate complains that staff actions "went too far." In a 1993 case, *LaMaire v. Maass*, 12 F.3d. 1444 (9th Circuit, 1993), a **malicious and sadistic test** was applied in the court deciding if restraints and other security measures taken to control an unruly inmate were not improper and punitive. Restraints were placed on an inmate who had committed the following acts:[50]

- Attacked a sergeant.
- Stabbed another prisoner that he thought was an informant.
- Attempted to cut two correctional officers.
- Made death threats to correctional officers.
- Used urine and feces to assault staff.
- Attacked correctional staff while in restraints.
- Committed 25 major disciplinary infractions in two years.

The correctional staff had attempted over time to temper the behavior of this inmate, including increasing efforts to administer discipline. The court noticed that the correctional staff kept good records on actions concerning this inmate and had conducted themselves in a professional manner. Due to the actions of this inmate and the efforts made by staff to control him, the malicious and sadistic test was found in favor of correctional staff. In another case, the federal circuit court approved the use of safety cells for short periods of time for unruly, out of control inmates who pose a danger to themselves and others—which includes other inmates and staff.[51]

What is interesting about this case was that the court approved the feeding of **nutra loaf,** which is a food product with vegetables and fruit baked in, served to inmates in lieu of meals, giving an inmate his or her entire daily nutritional requirements. Other methods that were approved by the court included using restraints in the inmate while in the shower, outdoor recreation being denied for extended periods, use of a quiet cell, and the occasional removal of clothes.[52]

Another case illustrated the improper treatment of an inmate with medical needs, which were found to be unconstitutional. A semi-quadriplegic inmate, without a colon or bladder, confined to a wheelchair, lived in a safety cell for three months. His wheelchair could not fit through the doorway of a regular cell. The cell had no running water, no bed, and no toilet. The inmate emptied waste from his colostomy and urostomy bags into an open floor drain. If he spilled human waste on his hands, he could not wash them until "bath day."[53]

Another use for the malicious and sadistic test is in use of force cases. Jail officers must maintain order, and frequently force is used to prevent an inmate from injuring himself/herself, other inmates, or staff. Inmates must be prevented from escaping, committing crimes, and destroying property. Putting "hands on" an inmate is part of the job. A well-run jail has a use of force policy that, if applied properly, can protect the officers from litigation alleging cruel and unusual punishment from the use of excessive force.

The position of the Supreme Court is clear concerning the improper use of force. In the landmark case of *Hudson v. McMillian*, 112 S.Ct. 995 (1992), the

Court said that force is unconstitutional when it is used "maliciously and sadistically for the very purpose of causing harm" as compared being used "in a good faith effort to maintain or restore discipline." Officials who know of a pattern or practice of excessive force and its possible consequences can be found deliberately indifferent if no action is taken to deal with the problem. The use of force can include use of restraint chairs, handcuffing, and applying body holds. Jail supervisors should ensure that decisions to use force are made carefully and that inmates concerned are examined by medical and mental health personnel.[54]

In the *Hudson* decision, the Supreme Court listed five factors in determining if force used against an inmate is unconstitutional under the malicious and sadistic test. They are:[55]

- *The need for the use of force:* Is the situation such that force has to be used? The inmate may not be obeying orders, is destroying property, is taking an aggressive stance, is committing acts of self-harm, is assaulting another inmate, visitor, or staff member, etc. Use of force may be necessary to protect lives, control the situation, and not let it escalate any further.
- *The amount of force used:* A good rule is only to use force necessary to overcome resistance and gain control of the situation.
- *The extent of any injuries suffered by the inmate:* Adrenalin runs high among both staff and inmates in use-of-force situations. Once the force used overcomes resistance and control of the situation is reached, force should decrease.
- *The threat perceived by the reasonable correctional officer:* If the officer was in fear for his life or feared serious bodily harm to a fellow staff member or an inmate or visitor, the force used to protect him and others may be justified.
- *Efforts made by staff to temper the use of force:* Efforts should be made, if possible to "talk the inmate" down and to reason with him or her. Commands may have to be repeated. Getting the inmate to comply peacefully with commands and use of force being avoided is always preferable to the employment of force.

These factors have been incorporated into training and policies in many jails, with emergency response teams using video documentation whenever possible. It would be extremely difficult for an inmate to litigate an excessive force complaint if a videotape shows him not responding to commands or cooperating with officers. At the very minimum in all cases of use of force, detailed reports and logs should be written and noted. All inmates who have been subjected to use of force should be examined and treated by medical staff. Restraints should be checked and discontinued once they are no longer deemed necessary.

## Conditions of Confinement and Overcrowding

Jails and prisons do not have enough space for the high numbers of offenders and inmates who are incarcerated in them. Overcrowding or confining inmates beyond the capacity of the facility is constitutional. The landmark case *Bell v. Wolfish*, 441, U.S. 520 (1979) discussed the double bunking of pretrial detainees at the Metropolitan Correctional Center (MCC) in New York City, a jail operated by the Federal government. Inmates filed suit challenging many conditions at the MCC, including the overcrowding. The Supreme Court said that pretrial detainees are not to be punished prior to court proceedings without due process of law. If a person is detained pretrial, and is not comfortable, that is not seen as punishment. Pretrial detention is accomplished through devices used by the government, such as confinement. If such confinement does not result in privations and hardships over a long period, then double bunking is allowed. Furthermore, the conditions at the time at the MCC were not such that any constitutional violations took place.[56]

This was further addressed by the Supreme Court in the 1981 case *Rhodes v. Chapman*, 101 S.Ct. 2392. The Supreme Court reversed a lower court ruling for the inmates saying that double-celling violated correctional standards. It ruled that inmates cannot claim an Eighth Amendment violation unless serious hardships can be shown. In the *Rhodes* decisions and related court decisions, the **totality of conditions,** or an examination of all aspects of the institution environment and practices, must be closely scrutinized. These conditions include length of stay, amount of time spent in the cell, sanitation, lighting, ventilation, noise, opportunities for programs, out-of-cell activities, plumbing (including showers), type of facility, safety issues (level of violence), and the facility's state of repair. If these conditions are below decency levels and are substandard, *and* the facility staff knew about them, then they are unconstitutional under the Eighth Amendment.[57] Subsequent rulings by the courts indicate that the following specific factors should be examined by the courts in deciding in totality of conditions suits:[58]

- Health and safety hazards resulting from the physical facilities.
- Overcrowding.
- Absence in the facility of a classification procedure.
- Conditions of segregation and isolation cells.
- Medical care facilities and treatment.
- Food service.
- Personal hygiene and sanitation.
- Incidence rates of violence and homosexual assaults.
- Quantity and training of institution staff.
- Lack of rehabilitation programs.
- Presence of any other constitutional violations.

These conditions are representative of the jail environment. If any are substandard, then adverse conditions result for the inmates and open the staff to liability. Jail administrators should ensure that all 11 factors are functioning at their optimum conditions.

## The Fourteenth Amendment: Due Process of Law

The due process of law right enjoyed by everyday citizens has found limited protection inside jails and prisons. Two areas concerning inmate rights of due process have been addressed by the courts: administrative hearings and access to the courts through prison and jail law libraries.

Concerning **due process,** the definition is clear: It is the exercise of power by the government (such as in a jail) in procedures that are prescribed by settled principles of law. At a minimum due process allows a person (inmate) to be heard, to assert their rights, *after* adequate advance notice of the proceedings (such as disciplinary charges or classification matter) before a person or panel authorized to hear and decide the matter per established rules of good order.[59]

Due process appears in two amendments to the U.S. Constitution: the Fourteenth Amendment, which says that no person shall be deprived by the State of due process of law or the equal protection of the laws; and the Fifth Amendment, which says that a person cannot be deprived of life, liberty, and property without due process of law. The purpose of due process is to ensure that there are justifications and fair procedures before something is taken away from someone.[60]

In other words, jail inmates are not placed in disciplinary segregation or administrative segregation without a "due process" hearing. In the hands off era, "kangaroo courts" decided inmates' fates inside some jails and prisons. Due process, when performed properly, safeguards the rights of the inmate and protects the staff in the event of litigation. Due process is crucial in **administrative hearings,** or hearings that are conducted by staff inside the jail to determine the status of an inmate, including custody level, housing status, program involvement, or the placement or removal of restraints and staff escorts.

## Inmate Discipline and Due Process

To keep order inside a jail, especially where jail staff is outnumbered by the inmates, jails must have a disciplinary code—offenses that if disobeyed, inmates will be punished for. This is essential for several reasons. One is deterrence, where inmates will see other inmates being punished and hopefully will decide not to disobey the rules; the other is segregation, where the troublemakers are removed from general population and isolated. In other words, a warning is sent to inmate in a deterrent fashion, and the "bad apples" are taken out of the barrel. Disciplinary segregation is not the only form of punishment. Depending on the severity of the offense, inmates may lose personal visiting, commissary privileges, personal phone calls, program participation, recreation, and library privileges. Inmates may also lose good time credits.

In the hands off era, inmate discipline in prisons and jails was a brutal, haphazard affair. The concept of fair and impartial due process was not given serious consideration. Inmates could be thrown into the "hole" or be tortured on a whim disguised with a "kangaroo court" type hearing.

The first case to take up the issue was *Wolff v. McDonnell*, 418 U.S. 539 (1974), where an inmate contested in a Section 1983 suit that the state of Nebraska was taking away his good time credits without due process for a serious disciplinary infraction. The U.S. Supreme Court rejected the position that inmates had no rights of due process. The Court said also that disciplinary hearings should not be like the adversarial procedures in criminal trials, as this would hamper the facility in administering discipline.[61]

The Supreme Court in the *Wolff* case ruled that inmate disciplinary actions must have the following procedures due to the state creating something valuable to the inmates (good time, privileges, etc.) and then taking it away. This is an administrative hearing and to take it away, disciplinary hearings should have:[62]

- Notice of charges given to the inmate.
- Adequate time for the inmate to prepare a response at a disciplinary hearing.
- Opportunity to present evidence and witnesses; witnesses are allowed if institution security is not threatened.
- Impartial panel.
- Written statement to the inmate containing the conclusion of the panel (verdict) and the reasons for reaching the decision.

There are two other areas: the right to assistants to help in a defense and the right to appeal. Under some circumstances, such as illiteracy or due to the complexity and seriousness of the charges, an inmate may be allowed to have, if he or she so chooses, assistance from another inmate or staff member. Although criminal charges may be pending, an inmate has no right to an attorney in a disciplinary hearing.[63]

Even though the courts have not said that inmates have a right under the Constitution to appeal the findings of a disciplinary hearing, most jails have an appeals process. The appeals process serves as a "double check" of disciplinary hearings, where errors can be corrected and it is made sure that the inmate's rights were not violated.[64] Jail staff has to be careful that any punishment does not start until the appeal is answered by a higher authority, such as a member of the jail command staff.

Disciplinary due process continues to be examined by the courts. In *Sandin v. Conner*, 115 S.Ct. 2293 (1995), the Supreme Court examined the case of an inmate who received a 30-day disciplinary segregation sentence. The Court said that such a disciplinary sentence does not create a deprivation that could be called a liberty interest. The action was discretionary and not entitled to due process; and the punishment did not exceed the inmate's sentence.[65] However, most jails continue to make *Wolff* type rights in disciplinary cases available to inmates, as a precaution.

Another area concerning due process is classification. While inmates may not be charged with disciplinary infractions, their conduct and criminal history, past and present, may necessitate the jail staff placing them in administrative segregation, removing them from programs and recreation, and placing staff escorts and restraints on them. These are critical, significant factors that create a special circumstance. This classification places a restriction on the freedoms and opportunities concerning programs, housing, and privileges that are afforded to other inmates. Some courts have said that these are liberty interests. Due process should include a notice of a hearing, the reason for the hearing, an opportunity to make a written or oral statement, and a written decision. There should be periodic reviews of the case. Like in disciplinary cases, there should be an avenue of appeal to a higher authority.[66]

Jails usually allow attorneys to be present in classification hearings (formal ICCs) at the request of either the inmate or the attorney. Attorneys should be advised that the classification hearing is not a trial, and they may observe the proceedings to ensure due process. To ensure the fairness of the hearing, the attorney should also be allowed to ask questions of the classification committee hearing members. However, the hearing is an administrative hearing, not a trial, and the decision will be made in the best interests of the jail.

## Access to Courts

Access to the courts by jail inmates takes several forms. One is visitation with an attorney. Jails can regulate the times that attorneys can come and see inmates. All inmates, even those on disciplinary segregation, have access to their attorneys. If an inmate's behavior is disruptive, mentally imbalanced, or unruly and an attorney visit does not occur, the jail staff should clearly document the inmate's behavior.

The other areas concerning access to the courts are the jail law library and inmates assisting each other with legal work. The courts have been protective of inmates having access to law books and other legal materials as a means of participating in their defense in court, filing appeals, and filing civil rights litigation that may challenge the conditions of confinement or allege that their rights have been violated. But, over time, the courts have modified their views of inmates and law libraries.

The first case to address the issue of inmates filing court papers interestingly happened during the hands off era. In *Ex parte Hull,* 312 U.S. 546 (1941), the Supreme Court struck down a Michigan regulation that prohibited inmates from mailing legal documents to court unless they were reviewed by the institution office. This prevented inmates for effectively filing court papers. The Supreme Court in this case said that corrections professionals are not to screen, censor, or interfere with an inmate's mailings of and submissions of legal papers to court.[67] Even if inmates are suing the jail or a particular jail staff member, the jail is not to interfere or harass the inmate in any way.

Inmates may assist other inmates in preparing court papers such as appeals, etc. This was the issue in *Johnson v. Avery,* 393 U.S. 482 (1969). An inmate was disciplined under a Tennessee prison regulation for aiding another inmate in preparing legal papers. The trial court said that the regulation was invalid, but the appeals court reversed the decision. The Supreme Court accepted the appeal of the case and addressed the issue of an inmate knowledgeable in the law assisting another inmate, known as **jailhouse lawyering.** The Supreme Court ruled in favor of these "legal-wise" inmates called **jailhouse lawyers** providing assistance to illiterate and poorly educated inmates because Tennessee did not have any alternatives for such assistance. Secondly, because the "jailhouse lawyering" system can be abused (inmate payoffs, etc.), the state can regulate the practice by establishing rules for time, place, and prohibiting inmates to pay for legal assistance in money, favors, etc.[68]

Law libraries inside jails are a crucial factor in inmates having access to the courts. The first important case concerning law libraries was *Bounds v. Smith,* 430 U.S. 817 (1977) that stated that the states must take measures to assist inmates if there were no alternative means to obtain legal assistance. The state involved, North Carolina devised a law library plan containing typewriters, writing paper, legal forms, and photocopying procedures. It is still used as a model. Inmates objected to this plan, and said that more was needed, including more law books and legal counsel assistance. The Supreme Court said that assistance is required by the states to inmates for "meaningful access" to the courts by providing adequate law libraries *or* having adequate assistance by persons trained in the law. If the state has alternative means of adequate legal assistance, then law libraries are not required under the Constitution.[69]

In 1996, the issue of prison and jail law libraries took a significant turn in the case of *Lewis v. Casey*, 64 U.S.L.W. 4587 (No. 94-1511, June 24, 1996). The Supreme Court overruled a lower Arizona federal district that said that the Arizona Department of Corrections (DOC) was not meeting legal assistance as outlined in *Bounds v. Smith*. An outside law professor from New York drew up a plan to correct the problem. The Supreme Court said that the Arizona DOC should have handled the problem and the plan devised had gone too far by expanding the operations of law libraries, training bilingual inmates to assist non-English-speaking inmates, etc. More significantly, only *two* inmates had been injured by not getting their legal papers into court. *Lewis* stated three important points: First, to challenge the constitutionality of a prison or jail law library, the inmate must show how the inadequacy of the law library and/or legal assistance program hindered his or her efforts to pursue a legal claim. Secondly, the *Bounds* opinion went too far and said that the State by providing expanded law libraries and related services had enabled inmates the means to become "litigating engines capable of filing everything from shareholder derivative actions to slip and fall claims." Third, the legal tools to be provided are only those materials that the inmates need to attack their sentences and to challenge the conditions of their confinement.[70]

For jail administrators and program director, the *Lewis* decision "put the brakes" on jail law libraries expanding to the point where materials would become too expensive, space would become used up, etc. Jails do not have to afford inmates training to turn them into lawyers. Realistically speaking, law libraries should contain the following materials and procedures:

- Typewriters or word processors
- Ample supply of paper and writing instruments
- State code
- Federal court reporters containing federal court decisions (case law): U.S. Supreme Court decisions are located in United States Reports (U.S.), Lawyer's Edition (L.Ed.) or Supreme Court Reporter (S.Ct.); U.S. District Court decisions are located in the Federal Supplement (F.Supp.) and U.S. Courts of Appeals are in the Federal Reporters (F.), F.2d is the second series, F.3d is the third, etc.[71]
- State Court of Appeals decisions, published in geographical reporters: Pacific Reporters (P), Atlantic Reporters (A), South Western Reporter (S.W.), South Eastern Reporter (S.E.), Southern Reporter (So.)[72]
- Law dictionaries
- Legal reference books
- Legal forms books

Some of these materials are available on CD-ROM, and inmates should have the choice of typewriters or word processors. It is customary to purchase legal materials and computers with inmate commissary funds. Jails can charge inmates for photocopying and can enforce procedures on how an inmate can request the law library, procedures how an inmate can obtain the assistance of another, and

Jail inmate law libraries take many forms; inmates may request legal materials from this law library, and they are delivered to them by staff.

Photo by author, courtesy Butler County Prison.

rules of conduct in the law library. Care must be exercised as some inmates may pass themselves off as "jailhouse lawyers" just to take advantage of other inmates. These inmates enjoy making excessive demands on the programs staff to provide copies and legal materials.

## RECENT LEGISLATIVE ACTS: IMPACT ON CORRECTIONS

In recent years, the United States Congress has enacted legislation that has significantly impacted the rights of inmates in jails and prisons. The goals of these acts have been several: to safeguard the rights of a small group of inmates (the disabled), to clarify the limitation of religious freedoms enjoyed by the incarcerated, to streamline the process of inmates filing litigation, and to establish inmate grievance procedures.

### Americans with Disabilities Act

Passed by Congress in 1990, the **Americans with Disabilities Act,** or ADA, protects people applying for jobs, people working in corrections, and inmates from unfair discrimination and treatment due to disabilities. Also, ADA extends protection to people who enter the institution—such as visitors to the jail staff and visitors who visit inmates, such as handicapped family members. ADA has changed employment procedures, the way in which correctional institutions are constructed (such as installing elevators and wide doorways for visitors and handicapped cells), and the way in which correctional programs are operated. Inmates receive government services, programs, and activities, so ADA protection with limitations extends to them.[73]

Under the ADA, an individual is disabled if he or she suffers from a "physical or mental impairment that substantially limits one or more of the major life activities of such individual; a record of such impairment, or being regarded as having such an impairment."[74] An inmate who walks with crutches, is restricted to a wheelchair, or suffers from a serious mental illness that severely limits life's activities are subject to ADA protection.

There are several aspects of the ADA that impact corrections. One aspect is physical access: Disabled inmates may not be denied access to jail activities and services because its facilities are inaccessible. This does not mean that existing jails have to undergo major remodeling and renovation, but new facilities that are built or remodeled must provide physical access. If providing physical access means that the program or service is significantly altered or it would incur a major financial burden or expense, ADA access is not required. The second is communication, such as the availability of telecommunications devices for the deaf (TDDs), so inmates who are deaf and hearing impaired can communicate. For the blind and or visually impaired, a recorded selection of jail library books or recorded jail rules, regulations, and orientations may be reasonable accommodations. Some materials can be in braille. In administrative hearings for hearing impaired inmates, interpreters may have to be brought into the jail to assist the inmate.[75]

A third impact on corrections is programming. Inmates with special disabilities should be permitted to participate in educational programs, substance abuse programs, work programs, work release, religious programs, self-help programs, and preparation for release programs and recreation whenever possible. Creative alternatives may have to be implemented. For example, a developmentally disabled inmate who wants to attend education classes may benefit from a citizen tutor volunteer with an education background. An inmate with a walker cannot play basketball in the gym, but should be given the opportunity to walk around the gym in order to benefit from some form of recreation.[76]

## Prison Litigation Reform Act

By the 1980s, the hands off era was in full gear. Inmates were filing numerous lawsuits against jails; some were apparently frivolous. **Frivolous law suits** are suits filed by inmates simply to harass corrections officials, are without merit, and often contain minor complaints that do not threaten the health, welfare, and safety of the inmate. Some examples of frivolous inmate lawsuits include:[77]

- An inmate ordered a jar of chunky peanut butter worth $2.50, paid for it, but did not receive it. He received a jar of creamy peanut butter after complaining to prison staff.
- The inmate shower area was too far from the cells, resulting in discomfort on cold days.
- Prison authorities would not sponsor an interracial chorus.
- The prison did not supply an adequate supply of matches.

In order to curb the amount of frivolous inmate lawsuits that were being filed, but still have in place an avenue where inmates could complain, Congress enacted the **Prison Litigation Reform Act of 1996, or PLRA.** The PLRA was a major step in corrections' efforts to curb the jailhouse lawyer, not in a way that discouraged inmates from filing serious litigation, but from filing litigation that would waste the time and efforts of correctional staff and the courts.

The PLRA has several conditions concerning the filing of litigation in federal court:[78]

- Requires all inmates filing suits in federal courts to pay a filing fee; other fees may be waived.
- Sets limits on attorneys' fees if an inmate successfully wins a lawsuit.
- Prohibits inmate suits against the federal government alleging psychological damages unless there are physical injuries suffered.
- Requires federal judges to screen inmate lawsuits and dismiss those suits that are frivolous and contain little merit.
- Provides for the rescinding of good time credits to penalize inmates who have used the courts to harass corrections officials.
- Expands the grievance requirements first established by the **Civil Rights of Institutionalized Persons Act, or CRIPA.** CRIPA was a law enacted by Congress authorizing the Justice Department to file civil rights litigation on behalf of all persons inside institutions, including prisons and jails. CRIPA also allowed the federal courts to postpone action on an inmate's civil rights litigation until the inmate exhausted all administrative remedies under grievance systems meeting federal court or Justice Department criteria. PLRA expanded the grievance stipulation; now inmates must exhaust *any* grievance or appeal system that is available to them, before filing a suit, not just those who meet federal guidelines.[79]

Many jail inmates, in an effort to frighten or harass staff, threaten lawsuits saying the "you are violating my civil rights" and request a "1983 form," or the form required by the federal courts to file a Section 1983 suit. They must exhaust the facility's grievance system first as required by the PLRA.

Inmates should be encouraged to use the tools that they have, such as request forms, to get their problems worked out with the jail staff before it gets to the grievance stage. Also, the jail staff should thank the inmates for using the grievance procedures, as this can promote harmony.

## Religious Land Use and Institutionalized Persons Act

Passed in 2000, the **Religious Land Use and Institutionalized Persons Act (RLUIPA)** replaced the Religious Freedom Reformation Act (RFRA), which was struck down by the U.S. Supreme Court as unconstitutional several years before. The two laws are similar. The RLUIPA makes it more difficult to justify imposing limitations and restrictions on inmate religious practices.[80]

To understand the RLUIPA, one must understand its predecessor, the RFRA. Passed in 1993, the RFRA required a correctional facility show that restrictions of inmate's religious practices are based on legitimate penological interests, and the restriction is the *least* restrictive means. In 1997, the Supreme Court struck down the RFRA, based on the opinion that RFRA had intruded on states' rights by creating a broader protection than the First Amendment. Also, there was a flood of lawsuits by inmates, who challenged religious restrictions in jails and prisons.[81]

Congress corrected these flaws in 2000, passing the RLUIPA. The RLUIPA states that any agency receiving federal funds that institutes a "substantial burden" on an inmate's exercise of religion must support a "compelling governmental interest" (or a legitimate penological interest). The institution must show that the restriction is the least restrictive means of furthering the compelling governmental interest. There are two parts to this issue. Courts most likely have no problem agreeing with facilities that security is a compelling governmental interest. That is clear; but a court deciding if a policy or procedure is the least restrictive measure invites courts to second guess jail administrators, which is something that the courts wish to avoid in the one hand on, one hand off era.[82]

A **grievance** is an inmate complaint filed through the channels to the appropriate staff in whose area the complaint is concerned. A grievance procedure includes a form where the inmate writes the details of his complaint or concern, an acknowledgment of receipt, assignment to the proper staff, a time limit for response, and an avenue of appeal to a higher authority.

An example of a well-written grievance procedure is in the Alexandria, Virginia Office of the Sheriff *Inmate Handbook*. It states:

**Inmate Grievance Procedures**

A grievance is a way for you to make a written complaint concerning your personal health or welfare, or about the operations and services in the Detention Center. Grievances will not become part of your inmate file and will not be held against you. The following issues are not grievable: disciplinary sanctions, housing assignment, and your classification.

Before you file a grievance, you must talk with the person involved about the problem. If you do not like the way the matter was settled, you may request an Inmate Grievance Form.

Fill out the form completely and return it to the Deputy. If the form is not filled out correctly, it will be returned to you. You may ask for help if you need assistance in completing the form. Staffs have four on-duty days to respond to your grievance.

The written response will be returned to you.

Grievances containing profanity, threats, and insults will not be accepted. The grievance procedure is not a tool to "write-up" or insult staff.

If you are dissatisfied with the response, you may appeal to the staff person's supervisor. Use the Inmate Grievance Appeal Form available from the Housing Unit or Floor Security Deputy. You must include your copy of the original grievance with your appeal. The supervisory staff has five on-duty days to respond to your grievance. Once the appeal process is completed, no further correspondence concerning the grievance will be accepted.

You may submit a grievance on behalf of a group of inmates. All inmates involved must sign the form. The response will be sent to the inmate who completed the form, and not to all members of the group.

**Alexandria Detention Center**

**INMATE GRIEVANCE FORM**

______________________________________________

Last Name First Name M.I. DEFN ID Housing Unit

Please read the section "Inmate Grievance Procedure" in the Inmate Handbook prior to completing this form. Forms will not be accepted for processing unless they are complete and signed. Use of the Grievance Procedure will not be held against the inmate.

I have tried to resolve this grievance verbally with Deputy ______________________ on
(name)

______________________ .
(date)

**INMATE'S STATEMENT**

What is your grievance?

Inmate's Signature: ______________________ Date ______________________

Received by Deputy/Serial Number ______________________ Date ____________

**DEPUTY'S RESPONSE/REASON:** (To be completed and returned within four (4) working days)

Deputy's Signature/Serial Number ______________________ Date ____________

Original: Master grievance file Copy 1: Returned to inmate with response Copy 2: Retained by inmate when grievance is filed

F-SHR-0045 (Rev. 1/94) INT: DLP

**ALEXANDRIA DETENTION CENTER**
**INMATE REQUEST FORM**

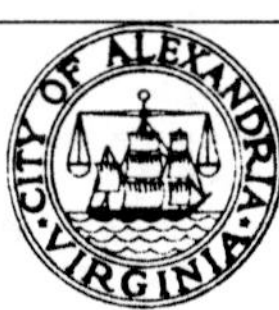


NAME ____________________

DATE ____________________ HOUSING ____________________

**INSTRUCTIONS:** Please check the problem or request area **Be specific** about what action you want. This is **not** a grievance form.

- ☐ Appeal of Discipline
- ☐ Classification Appeal
- ☐ CDI - Community Diversion
- ☐ Waive 24 hour hearing
- ☐ Waive hearing appearance
- ☐ Inmate Housing Unit Worker
- ☐ Inmate Work Force
- ☐ Property Bin No ____________
- ☐ Special Canteen
- ☐ Special Visit
- ☐ Inmate Accounts
- ☐ Hearing Assistant
- ☐ Other, Specify ____________

Request: ____________________

Staff Receiving the Request ____________________ Date ____________

Supervisory Review ____________________ Date ____________

Action Taken: ____________________

Response: ____________________

Signature ____________________ Date ____________

Original - Completed form forwarded to appropriate file
Copy 1 - Completed form returned to Inmate with Action Noted
Copy 2 - Retained by Inmate at Time of Request

F-SHR-0016 Rev. 2/91 Initials DLP

From: Inmate Grievance Procedures, in INMATE HANDBOOK, Alexandria Detention Center, Alexandria, VA Office of Sheriff, 2004. Reprinted by Permission, Alexandria Office of Sheriff. Thanks to Mondre Kornegay, Commander of Inmate Services, Alexandria Detention Center.

**FIGURE 9-3** Grievance Procedures

### Civil Rights of Institutionalized Persons Act (CRIPA)

This act, already mentioned in this chapter, has been used by the Justice Department to require jail administrators to make changes in conditions and policies. First enacted by Congress in 1980, CRIPA serves to protect the rights of persons housed or confined in state and local governmental institutions, including jails. Using the authority of CRIPA, the U.S. Justice Department began to investigate the Maricopa County, Arizona, jail system in 1995. This jail system is supervised by Sheriff Joe Arpaio, who believes that effective jail management should include Spartan conditions for inmates, including few amenities and housing in tents. In a four-year investigation, the Justice Department ruled that the 7,000-inmate capacity jail system failed to provide inmates with adequate medical and mental health care. Initially, the investigation also looked at allegations of officers using excessive force, but a 1997 settlement agreement resulted in revisions of the methods of force and use of mechanical restraints by officers.[83]

The agreement reached between the Justice Department and the Maricopa County Jail was filed in the U.S. District Court in Phoenix, Arizona. Maricopa County under this agreement must do the following:[84]

- Hire additional staff in the following areas: medical, mental health, physicians, dentists, psychiatrists, pharmacists, nurses, counselors, and an infection control manager. The agency is also to hire medical transport officers.
- Make improvements in medical evaluations, services, and staffing concerning newly admitted inmates.
- Improve the jails' physical plant in order to facilitate medical services. This includes providing additional space for medical intake evaluations, "suicide safe" cells, transition rooms for mentally disordered inmates, rooms for inmates with infectious diseases, and medial transport vans.
- Make improvements to the distribution by providing at a minimum twice-daily medication distribution runs and informing inmates of and monitoring possible medication side effects.
- Improve procedures for the processing of inmate requests for medical and/or mental health treatment.
- Institute the creation of an Infection Control Committee, which will maintain data and information about communicable and infectious diseases and take steps to protect both inmates and staff.
- Make improvements to quality assurance mechanisms to accurately assess through random audits of inmates' medical and mental health charts and to implement the county's existing quality assurance plans.

## RECENT TRENDS IN INMATE LITIGATION AND PROTECTIVE MEASURES FOR STAFF

Jails have made good progress in improving the confinement conditions of inmates, implementing grievance procedures, and providing training to jail staff concerning inmate rights. Inmate lawsuits will continue; there will always be jailhouse lawyers and inmates who feel that they have been wronged and are willing to take jails to court. Inmate lawsuits are not at the intensity that they were during the hands on era.

## Trends in Inmate Litigation

Some recent examples of inmate lawsuits show the power of the courts at times against jails, at times against the inmate, and taking surprising positions on issues. Personal safety, medical, and religious issues continue to keep the courts' attention.

The family of an inmate incarcerated in a Louisiana jail settled in court for $4.9 million. The 59-year-old man was targeted and beaten by an inmate who did not like his body odor. The lawsuit alleged that other inmates called for assistance from jail officers with negative results. The victim's head was "repeatedly stomped until tissue and fluid came out of his skull." The chief administrative officer in the jail's jurisdiction stated that the jail was deemed liable, and the victim was placed in an assisted care facility due to his injuries.[85]

Inmate lawsuits can "go back a ways." In a settlement approved by a U.S. District Court judge, more than 800 former inmates will receive $1,000 each, as part of an $800,000 settlement. Inmates in a class action lawsuit had claimed that from June 26, 1999 through July 1, 2002, jail officers had conducted thousands of "blanket" strip searches and body cavity searches. Also, the inmates claimed that jail officers ridiculed them about the size of their genitals, the shapes of their bodies, and odors while the searches were conducted. Besides the $800,000, the attorneys representing the inmates will receive $372,000.[86]

A woman had a broken arm when she was incarcerated in a Kentucky jail in December 1999. She was subsequently transferred to a state prison. She claimed that she asked the jail staff for medical attention to no avail. She claimed that jail personnel were deliberately indifferent to her medical needs. The U.S. District Court dismissed her suit, ruling that she did not exhaust available remedies under the PLRA. The woman appealed, saying that the only procedure in the jail for inmates needing medical care was to submit a request for medical treatment. This indicated a "flat rule" against medical grievances. The U.S. Circuit Court of Appeals reviewed the case and ruled that there was a "flat rule" against medical grievances, and this exempted the inmate from the exhaustion requirement under PLRA. The case was ordered to proceed.[87]

Some litigation against jails stems from restraining problem inmates or not recognizing how a "problem" inmate can die. In one case that resulted in a $10 million award, an unruly, big inmate was restrained by a team of correctional officers. They "hogtied" him, face down on the cell floor. The officers left the cell, and eventually returned to find the inmate had suffocated by his weight pressing down on his respiratory system. In another case, a "frequent visitor" was booked into the jail for his usual crime of public drunkenness. He made an interesting sight as he staggered and stumbled about the cell. The on-duty officer thought that this would make a good video for substance abuse classes. When the inmate shook, trembled, and collapsed, the camera was rolling. An hour later, the inmate died from DTs, or delirium tremens. The officer's stupidity concerning the inmate's right to medical care cost the jail $2 million.[88]

An inmate with a history of filing frivolous lawsuits against corrections officials was barred from filing any more civil lawsuits without getting the permission of a United States Court. Before he can file another suit in the district, he will have to pay a court clerk fee of $100.00. He had filed a suit in federal court claiming that the Comedy Central Network was responsible for racial violence that led to an African American customer being beaten in a Wal-Mart store. The network had aired an episode of *Mad TV*. Because he had filed four previous actions that were ruled frivolous, the court dismissed his case before determining the merits of the complaint. He had filed the suits as an indigent inmate at state expense, and the court said that the only way he could file another lawsuit was to show imminent danger of serious physical injury, which he had failed to show.[89]

Medical issues are prevalent in inmate suits and have the potential to work in the inmate's favor. An example of this occurred in 2004, where an inmate booked into a county jail for driving on a suspended license complained of abdominal pain within an hour of arrival at the jail. He complained to a deputy jailor and requested medical care. Jail officials did not obtain medical care and gave the inmates antacids. Two days after the first complaint, a jail nurse examined the inmate and diagnosed him as having classic symptoms of acute appendicitis. He was transferred that day and underwent a successful appendectomy. The inmate sued, alleging that the jail violated his constitutional and civil rights by denying him prompt medical attention for a serious medical condition. Additional allegations said that the jail failed to implement policies and train jail officers to respond to his serious medical need. The district court granted summary judgment for the jail, ruling that the inmate did not show any ill effects from not having his surgery performed earlier. The U.S. Court of Appeals reversed the summary judgment, saying that it was sufficient for the inmate to show that he had a serious medical problem, and that the jail did not address the problem within a reasonable length of time. The officers had a "sufficiently culpable state of mind." Finally, because the jail did not have any policies, practices, or adequate staff training for this type of problem, they were vulnerable for litigation.[90]

In June 2005, the Supreme Court ruled that unusual religions, such as Asatru (a Viking religion whose followers worship Thor), the Church of Jesus Christ Christian (which believes in racial separatism), Wicca (witches), and Satanism, must receive accommodation for prison officials. These are not "mainstream religions" such as Baptist, Lutheran, or Roman Catholic. Ohio prison inmates who were followers of these religions had complained that they were not permitted to receive religious literature and conduct services. The Court said that corrections officials must make accommodations for *sincere* followers of a religious faith or doctrine, *no matter how odd or unusual.* All accommodations on religious practices in a correctional facility could not be perceived as benefiting inmates in the sense that their incarceration is less restricted. The accommodations sought under the RLUIPA did not impose significant hardships and burdens on wardens. However, the Court's decision does not give "free reign" to inmates, and corrections officials have a compelling governmental interest to maintain institution order and security.[91]

In view of religious diets and practices, jails are adapting to prevent inmate litigation. For example, to avoid issues about religious diets as non-pork for Muslims, many jails simply take the step of eliminating all pork from prepared foods. When inmates complain that they are not receiving a pork-free diet in accordance with their religion, the jail can clearly inform them that no pork is used anywhere inside the jail.

Civil litigation by inmates against correctional personnel is most likely to occur on two levels—the line correctional officer and the supervisors and administrators of the facility. The litigating inmate(s) may assume that the supervisors, agency heads, and administrators may be responsible because they could have possibly prevented the conduct of the officer(s) named in the suit. As a result of this thinking, inmates file suits naming not only officers, but as many supervisors up the chain of command as they can. Sometimes the strategy is that if the more personnel named in the suit, the more successful the inmate will be.[92]

The other level is the individual jail officer—the one that works closer to the jail inmate than most other staff. By the nature of his or her job, the jail officer makes decisions relating directly to an inmate's confinement:[93]

- Deciding to search and/or seize a jail inmate's property.
- Using a level of force on an inmate.
- Deciding to protect an inmate in jail.
- Providing security.
- Providing proper medical care to inmates.

Jail staff should be aware that if they lose an inmate lawsuit, the payout or relief may come in many ways. Some relief is in money damages, and some types of relief are court orders. The main categories of relief are:[94]

- **Injunctive relief or injunction:** A court orders a jail to do or not to do something, such as taking steps to relieve overcrowding, improving the inmate law library, etc.
- **Declaratory relief:** The court rules or issues a statement that inmates have certain rights.
- **Nominal damages:** The defendant (jail) pays the plaintiff (inmate) a "token" sum because the damage done is extremely minor.
- **Compensatory damages:** The agency pays expenses incurred by the inmate that are "out of pocket," such as attorney fees, medical costs, lost wages, etc., either for a short or a long period of time.
- **Punitive damages:** These damages are meant to punish staff and deter staff from similar behavior; the officer found liable has to pay out of his or her pocket.

Another type of relief is the **consent decree,** which is different from an injunction. Where an injunction is simply a court order, a consent decree means that the jail agrees to the court having an order made against them and it is binding.[95] A consent decree may involve the jail consenting to devise measures to reduce the inmate population or make improvements to jail conditions.

Even with the passage in 1996 of the PLRA, inmate lawsuits are still hovering around corrections facilities. Writs of habeas corpus are increasing, while Section 1983 actions are decreasing. Habeas corpus petitions increased 50 percent from 1995 to 2000; 41,679 civil petitions were filed by inmates in 1995 compared with 25,504 filed in 2000.[96] Even with state-of-the-art law libraries and "savvy" jailhouse lawyers, it is evident that the PLRA has stemmed the flood tide of inmate litigation once experienced by the courts.

In 2001, a study of inmate litigation against Michigan jails was funded by the Michigan Municipal Risk Management Authority (MMRMA). The most common claims against Michigan jails were:[97]

- *Property:* losing property and personal clothing, inmate delayed from receiving property after a move, inmate's property being misplaced or destroyed, denial of property to an inmate while confined.

- *Medical:* inadequate care/treatment, failure to provide medical care, distribution of wrong medication, denial of medication.
- *Sexual assault/harassment:* sexual assault/harassment of female inmates.
- *Other harassment/discrimination:* allegations of defamation, slander, racial prejudice by jail officers toward inmates.
- *Personal injury:* slipping and falling, falling from an upper bunk, injury during recreation/exercise, falling off crutches.
- *Denial of access:* denied access to courts, access to jail law libraries, access to religious practices.
- *Excessive force:* while being searched by officers, officer medically intervening with a disruptive, combative inmate, officers shooting an inmate (two incidents).
- *Classification:* housing in the wrong cell, improper placement of female inmates with male inmates, juvenile detainees with adult inmates, overcrowding, denial of recreation time or recreation facilities, lack of drinking water.

Property complaints were the most often filed, followed by medical claims and sexual assault/harassment. The entire study listed 20 categories, and 3 closely related categories—completed suicides, attempted suicides, and wrongful death represented only 8 cases when combined but accounted for the highest total amount of costs incurred per claim, at almost half million dollars. This was followed by medical care claims at over $150,000 and a combined category of excessive force and charges of assault and battery at about $120,000.[98]

Inmate lawsuits are expensive. Insurance companies retained by the jail pay out if the inmate wins, and attorneys collect fees. If a jail is small and is located in a rural county with a limited tax base and funding, a major inmate lawsuit can create serious financial difficulty.

There are other effects of inmate litigation. Officers incurring punitive damages can be fired if their employment records and supervisors' evaluations reveal job performance problems that would cause future liability if the person is retained on the job. Policies and procedures must be re-examined and training curriculum revised due to a lawsuit. Finally, jails are visible institutions in the community, and sheriffs of them are public, elected officials. A successful inmate lawsuit painting a negative picture of jail conditions and staff practices can cause the jail a negative public image, especially through the media.

It is the responsibility of jail management and training officers to ensure that jail staffs who deal directly with inmates receive the best training in inmate rights and liability of jail staff. Jail staffs must be informed that if they violate inmates' constitutional rights granted to them by the courts, they may be disciplined or fired if they are found liable for punitive damages. The following is a suggested curriculum guide for trainers:

*Property claims:*

- Safeguarding inmate's property, clothing, possessions
- Delaying transfer/reception of property
- Destruction or misplacement of inmate's property

*Medical claims:*

- Inadequate medical care: treatment, response, follow up
- Medication: denial, delay, dispensing wrong medication
- Policies/procedures: sick call, reporting illness and injuries, and summoning assistance
- Recognition and acting on signs of distress and illness
- Emergencies: response, checking restraints
- Monitoring and observation

*Custodial Deaths, injuries, assaults, and mistreatment of inmates:*

- Booking forms and procedures
- Classification procedures
- Transportation of inmates
- Proper searching techniques of inmates
- Proper supervision and management of inmates
- Proper cross gender supervision
- Adherence to sexual harassment policy
- Use of force: policy, reasons, tactics, use of equipment, multiple officer response, cell extraction, handling of disturbances and riots medical interventions, use of deadly force

*General topics:*

- Ongoing training: roll call, in service in inmate constitutional rights and jail liability
- Use of grievance procedures and inmate request forms
- Jail inspections, reporting of substandard conditions and problems

DOCUMENTATION (of all routine and nonroutine interaction with inmates, proper use of logs, proper report training, stressing):

*If it was not written down, then it did not happen.*

*All documentation written by a jail officer has the potential of going to court.*

**FIGURE 9-4** Avoiding Inmate Lawsuits[99]

## SUMMARY

The courts have not always been involved in the operations of jails and issues concerning the welfare of inmates. Jails have always operated independent of court scrutiny, as evidenced by the "hands off era," during which inmates were referred to "slaves of the state." The two following eras, the "hands on" and the "one hand on, one hand off" resulted in more court scrutiny of jails. The civil rights movement of the 1960s influenced the hands on era, where the courts, without precedent, wrestled with inmate suits claiming constitutional rights. With the one hand off one hand on era, courts take a more realistic view—they balance the inmate's claimed need for constitutional rights against the needs of the jail, mainly security.

Inmates prefer to file civil rights litigation claiming that constitutional rights were violated in violation of 42 United States Code Section 1983. However, due to actions by Congress, mainly the Prison Litigation Reform Act, more emphasis is put on administrative remedies such as grievances being first used by inmates before any court action is filed. The provisions of the PLRA also combat frivolous lawsuits.

Inmate litigation can be successful if staff is found to be negligent, be deliberately indifferent, or violate several of the tests that recent cases have established concerning use of force. Inmates enjoy limited protection of constitutional rights under the First, Fourth, Eighth, and Fourteenth Amendments. Inmates are allowed due process, religious freedoms, protection against cruel and unusual punishment, and access to the courts that are subject to limitation under the balancing test and by case law.

Inmates prefer to file Section 1983 suits in the areas of medical care, due process, and physical security. Staff can take safeguards against liability in inmate suits, including being proactive concerning jail conditions and participating in training.

## REVIEW QUESTIONS

1. Describe the *hand off, hands on* and the *one hand on, one hand off* eras.
2. What type of litigation is preferred by inmates and why?
3. What areas are targeted by inmates in Section 1983 lawsuits?
4. What is a legitimate penological interest concerning mail?
5. What are the types of relief granted by the courts in inmate civil litigation cases?
6. What is the importance of inmate grievances?
7. How does a court determine if an inmate's complaint shows cruel and unusual punishment?
8. What are the different forms of negligence?
9. What materials should be in a jail law library?
10. How can jail staff protect themselves from inmate litigation?

## TERMS TO KNOW

42 United States Code 1983
administrative hearings
Americans with Disabilities Act
balancing test
case law
civil rights actions
Civil Rights of Institutionalized Persons Act, or CRIPA
compensatory damages
consent decree
declaratory relief
deliberate indifference
due process
federalism
frivolous law suits
grievance
gross negligence
habeas corpus actions
hands off era
hands on era
injunctive relief *or* injunction
jailhouse lawyering
jailhouse lawyers
legitimate penological interest
malicious and sadistic test
negligence
nominal damages
nutra loaf
Prison Litigation Reform Act of 1996, or PLRA
publishers only rules
punitive damages
religious cell visitation
Religious Land Use and Institutionalized Persons Act (RLUIPA)
restrained hands approach
slaves of the state
sincerity of belief
status call
torts
totality of conditions
Tucker Telephone
willful negligence

## ENDNOTES

1. Christopher E. Smith, *Law and Contemporary Corrections* (Belmont, CA: West/Wadsworth, 2000), pp. 18–20.
2. Gary F. Cornelius, *The Correctional Officer: A Practical Guide* (Durham, MD: Carolina Academic Press, 2001), pp. 233–235.
3. Ibid., pp. 235, 236.
4. Roger A. Hanson and Harry W.K. Daley, *Challenging the Conditions of Prisons and Jails: A Report on Section 1983 Litigation* (Washington, DC: U.S. Department of Justice, 1995), p. 6.
5. Clair A. Cripe, *Legal Aspects of Corrections Management* (Sudbury: Jones and Bartlett, 2003), p. 432.
6. Hanson and Daley, *Challenging the Conditions of Prisons and Jails*, pp. 8, 9, 17–19.
7. Cornelius, *The Correctional Officer*, p. 234.
8. Michael B. Mushlin, *Rights of Prisoners, 3rd Edition*, Vol 1 (Eagan, MN: Thomson-West, 2002), p. 10.
9. Christopher E. Smith, *Law and Contemporary Corrections* (Belmont, CA: West/Wadsworth, 2000), p. 24.

10. Ibid.
11. Mushlin, *Rights of Prisoners,* Vol 1, p. 10.
12. William C. Collins, J.D., *Correctional Law for the Correctional Officer, 4th Edition* (Lanham, MD: American Correctional Association, 2004), pp. 8, 24.
13. Ibid., p. 8.
14. Ibid., pp. 10–12.
15. Ibid., p. 9.
16. Mushlin, *Rights of Prisoners,* Vol 1, pp. 11, 12.
17. Ibid., pp. 15–18.
18. William C. Collins, *Jail Design and the Constitution* (Washington, DC: National Institution of Corrections, 1998), p. 11.
19. Collins, *Jail Design and the Constitution,* p. 11.
20. Ibid., pp. 11, 12.
21. David S. Sutty, *Legal Issues for Correctional Staff,* Book I (Lanham, MD: American Correctional Association, 1999), pp. 111, 112.
22. Ibid., p. 112.
23. Ibid.
24. Smith, *Law and Contemporary Corrections,* pp. 307, 308.
25. Collins, *Correctional Law,* p. 76.
26. Ibid., pp. 75, 76.
27. Ibid., pp. 77–79.
28. David S. Sutty, *Legal Issues for Correctional Staff,* Book II (Lanham, MD: American Correctional Association, 1999), p. 99.
29. Smith, *Law and Contemporary Corrections,* p. 92.
30. John W. Palmer, J.D., and Stephen E. Palmer, J.D., *Constitutional Rights of Prisoners, 7th Edition* (Cincinnati, OH: Anderson, 2004), pp. 37, 40.
31. Mushlin, *Rights of Prisoners,* Vol 1, pp. 706, 707.
32. Collins, *Correctional Law,* pp. 69, 70.
33. Mushlin, *Rights of Prisoners,* Vol 1, p. 713.
34. Collins, *Correctional Law,* p. 71.
35. Palmer and Palmer, *Constitutional Rights of Prisoners,* p. 109.
36. Ibid., p. 110.
37. Collins, *Correctional Law,* p. 73.
38. Palmer and Palmer, *Constitutional Rights of Prisoners,* p. 115.
39. Ibid., pp. 119, 120.
40. Michelle Gaseau, "Monitoring Extremist Groups and Maintaining Religious Rights," *corrections.com,* September 20, 2004, http://www.corrections.com/printNews.aspx?Zone=Homepage
41. Ibid.
42. Palmer and Palmer, *Constitutional Rights of Prisoners,* p. 334.
43. Ibid.
44. Ibid., p. 332.
45. Ibid., p. 333.
46. Ibid., pp. 331, 332.
47. Collins, *Correctional Law,* p. 106.
48. Collins, *Jail Design and the Constitution,* p. 34.
49. William C. Collins and John Hagar, "Jails and the Courts...Issues for Today, Issues for Tomorrow," *American Jails,* May–June 1995, 22.
50. Ibid., p. 25.
51. Ibid.
52. Ibid.
53. Ibid.
54. Ibid., p. 27.
55. Ibid.
56. Cripe, *Legal Aspects of Correctional Management,* pp. 242–246.
57. Michael B. Mushlin, *Rights of Prisoners, 3rd Edition,* Vol 2 (Eagan, MN: Thomson-West, 2002), pp. 286, 287, 299, 300.
58. Mushlin, *Rights of Prisoners,* Vol 1, p. 332.
59. Cripe, *Legal Aspects of Correctional Management,* pp. 423, 424.
60. Ibid., pp. 163, 164.
61. Ibid., pp. 169, 170.
62. Smith, *Law and Contemporary Corrections,* p. 140.
63. Collins, *Correctional Law,* p. 162.
64. Ibid., p. 163.
65. Cripe, *Legal Aspects of Correctional Management,* pp. 172, 173.
66. Mushlin, *Rights of Prisoners,* Vol 2, pp. 312, 313, 315–317, 319.
67. Cripe, *Legal Aspects of Correctional Management,* pp. 86, 87.
68. Ibid., pp. 87, 88.
69. Ibid., pp. 88–90.
70. Ibid., pp. 91–93.
71. Sutty, *Legal Issues,* Book I, pp. 101, 103, 104.
72. Ibid., p. 105.
73. Collins, *Correctional Law,* p. 211.
74. Cripe, *Legal Aspects of Correctional Management,* p. 337.
75. Ibid., pp. 339–341.
76. Ibid., pp. 340, 341.
77. James F. Quinn, *Corrections: A Concise Introduction* (Prospect Heights, IL: Waveland Press, Inc., 1999), p. 270.
78. Ibid., pp. 271, 272.
79. Collins, *Correctional Law,* p. 37.
80. Ibid., p. 73.
81. Cornelius, *The Correctional Officer,* p. 253.
82. Collins, *Correctional Law,* pp. 73, 74.
83. Press Release: "Maricopa County to Improve Medical and Mental Health Care for Inmates, Under Justice Department Agreement," December 6, 1999, http://www.usdoj.gov/opa/pr/1999/December/588cr.htm (accessed February 8, 2007).

84. Ibid.
85. Shreveport Times, "Shreveport Will Settle for $4.9 Million," http://www.corrections.com/news/justin/index.html (accessed December 3, 2002).
86. Newsday, "Renssalear County to Pay Jail Inmates for Illegal Strip Searches," http://www.corrections.com/news/didyouknow/ (accessed October 14, 2004).
87. "Jail's Grievance Procedure Must Exist to Require Exhaustion," *The Corrections Professional,* 10 (15) (April 29, 2005): 14.
88. Darrell L. Ross, Ph.D., and Bill Page, "Jail Liability: Reducing the Risk by Studying the Numbers," *American Jails,* January–February 2003, 9, 10.
89. "Court Sanctions Inmate Who Files Frivolous Lawsuits," *The Corrections Professional,* 10 (13) (March 25, 2005): 13.
90. "Lack of Training for Appendicitis Attack Subjects Jail to Suit," *The Corrections Professional,* 10 (9) (January 21, 2005): 13.
91. Alex Johnson, "Court Upholds Prisoners' Religious Rights: Justices Say Unusual Faiths Must Be Accommodated," *MSNBC.com,* http://www.msnbc.msn.com/id/8047388/fromRL.1/print/1/displaymode/1098/
92. Ross and Page, "Jail Liability," p. 10.
93. Ibid.
94. Cornelius, *The Correctional Officer,* pp. 241, 242.
95. Sutty, *Legal Issues,* Book II, p. 160.
96. Ross and Page, "Jail Liability," p. 10.
97. Ibid., pp. 11, 13.
98. Ibid., p. 14.
99. Ibid., p. 11.

## REFERENCES

Collins, William C. *Jail Design and the Constitution.* Washington, DC: National Institution of Corrections, 1998.

Collins, William C., J.D. *Correctional Law for the Correctional Officer, 4th Edition.* Lanham, MD: American Correctional Association, 2004.

Collins, William C. and John Hagar. "Jails and the Courts...Issues for Today, Issues for Tomorrow." *American Jails,* May–June 1995, 18–28.

Cornelius, Gary F. *The Correctional Officer: A Practical Guide.* Durham, MD: Carolina Academic Press, 2001.

"Court Sanctions Inmate Who Files Frivolous Lawsuits." *The Corrections Professional,* 10 (13) (March 25, 2005): 13.

Cripe, Clair A. *Legal Aspects of Corrections Management.* Sudbury: Jones and Bartlett, 2003.

Gaseau, Michelle. "Monitoring Extremist Groups and Maintaining Religious Rights." *corrections.com,* September 20, 2004, http://www.corrections.com/printNews.aspx?Zone=Homepage (accessed September 20, 2004).

Hanson, Roger A. and Harry W.K. Daley. *Challenging the Conditions of Prisons and Jails: A Report on Section 1983 Litigation.* Washington, DC: U.S. Department of Justice, 1995.

Hole, JacksonWY *Inmate Rules and Regulations.* Teton County Jail, Teton County Sheriff's Office, revised May 12, 2003.

INMATE HANDBOOK. *Inmate Grievance Procedures.* Alexandria, VA: Alexandria Detention Center, Office of Sheriff, 2004.

"Jail's Grievance Procedure Must Exist to Require Exhaustion." *The Corrections Professional,* 10 (15) (April 29, 2005): 14.

Johnson, Alex. "Court Upholds Prisoners' Religious Rights: Justices Say Unusual Faiths Must be Accommodated." *MSNBC.com,* http://www.msnbc.msn.com/id/8047388/fromRL.1/print/1/displaymode/1098/ (accessed June 11, 2005).

"Lack of Training for Appendicitis Attack Subjects Jail to Suit." *The Corrections Professional,* 10 (9) (January 21, 2005): 13.

Mushlin, Michael B. *Rights of Prisoners, 3rd Edition.* Vol 1. Eagan, MN: Thomson-West, 2002.

Mushlin, Michael B. *Rights of Prisoners, 3rd Edition.* Vol 2. Eagan, MN: Thomson-West, 2002.

Newsday. "Renssalear County to Pay Jail Inmates for Illegal Strip Searches." *corrections.com,* http://www.corrections.com/news/didyouknow/ (accessed October 14, 2004).

Palmer, John W., J.D., and Stephen E. Palmer, J.D. *Constitutional Rights of Prisoners, 7th Edition.* Cincinnati, OH: Anderson, 2004.

Press Release. US Department of Justice: "Maricopa County to Improve Medical and Mental Health Care for Inmates Under Justice Department Agreement." December 6, 1999, http://www.usdoj.gov/opa/pr/1999/December/588cr.htm (accessed February 8, 2007).

Quinn, James F. *Corrections: A Concise Introduction.* Prospect Heights, IL: Waveland Press, Inc., 1999.

Ross, Darrell L., Ph.D., and Bill Page. "Jail Liability: Reducing the Risk by Studying the Numbers." *American Jails,* January–February 2003, 9–15.

Shreveport Times, "Shreveport Will Settle for $4.9 Million." *corrections.com,* http://www.corrections.com/news/justin/index.html (accessed December 3, 2002).

Smith, Christopher E. *Law and Contemporary Corrections.* Belmont, CA: West/Wadsworth, 2000.

Sutty, David S. *Legal Issues for Correctional Staff.* Book I. Lanham, MD: American Correctional Association, 1999.

Sutty, David S. *Legal Issues for Correctional Staff.* Book II. Lanham, MD: American Correctional Association, 1999.

# JAIL STANDARDS 10

*Objectives of chapter*

The student will:

- Understand what jail standards are, their purpose and how adherence to standards is beneficial to the jail staff
- Understand the history and development of jail standards
- Gain an insight by examining an overview of standards in jail operations and health care
- Understand the process of how local jails comply with standards through policies and procedures, inspections and the audit process.

If a jail adheres to standards, whether it is by standards from the state or by recognized correctional organizations such as the American Correctional Association (ACA) or the National Commission on Correctional Health Care (NCCHC), it is operating in a professional manner. Standards are the basis for jail policies and procedures that govern the way the jail is operated and how inmates are treated. Jail standards can be viewed as the "glue" that holds a well-run jail together. Adherence to standards requires a lot of effort, documentation, and inspection by the jail staff. This chapter will present the reader with a concise view of the process of meeting jail standards.

## STANDARDS: DEFINITION, PURPOSE, AND BENEFITS

A **jail standard** is a statement that defines a required or essential condition to be achieved or maintained.[1] It must be included in jail policies from which procedures are derived, and jail staff to which the policies apply must be trained concerning meeting the standard. Proof that the standard is being met must be in the form of documentation, inspections, annual reports, and audits. For example, jail standards are not limited to standards set down from the state department of corrections. Jail standards also encompass guidelines from the local health department concerning food handling, the local fire department concerning fire inspections and conditions of fire equipment, a recognized medical organization dictating protocols for medical care for inmates, etc.

For example, a contemporary illustration of a jail standard is from the American Correctional Association (ACA). In the Safety section of ACA's current performance-based jail standards, a performance standard is:

**Emergency Preparedness/Response: 1C: "The number and severity of emergencies are minimized. When emergencies occur, the response minimizes the severity."** This is a condition—minimal number and severity of emergencies—for the jail to maintain.

The expected practice or what was more commonly known as "standard" is 4-ALDF-1C-07 from the ACA's *Performance-Based Standards for Adult Local Detention Facilities, Fourth Edition,* published by ACA in June, 2004. It incorporates fire safety guidelines:

> (Mandatory) The facility conforms to applicable federal, state, and/or local fire safety codes. The authority having jurisdiction documents compliance. A fire alarm and automatic detection system are required, as approved by the authority having jurisdiction, or there is a plan for addressing these or other deficiencies within a reasonable time period. The authority approves any variances, exceptions, or equivalencies and these must be a serious life-safety threat to the occupants of the facility.[2]

This standard does not involve just the jail; it also involves any federal, state, or local fire laws that may apply to the jail. Built into the standard is the fact that documentation must be maintained, and there are guidelines if the jail varies from this standard. Overall, the purpose of the standard is for the jail to have an effective fire prevention system. However, ACA has modified its standards, and what was previously known as a standard is now known as an expected practice, which will be explained later in this chapter. In the previously referenced example, the information written in 4-ADLF-1C-07 may be written as a state standard in a different format and not as an expected practice.

The purpose of jail standards is for the jail management staff to be proactive—to take an approach where problems are to be avoided and jail management flows easier and smoother. Standards are designed to prevent problems by being incorporated into agency practices, policies, and procedures.

Jail standards can provide the jail administrator and supervisors with several effective management tools:[3]

- Standards offer a perspective and benchmark against which the supervisors of the jail can judge staff performance.
- Standards offer a blueprint or guide for staff in many areas of jail operations.
- Standards provide a foundation on which to formulate acceptable policies and procedures.
- Training curriculum can be developed from jail standards.
- Standards can also be used to justify new staff, additional equipment, and services.
- Standards can "head off" inmate litigation and provide an effective defense if a lawsuit is filed.

Standards are good for staff supervisors. With the above management tools, staff performance can be judged, for example, by seeing if a policy in food handling is being met. If staff is not handling food properly, the problem can be measured against the food-handling procedure, in a policy based on a jail standard.

Concerning "blueprints," some standards involve how staff place inmates on segregation. A policy based on a jail classification standard that outlines the reasons for segregation gives the classification staff a guidepost.

In almost all sets of standards, training is mentioned, with a specified list of training subjects and the number of hours that have to be respectively taught and met. If a standard calls for new procedures in inmate medical or dental care, a jail administrator can make a budget request for additional medical staff to the local government citing the requirements of the standard. Standards are based on court decisions involving inmate lawsuits, acts by legislatures, consent decrees, injunctions, declaratory rulings, and opinions handed down from the federal or state attorney general.[4] The resulting policies and procedures can deter inmate suits and minimize their chances of success.

The process of an agency meeting and complying with jail standards is called **accreditation.** Accreditation is an involved process, and a jail is only deemed to be accredited after the standards agency completes an audit, or a detailed inspection of the jail's operations to determine whether such operations are in accordance with the standards incorporated into approved policies and procedures. The audit is performed by the agency granting the accreditation, such as the National Commission on Correctional Health Care (NCCHC), the ACA, state departments of corrections, the Federal Bureau of Prisons (if the jail is holding federal inmates), etc. Each agency has a time period of accreditation and a schedule of audits. For example, the ACA conducts an audit every three years.

A set of jail standards addresses all of the important areas of jail operations and focuses on the safety and welfare of both the staff and the inmates. A major step in the improvement of jail standards was the publication of the 2004 *Performance Based Standards for Adult Local Detention Facilities* by the ACA. They are divided into these major categories with supporting sub headings:[5]

- Safety: protection from injury and illness, vehicle safety, emergency preparedness, and response.
- Security: protection from harm, use of physical force, contraband, access to keys, tools, and utensils.
- Order: inmate discipline.
- Care: food service, hygiene, continuum of health care services, health services staff.
- Program and Activity: inmate opportunities for improvement, family and community ties, programs.
- Justice: inmate rights, fair treatment of inmates, due process for inmates, inmate responsibility.
- Administration and Management: legal status, recruitment, retention and promotion, staff ethics, facility administration, staff treatment, community relations.

The benefits for the jail if these standards are followed include current training, up-to-date medical practices, and a form of assurance to the inmate population that they will be treated properly and fairly. Standards are constantly being revised to reflect case law, legislative acts, new information, and ideas in inmate management and corrections that have been accepted by the jail community. Following standards facilitates the agency's efforts to keep up in the field.

Jail staffs in the field recognize the value and pride of being accredited, especially by the ACA. Writing in a 1996 issue of *Corrections Today,* Major Michael

Pinson of the Arlington County (VA) Detention Facility described the positive benefits of the accreditation process. In deciding to seek accreditation, the reasoning by the agency management was that accreditation would result in strict operational standards designed for the protection of life, safety, and health of all staff and inmates. Another benefit is accreditation would provide assistance in dealing with any possible inmate litigation. A third result is that through accreditation, the agency evaluates itself, which is a valuable management tool. Finally, accreditation facilitates a feeling of accomplishment, professionalism, and recognition.[6]

The Arlington jail management staff asked staff members "What does accreditation mean to you individually and as a member of this office?" One jail deputy, assigned to the Intake Housing Unit said:

> Being accredited means to me that the sheriff's office is always striving to meet and go beyond state and national standards and guidelines, it creates a professional attitude among staff members and creates a cleaner and safer environment for staff. It shows that the sheriff's office takes pride in being one of the few offices which meets accreditation standards. It also shows the dedication of the sheriff's office to providing Arlington County residents with the best service it can.[7]

Another jail deputy who was assigned to the female inmate general housing unit said in response to the accreditation question:

> Coming from the old jail system, I feel that being accredited holds me to a higher standard. Having had an opportunity to see the accreditation process, I understand that my department has met standards that not every department can meet.[8]

Operationally, a jail can benefit in preparing for accreditation. Training is one critical area. For example, if a standard mandates that jail officers receive annual training in suicide prevention, records must show that all jail officers did receive training in preventing suicides. Before the accreditation process, this training may have been conducted sporadically, but not documented. Another area is inspections. Standards may dictate that all caustic cleaning material is properly stored and inventoried. The procedures in this area may have been sloppy and haphazard, but due to the process of meeting standards, such materials can be stored in the right way, inventoried, and documented. The greatest benefit of accreditation is staff performing their duties in a professional and uniform manner resulting in many improvements to day-to-day operations in jail.

## JAIL STANDARDS: HISTORY AND DEVELOPMENT

Jail standards are relatively new, considering the long world history of jails, prisons, and local corrections. There have been attempts to bring safe and humane operations to jails throughout history. One of the earliest was John Howard's essay *The State of the Prisons,* written in 1777 in an effort to improve the conditions in the jails in England and Europe. Howard became aware of the squalid conditions in jails when he became the High Sheriff of Bedfordshire, and in 1775, he toured European jails and prisons. The *State of the Prisons* was Howard's far-reaching and visionary effort to reform penal institutions by setting forth guidelines for both standardized operations and staff conduct.[9]

Calling his standards "correct principles," Howard outlined many guidelines in the areas that jail standards cover now. His standards or "correct principles" included suggested location of the institution, sanitary practices, food and diets, housing of inmates (sleeping alone), alarm bells in cases of escapes, security, inmates clothing, and health care. What was revolutionary about Howard's views was the fact that he wrote about several important issues in jail operations that are taken very seriously now. They were:[10]

- Classification: "Women-felons" should be housed separately from the male prisoners. Also, young criminals (now called juveniles) were to be housed separately from "old and hardened" offenders.
- Staff: The "gaolors" (jailors) should be "honest, active and humane," be paid well, and be sober. The "turnkeys" should also be well paid and separately from the jailor.
- Security hardware and installation: Inmates should wear uniforms; there should be double doors, gaoler's window looking into the jail yard, and a high wall surrounding the jail. Attention to be paid to the number of turnkeys, or jail officer and their disposition or postings in the jail.
- Religious instruction: A chaplain should be present in the jail to minister and counsel young offenders.
- Disciplinary actions: A system is needed where inmate disputes are settled by the "keeper" or jailor; rules are in place "prohibiting quarreling or abusive language; nor the frequent occasion of them, gaming [gambling]." More serious offenses should be referred to a magistrate or inspector. Punishments should include dietary restrictions, solitary confinement, and the jail term lengthened on escape attempts. Rules should be intelligently written and publicly posted for the inmates to see.

Howard's views were far reaching and set a foundation for today's standards. The subsequent three major correctional systems, the Pennsylvania, Auburn, and Reformatory, had rules and regulations that promoted their respective correctional philosophies. However, the next milestone in the development of correctional standards was in 1870, nearly a century after Howard's *The State of the Prisons*. Penal institutions of the time had no clear standards of operation or goals for the humane treatment of inmates and the qualifications of staff.

By the late nineteenth century, some leaders in penology were aware of progressive ideas such as Sir Walter Crofton's Irish System and Captain Alexander Maconochie's Mark System, calling for steps to be taken in inmate rehabilitation and preparing the inmate for eventual release. Until this time, there had been public indifference as to the conditions of correctional institutions. Dr. Enoch Wines, a penal reformer, commenced a movement to reform corrections institutions after he toured several prisons in 1865. Dr. Wines advocated the formation of an international congress of prison reformers through an American penal reform organization that had the representation power to call a world meeting.[11]

In 1870, in Cincinnati, Ohio American prison administrators and penal reformers met in the first National Prison Congress. The convention was attended by 130 delegates from 24 states, countries in South America, and Canada. Forty papers were presented discussing such subjects as executive pardons, prison hygiene, indeterminate sentencing, and jails. As a result of this Congress, the National Prison Association was formed. This organization evolved into what is today known as the American Correctional Association (ACA). The 1870 National Prison Congress adopted a **"Declaration of Principles,"** promoting penal reform and giving birth to today's modern correctional standards.[12]

These declarations addressed such issues as the "treatment of insane criminals," what is called now the mentally ill in jails. Religion and education were deemed important, as they are in jail programs today. Today, policy is based on statistical research, which was called for in 1870. Classification was mentioned as separate institutions for different types of offenders. Rewards for good conduct were the forerunners of what is known as good time today. The physical plant concerning humane housing as to air and sunlight were deemed important. Job training for correctional staff was called for, and we see that per the correctional standards currently in place.

Adopted and Promulgated at the 1870 National Prison Congress

(A Summary)

The Declaration of Principles promoted:

1. Reformation, not vindictive suffering as the purpose of penal treatment of prisoners.
2. Classifications made on the basis of a mark system, patterned after the Irish System.
3. Rewards for good conduct.
4. Prisoners being made to realize that their destiny is in their own hands.
5. The chief obstacles to prison reform: the political appointment of prison officials and the instability of management.
6. Job training for prison officials.
7. Indeterminate sentences as substitutes for fixed sentences and removal of the gross disparities and inequities in prison sentences. Also, emphasis on the futility of repeated short sentences.
8. Religion and education as the most important agencies of reformation.
9. Prison discipline that gains the will of prisoners and conserves their self-respect.
10. Making industrious freemen rather than orderly and obedient prisoners as the prison's aim.
11. Full provision for industrial training.
12. Abolishing the system of contract labor in prisons.
13. Small prisons and separate institutions for different types of offenders.
14. Laws striking against the so-called "higher-ups" in crime, as well as against the lesser operatives.
15. Indemnifying prisoners who are afterwards found to be innocent.
16. Laws relating to the treatment of insane criminals be revised.
17. More judicious exercise of pardoning power.
18. Establishing a system for the collection of uniform penal statistics.

19. Developing a more adequate prison architecture, providing sufficiently for air and sunlight, as well as for prison hospitals, schoolrooms, etc.
20. Within each state, centralizing prison management.
21. Facilitating the social training of prisoners through proper associations and abolishing the silence rule.
22. Making society at large realize its responsibility for crime conditions.

"The Reformatory Era" from *The American Prison: From the Beginning . . . A Pictorial History*. Copyright 1983 by the American Correctional Association. Reprinted by permission of the American Correctional Association.

**FIGURE 10-1** Declaration of Principles

During the next century after the 1870 Congress, the ideas born by the Declaration of Principles stagnated; little was done by prison superintendents, courts, or government officials to bring these ideas to practical fruition. The principles lacked specifications that were precise and measurable, and prison administrators were "their own bosses" and felt comfortable doing things in their own way. The independent practices of these supervisors were not subject to inspection or oversight by governments or the courts.[13]

The lack of enthusiasm from the correctional management community was not the only reason for the inaction over a century concerning the 1870 principles. According to research by Paul Keve, there were three primary reasons why the 1870 principles failed to be implemented. First, the principles did not originate from efforts from representative practitioners in the correctional field but were drawn up by correctional leaders and *then* presented to the line staff. Second, according to the wardens, there were no adverse or threatening conditions in prisons that could be resolved by the adoption of the principles. Finally, accreditation as is known today did not exist. Prison administrators did not realize at the time a process would be needed to apply the principles.[14]

For most of the twentieth century, the courts took a "hands off" approach to prisons and jails. The administrators of jails had no guidelines or standards to follow; they were on their own. The subsequent "hands on" era found the courts involved in complaints from inmates and attorneys concerning brutal conditions, lack of health care, etc. Courts in the hands-on era began to deal with inmates' religious rights and disciplinary cases. With the court rulings, which could not be based on precedent case law (as there was none to speak of) a need for guidelines became clear.[15]

Another milestone in the development of correctional standards appeared in 1956. Mryl E. Alexander (1909–1993) was at that time the President of the ACA, and was also an Assistant Director at the Federal Bureau of Prisons. Later he would serve corrections as the Bureau's Director. In his ACA presidential address, he stated an inmates' "Bill of Rights" that supported the views of the Declaration of Principles at the 1870 National Prison Congress. These "Rights" would become more prevalent in the 1960s.[16]

Inmates have:

1. The *right* to clean, decent surroundings with competent attention to (the inmate's) physical and mental well-being.
2. The *right* to maintain and reinforce the strengthening ties which bind (inmates) to (their) family and to (their) community.
3. The *right* to develop and maintain skills as a productive worker in our economic system.
4. The *right* to fair, impartial, and intelligent treatment without special privilege or license for any (inmate).
5. The *right* to positive guidance and counsel from correctional personnel possessed of understanding and skill.



**FIGURE 10-2** Alexander's Bill of Rights for Inmates

With the involvement of the courts in correctional management and inmate rights during the hands on era, the issue of correctional standards began to move forward. In 1968, a project was undertaken to develop an accreditation plan for correctional standards that were specific and measurable. In 1970, the results of the project were presented to the Congress of Correction in Cincinnati, exactly 100 years after the ground-breaking 1870 Congress. The Board of Directors at the Congress approved the plan, and new correctional standards began to develop.[17]

Manuals of corrections standards for staff to follow are not a new concept. As early as 1946, the American Prison Association published its first edition of *Manual for Prison Standards*. By the 1960s, the Executive Secretary for ACA, E. Preston Sharp, and C. Winston Tanksley of the Colorado Prison System were working to develop a set of standards that were modern and comprehensive. One important aspect of the efforts at this time was the development of a voluntary standards compliance system and awarding of accreditation. In 1974, ACA created the Commission on Accreditation for Corrections (CAC), and it commenced to distribute standards to and also accepted applications from correctional institutions that wished to be accredited. The first accreditations by the CAC were granted in 1978, and by 1995, over 1,400 correctional facilities-prisons and jails had obtained accreditation or were seeking accreditation.[18]

When first implemented, accreditation was granted or withheld by the CAC based on inspections and evaluations, or audits on all aspects of a correctional facility's operations and staffing: the amount of minimum space per inmate, health (medical) service, diets and food service, recreation for inmates, educational programs for inmates, staff training, etc.[19]

In the area of jail accreditation and jail standards, there are other professional organizations that have professed an interest due to their related functions to jails. According to researcher Paul Keve, these interests by such agencies as the International Association of Chiefs of Police, the National Sheriff's Association, the

National Organization of Blacks in Law Enforcement, and the Police Executive Research Forum resulted in the formation of the Commission on Accreditation for Law Enforcement Agencies (CALEA) in 1979. This Commission developed standards for police lockups—a form of correctional facility—that were based on prison and jail standards developed by the CAC.[20]

Police officers in police lockups face the same problems and issues that jail officers face in many instances. If an offender is arrested and placed in police custody in a lock up, they may have health and safety issues as jail inmates have. Standards give the police guidance in the proper handling of offenders in their custody.

Another professional organization that has become prominent in jail standards is the NCCHC. The mission of the NCCHC is to "improve the quality of health care in jails, prisons and juvenile confinement facilities." NCCHC has separate volumes of its standards for prisons, jails, and juvenile facilities and covers such areas as care and treatment, health and medical records, medical administration, medical personnel and issues involving medical and legal issues.[21]

In the three decades since the 1970s, many states have formulated their own standards for jails, and jails' being accredited by NCCHC is a growing, positive trend. Correctional standards, whether they be through the ACA, a state board of corrections, or the National Association of Correctional Health Care are updated annually, reflecting the latest thought and good practices in local corrections. In reality, the primary jail standards that are the most advantageous to follow have originated from the ACA.

Standards have had an impact on the nation's jails, which for many years operated under little or no guidelines. Paul Keve in 1996 describes the "linkage" that correctional standards have had with the nation's sheriff's offices that operate many jails in the United States. Sheriffs have operated their departments, including the local jails with a "stout sense of independence," resisting outside influences. Faced with more complex issues in jail management, such as inmate health care and staff training, sheriffs are finding more interest and respect in jail standards that promote professionalism, a positive public image, and define "safe and competent" jail management practices.[22]

One area of progress in the past twenty years has been recognizing the problems of small jails. In some jurisdictions, funding may not be available for the construction, renovation, staffing, etc. of a large jail—the tax base cannot support them. In 1987, representatives from ACA, the American Jail Association (AJA), the National Sheriff's Association, and the National Institute of Corrections convened. Their goal was to examine the problem of small jails and accreditation. These organizations thought that a list of standards should be developed to meet two goals. The first was to have standards that met the needs of small jails throughout the United States. The second goal was to have small jails involved in an accreditation process. In 1988, 207 standards for small jails were approved by the 118th Congress of Correction.[23]

Many sheriffs' offices have multiple duties; some maintain the safety and security of the courts, serve court papers, operate the jail, *and* engage in police type law enforcement duties. The latter is commonly called "working the road." Deputies may be transferred between operational sections of a sheriff's department. As a result, personnel may have to be capable to perform many different duties.

Sheriffs of such multi-tasked departments may wonder which accreditation they should achieve—NCCHC, CAC, etc. If the state has jail standards, the local jail must meet them in order to be certified by the state to hold inmates. However, meeting standards from CAC or NCCHC is not mandatory. Accreditation is an expensive process. Accreditation by standards other than the state may be partial—the sheriff may elect only to have his or her jail's medical department certified by NCCHC. Some jails, according to Keve, attempt to attain **triple crown certification,** which is meeting the standards of three professional agencies: the CAC, the CALEA, and the NCCHC.[24] Some local detention facilities have the work release part of their jail systems accredited by the ACA through the Performance-Based Standards for Adult Community Residential Services[25] and not have the jail ACA accredited. It is an accomplishment for a jail to meet state jail standards *and* standards from other outside corrections organizations.

One question is that if the CAC or ACA standards are so progressive, why have not more jails been accredited? It is estimated that only a few of the nations' 3,000 plus jails are CAC accredited, due to sheriffs meeting what they feel are sufficient state standards. Sheriffs may elect to have only NCCHC certification because their standards represent the latest and the most protective guidelines in inmate health care and represent a cost savings by less hospital trips, etc. Another reason is that jails in the United States vary in size and characteristics, and many may not meet standards.[26]

## AN OVERVIEW OF JAIL STANDARDS

There are three main areas of jail standards: state standards, CAC or ACA standards, and NCCHC standards. State standards are the most basic and usually are not as detailed and strict as CAC or NCCHC standards. Probably the most effective accreditation for a jail involves being accredited in all three areas; in that way a jail is afforded maximum protection from both criticism and litigation.

### State Standards

In terms of consistency among the states and jail standards, the fact is that there is no consistency. Some states have no standards, some have correctional associations that oversee voluntary standards compliance, and some are operated by the state department of corrections who oversee standards compliance.

An example of clear and detailed state jail standards is in the state of Illinois. There are 29 sections to the standards, including three sections of standards addressing the detention of juvenile offenders remanded to the custody of a local jail on written authority of the court or probation officer, the temporary detention of juveniles in excess of 36 hours up to seven days, and the detention of youths prosecuted under Illinois Criminal Code of 1961.[27]

The Illinois standards list these sections of operations, each of which is supported by standards:[28]

- *Administration:* staff training, written procedures (manual), records, jail officer staffing, personnel rules.
- *Personnel:* provides for staffing, gender supervision guidelines, and personnel rules.

According to the National Institute of Corrections, the following listing indicates how each state deals with jail standards and inspections as of 2005:[29]

| *State* | *Inspections and Standards Compliance Authority* |
|---|---|
| Alabama | Alabama DOC responsible for jails inspections |
| Alaska | Unified system, DOC houses jail inmates |
| Arizona | No formal jail inspection program |
| Arkansas | Standards enforced by Criminal Detention Review Committee |
| California | Board of Corrections sets standards, inspects jails, no enforcement authority |
| Colorado | No state oversight of jail facilities. |
| Connecticut | Unified corrections system, no locally operated jail facilities |
| Delaware | Unified corrections system, no locally operated jail facilities |
| Florida | Inspections performed by Florida Sheriff's Association for compliance with standards |
| Georgia | Voluntary jail standards compliance managed by GA Sheriff's Association |
| Hawaii | Jails operated by State Division of Corrections |
| Idaho | Jail inspection, voluntary compliance operated by Idaho Sheriff's Association |
| Illinois | State DOC manages jails inspection and standards compliance |
| Indiana | State DOC inspects jails and enforces standard compliance |
| Iowa | State DOC inspects jails and enforces standard compliance |
| Kansas | No formal jail standards or jail inspection system |
| Kentucky | State DOC inspects jails for standards compliance |
| Louisiana | State DOC & LA Office of Public Health inspects jails for standards compliance |
| Maine | State DOC inspects jails for standards compliance |
| Maryland | MD Commission on Correctional Standards enforces jail standards compliance |
| Massachusetts | State DOC inspects jails for standards compliance |
| Michigan | State DOC inspects jails for standards compliance |
| Minnesota | State DOC inspects jails for standards compliance |
| Mississippi | MS Department of Public Safety inspects jails; compliance with standards is voluntary |
| Missouri | No jail inspections or standards programs |
| Montana | No jail inspections or standards programs |
| Nebraska | NE Crime Commission inspects jails, enforces compliance |
| Nevada | No jail inspections or standards programs |
| New Hampshire | No jail inspections or standards programs |
| New Jersey | State DOC inspects jails for standards compliance |
| New Mexico | No jail inspections or standards program |
| New York | NY State Commission of Corrections inspects jails for standard compliance |

**FIGURE 10-3** Continued

| | |
|---|---|
| North Carolina | NC Dept. of Health & Human Resources & NC Department of Justice responsible for jail standards compliance |
| North Dakota | ND Department of Corrections and Rehabilitation manages jail standards |
| Ohio | Ohio Bureau of Adult Detention, Dept. of Rehabilitation and Correction manages jail standards |
| Oklahoma | OK Department of Health conducts jail inspections |
| Oregon | Oregon DOC: Voluntary compliance with jail standards |
| Pennsylvania | State DOC inspects jails for standards compliance |
| Rhode Island | One jail for pre trial offenders operated by DOC |
| South Carolina | State DOC inspects jails for standards compliance |
| South Dakota | No jail inspections or standards program |
| Tennessee | Tennessee Corrections Institute inspects jails for standards compliance |
| Texas | TX Commission on Jail Standards inspect jails for standards compliance |
| Utah | UT Sheriff's Association: operates voluntary compliance program |
| Vermont | State DOC inspects jails for standards compliance |
| Virginia | State DOC inspects jails for standards compliance |
| Washington | No jail inspections or standards program |
| West Virginia | No jail inspections or standards program |
| Wisconsin | State DOC inspects jails for standards compliance |
| Wyoming | No jail inspections or standards program [DOC: Department of Corrections] |
| District of Columbia | Unified system, DOC houses jail inmates[30] |

**FIGURE 10-3** Jail Systems and Standards

- *Records:* booking, personal record, monthly reports to the Department of Corrections, reporting of extraordinary or unusual circumstances.
- *Admission procedures:* posting of rules, frisk/strip searching, identity of inmates, injuries, personal property, telephone calls, physical and mental health assessments, medication, booking and personal record information, medical records, showers, cell assignments, issues items to inmates.
- *Orientation:* inmate life, rules of conduct, disciplinary procedures, programs and work information, requests, complaints to the jail staff, the Department of Corrections and Judiciary, assisting illiterate and non-English-speaking inmates.
- *Release procedures:* identification, physical inspection of inmate for wounds and injuries, contraband search of inmates, personal property, discharge of mentally ill persons, transfers to the Illinois Department of Corrections.
- *Classification and separation:* information for classification files, categories of separation, classification review guidelines.
- *Housing:* space in cells and detention rooms, dormitories, housing area equipment, showers, ventilation, architectural plans, etc.
- *Medical and mental health care:* services, admission examinations, sick call, written records and logs, medical security, staff mental health training, tuberculosis (TB) isolation.

- *Clothing, personal hygiene and grooming:* cleanliness, grooming, maintaining personal hygiene.
- *Food services:* meal and food service, special religious diets, menus, food service staff, food preparation, and service.
- *Sanitation:* general sanitation guidelines, facility equipment, drinking equipment, supplies, food service sanitation, body pests, pest, and vermin control.
- *Supervision:* shift coverage, supervision and observation guidelines, shift records, night hour procedures.
- *Security:* searches, facility security measures, tools and equipment, maintenance, keys and record control, headcounts, firearms and other weapons, chemical agents, emergency power source.
- *Safety:* fire protection, fire plan, emergency exits.
- *Discipline:* written rules, distribution of rules procedures, complaints, staff disciplinary procedures (hearings, punishments, etc.) and use of restraints.
- *Employment of detainees:* inmate work opportunities and guidelines.
- *Mail procedures:* scope of inmate correspondence (whom inmate is allowed to correspond with), incoming mail, outgoing mail, special mail (certified, outgoing/incoming privileged mail, disciplinary denial of mail).
- *Use of telephone:* limited number of inmate calls, suspension of phone use.
- *Visiting:* limits and scheduling of inmate visits, visits by attorneys, probation officers, clergy, etc., security guidelines.
- *Social service programs:* encourages social services programs, such as Alcoholics Anonymous, Gambler's Anonymous, religious volunteers, and recruitment of citizens as volunteers.
- *Education:* discusses guidelines for Adult Basic education courses, elementary and high school courses, General Education Development (GED) correspondence courses, social education, vocational skills and life skills.
- *Library:* guidelines for both leisure library and law library.
- *Religious services:* affords inmates opportunities to participate in religious services and counseling on a voluntary basis.
- *Commissary:* jails will maintain a commissary system, with proceeds being used for inmate benefit and welfare, which is subject to audit.
- *Recreation and leisure time:* offers guidelines for exercising, time allotted for exercise, and general guidelines for leisure time activities.
- *Juvenile detention:* guidelines for the housing, checking, and security of minors being temporarily held in a jail, for up to six hours and no more than 36 hours.
- *Temporary detention standards:* guidelines for juveniles in the custody of the sheriff from 36 hours up to 7 days, housing, program, visiting, and recreation guidelines.
- *Standards for detention of youths prosecuted under the Criminal Code of 1961:* guidelines for the housing, recreation, programs, counseling services, and visiting of juveniles being prosecuted under the Criminal Code of 1961.

Another example of detailed standards is the state of Tennessee. Tennessee standards are applicable to the type of local correctional facility that is designated. For example, for purposes of the standards, adult jails or workhouses that hold prisoners which confine offenders over 72 hours are considered Type I; adult jails and workhouses that hold inmates no more than 72 hours are designated Type II, and adult jails that house inmates for no more than 12 hours are Type III. Each standard that is written lists the type of jail to which it applies.[31]

Like the Illinois standards, Tennessee standards are detailed. For example, all facilities shall have a special purpose cell for the temporary detention of offenders under the influence of intoxicants, and new facilities shall have at least one single cell for the separation and control of problem prisoners. In the medical standards, a more complete and detailed medical examination (than receiving screening) shall be conducted on prisoners within 14 days of their initial confinement date. When receiving and booking inmates, the mandatory intake form lists information that is very detailed.[32]

The more detailed and specific the standards are, the more beneficial it is for the jail. Jail policies and procedures are easier to write when the standards for compliance are clear, well written, and understandable. Another benefit is training, as training curriculum would be easier to develop. However, jail standards always should be updated in view of new case law and correctional practices.

Since the 1970s individual states have taken steps to improve the operation of small and large jails in their jurisdictions by creating standards that must be complied with. However, leaders in the corrections field see the state standards as "bare bones minimum" and prefer that our nation's jails seek to follow a higher set of

Food service is a critical area that must meet strict state standards as well as standards from the American Correctional Association.

Photo by author, courtesy Teton County Jail.

values and practices concerning jail operations and the treatment of inmates. For some jails accreditation by ACA may be too expensive, so efforts are being made to upgrade state jail standards and keep them current so that jails will operate at the optimum level.[33]

By not meeting jail standards, jail administrators and sheriffs can give political opponents ammunition in election bids, incur costly litigation, and suffer bad publicity. To avoid this, South Carolina is improving their system of state jail standard certification, and Orange County, Florida, is part of a consortium with six other Florida counties that pool resources such as inspections to facilitate the accreditation process. Orange County was working in 2004 to meet standards under the Florida Corrections Accreditation Commission—a combination of mandatory state standards and ACA standards.[34]

## ACA: Performance-Based Standards

In 2004, ACA published its revolutionary new version of jail standards, the *Performance-Based Standards for Adult Local Detention Facilities: Fourth Edition.* Due to the hard work over five years by many corrections professionals, what were called "standards" were reclassified to be called "expected practices." This changed the accreditation process to include summaries of significant incidents and a report that studies inmates' condition of confinement. In granting or denying accreditation, the CAC now looks at wide range of performances and events in the jail. This is the "New Generation" of jail standards.[35]

These standards are the "peak" of how a jail should be operated and provide the best guidance for jail administrators. The major contributors to this project represented several state and county departments of corrections and corrections experts from the National Sheriff's Association, the AJA, and the ACA. Rod Miller, consultant and founder of Community Resources Services, Inc. has been working on jail standards issues for over 30 years and assisted on the ACA jail standards project. Miller says that the best practices for our nation's jails are embodied in the latest ACA standards and change will be slow due to 3,200 (plus) jails and the differences in jail management and leadership.[36]

POINT OF VIEW

### Jail Standards

*Rod Miller*

The nation's jails are, in effect, independently owned and operated.

In this context, many states found it necessary to attempt to regulate jail conditions and operations by adopting minimum jail standards. In most instances, states also had enforcement authority to compel compliance. State jail standards are usually described as "minimum" standards. While many state jail standards represent minimums, national standards written by the ACA offer a much higher level of practice—"professional" standards and practices. Compliance with ACA standards is voluntary, and although ACA offers accreditation to local jails, less than 10 percent of jails are involved with the accreditation process.

Jails and prisons, contrary to most people's beliefs, are very different from each other. Over the years, there had been a widespread perception by jail practitioners that the ACA Adult Local Detention Facility standards were more geared to prison operations rather than jail operations. The AJA, which supports standards for jails as well as accreditation, offered its assistance to ACA to bring together jail practitioners to update the standards and, hopefully, help alleviate those perceptions. The result has been the recent publication of the Fourth Edition of ACA's jail standards.

Federal courts influence minimum jail standards by establishing "constitutional minima." Federal courts sometimes refer to ACA standards, but rarely rely on such professional standards to establish constitutional requirements, as in the following federal appeals court case suggests (from *Detention and Corrections Caselaw Catalog, 16th Edition*, Miller and Walter, CRS Inc., Gettysburg, Pa., 2004):

*Grayson v. Peed*, 195 F.3d 692 (4th Cir. 1999). The administrator for the estate of a deceased detainee sued officers and county officials under § 1983 asserting constitutional violations, negligence, gross negligence, negligent training, and negligent supervision. The district court granted summary judgment for the defendants on all § 1983 claims and declined to assume supplemental jurisdiction over state law claims. The appeals court affirmed. The court found that there were no actionable deficiencies in the sheriff's policies, customs, or training. According to the court, ". . . the appellant's own expert penologist conceded that [sheriff] Peed's policies met the standards of both the Virginia Board of Corrections and the American Correctional Association." The court also concluded, ". . . Appellant's claims that [sheriff] Peed provided inadequate training for his employees must also fail. As of the time of this incident, the Adult Detention Center had been accredited for more than ten years by both the American Correctional Association and the National Commission on Correctional Health Care, two organizations whose training requirements often surpass minimal constitutional standards." (Fairfax County Adult Detention Center, Virginia)

State jail standards have come under fire in recent years, and some states have retreated from their long-established regulatory roles with jails under pressure from local officials who assert that jail standards represent unfunded state mandates. While state standards are in decline, national standards are experiencing exciting new changes.

## ACA's *Performance-Based* Standards: New Generation Standards for Jails

After five years of development, the American Correctional Association published its first set of performance-based standards in 2001. Partially funded by the U.S. Department of Justice's Bureau of Justice Assistance (BJA), *Fourth Edition Standards for Adult Community Residential Services (ACRS)* are the prototype that has guided the revision of other existing ACA standards manuals—and several new sets of standards. In 2004, ACA adopted performance-based standards for jails (*Performance-Based Standards for Adult Local Detention Facilities, Fourth Edition*. American Correctional Association, Lanham, Maryland 2004).

For most jail practitioners who were familiar with the first three editions, at first blush, the fourth edition will look very different from what they have been used to seeing and following. However, most of the operational areas that are addressed in the new standards have not changed, only the format. In its new performance-based template, ACA acknowledged that most of the "old" standards prescribed *activities or practices*. A new performance-based standard describes a *condition* to be achieved and maintained.

ACA's performance-based standards are composed of several elements:

- **functional area** (7 areas total)
- **goal statement** (one for each functional area)
- **performance standards** (as many as needed to achieve the goal)
- **outcome measures** for each performance standard
- **expected practices** for each standard, and corresponding
- **protocols,** and
- **process indicators**

These elements are defined and described below.

## Definitions of Performance-Based Standards Terms

These "tracks" or "footprints" allow supervisory and management staff to monitor ongoing operations.

The *relationship* between the elements is shown below.

| *Element* | *Definition* |
|---|---|
| Functional Area | |
| *Goal Statement* | General statement of what is sought within the functional area (of a performance-based standard) |
| *Standard* | A statement that clearly defines a required or essential *condition* to be achieved and maintained.<br>A performance standard describes a "state of being," a condition, and does not describe the activities or practices that might be necessary to achieve compliance. Performance standards reflect the program's overall mission and purpose. |
| *Outcome Measure* | Measurable events, occurrences, conditions, behaviors, or attitudes that demonstrate the extent to which the condition described in the performance standard has been achieved.<br>Outcome measures describe the *consequences* of the program's activities, rather than describing the activities themselves.<br>Outcome measures can be compared *over time* to indicate changes in the conditions that are sought. Outcome measure data are collected continuously but are usually analyzed periodically. |
| *Expected Practice(s)* | Actions and activities that, if implemented properly (according to protocols), will produce the desired outcome (of a performance-based standard).<br>What we *think* is necessary to achieve and maintain compliance with the standard—but not necessarily the *only* way to do so.<br>These are activities that represent the current experience of the field but that are not necessarily supported by research. As the field learns and evolves, so will practices. |
| *protocol(s)* | Written instructions that guide implementation of expected practices, such as policies/procedures, post orders, training curriculum, formats to be used such as logs and forms, offender handbooks, diagrams such as fire exit plans, internal inspection forms. |
| *Process Indicators* | Documentation and other evidence that can be examined periodically and continuously to determine that *practices* are being implemented properly. |

## Functional Relationship of Performance-Based Standards

### *Element*

Two new elements of the ACA template are "outcome measures" and "process indicators." Understanding the difference between outcome measures and process indicators can be difficult.

Process indicators relate directly to expected practices. Process indicators tell jail managers if they are doing what they set out to do. Process indicators establish that various activities were actually implemented. But it is the outcome measures that determine whether these activities were actually effective.

Most process indicators refer to written documentation that can be consulted "after the fact." In addition to these "footprints" that are left by an organization, implementation of expected practices may be confirmed on-site by such activities as:

- observation
- interviews (staff, volunteers, offenders, others)
- measurement (e.g., light levels, noise levels)

Such activities are also central components of comprehensive self-audit and self-assessment systems. These additional activities (observation, interview, measurement) are also a central part of ACA's accreditation process, comprising much of the work that is conducted on-site during audits.

Observation, interview, and measurement activities are usually suggested *only* when other methods are not possible. Observation, interview, and measurement rely on an on-site "single point in time" activity, while the other methods have the ability to examine practices randomly, over a longer period of time. For example, *observing* a single admission of a new inmate does not confirm that procedures are properly implemented at other times, while randomly reviewing intake documentation from offender files provides a much broader sampling of actual activities.

Outcome measures look at the "bottom line"—not just whether expected practices were properly implemented, but rather whether the desired condition or state of being described in the performance standard was achieved. There are three basic ways to express outcome measures:

- as *rates* (the frequency of an occurrence over time, such as the number of serious fires/year);
- as *ratios* [comparing two numbers as a fraction or decimal, such as the number of serious fires *divided by* the average daily population (ADP)]; or
- as *proportions* (the relation of a part to the whole, such as the number of serious fires *divided by* the total number of fires). A *percentage* is a proportion multiplied by 100.

Whenever possible, denominators attempt to reflect the volume of activity. Therefore, it is preferable to divide by the ADP rather than simply counting the number of events per month. In the ALDF standards, two denominators are frequently used—the ADP and the number of admissions.

## How Will Performance-Based Standards Affect Jails?

The goal of professional standards—to elevate the level of practice in the field—should be advanced in the coming years through the implementation of the new performance-based standards. The new approach and format provides practitioners with more tools, and more options, for evaluating and improving correctional operations. And most important, this approach forces practitioners to look beyond the day-to-day mechanics of operations toward the larger picture of the results of their efforts—the outcomes.

As performance-based standards are developed for all facets of corrections, practitioners will become more comfortable with the new terminology. "Expected practices" used to be called "standards." This new term describes the former standards very well because almost all of the former "standards" actually prescribed specific practices. Perhaps practitioners will be more likely to experiment with new and different approaches.

In 1987, the National Institute of Justice (NIJ) commissioned a study of ACA's institutional standards for physical plant conditions (e.g., cell size, lighting, temperature). NIJ and ACA expected to identify many empirical foundations for the standards. Instead, the research team found that many of the standards were based on the experience of practitioners and their best estimates of what was warranted. The final report for the "Conditions of Confinement Standards" project recommended a move toward performance standards rather than prescriptive standards. It was this research initiative that suggested the new concept of "unencumbered space" that is now used to determine the adequacy of inmate cells and housing areas. Rather than requiring a specific amount of space to be provided (such as the former 70-square-foot standard), the focus was shifted toward the way in which a cell performed. In this way, designers were *encouraged* to experiment with cell layouts.

Because many expected practices are based on experience rather than research, practitioners should be encouraged to try new approaches. The new performance-based standards attempt to describe a condition to be achieved and maintained; this leaves more room for a variety of practices that may prove effective.

Hopefully, the new performance-based standards will increase overall support for professional standards. The new standards shift the focus from activities (practices) to actual results (outcomes), which should address earlier criticism that the standards were more concerned with policies and procedures than with actual practice.

The expanded format of ACA's performance-based standards template invites the development of new tools for the field. Standards and their corresponding expected practices can be delivered to the field in new ways. For example, the "process indicators" that are identified for each expected practice can easily be offered to practitioners as a management tool, such as an internal audit tool.

When correctional practitioners implement the new performance-based standards, they will find themselves collecting and analyzing an extraordinary amount of data. Although intended to be used to improve agency or facility operations, there will undoubtedly be an interest in *comparing* outcome measures externally. There has already been some discussion of the possibility of establishing national "benchmarks." In the opinion of this author, the prospect of national benchmarking is troubling. There are so many variables that comprise the context of each correctional operation that each one *must* be considered unique. Outcome measurements derived from such a unique context are extremely valuable as a management tool for the organization, but may be misleading if applied or compared to other operations. Furthermore, each agency will have its own definitions. For example, what constitutes an "incident" or a "rule violation" in one facility may not be identical to the practices and definitions in another. For now, such cross-agency comparisons will not be meaningful and could actually be counterproductive.

As organizations collect outcome measurement data over time, they will be creating a new element that may be used in the courts. Outcome measures can cut both ways when it comes to litigation. If collected, analyzed, and *acted upon*, outcome measures could offer proof of an organization's commitment to improvement. On the other hand, failing to act upon the "red flags" that outcome measures will sometimes raise might be interpreted by the courts as indifference to identified problems and conditions.

Thanks to Rod Miller, Community Consultant Resources, Inc., for lending his expertise on jail standards. Reprinted by permission.

Thanks to the American Correctional Association for permission to print charts, text and table from *Performance-Based Standards for Adult Local Detention Facilities: Fourth Edition.* Lanham: American Correctional Association, 2004.

The ACA standards have seven functional areas each with a supporting goal statement. They are[37]

- Safety
- Security
- Order
- Care
- Program and activity
- Justice
- Administration and management

An example of how the revised standards are set up would be to examine an area of jail operations (functional area) and apply the supporting logic and documentation.

In the above illustration, the supporting documents support the expected practices. To be accredited, a jail has to have accurate and well-written reports, logs, etc. The training and supervisory staff must ensure that all jail staff are well trained in documenting incidents and writing reports. Also, the documentation must be filed in an orderly system where documentation may be retrieved quickly if questions arise during an audit.

The ACA standards include some expected practices that are mandatory. If the standards are not through ACA, the term is mandatory standard. In any event, mandatory **standards/expected practices** are standards or expected practices that *must* be met in order for the jail to achieve accreditation. These are critical and usually deal with safety, security, and medical care. For example, in the ACA performance-based standards, an example of a mandatory expected practice is 4-ALDF-1C-10 that states: "Facility furnishings meet fire safety performance requirements." Another example is 4-ALDF-2D-01 that states: "The use of keys is controlled."[38]

At the time of this writing, concerning ACA performance-based standards, there are a total of 384 expected practices: 62 mandatory and 322 non-mandatory. When a jail administrator representing the agency believes that the jail has met or has exceeded the accreditation compliance levels, he or she can request a standards

Functional Area: IV. Care

Goal Statement: Provide the basic needs and personal care of inmates.

**Performance Standard**

*Food Service*
4A. Food Service provides a nutritionally balanced diet. Food service operations are hygienic and sanitary.

**Outcome Measures**

1. Number of documented inmate illnesses attributed to food service operations in the past 12 months divided by the ADP in the past 12 months.
2. Number of inmate grievances about food service decided in favor of the inmate in the past 12 months divided by the number of inmate grievances about food service in the past 12 months.
3. Number of violations cited by independent authorities for food service sanitation in the past 12 months.

**Expected Practices**

*Food Service*
4-ALDF-4A-01
Ref. 3-ALDF-2E-05: Dining space is large enough to allow meals to be served, affording each inmate the opportunity to have at least 20 minutes of dining time for each meal.

*Comment:* None.
*Protocols:* Written policy and procedure. Facility plans/specifications.
*Process Indicators:* Observation. Facility logs and records.
The supporting data are the jail's policies and procedures on food service, facility floor plans, and specification, so that the space that inmates have for eating can be determined. The inspection team may observe for themselves and look at post logs and records to see for themselves how inmates are fed.
Another example could involve the functional area of security.
*Functional Area:* II. Security
*GOAL:* Protect the community, staff, contractors, volunteers, and inmates from harm.
*Performance Standard:* Use of physical force

2B. Physical force is used only in instances of self-protection, protection of the inmate or others, prevention of property damage, or prevention of escape.

**Outcome Measures**

1. Number of instances in which force was used in the past 12 months divided by the ADP in the past 12 months.
2. Number of instances in which force was used in the past 12 months divided by the number of admissions in the past 12 months.
3. Number of times that staff uses of force was found to have been inappropriate in the past 12 months divided by the number of instances in which force was used.
4. Number of inmate grievances filed alleging inappropriate use of force in the past 12 months divided by the ADP in the past 12 months.

5. Number of grievances alleging inappropriate use of force decided in favor of the inmate in the past 12 months divided by the number of grievances alleging inappropriate use of force filed.
6. Number of injuries requiring medical treatment resulting from staff use of force in the past 12 months divided by the ADP in the past 12 months.

**Expected Practices**

*Use of Force*
4-ALDF-2B-01

(Ref. 3-ALDF-3A-30 and 3A-31)

(MANDATORY) The use of physical force is restricted to instances of justifiable self-defense, protection from others, protection of property, and prevention of escapes, and then only as a last resort and in accordance with appropriate statutory authority. In no event is physical force used as punishment.

*Comment:* None.
*Protocols:* Written policy and procedure. Staff training curriculum.
*Process Indicators:* Facility records and logs. Incident reports. Training records.

From Part IV. Care and Part II. Security in *Performance-Based Standards For Adult Local Detention Facilities,* Copyright 2004 by the American Correctional Association. Reprinted by Permission of the American Correctional Association.

**FIGURE 10-4** Examples of ACA Performance-Based Standards[39]

Jail living areas, no matter how small, must meet standards in health and safety.

Photo by author, courtesy Baltimore City Central Booking and Intake Center.

audit. The compliance levels for ACA accreditation are 100% of the mandatory expected practices and 90% of the non-mandatory expected practices. Accreditation is valid for three years.[40]

## Standards: National Commission on Correctional Health Care

The NCCHC was incorporated in 1983 and can trace its origin to the early 1970s. At that time, it was a project of the American Medical Association (AMA). The 2003 *Standards for Health Services in Jails* is the seventh revision of correctional health care services, which were first published by the AMA in 1977. The NCCHC standards represent recommendations to correctional facilities on the proper management of a correctional health care system.[41]

NCCHC also publishes position statements periodically on important issues in inmate health care. Correctional administrators find these valuable tools in order to provide the best health care to inmates. In the 2003 standards, the following issues were included in the position statement section:[42]

- *Administrative Management of HIV in Corrections:* Includes making voluntary HIV testing to inmates, including pregnant females, education about HIV, and opposes housing HIV-positive inmates separately. Inmates with AIDS may require medical isolation for their well-being as determined by the treating physician or the jail doctor. Other issues discuss confidentiality, Center for Disease Control (CDC) precautions, prevention, and problems concerning the HIV-positive health care worker.
- *Charging Inmates a Fee for Health Care Services:* NCCHC recommends that if inmates are charged a fee for health care, the access to such services will be available to all inmates regardless of their ability to pay a fee.
- *Licensed Health Care Providers in Correctional Institutions:* NCCHC and the Society of Correctional Physicians both advocate that physicians, nurses, and other licensed health care providers working in the field of corrections be fully licensed. These workers may be able to work freely in the community as well as inside a juvenile detention facility, prison or jail.
- *Management of Hepatitis B Virus (HBV) in Correctional Facilities:* All inmates should be screened for HBV and treated as necessary. HBV education should be provided to all inmates and staff in prisons, jails, and juvenile facilities.
- *Management of TB in Correctional Facilities:* All correctional staff should be tested initially and annually for TB as a condition of employment. All new adult and juvenile offenders admitted to correctional facilities should be screened for TB, including chest X ray and two-step examinations if necessary. All staff and inmates must receive the appropriate level of education about TB.
- *Mental Health Services in Correctional Settings:* All correctional facilities (including jails) should be required to meet recognized community standards for mental health services that are supported by standards from NCCHC, the American Psychiatric Association, and the American Public Health Association. Treatment protocols are also addressed.
- *Use of Automated External Defibrillators (AEDS) in Correctional Settings:* Correctional facilities considering using AEDS should conduct a needs analysis. If the decision is made to implement the installation of AEDS, it should be under the direction of

the responsible (jail) physician working with authorities in the facility. Both the physician and the facility authority should approve the locations of AEDs, considering the facility plan and staffing. All staff designated to use AEDs should receive initial and on going in-service training.

NCCHC standards are divided into nine general areas and total 72 standards. Standards are classified either as "essential" or "important." Essential standards are concerned with the health, safety, and welfare of inmates in a jail, and the critical components of a health care system, namely in the areas of receiving and medical screening of inmates, health assessment by staff, and quality of care assurance. NCCHC standards may not apply to a jail in all situations. In a jail that confines only male inmates, the NCCHC standards dealing with pregnant female inmates would not have to be met. To be accredited by NCCHC, all essential standards that are applicable must be met, and 85% of the important standards must be in compliance.[43]

Small jails with populations of fewer than 25 inmates have been accredited by NCCHC.[44] Small jails do not have the luxuries of medical staffing and funding that large jails do, and NCCHC accreditation can serve to make their health care the best as possible. Medical care for inmates is of primary importance, whether a jail is large or small.

NCCHC standards total 72, grouped into nine general areas.[45] All critical areas of jail inmate health care are covered. The categories are

- *Section A—Governance and Administration:* Included are eleven standards involving inmate access to health care, the medical authority responsible for health care, medical autonomy (decisions affecting health care of inmates are the sole responsibility of qualified health care professionals), administrative meetings and reports, emergency response plan, continuous quality improvement program, staff communications concerning special needs patients, privacy of health care, inmate death procedures, and an inmate grievance mechanism for health complaints.[46]
- *Section B—Managing a Safe and Healthy Environment:* Four standards concern infection control, environment health and safety, kitchen sanitation, food handler sanitation, and control of ectoparasites (scabies, etc.).[47]
- *Section C—Personnel and Training:* Nine standards addressing credentials, clinical performance enhancement, continuing education for health care professionals, correctional officer training, medication administration training, staffing, inmate workers (trusties), health care liaison, health staff orientation.[48]
- *Section D—Health Care Services and Support:* Five standards in the areas of pharmaceutical operations, medication services to inmates, clinic issues: space, equipment, and supplies, diagnostic services, hospital and specialty care.[49]
- *Section E—Inmate Care and Treatment:* Thirteen standards on health services information, screening: receiving, transfer, and mental health, mental health evaluation, health assessment, oral (dental) care, non-emergency health care requests and services, emergency services, segregated inmates, escort of patients, nursing assessment protocols, continuity of care while incarcerated, inmate discharge planning.[50]
- *Section F—Health Promotion and Disease Prevention:* Five standards addressing health education and promotion for inmates, nutrition and medical diets, exercise, personal hygiene, and tobacco usage.[51]
- *Section G—Special Needs and Services:* Twelve standards concerning special needs treatment plans, chronic disease management, infirmary care, mental health services,

suicide prevention program, intoxication and withdrawal, pregnant inmate care, pregnancy counseling, inmates with substance abuse problems, procedures in the event of sexual assault, aids to impairment including orthoses, prostheses, and care for the terminally ill.[52]

- *Section H—Health Records:* Six standards addressing format and content of health records, confidentiality of health records and information, access to custody information, health records: availability and use, transfer and retention.[53]
- *Section I—Medical–Legal Issues:* Seven standards that deal with use of restraint and seclusion in a correctional facility, emergency psychotropic medication, forensic information, end-of-life decision making, informed consent, inmates' right to refuse treatment, and medical and other research issues.[54]

The NCCHC standards both keep up with the times in corrections as well as address frequently asked questions. Many criminal justice college students and correctional officer trainees ask, for example, whether an inmate who is mentally disordered can be forced to take psychotropic medication or forced medication, that is addressed in NCCHC standard J-1–02, which refers the issue to the laws applicable in the jail's jurisdiction. However, in the discussion section of the standard, the issue is clarified. Even though state laws vary on this subject, the rule is that forced psychotropic medication "is employed only when the inmate is imminently dangerous to self or others due to mental disease or defect."[55]

While improvements have been made in both inmate health care and inmate suicide prevention, inmates do die in jail, NCCHC standard J-A-10 discusses what the mental health and health care staff should examine after the death: appropriateness of clinical care and an examination of procedures, policies, and practices. In the definition section of the standard, two procedures are recommended: a clinical mortality review, which is an assessment of the clinical care provided to the deceased inmate and circumstances leading up to his or her death; and a psychological autopsy, which is a reconstruction of the deceased inmate's life focusing on factors that may have played a role in the inmate's death.[56] These practices can also be valuable in training and revising procedures and staff work practices in good faith efforts to prevent such catastrophic events.

NCCHC standards in conjunction with ACA performance-based standards will continue to improve the quality of confinement and treatment for inmates. Local correctional facilities should model procedures after them, if accreditation is not feasible.

## MEETING STANDARDS: CHALLENGES FOR THE LOCAL JAIL

Some jail staff is of the opinion that meeting anything but state jail standards are a bothersome waste of time. It is true that meeting standards is a lengthy and intricate procedure. If jail staff are new to the process, or are not prepared, the values of accreditation can be lost due to criticism. However, it does have its benefits, most importantly ensuring that inmates receive the best care while confined while receiving treatment from staff that is professional. Jail policies and procedures are based on standards, and they are only as effective if they are adhered to willingly by the rank and file jail staff.

Agency managers, supervisors, and accreditation managers must educate the line staff as to the reasoning of the standards—what their purposes are and the benefits to the jail for following them. One way is to get staff involved in the development of policies and procedures. Marty Drapkin of the Wisconsin Department of Justice Training and Standards Bureau makes these suggestions:[57]

- Staff members should be permitted to conduct research into policy contents such as legal requirements, state and federal laws, case law, state jail standards, ACA and NCCHC standards, etc.
- Staff members should be encouraged to provide input concerning specific items and issues to be included in policies and procedures, including their ideas on how something should be done.
- Staff members should write drafts for policies and procedures, and also critique and make suggestions to policy and procedure drafts.

The backbone of any jail's compliance with standards—whether state, ACA, or NCCHC—is its policies and procedures manual. The standards are incorporated into the policies and the procedures are what the staff does in the jail to make sure that the policy is carried out.

A **policy** is:[58]

- A course of action adopted and pursued by the agency that serves as a guide and determines present and future courses of actions and decisions. Policies guide the agency, and in turn decisions are made affecting the jail. In the accreditation process, policy compliance with standards is necessary.

A **procedure** is:[59]

- The actions, sequential and in detail, that must be carried out to ensure that a policy is implemented; procedures give staff direction.
- For example, if the jail's policy is that "inmates shall be afforded access to the jail law library," the procedure is a general order that specifies the times that an inmate can go, how long he or she is in the law library, etc. Another example would be a policy that inmates will be afforded opportunities for recreation. The procedure would be when the gym operates, when inmates will be taken there, what is available to them in terms of recreation, etc.
- To meet standards, the jail management must realize that compliance is needed and take steps to plan how it is to be done. The following staff and events are essential in planning how to meet standards:
- **Accreditation Manager:** An employee of the agency, sworn or civilian, designated by the agency head or jail administrator to supervise and plan the accreditation activities in the agency, including the jail. This person must have a good working knowledge of jail operations and authority to obtain documentation, assign tasks, etc.[60] This staff member examines standards, obtains the supporting documentation, and keeps the agency up to date with revisions to standards or new standards.
- **Quarterly Documentation:** Each accreditation manager and agency has different methods of meeting an audit. However, many agencies use quarterly documentation for accreditation compliance. Each standard's supporting documentations—logs, reports, etc.—are gathered by quarter.

- **Audit:** An audit is a detailed examination of the agency's policies, procedures, and facility records and/or accounts to see whether they are in compliance with the standards.[61] The state agency or organization granting accreditation will communicate to the accreditation manager when an audit is being scheduled.
- **Audit team:** An audit team is a panel of corrections professionals from outside the agency that conducts the audit and reports their findings both to the agency and to the accrediting organization.
- **Self audit report,** which is an in-house evaluation of all policies, procedures, and operational practices to ascertain whether they are being practiced by staff in a synonymous and uniform manner.[62] The importance of this cannot be underestimated as it may show glaring deficiencies in the jail operations. This is conducted in preparation for the actual audit.
- **Internal mock audit,** which can be termed a "dry" or "practice run." This type of audit is usually conducted by corrections professionals from outside the agency, who work in nearby accredited jails[63] in order to have a more non-partisan, objective type view of the jail's policies and procedures as they relate to the standards. Input from these outside professionals is invaluable, and in a progressive agency are very much appreciated.
- **Plan of action:** If a standard is found to be in non-compliance, the action steps that are taken to correct the deficiency are called the plan of action.

A thorough audit can take several days and involves a facility inspection, review of the documentation on file, and interviews with staff members and

Staff should be familiar with their jail policies and procedures that are in accordance with jail standards.

Photo reprinted with permission, American Correctional Association.

inmates. An audit team can be very inquisitive and may ask for more than the documentation on file. The best guide for an audit team is the jail policies and procedures manual. A good policy and procedures manual will contain general orders or standard operating procedures (SOPs) that guide the jail staff in operations that are in compliance with the standards. Each procedure should have applicable standards for that policy listed for easy reference. All jail staff should be issued a manual, be instructed in how policies and procedures are set up, and have access to the applicable standards for further clarification. In some of the larger jails, the amount of SOPs are so numerous, that the SOPs are put in a computer networking for viewing or placed on a CD-ROM disk for staff distribution.

## SUMMARY

Jail standards are designed for the optimal operational benefit of jails, because when followed they provide the best guidance from up-to-date correctional practices, court decisions, etc. Jail standards originated from corrections reformers in the 1870s, and later in the mid-twentieth century. Most states have some version of jail standards and inspection authority to ensure compliance. Some jails only have standards with voluntary compliance. Many state jail standards are overseen by the state department of corrections.

In recent years, jail standards have been revolutionized by the ACA, whose standards are performance based requiring documentation that show actual conditions and staff practices. The NCCHC has made great strides in improving jail health care standards first promulgated by the ACA in the 1970s. To supplement their standards, NCCHC has published position statements on timely jail health care issues.

The process of standards accreditation is intricate and detailed, involving several types of audits, and documentation to show that the standard is being followed. Staff should be involved in policy development based on standards and as a result will see standards as necessary and beneficial and not as a hindrance.

## REVIEW QUESTIONS

1. What is a jail standard?
2. Discuss the origins of jail standards.
3. Name and discuss five Principles from the 1870 National Prison Congress.
4. How has jail standards changed in recent years?
5. Discuss Alexander's Bill of Rights for Inmates.
6. Name and discuss the seven elements of ACA's Performance-Based Standards.
7. What is the importance of the NCCHC standards?
8. Discuss three NCCHC Position statements.
9. Why don't some sheriffs or jail administrators seek ACA or NCCHC accreditation?
10. Discuss the basic parts of the accreditation process in a jail, including staffing.

## TERMS TO KNOW

accreditation
accreditation manager
audit
audit team
Declaration of Principles
expected practices
goal statement
internal mock audit
jail standard
mandatory standards/expected practices
outcome measure
plan of action
policy
procedure
process indicators
protocol(s)
quarterly documentation
self audit report
triple crown certification

# ENDNOTES

1. *Performance-Based Standards for Adult Local Detention Facilities, 4th Edition* (Lanham, MD: American Correctional Association, 2004), p. 185.
2. Ibid., p. 12.
3. Daniel Evans, "Jail Standards," *Jail Managers Bulletin,* 2 (11) (1991): 2.
4. Ibid., p. 2.
5. *Performance-Based Standards,* pp. iii–ix.
6. Michael Pinson, "Jails: Accreditation is Worth the Effort," *Corrections Today* (December 1996): 73.
7. Ibid.
8. Ibid.
9. John Howard, "The State of the Prisons, 1777," in *Penology: The Evolution of Corrections in America,* ed. George G. Killer and Paul F. Cromwell, Jr. (St. Paul: West, 1973).
10. Ibid., pp. 6–11.
11. Julie N. Tucker, ed., *The American Prison: from the beginning . . . A Pictorial History* (Lanham, MD: American Correctional Association, 1983), pp. 66–70.
12. Ibid., pp. 71, 72.
13. Paul W. Keve, *Measuring Excellence: The History of Correctional Standards and Accreditation* (Lanham, MD: American Correctional Association, 1996), p. 6.
14. Ibid.
15. William C. Collins, *Correctional Law for the Correctional Officers 4th Edition* (Lanham, MD: American Correctional Association, 2004), pp. 12, 13.
16. John W. Roberts, *Reform and Retribution: An Illustrated History of American Prisons* (Lanham, MD: American Correctional Association, 1997), p. 193.
17. Keve, *Measuring Excellence,* p. 7.
18. Roberts, *Reform and Retribution,* p. 219.
19. Ibid.
20. Keve, *Measuring Excellence,* pp. 56, 57.
21. National Commission on Correctional Health Care, http://www.ncchc.org
22. Keve, *Measuring Excellence,* p. 57.
23. Jeffrey Washington, "ACA's Standards: Tailoring the Process to Fit Small Jails," *Corrections Today* (December 1988), pp. 42, 43.
24. Keve, *Measuring Excellence,* pp. 57, 58.
25. *Performanbce Based Standards,* p. x.
26. Keve, *Measuring Excellence,* pp. 58, 59.
27. Illinois Department of Corrections, *Illinois County Jail Standards* (Springfield, III: Department of Corrections, 2004), pp. 2, 52, 56–58.
28. Ibid., p. 2.
29. National Institute of Corrections, http://www.nicic.org/StateCorrectionsStatistics/AL.htm
30. *National Jail and Adult Detention Directory, 2002–2004* (Lanham, MD: American Correctional Association, 2002), p. 93.
31. Rules of the Tennessee Corrections Institute: *Correctional Facilities Inspection,* Chapter 1400–1: Minimum Standards for Local Correctional Facilities, November 2004, (Revised).
32. Ibid., pp. 8, 21–23.
33. Michelle Gaseau, "Raising the Bar: Jails Work Toward a Higher Standard," *corrections.com,* April 4, 2004, http://database.corrections.com/news/results2_new.asp?ID-10154 (accessed April 4, 2004).
34. Ibid.
35. *Performance-Based Standards,* pp. xxix, xxx.
36. Gaseau, "Raising the Bar."
37. *Performance-Based Standards,* pp. iii–ix.
38. Ibid., p. 37.
39. Ibid., pp. 15, 31, 41.
40. Ibid., pp. xix, xxviii.
41. *Standards for Health Services in Jails, 2003* (Chicago: National Commission on Correctional Health Care, 2003), p. vii.
42. Ibid., pp. xi, 187–189, 193, 204, 208, 209, 214, 215, 219, 224.
43. Ibid., p. viii.
44. Ibid., p. xi.
45. Ibid., p. viii.
46. Ibid., pp. 1, 3, 5.
47. Ibid., pp. 21, 29.
48. Ibid., p. 31.
49. Ibid., p. 45.
50. Ibid., p. 55.
51. Ibid., p. 79.
52. Ibid., p. 89.
53. *Standards for Health Care,* p. 115.
54. *Standards for Health Care,* p. 123.
55. *Standards for Health Care,* p. 127.
56. *Standards for Health Care,* p. 17.
57. Marty Drapkin, "Involving Jail Staff Members in Policies and Procedures Development," *American Jails* (November–December 2002): 36.
58. *Performance Based Standards,* p. 182.
59. Ibid.
60. Ibid., p. 171.
61. Ibid., p. 172.
62. Pinson, "Accreditation is Worth the Effort," p. 73.
63. Ibid.

## REFERENCES


Collins, William C. *Correctional Law for the Correctional Officer, 4th Edition.* Lanham, MD: American Correctional Association, 2004.

Drapkin, Marty. "Involving Jail Staff Members in Policies and Procedures Development." *American Jails,* November–December 2002, 35–38.

Evans, Daniel, "Jail Standards," *Jail Managers Bulletin* (American Jail Association) 2 (11) (1991).

Gaseau, Michelle. "Raising the Bar: Jails Work Toward a Higher Standard," *corrections.com,* April 4, 2004, http://database.corrections.com/news/results2_new.asp ?ID-10154.

Howard, John. *"The State of the Prisons, 1777."* In *Penology: The Evolution of Corrections in America,* ed. George G. Killinger and Paul F. Cromwell, Jr., 5–11. St. Paul: West, 1973.

Illinois Department of Corrections, *Illinois County Jail Standards.* Springfield, Ill: Department of Corrections, October 1, 2004.

Keve, Paul A. *Measuring Excellence: The History of Correctional Standards and Accreditation.* Lanham, MD: American Correctional Association, 1996.

Miller and Walter, *Detention and Corrections Caselaw Catalog, 16th Edition.* Gettysburg, PA: CRS Inc., 2004.

*National Jail and Adult Detention Directory, 2002–2004.* Lanham, MD: American Correctional Association, 2002.

National Commission on Correctional Health Care: http://www.ncchc.org

National Institute of Corrections: http://ww.nicic.org/StateCorrectionsStatistics/AL.htm

*Performance-Based Standards for Adult Local Detention Facilities: 4th Edition.* Lanham, MD: American Correctional Association, 2004.

Pinson, Michael. "Jails: Accreditation is Worth the Effort." *Corrections Today,* December 1996, 72–75.

Roberts, John W. *Reform and Retribution: An Illustrated History of American Prisons.* Lanham, MD: American Correctional Association, 1997.

*Standards for Health Services in Jails, 2003.* Chicago: National Commission on Correctional Health Care, 2003.

Tennessee Corrections Institute: *Rules: Correctional Facilities Inspection, Chapter 1400–1: Minimum Standards for Local Correctional Facilities,* November 2004 (Revised).

Tucker, Julie N., ed. *The American Prison: from the beginning . . . A Pictorial History.* Lanham, MD: American Correctional Association, 1983.

Washington, Jeffrey. "ACA Standards: Tailoring the Process to Fit Small Jails." *Corrections Today,* December 1988, 42–43.

# 11 JAILS AND COMMUNITY CORRECTIONS

***Objectives of chapter***

The student will:

- Learn an overview of the philosophy and goals of jail community corrections programs
- Describe the various community corrections programs and the agencies that support them
- Gain insight into the security concerns of community corrections programs including the screening of offenders and security methods employed by the jail staff

One of the basic goals of corrections, whether at the federal, state, or local level, is the effort to *change* the offender—from a lawbreaking person to a law-abiding citizen. At the local level, many jails engage in programs that afford the jail inmate opportunities to get out of jail—and stay out. These programs are very beneficial to the jail system, the community, and the inmate. The jail collects money from inmates participating in certain types of programs, space is made more available inside the jail, the community benefits by employing new and sometimes very skillful workers, and the inmate can re-enter his or her community and family situation on a positive note.

Jail community corrections programs are numerous and interact with many local agencies such as the courts and local government service agencies and community organizations. Additionally, security is a primary concern. Jail inmates entering the community as part of community corrections programs are still lawbreakers; the temptations to misbehave and slip back into criminal old habits are still there. As a result, jail community corrections staff must be vigilant and innovative when checking offenders in the community.

## JAIL COMMUNITY CORRECTIONS: PHILOSOPHY AND GOALS

Jail community corrections programs try, at the local level, to reintegrate low-risk jail offenders back into their communities. The focus of inmates being released from incarceration and "back to the streets" has primarily involved inmates being released from federal and state prisons.

The Bureau of Justice Statistics reported that approximately 592,000 state prison inmates were released into the community in 2001 after serving time, and that at a minimum, 95 percent of state prison inmates will be released at some point, and almost 80 percent will be released to supervision by parole.[1] The aforementioned figures do not count the number of federal and local jail inmates. In 2000, media attention began to focus on the problem of criminals returning to the streets. In the December 27, 2000 issue of the *USA Today*, it was reported that in 2001, a record high of 585,000 felons would be released from state and federal prisons. This figure represents three times the number of felons being released 20 years previously in 1980. This trend reportedly began in 1996, when the number of inmates being released from prison was over 500,000. Authorities did predict at that time that this trend would continue over the course of the next several years, and it did.[2]

Recently, inmates being released from prison has annually stayed over the 600,000 mark. According to the Bureau of Justice Statistics, the following releases were reported from state *and* federal prisons:[3]

- 2000: 604,858
- 2003: 656,384
- 2004: 672,202

The releases from local jails are not that clearly reported. Jails vary in size and also the rates of release of inmates. Where a large jail may release into the community several thousand inmates per year, a small jail may release a fraction of that number. Whether it is a release from prison or jail, corrections' hope is that inmates have "learned their lesson" and will stay out.

Community corrections can also be termed "preparation for release." While some jail inmates are released from doing time because their sentences are served, not all are involved in community corrections programs. Jail programs such as substance abuse, education, and vocational skills inside the jail are generally attended by inmates on a voluntary basis. If the inmate is fortunate enough to connect with an organization in the community to continue the rehabilitative process, then he or she has a chance at staying crime free. An example would be a jail volunteer who is tutoring the inmate in GED development. When the inmate gets out, the volunteer may continue contact with the inmate and assist him or her in enrolling in a local high school adult education program.

Community corrections programs take this concept a step further. Organized sections in the local corrections agency can structure and supervise offender participation in community corrections programs and allow the inmate to actually go out into the community for employment and program participation. By doing so, the inmate gets a chance to prove him or herself on the outside.

## Restorative Justice

Historically, the criminal justice system has followed these concepts in dealing with offenders:[4]

- A crime is a violation of the law and against the state.
- What specific laws have been broken?
- Who broke the law?

- A crime or violation creates guilt.
- The criminal justice system is required to determine guilt and impose a harsh, painful punishment.
- The central focus of the criminal justice system is that the offender, by violating the law, gets what he or she deserves.

The traditional criminal justice system concerns itself with punishment, and in some cases, the more harsh the better.

For one to understand what community corrections programs are trying to accomplish, one must understand the underlying philosophy of community corrections—the concept of **restorative justice.** This concept takes the view that a crime violates people and interpersonal relationships, it creates obligations by the offender, and the fundamental obligation is for the offender to right the wrong that he or she has done.[5]

Simplistically, restorative justice takes these views, which differ from the traditional criminal justice approach:[6]

- A crime or violation is a violation against people and relationships.
- Crimes create obligations to be repaid on the part of the offender.
- The administration of justice involves victims, offenders, and the community all working to "put things right."
- The central focus is on meeting victims' needs and the offender taking the responsibility for repairing the harm that he or she (the offender) has committed.
- Who has been hurt by the offender?
- What are their (offenders) needs?
- Whose obligations are these?

Restorative justice, through the offender being involved in community corrections programs, focuses on the offender becoming a better person by getting a "handle" on the problems that resulted in criminal behavior. Part of this process is to make amends to the victim and the community that he or she has wronged.

The concerns of the community when discussing the approximately half a million plus offenders being released every year can be addressed by restorative justice. The following problems predicted several years ago by law enforcement and health officials include:[7]

- *Increasing crime rates:* Criminals, especially felons, being released into communities that have enjoyed low crime rates are a concern.
- *Negative social consequences:* Returning criminals are faced with domestic family situations when they try to reconnect with spouses, significant others, parents, siblings, and children. After being incarcerated, financial and emotional hardships as well as dysfunctional relationships result. The "homecoming" of the offender may not be a smooth one. Many families move on with their lives, and the offender may have nowhere to live. As a result, the number of ex-offenders who find themselves homeless or living in shelters may increase, or the number getting food and clothing from charitable organizations increases.

The problems of inmates re-entering the community are serious, according to the Re-Entry Policy Council, an organization that works to promote and facilitate the safe and successful return of offenders into their communities. The Council was established by the Council of State Governments and is comprised of 100 key leaders in communities, state, federal, and local governments, state lawmakers' criminal justice policy makers, criminal justice practitioners, employment services officials, workforce developers, housing providers, and housing officials. Also represented are health, mental health, and substance abuse treatment staff, victim advocates, formerly incarcerated offenders and their families, and members of the clergy and those working in faith-based facilities.

In its Executive Summary, it is noted that "virtually every person incarcerated in a jail in this country—and 97 percent of those incarcerated in prisons—will eventually be released." This results in "nearly 650,000 people being released from prisons and over 7 million different individuals being released from jails in this country each year."*

The Council notes the following issues in the examination of offenders re-entering the community:*

- Approximately two of every three people released from prison are re-arrested within the first three years after being released.
- The number of offenders re-entering the community in the past two decades has increased four times, and they have not been adequately prepared to successfully reintegrate into society.
- Three quarters of offenders being released from prisons have a history of drug and/or alcohol abuse, and two thirds do not have a high school diploma.
- Vocationally, almost half of offenders being released from jail earned less than $600.00 per month immediately prior to their incarceration. The chances for gainful employment decrease once they incur a criminal record.
- Concerning mental/physical health, more than one third of jail inmates report that they have some type of physical or mental disability; the rate of inmates with serious metal illness is approximately three to four times the rate of mental illness in the nonincarcerated general population.
- Fifty-five percent of adult offenders re-entering the community have children under age 18, and incarcerated parents owe an average debt of over $20,000 upon release.

*Data from Esther Griswold, Jessica Pearson and Lanae Davis, *Testing a Modification Process for Incarcerated Parents*, Denver, CO: Center For Policy Research, pp. 11–12.

**FIGURE 11-1** The Problem of Inmate Re-Entry[8]

- *Increased load on public health and social services:* Many offenders being released have HIV infection, tuberculosis, hepatitis C, or substance-abuse-related problems.

Community corrections programs address the well-known causes of criminality: substance abuse, lack of education, and criminal thinking. Also addressed are where in the community the offender can go to seek help with medical problems, assistance for substance abuse problems, and mental health counseling.

Certain basic principles or tenets must be in place for community corrections programs to be effective both at the state and local levels. Most of the public thinks that wrongdoers belong in jails and prisons and are uninformed about community corrections programs. According to Dennis S. Schrantz, executive director of Michigan's Office of Community Corrections, these five tenets are:[9]

- *Decentralization:* Local governments are given the authority to administer community corrections programs. The state can provide guidelines for policy development, and the authority can be through state statutes and acts allowing sheriffs and local jails to permit certain offenders to participate in community corrections programs such as work release and work programs.
- *Linking overcrowding in jails and prisons:* Community corrections programs if implemented properly can relieve overcrowding in jails by housing low-risk and carefully screened offenders in such housing as work release dormitories or separate facilities. By doing so, cells are made available for more serious offenders. Another option is to have pretrial release options where some offenders can be released pending court. In Michigan, incentives are offered by the state to local jails; a jail reimbursement program is in place that provides funding to local jails holding felons with sentences of 12 months or more. A condition exists known as **system crowding,** where the courts, probation offices, public defender offices, district attorneys, police agencies, and jails all have more offenders than they have the capacity to handle.
- *Fiscal responsibility:* Tax dollars cannot be misspent, especially concerning community corrections offenders. Planning is a must, often with the help of outside consultants. Some community corrections programs, such as work release, actually save money due to offenders paying for their room and board.
- *Effective decision making:* Decisions must be made with as much information as possible about community corrections using sound policies based on data about the offenders to be placed in community corrections programs, as well as tools to evaluate the programs' effectiveness. For example, in Michigan, some communities were in the process of developing programs to deal with hard-core offender drug addictions. Their policies changed when data revealed that the primary addiction of the target population was alcohol.
- *Public education:* Jurisdictions that establish community corrections programs must be prepared to explain the philosophy, goals, and benefits of such programs to the general population, who may not understand what community corrections is, perhaps as a result of the "get tough" approaches to crime and offenders from politicians. Studies do indicate that once the general public is aware of the costs associated with incarceration, operating jails, and implementing programs that save money by motivating offenders to stay crime free, many are more likely to support community corrections.

Community corrections initiatives are not a new phenomenon. As far back as 1973, the state of Minnesota enacted its Community Corrections Act, which when combined with sentencing guidelines enables jurisdictions to use more appropriate intermediate sanctions for low-risk, less serious offenders, such as probation, restitution, community service, and local jail sentences. Minnesota incorporates annual funding to local jurisdictions to establish and operate community corrections programs tailored for their needs. The goal of this system is to reserve state prison cells for serious offenders.[10]

Community corrections involve both the removal of the sentenced jail inmate from the confines and structure of a secure facility to the outside: the "street." It also involves another type of sentenced offender—those who are not sentenced to jail time, but may have to perform community service, labor, work off fines, or do their time on weekends or at home through electronic incarceration. The jail community corrections staff must be professionally flexible enough to deal with these various types of offenders. The most important goal of community corrections is not so much the rehabilitation of the weekend offender or the person performing community service, but targeting the serious problems of the offenders in structured, regulated programs such as work release and electronic incarceration.

While much has been written and documented about community corrections, the term **community corrections** simply means several types of programs that manage and supervise offenders in the outside community instead of within the secure confines of a jail.[11] These programs include work release, weekend confinement, home electronic incarceration, community service, fines options programs, and labor programs.

Another concise definition of community corrections is the offering of a variety of human services and employment opportunities to offenders in natural, noninstitutional settings instead of jail, in order to facilitate the offender's reintegration back to the community as a law-abiding citizen. The offender reintegrates with a "grip" on the problems that caused criminal behavior. The services will be identified, developed, and administered by members of the community in which the offender is being served, or more importantly will be relocating to. Corrections professionals (the jail community corrections staff) will provide assistance in the selection of low-risk, appropriate offenders, training, and acting as liaison between the community program and the jail.[12]

In breaking this definition down, some basics in community corrections emerge. A variety of human services can involve many agencies in the community that could help offenders, such as Alcoholics Anonymous (AA), Narcotics Anonymous (NA), the local school board/adult education, community mental health services, etc. The setting for this involvement is natural—out in the community—like everyday citizens, and not artificial, such as in a jail classroom. This is a nonrestrictive environment, where correctional officers are not present.

The services, whether they are substance abuse, educational, or vocational, are administered by people in the community in which the offender will be released to and may be residing in, either alone or with family. The purpose here is to give the offender resources in the community that he or she can turn to in times of need, crisis, or impending relapse. For example, many work release programs require offenders with substance abuse problems to go to local AA or NA groups, often with a sponsor who has been cleared to come into the work release center to work with the offender.

Members of the community, such as recovering substance abusers in AA and NA, GED tutors, or volunteers, may be involved after proper training by the community corrections staff. These are everyday citizens who can show the offender that they can get their lives turned around. Other agencies, such as substance abuse services, school district educators, etc., can also work with the offenders.

Finally, the jail community corrections staffs work with community resources by selecting low-risk offenders with nonserious crimes, training community agency staff and volunteers, and acting as a liaison between them, the offender and the jail community corrections unit. Employers are also included, as they are briefed fully about work release, etc., when they hire an offender. Training is important, as the community corrections staffs deal with inmates on a daily basis. As a rule, employers, community agency staff, and volunteers must be "clued in" as to the type of person (inmates) that they will be dealing with.

POINT OF VIEW

## Community Corrections

***Blake Poindexter***
Director, Wells County (Indiana)
Community Corrections Department

The face of local corrections has changed significantly in the past 20 years. The development of technology, risk assessment tools, and a greater understanding of the criminal offender have caused local communities to see that containment in jails and prisons does not work effectively on certain offender populations. I started in 1990 in a new concept in Indiana. It was called community corrections.

I was hired as the first full-time field officer in 1990 and then became the first full-time director in 1993. The reason our county started this department was very simple; we ran out of space in our local jails and the state prison system. So our state legislators asked for a better local solution, hence the creation of community corrections on a statewide level. Our first programs were Electronic Monitoring Home Detention and Community Service Restitution.

In trying to explain what and where community corrections fits in the criminal justice system, I have always said we are parallel to probation, only more intensive, and to the jail. The marvel of community corrections is that these offenders serve their court-issued sentence while living at home and obtaining or maintaining employment. This allows for the ability to get needed services referred for drug and alcohol addictions or other mental or medical deficiencies. The last 14 years have proven that local community corrections programs can successfully and more efficiently deal with the certain populations that are nonviolent.

It was in 1991 that I asked the question of how we could help modernize our county Work Release Program. My first observations were that the jail commander and jail staff were already stretched beyond their duties. We had difficulties verifying (offender) work schedules and their (offenders') whereabouts. I then thought, why could we not put ankle transmitters on this group of offenders like we do with Electronic Monitoring Home Detention offenders? This allowed one community corrections officer to spot check and track work release inmates on their way to and from work and at the work site. This also made a better relationship for their employers and the court system. We also identified a level of education issue during this process.

I did some interviews with our offenders and inmates. I found an alarming consistency of low education levels achieved that averaged from junior high school to those who never completed high school. This is where we did our first collaboration effort outside of the criminal justice system. I worked with our local school system, which coordinated our county's adult education program. In the summer of 1995, we established the first in-house General Education Diploma (GED) program. This was the start of evaluating our local response to the criminal offender.

In our first five years, we had developed new programs and identified many behavioral and environmental issues that contributed to these individuals. The other thing we noticed was that this behavior and other issues were being handed down to our offenders' children. These children started to show up in the court system as a result of expulsion from school or with an addictions issue that led to other criminal activities, like property destruction and theft crimes.

In the years since, we have developed a very communicative relationship with all local law enforcement agencies, the welfare department, courts, and the probation department. We are also having an open dialog with mental health agencies, churches, business leaders, schools, and family service providers.

I often tell people that we have a lot of help thanks to technological advancement, but we also have developed a new technology including Risk Assessment and behavioral systems that analyze what these offenders have as a risk to themselves and the community. By evaluating the causes of "Why" they do the same repeated mistakes, we found the fact that many of the issues can be traced to the cognitive mistakes or a large part to core decision-making errors. Many times during an intake for a program, my staff and I have heard that "I guess I really didn't think before I did it!" This has brought about our plans to launch a new program that is called "Thinking for a Change," which is being pursued by the Indiana Department of Corrections.

Some other areas of technology have been introduced for the improvement of monitoring offenders, such as equipment that allows us to observe offenders in their homes for the use of alcohol, or the employment of satellite monitoring so that we can have a real-time accounting of offenders. The innovations of computers in the office and in the field have aided in the efficiency of officers and case mangers to work in a timely manner. This gives staff a continuous stream of information that allows adjustment of the incarceration and the treatment plan for each individual offender.

This is not a perfect system that the courts and the community have implemented, but it is an ongoing process and requires the support of all who are involved in the criminal justice system. We must always remember that we do have some limitations as to what can be done, but this should never stop us from thinking outside of what is currently being attempted. It has been this kind of unconventional thinking that we in Wells County and the State of Indiana have been able to achieve the level of success in alternative sentencing that we see today.

Courtesy: Blake Poindexter, Director, Wells County (Indiana) Community Corrections Department.

## Main Objectives of Community Corrections

While much as been published in correctional literature about community corrections, the simple, main goals of any community corrections programs, especially at the jail level, are punishment of the offender, cost savings to the local correctional agency and taxpayers, and the successful reintegration of the offender to the community.[13]

### *Punishment*

To the average citizen, an offender participating in a community corrections program may not appear to be punishment. To some, it may look like the criminal is getting off easy. Public relations—staff getting out and speaking to community organizations and civic groups—is a priority. What is important to be stressed is that offenders, while in the community, have been screened and selected carefully. Also important is the public knowing that correctional staff will be checking offenders in the community, whether it is at the workplace or at home, in cases of electronic monitoring.

Advocates of community corrections, such as local corrections or sheriff's personnel who are in contact with the public, are frequently asked to explain how a criminal who is in a community corrections program is being punished. To the outside observer, an offender who is in a jail work release program may be viewed as getting a lenient form of punishment. Also, this offender and one who is on electronic incarceration at home could be viewed as subverting the creditability of the law.[14]

Offenders placed by the courts or through a jail screening process *are* being punished, but not in the traditional sense. Offenders under community supervision are not free to come and go as they please, are not free to do as they wish, and must be held accountable for their actions. Also, they may have special conditions placed on them that the staff member supervising them may think are prudent. Many of the security limitations and restrictions that they must adhere to are aspects of life that the ordinary citizen takes for granted. More importantly if any of these restrictions are violated, the offender can be revoked from the program, the court can be notified, and the offender can be incarcerated. The threat of being returned to jail is constantly over the offender's head.[15]

The following lists of restrictions that are placed on offenders in jail community corrections programs clearly illustrate that the offenders are not "free."[16]

- *Nightly curfews:* Offenders on home electronic incarceration must be at home by a certain time, such as 10 P.M., for example.
- *Weekend lockup:* Offender is sentenced to serve time in the local jails on weekends until his sentence is satisfied.
- *Weekly drug/alcohol testing:* The offender is subject to random, unannounced tests of urine for drug usage. Also, the offenders' breath can be tested to ascertain if they have been drinking alcoholic beverages. Programs have rules against the usage of illegal drugs and alcohol.
- *Reporting to community corrections staff* (monthly, weekly, or at the staff's discretion): Offenders on community corrections programs are subject to be called in to meet with the staff at any time, from a job site, or from home in cases of home incarceration.
- *Restrictions on travel, associations, living situations, and romantic involvements:* Offenders under the supervision of a probation officer and not jail community corrections staff may be restricted on travel out of the jurisdiction of supervision, who they can live with because of possible criminal ties or behavior, etc. Offenders under jail community corrections supervision are also restricted on routes of travel, leaving the work site, the site of a furlough or pass, or the home under certain conditions of electronic incarceration, etc.
- *Financial penalties and restitution:* Offenders may be ordered by the court or be directed by the jail community corrections staff to pay court costs, pay fines, and make restitution to the victim. In a jail work release program, the offender's wages can be taken by the staff and these costs deducted.
- *Unpaid community service:* Offenders may be required to perform community service per court order as part of their sentence and under the instructions and supervision of the jail community service staff.
- *Regular submission to searches:* Offenders in community corrections programs are subject to search upon returning to the jail from the community, including what belongings they have with them, and submitting to a breath test for alcohol use and/or a urine test for illegal drug usage; for practical purposes, both are considered searches. Also, their living units—cells, bunks, or rooms—are subject to search by correctional staff.
- *Unannounced visits from correctional staff:* Offenders can be visited at their job sites if on work release, or at their homes if on electronic incarceration. Offenders on electronic incarceration can also be visited in their homes by correctional staff.
- *Employer reporting to the community corrections staff an offender's work progress:* Offenders on work release are required to maintain a job in good standing. This

involves the employer communicating to the jail community corrections staff the job performance (or lack thereof) of the offender.

- *Required attendance at treatment and rehabilitation programs:* As part of their involvement in a jail community corrections program, offenders may be required to attend one or more programs such as AA, NA, community substance abuse treatment, life skills, etc.

## Cost Savings

The financial advantages of community corrections are clear. It is less expensive to maintain custody of an offender housed or participating in a community corrections program than to house him or her inside the local jail. Also, if the offender is allowed to go into the community, he or she spends money in the community as a purchaser of good and services. Finally, some community corrections programs "get work" out of the offender, instead of the local government having to hire someone to perform the same tasks.

In addition, offenders in community corrections programs such as work release are required to pay room and board fees to the jail, pay court costs, make restitution to victims, and maintain a financial lifeline to dependents. Offenders in home electronic incarceration programs are generally charged a fee for the lease of the equipment. All of these financial requirements serve to remind offenders that committing crimes have financial obligations, as well as off setting the agency's expenses in administering the programs.

Community corrections programs in whatever form all save money by reducing of the number of inmates incarcerated in the local jail. If low-risk offenders are sentenced to community corrections programs, jail cell space is reserved for the more serious type of offender. For example, the Bureau of Justice Statistics reported that at midyear 2005, jails in the United States held a total of 819,434 inmates. The number being held in jail totaled 747,529, while 71,905 offenders were supervised outside a jail facility in community corrections programs. This figure represents almost 10 percent of the total of jail inmates who are not confined under increased security and do not all have to be fed and provided for around the clock.[17]

Community corrections save jurisdictions money. Correctional systems in the United States spend approximately $15,000 to $25,000 per inmate per year in prisons. Jail costs are about half that amount or more. Traditional probation may cost anywhere from $500 to $1,000 per year, and intensive or special community corrections programs may cost about three times as much; from $1,500 to $3,000 per offender per year.[18] No matter how it is looked at, putting an offender into a community corrections program is always cheaper than putting him or her in jail.

## Successful Reintegration

Reintegration along with restorative justice is at the core of community corrections. Almost all community corrections programs offered by jail systems reference the benefits of rehabilitation. While these programs place the offender under some types of control and surveillance, they incorporate other strategies to permit the offender to both maintain ties to the community and develop new ones to facilitate a crime-free, positive lifestyle. These strategies are known as **reintegration.**[19]

The strategies of reintegration focus on several areas in offenders' lives, namely work, family, and social connections. To work these strategies, programs are **graduated release** in nature, where the offender is eased into the community and is spared the "culture shock" or impact of an abrupt transition from being incarcerated in the jail to life on the outside.[20]

Work, family, and social connections are central to the offender staying crime free. Logically, if an offender has a legitimate trade or vocation, he or she can make a decent living and support a family. Family strife can be decreased significantly if the offender is legitimately assisting with the basic necessities of housing, food, shelter, paying the bills, etc.

Social connections include the interaction with law-abiding citizens, who can serve as positive role models and exert positive influences. Many offenders for the first time in their lives may be exposed to a positive, mature role model who may show them proper ways to deal with problems.

Social connections can also include people in rehabilitative programs, such as AA and NA, tutors, church members, etc. In many pre-release programs, social connections are established with citizens who are involved in AA or NA. These recovering substance abusers can serve to sponsor an offender into a neighborhood AA or NA group. The jail community corrections staff can work with both the offender and the citizen by granting the offender permission to attend AA or NA meetings in the community with the help of a citizen sponsor.

Meeting the objectives of reintegration requires more than just clearing the offender to walk out of the jail and go to a job. In order to achieve reintegration, jail community corrections programs must meet the following requirements:[21]

- *Being located and having offenders interact within a "meaningful community."* A **meaningful community** is a community that can meet the offender's needs—such as employment, programs to combat problems (such as substance abuse, etc.), and a stable home environment. The goal is to be living and working in a community that is appropriate to maintaining a crime-free lifestyle. For example, a jail offender with a drinking problem who has not been able to keep a job should be returning to a community that has job opportunities, substance abuse self-help and recovery programs, and suitable housing for him and his family.
- *Authorized to leave the jail community corrections program and go into a nonsupervised environment.* A **nonsupervised environment** is an environment with minimal physical restrictions, such as staying at home if on home detention, or being confined to a job site. It also means minimal staff surveillance. The offender is on his or her own.
- *The availability of community-based education, training, counseling, and support services.* As part of the meaningful community, these services can be coordinated with the jail community corrections staff as part of correctional agencies or be noncorrectional such as private or public programs.
- *The offender has opportunities to assume the roles of law-abiding citizen, family member, student, or employee.* If the offender can function within these social roles, then he or she has taken a big step in the road to becoming a law-abiding citizen. This change is not automatic, and requires the ongoing guidance of jail community corrections staff.
- *The offender has opportunities for personal growth and change.* In any pre-release type program, the offender is tested. For example, an offender in a work release

program is employed in a department store. The rules of the program state that offenders are not permitted to have personal visitors at the job site. However, his girlfriend walks into the store and asks him to take a break and go out and sit in her car for a while. The test for him is should he or shouldn't he? Another offender has a drinking problem and is on a construction site. At lunchtime, a coworker takes out a six pack of cold beer and offers one to the offender. He says to the offender that no one will know. The offender knows that the ingestion of alcoholic beverages is against the work release program rules and that he is subject to random breath tests. The test is should he drink the beer or pass it up? There are other situations that constantly pit the offender against the lure of criminal behavior and being a law-abiding participant who follows the rules of the program. Jail community corrections staff are very familiar with these situations, ranging from leaving the job site, visiting friends (some who may be engaged in criminal activity), using drugs, drinking alcohol, stealing money and property, not performing job tasks and being lazy, or the most serious test—walking off the assigned job area and by doing so, escaping. Every time the offender walks out the facility door to go to work, there is a risk of escape.

## TYPES OF LOCAL JAIL COMMUNITY CORRECTIONS PROGRAMS

Recent statistics from the U.S. Bureau of Justice Statistics indicate that on any one day, approximately one half of the jail population in the United States is incarcerated as a result of failed re-entry into the community. Jails are important in any attack on this very serious problem. Jails are the initial point of entry into the correctional system as well as the point of release and return to the community. Also, jails are providing more community-based programs for inmates as alternatives for jail incarceration as well as assessing and intervening concerning offender's needs, problems, and behavior.[22]

Throughout the United States, there are a variety of community corrections programs that are operated by local correctional authorities in conjunction with local rehabilitative agencies. The main types of programs are:

- Work Release
- Home Detention/Electronic Monitoring
- Day Reporting Center Programs
- Weekend Confinement
- Community Service
- Community Offender Labor Programs
- Boot Camps

### Work Release

Probably the most well known type of community corrections program is **Work Release.** It is defined as a temporary release program in which the offender resides in the community corrections facility and is authorized to work, study, or visit in the community. Offenders work for the prevailing minimum wage under the same working conditions as free citizens. Also, offenders are supervised by civilians, work with civilians, and must meet the same requirements for the job as civilians do.[23]

The focal point of any offender work release program is to instill in the offender a sense of responsibility by functioning as a normal citizen, meeting obligations, and dealing with serious issues *without* resorting to criminal behavior. Offenders in work release, under staff guidance and limited supervision, must:[24]

- Locate or find employment.
- Arrange for transportation to and from the job location.
- Turn in their paychecks to the jail community corrections staff so deductions can be made for room and board, support of dependents, restitutions, fines, court costs, etc. Generally, 5–10 percent of an offender's pay is charged for room and board, but this varies among jurisdictions.
- Agree to save money for final release. Monies from their accounts may be withdrawn for legitimate expenses such as toiletries, clothes, and necessary personal items.

In keeping with the learning of mature responsibility, offenders are required in many programs to work out a job schedule with the staff, an approved means of transportation, and inform the staff if any problems are encountered on the job, such as conflicts with the supervisors, conflicts with the other employees, injuries, etc. Offenders are not permitted to change jobs or work schedules without the permission of staff. However, offenders on work release may complain to the staff that employers are paying less per hour to them because they are "convicts" or "jailbirds," and as a result are not worthy of the same wages as other employees. In such cases the staff will advise the offender to quit in a mature way, giving ample notice, and seek more gainful employment. In most community corrections centers, that type of employer will not be used again to employ offenders.

Another problem in work release concerning the employer is how the offenders are used on the job site. If the employer uses offenders in demeaning ways because they are criminals, then that employer should not have any dealings with the work release center. Also, there occurs in some cases a "twinge of conscience" with some offenders who wish to leave a job because the job may be demeaning to his or her job skills and abilities. In one work release center, an offender who was a certified master auto mechanic returned to the center and asked the staff if he could quit and look for another job. He was employed at a local gas station, and he stated that the mechanics there were not certified, sloppy, and did the customers injustices by not doing good work. He felt that he could not work in that type of environment, and could better himself. He worked the problem out with his counselor and found a better job. Such signs of maturity must be complimented and nurtured by the staff.

A similar type of temporary release is **study release,** where offenders are permitted to reside in a community corrections facility and attend educational classes in the community. This is crucial to the rehabilitation of the offender if the court's opinion of him or her is a favorable one; or in simpler terms, he or she is "salvageable." An offender, who may be a first-time offender, is remorseful, and nearing graduation from college or a specialized training school can benefit from study release. However, the same security precautions for all offenders in the community apply. The offender must have an approved class schedule, must account at all times to staff his or her whereabouts, etc. Teachers may be asked to sign documentation that the offender was in class; this paperwork must be submitted to the jail staff for verification.

### *Screening Offenders for Work Release*

Because the potential for liability is great—a criminal offender being released into the community—staff must be extremely careful in selecting offenders. Each jurisdiction establishes its own criteria for the selection of offenders, including eligibility. At the core of this criteria are offenders who are convicted of nonviolent and petty crimes, have minimum security custody levels, and have good jail records. Prime candidates who could benefit from work release are those offenders convicted of misdemeanors or nonviolent felonies such as theft, nonsupport of dependents, traffic offenses, property offenses, and lesser drug offenses such as first-time distribution or possession of drugs.[25]

More specifically, ideal work release offenders must have the following criteria so sentencing judges can order them into a work release program or be recommended to the judge by the jail community corrections staff:[26]

- Have an acceptable criminal history: no violent crimes, sex offenses, or escapes or attempted escapes from custody or incarceration. Misdemeanor violent crimes such as assaults can be examined on a case-by-case basis. Many of these types of offenses may be attributed to alcohol and/or drug abuse.
- Have no detainers or outstanding charges.
- Be within a few months of release or parole.
- Have maintained a good jail record: no major infractions, have participated in programs, have no incompatibilities with other inmates, have good relations with staff. Also, trusty work is desirable, as this shows the staff and court that the inmate is not a management problem.
- Have clearance by medical staff and mental health staff; there are no physical or psychological problems that would cause any difficulties in work release participation or result in a risk to the community.
- Have close ties to the community: family, friends, employment.
- Have an understanding of the purpose of the work release program, its rules and regulations, are apparently willing and able to participate, and have an overall good attitude about it. Some offenders may say that the program is too restrictive, has too many rules, etc., and may elect to do their time "straight" in jail.

Offenders can be sentenced to work release by the sentencing judge if the criminal code in the state allows such actions. This is a type of a "checks and balances" system; if the jail community corrections staff receives the court order but the offender may be at risk, they have a duty to inform the court. The court order can be amended based on newly received information. The most effective way to screen inmates for work release is through the use of the **screening board,** which may consist of a jail community corrections staff member, a mental health staff member, and a treatment counselor. Besides the general criteria described above, the board may ask the offender more direct questions about his or her criminal activity, their record, and their problems, and get an idea how serious the offender is about change, rehabilitation, and staying crime free. The best work release inmates are those who exhibit a sense of maturity, and the screening board can get a sense of just how mature and committed to change the offender is. The screening board makes its recommendation to the head of the jail community corrections section; from there it goes up the chain of command and over to the court where the sentencing judge can review the case for placement in work release.

An example of a local corrections department tasked with operating several community corrections programs is Wells County (Indiana) Community Corrections Department. All information is made very clear to the offender.

**General Rules and Regulations**

Community Service is a privilege. Participants are offenders serving a sentence in a special arrangement. Failure to observe the rules strictly may result in termination. If, in the judgment of the Community Corrections Officer, there is reason to believe a violation has occurred, participants will be terminated from the program and returned to the referring agency or returned to Court for a hearing.

PLEASE INITIAL BESIDE EACH RULE AFTER YOU HAVE READ IT.

**1. Financial:**

You are required to pay a user fee to Wells County Community Corrections at the rate of $1.00 per assigned hour. You are also required to pay the sum of $4.50 to cover the insurance cost of your participation in this program. All payments are to be made at the time of the intake appointment and must be paid by money order or cashier's check.

*If you are terminated from the program for failure to comply with the rules, there will be a $50.00 re-admittance fee if you are re-referred by the sentencing court.*

**2. Agency Assignment:**

You are required to report to the agency as assigned by Wells County Community Corrections at the designated time and date.

You are required to perform the hours of work in a satisfactory manner (without disciplinary or attitude problems) or you will be required to repeat those hours.

If you must reschedule or miss a scheduled work date, you must notify the assigned agency in advance and request permission. Permission will be granted based on your work performance and the reason for the request.

Failure to appear on any date scheduled on your weekly work schedule will result in your number of hours/days being extended three (3) for one, i.e., 24 hours for each 8 hours missed/3 days for each day missed. Since rescheduling in advance is possible, almost no excuse will be accepted for an absence without prior approval.

You are required to comply with all reasonable requests or directives of your agency supervisor. You are subject to and will obey all work rules in effect at the assigned agency.

You are required to perform the hours of work without any payment or compensation.

The agency to which you are assigned can terminate your work assignment at any time without notice or without reason. If that should occur, you are to report to Wells County Community Corrections immediately.

Your friends or acquaintances are not allowed to visit you at your assigned agency at any time during your work hours.

**3. Photo Identification:**

At the time of your appointment with Wells County Community Corrections, you will need some form of picture identification. You must take this identification with you when you perform Community Service hours.

*You must also bring this identification to all Community Service check-ins.*

**4. Clothing:**

You are required to dress in a manner and style appropriate for the work to which you have been assigned.

**5. Employment:**

It is your responsibility to advise Wells County Community Corrections of any change of address, employment, or telephone number.

**6. Check-in:**

You shall report to each designated check-in at the proper location, and at the appointed time, as directed by the Wells County Community Corrections Office. You shall then submit your time card for verification and make any payments necessary. *You must also bring picture identification to check-in.*

**7. Illness or injury:**

If you are unable to work due to illness, you must call the agency prior to missing and you must provide a doctor's statement to Wells County Community Corrections. *If you are injured at a Community Service site, you must immediately report it to your supervisor and after receiving medical attention report to the Community Corrections Office in the Court House and fill out all necessary paper work. If you fail to report any injuries within four hours of the accident to Wells County Community Corrections, we will not be responsible for any medical expense that is the result of your accident.*

**8. Transportation:**

Transportation to and from the agency assigned is solely your responsibility.

**9. Conduct:**

You are to obey all laws of the United States and the State of Indiana and behave well in society. Providing false information, or altering or falsifying employment records or other documentation will result in your termination from the program.

**10. Discipline:**

Any offender may be written up by a Community Service Supervisor for any violation. Serious violations may result in removal from the program and referral back to the referring agency or Court.

**11. Drugs and Alcohol:**

Any use of a mind-altering substance (drugs or alcohol), in any form or any amount, is strictly prohibited.

Any use of any product containing poppy seeds, all hemp products, including hemp seed oil, and the Vicks Inhaler is also strictly prohibited.

You shall agree to submit to a test for the presence of drugs or alcohol at any time and to pay for such testing, if required. If you fail to give a sample within a two-hour period after being asked to provide one, your refusal will be considered the same as a positive test. If a test returns twice as a diluted sample, it will be considered a positive test. Failure or refusal to submit to such testing or tampering with a test sample shall

**FIGURE 11-2** Continued

be considered the same as a positive test and you will be referred back to the referring agency or Court for a hearing.

**12. Weapons:**

You shall not possess or use any firearm, destructive device, or other dangerous weapon unless granted written permission from the Wells County Community Corrections Director.

If you have any questions or problems, contact the Wells County Community Corrections Office at 219–824–6405. If no one is in the office, leave your name and phone number on the answering machine so the staff member can reach you.

I, the undersigned, hereby acknowledge that I have read and fully understand these rules and further agree to abide by them. I understand that my failure to comply may result either in termination and referral back to the referring agency or in a Court hearing. I understand and agree that I will not hold Wells County Community Corrections or any employee liable for any injuries or illness I may suffer while I am a participant of the Community Service Program, and I agree to indemnify and hold said agency and individuals harmless from claims for damages or injuries incurred by others resulting from my actions.

Offender's signature:____________________ Date:____________________

Courtesy: Blake Poindexter, Director Wells County Community Corrections.

Reprinted by Permission.

**FIGURE 11-2** Wells County Community Corrections Community Service

### *Treatment in Work Release*

While incarcerated in a work release program, an offender may be required to participate in treatment and other rehabilitative programs if deemed necessary by the jail community corrections staff. Part of the initial process in bringing an offender into work release is identifying and assessing what problems and lack of skills led the offender to crime. While this sounds utopist and philosophical, in reality all offenders have problems in one form or another which have resulted in committing crime. As a requirement for participation in a work release program, offenders may be required to complete a series of **life skills classes,** or classes that instruct the offender in the areas of good decision making, budget management and financial responsibility, communications, mental health, stress management, workplace adjustment, and transitioning back into the community. These classes are mandatory in many jurisdictions and are also known as "survival skills classes."[27]

Work release staff members who are assigned to assist offenders through the program may have the offender attend substance abuse services in the community, including participation in AA and NA. The advantage to incorporating these programs into a work release program is that the offender can participate in the community with law-abiding citizens, some of who may serve as sponsors to AA and NA. These concerned citizens may assist the offender in staying clean and sober, and preventing relapse. This is not to say that programs in the jail setting are no less important, but jail programs are conducted in a somewhat artificial environment—the confines of a secure jail.

Each inmate on a work release program is unique in terms of vocational talent and work background. Inmates in work release come from a variety of occupations, such as priests, doctors, lawyers, military, sales, etc. Some employers in the community say that they are open to hiring offenders because often they are sober and punctual. Inmates participating in work release programs say that the programs teach responsibility and how to hold down a job.[28]

### A Profile of Several Work Release Programs

One of the most progressive local community corrections programs is the Montgomery County, Maryland Pre-Release Center (PRC), which serves as a key transition program for almost 500 criminal offenders annually. The PRC offers a wide variety of employment services for offenders, education programs, life skills classes, and substance abuse treatment programs, all in an effort to assist offenders in a successful return to their neighborhoods. Each year, nearly 500 criminal offenders are placed into suitable employment in the community.[29]

Another example is the work release program in Lake County, Illinois. The work release center there houses 110 offenders, called residents, with the average daily population numbering about 106 residents. Residents at the Lake County facility, as in other work release programs, are financially responsible for the cost of the work release program, and must pay room and board fees. Additionally, they must pay court costs and restitution. Annually, approximately $550,000 is collected from residents for room and board fees, and an additional $42,000 is collected for court costs and restitution. Overall, 61 percent of residents complete the program with no further violations. When in the community, residents are supervised by resident field coordinators; when inside the work release facility, they are under the supervision of correctional sergeants and correctional technicians.[30]

In Oakland County, Michigan, the practice is to admit offenders who are already employed. Offenders must be sentenced and granted work release by a judge on all charges. Offenders must be currently employed and must produce a current valid letter indicating their employment. The letter must contain the following information:[31]

- Name of offender.
- Name and address of employer or company.
- Telephone number for the employer or direct supervisor/person completing the letter (for verification purposes) and signatures of same.
- Current salary or rate of pay.
- Work schedule: The schedule must list the exact days and hours of work, and must not exceed 10 hours per day or 6 days in a row. Offenders must be in the work release facilities for at least 11 hours between work shifts. Additional documentation is required for a family-owned business or if the offender has his or her own business.

In Pitkin County, Colorado, offenders sentenced by a judge to work release are advised to contact the jail administrator because work release is often full and reservations may have to be made. Candidates for work release are required to provide a letter from their employers. Any changes to their work schedule must be submitted in writing for staff approval. Offenders must pay room and board fees on paydays; for Pitkin County residents, the fee is $15 per day. For offenders from other jurisdictions, the fee is $50 per day.[32]

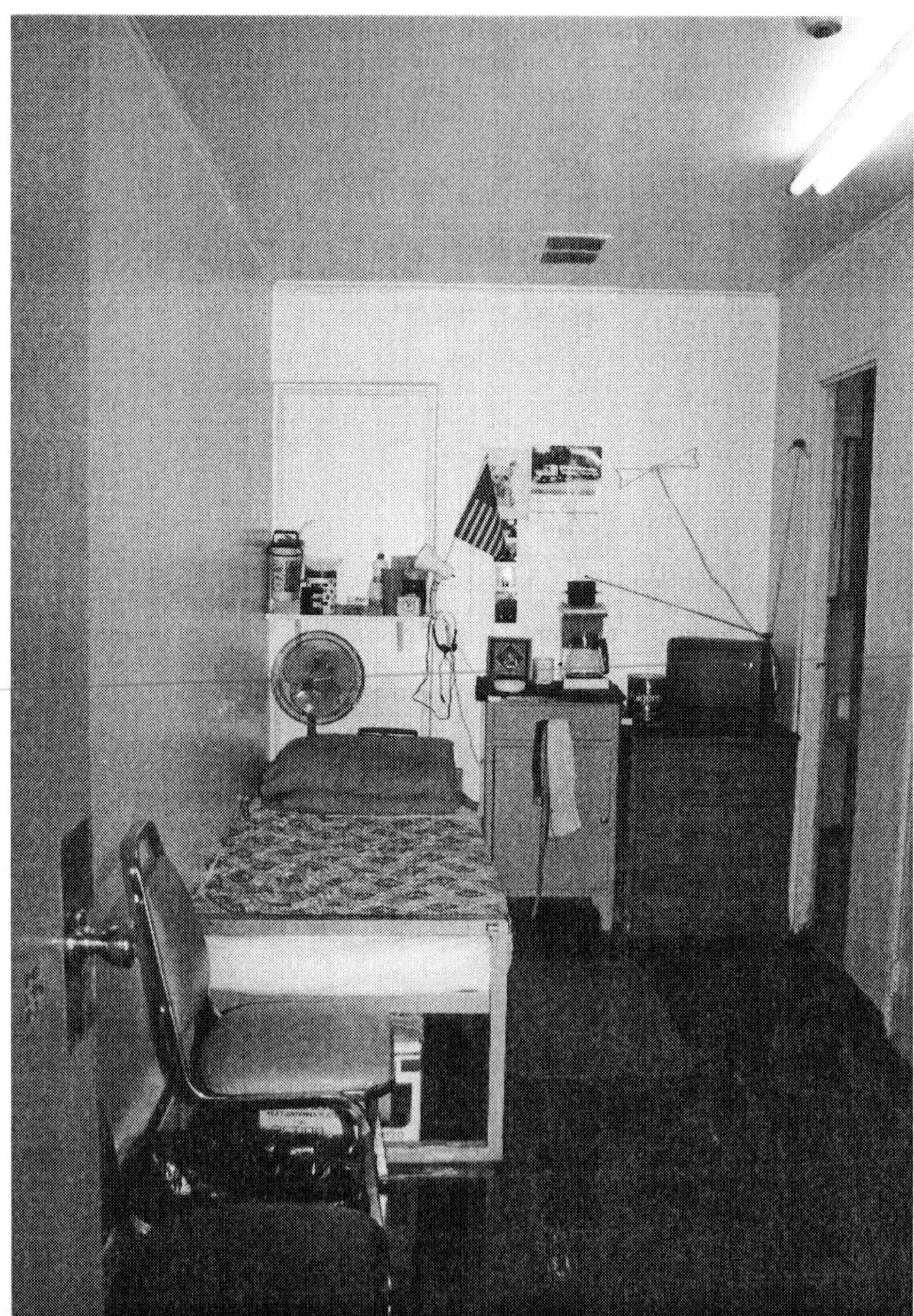

Local corrections work release quarters for inmates are much more comfortable than cells in the jail.

Photo reprinted with permission, American Correctional Association.

For the most part, life for an offender in a work release unit means adhering to mature responsibility. Offenders are assigned to either a bunk (in older facilities) or a room. Offenders are given a key and it is up to them to safeguard their property. Staff does not usually awaken an offender for work; the offender is allowed to keep an alarm clock or radio and they must get up and get to work on time. Many facilities observe "quiet hours," when offenders in residence must be quiet so others can sleep. Also, they must get to their classes and programs, either in or out of the facility, on time. Offenders who are working are allowed to wear their own clothes, and must keep them, themselves, and their room/bunk clean. Many work release facilities are crowded, and offenders in them, like in an overcrowded jail, must learn to get along with others. Finally, in modern work release facilities meals are served during specific hours in a dining hall, and it is up to the offender to get there for meals.

Not all offenders in jail work release programs are local jail inmates; some are state department of corrections inmates. By jails taking state inmates, they are both aiding in inmate reintegration and helping to relieve crowding in state corrections systems. For example, in 1997 the Virginia Department of Corrections (VDOC) entered into a cooperative agreement with local jails called the "Jail Contract Bed Work Release" or JCB program, which allows eligible VDOC work release inmates to participate in local jail work release programs. This allowed the closure of the few remaining state work release facilities. State inmates must be nearing the end of their sentence and are screened by VDOC staff. Since 1995, 32 local Virginia jails had contracted into the JCB program. In fiscal year 2003, 814 local jail beds were contracted under the JCB program.[33]

## Home Detention/Electronic Monitoring

Allowing offenders through court order or screening to serve their sentences at home has been one of the most innovative and somewhat controversial programs in local corrections in the past 25 years. Often used interchangeably due to the technology employed, **home detention/electronic monitoring** (also called Electronic Incarceration Program, or EIP) is defined as a process where offenders serve their sentences at home, under electronic surveillance, and are allowed access to the community only for employment, rehabilitative programs, or any reason of importance (such as medical treatment) with prior approval of corrections staff. They are also subject to frequent visits by staff.[34]

In such a program, offenders' homes become the jail, but with three distinct advantages. First, the offender is not isolated from society as he or she would be inside a jail. Second, he or she is not spending time with other inmates, but is interacting with citizens who can have positive influences on the offender. Third, the offender does not occupy a cell in an overcrowded jail.[35] Home detention/electronic incarceration programs can benefit first-time offenders who may have a difficult time adjusting to jail, elderly offenders, and offenders with critical medical conditions such as pregnancy or a physical handicap. Like work release, the offender can keep family and community ties strong, and by being home and working, can maintain family unity.

The controversy surrounding the usage of electronic monitoring is one of concern by the general public. On its face, offenders are being released into the community, and are not under the "eyeball" supervision of correctional staff. The first step in alleviating these fears is through the selection and screening process. The public must

WELLS COUNTY SHERIFF'S DEPARTMENT

**Work Release Program Admittance Guidelines**

In order to qualify for admittance into the work release program, you must meet certain guidelines for admission as follows:

- Must be physically fit and able to work full time.
- Must be over 18 years of age, or convicted in an adult court.
- Must have no conviction (past or present) of a violent crime.
- Must have no conviction (past or present) of a sex crime (this rule is at the discretion of the program administrators, also to possibly include compulsory attendance of a Court certified counseling agency).
- Must be reviewed by the program administrators for any battery conviction before being placed on the Wells County Work Release Program.
- Must have or be able to secure full time employment prior to admittance.
- Must have transportation to and from work.
- No offender convicted of a drug dealing charge, misdemeanor or felony, will be allowed to be on Work Release in the Wells County Jail.
- No offender can be admitted to the Work Release Program if they have a pending open case or hold, or an outstanding warrant (pending Departmental review).
- The employer of any Work Release inmate must be an approved place of employment by the Wells County Jail Work Release Program.

**Procedures for Admission**

- Directly after sentencing by Court, the applicant should report to Community Corrections.
- Applicant needs to bring a letter from the employer, on company letterhead, stating the days worked, the shift hours, and the supervisor's name and work phone number.
- Interview with Community Corrections.
- Fill out the written application and submit it to the Director. Once the applicant has been interviewed by Community Corrections and the application filled out and returned, an admission review will be conducted. This review may include interviews with police, probation officers, family, friends, neighbors, employers, and coworkers.

If a sentence is 14 days or less, the applicant will pay all required fees when reporting to begin serving the sentence.

All work release fees must be paid before an inmate is released from jail.

**Commonly Asked Questions by Work Release Inmates**

Q. Can you help me get an early release?

A. No. Work Release is a privilege to begin with. The only way you may obtain an early release is through a sentence modification, which must be obtained through your attorney, and appropriate court judge.

Q. How far away can I go to work?

A. Generally, you must work within Wells County, Huntington County, Grant County, Blackford County, Jay County, Adams County, and Allen County.

Q. If I get paid every two weeks, do I still have to pay my Work Release fee every week?

A. Yes. You must allot enough money from your check to be able to pay your fee each week.

Q. Can I do my personal laundry at home?

A. No. You must make arrangements with the jail for your laundry.

Q. What happens if I cannot, or do not, pay my fee on Friday each week?

A. You will not be allowed to go to work until it is paid.

*Note:* Now that you have read and understood the answers to these questions in advance, there should be no need for you to ask them of the staff. Please, do not embarrass yourself or take up the staff's time by asking them.

---

**Drug Use Questionnaire**

Date:________________ NAME:________________

During the past 30 days, I have used the following drugs and/or medications:

I. Prescription:

Prescribed by Dr. ________________ telephone #: ____________

for: ____________________

| Drug | Dose | Frequency | Date last used |
|---|---|---|---|
| A. | | | |
| B. | | | |
| C. | | | |

II. Over-the-counter medication:

| Medication | Dose | Frequency | Date last used |
|---|---|---|---|
| A. | | | |
| B. | | | |
| C. | | | |

III. Illegal drugs:

| Drug | Dose | Frequency | Date last used |
|---|---|---|---|
| A. | | | |
| B. | | | |
| C. | | | |

Offender's signature: ________________ Date: ____________

**FIGURE 11-3** Continued

**Drug Admission Form**

I hereby admit that I have used the following drug(s):

on the following date(s):

without proper medical authorization in the form of a valid prescription or physician's instructions.

This admission of drug use is made voluntarily without threat or promise, and I understand that it can be used against me in a court of law.

Signed: ____________________________

Date: ____________________

Witness: ____________________________

---

**Work Release Policy Concerning Drugs and Alcohol**

Caution: The following document is legally binding. Read and understand it before signing. If you have any doubts about any part of it, consult an attorney before signing.

Participation in the Wells County Work Release Program is voluntary. Those who apply must understand that they do so of their own free will. Additionally, those who apply must understand that the program has a zero tolerance of alcohol and drugs. Therefore every applicant for the Work Release Program is required to sign the following document prior to being accepted into the program.

If admitted into the Wells County Work Release Program, I understand and agree to the following terms, without the right of a disciplinary hearing.

A. That if I test positive for marijuana or any other illegal drug, or possess or consume alcohol, I will immediately be taken back to jail and removed from the program. In addition, I may also lose all good time credit toward my sentence.
B. If I am on probation while in the work release program, I also understand that a formal charge of probation violation may be filed with the court.
C. If I am removed from the work release program for any of the above reasons, I understand that I will not be eligible for the program for two years from the date of the violation.

By my signature below, I acknowledge that I have read and understood all of the above, and agree to all the disciplinary terms as stated.

Signature: ____________________ Date: ____________________

Reviewed with Inmate by: ________________________________________________

Date of review: ____________________

Courtesy: Blake Poindexter, Director Wells County Community Corrections.

Reprinted by Permission.

**FIGURE 11-3** Work Release Guidelines

The Cook County Sheriff's Department operates the world's largest pretrial offender monitoring program. Electronic monitoring or EM can be used for both sentenced offenders and those who are considered low risk and are awaiting trial. It is more cost effective to have low-risk offenders on EM outside of jail than inside overcrowded facilities.

The Cook County program allows nonviolent pretrial and short time sentenced offenders to remain in the community in lieu of being incarcerated in jail. The average daily population of the program is approximately 1,200 offenders. Eighty five percent of those offenders are in a pretrial status.

The program is divided into five sections: A *Monitoring Section* is responsible for the program's daily operations, the monitoring center, the dispatch desk, and the permissions desk. Offenders are monitored, staff can be dispatched to a residence or job site, and permissions can be granted to offenders to leave their homes for legitimate reasons. The *Patrol Section* conducts field investigations concerning EM offender violations, and returns to jail the offenders who have violated the program. An average of 150 unannounced home visits is conducted each day. The *Records Section* screens and evaluates files of Cook County Department of Corrections general population inmates for possible participation in the program. The *Work/School Section* verifies and maintains EM offender's work and school schedules. Finally, the *Technical Service Section* performs processing duties placing inmates on EM, repairs and replaces damaged EM equipment, and recovers EM equipment that has been lost and/or stolen.

Each offender is fitted with an ankle bracelet that is the unit transmitter; the transmitter is worn by the offender 24 hours per day. A constant radio signal is emitted from the ankle bracelet transmitter to the Home Monitoring Receiving Unit (HMRU), which is a box-like receiver that is attached to the offender's home telephone. The HMRU sends a signal over the telephone line to the program's Monitoring Center, informing the staff when the offender leaves and enters his or her home. The HMRU will also inform the Center if the offender tampers with the equipment. This is typical of many EM programs: a signal is sent saying that the offender is home or if he or she has left home without permission.

Jail inmates are evaluated for the program, and the seriousness of the crime and bond amounts may exclude an offender. Inmates in the Psychiatric Unit, those with violent criminal histories, offenders having sex offenses, and domestic violence offenders are excluded from consideration.

EM offenders can work, attend school, and participate in vocational training programs. There are other circumstances under which EM offenders can leave their homes with approval from staff: obtain food stamps, go to public aid or assistance, cash aid checks, go on job interviews, and attend meetings with their probation officers and attorneys.

**FIGURE 11-4** Cook County, Illinois Electronic Monitoring Program[36]

be made to realize that electronic monitoring program (or EIP) can benefit the taxpayer; holds offenders accountable in an effort to facilitate responsibility, and carefully selects offenders.

The more strict the criteria for allowing an offender into an EIP, the easier it is for sheriffs and local correctional supervisors to both "sell" the program to the public and answer inquiries and criticisms. Also, there may be personnel in the local judiciary, such as in the prosecutor's offices, who feel that increased usage of incarceration promotes less of a risk to the community.

Community Corrections staff must be very careful in the selection and supervision of offenders who will be "doing time at home." Information on what is required and expected of the offender must be made very clear.

WELLS COUNTY COMMUNITY CORRECTIONS

**Electronic Monitoring/House Arrest Program**
**Admittance Guidelines**

In order to qualify for admittance into the Electronic Monitoring/House Arrest program, you must meet certain guidelines for admission as follows:

- Must have no conviction (past or present) of a violent crime (subject to Departmental review).
- Must have no conviction (past or present) of a sex crime (subject to Departmental review).
- Must be reviewed by the Program Director for any battery conviction before being placed on the program.
- No offender convicted of a drug dealing charge, misdemeanor or felony, will be allowed to be on the Electronic Monitoring/House Arrest Program (subject to Departmental review).
- Must have secured or have been able to secure full-time employment prior to admittance (subject to Departmental review).
- The employer of any offender on the program may be contacted and the offender may be checked on while at work.
- Must have transportation to and from check-ins.
- Must have installation fee and the first weeks' monitoring fee paid prior to installation of the monitoring equipment (subject to Departmental financial review).

**General Rules and Regulations**

Electronic Monitoring/House Arrest is a privilege. Participants are offenders serving a sentence in a special arrangement. Failure to observe the rules strictly may result in termination. If, in the judgment of the Community Corrections Officer, there is reason to believe a violation has occurred, participants will be terminated from the program and returned to the referring agency or returned to Court for a hearing.

PLEASE INITIAL BESIDE EACH RULE AFTER YOU HAVE READ IT.

**1. Electronic Monitoring:**

An electronic monitoring transmitter will be installed on your person so that your activities outside the home can be monitored. A daily fee of $11.00 to $17.00 will be charged for the use of the transmitter and all fees are to be paid prior to your release. This fee is subject to change at any time. You will be responsible for the care of this unit. If it is damaged, you will reimburse Wells County Community Corrections anywhere from $500.00 to $3,500.00 for the cost of the unit. Tampering with or destroying your monitoring equipment will result in termination from the program and a charge of Criminal Mischief.

**2. Financial:**

Electronic Monitoring/House Arrest charges shall be paid by money order or cashier's check only and will be made payable to the Wells County Community Corrections Office.

There is a one-time installation fee of $50.00 along with a monitoring fee of $11.00 to $17.00 per day, which is subject to change at any time. All fees are to be paid prior to your release from this Department.

*You will have an intake appointment at the Wells County Community Corrections office.* At that time you must have a payment of $127.00 to $169.00, which is for installation and the first week of fees.

If you are placed on a Satellite Monitoring System, the fees will be $17.00 per day, with possible additional fees assessed dependent upon the amount of cell phone charges assessed from the unit.

Monitoring fees will be paid weekly at check-in. Failure to abide by this rule is considered a violation.

**3. Medical:**

You will be financially responsible for any medications, medical care, including dental care, while on the program. Medical appointments shall be arranged in advance with the Community Corrections Officer.

Over-the-counter medicines, as well as prescribed medications, shall be checked in with the Community Corrections Officer. You will not be allowed to have in your possession an over-the-counter medication, nor prescribed medication, without the consent of the Director or Community Correction Officer. Any prescription medication found in your possession, without prior staff approval, shall result in referral back to the referring agency.

**4. Check-in:**

You shall report each week, to the proper location, at the appointed time, as directed by the Wells County Community Corrections Office. You shall then (a) provide a printed and legible schedule for the upcoming week; (b) make weekly payments as set forth; (c) have the ankle transmitter inspected; and (d) turn in any documents that verify times away from home for the week that was just completed.

**5. Employment:**

Your employer must have knowledge of the limitations placed upon you and you must expect that a Community Corrections Officer will check with your employer to verify schedules.

Electronic Monitoring/House Arrest requires a set schedule of working hours; open-ended job assignments are not acceptable. The only acceptable activities are limited to employment and Court-ordered activities.

It is your responsibility to advise Wells County Community Corrections of any changes of address, employment, or telephone numbers.

You will be required to advise your employer to submit copies of your time cards or time sheets to Wells County Community Corrections either by mail or by fax (219)824–6406. It is required that these copies be submitted every Monday, unless another time has been allowed by the Director, and should be for the prior week of work.

Providing false information, altering, or falsifying employment records or other documentation used for verification of your whereabouts, will result in your termination from the program.

If, for any reason, your employment is temporarily terminated, you must return to your residence and immediately notify Wells County Community Corrections. For example, if you work outside and weather conditions prevent you from being able to work, you must return home.

**FIGURE 11-5** Continued

Schedule changes after 6:00 P.M. are restricted to genuine emergencies only. If your employer requires mandatory overtime, you are to contact Wells County Community Corrections. Voluntary overtime must be approved at least 24 hours in advance. The maximum amount of hours you are allowed to work in one week is 60 hours, unless approved by Community Corrections.

You will not be allowed to change employment while participating in the program without prior approval from Wells County Community Corrections.

**6. Verification of Daily Activities:**

You will be punctual and accountable to Wells County Community Corrections for your whereabouts at all times.

You are not to stop while going to or from work, unless permission has been granted in advance by Wells County Community Corrections or in a genuine emergency, i.e., car trouble or accident. Travel time will be reasonable and based on the assumption that no stop has occurred.

Any departure from the approved daily schedule must have prior approval by Wells County Community Corrections.

**7. Phone Calls:**

No one shall use your phone for more than 15 minutes at one time. You must maintain a working phone at all times. You need to check with the telephone company to make sure that you have a 48-volt line instead of a 24-volt line.

You shall not have anything other than basic phone service, such as the following:

a. Call forwarding
b. Call waiting
c. Caller I.D.
d. Or any other services available from the telephone companies
e. Wireless phone
f. Answering machine
g. Computer modem

**8. Conduct:**

You are to obey all laws of the United States and the State of Indiana and behave well in society.

You are expected to fully cooperate with the staff of the monitoring company in their efforts to properly monitor your activity. Failure to do so could result in your being terminated from the program.

**9. Drugs and Alcohol:**

Any use of a mind-altering substance (drugs or alcohol), in any form or any amount, is strictly prohibited. Any use of any product containing poppy seeds, all hemp products, including hemp seed oil, and the Vicks Inhaler is also strictly prohibited. You will not have any alcoholic beverage on your premise (opened, unopened, or any empty container) unless otherwise stated in the Order of the Court.

You shall agree to submit to a test for the presence of drugs or alcohol at any time and to pay for such testing, if required. If you fail to give a sample within a two-hour period after being asked to provide one, your refusal will be considered the same as a positive test. If a test returns twice as a diluted sample, it will be considered a positive test. Failure or refusal to submit to such testing or tampering with a test sample shall be considered the same as a positive test and you will be referred back to the referring agency or Court for a hearing.

**10. Searches:**

You shall be subject to a search of your person or belongings at any time while on the Electronic Monitoring program. However, no member of the opposite sex shall be authorized to conduct a strip search of you, and any strip searches will be conducted only according to staff policy. Two staff members will be present, unless exigent circumstances warrant. This includes your vehicle, any designated locker space or location at a place of employment where your personal belongings are kept, and any dwelling that you reside in. A K-9 unit can be used where it is deemed necessary by the Community Corrections Director or Field Officer.

**11. Vehicles:**

It is understood that any vehicle driven by you shall be subject to search at any time by the Community Corrections staff. A K-9 unit can be used where it is deemed necessary by the Community Corrections Director or Field Officer. You shall be held accountable for any contraband found in the vehicle. For the purposes of this rule, the following items will be considered contraband:

1. Any alcoholic beverage
2. Any alcoholic beverage container
3. Any type of firearm (including a toy firearm)
4. Any type of fireworks
5. Any bow or arrow
6. Any type of knife
7. Any controlled substance

**12. Weapons:**

You shall not possess or use any firearm, destructive device, or other dangerous weapon unless granted written permission from the Wells County Community Corrections Director.

**13. Escape:**

Being in an unauthorized place, or leaving your residence or place of employment without authorization, could result in your being charged with the crime of escape [IC 35–38–2.5–6, IC 35–44–3–5].

If you have any questions or problems, contact the Wells County Community Corrections Office at 219–824–6405. If no one is in the office, leave your name and phone number on the answering machine so the staff member can reach you. In the case of an extreme emergency, contact the Wells County Sheriff's Department at 219–824–3426 and they will contact the on-call staff member.

I, the undersigned, hereby acknowledge that I have read and fully understand these rules and further agree to abide by them. I understand that my failure to comply may result either in termination and referral back to the referring agency or in a Court hearing. I understand and agree that I will not hold Wells County Community Corrections or any employee liable for any injuries or illness I may suffer while I am a participant of the Electronic Monitoring/House Arrest Program, and I agree to indemnify and hold said agency and individuals harmless from claims for damages or injuries incurred by others resulting from my actions.

Offender's signature: ______________________ Date: __________________

**FIGURE 11-5** Continued

**Co-Resident's Agreement**

I understand that all persons residing in my residence must be aware of my placement in the Electronic Monitoring/Home Detention Program. They must be aware of my program requirements and agree to support my responsibilities during my Electronic Monitoring/Home Detention period.

While the people with whom I reside are not directly responsible for me, they understand the consequences I must face if any violations occur in my program.

I further understand that any person using the phone must limit calls to under 15 minutes.

The following is a list of those persons living with me.

| | |
|---|---|
| 1. ____________________ | 1. ____________________ |
| (Printed name) | (Signature) |
| 2. ____________________ | 2. ____________________ |
| (Printed name) | (Signature) |
| 3. ____________________ | 3. ____________________ |
| (Printed name) | (Signature) |
| 4. ____________________ | 4. ____________________ |
| (Printed name) | (Signature) |
| 5. ____________________ | 5. ____________________ |
| (Printed name) | (Signature) |

Offender's signature: ____________________ Date: ______________

PRODUCTS THAT DO NOT CONTAIN ALCOHOL ARE LISTED BELOW. MOST CAPSULE AND TABLET FORMS ARE SAFE. ALWAYS CHECK WITH YOUR PHARMACIST.

| *Cough–Cold–Allergy* | *Antidiarrheals* | *Oral Products* |
|---|---|---|
| Actifed | Kaopectate | Chloraspectic |
| Wal-Act | Kaolin-Pectin | Ora-Relief |
| Drixoral | Rheaban | Proxigel |
| Delsym | Dia-Eze | |
| Efficol Cough Whips | Pepto Bismol | |
| Mediquel | | |
| Ryna | | |
| Sudafed | | |
| Sudafed Plus | | |
| Wal-Phed | | |
| Triaminic DM | | |
| Wal-Minic DM | | |
| Triaminic Cold Syrup | | |
| Wal-Minic Cold Relief | | |
| Codimal Expectorant | | |
| Orthoxical | | |
| Coricidin | | |
| Triaminicol | | |
| Naldecon-DX Adult Liquid | | |

Courtesy: Blake Poindexter, Director Wells County Community Corrections.

Reprinted by Permission.

**FIGURE 11-5** House Arrest

At the Fairfax County, Virginia Sheriff's Office, the criteria for offenders to be placed into both the work release and the EIP are strict. The EIP is an extension of the Work Release Program; both are based out of the Fairfax County Pre-Release Center (PRC). Detailed and strict criteria narrow the field of applicants, helping to ensure that only the lowest risk offenders in terms of criminality are considered. The criteria for EIP are:[37]

- Offenders must be sentenced to a term of two years or less.
- Offenders must be within 180 days of their release before they can begin the program, with a minimum of 30 days left to serve.
- Offenders are not to have any outstanding charges, detainers from other jurisdiction, or out-of-state sentences to serve.
- No convictions for sex and/or child related crimes.
- No criminal history of violent crime, or any pattern of violent crime.
- Cannot be currently incarcerated for the distribution of a controlled drug(s).
- No record of escapes from custody.
- Not previously revoked from the EIP during the current period of incarceration.
- Place of primary residence is in Virginia.
- Offenders may be required by Sheriff's staff to complete the residential segment of the Intensive Addictions Program (IAP) prior to work release participation. Also may be required to participate in PRC or community rehabilitation and treatment programs as a condition of work release.
- Offenders must agree to submit to random and unannounced home checks by staff and screenings for drug and alcohol usage.

Home detention and EIPs can require that the offender pay a fee for the usage of the equipment, thus defraying the costs of the program. For example, in Fairfax County, these fees are placed into a General Account Fund for Fairfax County. Together with Work Release fees, the programs generate an average of $350,000 per year.[38]

In the above illustration of the Fairfax County programs, the criteria for work release are very similar to the EIP, with several exceptions. The offender must reside in the Washington, DC metropolitan area. Also, there is no restriction on a charge of distribution of drugs.[39]

Community corrections staff has a duty to inform the court of unusual circumstances concerning offenders who are ordered into such programs as work release or home detention/electronic monitoring. An inmate can meet the eligibility criteria but may be a management problem in the jail, such as having a record of incompatibilities and/or disciplinary infractions. If the staff has reason to believe that the offender may not be able to follow program rules and regulations, the court must be informed. This serves as part of the "checks and balances" of screening. Judges are not bound by local correctional agency criteria, but court orders placing risky and questionable offenders in community corrections programs can be rescinded. For example, in Fairfax County, the sheriff's office staff may provide the court with additional information about an offender who may have been ordered into a work release or home detention program. As a result of this action, the sentencing judge can rescind the court order.[40]

A new trend in electronic monitoring is called **electronic tethering,** which uses electronic monitoring to map an offender's movements using of Global Positioning Systems (or GPS). Tethering can make sure an offender is where he or she is supposed to be at specific times. According to national jail research organizations, Michigan was the first state to propose using such technology to deal with the problem of jail overcrowding. In the metropolitan Detroit area, offenders carry a purse-like device that maps where they are allowing some offenders to serve their time outside of jail. Other offenders, such as those in a pretrial status and are considered low safety and flight risks, are permitted by the courts to be "tethered." Offenders on electronic monitoring pay as much as $102 per week on the program.[41]

Other revolutionary devices are being used, such as an ankle bracelet that measures the blood alcohol level through the offender's skin. If the level is too high, notification is made to the judge. Another device is a voice verification device that for $6.50 per day calls offenders who are supposed to remain at home. The device asks the offender to repeat numbers, and verifies that it is the offender on the phone. Perhaps the most unique tether is used in stalking cases; if the defendant comes within a specified distance of a victim, the monitoring company notifies the court.[42]

**FIGURE 11-6** New Trends in Electronic Monitoring

## Day Reporting Center Programs

An innovative way to keep the jail counts down is through the use of the **day reporting center, or DRC.** At these centers, offenders who are in a pretrial release status, on probation, or on parole are ordered to appear on a regular schedule in order to receive supervision and take part in rehabilitative programs.[43]

When properly operated, DRCs are not a "free ride" for the criminal offender. DRCs may require the offender to make a full accounting of their daily activities, call in via telephone throughout the day, submit to frequent home checks, and submit to random substance abuse tests. Offenders are required to take advantage of a variety of services, such as job-seeking classes, substance abuse education and treatment, counseling, and life skills classes.[44]

In Cook County, Illinois, the DRC operated by the Cook County Sheriff's Office has inducted over 11,000 offenders since it began operations in March 1993. The Cook County DRC offender is typically a pretrial nonviolent male offender with drug-related charges.[45]

Participants in the Cook County DRC must undergo an eight-day orientation period when entering the program. After a staff evaluation, the offender is placed in a specific program track that addresses his or her specific problems and needs. The length of the program track is dependent on the seriousness of the offender's problem(s). Program tracks vary from three to nine hours per day; a DRC program day lasts ten hours. The ideal goal for the track system is for the offender to move successfully through a continuum of services to the point where they are gainfully employed, are not dependent on drugs, and are attending school or a job training program. Eligible offenders who are drug free for at least 30 days can be enrolled in off center training and take part in job opportunities developed by staff. The program is not without rules and punishments; offenders who fail to follow rules are reincarcerated in jail. Rule violations include being arrested for a new crime, excessive tardiness, absenteeism, and disregard for DRC rules.[46]

The DRC provides some services that are sorely needed by offenders. They include the following:[47]

- Drug and Alcohol Education and Treatment
- Drug testing
- GED
- Adult Basic Education
- Literacy classes
- Life Skills classes
- Violence Interruption
- HIV and AIDS Education
- Job Readiness
- Vocational Placement
- Job Placement
- Parenting

## Weekend Confinement

In an effort to keep the populations of overcrowded jails down, courts are turning to the use of **weekend confinement.** Weekend confinement simply means that the offender serves a type of "divided sentence" over the course of several weekends. These sentences are for minor crimes, and the judge is giving the offender leniency, in so far as the offender can keep his or her job and live at home.

Weekend offenders, or informally known as "weekenders," must report to the jail complex at a certain time, usually on a Friday evening. Because they have to be placed on the jail count and are jail inmates, weekenders must be booked in, searched, and housed. Local jails have authority over the procedures; weekenders serve Saturdays and Sundays and are released on Sundays. Local jail procedures determine the time of release, and each weekend served counts toward the completion of the sentence.

Being a "weekender" does not mean that the jail staff should not view that offender as an inmate. Weekenders must be booked in properly and searched. Their medical problems must be addressed like as with any other inmate. Weekenders can also smuggle in contraband and messages to inmates in the jail general population.

Inmates doing time on weekends were often housed in jail with nothing to do. A growing trend in today's jail is to put weekenders to work in the community with other offender labor. Weekenders are considered low risk due to the nature of their charges and the trust that the court has placed in them. However, weekenders can be incarcerated in jail to serve their sentences as "straight" time if they disobey the orders of staff or violate a rule. In such cases, the local jail staff notifies the court and the sentence can be amended, removing the weekend condition.

## Community Service Programs

Many minor offenders are sentenced to perform a set number of hours performing **community service,** which is a form of community corrections. Community service is defined as a condition that the offender performs a required number of hours of free labor in some type of public service job.[48] These jobs can include cleaning up playgrounds and parks, washing government vehicles, cleaning offices, rooms and restrooms in public buildings, picking up trash on public roads, etc. In some localities, indigent offenders can work off their fines (with court and local correctional agency approval) by performing community service that has an hourly monetary value. The hourly rate multiplied by the number of hours is applied toward the total of the fine.

In Genesee County, New York, the authorities have put the concept of restorative justice into practice with its felony diversion track. It targets the offender's conscience, and unites county judges, prosecutors, and law enforcement officials into devising punishments that force the criminal to face up to his or her responsibilities of their crimes both to the victims and to the community. The programs are operated by the sheriff's office in Batavia, New York, and were formed over 15 years ago as a result of a sheriff's election in 1980, where the new sheriff did not want to build a new maximum security prison.

The Genesee County program offers assistance to the victims and involvement throughout the criminal justice process, and arranges face-to-face meetings to bridge the gap between victims and offenders, forcing the offenders to face up to what they have done.

After admitting guilt, the offender meets with his or her victim, who tells the offender how the crime has impacted him or her. A mediator is present and a plan is worked out to repair the damage. Examples of such plans that are strictly enforced by the county sheriff's office or county probation office include:

- An offender convicted of negligent homicide paying $4,000 to an educational memorial fund.
- An offender convicted of driving under the influence (DUI) paying $200 to Mothers Against Drunk Driving (MADD).
- A convicted drug offender paying $500 to two local hospitals.

Each crime can have a unique plan, and can be utilized to keep offenders out of jail before their trial. In one example, a six-time DUI offender, arrested for his seventh DUI, was placed in Genesee County's pretrial diversion program. The offender was under house arrest for six months, from 10 P.M. to 7 A.M. daily. Other conditions included:

- Unannounced visits by deputy sheriffs to his home.
- Visits from program counselors to monitor progress and to administer random urine tests for substance abuse.
- Ordered to perform 200 hours of community service for the American Red Cross.
- Attendance at two AA meetings per week.
- Weekly meetings with a minister.
- Participation in group counseling.
- Attending victim impact meetings at MADD.

Monthly progress reports were sent by the sheriff's office to the judge, the district attorney, the offender's attorney, and the president of MADD.

The statistics and support of this program are impressive. Besides diverting offenders from incarceration in the local jail, either pretrial or post-trial, the program has had the following results:

- In the five-year period prior to 1998, the program has saved the jurisdiction over $2 million, or approximately $55 per inmate per day, due to keeping hundreds of nonviolent criminals out of jail.
- Over the same five-year period, the county was paid $3 million in fees due to accepting federal inmates, thus using the available empty cell space. In a neighboring county, the jail is overcrowded and faces both renovation and expansion of its county jail.
- Offenders have paid thousands of dollars in restitution to both victims and community groups.
- Offenders in alternative sentencing programs have performed over 250,000 hours of community service, such as the restoration of a town hall, the expansion of a local church, and thousands of man hours in such projects as painting, cleaning, and construction.
- From 1982 to 1998, Genesee County has handled over 400 criminal cases of violent or serious offenses.
- From 1985 to 1998, about 3,200 adult offenders have been given community-based sentences by the court, instead of being incarcerated in jail or fined. Many of these sentences have been a condition of probation. Most of these offenders—92 percent—met all of the conditions of their sentences, and few have re-entered the criminal justice system.
- Genesee County also gave approval to approximately 150 felony diversions from 1985 to 1998, and all but a few offenders completed their programs without serious incident; of those cases, only 20 percent were re-arrested.
- An estimated 120 agencies in Genesee County have enacted agreements to employ offenders in community-based work programs such as performing park clean up, painting local churches, filing books in libraries, and mopping floors in local hospitals—all at a savings to the taxpayers.
- Over 100 citizen volunteers have been recruited to work with offenders while they are on diversion.
- Road patrol officers are assigned from the sheriff's office to check on offenders to see if they are following the conditions of their agreements, including late evening checks at 11 P.M.

In summary, this unique approach, with the backing of local agency heads and the citizens, can have a great deal of impact on keeping local jail overcrowding at a minimum.

**FIGURE 11-7** Restorative Justice: The Genesee County Approach[49]

## Community Offender Labor Programs

One of the best uses for inmates in terms of repaying society in combination with cost savings is the formulation of **community offender labor programs.** These programs take carefully screened, low-risk, and minor offenders and work them in the public sector under supervision. This is not work release, where the offender is gainfully employed and not under constant supervision. In offender labor programs, offenders are assigned to crews supervised by a sworn officer and are transported to the job site.

This type of community corrections operation is not without risk. Not only do offenders have to be carefully selected, but the potential is also present for escape from custody and the picking up and smuggling of contraband into the facility. As in jail trusty programs, inmates may not be the most industrious and hard working. Staff must reassign "slackers" back into the jail.

Labor program should address the following issues, which serve to educate both the public and the judiciary as to their value:[50]

- Addresses the expectation from the public that offenders will be under some form of punishment.
- Addresses concerns about public safety.
- Reduces the costs of operating the jail.
- Provides an alternative sentence that judges can use.
- Takes measures to prevent contraband from being smuggled into the jail or community corrections facility.

An example of a labor program meeting these conditions can be found in Broome County, New York. The sheriff's office manages the Broome County Sheriff's Office Intermittent Work Program. In 1994, inmates in this program

**Many jail community corrections programs make use of inmate labor to benefit taxpayers.**

Photo reprinted with permission, American Correctional Association.

produced over 7,000 hours of labor for the local community. Also, in 1994, the cost to house an inmate in the Broome County Jail was $77.44 per inmate per day. The cost of maintaining an offender in the Intermittent Prisoner Work Program was $9.08 per offender per day. In the first eight months of the program's operations, the net savings of $68.36 per offender per day resulted in savings of over $41,000 to the county taxpayers.[51]

The Broome County program is for "intermittent offenders" or weekenders as defined by New York law. Offenders are referred to the programs by the court and are ordered to report to the sheriff's office staff each Saturday and Sunday on the weekends to be served, from 8 A.M. to 4 P.M. On the first reporting Saturday, the offender is booked in like any other jail inmate, with fingerprints and photographs, and his or her sentence is calculated by figuring how many weekends will have to be served. Offenders are medically screened to ascertain their ability to work; those found medically unsuitable for the type of work are assigned to nonconfidential office work: filing, sorting, etc. The only meal provided is lunch, at the cost of $1.08 per offender.[52]

The program has been "marketed" by the Broome County Sheriff's Office to the local courts and agencies. All local municipal governments such as towns, boroughs, etc. and public agencies may request free inmate labor. Also, nonprofit groups may also request services. Private citizens and profit-making organizations or groups are prohibited by law from receiving free inmate labor. Such projects have included snow removal in public areas, working on highways and in public parks, interior renovations, brush removal, etc. The program always has work available.[53]

Staff must keep in mind that intermittent offenders are criminal violators and are not above escape, breaking the rules, or trafficking in contraband. As is typical in other programs of this type, offenders are taken to the job site by staff and supervised by officers in a ten-offenders-to-one-officer ratio. Officers are well trained in adhering to professional standards plus possessing keen observation skills and report writing skills. Offenders wear easily identifiable and visible facility issued garments. All offenders are subject to physical searches, as well as random testing for drugs and alcohol usage. Offenders who violate the rules of the program are reported to the courts, which can impose a determinate sentence, or have the offender do "straight time."[54]

Another example is the Arlington County, Virginia Sheriff's Office Jail Industries Program (JIP), which was established within the Arlington County Sheriff's Office Corrections Division in 1994. The JIP program develops and provides work opportunities and vocational training for inmates under sheriff's office supervision. Inmates experience real-life work situations while working for county agencies, other government jurisdictions, and eligible nonprofit organizations.[55]

The Arlington program deals with a variety of jobs, mixing routine, menial tasks with some tasks in which inmates can learn a skill. These jobs include:[56]

- Department of Human Services (DHS): catering meals for the Residential Center, laundering blankets for the Homeless Shelter.
- Department of Public Works (DPW): sign fabrication, joint cleanup projects, and snow removal with the jail Inmate Work Program and the Traffic Sign Maintenance Program.

Inmate labor programs can be used in a variety of ways, such as road clean up etc.

Photo reprinted with permission, American Correctional Association.

- Department of Parks, Recreation, and Community Resource: Parks Maintenance Project.
- Working in the Bindery Shop through an agreement with the Arlington County Print Shop.
- Working in the Aramark/Inmate Commissary.
- Job Shop: short-term work—dry mounting pictures for the Arlington County Fair, stuffing envelopes for mailings from County agencies, and the making of posters.

It is not unusual to observe that a local jail may term its inmate work program as a work release program. In Oregon, inmates at the Coos County Jail provide over 40,000 hours of inmate labor annually to the local community. Projects include washing county vehicles twice per week. Inmates have assisted at the Coos County Fair, local parks, and perform labor at the local police department and school system.[57]

## Boot Camps

One type of community corrections program that has caught the public eye in the last two decades is the **boot camp.** A boot camp is a short-term reintegration program for selected offenders that employs the methods of military discipline, strict programming, and physical conditioning to prepare the offender for a return to the community with the ability to resist criminal behavior.

The *Gateway Through The Rockies* program of the El Paso County, Colorado Sheriff's Office asks a fundamental question: "What are we to do with the criminal element, in this case the offender, to reduce the likelihood of reoccurrence?" Realizing that the criminal is convicted, serves his or her time, and is released back into the influences and environment that caused criminality in the first place, the program seeks to provide treatment and educational opportunities to offenders. These serve to give the offender a "fighting chance for success."

Implemented in October 1996, the program targets low-risk, nonsexual offenders and places them in a four-phase transitional program that combines traditional education and vocational experience. The instructional phases target the offenses and behaviors that led to committing crimes. The phases are:

Phase I—Introductory Classes: During a three-week period, offenders attend classes in life skills, anger management, hygiene, nutrition, parenting, drug and alcohol education, employability, and writing a resume.

Phase II—Supervised Work Projects: Offenders who successfully complete Phase I work full time hours and receive wages. Portions of the offenders' wages are contributed to the Fourth Judicial District Victim's Compensation Fund, and the remainder of their pay is placed in a savings account for them. Offenders must maintain high levels of work ethics and demonstrate abilities to put into practice what they have learned in Phase I as well as in the workplace. Offenders are required to work at community nonprofit organizations.

Phase III—Work Release: Phase III is a modified work release program where businesses in the community who have entered into a partnership with *Gateways* make employment opportunities available to offenders. The goal here is to make the offender realize that hard work and law-abiding behavior ensure success, and not committing crimes. Many companies who are involved in Phase III have gone on to hire offenders.

Phase IV—Reintegration: The offender is released from custody and participates in follow-up care, such as substance abuse counseling and education classes. Staff also assists the offenders with temporary housing needs until they can secure more permanent housing. Also in Phase IV, "Quarterly Reunions" are held where *Gateway* graduates can share their successes with other graduates and find mutual support.

The program staff reports such benefits as lower levels of tension in the jail in units where *Gateway* offenders are housed, more sentencing options for the local judiciary, and community benefits such as inmates returning to the community sober, with good work histories and enhanced life skills. The community also benefits from inmates working and paying taxes, plus making restitution to victims and contributing to the victim contribution fund. Statistically, from 1997 to 2000, offenders performed 1,311 unpaid hours of community service and contributed $52,348.04 to the Victim Compensation Contribution Fund. In 1999 and 2000, the recidivism rate of the *Gateways* program averaged only 33 percent.[58]

**FIGURE 11-8** *Gateways Through the Rockies* Program

Not all local jail systems have boot camps. Research conducted by Camp and Camp in 2003 indicated that 20 local jail systems were operating boot camps in 2002, serving an offender population of 3,004. The goals of boot camps are to afford offenders opportunities for rehabilitation and reintegration; to provide discipline, to promote deterrence from future criminal behavior; to provide opportunities for participation in vocational and rehabilitative services and programs, and as a result, divert offenders from the local jail and ease overcrowding.[59]

Boot camps work with the courts and other agencies in an effort to "turn around" young offenders. An example of this is the Polk County, Florida Juvenile Boot Camp Program, a joint partnership between the Polk County Sheriff's Office, the Board of Polk County Commissioners, the Florida Department of Juvenile Justice, the Polk County School Board, and the citizens of Polk County, Florida. The program is the largest in Florida and began operations in 1994. With additions since 1994, the facility contains four 20-bed wings, a transition dormitory, an aftercare office, classroom facilities, a general-purpose hall, a control center, and an obstacle course. The target population consists of males who have been found guilty in court and are aged 14–18. The boot camp curriculum runs for a total of 12 months and includes military-style physical training and conditioning, education, vocational training, and psychological counseling. The 12-month program is divided into components: six months in the boot camp, three months of transition programming, and three months of aftercare, which is closely monitored by staff. Inmates experience military life, including military haircuts, marching, and discipline. The program blends traditional methods such as parade ground calisthenics with state-of-the-art classroom computers.[60]

While boot camps look favorable to those who maintain a view that the criminal justice system needs to get tough on offenders, the boot camp method of corrections is not without its critics. One of the main selling points is that boot camps will relieve jail overcrowding, which may appear attractive to a cash-strapped jurisdiction.

Some researchers are of the opinion that boot camps suffer from flaws in their designs. To relieve jail overcrowding, jurisdictions must admit offenders to boot camps who would normally be incarcerated in jail for long periods of time if there were not the alternatives of boot camps. In reality, boot camps target and admit offenders who would otherwise be sentenced to short sentences in the jail. As a result, the boot camp inmates serve longer sentences than inmates who are not sent to boot camps. Generally, boot camps accept volunteers from the offender population, and the length of the program may reduce the offender's incentives and enthusiasm to participate. Offenders are generally impatient; some want a "quick fix." Admissions may decrease, and the ability to have a favorable impact on the reduction of jail crowding may decline. Other concerns include the admittance of "lightweight offenders"—nonviolent first-time offenders. By concentrating on lightweight offenders, the hard-core repeat offenders who may benefit from the boot camp regimen are excluded. Reducing criminality in hard-core offenders would better serve the reduction of jail populations. Lightweight offenders who would usually be on probation may incur technical violations in a boot camp program, which may result in their being incarcerated in the jail. A final criticism is the aspect of many "players" in the system, especially in court where plea bargaining is constantly exercised. Subsequently, the most appropriate sanctions, including boot camps, may not be imposed to best suit some offenders. Prosecutors and judges may have to become involved in the design of intermediate sanction programs, including boot camps.[61]

While the final verdict on the effectiveness of boot camps is apparently not in, the components of aftercare once a young offender is released back to his or her neighborhood are critical to rehabilitation. Also important is the type of jail staff member selected to be drill instructors. It is important that such staff can exercise discipline and authority without going "overboard" and being overbearing to the point that offenders are physically injured, emotionally abused, or intimidated to the point of being so fearful that the program's goals cannot be attained. Common sense, a balanced view of the boot camp philosophy (discipline plus reintegration), and an empathetic view of offenders must all be evident in the drill instructors and discussed in the staff applicant and transfer processes.

## SECURITY CONCERNS OF COMMUNITY CORRECTIONS PROGRAMS

Community corrections staff must realize that the administration of security with community corrections offenders follow the same principles of maintaining security inside the jail. The offenders are still criminals; they may use various ploys and schemes to do time "their way" and continue to use and traffic in contraband. Criminal offenses can be committed in the community while the offender is on the street, just as they can be committed by inmates incarcerated inside the jail.

The most risk in community corrections security is if an offender absconds, or escapes from a work crew, work release, or home detention/electronic monitoring. For example, a Colorado county jail work release inmate failed to return to the jail at his scheduled return time. He was serving a 90-day jail sentence for misdemeanor harassment/ethnic intimidation, misdemeanor assault, and a felony possession of a weapon charge. He had a prior record on various charges including child abuse, theft, assault, and assault with a knife.[62]

The above type of escape can be termed a **walk off,** where the inmate simply walks away from his or her job or, in the case of home detention, his or her home. There is no violence, just a simple disappearance. Often, the community corrections staff does not become aware of the escape until it is noticed that the inmate has not returned. These escapes can be embarrassing to the local corrections agency, especially if the story makes it into the local media—television, radio, and newspapers.

### Selection

No manner of selecting inmates for a community corrections program is foolproof. Inmates who appear to be "model inmates" may fail to return for many reasons, such as fearing detection of illegal drug or alcohol use, going home and getting into a domestic dispute, or committing a new crime and "going on the run." The risky aspect of any community corrections program is the staff not knowing if the inmate will be where he or she is supposed to be or the inmate leaving the jail or work release facility and failing to return.

The use of a screening board is highly recommended, along with a careful examination of the inmate's criminal and jail record. A screening board with several professionals can discuss the inmate from multiple perspectives. Security concerns about the offender should be addressed, such as the type and frequency of offenses in the criminal record. For example, if a male inmate has a history of domestic assaults and/or disorderly conduct, he may not be a good risk in the community. The screening board may ask themselves if this particular inmate may be tempted to go home without authorization.

If the offense falls within the admittance criteria, such as having a non-sex offense, the screening board must examine the offender's entire make up. Questions put to the inmate by the board are crucial. The inmate should receive a straightforward, blunt explanation of the program, its rules and conditions, and the consequences for violations including the placement of additional criminal charges. No community corrections offender should enter the program "blind," even if the program is inmate labor or weekend confinement.

The classification file that contains incident reports is a good resource. The screening board must attempt to paint an accurate picture of the offender. One important aspect of this is knowing the inmate's extent of illegal drug and alcohol use, and the inmate's **drug of choice.** The drug of choice is the primary substance that the inmate prefers to use, and is indicated on record (jail, classification interview, pre-sentence report, criminal history, etc.)

## Security Concerns Outside Facility

Offenders on work release and home detention/electronic monitoring are in effect still incarcerated. The areas where they are permitted to be outside the facility are termed the **authorized extended areas of incarceration.** Per the offender's work release condition or the conditions of his or her home detention/electronic monitoring, the home, job site, etc. are areas where he or she is permitted to be with staff authorization.

For example, a work release offender is permitted to work in a gas station two miles from the jail. His authorized extended area of incarceration is the workplace, and the direct route to the gas station and back to the jail. This route cannot be deviated from unless there is authorization in advance by staff. If the offender is on home detention/electronic monitoring, his authorized extended area of incarceration is the home and his job. It also may include any treatment or educational programs in the community that are authorized in advance by staff.

Security in community corrections, especially in work release and home detention, depends heavily on documentation. The most important document is the agreement that officially allows the offender access into the community or places him or her on home detention. While the format and names vary among jurisdictions, the basic documentation allowing community access should contain the following:

- Agency address, phone number.
- Name of offender.
- Name, address, and phone number of employer.
- Title of job assignment.
- Immediate supervisor.
- Work schedule: days and hours of employment, offender sign out and in times.
- Authorizing signature: local correctional staff.

The offender's immediate supervisor should be the only supervisor who can authorize overtime. Inmates have escaped or walked off their jobs by calling the work release center and telling staff that they have to work overtime, and as a result gaining a "head start." The immediate supervisor should be the primary supervisor with whom the staff works out the employment details for the offender—and is termed the **supervisor of record.** This serves two purposes: he or she is the *only* supervisor who can contact the staff and authorize extra work days, schedule variations or overtime. Offenders should *never* adjust their own schedules. Many work release/home detention programs require the supervisor of record to submit to staff in advance written schedule changes. One ploy of work release offenders is to convince a new staff member of a bogus change in the schedule which originated from the offender and not the supervisor of record.

Other critical areas to document include the mode of transportation. Some citizens mistakenly think that the jail staffs transport the offenders to their jobs. Most work release programs work out with the offender an approved mode of transportation, figuring in a sufficient amount of travel time. If offenders have a valid driver's license, vehicle registration, and current insurance, they usually are permitted to drive to and from their workplace and also to any approved community program. Caution has to be exercised if the offender wants his or her spouse, close friend, etc. to drive him or her. The temptation to violate the rules could be too great, causing the offender to take an unauthorized "side trip" or not to go to work at all.

## Furloughs and Passes

Depending on the rules and policies of the program, an offender may earn the privilege of going into the community on a **shopping pass.** This is a temporary pass of only a few hours duration with which the offender can purchase necessities such as work clothes, toiletries, etc. As with other official documents allowing an offender access to the community, the shopping pass must have an authorizing signature, a sign out and sign in time, and itinerary that accounts for the total time, including travel in which the offender is out of the facility. A good security rule is to have an offender returning from a shopping pass show the staff the items bought and the receipt from the store.

Depending on the program, a work release offender can also earn a **furlough.** A furlough is an authorized pass into the community for specific purposes such as visiting family, friends, or engaging in activities to strengthen ties to the family and community before release. Unlike shopping passes, furloughs require a **furlough sponsor,** who is a responsible citizen who can verify the offender's activities while on furlough and agrees to maintain responsibility of the offender while out in the community.[63] Sponsors of furloughs must be upstanding citizens and staff may request that they meet with the sponsor before granting a furlough.

Furloughs can be granted for different durations of time, depending on the progress the offender has made in the program. An initial furlough can last for 12 hours, and gradually be increased to overnight or over the duration of a weekend.

Furloughs can be granted by the jail's community corrections staff for various reasons. However, the most common reasons for furloughs are:[64]

- Maintain or reestablish ties with the family, especially in cases of dependent children.
- To resolve problems and issues in the family.
- To prepare for the offender's final release, attend job interviews, to search for suitable housing, to obtain a driver's license, etc.

- To attend a short-term educational or vocational program that is offered in the community.
- To attend a special event in the community, such as speaking publicly to a group of students, a civic organization, etc.

### *Community Checks*

An effective tool to monitor the activities of offenders in work release and home detention programs is the **community check.** This is defined as an on-site, personal check by staff at the home, job site, or furlough site to make sure that the offender is where he or she is supposed to be and is not engaging in illegal activity, breaking any program rules, or using any illegal drugs or alcohol.

Offenders on work release or home detention should always be guessing as to if they are to be checked by staff at any given moment. Staff can also wear plain clothes and use unmarked vehicles that are recommended by veteran corrections staff. Staff checking on offenders wearing plain clothes serves as to not embarrass the offender in front of work colleagues, many who may not know that he or she is a convicted offender serving time. Community checks may just involve the corrections officer checking only with the supervisor to see if the offender is at work, or the offender can meet personally with the correction officer. The key to an effective system of offender community checks is to be random and frequent. An officer may decide to check on an offender two days in a row, or every week on different days.

With today's technology, officers can use portable devices to check breath for alcohol use and collect urine samples (by staff of the same sex) for drug screening. Both methods can result in immediate verification of drug or alcohol use.

Another type of community check is simply using the phone; calling the offender at home or at work to verify that he or she is at work or at home. Home detention devices that perform this task are computerized and randomly select the times. On the work site, an offender should be accessible by phone at all times.

## Security Inside the Facility

The work release facility is a secure correctional institution facing a unique challenge—combating contraband in a facility where the inmates are allowed out part of the time. The work release or community corrections facility should be separate from the main jail facility, but due to the original design of the jail, its age, funding, and staffing, this may not be possible in some jurisdictions.

There are several effective methods of security, and they must be practiced aggressively by staff. Every offender, no matter if they are on work release, a weekender, or in an inmate labor program, should be searched thoroughly along with anything they are bringing back into the facility. Strip search guidelines should follow agency policy, but offenders should be patted down, and anything purchased or in their possession, even a lunch pail, should be searched.

In one U.S. jail in 2005, an offender in a local jail work release program was found near death in a facility shower stall. The offender was not breathing and was rushed to a local hospital. Further medical tests revealed the presence of heroin and amphetamines in the offender's system. He had nearly died due to a drug overdose. Another work release offender was arrested on suspicion of selling drugs to the offender who had overdosed. The suspected drug dealer was allegedly hiding the drugs in his shoe.[65] Searches of community corrections dayrooms and offender rooms can be performed in the same manner and frequency of searches in the jail. Visiting in many community corrections facilities are open contact visits, and these areas, such as dining halls and lobbies, must be searched after visiting hours.

To combat the usage of drugs and alcohol, community corrections staffs employ the use of security equipment that detects drug use through urine samples of offenders. These are collected by staff trained in collection of urine and the administration of both urine and breath tests. Technology has improved in this area; urine tests now can tell staff in a matter of minutes if the offender has been using marijuana, cocaine, heroin, etc. The levels of use are not important, just if the offender has been using at all. Urine samples must be collected into a sterile container in the presence of a staff member of the same sex, labeled properly, and tested. During the procedure, the staff member must maintain a chain of custody—safeguarding the sample by logging the sample collected, taking it to storage, testing for results, and sending it for a back up check to a local laboratory used by the agency in case of a positive result. In positive result cases, the offender will have a due process disciplinary hearing and most likely will be found guilty of violating program rules and will be reincarcerated.

The effectiveness of such procedures depends on the element of surprise. Some community corrections agencies and facilities use a system that lists offenders' booking or inmate numbers on a list that is posted in plain sight for offenders to check. If they are scheduled, usually they have a fixed amount of time to report to a staff member to give a sample. Another system is the color code system; offenders are assigned a color, and the color for the day's testing is announced. If the staff has reliable information and reasonably suspects drug or alcohol usage with a particular offender or offenders, it is easy to conduct tests on site.

Alcohol testing can be "blanket" in nature where all offenders re-entering the facility must submit to a breath test. All offenders should be given a clear orientation as to the rules and regulations governing testing for drugs and alcohol; they should also be informed of the consequences of refusal—revocation and reincarceration. The temptations of the street are powerful. All offenders returning from any type of pass or furlough should be tested for drug or alcohol ingestion without exception.

While many community corrections programs vary in operation and scope, rules are essential in all types of programs. At the Livingston County, Michigan Sheriff's Department, the work release program is governed by 15 rules, and any violation by the offender will result in removal from the work release program, the violation reported back to the court, completion of sentence by "straight time," and loss of any accumulated good time. Offenders in the Livingston County program are not allowed to possess any personal property except work clothes, approved educational material, and a wallet. All hygiene items must be purchased by the inmate through the jail commissary. No beverage or food containers are allowed to be brought in, use of alcohol and drug is prohibited, and offenders are subject to random testing. Offenders are not allowed to receive or send any mail or packages from the jail.[66]

## SUMMARY

The focus of jail and local community corrections is on the concept of restorative justice, where the community works with the offender. The criminal offender has to deal with the needs and obligations to the victim of his or her crime plus be accountable to the community for his or her crime.

There are a high number of offenders returning to the community from incarceration every year; community corrections attempts to prepare them for a crime-free life in the community. Many have substance abuse and other types of problems, and community corrections programs attempt to link them with resources and people who can help.

Community corrections programs also relieve jail overcrowding and are cost effective. They do serve to punish the offender but not in the traditional sense. Offenders are still criminals, but the type of security is different. Also, the offender functions in a meaningful community with resources and opportunities, in a nonsecure environment, and undergoes testing of behavior.

While the types of community corrections programs vary by jurisdiction, the main ones that are operated by jails and local correctional agencies are work release, home detention/electronic monitoring, DRCs, weekend confinement, community service, and community offender labor. Boot camps are operated in some jail systems, and target youthful offenders. Military discipline and rehabilitation are the goals of the boot camps. However, boot camp program design, the selection of "lightweight" offenders, and the fact that there are many players that influence boot camp sentences may detract from any benefit that boot camps may attain. Finally, staff for boot camps must be carefully selected.

Because community corrections offenders enter the community and return to the facility, searches are important and should be conducted just as in the main jail. Also, offenders should be subjected to urine screens for drug use and breath tests for alcohol use.

## REVIEW QUESTIONS

1. Why is the problem of inmate re-entry a serious one?
2. What are the views of restorative justice?
3. What are five tenets of effective community corrections programs?
4. What are the requirements for a community corrections program to achieve positive reintegration for the offender?
5. How are offenders tested in the community?
6. Explain what work release offenders must do when participating in a work release program.
7. What are some security concerns of community corrections staff when offenders are out of the facility?
8. Discuss some security measures both inside and outside the work release facility.
9. Why is the selection of offenders for community corrections programs so important?

## TERMS TO KNOW

authorized extended areas of incarceration
boot camp
community check
community corrections
community offender labor programs
community service
furlough
furlough sponsor
day reporting center, or DRC
drug of choice
electronic tethering
graduated release
home detention/electronic monitoring
life skills classes
meaningful community
nonsupervised environment
reintegration
restorative justice
screening board
shopping pass
study release
supervisor of record
system crowding
walk off
weekend confinement
work release

## ENDNOTES


1. Timothy Hughes and Doris James Wilson, BJS Statisticians, "Reentry Trends in the United States," Bureau of Justice Statistics, http://www.ojp.usdoj.gov/bjs/reentry/reentry.htm (accessed February 16, 2007).
2. Tony Locy, "Prisons Release Record Numbers of Ex-Convicts," *USA Today* (December 27) 2000: 1A.
3. Paige M. Harrison and Allen J. Beck, Ph.D., Bureau of Justice Statistics, *Prison and Jail Inmates at Mid year 2005*, May, 2006, p. 6.
4. Howard Zehr, *The Little Book of Restorative Justice* (Intercourse, PA: Good Books, 2002), p. 21.
5. Ibid., p. 19.
6. Ibid.
7. Locy, "Prisons Release Record Numbers," pp. 1A, 2A.
8. Re-Entry Policy Council. *Executive Summary*, http://www.reentrypolicy.org/report/executive-summary.php (accessed November 5, 2005).
9. Dennis R. Schrantz, "The Five Tenets of Effective Community Corrections," *Corrections Today* (February 1995): 40, 42, 44, 45.
10. Frank W. Wood, "The Minnesota Approach," *Corrections Today*, February 1996, 52, 54.
11. Dean John Champion, *Probation, Parole, and Community Corrections, 5th Edition* (Upper Saddle River, NJ: Pearson Prentice Hall, 2005), p. 645.
12. Roger J. Lauren, Ph.D., *Community Managed Corrections and Other Solutions to America's Prison Crisis* (Lanham, MD: American Correctional Association, 1988), pp. 20, 21.
13. Todd R. Clear and Harry R. Dammer, *The Offender in the Community* (Belmont, CA: Wadsworth, 2000), p. 32.
14. Ibid., p. 33.
15. Ibid.
16. Ibid.
17. Paige M. Harrison and Allen J. Beck, Ph.D. *Prison and Jail Inmates at Mid year 2005*, p. 7.
18. Clear and Dammer, *The Offender in the Community*, p. 34.
19. Belinda Rogers McCarthy, Bernard J. McCarthy, Jr., and Matthew Leone, *Community Based Corrections, 4th Edition* (Belmont, CA: Wadsworth, 2001), p. 4.
20. Ibid.
21. Ibid., pp. 4, 5.
22. Vanessa St. Gerard, *New Study Proves Jails Are An Important Component of the Reentry Equation*, On the Line, American Correctional Association March 2005 (28) 2 (1).
23. McCarthy, McCarthy, and Leone, *Community Based Corrections, 4th Edition*, p. 149.
24. Ibid., pp. 149, 150.
25. Gary F. Cornelius, "Work Release: An Overview," *Jail Operations Bulletin* (American Jail Association) 4, (3) (1992): 3.
26. Ibid.
27. Ibid.
28. Justin Blum, "Learning the Confines of Life Outside of Jail," *The Washington Post*, August 16 (1993): D1, D4.
29. Website: http://www.montgomeryworks.net/E/00024/Detail.cfm?ID=19
30. Website: http://www.co.lake.il.us/sheriff/divisions/work.asp
31. Website: http://www.co.oakland.mi.us/sheriff/faq/work_release.html
32. Website: http://www.aspenpitkin.com/depts/28/jail_workrelease.cfm
33. Website: http://www.vadoc.state.va.us/offenders/institutions/programs/reentry.htm
34. Patricia A. Marshall, "Electronic Incarceration Programs," *Jail Operations Bulletin* (American Jail Association) 7 (12), 1996, 2.
35. Ibid.
36. Website: http://www.cookcountysheriff.org/dcsi/em.html
37. Website: http://www.co.fairfax.va.us/sheriff/eip.htm
38. Ibid.
39. Website: http://www.co.fairfax.va.us/sheriff/workrelease.htm
40. Ibid.
41. Nancy A. Youseff, "Tethers May Ease Jail Crowding, State Budget." Detroit Free Press, free/news/Michigan, February 10, 2003, http://www.freepcom/news.mich/alter10_20030210.htm (accessed February 13, 2003).
42. Ibid.
43. Clear and Dammer, *The Offender in the Community*, p. 247.
44. Ibid., pp. 247, 248.
45. Website: http://www.cookcountysheriff.org/dcsi/day.html
46. Ibid.
47. Ibid.
48. Todd R. Clear and George F. Cole, *American Corrections, 5th Edition* (Belmont, CA: West Wadsworth, 2000), p. 206.
49. Joe Loconte, "Making Criminals Pay," *Policy Review*, January–February, 1998, no. 87. http://www.policyreview.org/jan98/criminal.html
50. Larry S. Fischer and Robert Martone, "Putting Intermittent Prisoners to Work: A New Look at an Old Ideal," *American Jails*, March–April 1996, 43.
51. Ibid., pp. 43, 45.

52. Ibid., p. 44.
53. Ibid.
54. Ibid., pp. 44, 45.
55. Website: http://www.arlingtonva.us/Departments/Sheriff/SheriffJailIndustries.aspx?InsLinkID=870
56. Ibid.
57. Website: http://www.cooscountysheriff.com/work_release.htm
58. Carmen N. Santiago, "Give Success a Chance," *American Jails*, March–April 2002, pp. 15–18.
59. Champion, *Probation, Parole and Community Corrections*, pp. 198, 199.
60. Website: Polk County Sheriff's Office.
61. Dale Parent, Terence Dunworth, Douglas McDonald, and William Rhodes, National Institute of Justice, Research in Action, *Key Legislative Issues in Criminal Justice: Intermediate Sanctions*, Washington, DC, January, 1997, pp. 2–4.
62. "Inmate Fails to Return to Jail While on Work Release," *Summit Daily News*, October 5, 2005, http://www.summitdaily.com/article20051005/NEWS/51005007
63. Gary F. Cornelius, *Work Release: An Overview*, pp. 4, 5.
64. McCarthy, McCarthy, and Leone, *Community Based Corrections, 4th Edition*, p. 151.
65. Brad Turner, "Work Release Inmate Overdoses on Heroin," *The Daily Times-Call, Longmont FYI*, October 16, 2005, http://www.longmontfyi.com/Local-Story.asp?id=4162
66. Website: Livingston County Sheriff's Department Work Release: http://members.ismi.net/sheriff/work_release.htm

## REFERENCES


Blum, Justin. "Learning the Confines of Life Outside of Jail." *The Washington Post*, August 16, 1993, D1, D4.

Champion, Dean John. *Probation, Parole and Community Corrections, 5th Edition*. Upper Saddle River, NJ: Pearson Prentice Hall, 2005.

Clear, Todd R. and George F. Cole. *American Corrections, 5th Edition*. Belmont, CA: West Wadsworth, 2000.

Clear, Todd R. and Harry R. Dammer. *The Offender in the Community*. Belmont, CA: Wadsworth, 2000.

Cornelius, Gary F. "Work Release: An Overview." *Jail Operations Bulletin* (American Jail Association) 4, (3), 1992, 3.

Fischer, Larry S. and Robert Martone. "Putting Intermittent Prisoners to Work: A New Look at an Old Ideal." *American Jails*, March–April 1996, 43–45.

Harrison, Paige M. and Allen J. Beck, Ph.D., Bureau of Justice Statistics. *Prison and Jail Inmates at Mid year 2005*. Washington, DC: U.S. Department of Justice, May, 2006.

Hughes, Timothy and Doris James Wilson, BJS Statisticians. "Reentry Trends in the United States." Bureau of Justice Statistics, http://www.ojp.usdoj.gov/bjs/reentry/reentry.htm (accessed March 1, 2007).

"Inmate Fails to Return to Jail While on Work Release." *Summit Daily News*, October 5, 2005, http://www.summitdaily.com/article20051005/NEWS/51005007 (accessed October 29, 2005).

Lauren, Roger J., Ph.D. *Community Managed Corrections and Other Solutions to America's Prison Crisis*. Lanham, MD: American Correctional Association, 1988.

Loconte, Joe. "Making Criminals Pay." *Policy Review*, January–February 1998, no. 87, http://www.policyreview.org/jan98/criminal.html (Accessed January 10, 2004).

Locy, Tony. "Prisons Release Record Numbers of Ex-Convicts." *USA Today*, December 27, 2000, 1A–2A.

Marshall, Patricia A. "Electronic Incarceration Programs." *Jail Operations Bulletin* (American Jail Association) 7, (12), 1996, 2.

McCarthy, Belinda Rogers, Bernard J. McCarthy, Jr. and Matthew Leone. *Community Based Corrections, 4th Edition*. Belmont, CA: Wadsworth, 2001.

Parent, Dale, Terence Dunworth, Douglas McDonald and William Rhodes, National Institute of Justice. *Key Legislative Issues in Criminal Justice: Intermediate Sanctions*. Washington, DC: U.S. Department of Justice, January 1997.

Re-Entry Policy Council. *Executive Summary*, http://www.reentrypolicy.org/report/executive-summary.php (accessed November 5, 2005).

Santiago, Carmen N. "Give Success a Chance." *American Jails*, March–April 2002, 15–18.

St. Gerard, Vanessa. *New Study Proves Jails Are An Important Component of the Reentry Equation*, On the Line, American Correctional Association, March 2005, Volume 28, No. 2, 1–2.

Schrantz, Dennis S. "The Five Tenets of Effective Community Corrections." *Corrections Today*, February 1995, 40–45.

Turner, Brad. "Work Release Inmate Overdoses on Heroin." *The Daily Times-Call, Longmont FYI*, October 16, 2005, http://www.longmontfyi.com/Local-Story.asp?id=4162 (accessed October 29, 2005).

Website: http://www.arlingtonva.us/Departments/Sheriff/SheriffJailIndustries.aspx?InsLinkID=870 (accessed October 29, 2005).

Website: http://www.montgomeryworks.net/E/00024/Detail.cfm?ID=19 (accessed October 29, 2005).

Website: http://www.co.lake.il.us/sheriff/divisions/work.asp (accessed October 29, 2005).

Website: http://www.cooscountysheriff.com/work_release.htm (accessed October 29, 2005).

Website: http://www.co.oakland.mi.us/sheriff/faq/work_release.html (accessed October 29, 2005).

Website: http://www.aspenpitkin.com/depts/28/jail_work release.cfm (accessed March 3, 2007).

Website: http://www.vadoc.state.va.us/offenders/institutions/programs/reentry.htm (accessed October 29, 2005).

Website: http://www.co.fairfax.va.us/sheriff/eip.htm (accessed December 4, 2005).

Website: http://www.co.fairfax.va.us/sheriff/workrelease.htm (accessed December 4, 2005).

Website: http://www.cookcountysheriff.org/dcsi/day.html (accessed October 29, 2005).

Website: Livingston County Sheriff's Department Work Release: http://members.ismi.net/sheriff/work_release.htm (accessed October 29, 2005).

Website: http://www.cookcountysheriff.org/dcsi/em.html (accessed October 29, 2005).

Website: Polk County Juvenile Boot Camp Program, Polk County Sheriff's Office: http://www.polksheriff.org/detention/bootcamp.html (accessed April 14, 2006).

Wells County, Indiana Community Corrections Forms: Community Service, Work Release, EM.

Wood, Frank W. "The Minnesota Approach." *Corrections Today*, February 1996, 52–56.

Youseff, Nancy A. "Tethers May Ease Jail Crowding, State Budget." Detroit Free Press, free/news/Michigan, February 10, 2003, http://www.freepcom/news.mich/alter10_20030210.htm (accessed February 13, 2003).

Zehr, Howard. *The Little Book of Restorative Justice*. Intercourse, PA: Good Books, 2002.

# 12 THE FUTURE OF THE AMERICAN JAIL

*Objectives of chapter*

The student will:

- Understand why jails must keep up and be current with changes in both the correctional system and society.
- Be able to understand why overcrowding continues to have an impact on the local jail.
- Learn how security is becoming more advanced and sophisticated plus understand the need for jail staff to be more computer proficient.
- Understand that special inmate populations will continue to be a concern.
- Understand the need for innovative training and education for staff.
- Learn the importance of continuing good relations with the local community.

## KEEPING UP WITH CHANGE

Jails are an integral part of the local community and what happens in the local community can directly impact the jail. For example, a county has been rural for many years, and due to expanded growth, more homes are being built, and businesses are establishing themselves in the community. The population increases as more people move to that area. With an increase in population comes the potential for increases in arrests, etc. The local jail, which for years has "gotten by" with a small capacity and a small staff, now faces growing pains as local police bring more offenders to the jail.

Community expansion is but one area that will have a future impact on the local jail. Advances are being made in all areas of jail operations: security, classification, records, medical/dental care, commissary, handling of special populations, etc. More emphasis is being placed in some jails on the expansion of their community corrections operations in order to reserve their jail cells for the more serious offenders. Initiatives are being planned for diverting special needs offenders away from the local jail.

## Predicting the Future

In 1988, Barbara Bostick, then commissioner of the Baltimore City Jail, wrote in *Corrections Today* that small jails (and larger ones) faced a number of problems that were "seriously testing their ability to become or remain safe and humane."[1] The fact was and is that jails have become "multifaceted operations" with problems that may make it difficult for them to cope. Commissioner Bostick described five problems:[2]

- Chronic overcrowding
- Inmate litigation
- Specialty classification and services
- Human resources management
- Need for compliance with nationally mandated standards

A more recent view of the future of corrections has been stated by Dr. Richard Seiter, Director, Criminal Justice Program at Saint Louis University. His view is a mixture of both positive and negative views. Due to research in the early 1990s, Seiter suggests that a **"new penology"** has developed where corrections administration has changed from making clinical judgments about the rehabilitative needs of offenders and combating recidivism to the identification of high-risk groups and offenders.[3] Through incarceration, these groups, which include sex offenders, parole violators, gangs, etc., are controlled and theoretically prevented from committing new crimes. Strategies in the recognition and control of these offenders as they are incarcerated in jail must be a crucial component of any jail staff training program.

The five problem areas discussed by Commissioner Bostick have been dealt with in mostly positive ways by jail administrators, courts, and local jurisdictions. While overcrowding remains a problem in many jails, other problems have been acted upon.

Inmate litigation has been curtailed by the provisions of the Prison Litigation Reform Act (see Chapter 9). While inmate lawsuits are still filed, both the frivolous lawsuits and the ease of which these types of lawsuits were filed have been thwarted by this Act. Grievance procedures have been streamlined and improved, and in most cases, inmates are required to submit complaints to the jail administration and exhaust administrative remedies.

With more information now known about security threat groups (STGs), gangs, foreign inmates, mentally disordered inmates, etc., classification in jails is more thorough, precise, and able to properly house such inmates and refer them to qualified staff for dealing with their problems. Computer databases, thorough questionnaires, proper referrals, and use of administrative tools such as hearings have improved classification significantly. Food and medical services in jails have improved greatly in the past 25 years.

Jail staffs are better trained than they were 25–30 years ago. From two-week "jailor schools" to sixteen-week courses in some jurisdictions, jail officers are trained in more diverse subjects, as well as first responder/first aid/CPR, cultural diversity, non-lethal use of force, more advanced firearms, etc. In terms of human resource management, more jurisdictions have offered better benefits when hiring jail staff, as well as employee assistance programs. Jail staffs are more diverse in terms of gender and ethnicity. In jail teams or squads, more female officers and supervisors are present, and it is common to find officers from many different ethnic backgrounds who can speak several languages. Such diversity and bilingual skills aid many processes in the jail, from medical screening, booking, and classification.

It is important for local jails to keep up with advances in technology and training. Jails play a critical role in keeping communities safe by keeping inmates securely incarcerated. There are better products in security, closed-circuit television, radio communications, computer-based data and booking, and training. To better perform the task of secure confinement, jails are making an effort to keep up, if funding is available.

It is not known what local jails will exactly look like a century from now. With the aforementioned advances, no one can predict for sure. However, the following list can serve as a "thumbnail guide" to the jail of the future:

- Crowding and finding alternatives to incarceration.
- Planning new types of facilities to meet demands of the jail.
- Advances in security equipment, including computer technology.
- Management of special populations.
- Advancements in staff training and education.
- Importance of maintaining good community relations.

According to noted jail expert Ken Kerle of the American Jail Association (AJA), jails will be affected by demographics and minorities. Data on jails at the close of the twentieth century indicated that the numbers of African Americans and Hispanics in jails continued to increase, but not at the same rate as was seen in the mid 1990s. Both minorities as represented in the U.S. jail population come from the lower end of society's economic scale; Kerle thinks it is likely that increased numbers of them will do time in jail. The problems that these minorities face in the poverty stricken and dysfunctional areas of the inner cities are not being seriously addressed, which may contribute to the incarceration of African Americans, Hispanics, and other minorities who live there and become involved in crime. Education and vocational opportunities including computer training can serve to assist these groups; if not, their job futures are bleak that they may find a home in jail—either for long stretches or going in and out the jail "revolving door."[4]

Another change in society that will affect local corrections is the advancement of female staff in the local jail. Twenty-five years ago, female jail officers were often regulated to clerical duties, confined only to duties in female confinement sections or passed the time waiting for female offenders to be booked into the jail and processed. Permitting females to work in all male confinement areas was unheard of. Recently, the number of female administrators in U.S. jails has increased from 1991 to 2003, proving that female jail officers and staff have been always able to handle the job. Jail management has a challenge: how to recruit and retain high-caliber women into what was a predominantly male field.[5] In addition, the revolutionary idea of cross gender supervision has taken hold and continues to be practiced in jails, giving female jail officers more opportunities for both a variety of duties and assignments in the jail, as well as opportunities for promotion and advancement. Female jail officers supervise jail squads, sections, and branches, and females are providing specialized assistance to jails, such as in the area of computer technology.

## OVERCROWDING AND ALTERNATIVES TO INCARCERATION

Even though jails are operating below their capacity that does not mean that they are not crowded. The recent statistics published by the Bureau of Justice Statistics (BJS) in May 2006 shows a trend in the last several years concerning jail populations.

It is clear from the below statistics that the jail count is steadily increasing rather than decreasing. In the year ending on June 30, 2005, local jails were operating at a rate of 5% below their rated capacity. That percentage cannot be viewed as flexibility; any significant upsurge in the local arrest rate or the number of inmates being sentenced to incarceration from the local court can narrow that gap quickly. Also, if the jail encounters maintenance problems, etc., cells are lost for inmate use until repairs are made. What is significant is that a range of 90–95 percent of jail capacity is occupied. It is clear that the percentage rate of jail capacity that is occupied is steadily increasing.[6]

These numbers are high, and the trend appears to be heading in a few years to possibly one million offenders housed in local jails. It is apparent that finding alternatives to incarceration is a logical solution to local jail overcrowding. The statistics appear to be heading that way. Even weekender programs only temporarily increase the jail count a few days per week. Offenders in alternative programs that are supervised by jail staff do free up critically needed cell space. One concern in smaller jails is if staff can be allocated for such programs, while in larger jails entire squads, branches, or sections can be designated to provide supervision for alternatives to incarceration programs.

Statistically, it appears that more offenders are being placed in alternative programs that are supervised by jail staff. This is beneficial for the offenders and allows them to remain in the community to work and be with their families, while avoiding the stigma of being in jail. Note the trends of the last several years concerning the number of inmates held in custody inside the jail as compared to being supervised outside the jail facility in alternative programs (Figure 12.2):

| *Year* | *Number of Inmates* | *Incarceration Rate per 100,000 g.p.* | *% Capacity Occupied* |
|---|---|---|---|
| 2000 | 621,149 | 220 | 92 |
| 2001 | 631,240 | 222 | 90 |
| 2002 | 655,475 | 231 | 93 |
| 2003 | 691,301 | 238 | 94 |
| 2004 | 713,990 | 243 | 94 |
| 2005 | 747,529 | 252 | 95 |

Percentage of change mid-2004 to mid-2005: 4.7%
Annual average increase from mid-1995 to mid-2005: 3.9%
g.p. indicates 100,000 residents in general population.

*Source: Prison and Jail Inmates at Midyear 2005,* Bureau of Justice Statistics Bulletin NCJ 213133, May, 2006, by Paige M. Harrison and Allen Beck, Ph.D.

**FIGURE 12-1** Inmates Held in Local Jails/Capacity Occupied 2000–2005[7]

| Year | Number of Inmates in Held in Jail Custody | Inmates Supervised Outside Programs* |
|---|---|---|
| 1995 | 507,044 | 34,869 |
| 2000 | 621,149 | 65,884 |
| 2004 | 713,990 | 70,548 |
| 2005 | 747,529 | 71,905 |

*Outside programs: weekender, electronic monitoring, home detention (non-electronic monitoring), day reporting, community service, other pre-trial and work programs, treatment, and unspecified.

From 2000 to 2005, the number of inmates supervised by the local jail but *not* incarcerated inside the jail has been in 65,000–72,000 range and is increasing.

*Source: Prison and Jail Inmates at Midyear 2005,* Bureau of Justice Statistics Bulletin NCJ 213133, May, 2006, by Paige M. Harrison and Allen Beck, Ph.D.

**FIGURE 12-2** Jail Inmates Incarcerated versus Supervised in Alternative Programs[8]

Jail crowding can be attributed to sentencing and criminal justice practices that place more offenders in jail for longer periods of time, or inmates making rehabilitation a low priority to the point of re-offending. According to the BJS in 2003, the increase in inmate population in the United States—prisons and jails—was mainly because of mandatory sentences for non-violent drug offenders. This hurts correctional budgets due to both overcrowding and costs—an estimated 40 billion dollars in 2003.[9]

Other factors can affect a jail's headcount. Task force operations by specialized units, such as vice, gang, illegal immigration enforcement, etc., may result in raids and mass arrests. It is impossible to predict a jail's exact count at any one moment because of the frequency of inmates being booked in and released. Jails have to take in and house whoever comes in through the intake area.

Some jurisdictions are adopting more flexible policies. In Washington State, several counties tried a novel approach to deal with jail overcrowding. Increasing the use of bail for minor offenses significantly reduced jail overcrowding. Police officers were advised to take the following actions when possible, which reduced the Spokane County jail admission rate by 29 percent:[10]

- Not to bring to jail out of county misdemeanant warrant arrests.
- Not to bring to jail misdemeanor charges except if required by state law or district court bail schedule.
- Not to bring to jail traffic charges other than driving under the influence (DUI).

Through diversion, many post-conviction and traffic offenders did not go to jail, reducing the average length of stay from 14 to 12 days. To a crowded jail, this is significant when staff is struggling to find every bed available.[11]

Regional jails (see Chapter 1) are another option, where jurisdictions pool money and resources to build one jail to serve the needs of all jurisdictions involved. This trend is continuing. To financially strapped jurisdictions, this makes good operational and fiscal sense. Small populated counties find it uneconomical to operate small jails around the clock every day of the year. A comparison of rated capacities in regional jails in the directories of *Who's Who in Jail Management 1991 and 2003* revealed an increase of a little over 2,000 to almost 17,000 inmates. One state that has taken a proactive approach in using the regional jail concept is West Virginia, where the local jails in the state's 50 plus counties will be condensed into an arrangement of 10 regional jails. In nearby Virginia, the commonwealth encouraged local jurisdictions to build new regional jails by offering to them a higher state subsidy. There are also economic advantages to regionalization of jails. Regional jails can offer career opportunities in many areas of corrections, including community corrections.[12]

The problem of offenders committing new crimes and returning to jail is a recurring problem. According to Mark Mauer, director of the Sentencing Project, this problem is further complicated by what he calls **"invisible punishments."** These are defined as laws that make a certain group of offenders, such as drug offenders, ineligible for certain types of employment and services. In Pennsylvania, persons with criminal histories cannot get a job in health care; in Delaware, drug offenders are ineligible for food stamps and welfare. With over a half million inmates being released from prisons and jails every year, these roadblocks may cause them to commit crimes to survive. If they do, the local jail will have to take them back in. Clearly, these types of laws and policies may need to be reexamined in order to reduce local jail overcrowding.[13]

## New Jail Designs

As jails in the United States age and are feeling the effects of overcrowding, many jurisdictions are faced with the problem of either renovating existing jails or building new facilities. In counties and cities where available funds are sought by many different groups and government departments, funding a jail renovation or the construction of a new jail may not be popular. Both renovations and construction take long periods of time, and jail administrators are faced with the possibility that the jail will be full on the same day that it opens. The fundamental questions are: How can a jail be renovated or built to serve the community for a long period of time and still be cost effective?

An example of strategic jail planning is in Orange County, California. The community demographics changed in the 1980s, and the sheriff began a comprehensive planning process to plan for the needs of the jail for the next 20 years. The far ranging plan called for a centrally located facility to meet the demands of the fast growing community. The final result was the Theo Lacy site, centrally located in the county, near the juvenile courthouse and within minimal travel time from several other courthouses.[14]

In this facility, there are several unique security improvements. No inmate cells are located on exterior walls, and the entire exterior wall is bordered by a service corridor with high-view windows. Maintenance is performed without displacing the inmate from the cell. Access points and cells in the facility can be unlocked from 50 yards away, thus minimizing the danger that jail officers face when going to a cell and getting an inmate.[15]

Another example of far-reaching design is the $47.6 million, 475-bed Ramsey County Law Enforcement Center in St. Paul, Minnesota. Completed in

October 2003, the Center features open arraignment booking courts, an ergonomic video display in arraignment showing the judges the defendants and inmates on the docket waiting for court, which allows the handling of up to 150–200 cases per day. It has a six-story inmate-housing tower for sentenced inmates. The firing range, training areas, sheriff's offices, warrants, and investigations are contained within the complex. The goal of the project was greater longevity of the facility.[16]

Expansions are also an option for future operations of jails. In South Carolina, plans are underway to expand the Charleston County Jail by 1,372 beds at a cost of almost $58 million, along with a new juvenile detention facility at a cost of almost $10 million. In Sebastian County, Arkansas, the 10-year-old jail will have an additional pair of 48 bed wings at a cost of $3.5 million. In Gibson County, Tennessee, a new 330-bed facility will connect to the existing jail.[17]

As jails expand or undergo renovations, more creative methods will have to be devised by staff to give the inmates positive activities such as programs and recreation. Jail officers will say that recreation and programs do help to keep the tensions down. As jails become crowded, and staffing is chronically short in many facilities, inmate activities must continue despite these hindrances. Direct supervision types of housing unit appears to be the way of the future, as inmates behave better and the climate is more beneficial to the jail officer.

While the concept of privatization of local jails is discussed in Chapter 1, jurisdictions are exploring ways to bring in private correctional companies to operate jails. This is a trend of the future. In Galveston, Texas, a new criminal justice center is being built. Rather than let the old existing jail sit empty, the county is seeking proposals from private companies to provide staffing, transport, and building costs. The privatization factor is controversial. While supporters hope that revenue will be generated and costs kept down, critics argue that private jail officers are paid less and inadequately trained.[18]

## ADVANCES IN SECURITY EQUIPMENT AND COMPUTER TECHNOLOGY

As jails progress into the twenty-first century, developments in technology on the outside are mirrored inside the local jail. Some jails have personal computers on posts where deputies can access e-mails, check inmate booking screens for information, and access forms. Computer proficiency is required to type incident reports, access information, and to participate in online training. It is rare to see a jail booking in a prisoner by the old "booking card" method where all data and charges, including court dispositions, are handwritten on a card or in a paper file, The preferred method of booking uses computer screens and forms. Checking for criminal histories, fingerprinting and photographing have all advanced in the last 25 years. In a control booth, doors are activated with a computer mouse or by a touch screen. Instead of typewriters, incident reports are written on word processors and sent online to the supervisor for further action. The computer skills learned in today's schools can well serve the jail officer.

There have been some significant advances in corrections security technology. Besides the more routine innovations such as pepper spray, video monitoring, the expandable baton, better radio communications, and personal alarm devices, jails officers now may be using the following new devices:[19]

- *Layered voice analysis:* **Layered voice analysis** uses software to track and analyze thoughts, to show stress, inaccuracies, and deceptions. It has potential uses in investigations of inmate assaults, contraband, escapes, rule breaking, and in the monitoring of sex offenders, probationers, and parolees. Other uses for the software include analyzing inmate telephone conversations to see whether any illegal activities are planned or are occurring. The Wisconsin Department of Corrections is currently using this software.
- *Automated light survey:* The **automated light survey** detects deficient lighting in outdoor areas and perimeters of correctional facilities. The portable system uses Global Positioning System (GPS) technology, a light meter and a computer interface to determine which areas need more lighting. It is portable and can be easily carried by a jail officer on rounds.

Being forewarned about inmates is being forearmed. The more that is known about an inmate, the safer the jail officer can be. In Littleton, Massachusetts, jail officers at the Essex County Sheriff's Department correctional facilities use the **wearable computer.** This small computer, about the size of a brick, can be worn inside the officer's body armor, in the belt, and can be adapted with microphones and headphones for hands-free use with speech recognition software. This speech recognition software allows the officer to speak verbal commands to the computer instead of scrolling through a menu. It has full intranet, Internet, and networking capabilities, and a touchpad for input. A small video camera can be attached to transmit both still images and streaming video. Its uses include allowing the officer wearing it to see through a wireless connection an inmate's complete history, including medical and disciplinary. This information can be accessed on the way to a critical incident such as a disturbance, barricade situation, inmate fight, suicide threats, etc. By way of a monitor that can be attached to the computer and link capability to the facility's closed-circuit television system, officers can view fights, actions by inmates and staff, etc. before arrival at the scene. With this information, good decisions on what to do can be made. Officers can also use the video and digital photos to write accurate incident reports. One company sets the price of one wearable computer at $4,500, which means that an agency with budgetary limits may only be able to afford one or two.[20]

One concern of security and the future is the trend of anti-terrorist security because the tragic events of September 11, 2001 (attacks on the World Trade Center) and the Oklahoma City bombings in April 1995. Jails are government buildings, and many are connected to police departments, courthouses, and other government offices. Jails have held inmates accused of terrorist acts. When doing so, extra security precautions are put into place. Like all government buildings, jails can be a target for terrorist groups for whatever reason that they devise. The future of jails may include these security hardware materials and placements:[21]

- *Ballistic glass:* **Ballistic glass** or sometimes called "bullet proof glass" is bullet-resistant glass that should be installed in ground-level jail windows to protect staff and inmates from drive by shootings.

- *Screening:* Walls and trees can be used to block a straight line of sight to lobbies and windows, which may protect against drive by shootings.
- *Barriers:* **Barriers** are objects such as concrete planters, steel girders, concrete or steel pilings sunk into the ground, or the commonly seen "Jersey" barriers that can help to prevent a vehicle laden with explosives (such as a "truck bomb" from getting close to the side of the building and detonating).

Other common sense security guidelines that reflect this trend are more thorough checking of identification, outside perimeter patrols, improved lighting, video surveillance, and bomb threat training. The future trend is that jails will eventually be more secure within their perimeters.

The future of the American jail security must include the concept of direct supervision. When properly implemented, direct supervision allows for low-risk and carefully classified inmates to be moved from a jail's overcrowded sections into the more positive surroundings of direct supervision. This can serve to maintain a positive atmosphere in the jail, which assists in maintaining security and lowers tension. Several things about this concept have to be addressed: citizens, government, and academics must more fully understand the goals of direct supervision, and direct supervision units should be used for what they were intended for—housing inmates per the concept of direct supervision and not double bunking inmates in a "just another crowded jail" type of scenario. Double-bunking inmates in direct supervision units violate the very principles upon what direct supervision is based. Also, more training in direct supervision continues to be requested of regional jail training seminars conducted by the AJA.[22]

The future of jails includes spacious, modern living areas for inmates.

Photo by author, Courtesy Butler County Prison.

On a related note, training in direct supervision and its communication and assertiveness techniques must be taken seriously. It is still a new concept, and many jail officers are more comfortable with the traditional linear and podular styles of jail inmate supervision, in which interaction and communication with inmates are minimal and very limited. Agency heads and jail officer supervisors must recognize the value of direct supervision and do whatever it takes to get their subordinates to buy into the concept. It is highly recommended that only the best instructors and veteran staff be used in training and instruction on direct supervision, as well as allowing jail officers to tour other jails where direct supervision is used and is working well.

## DEALING WITH SPECIAL POPULATIONS

With advances in knowledge about mentally disordered inmates, substance abusers, female inmates, and the elderly, to name but a few, future trends in jails will include the special management and handling of these inmates. Classification, medical care, programs, and services will all be impacted by elderly inmates, pregnant females, and foreign inmates that do not speak English. Ray Coleman, Division Manager at the King County, Washington, Department of Adult Detention, wrote in 1999 of the challenges facing jails in the twenty-first century concerning special populations:[23]

- *Elderly:* With the onset of aging baby boomers, many elderly offenders will be arrested and housed in the local jail. Many will be first-timers, and the cause of their crimes may be Alzheimer's, domestic violence, lack of income and retirement planning, and homelessness. Some will have a mental condition that makes it difficult to be law abiding. Dietary needs, medical care, classification and housing, and programs will have to adjust to the needs of the elderly inmate.
- *Juveniles:* Many jurisdictions are taking another look at juvenile offenders and are certifying some as adults. Certification means that they come to jail and will be housed as adults. However, with juveniles under certain conditions being placed in a local jail, the jail will have challenges in separating juveniles from adult inmates, classification, etc.
- *Females:* According to Coleman, the female offender population will increase in the next century. Welfare reform and not necessarily crime will contribute to this, as women offenders look to crime for survival as their welfare status ends. Jails will have to deal with mentally ill female offenders, pregnant females, etc.
- *Mentally ill:* Mentally ill offenders will still be a factor in the jail population. With community resources unable to handle the problems of the mentally disordered, those who commit crimes will still have to be dealt with in the jail.
- *Substance abuse:* Offenders who abuse drugs and alcohol should receive treatment, but many jails do not have the resources to operate and fund programs to address substance abuse issues. Collaboration with community resources including the involvement of volunteers should be explored.

- *Foreign/culturally diverse inmates:* With the problem of illegal immigration and the increase of foreign nationals settling in the United States, more emphasis will be needed in operations and training to deal with the foreign/culturally diverse inmate. Two areas that are important are communication and training. A more culturally diverse staff is also needed.

Jail officers will not be able to handle these diverse types of inmates alone. With special populations comes the need for specialized staff, which will become an integral part of the jail staff: mental health personnel, substance abuse counselors, chaplains, teachers, including those proficient in several languages, medical personnel familiar with geriatrics, instructors in specialized subjects such as sexually transmitted diseases, parenting, etc., and volunteers.

One program that illustrates the possible future handling of mentally ill offenders is the Crisis Intervention Training (CIT) course in Las Vegas, Nevada. Adopted by the Las Vegas Metropolitan Police Department in 2003, 151 police officers and 52 correctional officers were trained in proper responses of handling psychologically unstable and/or mentally ill individuals. Incidents with these individuals have been de-escalated to reasonable resolutions, and as a result both the community and the Clark County, Nevada, Detention Center are benefited. The Clark County Detention Center is a large facility with a daily inmate count of over 3,200 and handles over 59,000 bookings per year, taking offenders from 30 state and local agencies. In conjunction with jail mental health personnel, social workers, and physicians, CIT-trained officers have stabilized and handled approximately 700 mentally ill offenders. The jail has 57 housing units, and 2 units are designated for mentally ill offenders; these inmates benefit from CIT-trained jail officers. As a result, the jail has experienced a reduction in violent incidents in the jail. Also, once the mentally ill inmates are stabilized, they may be able to be reclassified into the jail's general inmate population.[24]

In 2003, Clark County established a Mental Health Court Advisory Committee, which developed a grant to fund the eighth Judicial District Mental Health Court. This court works with the personnel in the jail and community mental health agencies to divert screened offenders from the criminal justice system. This approach also involves the prosecutor and the public defender's office, which negotiate a plea agreement acceptable in the mental health court.[25] This is unique approach that many jails should examine in dealing with the high numbers of mentally ill offenders; it will require a fresh look at the problem and the commitment from agencies to make such solutions feasible.

Another jail that is expanding services to mentally ill inmates is the Brevard Jail Complex located in Sharpes, Florida. This jail has struggled with overcrowding, jail suicides, and inmate safety. The jail in November 2006 housed 1,763 inmates—55 percent over capacity. Five inmates attempted suicide during two months in 2004 and 2005, resulting in four inmate fatalities. The county government sold bonds, resulting in funding for a $17 million Medical and Mental Health Facility, due to be completed by 2008. In the interim, the first of four 7,000-square foot, reinforced, air-conditioned tents has been erected to house 288 inmates. Authorities say that it will allow jail staff expedient access to inmates having mental health and medical issues.[26]

One special type of jail inmate who will become necessary to handle carefully in the future is the high-profile offender. The War on Terror that commenced after the terrorist attacks of September 11, 2001, have brought the law enforcement actions including the arrest, incarceration, and conviction of suspected terrorists into the spotlight. More than ever, the American public wants to feel safe, which means that the local jails have to keep these inmates securely confined. The offenders arrested in the War on Terror are not the only high-profile offenders that jails will have to deal with. As law enforcement techniques continue to improve resulting in increased media exposure, jails will deal more with serial killers, child molesters, and other offenders of note. Examples include O. J. Simpson, on trial for murder in the early 1990s, Timothy McVeigh, the Oklahoma City bomber of 1995, and the D.C. area snipers, Lee Boyd Malvo and John Muhammad, in 2002.

The distinction between a "high profile inmate" and the everyday jail inmate is based on perceptions: he or she is famous and special precautions must be taken. A **high-profile inmate** is a highly visible inmate due to the perceptions of staff, other inmates, and the public, thanks mostly in part to the advances in media coverage. Jails have to devise special ways to deal with these offenders while maintaining security, because as a general rule, jails are at the mercy of whoever the police or another law enforcement agency brings through the jail house door. There are four considerations in dealing with these types of inmates; considerations that the jail operations of the future will have to contend with: physical security of the facility, physical security of the inmate, behavior of the inmate in the jail, and jail compliance with court orders and transportation of the inmate.[27] Special conditions of confinement must be imposed and precautions taken to ensure that the inmate's incarceration is uneventful while security is maintained.

A good example of how a jail should handle a high-profile inmate or inmates can be found in Wichita, Kansas, at the Sedgewick County Sheriff's Office. Sedgewick County has housed several high-profile inmates since the mid-1990s, namely Terry Nichols, convicted in the Oklahoma City bombing case, brothers Jonathan and Reginald Carr, who committed a crime spree resulting in five people dead, and one person severely wounded. Several of the Carrs' victims were sexually abused, and the crimes were described as extensively cruel. The Carr brothers' trial lasted almost two years; they were confined for 700 days. Sedgewick County also confined Dennis Rader, the self-named "BTK" serial killer for 174 days. Each case was unique. Terry Nichols and Dennis Rader were both segregated, while the Carrs were placed in general population.[28]

The future of jails managing the high-profile inmate includes different ways of doing "business as usual" in the jail. Jail staff will have to adapt to changes in duties and perform special tasks. In the aforementioned three cases of high-profile inmates, the Sedgewick County jail ordered special precautions to be taken by staff, and the conditions under which these inmates were housed reflected the seriousness of security. Terry Nichols was segregated and monitored 24 hours per day, seven days per week by jail deputies who were instructed to engage in minimal conversation with him. Deputies were also instructed to record anything that Nichols said and all conversations with him. Any time that Nichols was moved, he was in leg restraints, escorted by two deputies; hallways were cleared of all traffic. Deputies escorted Nichols everywhere he went in the jail, and he ate his meals in his cell. Due to the nature of his crime and the possibility that an external threat existed, all jail deputies were ordered to keep an extra watch on the jail's exterior for any type of suspicious activity.[29]

In the BTK Killer Dennis Rader's case, the jail had a unique advantage of advance notification. While in many cases the jail staff is alerted only a very short time after a high-profile offender's arrival, selected Sedgewick County Jail staff was advised that a suspect was going to be arrested in the BTK case; the advance notice allowed the staff to plan. Each security watch had designated personnel to supervise Rader, and the medical section limited contact with him to selected staff. Rader was placed in a housing unit with 11 other inmates who were carefully interviewed and reclassified by a classification sergeant. Rader's inmate file and medical file were both maintained by watch commanders and medical administrators respectively to further safeguard information about the inmate. Sealed court orders mandated that Rader's mail, both incoming and outgoing, be read by staff for threats or escape plans.[30]

Concerning the Carr brothers, they were housed in the jail's general population but were a management problem due to physical altercations with jail inmates and staff; one brother attempted to bribe a deputy into bringing in marijuana (which the deputy reported) and one brother possessed another inmate's identity card. The Carrs were not white but their victims were, which fueled demonstrations by white supremacist groups. One condition was a gag order from the court, applicable to all participants in the trial and the deputies of the Sedgewick County Sheriff's Office.[31]

## ADVANCEMENTS IN STAFF TRAINING AND EDUCATION

With jails changing, jail officers will have to keep up with advancements in computer technology and in specialized subjects such as handling high-profile inmates, anti-terrorism, special populations, and because of direct supervision, interpersonal communications. With every change in technical procedures such as in booking, classification, electronic monitoring, etc., training will have to be conducted and documented. Probably the most unique advancement in training has been the development of online classes offered by such organizations as the American Jail Association (ACA), the AJA, and the Corrections Connection.

Firearms training is undergoing a change as jail officers are being trained in non-lethal ammunition and transitioning from revolvers to semi-automatic side arms. Simulated firearms' training is also gaining popularity with training academies. With more safeguards on criminal histories and faster, more expedient online ways to access criminal history records and wanted checks, training is improving in the areas of criminal records.

With the advent of gangs and STGs, more seminars and such specialized topics are being offered on gangs, STGs, weapons of mass destruction, anti-terrorist training, bio-hazard materials, and handling high-risk inmates.

New laws and the messages that they send to the jail staff will have to be addressed in training. For example, the Americans with Disabilities Act passed by Congress in the 1990s necessitated training for jail staff on issues of inmates with disabilities. The Prison Rape Elimination Act of 2003 will have an impact on jail staff as they must learn to prevent, report, and investigate sexual assaults of inmates. Twenty-five years ago, it is safe to say that such a law and the ramifications for staff training could not have been envisioned.

There are "common sense" areas of training concerning inmates who must continue to be offered to the jail staff. Suicides in jail are a continuing problem,

Modern state of the art jail booking areas continue to mark the progress of jails.

Photo by author, courtesy of Sheriff Michael G. Bellotti and Deputy Superintendent David Reilly of the Norfolk County Sheriff's Office.

as are the mentally disordered inmates. More information is now being put forth concerning sexually transmitted diseases and bloodborne pathogens, and training is required.

Inmate manipulation is a popular subject and is necessary to be presented occasionally, especially to new staff who is not "seasoned" in interacting with and controlling inmates. As new information and intervention strategies are introduced to these and other subjects, training seminars will have to be offered at the in-service level in order for jail officers to be kept current.

There are common sense subjects among staff, also. Ethics and professionalism is important especially combined with sexual harassment. Training in these subjects can only serve to enhance the workplace. Legal rights of inmates is a subject that constantly changes, thanks to ongoing court decisions and laws such as the Americans with Disabilities Act, the Prison Litigation Reform Act, and the Prison Rape Elimination Act. Training is offered at the in-service level, but more jail officers have to keep up with these important issues to avoid liability.

There has never been a better time for jail officers to advance their education through the convenience of **online college classes.** These classes are offered by accredited universities and colleges. Jail officers study online, complete class work, and by doing so can obtain a bachelor's degree or master's degree. Online classes are part of the new training concept of **distance learning.** Distance learning encompasses students completing course work and sending it to an accredited college for the evaluation and grading for credit toward a degree.

Distance learning and online learning present several advantages to both the jail officer and the jail supervisor. First, the officer can take courses on his or her off duty time or during a midnight shift with the supervisor's permission. Second, the jail officer does not have to worry about getting approved leave to go to class. However, some jails do allow officers time off to take classes. In any event, an officer taking classes at a nearby college or community college is striving to improve his or her job performance.

Correspondence courses can also be advantageous to the jail staff member looking to broaden his or her knowledge base. Organizations such as the ACA offer a variety of courses in inmates' legal rights, suicide prevention, staff supervision, report writing, just to name a few. Successful completion of such courses can earn educational/training credit with the organization.

Education for jail officers can serve to enhance professionalism and job skills. According to Dr. David R. Struckhoff of Loyola University, the jail staff of the future "must combine the skill of hi-tech/net surfers with the interpersonal skills of a counselor." Dr. Struckhoff advocates that because jail staff are more career minded, academia should move into the mainstream of law enforcement training through relevant, accredited seminars. Also, government agencies must understand the importance of the local jail and its staff in "enhancing the stability of society and progress in understanding human (mis) behavior." Jails and academia—the local colleges and universities—should combine resources. Courses should be diverse, such as political science, psychology, social work, criminal diagnostics, and business management. In other words, combine the knowledge of higher learning with the practical knowledge of dealing with jail inmates and operations. This is a "down to earth" grass roots approach to career development.[32]

Dr. Struckhoff also wrote that the Commission on Correctional Curriculum in Higher Education suggested that the college curricula for jail officers include 18 hours of credits for the following six courses: Corrections in the Criminal Justice System, Correctional Practices, Communication in Corrections, Offender Behavior and Development, Juvenile Justice and Corrections, and Ethical and Legal issues in Corrections.[33]

This approach to combine both jail staff career development and academics was adapted by the Cook County, Illinois Sheriff's Office. In an agreement with Governors State University, Triton College, and the Cook County Sheriff's Office, undergraduate and graduate classes are offered at both a sheriff's learning campus located near the Cook County Jail and the college campuses. The program that developed is called the Leadership and Development Program and was designed to assist jail staff who wishes to advance their careers.[34]

George Mason University in northern Virginia has also made great strides in providing criminal justice education. Many of the courses offered, including the Sociology of Punishment and Corrections, Community Corrections, and Jails and Local Corrections, are instructed by corrections professionals. A novel program under development is "Straight Talk from America's Students." The Corrections Connection (www.corrections.com) and Eastern Kentucky University have devised this program where criminal justice college students can design and research their own Web sites on any number of law enforcement and correctional issues. Students analyze data and present issues and findings to over 500,000 industry professionals and practitioners while earning college credit.[35]

In this age of fast information, there are many online Internet sites for jail staff to access. One of the most widely known is the Corrections Connection, from Screened Images Multimedia (SIM) based in Quincy, Massachusetts. It features news articles from all areas of corrections: Juvenile, state, federal, and local. These articles are gleaned from reputable wire news services, television stations and newspapers from across the United States and abroad. Also, the Web site features link to many organizations, such as the ACA, the AJA, and the International Association of Correctional Training Personnel (IACTP). New products and correctional programs can be viewed, as well as live Web casts featuring interviews with corrections professionals on a variety of topics. News articles are archived, and college professors who teach corrections have urged their students to access this site. Training events and conferences are posted, and an online directory allows the user access to the latest information in such areas as food service, juvenile, and privatization. The Corrections Connection is truly a one-stop resource for the corrections professional, student, and training instructor and represents the technological advancement concerning up-to-date useful information in corrections.

Information courtesy of The Corrections Connection Network News at www.corrections.com—Eye on Corrections.

Special thanks to Laura and Joe Noonan, the Corrections Connection, at www.corrections.com.

**FIGURE 12-3** The Corrections Connection

## IMPORTANCE OF MAINTAINING GOOD COMMUNITY RELATIONS

Jails are visible to the citizens of the jurisdiction of which they serve. These citizens realize that circumstances may place a friend or family member inside the jail. The public wants a well-run and humane jail. News of jail suicides and assaults are unsettling and bring negative publicity to both the agency and the facility. Through the Internet, sheriff's offices have Web pages that tell the public about the jail and the professionalism of its staff. Sheriffs and jail officials must be able to "sell" to taxpayers plans for funding a new jail, renovating an existing jail, implementing new inmate programs, obtaining funding for staff training and equipment, and hiring new jail staff.

Colleges and universities are benefiting from good community relations with local jails. George Mason University in Fairfax, Virginia, for example, allows college students to participate in internships for credit in local criminal justice agencies, including local jails. Another internship program for junior and senior college students is administered by the Department of Sociology and Corrections at Minnesota State University. The goal of the MSU internship program, which has been in place for 30 years, is to turn out students who have an understanding of corrections and can easily enter the corrections field. All corrections majors must complete the 450-hour internship class while also participating in a seminar class. The intern gives a report at the conclusion of the internship with their supervisors present. Internship sites include prisons, halfway houses, probation agencies, and county courts. Blue Earth County Community Corrections has interns performing administrative tasks, going to court, and visiting offenders in the local jail. Interns gain valuable experience and also increase their chances of finding a job in the corrections field.[36]

Jails getting involved in the community will also be a trend of the future. One jail that has taken a lead in this is Pike County Correctional Facility in Pennsylvania. Warden Richard A. Caridi wanted to get across to young people the dangers of the criminal lifestyle that results in people coming to jail. Not wanting to use inmates to "scare" youths, like in the traditional Scared Straight Program, he started a program that uses the jail staff who reflects positive role models. Called the "Reality Check Program," students and chaperones are brought into the jail and are instructed in what to do, where to go, etc.—just like being incarcerated. Staff then speaks to the group about giving respect to get respect. Positive behavior is discussed, as students realize in the tour that when incarcerated in a jail one's individuality is gone, and being an inmate is not a very pleasant experience. Students tour inmate living areas and the secure visiting booths. There they are told to sit, pick up the phone, and say hello to their mother. They are informed that when in jail, life is hard as one is separated from family and things in their lives. The tour concludes with the students going to the conference room with the warden, sampling the jail "Nutraloaf" and asking any questions, all which are answered directly and sternly. Students are then instructed to write a brief summary of their experience and thank the jail staff. As of January 2003, over 750 Pike County students had participated in the "Reality Check Program."[37]

Another area of maintaining positive community relations is victim notification. In Los Angeles County, the sheriff's department provides the Victim Information and Notification Everyday or VINE program. VINE is an anonymous, computer-based telephone program with which victims can get information about an inmate's incarceration status and notification when an inmate is released or transferred. To ascertain whether an inmate is still in custody and be informed of his or her custody location, callers can call a main telephone number and follow the prompts. To be notified if the inmate is transferred or released, the victim can enter a four-digit personal identification number (PIN). The service will automatically call the victim and will try to reach the victim every half hour for 24 hours if no one answers the phone or the line is busy. VINE will also leave messages on an answering machine.[38]

POINT OF VIEW

## Jails of the Future

*William "Bill" Sturgeon, MA*

The jails of the future will have to face challenges that are similar to those that they are now facing; this is just part of the normal day-to-day evolution of jail operations. These include retirement of the baby boomer generation, lack of trained and experienced staff, continuous funding issues, younger, more violent offenders, repeat offenders who will be facing a long sentence in the state's prison, and more inmates with serious or chronic illnesses, etc. Unfortunately, the jails of the future will lose their abilities to be safe havens for some of society's forgotten people. There will not be the "bed space" to house these individuals and keep them safe from predators. The jails of the future will be, as some currently are, "hardcore" operations. In a way it is too bad that trend has already started to occur because society has yet to fill the void. An analogy that could be used is hospitals. In years past, people were permitted to stay in the hospital a day or two longer if their physician ordered it. Now, the only people permitted to stay in today are those who are really sick and for which we can do something.

There will be other challenges that jails of the future will encounter that are outside our current scope of knowledge and awareness. These challenges will manifest themselves as society progresses through this new millennium. They could involve medical issues for example, new strains of diseases and infections, an entirely new series of illicit "designer" drugs that are highly addictive and that could have serious side affects such as violent behavior, impaired cognitive functions, etc. There could be terrorist events so catastrophic as to affect the way Americans conduct their daily affairs. The future is exciting and challenging because of the unknowns it holds. Those who will be responsible for managing and operating the jails of the future will have to embrace the reality of "constant change" and have the ability to respond, adapt, and implement changes to the operation of the jail to meet the demands of society.

Administrators, unions, managers, supervisors, and line staff will have to be able to change relatively quickly to meet whatever new challenges should arise. Since the beginning of the 1990s, the pace of the change that has taken place in all of society, to include jails, has accelerated to a pace that often leaves those unwilling to change and/or adapt playing catch-up or out of the game. As an example, the onset of larger numbers of juveniles who were committing violent crimes started to increase in the early 1990s. State legislatures across America started to "change" the laws about incarcerating juveniles in adult jails and prisons. In a short period of time, jails and prisons were experiencing a new type of prisoner whom they were ill prepared to properly manage. It took until the mid-1990s for staff training programs to be developed and for specialized youthful offender programs to be implemented to manage this "specialized" population.

Those in leadership positions in the jails of the future will not have the luxury of three to four years to spot trends; develop policies and procedures to deal with the new trends, to train staff, and to implement new programs or operations changes. They will have to be ready to change to meet and manage any new challenges almost instantaneously. The events of September 11, 2001, taught the nation that the game has changed, and to be effective and efficient, agencies, departments, and individuals have to be able to think quickly and implement the necessary actions that need to take place.

The jails of the future will continue to incarcerate those being held for trial and those who have been sentenced. Also, in some cases, they will also continue to act as a "temporary home" for those individuals who have mental disorders that lead them to commit "public nuisance" crimes for which they end up in jail.

Jails have adapted to the introduction of street and prison gangs, HIV/AIDS, elderly inmates and inmates with serious mental health issues, shrinking budgets, etc. These and many other factors have helped to develop the characteristics of today's prisoners.

What is not known is: What are the characteristics of the inmates of the future? As mentioned previously, new drugs could hit the "streets" making managing inmates more difficult. This is because of the resulting aggressive, violent behavior, and/or impaired cognitive abilities, similar to those inmates who were on LSD in years past. A new sexually transmitted disease could appear and cause additional medical problems and costs for the jail. The incarceration of terrorists as prisoners will add new and unique challenges to prisoner management techniques. It will be difficult to try to secure and manage a prisoner population that will sacrifice their own lives on the promise of a better life/status in the afterlife. Managing a prisoners population that would kill/injure a staff person to make a political statement, kill perceived enemies, and/or gain status in the eyes of their fellow terrorists presents hard challenges.

It is almost a certainty that jails will have to play a more active role in the public health arena. Because of the lifestyle of the majority of people who go to jails across the country, they are susceptible to become the first victims and hosts of any new diseases, drugs, infections, etc.

The lurking unknown since 9/11 is terrorism and its effects on the American way of life. Jails are microcosms of society as a whole and as an example; government will become directly affected by any terrorist events. When dealing with the issue(s) of terrorism, jails of the future will have to have a multidisciplinary approach because of the many functions they could be asked to fulfill. Jails could be required to incarcerate suspected terrorists. The jail building(s) could be used to treat injured citizens, first responders, or as a gathering place for additional help. The jail grounds could be used as decontamination areas. Jail staff could be called upon to fulfill functions for the community that are outside the scope of their normal duties, such as deliver food and water to rescue workers, the elderly, etc., assist in delivering medical treatment and to help with search and rescue efforts. A future reality could be that jails open up their doors to bring civilians in to care for them and for their staffs to deliver to their fellow citizens. Even with the potential of all these added duties and responsibilities, they will still have to ensure the safe, secure, and humane treatment of those prisoners who are incarcerated in the jail.

Jails themselves could become targets for terrorist events, ranging from attacking the physical building(s) and recruiting both staff and prisoners to intimidate jail staff and their families. In some countries, jails or the equivalent are targets for terrorists because they represent the government. There was a period in America in the 1980s when country jails and sheriffs' departments were themselves targets of some domestic terrorist groups.

In the majority of cases, it will be the local jail where newly arrested terrorists will be incarcerated on their way through the American criminal justice system. Just as Richard Reid, also known as the "Shoe Bomber," was held initially at the Plymouth County House of Corrections and Jail (Massachusetts); so too will other jails hold other terrorists. It should also be noted that some terrorist arrests have been made in non-metropolitan areas such as Lackawanna, NY, Albany NY, and Port Angelous, WA. One thing that those who will be responsible for managing jails of the future will have to overcome is the "it won't happen here" syndrome. That type of thought process is in part, some say, what permitted the terrorist attacks of September 11, 2001.

As more terrorist events occur, and there will be more because this is the beginning of a long worldwide struggle, terrorists of every ilk, domestic, international, religious, and cause will end up incarcerated in local jails. As jails develop new strategies for incarcerating terrorists, they will have to develop comprehensive plans for taking defensive posture. As part of the defensive posture, jails will have to be as prepared for attack from the outside as they are for escape from the inside.

The locations of some of the jails of the future will move from metropolitan, urban, and downtown areas to rural areas where they install exterior defensive perimeters. These exterior perimeters will be established to protect the building(s) from outside attacks, to include bomb blasts, direct assaults by para-military-type teams, etc. These extended exteriors perimeters will add additional boundaries to the jail's overall security envelopes lengthening the distance between the building(s) and the perimeter walls or fences. Also included in these extended perimeters would be additional intrusion detection technology. In fact, exterior perimeters of the jails will incorporate the most advanced "high tech" security devices to provide the best security possible.

For those localities where moving the jail to a rural location would be too difficult, those jails of the future will be constructed subterranean (underground). Using this type of construction will help establish another type of defensive perimeter from outside attack and bomb blasts and will add to the jail's internal security envelopes. The design of the jails will be similar to some of the new federal prisons and will incorporate a series of underground levels (stories). The most dangerous will be housed on the lowest level of the facility.

The jails of the future will permit little internal movement of prisoners. Arraignments, lawyer visits, will be via secure link closed-circuit television or whatever replaces television. A majority of the prisoners' programming will be conducted via in-cell multimedia communications controlled by clinicians and educators located in transmission studios. Prisoners will be able to take educational courses, interact in group therapy sessions, and have visits via this communication methodology. The facilities will be designed with exercise equipment and recreational space close to the prisoners' living areas. The prisoners will have access to the exercise equipment and recreational space as many times a day his or her individual program allows. The entire concept will serve to develop staff safety, the use of appropriate technology that compliments the mission of the jail, and the daily operational needs of the jail.

The movement of prisoners will be accomplished with little to no direct contact with security staff. Prisoners who prove to be disciplinary problems or refuse to go along with their individual programs will be removed to a living area that is very restrictive. These restrictive living areas will have little human comforts with the exception of programs especially designed to specifically address the individual inmate's issues. Special attention will be given to those inmates who suffer from mental illness and/or who have medical issues. Every effort will be made to house these prisoners in an area (medical/mental health) where they can get the treatment that they need.

The staffing of the jails of the future will change significantly. There will be less staff because of the cost of staffing jails. As mentioned above, facilities designers will work to incorporate operationally functional and sound technologies into their designs of new jails, so that the need for staff will be reduced. In the 1980s and 1990s, jail designers worked toward designing a new model for jails and from their efforts "Direct Supervision" jails became a reality throughout the country. Looking back "Direct Supervision" jails were the future then.

The overall philosophy that society takes toward jails in general and the treatment of prisoners will determine the baseline purpose of jails and therefore will dictate the makeup of its staff. There are basically two ways that the society will approach jails. It will drop all pretense of providing rehabilitative service except for those required by law, for example, medical, education, etc. Or it will restructure its staffing patterns to include more "service" providers such as social workers, teachers, psychologists, and rehabilitation specialists/counselors.

Public opinion will be the driving force behind what route the jails will follow. But be assured that there will have to be some decisions made as to staffing because communities will not continue to support the continuous budgetary increases. If society decides to follow the programming route, then inmate programs will have to produce. Every program will have to have measurable goals and objectives. Society will have to be educated to understand that because one or more inmates commit a crime after completing a program does not mean that the program is a failure. Jails will have to work hard to identify what programs they will need, what the appropriate staffing should be, what specifically that staff should be doing, what specific expectation there are for the prisoners who are in the various programs, and a method for evaluating each program's effectiveness.

As an example, maybe the jail does not need a GED program. Perhaps what it needs is an educational program that teaches middle school curriculum or earlier levels for some of the prisoners.

The jail programs of the future will be strictly monitored by outside agencies (department of education, mental health, public health, etc.) because the jails will have to depend on these agencies for funding.

Consider also the great unknown of terrorism. Society might want to take a more progressive rehabilitative role, but the overall economic conditions of the country preclude treatment purely because of the "direct" cost. Of course, there will be those who will expound on the long-term benefits and the need for rehabilitation, but if the money is being spent to protect the immediate needs of the general public, then it is a safe bet that money will not be going to inmate programs.

There will be some regions of the country that will have to consider entering into regional jails. It will not be long before the small county jails will become extinct due to the cost of day-to-day operations and the practicality of continuing their operations. The majority of the operational cost today is and will be staffing and inmate medical care, to include prescription drugs. There are counties today that struggle to pay the costs associated with inmate medical costs. In the future, their operational budgets will be so structured (tight) that there will not be any options for some counties but to enter into regional jails. Another factor that will facilitate the use of regional jails is that sheriffs' departments (who operate the majority of the country's jails) will be required to increase their law enforcement endeavors to meet the potential demands placed upon them by terrorist events.

The training of jail staff will be expanded to include a variety of topics that will be needed to work in the jails of the future. There will be training courses in the high-tech equipment that will be an integral part of the overall and security operations of the jails. The jail personnel will have to develop a mastery of how the technology operates. No longer will it be good enough to have just a basic knowledge of the technology used in the jail. Jail staff will have to have a mastery of all the technology that they come into contact with in the performance of their duties. Staff training will also have to ensure that every person who works or volunteers at the jails of the future will have to know what they are to do in the event of an emergency, whether that emergency is a natural disaster or a terrorist event. The staff will have to know exactly what their individual jobs are and how to use any equipment associated with their job and the specific emergency.

Additional training will be required to learn how to manage those inmates with mental health issues. As more funding evaporates for mental health, halfway houses, and institutions, many of these individuals will end up in jails.

The methods and techniques that will be used to train jail personnel in the future will have to be expanded to include "on job site, distance instruction, and testing," practical "hands on" training and testing, advanced first aid, including how to deal with people who have been exposed to or injured by weapons of mass destruction. Also included is the usage of decontamination equipment, semi and automatic weapons, equipment and tactics.

In reality, the future is NOW, and the jails of the future have already started to evolve. In many parts of the country, jails have been catapulted into the future because of their locations. Those jails have to be careful to continue on the path to the future and not fall back into the paradigms of the past.

As America faces the challenges of the future, the nation's jails must be prepared to respond to society's needs. The men and women who manage and operate the nation's jails have always been able to respond to the needs of their nation and their individual communities. These challenges should not be underestimated or dismissed by those who operate jails that are not located in metropolitan areas. The jails of the future will need sufficient funding, meticulous planning, comprehensive staff training, and precise implementation of operational policies and procedures to operate.

The jails of the future will be more clearly defined by the way society as a whole and the economic situation of the nation unfolds. If society moves in the direction of rehabilitation and treatment and the economic situation of the country supports the costs of treatment, then jails will become treatment centers. If the pendulum swings in this direction, there could be some revolutionary changes in design, staffing models, technology, operations, and program delivery.

On the other hand, if society believes that jails are places of punishment and where harsh living conditions should be the norm, void of all but legally mandated programs, or the economic conditions are not conducive to supporting treatment programs, then jails will become warehouses for society's less desirables.

Then there is the "wild card" of private jails. The first wild card is the degree to which private corrections will grow. Will the political entities, who ultimately approve the operational budgets for jails opt out to paying private companies to operate their jails? Every year, private companies play an increasing role in the operations of jails. These private companies and the services they provide span the gamut. In some cases, the private companies actually have full responsibility for operating the jail. In others situations, these private companies provide services such as medical care, food service, transportation of inmates, etc.

The second wild card is terrorism and what factor will terrorism play on society as whole. If there are additional acts of terrorism on American soil, society's paradigm will change to one of survival and defeating those groups who would do us harm. Funding for jail operations will become very difficult.

Thanks to William Bill Sturgeon, Director, The Center for Rural Preparedness and Emergency Services, Southern Vermont College, Bennington, Vermont.

## SUMMARY

Jails of the future are moving into unknown territory where they will be facing new challenges on existing problems and concerns. Jails must keep up with the events of society, namely in the areas of minorities coming into jails and the high-profile inmate. New security methods will have to be employed by jail staff to deal with inmates whose crimes and notoriety have made it necessary to take special precautions.

Overcrowding and finding alternatives for offenders will still be major hurdles. New alternatives must be found to lower the rates of jail overcrowding. Direct supervision can continue to play a role in jail safety, but only if used properly. New security hardware will make the job of jail staff safer, but specialized training will be required. New hardware will aid in investigations and preparation for serious incidents. Jail officers are expected to continue handle special populations such as the mentally ill, but new approaches are being tried. New concerns and problems will arise in special populations due to the incarceration of the elderly, females, juveniles, foreign inmates, substance abusers, and gangs/STGs. Jails may assume additional roles due to anti-terrorist law enforcement activities.

Jail officers are moving away from the traditional "jail guard" role and will be in need of more specialized training, including training in anti-terrorism and direct supervision. To improve their job performance and chances for advancement, jail staff will be able to take advantage of online training in corrections subject both in service and at the college level. Female staffs are making advancements in the jail workplace, including supervision, administration, and working in cross-gender supervision.

Finally, jails are a visible part of the community, and many have programs underway to assist young people and be more visible to the citizens.

## REVIEW QUESTIONS

1. What are the current and future trends concerning jail overcrowding?
2. What are some jails doing to reduce overcrowding?
3. Discuss two examples of new security technology/hardware.
4. What special populations will be a concern in the jails of the future?
5. Describe advancements in jail officer training and education.
6. Why should good community relations be important to the local jail?

## TERMS TO KNOW

automated light survey
ballistic glass
barriers
distance learning
high-profile inmate
invisible punishments
layered voice analysis
new penology
online college classes
wearable computer

## ENDNOTES


1. Barbara Bostick, "Facing the Future: Challenges for Small Jails," *Corrections Today* (December 1988): 6.
2. Ibid.
3. Richard Seiter, *Correctional Administration* (Upper Saddle River: Prentice Hall, 2002), p. 473.
4. Kenneth E. Kerle, *Exploring Jail Operations* (Lanham, Hagerstown, MD: American Jail Association, 2003), pp. 273–274.
5. Ibid., p. 275.
6. Ibid., pp. 1, 9.
7. Paige Harrison and Allen Beck, Bureau of Justice Statistics Bulletin, *Prison and Jail Inmate at Midyear 2005*, NCJ 213133, Washington, DC (May 2006): 1, 7, 9.
8. Ibid., p. 7.
9. "Drug Sentences Continue to Drive Growth of Inmate Populations," *The Corrections Professional*, 9 (1) (August 22, 2003): 1, 6.
10. Dean J. Champion, *Corrections in the United States: A Contemporary Perspective, 4th Edition* (Upper Saddle River: Prentice Hall, 2005), p. 249.
11. Ibid.
12. Kerle, *Exploring Jail Operations*, pp. 276, 277.
13. "Drug Sentences Continue to Drive Growth of Inmate Populations," p. 6.
14. Kristina Feller and Mike Brenchley, "Planning Strategic Growth: Correctional Campus Design Can Benefit from Far Sighted Thinking," *American Jails* (September–October 2003): 50–52.
15. Ibid., p. 52.
16. Morgan Jones, "Saving by Design," *Correctional News* (January–February 2005): 26–30.
17. "In the News," *Correctional News*, 11 (1) (January–February, 2005): 1.
18. Carter Thompson, "County Explores Privatizing Old Jail," *Galveston Daily News*, August 29, 2004, http://www.galvestondailynews.com/print.lasso??ewcd=b 1af78d45 401b95b (accessed August 30, 2004).
19. Michelle Gaseau and Meghan Mandeville, "Assessing Technology for Corrections and Security," *corrections.com*, http://www.corrections.com/printNews.aspx?Zone=Homepage (accessed September 28, 2004).
20. Bill Siuru, "Wearable Computers," *Correctional Technology and Management*, 7 (1) (Spring 2003): 12–14.
21. Donald F. Olson, "Who is Breaking into America's Jails?" *American Jails* (March–April 2002): 59–61.
22. Kerle, *Exploring Jail Operations*, pp. 274, 275.
23. Ray Coleman, "Corrections in the 21st Century," *American Jails* (January–February 1999): 47–49.
24. Howard L. Skolnick and Henry C. H. Hoogland, "Mental Health Issues: The Impact of Explosive Growth," *Corrections Today* (August 2005): 63, 64.
25. Ibid., p. 64.
26. John Torres, "Medical Jail Tent Program Expands: Sick Prisoners Need More Room," *floridatoday.com*, November 6, 2006, www.floridatoday.com/apps/pbcs.dll/artikkel?Dato=20061109&Kategori=NEWS01 (accessed November 9, 2006).

27. Gregg W. Etter, Sr. and Robert L. Hinshaw, "Managing High Profile Inmates in a Jail Setting," *Corrections Today* (February 2006): 28.
28. Ibid., pp. 28, 29.
29. Ibid.
30. Ibid., pp. 29, 31.
31. Ibid., p. 29.
32. David R. Struckhoff, "Éducation for Jail Staff at the Millenium," *American Jails* (November–December 1996): 25–29.
33. Ibid., p. 28.
34. Ibid., p. 29.
35. Laura Noonan, memorandum to author, *Corrections Connection*, January 13, 2005.
36. Michelle Gaseau, "Corrections Interns Get Real Life Experiences," *corrections.com*, http://www.corrections.com/printNews.aspx?Zone=Program Profile (accessed March 2, 2005).
37. Craig A. Lowe, "Reality Check: Give Respect to Get Respect," *American Jails* (July–August 2003): 54–57.
38. Los Angeles County Sheriff's Department-VINE Program, www.lasd.org/lasd_services/vine.html (accessed January 17, 2007).

## REFERENCES


Bostick, Barbara. "Facing the Future: Challenges for Small Jails." *Corrections Today*, December 1988, 6.

Champion, Dean J. *Corrections in the United States: A Contemporary Perspective, 4th Edition*. Upper Saddle River: Prentice Hall, 2005.

Coleman, Ray. "Corrections in the 21st Century." *American Jails*, January–February 1999, 47–49.

"In the News." *Correctional News*, 11 (1) January–February, 2005, 1.

"Drug Sentences Continue to Drive Growth of Inmate Populations." *The Corrections Professional*, 9 (1) August 22, 2003, 1, 6.

Etter, Gregg W., Sr. and Robert L. Hinshaw. "Managing High Profile Inmates in a Jail Setting," *Corrections Today*, February 2006, 28–31, 41.

Feller, Kristina and Mike Brenchley. "Planning Strategic Growth: Correctional Campus Design Can Benefit from Far Sighted Thinking." *American Jails*, September–October 2003, 50–52.

Gaseau, Michelle and Meghan Mandeville, "Assessing Technology for Corrections and Security," *corrections.com*, http://www.corrections.com/printNews.aspx?Zone=Homepage (accessed September 28, 2004).

Gaseau, Michelle, "Corrections Interns Get Real Life Experiences," *corrections.com*, http://www.corrections.com/printNews.aspx?Zone=Program Profile (accessed March 2, 2005).

Harrison, Paige and Allen Beck, Bureau of Justice Statistics Bulletin, *Prison and Jail Inmates at Midyear 2005*, NCJ 213133, Washington DC, May 2006.

Jones, Morgan. "Saving By Design." *Correctional News*, January–February 2005, 26–30.

Kerle, Kenneth E. *Exploring Jail Operations*. Hagerstown, MD: American Jail Association, 2003.

Los Angeles County Sheriff's Department-VINE Program, www.lasd.org/lasd_services/vine.html (accessed January 17, 2007).

Lowe, Craig A. "Reality Check: Give Respect to Get Respect." *American Jails*, July–August 2003, 54–57.

Noonan, Laura. Memorandum to author, *Corrections Connection*, January 13, 2005.

Olson, Donald F. "Who Is Breaking into America's jails?" *American Jails*, March–April 2002, 59–61.

Seiter, Richard. *Correctional Administration*. Upper Saddle River, NJ: Prentice Hall, 2002.

Skolnick, Howard L. and Henry C. H. Hoogland. "Mental Health Issues: The Impact of Explosive Growth." *Corrections Today*, August 2005, 62–64, 102.

Siuru, Bill. "Wearable Computers." *Correctional Technology and Management*, 7 (1) Spring 2003, 12–14.

Struckhoff, David R. "Éducation for Jail Staff at the Millennium." *American Jails*, November–December 1996, 25–29.

Thompson, Carter. "County Explores Privatizing Old Jail," *Galveston Daily News*, August 29, 2004. http://www.galvestondailynews.com/print.lasso??ewcd=b 1af78d45 401b95b (accessed August 30, 2004)

Torres, John. "Medical Jail Tent Program Expands: Sick Prisoners Need More Room," *floridatoday.com*, November 6, 2006, www.floridatoday.com/apps/pbcs.dll/artikkel?Dato=20061109&Kategori=NEWS01 (accessed November 9, 2006).

# GLOSSARY OF TERMS

**4/10 approach:** revolutionary approach to staff scheduling, staff member works four 10-hour days.

**42 United States Code 1983:** also known as 42 USC 1983 and to inmates as "Section 1983," states that a government official such as a jail officer is liable for monetary damage if found guilty of violating the civil rights of an inmate.

**Accreditation:** the process, by audit and inspection, of an agency meeting and complying with jail standards.

**Accreditation manager:** sworn or civilian agency employee that supervises and plans agency accreditation, examines standards, provides documentation, and keeps agency up to date.

**Active recreation:** recreation involving inmates engaging in physical activities.

**administrative hearings:** hearings in jail conducted by staff determining an inmate's status, including custody levels, housing status, program involvement, staff escorts, and the usage of restraints.

**Administrative segregation or A/S:** removal from general population and placement of inmates in segregation or isolation for reasons other than disciplinary, not a punishment status, and can receive privileges and services afforded to general population inmates.

**Adult Basic Education:** classes designed to prepare an inmate for the GED test, to continue high school education, and to continue in a specialized education plan.

**adult certified:** concerning a juvenile in an adult jail, a court order from a judge stating that the juvenile offender is certified as an adult, to be tried as an adult, be sentenced as an adult, and be housed in the jail's adult population.

**AKAs:** acronym for Also Known As, or aliases, nicknames and "street names" that can be compared to names in the inmate's criminal history.

**amelioration of pain:** based on research by Gresham Sykes, the process of depriving the jailed inmate of five important things in life—liberty, goods and services, heterosexual contact, autonomy, and security.

**Americans with Disabilities Act or ADA:** act passed by U.S. Congress in 1990, protects people who are disabled who apply for correctional jobs, that work in corrections, and are inmates, protections include access of handicapped visitors, access to programs and services by disabled inmates, and modification of the physical plant to accommodate disabled inmates and visitors.

**anxiety disorders:** mental disorder in which inmate appears overly anxious and engages in repetitive behavior, examples include post-traumatic stress disorder (PTSD), phobias, and obsessive compulsive disorders.

**Assistant squad commander:** assistant to squad commander, reviews and signs off on shift logs, reports, participates in disciplinary actions, counseling, and evaluations, liaison to classification, acts as on scene supervisor in emergency cell extractions, rank is below squad leader's rank at sergeant, corporal, etc.

**Audit:** detailed examination of an agency's policies, procedures, facility records, and accounts to see whether they are in compliance with standards.

**Audit team:** panel of correctional experts from outside the agency, conducts audits, and reports findings to the agency and the accrediting organization.

**authorized extended areas of incarceration:** areas where offenders are permitted to be outside the correctional facility in the community such as a job site, home, program, etc. per the conditions of the work release or home incarceration/electronic monitoring program.

**Automated light survey:** detection of insufficient lighting in outdoor areas and perimeters of correctional facilities.

**Back-tracking:** practice of the jail officer on patrol immediately returning to the area that he or she just checked; keeps inmates from thinking that they are "in the clear".

**Backdoor classification:** dangerous practice of a jail officer(s) moving an inmate to administrative segregation without the approval from a supervisor, may be viewed as harassment.

**backup keys:** jail keys to limited areas such as the laundry, lock shop, maintenance shop, control center, etc.

**Bail:** amount of money set by the court that an offender pays to endure his or her appearance in court.

**balancing test:** a four-part test applied by a court that balances the needs of the correctional facility against the constitutional rights needs of the inmate.

**Ballistic glass:.** known also as "bullet proof glass," bullet-resistant glass than serves as protection to inmates and staff from drive by shootings.

**Barriers:** objects such as concrete planners, steel girders, etc. that protect the facility from explosive laden vehicles, such as "truck bombs."

**Basic training:** training that newly hired jail officers undergo within their first year of employment which instill the organizational culture and makeup, as well develop skills for job performance.

**Behavior modification:** approach that attempts to change the offender's criminal behavior by using a system of rewards and punishments; believes criminal behavior is the result of a defect in learning.

**body (or strip search):** search that examines the skin surface of the inmate without clothing, performed when an inmate returns to the jail from an outside transportation run, from another institution and contraband is suspected, or whether there is reason to believe that the inmate is concealing drugs or a weapon.

**body cavity search:** most intrusive of all searches of an inmate, inspects the body's openings, the anus and vagina; it is based on reasonable suspicion and should only be conducted by medical personnel, authorized by a supervisor and documented.

**Bond:** written agreement by a bonding company pledging that the offender will appear in court.

**Bond surrender:** apprehension of and return to the jail of an offender by a bondsman for violating the conditions of the bond, not cooperating with the bonding company, etc.

**Booking (inmate) number:** also called the inmate identification number; the official number that appears on all jail paperwork relating to that inmate.

**Boot Camp:** short-term reintegration program for selected offenders that employs the method of military discipline, strict programming, and physical conditioning to prepare the offender for a return to the community with the ability to resist criminal behavior.

**Calaboose:** informal term used in rural Iowa to describe the local jail.

**Capital punishment:** severe punishment given to wrongdoers that caused death, methods include(d) hanging, beheading, stoning, burning at the stake, etc.

**case law:** sometimes known as precedent, defined as law made through court rulings and decisions rather than by acts of the legislature.

**Case manager:** key person in the unit management team, acts as liaison between the inmates, the jail staff, rehabilitation agencies, and the unit management team; deals with inmates in the unit and prepares them for release.

**census count:** counts taken to verify inmates' presence at recreation, programs, work details, etc.

**Central intake processing:** new trend in jail booking procedures, performed in a specific facility, centralizes the booking procedures, inmate processing and transfer to a main jail, concentrates more staff on booking, safe processing, and proper release of inmates.

**Change-up:** part of the jail intake process, inmate is given the opportunity to shower, and civilian clothes will be exchanged for the jail inmate uniform.

**CHUMPS:** acronym that changes an inmate slang word describing gullible staff into an easy to remember strategy for combating inmate manipulation—control yourself and do not be complacent, help the inmate help themselves, understand the offender sub-culture and understanding yourself, maintain a safe distance, practicing professionalism in adhering to policies and procedures, and stop yourself from being stressed out so you are not vulnerable.

**civil rights actions:** legal actions filed by inmates alleging that their civil rights under the U.S. Constitution were violated; preferred method is to file under 42 USC 1983 in federal court.

**Civil Rights of Institutionalized Persons Act or CRIPA:** law enacted by U.S. Congress authorizing the Justice Department to file civil rights litigation on behalf of persons confined in institutions, including prisons and jails.

**Civilian jail staff:** jail staff that has no law enforcement authority but provide services to the jail such as medical services, food services, programs, maintenance, and substance abuse/mental health counseling.

**Classification:** ongoing process and management, based on staff analysis and diagnosis of inmate information, allowing staff to have the tools necessary to both predict and control inmates' behavior.

**Classification file:** file generated by the classification section, central repository from critical information about a jail inmate, contains inmate classification interview, criminal history, mental health reports, incident reports, etc.

**Classification initial interview:** interview of the jail inmate conducted by a classification officer that obtains detailed social, criminal, substance abuse, medical, mental health information, and any information about the inmate can be used to formulate classification decisions.

**Co-defendants:** inmates who are involved in the same offense, not recommended to house them together due to damaging prosecution's case and one may be cooperating with police about the other.

**command center:** central headquarters for the staff in charge of an emergency to meet, plan, evaluate the situation, communicate with all involved, and issue orders and media statements.

**Command staff:** small group of senior supervisors, depending on the size of the jail, ranks can vary from captain down to sergeant, reports to the jail administrator, and supervises jail staff to ensure that all policies are correctly carried out.

**Commissary:** also known as canteen, is a privilege by which the inmates can purchase snacks, over the counter medications, or toilet articles.

**community check:** on site, personal check performed by staff at the home, job site, or furlough site to ensure that the offender is in the proper location, not engaging in illegal activity/substance abuse, or breaking any program rules.

**community corrections:** correctional system that manages and supervises offenders in the community in lieu of jail incarceration; includes work release, weekend confinement, home electronic incarceration, community service, fine options programs, and labor programs.

**community offender labor programs:** program in which carefully screened, low-risk and minor offenders perform public sector work under sworn staff supervision.

**community service:** condition or sentence that the offender perform a required number of hours in free labor in the community, such as parks maintenance, picking up trash, etc.

**Compensatory damages:** in an inmate lawsuit, the agency pays for "out of pocket" expenses that are incurred by the inmate, such as medical bills, lost wages, etc.

**confidential informants:** inmates who supply critical information to correctional officers or staff members with the understanding that their identities will not be revealed, also called "snitch."

**Confinement branch or custody branch:** branch of the jail staff responsible for the 24 hours per day/7 days per week operation and security of the jail, responsible for the enforcement of all jail rules and regulations and laws of the jurisdiction

**Congregate System:** system of prisoner confinement developed in New York in 1816 to 1825; inmates were confined separately at night but ate and worked (in congregate groups) together during the day.

**consent decree:** different than an injunction, the jail agrees to the court having a binding ruling against them, ordering that certain actions be taken.

**Contraband:** unauthorized items or materials either manufactured or introduced into the jail that could disrupt security, safety, aid escape, and facilitate criminal behavior; also items that are authorized but are altered, modified, or possessed in excess.

**contract system:** early form of prison labor where inmates in prison workshops were made to work for private businesses who entered into a contract with the prison for the use of inmate labor, primarily used in the northern U.S.

**convicted status:** status of jail inmates who have been adjudicated in court, are sentenced or awaiting sentencing, and are awaiting transfer to a state or federal prison system; they are finished with court.

**Copycats:** informal term denoting inmates who imitate being involved in religions that other inmates are practicing, goals made may be to enhance their status or convince a religious volunteer to bring in contraband, perform favors or to break the rules.

**Corporal punishment:** actions carried out against wrongdoers designed to inflict pain and suffering, but not death.

**Correct assertiveness:** jail officers getting their points across to inmates without arguments, tension, and stress, thus ensuring compliance from the inmates.

**Criminal justice information system:** system that links the jail booking system with computerized criminal records, warrant databases, identification data, and the National Crime Information Center (NCIC).

**criminal justice status:** status of the offender in the criminal justice system—convicted, un convicted, has a detainer lodged, etc.

**cross-gender supervision:** type of jail housing where staff members of opposite genders supervise inmates.

**custody section:** also known as security, confinement branch, etc., the section of the jail staff composed of teams or squads that provide round the clock jail security, keeping inmates properly confined and the staff and inmates safe.

**Daily life questions:** questions asked by interviewers to prospective jail staff applicants that ask about themselves, their views of life, and their responses to obstacles and responses in real life.

**day reporting center or DRC:** centers where offenders on pre-trial status, on probation or parole must report to receive supervision and to take part in rehabilitative programs.

**Debtors:** private citizen confined incarcerated through a civil process until a debt was paid, used in early European corrections history.

**Decision-tree instrument:** one of two processes that the ICC uses to make a housing decision; inmate is asked a series of yes or no questions containing risk factors.

**Declaration of Principles:** principles for penal reform adopted in 1870 by the National Prison Congress and served as a foundation for modern jail standards.

**Declaratory relief:** ruling or statement by the courts stating that inmates are to be afforded certain rights.

**deliberate indifference:** situation where staff are indifferent to the serious needs of the inmate, such as medical care, safety, etc.; combined with staff awareness that infers a substantial risk of serious harm to the inmate exists.

**Detainers:** charges on file from other jurisdictions that can hold the inmate in jail awaiting transfer to the other jurisdiction.

**Diagnostic and treatment staffs:** classification, medical, and mental health staff who diagnose inmate characteristics and problems and decide on inmate housing, medical care, and mental health intervention. Staff may also include inmate programs staff.

**Dimensions of classification:** five areas in which new offenders are classified in the jail—custody, security, housing, programs, and reclassification.

**direct supervision:** third generation of jail design where the jail officer is placed inside the inmate housing unit with no physical barriers; officer acts as a "behavior manager."

**Disciplinary segregation:** also known as D/S, housing an inmate in segregation or isolation for rule breaking and have privileges removed.

**Distance learning:** courses where students complete course work and send to an accredited college for evaluation and grading.

**Disturbance:** smaller in scale than a riot, defined as a disruptive or violent act or acts by a small group of inmates and is confined to a much smaller area.

**drug of choice:** illegal drug or substance that the inmate prefers to use and is indicated in jail records such as jail classification interview, pre-release report, criminal history, etc.

**Dually diagnosed:** diagnosis of two problems—a substance abuse problem combined with a mental illness; treatment must address both areas.

**dubious informant:** opposite of the respected informant, inmate informant that may have underlying, self-serving motives in giving staff information.

**due process:** exercise of power by the government in procedures that are prescribed by principles of law, in jails allowing an inmate advance notice of proceedings, to have rights, and to be heard before a panel, etc.

**early release:** procedure by which a jail relieves overcrowding by the authorized release of minor offenders, usually with the cooperation of the courts or other governmental authority.

**elderly or mature inmates:** offenders who are age 50 or older; health conditions may become more serious, visible, and chronic.

**electronic tethering:** system that uses Global Positioning Systems (GPS) to map and track offenders' movements.

**emergency count:** count of inmate population taken due to an emergency such as a power outage, fire, riot, disturbance, etc.

**Emergency keys:** keys that allow staff access to all areas in the event of a computer malfunction, a riot, fire, etc. or other serious emergency.

**Emergency response team (ERT):** also known as the Sheriff's Emergency Response Team or the Corrections Emergency Response Team, a team of highly trained, carefully selected correctional officers who through special tactics and security equipment respond to and resolve volatile situations in the jail.

**Escape:** breach of the security perimeter of a correctional facility or an authorized extended area of incarceration (such as by an inmate on work release or work detail).

**Expected practices:** properly implemented practices and activities that produce the desired outcome of a performance-based standard.

**Farmed out:** informal jail term meaning the transfer of inmates from one jail to another to relieve overcrowding or for security reasons.

**Federalism:** belief that federal courts should not be involved in state and local affairs, such as the operations of state prisons and local jails.

**fee system:** practice in early jails of charging inmates money for services in the jail; used to finance the jail and pay the keepers.

**Field training officer (FTO):** veteran staff member who serves as the training supervisor of the new jail officer for a specific number of hours and requires the new officer to perform tasks such as searches and headcounts, etc.; the FTO also observes and rates the trainee's job performance in these tasks.

**File reviews:** process by which the informal ICC reviews the files of inmates who are on administrative or disciplinary segregation status, determines whether the inmate can be removed from administrative segregation, whether any restrictions change, addresses inmate requests, and reviews the latest medical or mental health information about the inmate.

**first timers:** offenders experiencing their first incarceration.

**flagellum:** forerunner of the "cat o nine tails," flogging device used by the Romans to flog criminals, made of ox-hide thongs knotted and weighed with bone slivers, metal balls or hooks, instrument of corporal punishment.

**Flex time:** flexible scheduling where a staff member works overtime and can use the extra hours to leave early, come in later, etc.

**Floater:** jail correctional officer who is mobile throughout the jail, performs such duties as post relief, visitor escorts, inspections, special tasks, etc.

**formal count:** a count of the inmate population that is required by the jail's policy and procedures and are conducted at mandatory specific times.

**Formal ICC:** formal convening of the ICC to hold a hearing to discuss an inmates' status and housing and decide whether administrative segregation or any other restrictions are justified; the inmate concerned is afforded due process including an advance notice of the hearing.

**frisks (pat downs):** most common type of search; the jail officer inspects the inmate's clothing and body by feeling through the clothing, feet and footwear are searched, and the pockets are emptied.

**Frivolous law suits:** lawsuits filed in courts by inmates that have no merit and aim to harass correctional officials; often the complaints are minor and do not threaten the safety, health, or welfare of the inmate.

**Furlough:** authorized pass into the community for specific purposes such as offender visiting family, friends and engaging in positive activities to strengthen family and community ties.

**Furlough sponsor:** required for a furlough; a responsible citizen who can verify an offender's furlough activities and agrees to maintain responsibility of the offender while in the community.

**General Educational Development (GED):** nationally recognized alternative to the high school diploma; test to obtain a GED consists of five sections—Reading, Science, Social Studies, Math, and Writing; inmate must pass a practice GED test to be qualified for the formal GED test.

**General population:** sometimes called the jail population, housing of all classified inmates who are suitable per the classification staff or ICC to live with other inmates.

**Goal statement:** general statement of what is to be achieved within the functional area (safety, security, etc.) of a performance-based standard.

**Good time:** time off, per statute, of an inmate sentence for participation in programs and engaging in positive behavior while incarcerated, successful tool in combating jail overcrowding.

**graduated release:** a process where the offender is eased into the community, avoiding the culture shock of abruptly transitioning from jail into life outside jail.

**Grandstanding:** action by which an inmate is acting "big" in front of the other inmates or is "showing off."

**Great Code:** set of laws in Colonial Pennsylvania, promulgated by William Penn, that made sweeping reforms to corrections in the colony, including capital punishment only for murder, establishment of houses of corrections without fees, abolishing pillories and stocks, introducing bail and requiring inmates to perform useful work.

**Grievance:** complaint filed by an inmate through channels to the appropriate jail staff in whose area of responsibility the complaint is concerned.

**Grievance flooding:** increase in the number of grievances by inmates, especially about an unpopular policy change, one of the signs of increasing frustration and tension in the jail.

**Gross negligence:** legal term involving actions by correctional staff having reckless disregard of the consequences.

**Group therapy:** group of clients (inmates) work together with a therapist, who acts as group leader; clients give each other support and advice while also challenging each other's defense mechanisms.

**Habeas corpus actions:** legal actions filed by inmates claiming that they are being confined illegally, can name a court, agency or jail personnel.

**hands off era:** first of three eras in the development of inmate legal rights where the courts took no action concerning inmate complaints filed concerning conditions or treatment in jails or prisons.

**hands on era:** era in the development of inmate rights where the courts took a very active and overbearing role concerning corrections and inmate rights.

**Headcount:** a primary tool of jail officers, where inmates are located and counted no matter where they are and what activity they are engaged in.

**High-profile inmate:** a highly visible jail inmate due to the perceptions of staff, other inmates, and the public, due to advances in media coverage; jails must devise special ways to deal with these inmates while maintaining security.

**High-risk prisoner:** inmate who due to charge, criminal history, prior escape attempts, conviction status, mental state, and criminal affiliations is at high risk to attempt escape or to assault staff.

**home brew:** informal term for alcohol manufactured by inmates or homemade alcohol.

**home detention/electronic monitoring:** process where offenders are incarcerated in their homes, subject to staff checks, under electronic surveillance, but are allowed to enter the community to attend programs and to work.

**Hulks:** practice in eighteenth-century England of using old ships to confine prisoners; conditions were horrible, used to relieve prison and jail overcrowding.

**Human relations skills:** skills that enable the jail officer to interact with the inmate population in a positive way.

**Human Services Officer:** approach advocated by some correctional officers; inmates are treated like people, giving them what they need, helping them adjust and assisting them if possible.

**inactive keys:** keys no longer used by staff, retained as spare, and backup keys for unused locking devices.

**incident report:** reports that document unusual events in the jail, inmate rules violations, security problems, critical information received about an inmate and observations of inmate behavior.

**Incompatible:** situation where an inmate or inmates have difficulty living in a group setting with other inmates due to various reasons such as personality clashes, threats of sexual assaults, etc.

**indentured servant:** form of punishment in early European colonies where the offender worked off his or her sentence by serving a master.

**indeterminate sentence:** originally developed in the Reformatory System of the 1870s; inmates were given a minimum sentence without a maximum term indicated, the goal was for the inmate to earn a release through their efforts to reform themselves.

**Individual therapy:** therapy where the client or inmate enters a therapeutic relationship with a trained and qualified therapist or counselor.

**Injunctive relief or injunction:** order by the court that compels a jail to do or not to something, such as taking steps to relieve overcrowding, make improvements to the inmate law library, etc.

**inmate code:** set of informal social rules that inmates learn to live by, violation of the code could mean physical assault or death from other inmates, ostracism, or being labeled a "snitch" or weak.

**Inmate commissary funds:** monies made from the inmates buying items in the jail commissary; can be used for inmate programs, recreation, leisure, and law library services, etc.

**Inmate Handbook:** handbook given to jail inmates containing information about the jail that is necessary for the inmate to know.

**inmate leader:** inmate who becomes known to the jail staff and inmates as an inmate who exerts his or her will and influence over a group of inmates.

**Inmate move list:** list showing where inmates are moving from, their destination inside the jail, and the reason for the move; list must be approved by a supervisor.

**Inmate orientation:** orientation that informs the jail inmate about what is expected from him or her, respecting others, following the rules, obtaining staff assistance, etc., may be conducted in person by a jail staff person or shown in a video.

**Inmate request form:** most common form of communication from jail inmates to various sections of the jail staff; common versions contain a checklist or boxes that the inmate can use to address his or her message and staff can write a response.

**inmate transport:** removal of the inmate from secure confines of the jail under escort by correctional officers for official and authorized reasons such as court, medical/psychiatric visits, etc.

**Inmate-staff fraternization:** acts of staff and inmates engaging in sexual relations; repercussions can be serious to include contraband smuggling, escape, breakdown of staff efficiency, criminal charges, and the transmission of sexually transmitted diseases.

**inner perimeter:** next barrier inside the jail complex from the outer perimeter, entrances to the inside of the jail are controlled through lobby checkpoints, secure doors, limited access for staff and visitors, and the sally port.

**In-service training:** corrections/law enforcement training designed to maintain certification of the jail officer by requiring that a specific number of training hours in applicable subjects are attended during a specific time.

**inside cells (interior cellblock):** type of prison housing design developed in Auburn type prisons; cellblocks were stacked upon one another in tiered layers in a type of cellblock building contained inside a larger one.

**Institutional Classification Committee or ICC:** committee that meets daily in the jail; performs several functions such as reviewing classification files of inmates for placement, changes in inmate housing, placing inmates on and reassigning them from administrative segregation, placing security restrictions on inmates, etc.

**Inter-facility-training programs:** training where jails in the same area or locality can assist each other in training staff; trainees are sent to another jail to assist in such operations as searches; gives trainees a broad picture of how other jails operate.

**Internal classification:** classification approach of placing an inmate with other inmates having similar custody levels and backgrounds.

**Internal mock audit:** "dry" or practice run audit conducted by correctional professionals outside the agency in order to have an objective and impartial view.

**Invisible punishments:** laws that make certain types of offenders ineligible for certain types of employment and services, such as offenders with criminal histories and substance abusers.

**Jail:** correctional facility administered by a local law enforcement agency, such as a sheriff's office or local corrections department; confines adult offenders and juveniles under certain circumstances awaiting trial or sentenced to one year (12 months) or less.

**Jail administrator:** also known as the warden or chief jailor, responsible for the supervision of all sections and staff who work in the jail.

**Jail booking form:** form that contains crucial information obtained from the offender, arresting officer, court, and transporting officer; establishes the legal commitment and the official jail record.

**jail climate:** the overall mood of the jail in terms of inmate behavior, actions and the level of tension experienced both by the inmates and the staff.

**Jail correctional officer:** corrections officer assigned to a jail post, responsible for the smooth operations of the post, safety and welfare of inmates, conducts counts, searches and inspections, enforces jail rules, acts in emergencies and perform other duties as assigned.

**jail house lawyering:** practice of "legal-wise" inmates assisting other inmates.

**Jail programs:** rehabilitative programs that eligible inmates can attend in the jail during specific times and in specific places.

**Jail services:** services offered to inmates to aid in rehabilitation or to provide some sort of assistance, such as health care, food services, recreation, mail, commissary, barber, property, and the leisure and law libraries.

**Jail standard:** a statement that defines a required or essential condition that has to be maintained in the jail; must meet the criteria of a correctional authority or organization and be supported and documented by policies and procedures.

**Jail-wise inmates:** inmates who have done occasional stints of varying length in local jails.

**Jailhouse lawyers:** inmates knowledgeable in the law, provide assistance to illiterate and poorly educated inmates.

**Job fairs:** events where representatives from local correctional agencies attend employment activities on local college campuses and in the community, goals are to meet prospective applicants and inform them about their departments' employment opportunities, wages, and benefits.

**Judicial intervention:** period between 1970 and 1990 where the courts through court orders and consent decrees, dictated changes in local jails, addressing overcrowding, staff increases, and services.

**Keep separate list:** list that identifies all inmates who should be housed separately due to being enemies, co-defendants, gang members, members of security threat groups, etc.

**Law library:** library that affords inmates access to up-to-date legal references, court decisions, statues and opinions so that they can participate in court defense, pursue civil rights litigation, and conduct legal research.

**Layered voice analysis:** analysis using special software to analyze thoughts, shows stress, inaccuracies, and deceptions; useful in inmate investigations and analyzing inmate phone conversations.

**lease system:** prison labor system where inmates were rented out to businesses, working in mines, farms, plantations, etc.; used in southern and western U.S.

**legitimate penological interest:** part of the court balancing test, means areas of vital concern to the operation of the correctional facility—security, order, discipline, etc.

**Leisure library:** services that make quality reading material available to the inmate general and administrative segregation population through citizen donations, civic groups, subscriptions, or acquisitions form the local library.

**Life skills:** proper and correct things that law abiding citizens do daily to provide for themselves and their families, including completing a job application, balancing a checkbook, paying bills, etc.

**life skills classes:** also known as survival skills, a series of classes that instruct offenders in various subjects in order to ease transition back into the community, generally mandatory.

**linear design:** first generation or traditional jail housing design where cellblocks are aligned in rows running down a central corridor; officer contact is limited except through a food slot located in the cellblock door.

**Local county corrections department:** county or local agency that operates the local jail, is not a sheriff's office.

**Lockbox:** in older jails, large steel cabinets that are located at the end of a cellblock outside the main cellblock door, contains levers that unlock the individual cells.

**Lockout:** inmate management practice in some jails where general population inmates are locked out of their cells during the day and confined to the dayroom; goal is to have inmates accessible for counts, visiting, programs, etc., and visible by staff.

**Lockup:** temporary holding facility used to confine offenders who have just been arrested; located adjacent to or inside a police station.

**malicious and sadistic test:.** court test that decides whether restraints and other security measures used to control an unruly inmate were justified and not punitive and improper.

**Mamartime Prison:** series of underground dungeons used to confine prisoners, built by the ancient Romans in 64 B.C.

**Mandatory overtime:** overtime requiring that officers are held over on duty, must work a special detail for extra hours, or are called in on days off.

**Mandatory standards/expected practices:** standards or expected practices that a jail *must* meet in order that the jail can be accredited; usually deal with safety, security, and medical care.

**master keys:** jail keys that are cut so that one key may unlock many locks throughout the jail that are made by a single manufacturer.

**Maximum custody:** jail custody level requiring constant supervision in the most secure general housing population possible, reserved for hard core, violent, very institutionalized, dangerous, and escape risk inmates.

**meaningful community:** a community environment that meets offenders' needs in such areas as employment, substance abuse, and stability in a home environment.

**Medical dispensary:** a "mini hospital" inside the jail housing inmates with medical problems per the authority of the jail medical staff.

**Medication runs:** period of time when the jail medical staff makes rounds in the jail living areas to dispense medication.

**Medium custody:** jail custody level requiring constant supervision, but some inmate freedom of movement is permitted, inmates are non-violent, low escape risk and trusty eligible.

**Memorandums of Agreement (MOA):** agreements between jails and agencies and organizations supporting programming in the jail, such as religious organizations, local school boards, substance abuse services, mental health services, etc. MOAs specify in writing responsibilities of all concerned, goals, equipment needed, etc.

**Mentally ill diversion:** process where low-risk mentally ill offenders are evaluated and diverting them from the jail and placing them with treatment resources in the community.

**Minimum custody:** jail custody level where periodic supervision is required; inmates allowed maximum freedom of movement, inmates are short term and non-security risks.

**Mock cellblock:** in a training academy, a room remodeled and redecorated to look like a jail living area, complete with inmates' possessions and furnishings; trainees must secure the area and search for contraband.

**mood disorders:** mental disorder characterized by the offender having extreme mood changes that are not considered normal, such as depression, mania, and bi-polar.

**Negative discipline:** form of discipline where the jail staff attempts to teach the inmate the correct way to behave through punishments and sanctions.

**Negligence:** failure to exercise care as a reasonably prudent person would in a similar situation, or failure to conduct one's self per standards designed to protect a person from harm.

**New penology:** school of correctional thought where corrections administrators have changed from making clinical judgments about offender rehabilitative needs and combating recidivism to identification of high-risk groups and offenders.

**Nominal damages:** in an inmate lawsuit, the defendant (jail) pays the plaintiff (inmate) a "token sum" (such as one dollar, one hundred dollars, etc.) due to the damage done to the inmate is extremely minor in scope.

**Non-denominational chaplain's staff:** chaplain's staff who does not promote any one particular faith and is knowledgeable in most religions.

**Non-supervised environment:** environment where the offender is under minimal physical restriction or staff supervision; the offender is "on his or her own."

**Nutra loaf:** food product containing vegetables and fruits baked in, served to unruly inmates in lieu of meals, designed to meet daily nutritional requirements.

**Objective jail classification:** classification system that uses measurable factors and applies them in the same way to all inmates, by scoring, has replaced subjective classification in nearly all prison systems.

**Observation log:** log containing information about a segregated inmate including status (A/S, D/S, etc.), staff interactions (meals, showers, medical staff visits, staff precautions, etc.); it is posted on the cell door or kept in a binder at the jail officer's post where the inmate is housed.

**Officer comportment:** how jail officers carry themselves and perform their duties; negative comportment adds to the tension levels in the jail, while positive comportment reduces tension.

**Online college classes:** online (Internet) college classes offered by accredited universities and colleges, enables jail officers to advance their education.

**Operational capacity:** level of population that the jail can safely function at day to day.

**Oral reprimand:** first level of jail discipline where the inmate is verbally counseled by the jail officer, who does not generate written documentation.

**Outcome measure:** events, occurrences, conditions, behaviors, and attitudes that can be measured and indicate whether or not the condition described in the performance standard has been achieved.

**outer perimeter:** security perimeter that encompasses the outer grounds of the jail and both vehicle and pedestrian approaches to the jail, may be walled or fenced.

**outside patrols:** roving patrols by jail officers in vehicles or on foot looking for any security breaches, suspicious persons or activities, or contraband.

**Pacification of inmates:** process where programs and activities fill inmates' time constructively, gives inmates incentive to follow rules so that privileges are not lost, assists the jail staff in inmate management.

**Panopticon:** circular design for prisons developed by eighteenth-century English scholar and philosopher Jeremy Bentham, outside prison cells constructed in a wheel like circle facing an interior courtyard with the prison guard's station in the center or hub, forerunner of circular jail and prison inmate housing.

**Passive recreation:** recreation that is non-physical; includes board games such as checkers, chess, playing cards, etc.

**pass-on:** staff passing on vital, critical information from a post jail officer to a relieving officer, also at the section and shift levels.

**pattern keys:** keys from which all other keys for a certain lock or series of locks are cut.

**Pennsylvania Prison Society:** penal reform organization evolved from the Philadelphia Prison Society of the late 1700s, founded by Dr. Benjamin Rush, worked to reform penal institutions and to aid prisoners.

**personal contact visit:** type of visit that allows the inmate to visit with a family member or significant other in the same room under strict rules as only holding hands, no sexual misconduct, set time limit, a beginning and ending kiss, etc.

**personal location systems:** technology that pinpoints an officer's location inside the jail, can be activated to alert the staff if the officer is in trouble.

**Personal recognizance:** release of an offender before trial without posting bail or bond; offender promises to appear in court; decision is made after offender is interviewed by court personnel.

**personal visits:** inmate visits with family and/or friends, usually through glass window using a telephone, no contact is allowed.

**personality disorders:** mental disorder caused by environmental influences and inherited traits, and are part of who the inmate actually is; examples are anti-social personality disorder, borderline personality disorder, and paranoid personality disorder.

**Plan of action:** action taken to meet a standard that is found to be in non-compliance.

**Pocket guide:** a compact summary of vital information and procedures concerning inmates in the jail, carried on the jail officer's person.

**podular remote surveillance (podular):** second generation of jail design where the jail officer control booth is centrally located and surrounded by inmate housing units called "pods"; visual observation is increased and verbal communication is limited to intercom.

**Point additive instrument:** more popular method of ICC housing decision making; classification staff assigns weights and numbers to a variety of risk factors and computes a score, which guides the decision.

**Policy:** course of action adopted and pursued by an agency that serves as a guide, determines present and future courses of actions and decisions.

**Population adjustment:** classification process of adjusting inmate living areas for several reasons, including balancing out custody levels or separating inmates who are not getting along.

**Positive discipline:** discipline (reprimands) exercised by jail staff who attempts to teach and instruct the inmate; takes a training approach encouraging inmates to think maturely and use common sense.

**power plays:** actions where an inmate or a group of inmates attempt by fear, violence, and intimidation, to "run" a cellblock.

**Pre-disposing factors of unrest:** conditions of the jail environment and population that tend to reinforce the potential for trouble in the jail, including environment, overcrowding, inadequate staffing, and idleness/lack of programs.

**Precipitation:** early form of capital punishment performed by ancient Greeks; offenders were thrown off cliffs.

**Principles of Collective Behavior:** circumstances that may bring inmates together in a riot or disturbance situation—unity, frustration, and a highly charged atmosphere.

**Prison:** correctional facility funded and operated by the federal or state government; confines inmates sentenced to longer than one year for serious offenses.

**Prison Litigation Reform Act of 1996 or PLRA:** act passed by U.S. Congress in 1996, purpose is to curb frivolous inmate lawsuits by jailhouse lawyers, contains several strict conditions concerning filing of lawsuits in Federal courts.

**Prison Rape Elimination Act:** act of U.S. Congress, passed in 2003, to combat the problem of inmate sexual assault in corrections facilities, purpose is to establish a zero tolerance policy for prison rape and sexual assault, prioritizing prevention and the development of standards for detection, prevention, reduction, and punishment of perpetrators.

**Prison-wise inmates:** offenders who have done time in federal and state penitentiaries and because they have committed new crimes, are incarcerated in the local jail.

**Prisonization:** process by which the jail inmate learns the formal rules, regulations, and routine of the jail, as well as the informal values, customs, and rules of the inmate sub-culture.

**Private Sector Prison Industries Enhancement Act Certification Program (PIECP):** act passed nearly 20 years ago by the U.S. Congress, authorizes correctional agencies to ship goods manufactured in jail or prison for sale on the open market; conditions are stated in the act for inmate wages, worker displacement, and informing local labor organizations and competitor manufacturers.

**Privatization:** process by which private corporations take over the responsibility, staffing, and operations of local jails per agreement with the local jurisdiction(s).

**Probationary period:** a specific time period (usually 12 months) after being hired where the new jail officer can be dismissed if supervisors and/or training staff have reason to believe that the new officer is not suitable for jail work.

**Procedure:** actions, sequential and in detail, that must be carried out to ensure the implementation of a policy, provides direction for staff.

**Process indicators:** documentation and other supportive evidence that is periodically examined to ensure that practices are being properly followed.

**professional visits:** visits to the inmates such as with attorneys, bail bond personnel, law enforcement officers, clergy, social workers, counselors, etc., occur in secure rooms with inmate.

**Property receipt:** document that states what items and monies were taken from the inmate, and what items and monies were brought to the jail by family and friends for the inmate.

**Protective custody (PC):** non-punitive form of administrative segregation where the inmate is due to safety concerns, such as weak inmates, witnesses, notable inmates due to charge, etc.

**Protocol(s):** a written instructions such as an agency policies/procedures, post orders, training curriculum, formats applicable to logs and forms, offender handbooks, fire evacuation diagrams, etc. that guide staff in implementation of expected practices.

**Public relations officer:** also known as the public information officer, a civilian or sworn position that serves as the agency representative to the media and the public; duties include press conferences, press releases, public events, public speaking, media presentations, tours, etc.

**publishers only rules:** requirement that inmates obtain publications only from the publisher; purpose is to further security.

**Punitive damages:** court ordered damages meant to punish staff, staff found liable in an inmate lawsuit have to pay damages "out of his or her pocket."

**Quarterly documentation:** gathering documentation, logs, reports, etc. by quarter, which supports standards compliance.

**rated capacity:** capacity of a jail based on the number of beds placed or built inside the jail when it was built and constructed.

**razor wire:** coiled barbed wire topped with razor-like blades.

**reasonable suspicion:** existence of objective, not subjective information that could likely predict the presence of weapons, drugs or any items of contraband.

**Receiving:** post in the jail manned by jail officers that take control of inmates as soon as they enter the jail and process them after completion of the booking procedure.

**Recontamination:** situation where an inmate may be contraband free when a transport begins, but may pick up something such as objects that convert to weapons, civilian clothes, drugs, while outside of the jail.

**Recreation:** commonly known as "gym," is an opportunity for inmates to engage in physical activity, sports, and games provided by the jail staff; the two types of recreation are active recreation and passive recreation.

**Reformatory System:** prison system based on the philosophy of Zebulon Brockway where young offenders between ages 16 and 26 could be reformed through the efforts of personnel in the social sciences, such as education, job training, etc.

**regional jails:** jails that are operated by several jurisdictions jointly by mutual agreement with each jurisdiction contributing funds for operations and staffing.

**Regional processing:** new trend in jail booking, offenders are booked into the jail system from locations in the community such as police substations or processing centers; relieves the load on jail processing centers and uses correctional personnel in the field.

**Rehabilitation:** the process whereby inmates change their criminal behavior through programs that help them to identify their needs, weaknesses, and problems; attempt to strengthen weaknesses through law abiding behavior, and improve abilities to solve problems and meet life's future challenges.

**Reintegration:** basic principle of community corrections that focuses on several areas in offenders' lives to facilitate developing positive ties to maintain a crime-free, positive lifestyle.

**religious cell visitation:** alternative to inmates attending formal religious services, jail chaplains and/or approved clergy may visit a segregated inmate at his or her cell to attend to religious needs.

**Religious Land Use and Institutionalized Persons Act (RLUIPA):** law passed by the U.S. Congress in 2000, states that any agency that exercises a "substantial burden" on inmates' exercise of religion must support a "compelling governmental interest" and that such restriction is of the least restrictive means.

**respected informant:** informant most relied on by jail officers, generally an older inmate who has done a lot of time in prison and jail, and wants to stay out of trouble; will inform so that his or her stable environment will not be compromised.

**restorative justice:** view that crime violates people and interpersonal relationships, the offender is obligated to right the wrongs that he or she has committed; victims needs are met.

**restrained hands approach:** current era of inmate rights that jails are in, holds that courts will only be involved if absolutely necessary and the administration of corrections facilities are left to qualified staff.

**restricted issue (R/I):** method of supervising suicidal inmates in jail, they are issued nothing that could be used for self-harm—no sheets or towels to devise nooses for hanging, etc.

**restricted keys:** keys that allow access to sensitive areas of the facility; examples include the pharmaceutical storage area, evidence locker, firearms storage area, etc.

**Riot:** a series of violent acts by a large group of inmates whose purpose is to disrupt to the greatest extent possible the security and operation of the facility.

**Risk and needs assessment:** classification tool to measure the danger level an inmate poses to himself/herself, to others, in conjunction with the likelihood of escape; physiological and psychological needs are measured concerning medical care, mental health care, and educational and vocational needs.

**Role players:** selected veteran staff who participates in scenario-based training by playing different roles to enhance the reality of the training scenario.

**Roll call:** 20- to 30-minute meeting that precedes a jail squad's or team's tour of duty; command staff directives and memos are read, posts are assigned, training is conducted, etc., and any officer questions are answered.

**Roll call training:** training conducted during a 20- or 30-minute roll call, either in video format or broken down into components; guest speakers can also be utilized.

**sally port:** entrance/exit point for vehicles delivering supplies, doing maintenance, bringing official visitors to the jail, and transporting inmates in and out of the jail.

**Scenario-based training:** non-traditional training that places trainees in certain situations, either by electronic means or through involvement of role players.

**screening board:** method of screening jail inmates for work release or electronic incarceration, board consists of jail community corrections staff, a mental health counselor and a treatment counselor.

**security audits:** self-analysis by the jail administration of all security policies, practices, and equipment, also includes a close inspection of the physical plant of the jail.

**security keys:** jail keys that may facilitate an escape or breach of security by inmates if lost or duplicated.

**security network:** system that operates jail security through staff following procedures, post orders, sharing information in writing and verbally, properly using security equipment, reporting security problems for follow up and taking action in serious incidents.

**Security/procedural skills:** jail officer skills that involve the carrying out of day-to-day operational procedures.

**security threat groups:** groups, because of their organization, views, ability to recruit new members and carry out actions and illegal activities disrupt jail operations.

**Self-audit report:** in-house evaluation of all policies, procedures, and operational practices to ascertain whether staff is practicing them in a synonymous and uniform manner; used in preparation for a formal audit.

**Separate System:** also known as the Pennsylvania System, style of inmate management in the early 1800s; cells were built at right angles off of long central corridors and inmates were housed alone and not permitted to communicate with other inmates, small work projects were performed in their cells.

**sexual disorders:** mental disorders that exhibit sexual behaviors such as exhibitionism, pedophilia, and voyeurism.

**Shakedowns:** informal term meaning the search of inmate areas—cells, dayrooms, etc., and anywhere that the inmates have access.

**shanks:** informal term for knives manufactured by inmates or homemade knives.

**shire reeves:** English forerunner of the modern day sheriff, governed localities or "shires," and were responsible for establishing and operating the local "gaol" (jail).

**shopping pass:** temporary pass of a few hours duration granted to work release offenders enabling them to purchase necessary items such as work clothes, toiletries, etc.

**Short/long schedule:** system of scheduling jail staff to work a short week followed by a long week of 12-hour days, resulting in an 84-hour two-week pay period and every other weekend off duty.

**Sick call:** designated time in the jail operational schedule when inmates see the medical staff, nurse, and/or doctor for any observed and reported (by staff or inmate) medical problem.

**sincerity of belief:** demonstration by an inmate that he or she is acquainted with a religion's teachings, beliefs, and basic foundations.

**slaves of the state:** court opinion in *Ruffin v. Commonwealth*, an 1871 Virginia case basically stating that inmates are in penal servitude to the state and have no personal rights. One of the foundations of the hands off era.

**Snitch:** informal jail slang term for confidential informant.

**Social therapy:** combination of traditional therapy and behavior modification; inmate must exist within a pro-social environment and is rewarded for good behavior and challenged if he/she acts inappropriately; approach uses educational programming and group therapy.

**Special housing roster:** a document that is distributed to the jail staff that lists the inmates on special segregation, what types of segregation (A/S, PC, D/S), the reason for the segregation, the authority placing them in segregation (such as "per ICC." "per Medical"), release dates from disciplinary segregation, caution alerts for staff, and the dates of file reviews.

**Special management inmates:** inmates who are on administrative or disciplinary segregation; the reasons for their segregation status dictates the condition, privileges, and locations of their confinement.

**Squad leader:** supervises the operations of a jail squad, delegates authority to subordinate supervisors, has final authority on assignments, authorizes leave, carries out instructions from branch supervisor, reviews and signs off in reports, responds to emergencies, etc.; usually is the rank of sergeant or higher.

**squirrel cage jails:** nineteenth-century rotary design, where the jail was a three-level jail built inside a cage; each floor had revolving pie-shaped cells that could be turned for easy staff access to inmates.

**staff duty officer (SDO):** supervisor of high rank, usually a captain or higher who is on call to give advice, take charge, or make decisions in critical emergencies or unusual situations.

**Staff escort:** jail inmate is escorted by staff whenever he or she is out of his or her cell; inmate's behavior and attitude may necessitate the presence of two officers and the usage off-hand and leg restraints.

**Staff support groups:** groups that allow new jail officers to discuss among themselves any problems and concerns, and ways to deal with them including giving feedback to supervisors; enhance morale and builds good relations with fellow trainees.

**status call:** telephone call afforded an inmate entering disciplinary segregation to inform family of his or her status and that no personal visiting is permitted.

**STG intelligence unit:** unit in the agency that works with federal, state, and local law enforcement agencies and other jails to gather intelligence about security threat groups (STG), investigates inmate STG activity inside the jail, recommends actions to staff, and provides staff training.

**street wise:** offenders who are well versed in the criminal lifestyle, breaking the law, and associating with other criminals.

**study release:** similar to work release; offenders are permitted to reside in a community corrections facility and attend classes in the community.

**Subjective jail classification:** classification that relies on the "gut" feeling of classification staff when making decisions, especially housing decisions.

**substance abuse disorders:** mental disorder where the offender has a dependency on drugs and/or alcohol which affects the offender's functioning; symptoms include depression, mania, and schizophrenia; most common mental disorder found in jail.

**Substance abuse searches:** utilization of devices such as urine and breath tests to determine whether inmates are using illegal drugs or alcohol; urine should be collected by officers as the same gender as the inmate and testing performed by trained and certified personnel.

**supervisor of record:** primary supervisor, usually the offender's immediate supervisor, who works out the offender's employment details with the jail staff.

**Sworn jail staff:** uniformed jail staff who have law enforcement powers, such as the power of arrest and receive training that meet state and agency standards.

**system crowding:** condition where the courts, probation offices, public defender offices, district attorneys, police agencies, and jails are taxed due to having more offenders to deal with than they can handle.

**systematically unsystematic:** varying the jail officer's patrol techniques in order to keep inmates from predicting where the officer will patrol and will not be able to accurately clock his or her movements.

**Test of Adult Basic Education (TABE):** used by most GED test centers, including jail programs sections, it is an initial assessment tool of student math and reading proficiency.

**Therapeutic community:** jail housing unit designated as a "program unit," has a social therapy setting for a select group of inmates needing or requesting treatment.

**thought disorders:** identified as schizophrenia, delusional disorder, and related mental illnesses; inmates with this disorder will not respond when spoken to, may speak to a non-existent person or thing, or may talk to themselves.

**Tie off points:** points such as light fixtures and bars where a noose could be tied by an inmate for hanging and strangulation.

**Torts:** legal actions filed in state courts seeking damages, alleging medical malpractice, lack of staff training resulting in harm to the inmate (plaintiff), etc.

**totality of conditions:** an examination by a court of all aspects of the jail's environment and practices, such as inmate length of stay, sanitation, lighting, programs, safety issues, etc.

**Transaction:** the act of booking an offender in or out of the jail.

**trick bag:** an easy way for jail-wise inmates to trap other inmates by lending a naïve inmate an item that the jail-wise inmate claims is broken when returned, forcing the naive inmate to repay by sexual favors, etc.

**triple crown certification:** the process of a jail meeting the certification of three agencies: Commission on Accreditation for Corrections, Commission on Accreditation for Law Enforcement Agencies, and the National Commission on Correctional Health Care.

**Trusties:** informal term for jail inmate work force; inmates working in kitchen, as janitors, laundry, etc.

**Tucker Telephone:** torture device that delivered electric shocks to inmates, indicative of prison conditions in the hands off era.

**unconvicted status:** jail inmates who are in a pre-trial status awaiting court.

**Unit management:** type of inmate management where the jail's living areas are divided into smaller units that are supervised by a unit management team that make very informed decisions similar to ones made by an ICC; confinement staff rotate in and out of the unit.

**Universal precautions rule:** precautionary rule by jail staff in which they treat *all* inmates as if they have a communicable disease, such as HIV, AIDS, etc.

**Utilitarianism:** view of eighteenth-century Italian scholar Cesare Beccaria that says the laws should be designed to bring the greatest good benefit to the greatest number of people.

**vehicle keys:** keys to vehicles, such as transport vehicles, cruisers, supply vehicles, etc.

**walk off:** a type of escape in which the offender simply "walks away" from the job site in cases of work release, and away from home in cases of home incarceration/electronic monitoring.

**Wearable computer:** small computer that can be worn inside a correctional officer's body armor, can be adapted with microphones and headphones allowing the officer hands-free use; has speech recognition software, has intranet/Internet capabilities, inmate data access and video transmitting capability.

**weekend confinement:** sentence in which offenders serve their sentences divided over a specific number of weekends; reduces jail overcrowding.

**Weekenders:** inmates under court order to do time on the weekends from Friday to Sunday with each weekend served being credited toward the completion of their sentence.

**willful negligence:** occurs when a staff member intentionally does something that causes harm to the inmate, such as retaliatory actions designed to "get back" at the inmate.

**Work Release:** a temporary release program in which the offender is authorized to work, study, or visit in the community.

**Written reprimand:** documentation is generated by the jail officer that an inmate has been warned about breaking rules; documentation is placed in the inmate's classification file.

**Zero tolerance policy:** policy of the jail concerning security threat group (STG) activity; all STG activity as well as inmate rule violations will be dealt with through disciplinary hearings, administrative hearings (for administrative segregation), and/or criminal prosecution.

# INDEX